"Craig Shirley is that rare combination of a superb writer perfectly matched to his subject. His books on Ronald Reagan brought a freshness and perspective to a man he knew well and helped us know better. His examination of Newt Gingrich and the role the former Speaker of the House has played in the modern American political life is fascinating and hugely entertaining. This is not an easy subject; Newt Gingrich is a complex figure of many paradoxes who defies easy characterization. Craig Shirley embraces the contradictions of Gingrich's life and delivers a rich portrait of a man many know and few understand."

—STUART STEVENS, POLITICAL CONSULTANT, COMMENTATOR, WRITER, AND AUTHOR OF *THE INNOCENT HAVE NOTHING TO FEAR*

"Craig Shirley has become the leading biographer of America's political leaders. He did it first with Ronald Reagan and now with Newt Gingrich. *Citizen Newt* chronicles the rise and fall of Gingrich—and his rise again as a strategist, reformer, and commentator. Shirley captures the indispensable Newt, whose influence on politics and government never fades."

—FRED BARNES, EXECUTIVE EDITOR, *THE WEEKLY STANDARD*; AUTHOR, *JACK KEMP: THE BLEEDING HEART CONSERVATIVE WHO CHANGED AMERICA*

"*Citizen Newt* is a must-read for anyone interested in politics or how their government works. Craig Shirley, the brilliant strategist turned gifted biographer, has captured the unique, revolutionary movement led by a man who went from being a gadfly backbencher to the Speaker of the House. As he did with his Reagan books, Shirley takes it all in, making you feel as if you're in the room when the plots are laid and the comebacks seem impossible. Fascinating, well written, and well researched, this is a book you will treasure!"

—ED ROLLINS, REAGAN WHITE HOUSE POLITICAL DIRECTOR, 1984 REAGAN CAMPAIGN MANAGER, COMMENTATOR, AND CONSULTANT

"Newt Gingrich is one of the most fascinating and important conservatives in the post-Reagan era. Craig Shirley's volume represents a deep dive into the rise and continuing relevance of one of the key figures of the modern conservative movement."

—FRANK DONATELLI, REAGAN CAMPAIGNS, 1976, 1980, 1984; REAGAN WHITE HOUSE POLITICAL DIRECTOR; CHAIRMAN, THE REAGAN RANCH

"Craig Shirley has become our leading historian of modern conservative leaders. In *Citizen Newt*, he follows up his accounts of how Ronald Reagan brought conservatism to the White House with a sparkling account of how Newt Gingrich brought conservatism to the House of Representatives."

—MICHAEL BARONE, SENIOR POLITICAL ANALYST, *WASHINGTON EXAMINER*; RESIDENT FELLOW, AMERICAN ENTERPRISE INSTITUTE; COAUTHOR, *THE ALMANAC OF AMERICAN POLITICS*

"Craig Shirley is one of most insightful and informed historians of modern American politics, and he doesn't disappoint here. What a great book, about a man many have covered but until now few have understood. When future generations seek to assess Newt Gingrich, they'll read this first."

—TUCKER CARLSON, EDITOR, THE *DAILY CALLER*; HOST OF *TUCKER CARLSON TONIGHT*, FOX NEWS

PRAISE FOR *LAST ACT*

"In this affectionate and often moving book, Craig Shirley has given us a remarkable account of Ronald Reagan's 'long goodbye,' chronicling the final years of an American original who bent history in the service of freedom. This is an invaluable book about an invaluable man."

—JON MEACHAM, PULITZER PRIZE–WINNING AUTHOR OF *AMERICAN LION*

"Craig Shirley is a walking encyclopedia on all things Ronald Reagan. His latest, *Last Act*, delves into Reagan's post-presidential life with verve and insight, breaking plenty of new ground. The story of Reagan's battling the curse of Alzheimer's disease is utterly riveting. Highly recommended!"

—DOUG BRINKLEY, EDITOR OF THE *REAGAN DIARIES*

"With this book, Craig Shirley cements his place as the premier Reagan biographer. As revealing as his earlier volumes on Reagan were, this one is especially fascinating, chock full of new revelations and captivating observations about the former president's twilight years."

—DR. LARRY J. SABATO, FOUNDER AND DIRECTOR OF THE CENTER FOR POLITICS AT THE UNIVERSITY OF VIRGINIA; AUTHOR OF *THE KENNEDY HALF CENTURY*

"Through never-before revealed interviews and expert analysis, *Last Act* by Craig Shirley pulls back the curtain on the life, last days, and legacy of Ronald Reagan—an exceptional president who believed in American exceptionalism above all else. Important. Essential. Bravo."

—JANE HAMPTON COOK, AUTHOR OF *AMERICAN PHOENIX*

PRAISE FOR *DECEMBER 1941*

"I love historical nonfiction. I read it everywhere, in the bathroom, wherever I am. But typically it's written from sort of a distant perspective. You went through newspapers and magazines, and all the accounts of time. It gives an immediacy that I think it's difficult to find in these types of things."

—JON STEWART, *THE DAILY SHOW*

"I'm confident it'll be a bestseller."

—DON IMUS

"Masterful new book . . . Shirley not only transports us back to that tumultuous time, but reminds this generation that denial about an enemy's intentions can have grave consequences."

—CAL THOMAS, SYNDICATED COLUMNIST

"Folks, if you want a good read this Christmas season check it out."

—STEVE DOOCY, FOX NEWS

"The book also reveals . . . blockbuster historical moment[s]. Shirley . . . takes a new tack in his book about Pearl Harbor. Instead of just writing how it all went down, his book attempts to give readers a feel for how the country felt 70 years ago. He accomplishes that by providing anecdotal information from nearly 2,000 newspapers and magazines."

—US NEWS & WORLD REPORT

PRAISE FOR *RENDEZVOUS WITH DESTINY*

"An unbelievable book . . . I was part of the Reagan Revolution and I didn't know 80 percent of this stuff! . . . It's worth reading, and reading right now."

—MARK LEVIN, BESTSELLING AUTHOR OF *LIBERTY AND TYRANNY*

"This exhilarating history . . . arrives, serendipitously, at a moment when conservatives are much in need of an inspiriting examination of their finest hour."

— GEORGE F. WILL, FROM THE FOREWORD

"There have been hundreds of books written about Ronald Reagan and this is the question that always irritates an author, why do we need another one? Well, we don't have to get very far in Craig Shirley's new book about Reagan to know that, yes, there is still a lot we don't know about Reagan and how he came to the White House. . . . It is a fascinating book!"

— BOB SCHIEFFER, CBS

"Shirley puts to rest one of the great political mysteries: who stole Carter's debate briefing books? . . . Shirley also reveals that the Kennedy family had a long memory on Election Day. . . . when it came time for the election, virtually all of them voted for Ronald Reagan."

— NEWSMAX

PRAISE FOR *REAGAN'S REVOLUTION*

"All in all, Shirley's work has much to commend it. His book should be read by anyone interested in Reagan, the rise of conservatism in the Republican Party, or American politics in the mid-1970s."

— ANDREW E. BUSCH, *CLAREMONT REVIEW OF BOOKS*

"An indispensible resource for anybody who wants to understand just how Mr. Reagan lost and why his defeat set the stage for victory four years later, upending history's supposed dialectic."

— QUIN HILLYER, *WALL STREET JOURNAL*

". . . a vividly written tale of this largely forgotten campaign."

— MATTHEW DALLEK, *WASHINGTON POST, BOOK WORLD*

"One of the season's most exciting political books . . ."

— MICHAEL POTEMRA, *THE NATIONAL REVIEW, SHELF LIFE*

CITIZEN NEWT

OTHER BOOKS BY CRAIG SHIRLEY

CITIZEN NEWT

THE MAKING OF A REAGAN CONSERVATIVE

CRAIG SHIRLEY

NELSON
BOOKS

An Imprint of Thomas Nelson

Published in Nashville, Tennessee, by Nelson Books, an imprint of Thomas Nelson. Nelson Books and Thomas Nelson are registered trademarks of HarperCollins Christian Publishing, Inc.

Thomas Nelson titles may be purchased in bulk for educational, business, fund-raising, or sales promotional use. For information, please e-mail SpecialMarkets@ThomasNelson.com.

Any Internet addresses, phone numbers, or company or product information printed in this book are offered as a resource and are not intended in any way to be or to imply an endorsement by Thomas Nelson, nor does Thomas Nelson vouch for the existence, content, or services of these sites, phone numbers, companies, or products beyond the life of this book.

ISBN 978-1-59555-449-9 (eBook)

Library of Congress Control Number: 2017933630
ISBN 978-1-59555-448-2

Printed in the United States of America
17 18 19 20 21 LSC 10 9 8 7 6 5 4 3 2 1

For Zorine

He was a bold man that first ate an oyster.
—Jonathan Swift

CONTENTS

PROLOGUE

*"Ronnie turned that torch over to Newt and the
Republican members of Congress to keep that dream alive."*

American history has the almost supernatural habit of mirroring itself. Thomas Jefferson and John Adams died on the same day exactly fifty years after adopting the Declaration of Independence. The Civil War began and ended on the same man's property. And the two most important intellectual revolutions in this country took place in the same decade, the '70s—separated by exactly two hundred years.

Just as the American Revolution was a conservative one—unlike the French Revolution and the Russian Revolution, as every schoolchild used to be taught—a second conservative revolution took place in the 1970s, once again challenging dictatorial and big, corrupt government with new ideas and a renewed vigor.

American conservatism is a truly unique and singular philosophy in the world, vastly different from British conservatism. American conservatism takes its inspiration from John Locke, Thomas Paine, Thomas Jefferson, the Declaration of Independence, and the Constitution, and believes that the individual bearing God's image is at the center of creation because God wants him there.

American conservatism stands in stark contrast to that of Edmund Burke, the father of British conservatism, who believed in the divine right of kings and that power flowed downward from London and the British Empire to the people rather than the reverse, as the American expression holds. The distinction is crucial, and only the mistaken claim that Burke is the father of American conservatism.

Despite being a mostly dark tale, the 1970s saw the rise and rebirth of modern American conservatism, which came to full fruition less than ten years later. Thereafter, American conservatism quite literally changed America and changed the world by spreading rock-solid beliefs such as freedom was good. Godless Communism was bad. More was generally better than less. A Judeo-Christian heritage is better than atheism, because faith teaches us about mercy, love, understanding, and forgiveness. And, finally, winning is better than losing. All these precepts came alive again beginning in the 1970s, after a long, rationally draining era, most especially the drug-addled 1960s.

The explosion of creative thought in American conservatism in the 1970s centered on the expansion of freedom for the individual while pushing back on the illicit authority of the State. It was the first time serious attempts were made to create arguments against the New Deal, the New Frontier, and the Great Society. Conservatives defeated the idea of corrupt collectivism with the superior argument of maximum freedom to the states, localities, and individuals, consistent with law and order.

Of course, all this would have been irrelevant without dynamic leadership giving voice to rising conservatism, and there are none more important than Ronald Reagan, and few more important than Newt Gingrich.

Ronald Reagan's place in history is secure, notwithstanding liberal attempts to mischaracterize, hijack, or write poorly researched books about him. There have been some fine books written about President Reagan, but there have been few about Gingrich that are honest and accurate, though many have been written. Most books about Gingrich have been deeply flawed, biased, and downright hostile. The preservation of honest, fact-based, and objective history is too important to be left to people with more interest in an agenda than the facts.

Citizen Newt takes the reader from the threadbare days of his early and failing campaigns for Congress to his startling election in 1978 and his steady but sure climb up the ladder in the leadership of the GOP and the leadership of the conservative movement.

This volume is the only factual account of the twenty-year rise of a first-generation Reaganite. Operationally, wrote respected Democratic pollster John Zogby, what Bill Buckley was to scholarly conservatism, what Reagan was to the leadership of conservatism, what Antonin Scalia was to the legal arguments of conservatism, Newt Gingrich was to its tactical and legislative and political successes. Nancy Reagan once said that Gingrich helped complete the Reagan Revolution, that "Ronnie turned that torch over to Newt and the Republican members of Congress to keep that dream alive."[1]

That makes Gingrich and—it is to be hoped—this book important.

Craig Shirley
Ben Lomond, Virginia
2016

INTRODUCTION

"I felt this was the time you had to put yourself on the line."

They began in old shoeboxes, Newt Gingrich's ideas. Some good, some cockamamie, some off-the-wall, some sound as a dollar, some, well, intriguing. All held his youthful and undiscriminating attention.

Over the years, Newton Leroy Gingrich had gathered up newspaper articles, columns, letters he'd received, academic papers . . . along with the notes he was forever jotting to himself. All these scraps of paper went into shoeboxes to be retrieved later for review, for lectures and talks, for college bull sessions, for the occasional interview. To be used for whatever. He didn't keep a diary, but this flow of information sufficed for an intellectual chronology of the sometimes desperately modish academic.

It was 1974, a dying era in which educated men, autodidact and otherwise, were still truly men of letters, even if they were only posting notes to themselves. Gingrich, a young and exuberantly curious college professor, age thirty-one, stood just under six foot, though he seemed taller, with his thick mound of hair, prematurely flecked with grey. He had the requisite long sideburns of most trendy young men of the era, wore steel-rimmed glasses and longish, though not unkempt, hair. "He looked like Roy Orbison," quipped Bob Livingston, a later soldier in arms as a House revolutionary.[1]

His tastes in fashion ran to paisley ties and paisley short-sleeved shirts, made of the same polyester that everybody else was sporting. The 1970s were known for many things, including recreational drugs, gratuitous sex, and mostly good music. Not all. Maureen McGovern's idiotic song "The

Morning After" was ostensibly about a capsized bourgeois cruise ship, the *Poseidon*, but it also could have been about waking up hung over or rolling over not knowing the name of last night's sex partner.

He was not an Aquarian and though he'd smoked marijuana once,[2] Gingrich eschewed sit-ins and other faddish protests. Newt was an odd blending of middle class, academia, tree hugger, animal lover, alternative energy devotee, and budding moderate-to-conservative; but he was moving away from the "New Generation" ideas of most of his colleagues and students. He was well above average in intellect, charm (when he so chose), and most certainly ambition, including politics.

West Georgia College, located in Carrollton, was at best a second-tier school in a sleepy, red-clay, dusty town. Gingrich was an "assistant professor of history and coordinator of the environmental studies program." It did have its "real hippie aspects . . . weird psychology . . . touchy feely stuff," said Chip Kahn, an eventual campaign aide.[3] "The student body was not the cream of the crop. So it was a party school . . . [it was] funky." And "there was a town-gown issue."[4]

Carrollton was dominated by the college, the Baptist church, and Southwire, a copper manufacturing company. The company and the church overlapped easily, as they often did in the South.

Gingrich's plans had never included the quiet academic life: a tenured sinecure, teaching lounges, lecture halls, endless seminars, the occasional sabbatical, the approval of peers, watching the country from the sidelines. But Gingrich was a very popular teacher at West Georgia College (later to be renamed the University of West Georgia). On Sundays he taught Bible studies at the First Baptist Church in Carrollton. He enjoyed these days "rapping" with students but wanted more.[5] Indeed, his student reviews were uniformly glowing, praiseworthy. The only complaint he received was from one student who wanted more reading assignments given out. A fellow professor, Steve Hanser, said, "He was very active in school politics and in helping to reorganize the structure of the college . . . irritating many of his colleagues." But, "he was extremely charming." And in the classroom, Gingrich was "first class."[6]

He had won his undergraduate degree from Emory University with a

GPA average of only 2.8, but he thrived in getting his doctorate from Tulane, earning mostly A's.[7] During his time at Tulane, Gingrich began attending the St. Charles Avenue Baptist Church, where he would later be baptized into the denomination. His three-hundred-page doctorial thesis, *Belgian Education Policy in the Congo, 1945–1960*, was, mercifully, not published in book form, though boasted Gingrich, "I had an offer to publish a book based on my dissertation from Boston University Press, which was the leading African studies academic press at the time, [but] turned it down to run for Congress."[8] As of early 1974, he was thinking audaciously about running for Congress.

Running for Congress as a Republican in the yellowest of yellow-dog states—Georgia—in the year of Watergate, when the Republican Party seemed on the verge of extinction, was not going to be easy for the bespectacled young man immersed in the culture of the campus. In his favor, Gingrich had been working for several years attempting to help other GOP candidates breathe life into a state party more dead than alive. Working against him was the state of William Tecumseh Sherman's "March to the Sea" amid the recent unpleasantness, as some locals still told it.

The only Republican in the Georgia delegation was Ben Blackburn, but he, too, was fighting for his political life against the anti-Republican tide of 1974.[9] Despite the odds, Gingrich decided he'd been on the sidelines long enough.

"I felt this was the time you had to put yourself on the line," he told David Broder of the *Washington Post*. "As a conservative, I believe in organic growth."[10] He'd thought briefly about running for lieutenant governor, according to campaign aide Chip Kahn, but had decided on Congress instead.[11] At the time, Kahn and Gingrich played a football board game, but for Newt, it wasn't just about the game itself but the tactics and the strategy.[12] Kahn was so dedicated to the eventual campaign, he actually loaned it $10,000, having inherited a sum from his grandfather. He was eventually repaid most of it, but it took a while.[13]

The outgoing governor, Jimmy Carter, was fading from the scene after a lackluster term. Carter had fiddled at the edges of government reform and race relations but had left no real legacy. He had championed "sunshine laws," which would allow citizens to know what their government was up to, though one opponent told the governor: "There are two things a person should never watch being made. One is potted meat, and the other is laws."[14]

Mel Steely, a local Georgian author, said if the state hadn't had a one-term limit, then Carter would not have been reelected anyway. He was that unpopular.[15] Georgia governors were charismatic backslappers, went to barbecues and Little League games, and socialized after church on Sundays. Carter did none of these things and the word spread quickly in the Peach State that Carter just wasn't one of them. Zell Miller—a former Georgia governor and senator, college professor, and US Marine, as well as an utterly charming man—agreed that Carter never would have won reelection.[16] When Carter was running for president, a used car lot full of local politicians did not like him, but they saw his candidacy as a referendum on Georgia and indeed the whole South, so they took a vow of omerta, staying silent throughout the campaign of 1976.

Meanwhile, out in California, another governor, Ronald Reagan, was also exiting the stage after his own uninspiring second term. Unlike Carter, who was one-term limited, Reagan could have sought a third, but given the anti-Republican mood in the country and Reagan's waning interest in Sacramento, it was open to question whether he would have won against the young attorney general, Jerry Brown, whose father Reagan had crushed in 1966. In June, at a meeting of the nation's governors in Seattle, David Broder haughtily observed, "As for Reagan, who suddenly looks every one of his 63 years, he was put down, not only by Kennedy but by fellow Republicans and some reporters, as he tried to milk his last meeting for maximum publicity."[17]

No one was talking in 1974 about a Reagan presidential bid in '76. Gone was the small and brief hype over Reagan seeking the White House that had pushed him into a late-starting and ill-fated challenge to Richard Nixon in 1968. Reagan's star was fading fast.

Then Richard Nixon resigned in ignominy in the summer of 1974.

A brief, freshening breeze swept across the party when Gerald Ford assumed the presidency. In his first post-Watergate address to the country before a joint session of Congress, he called inflation "Public Enemy No. 1."[18] At last, a president was talking about what was on everybody else's mind.

Still to be addressed was filling the vacant vice presidency. After only a few weeks, Ford chose former New York governor Nelson Rockefeller, who conservatives couldn't stand because of his politics, who liberals couldn't stand because of what they perceived as his heavy-handed tactics at the Attica prison riot several years earlier, and who anybody who was not a multimillionaire couldn't stand because of his massive, inherited wealth. His nomination was not well received. In the US House, 128 members voted against his confirmation.[19]

One month later, President Ford pardoned former president Nixon for all crimes, for all time. Screams of "political fix" and "corrupt bargain" echoed across Washington and the country, and Ford sank into his own quagmire of questions and accusations. The moment of post-Watergate bipartisanship and unity had passed.

At his first press conference after the pardon, President Ford opened with a bland statement about the Jewish New Year, but he was peppered with twenty-one questions, fifteen of which dealt with Nixon, Watergate, the Watergate tapes, and Nixon's health. Two of the other questions were about Secretary of State Henry Kissinger's recent attempts to destabilize the government of Chile.[20]

Despite all of this, national Republicans were modestly hopeful about the uphill chances for young Gingrich. Gingrich, for his part, had gone public in his call for Nixon to resign as early as January 1974. Plus some minor scandals had attached themselves to the Georgia Sixth Congressional District incumbent, Democrat John J. "Jack" Flynt Jr., who hadn't even had an opponent in 1972,[21] even as Nixon was crushing George McGovern in Georgia by an astonishing margin of 75–25 percent.[22] So into 1974 stepped Newton Leroy Gingrich: "Newton" for his birth father, "Leroy" for his mother's brother, and "Gingrich" for his adoptive father. He was fresh-faced, articulate, boundlessly energetic, "a self-described 'moderate conservative.'"[23] To run, he took a leave of absence from his teaching position and a cut in pay by one-third of his annual eleven-thousand-dollar salary.[24]

The Washington-based GOP organizations threw their nominee for Georgia's Sixth District a few meager resources, though they themselves were scraping along, trying to help dozens of endangered Republican incumbents who hoped to avoid the Watergate undertow. Since no other Republican came forward to challenge him for the nomination, Gingrich could focus on Flynt. Meanwhile, Gingrich had channeled the hit movie *The Candidate* about a young outside reformer running against an entrenched and odious old incumbent.

The *Atlanta Daily World* covered Gingrich extensively and avidly, even though it catered predominately to the region's black community. The paper was founded in 1928, and was owned and operated by black Republicans, heirs to the post–Civil War party of the Great Emancipator, Abraham Lincoln. At its founding, the paper "served as a voice against the Jim Crow laws and lynchings prevalent in the South at that time" and was closely aligned with the Republican Party, and "resented the racial demagoguery of white southern Democrats." But by 1974, Republicans had lost their historic moorings, defending "Big Brother" government in Washington, which was running amok, spying on private citizens. Only liberals seemed interested in civil liberties, and the *Atlanta Daily World*, though still Republican-leaning, was less reliably partisan than it had been in 1960, when it endorsed Richard Nixon.[25]

Gingrich's opponent, the sixty-year-old Flynt, had been in Congress since Dwight Eisenhower had clacked his golf shoes across the parquet floors of the Oval Office. Flynt was a run-of-the-mill Southern Democrat, more or less a supporter of Jim Crow. A Dixiecrat, Flynt had never been seriously challenged for the House seat; some years the local Republicans couldn't even find a sacrificial lamb to put his name on the ballot against him.

Gingrich was an underdog, but that was nothing new to "Newtie," as his mother, Kathleen, affectionately called him. He'd been an underdog his whole life. His young parents divorced when he was just a small child. His mother remarried a recently discharged army enlisted man, Bob Gingrich, in 1946, when Newtie was three years old. Five years later, when he was eight, his adoptive father, with a newly minted college degree, rejoined the army, this time as an officer.[26]

Newtie grew up an atypical "army brat" in the shadow of the Cold War, spending his summers with his father, embraced—somewhat—by his adoptive father, a newcomer at school, once having to defend himself with his fists against boys challenging the new kid on the block. He'd lived on a half dozen different military bases as a child, including ones in France and Germany. While in France, he visited a macabre World War I memorial as a child, which had a lifetime effect on him. "I had two fights in my life—once with a bunch of kids at Junction City in the fifth or sixth grade and once I held a guy to prevent him fighting when I was a junior in high school," he recalled.[27]

He said, "[For a time] I was raised by Aunt Loma and Uncle Cal [on his father's side] and by my grandmother on my mother's side." Despite the constant moving around and growing up poor, Gingrich said, "I had an idyllic childhood." Maybe. As a child and when moving from his father's post in Kansas, the young Gingrich discovered to his horror that his box filled with his favorite toys—airplanes, fossils, books, and other things that delighted the young, intellectual, if sometimes lonely, boy—had been lost in shipment. Little Newt was devastated for a time, but thereafter learned not to like things too much.[28]

He hadn't grown up friendless, but moving year after year, the nearsighted kid found joy and happiness in books. At one time he'd thought about being a palaeontologist or a zookeeper. But reading and animals were just a few of his hobbies. Certainly politics, military history, American history, and writing had also animated the youngster.

And ideas.

PART I

THE CANDIDATE

(1974–1978)

CHAPTER 1

PROFESSOR GINGRICH

"If he gets elected, he would be the only anti-establishment
Republican in the House of Representatives."

1974

R ace and race relations were part of the backdrop of American politics
in 1974. The Supreme Court had ordered "forced busing" as a means
of achieving racial integration in public schools, and many communities—
black and white—had risen up in protest. Curiously, this controversial
order had gone down easier in some places in the South—where one might
have expected trouble—than in the North, where terrible riots broke out
in Boston, the very seat of liberalism, a clear sign that the "New South" of
1974 was different from the "Jim Crow South" of earlier decades. Beantown
officials asked for federal marshals to come in and help restore order. One
national newspaper went so far as to proclaim, "Race is no longer the leading
overt issue in the South."[1]

Everybody knew this was bull.

Other issues dominating the national debate included nuclear prolifera-
tion, the environment, and world hunger—a cause popularized by the late
singer Harry Chapin.[2] In bars and over kitchen tables, however, more immediate issues dominated. Feeding a family and gassing up the car were becoming
problematic propositions with wages stagnating. To combat the growing
recession, Senators Ted Kennedy and Walter Mondale proposed a personal
income tax cut of nearly $6 billion.[3] Their bill was folded as a rider into a
larger package of tax cuts being offered by the Democrats, but Richard Nixon
and most Republicans opposed it as "a dangerous step."[4] Instead, the Nixon

Administration had been poised to "pour out as much [federal] money as necessary to avoid a recession."[5]

Georgia voters were just as affected by these problems as everybody else in the nation, in some cases more acutely, with its high rural population of farmers and working poor. Unemployment was slightly lower than the national average, but so, too, was household income. Though still an agrarian-based state, Georgia was slowly emerging from her rough-and-tumble past. Newt Gingrich recalled a "[h]uge military presence beginning with World War II, a lot of textile mills, Lockheed had a huge aircraft plant, there were Ford and General Motors plants in the Atlanta area, the Atlanta Airport was already the dominant airport in the South."[6]

Gingrich formally entered the race at 7:30 in the evening on April 8, 1974, with a statement issued at his campaign's headquarters in Carrollton. Earlier, he'd kicked off his campaign with a 10:00 a.m. press conference at his headquarters in South Fulton.[7] It did not begin softly. He lashed the "incompetency and indifference" of Washington, and a Congress "more interested in party squabbling than in problem solving."[8]

Gingrich struck a decidedly populist pose, attacking an insular Congress that no longer held its doors open for the citizenry: "I can no longer sit idly by while my future—and the future of this country—is endangered by political hacks who do not understand what is happening to the people they supposedly represent." He promised the Georgia media press conferences every week.[9] The campaign's photo of the candidate had him in a garish plaid sports coat, dark purple shirt, and a wide plaid tie. He sported a broad and friendly, slightly lopsided grin.

There was a charming amateurishness to Gingrich's 1974 quest. The budget, all told, was around $90,000, which was respectable, but Gingrich insisted all his materials be produced in green, to signal his concern for the environment. Even his bumper stickers were green and white and simply proclaimed, "NEWT!" When asked about using just his first name, he quipped, "No one will remember the last name!"[10] His brochures declared, "The Politicians Had Their Chance. Now You Can Have Yours," "His Only Special Interest Is You!" and "We need a congressman that's as angry about the current mess as you are." The bureaucrats also came in for some good licks in Newt's campaign material.[11] It wasn't infrequent that Newt would call a press conference and no one would show up, according to Chip Kahn.[12]

This campaign was the longest of long shots. The last time anybody had seriously tried to take on Flynt was in 1966, and G. Paul Jones of Macon had gotten waxed by a 2–1 margin.[13] Newt's lackluster athletic record, rather than his burgeoning academic career, was the most relevant preparation for his "Hail Mary" political challenge. He had been a high school football player but frankly was not very good. "At that stage," he admitted, "I became a punching bag, but it was good training."[14] Indeed.

Newt's announcement was picked up verbatim in the *Atlanta Daily World* but was relegated to the bottom of page 3, which was essentially the black society page, with other stories covering PTA meetings[15] and a "Big Easter Show" featuring the Chi-Lites.[16]

A print ad—timed the day before the election—appeared in the *Atlanta Daily World* headlined "The 6th District Needs Newt." It states that "Newt Gingrich is a 31-year-old college teacher who is running against a 60-year-old rural oriented man who has been in Congress 20 years. Vote for Newt and give a chance to a young man with fresh ideas. Elect Newt Gingrich. Punch 74 on Nov. 5." A pleasant photo of the candidate accompanied the ad, though the disclaimer spelled his name "Gingrick."[17]

The district—much of it covering Fulton County—had changed since the 1970 census; by 1974 it included some of the suburbs of Atlanta and stretched to the Alabama border. Gingrich took note of this and stressed the need to understand "Metropolitan problems." In his campaign, he also promised to install a toll-free number for constituents to call at a district office at the Atlanta Airport.[18]

Though Atlanta was becoming more cosmopolitan, the *Atlanta Daily World*—the poor country mouse to the powerhouses *Atlanta Journal* and *Atlanta Constitution*—still ran candidates' press releases verbatim. On page 2, they ran one of Gingrich's. The "story" contained quotes, including that he was "presenting a serious challenger to [a] 20-year incumbent . . ." and saying that "Gingrich . . . has used youthful energy to develop a major campaign based on honesty and candidate availability."[19]

The paper somewhat surprisingly endorsed the Republican Gingrich over the Democrat Flynt in an editorial, saying he was "fair-minded on racial issues. His election would give President Ford more support and it is important that there be closer cooperation between the President and the Congress."[20] Gingrich was far more progressive on racial matters than Flynt.

Coming in to endorse Gingrich was Governor Ronald Reagan, doing what he could do to shore up the GOP's fading chances. According to Paul West of the *Atlanta Constitution*, Reagan was there "to boost" Gingrich's candidacy.[21] "Although a roomful of Republican candidates were gathered in hopes of receiving a blessing from Reagan, the California chief executive mentioned only Gingrich and [one other candidate] by name during his 30-minute appearance."[22] Reagan got bollixed by reporters when he defended President Ford's economic policies, but he also blasted the Treasury Department for selling too many high-yield notes, which he said would spur inflation on even more. He took a pass on saying whether he'd challenge Gerald Ford or whether he would support the nomination of Rockefeller, but he went especially hard after "McGovernite Democrats," whom he said had politicized the whole Watergate mess.[23]

Gingrich later accompanied Reagan to the airport. "He had one state trooper where there was no staff that I remember . . . and he got tired of chit chat and he said, 'How would you like to see how I did in the speeches?' I said, sure, yeah. So he put out his cards and he walked me through his theory.'" And Reagan explained to the young man how he put together a speech, how he told a story, how he mixed it up and worked in current material to keep the speech fresh and keep his own interest, along with that of his audience. "If I were to give exactly the same speech every time, I would get bored. They would sense I was bored and then they would get bored."[24]

A day later, Gingrich went solid after his opponent, charging Flynt with "using tax dollars to subsidize his own farm." Flynt had been employing an old political crony, Joe Akin, on his congressional payroll for years at an annual salary of $10,500. But Akin's real responsibility was managing Flynt's six-hundred-acre farm in Spalding County. Akin tried to pooh-pooh Gingrich's charges, admitting that while he did both jobs, managing the farm wasn't all that hard because "the only thing we have is about 100 head of cattle and some corn."[25]

It had been suspected for a long time that the farm was a major profit center for Flynt. Not only was he profiting from the cattle and crops, he was also receiving federal farm aid and, as a bonus, picked up a check from the Ford Motor Company for $12,500 for allowing the auto manufacturer to "park 14,000 Torinos" on the land.[26] Not surprisingly, Gingrich also discovered that both Henry Ford II and Benson Ford, scions of the fabled Detroit company, had each contributed $200 to his opponent's campaign.[27]

The sweetheart deal was appalling in part because it was so crass, so out in the open. There was plenty of land closer to the Ford plant on which to store cars, but Flynt was an influential member of Congress whose committee had oversight on emissions regulations. He was also on the committee that handled congressional ethics—a committee the *Atlanta Constitution* described as "largely dormant."[28]

All of Gingrich's charges were backed up with documentation, but he may have gone too hard after his older, though popular, opponent by calling him a "moral coward." Flynt, who had been ducking the Republican for months, finally responded by calling Gingrich a "desperate liar"[29] in his advertising, but again refused to meet him in any open debate. Gingrich responded in kind with TV and radio ads blasting the Democrat. The charges—which Flynt never really addressed—resonated in the Georgia media for days.

Only a few days earlier, Gingrich had stormed, "I am amazed and appalled that a member of the House of Representatives Ethics Committee would be engaged in activities that, if not illegal, are so clearly on the borderline of conflict of interest."[30] Flynt took the bait and denied that his decisions in Congress were at all affected by his business dealings with Ford Motor Company. Finally, Gingrich had an issue he could sink his teeth into. "And boy, did he p--s off Flynt, oh wow," said campaign aide Kahn.[31]

One day later, Gingrich proposed "a four-point program to stop special interests from exploiting the American people." His four points were pure William Jennings Bryan. He called for stricter government oversight of corporate America and "strengthening" antitrust legislation.[32]

Just a few days before the election, a leading columnist for the *Atlanta Constitution*, "Reg" Murphy, reviewed the race and said it was not outside the realm of possibility that the young upstart could win. Murphy clearly understood the anti-Watergate mood, aligning Flynt with the Washington crowd but Gingrich with "new faces, new ideas, fresh beginnings." He continued,

"Seniority is a dirty word. Experience is not prized." He also noted that while conservatives were siding with Gingrich, so, too, were labor unions, including the powerful Communications Workers of America and, most astonishingly, the local chapter of the United Auto Workers (UAW). Gingrich was also receiving the support of the airline pilots (of which there were many because Atlanta was a major hub for Delta) as well as churches and farm groups.[33]

"If he gets elected, he would be the only anti-establishment Republican in the House of Representatives," Murphy presciently wrote.[34] Gingrich wanted no less than to replace the "people who were in power. And at a secondary level, a replacement of the principles by which power is exercised."[35]

In the waning days, Gingrich went hard after the corruption of Congress and corporate America, bashing the real or imagined special interests and "the bureaucratic power wielders . . . the entrenched leadership . . . the lobbyists."[36] He was in the local media on a daily basis, making news, making charges, storming the gates of the good ol' boy establishment. One reporter noted the most obvious fact: Gingrich's "flair for gaining publicity."[37]

He'd already picked up the endorsement of the African American *Atlanta Daily World*[38] and the *Atlanta Suburban Reporter*.[39] On November 4, the day before the election, he also surprisingly garnered the support of the powerful *Atlanta Journal*, though its sister paper, the *Atlanta Constitution*, did not endorse either candidate, only giving Flynt "the little edge." Though Flynt was being cast as the old man in the race, he would not turn sixty until November 8, three days after Election Day.[40] He was still nearly twice his opponent's age.

In its endorsement, the *Journal* wrote, ". . . Gingrich [is] a relatively young man with the proper amount of maturity and comprehension of the problems bothering Georgians today. He is serious about serious matters, but at the same time he has a sense of humor."[41]

Yet another writer for the *Constitution* wrote, "Most political observers give Gingrich a good chance at taking Flynt's seat."[42] The challenger confidently predicted victory, telling his supporters in Hapeville he would win "because of a base of support that embraces conservatives, liberals, Republicans, Democrats, whites, and blacks." Issuing the most understated line of the campaign, Gingrich called it an "odd coalition."[43] Adding to the odd coalition was Bob Beckel, a hard-drinking Democratic operative, working on behalf of a liberal group who gave Gingrich a generous donation.[44]

PROFESSOR GINGRICH | 9

Kahn recalled many knock-down, drag-out fights with Newt over how to run his campaign and how to present him, as a moderate reformer, as post-partisan or something else. "You couldn't be an animal of both schools." Truth be told, Gingrich was hard to categorize, but he mistakenly thought "he could please everyone because he was Newt Gingrich." Still, "When Newt . . . talked about doing things outside the box, people saw in that something different . . . 'Well, this guy looks at things in a new way.'" Kahn was certain that Newt's wife Jackie was pro-choice in 1974, and Newt may have been, although when the issue came up, he simply said he was pro-life and quickly moved on.[45]

The race was not settled until the day after the election, when all the precincts had been counted. Alas, it was not to be for Gingrich, but he had lost by the slimmest of margins, a bit less than 3,000 votes: 49,082 for the incumbent Flynt, and 46,308 for the young Republican challenger. He lost by less than 3 percent and had won several counties.[46] Two years earlier, with no real opponent, Flynt had won more than 99 percent of the vote. As of Election Day, Flynt had said he thought he'd win by 70 percent; he later offered a more modest assessment of 62.[47] He was appalled to have come so shockingly close to losing.

Gingrich called his loss a "moral victory,"[48] a line often associated with narrowly losing candidates. Still, he'd been outspent and out-incumbented and out-Watergated and out-registered and yet he came amazingly close. As a result, he would live to fight another day if he chose to, and Newt chose to do so.

The rest of the Republicans were wiped out across the country, losing governorships, dozens of House incumbents, more senators, and hundreds of locally elected officials. As a result, the US House was controlled by the Democrats by a more than 2–1 margin. Having lost 4 seats in the Senate, the GOP was at 38, below the number needed to block legislation.[49] The Republicans were especially battered in the South, where they had made tiny gains since 1964—now these were gone as well.

The famed "Southern Strategy" of Richard Nixon had faltered badly.[50]

Georgia's lone House Republican, Ben Blackburn, was also easily defeated.[51] That is not to say there were not conservatives in the Georgia delegation. The congressional Democrats there were all by and large to the right of center on most issues.

Democrats now controlled two-thirds of the governorships and most of the state legislatures. Indeed, after November 1974, only in Kansas, Wyoming, and New Hampshire did the Republican Party control the governorship and both houses of their state legislature.[52] The Sunflower State's incumbent, Bob Dole, barely squeaked by reelection in one of the bloodiest campaigns in recent memory.

No one had forecast that November would be this horrific.

It was so bad that in Ohio, Jim Rhodes, who was attempting a comeback of sorts by throwing his hat in the ring against the incumbent Democrat, John Gilligan, conceded on election night, only to learn in the early morning after the election that he'd won the governorship back. Rhodes, like most Republicans, had expected to lose.[53]

Republicans on the House Judiciary Committee, who had defended Nixon through Watergate, were cut down left and right.

About the only office the Republicans still controlled was the presidency, yet they still did not control the second in command, as Congress had yet, as of late November 1974, to approve Ford's nomination of Nelson Rockefeller.

One month after the off-year elections, the fifty-year-old Jimmy Carter declared his candidacy for the 1976 nomination of his party. As reported in the *New York Times*, his announcement was greeted "by skeptics as just another Democratic dark horse . . ."[54] Carter said he would enter all the primaries and caucuses. *Time* magazine said the Georgian bore "a slight physical resemblance to John F. Kennedy."[55]

The Democratic field would grow very quickly, including former senator Fred Harris of Oklahoma, a true Prairie Populist who promised to take it to "the rich people and big corporations."[56]

While the number of contenders among the Democrats was growing, the congressional committee created to investigate Watergate—the Senate Select Committee on Presidential Campaign Activities—was shrinking. At one point, its staff had numbered more than one hundred, but by December 1974 it had dwindled down to thirty. They would soon be out of jobs. The final report was scheduled to be released in July.[57] One of its most unyielding in hating Richard Nixon was a young attorney and committed leftist, Hillary Rodham.

Though he'd been pardoned by Ford, Watergate still haunted Nixon. Time and again, the idea of his testifying at the trials of his former White House staff was floated in the nation's newspapers. His enemies in the media and the Democratic Party would not rest until they utterly broke the man and frog-marched him in an orange jump suit to jail. They hated Nixon and they would always hate Nixon.

Also, he was fighting with the government over ownership of his secret Oval Office tapes. Since his resignation, Nixon had been in and out of hospitals, ailing with phlebitis, a potentially life-threatening condition in which blood clots could form in the legs and thighs. Were clots to break loose, they could travel to his heart and lungs, killing the severely depressed, reclusive, and heavily drinking former president. Gerald Ford made a quiet visit to the ailing Nixon in the hospital in California. The press howled. For Nixon there was little end in sight, but for the American people Watergate had faded into a sideshow.

Gingrich had run far ahead of most other Republicans in the Watergate year of 1974, despite being heavily outspent by his Democratic opponent. Still, he'd lost. Of Gingrich's candidacy, the *Christian Science Monitor* wrote:

> In Georgia, a young Republican college professor, Newt Gingrich, came within an eyelash of upsetting conservative veteran Democratic Rep. John J. Flynt Jr. The Republican ran as a reformer and an environmentalist. The outcome indicated that if Republicans can recruit young, attractive candidates, they can challenge even Democratic incumbents head-on.
>
> Yet Gingrich-style, apolitical candidates are those usually being attracted to the Democratic Party because of the scandals that have racked the Republican White House. Republicans must reverse this trend—and quickly—or lose some of their most promising talent.[58]

The silver lining for the slightly graying thirty-one-year-old was that Watergate was fading as a national issue. Inflation topped 11 percent for

1974.[59] Everything was going up in cost, outstripping wages. By late 1974, unemployment had climbed to 6.5 percent, its highest level in ten years.[60] It was a bad forecast for incumbents. There would be few impediments coming down from the national level to stop Gingrich from winning when he tried again in two years.

Or would there?

CHAPTER 2

AGAIN UNTO THE BREACH

*"I knew I was in trouble when three people in line ahead
of me were voting as revenge for Sherman's March."*

1975–1976

Like most taxpayers, I just finished wading through the ridiculously complicated and inefficient U.S. Tax Forms." So began a less-than-mild-mannered letter to the editor of the *Atlanta Daily World* on May 8, 1975, authored by one Newt Gingrich of Atlanta.

The long letter was shot through with "outrage," "mish-mash," and other pejoratives. Gingrich took a very populist stance, urging that all deductions be eliminated, "except for one standard $2,000 for each individual taxpayer and each dependent and contributions to charities and religions." And that the existing tax code "must stop allowing the privileged few to escape with little or no tax bills while the great mass of hard-working, middle class taxpayers bear the bulk of the burden in our nation today."[1]

It was early in 1975, just months after Newt's razor-thin loss to Congressman John James Flynt. He blamed Gerald Ford for his loss, citing the Nixon pardon as what wrecked his candidacy. He may have been right, but Gingrich moved on.

At the end of May, the Peach State's GOP held their convention and easily snagged Gingrich as a speaker—it didn't take much convincing. They also attracted the former governor of California, Ronald Reagan. As there were virtually no elected Republican officials in the state—and none in their congressional delegation—Gingrich was already seen as a rising star, while Reagan had always made Georgia's GOP hearts go pitter-patter. And a lot of Democrat hearts too.

13

At the packed event, Reagan first held a 9:30 press breakfast and then spoke to nearly one thousand at the gathering, bringing them repeatedly to their feet.[2] The grateful Republicans gave Reagan a stuffed elephant, though they ducked in an attempt by some of the Gipper's more resolute supporters to pass a resolution endorsing him for president. The state party did, however, call for an open convention, which was a setback for those boosting a Ford candidacy.[3] Gerald Ford had not said if he would seek a term in his own right, though he had written a piece the year before—while still suffering as Richard Nixon's second in command—stating that if he became president through the Twenty-Fifth Amendment, he would not seek a full term of his own.[4]

But that was then. Living in a twenty-five-room private mansion, having jets and helicopters and staff at your beck and call, and having a kitchen that could whip up anything you wanted to eat at a moment's notice, all while having your own personal army and navy to command and people constantly taking your photos, having a national press corps scribbling down every utterance, holding your daughter's prom in the East Room of the White House, never worrying about a tee time or somebody playing through, having a heated indoor pool to relax in, traveling the world on a private plane without dealing with passports and visas, admiring a lovely garden full of roses just off your oval-shaped office, knowing that with one push of a button you could destroy the world . . . all this had been known to turn the heads of others who occupied the office of "The Most Powerful Man in the World." Ford was only human.

The two-day Georgia GOP confab also produced a platform that was tough on "armed robbers, murderers and rapists" and welfare cheats; the platform warned that "America is in danger of decaying into a jungle of violent crimes." Gingrich was a key member of the committee that drafted the hard-hitting, if also somewhat jingoistic, document.[5]

His ideology was already evolving. He'd begun as a run-of-the-mill Republican, more comfortable with the moderate elements in the GOP. In 1968, he'd supported Nelson Rockefeller over Richard Nixon at a time when most conservatives like Bill Buckley and Senator Strom Thurmond of South Carolina were supporting "Tricky Dick." Gingrich had always claimed he only supported Rockefeller because his first choice, Reagan, was not in the race, but when Reagan made a late charge for the nomination in Miami Beach, Gingrich stuck with Rocky.

Still, there was no doubt that Gingrich held the Gipper in high esteem. Newt's own populist conservatism, lightly seasoned with small-L libertarianism and drenched in optimism, closely resembled Reagan's. When Reagan had singled out Newt for praise the previous year, the college professor had become a firm admirer. He expressed his admiration in an op-ed for the *Baltimore Sun*, slamming Ford, praising Reagan, and talking up a 1976 primary challenge by the Gipper:

> "The simple reality is that only the ex–movie star has the charisma, national name recognition and professional staff to develop a serious challenge for the nomination." Gingrich accurately forecast that Ford and Nelson Rockefeller would antagonize the conservatives in the party, saying they were in "grave danger of overestimating conservative . . . goodwill."[6]

Outside of the conservative house organs *Human Events* and *National Review*—Bill Buckley's *National Review* was initially lukewarm to a Reagan challenge to Ford in 1976—Gingrich's piece was one of the first in the national media to openly speculate that Reagan could—and should—challenge a sitting president in his own party. Gingrich saw Reagan's appeal to young Americans, even as this eluded others in the political classes.[7]

The editorial pages of the *Wall Street Journal* seemed to have difficulty grasping the concept of Reaganism, comparing Reagan's worldview with that of George Wallace and Gerald Ford: "Each will have to strain mightily if he wishes to present a program for the rest of the decade that is readily distinguishable from the others."[8]

By August 1975, Gingrich was sprinting for Congress again. Though not an announced candidate, and though the newspapers said it was only "rumored" he was running again, there was no rumor to the rumor.

He bashed Congress for voting itself a pay raise of $3,350 per year to an annual $42,500. "Their salary alone is 4 1/2 times the income of the average Georgia family." He said the raise was "immoral and should be illegal."[9]

There was also no rumor about former Georgia governor Jimmy Carter's bid for the White House. Five others had joined him by May 1975, including former North Carolina governor Terry Sanford, Senator Lloyd Bentsen of Texas, as well as Senator Henry "Scoop" Jackson of Washington State.

On the sidelines, biding his time, was George Wallace, just waiting to jump in and savage the "pointy headed intellectuals" in his own party. He especially loathed Carter, as he saw him as an interloper on his turf, the South. Carter returned the loathing in kind.

By December, Carter was leading Wallace among Democrats in Florida, something unthinkable just months before. Carter was impossible to categorize. He was opposed to the death penalty, but also suggested he opposed abortion. Culturally he was a conservative, a "severe" lay Baptist preacher who did not smoke, drink, or play cards. Politically he was a moderate, but was also running as a fiscally conservative outside reformer who would clean up Washington. Americans had heard that before, but Carter was still one of the most unusual candidates ever to seek the presidency.

He wore his religiosity on his sleeve, campaigned openly from church pulpits, and spoke often of "a deeply profound religious experience that changed [his] life dramatically" in the late 1960s.[10] On the eve of the 1976 election, the Democratic nominee appeared in a nationally televised broadcast with the Reverend Pat Robertson.

In an effort to jumpstart his own political fortunes, President Ford chose army secretary Howard "Bo" Callaway of Georgia as his campaign chairman. Ford had decided to run for his own term, and the selection of the well-regarded Callaway was seen by many as a master stroke. Callaway was a native Georgian, talked Southern, and was a legitimate conservative who—it was hoped—would serve as Ford's Squanto to the native conservatives in their party. The move was also widely seen as an attempt to forestall the Gipper. More and more Southerners were actively touting a Reagan insurgency, but they'd heard nothing from California. Reagan was still on his mountaintop, undecided.

Callaway immediately mishandled the Rockefeller issue, telling reporters that the vice president was Ford's "No. 1 problem."[11] Callaway was forced to publicly backtrack on his comments, and his stock quickly fell in Washington political circles, as he too often spoke before organizing his thoughts.

One of Ford's "most active and vociferous critic[s]" was the South's "Mr. Republican," Clarke Reed, the chairman of the Mississippi GOP. According to the syndicated duo Rowland Evans and Robert Novak, Reed considered Ford "insufficiently conservative."[12]

Evans and Novak had the inside scoop on some of the early developments in the Ford campaign, including the role of the young and inexperienced Richard Cheney as the liaison between the White House and what eventually became known as "PFC": the President Ford Committee. Cheney was at the time deputy to Ford's nominal chief of staff, Donald Rumsfeld.

In May 1976, Reagan swept three Southern primaries, including Georgia, where he thrashed the incumbent Ford. Gingrich wisely remained neutral. He was looking out for his own political fortunes, and many Georgia Republicans—especially those in positions of power inside the party apparatus—were supporting Ford.

RNC chairman Bill Brock took a special interest in the young man's campaign. In College Park—a tiny suburb of Atlanta—Brock was the featured guest at a fifteen-dollar-per-head fund-raiser for Gingrich, which around two hundred people attended. Brock told the crowd, "I didn't come here to help a loser. Newt Gingrich is a winner."[13]

Brock had other things on his mind, though, including the Republican convention scheduled for the following month in Kansas City. The battle was yet to be decided, and Gerald Ford and Ronald Reagan were locked in a fight-to-the-death struggle for the party's nomination. Brock knew that if Ford was not nominated on the first ballot, then it would be "Katie bar the door" and Reagan's insurgents, in winning the nomination, would seize control of everything, including the RNC.

Jack Flynt still refused to debate his young opponent. Gingrich called him a "tough bird to flush into open ground," and Flynt's press aide, Martheana Burn, said flat-out that the man would not debate because "he has a great deal to lose." She was even more frank when she told the *West Georgian*, "Gingrich has no basis for debate because he has no platform." When a writer for the newspaper pointed out that if anybody had an opinion about everything, it was Gingrich, she replied there would be no debate because "that's the name of the game."[14]

Gingrich had sought the endorsement of the National Right to Work Committee, a powerful anti-compulsory union organization headquartered in Washington. But in their questionnaire, he answered two queries contrary to their policies: (1) regarding the forced unionization of farm workers (which Gingrich supported) and (2) regarding non-union construction workers' compulsory participation in common situs picketing (which Gingrich also supported). Gingrich did not receive the endorsement of the powerful organization, denying himself the contributions of businessmen and women who had fought the unions for years. Nonetheless, he concluded: "The right to work is a basic American freedom, and I will fight to preserve Georgia's right to work law. There is no reason to compel a person to join a union in order to earn a living."[15]

The candidate left few stones unturned. In late June 1976, he journeyed to Washington to attend a candidate workshop assembled by the National Republican Congressional Committee. But before heading north, he sent out dozens of letters ahead of him to political leaders and prominent journalists, reaching out for meetings with each. He was going to squeeze as much useful time as possible out of the trip. His letter to Robert Novak was addressed to "Robert Novack."[16]

He heard from an old friend, Nando Amabile, now with the Secret Service: "Dear Newt, Sixteen years ago you laid out to me a campaign for political life that included joining the Republican Party in Georgia and running for Congress." Amabile asked Gingrich to send him some material to update the files at the United States Information Agency (USIA), where the only information available on the long-plotting candidate was under the file "Knute Gringrich." The letter concluded, "I'm looking forward to seeing you when you visit Washington and to meeting your wife. If your schedule allows it, Helen and I would like to take you and your wife to dinner. My very best regards, Nando A. Amabile."[17]

His days on the campaign trail were frenetic and hectic, though Sundays were almost always reserved for Jackie and the girls.

Typically, his day would begin as early as 7:00 a.m. at a businessman's breakfast meeting. Woven into the schedule throughout the spring were his classes at West Georgia. Gingrich needed the money, and as a result his days were jam-packed, yet according to all staffers and observers he never lost his temper. Most campaign operatives had stories as long as their arms about freaked-out candidates who threw anything handy, screamed, yelled, and abused staff. One congressional aide remembered her old boss, Congressman Silvio Conte of Massachusetts, jumping up and down and screaming like a child when things did not go his way.

Gingrich spoke to the Amalgamated Clothing Workers, Lion's International, Masonic halls, the Jaycees, bank employees, the East Point

Women's Club. He excelled at speaking before groups—whether Girl Scouts or steel workers—though he never read from a prepared text. Instead, he would arrive a few minutes early and meet with the mill foreman or bank manager and listen to their issues and the issues of concern to the workers. He'd then go out and give an impressive talk, as if he knew all about their issues and their lives.

Direct mail was an important part of the campaign, as he couldn't raise the money to keep up with Flynt on television. In rural parts of the district there was no cable, and reception via antenna could be spotty at best. Letters went out to interest groups including "Doctors, Optometrists, Druggists, Dentists, Teachers" and the CWA—the Communications Workers of America.

"Environmentalists" were targeted for a letter signed by Alvin Toffler, patron saint of environmentalists and futurists.[18] Barry Goldwater came through the district in early October, not to stump for Gingrich per se, but to try to rally the few Republican faithful. Goldwater had carried Georgia in 1964 and he still carried a lot of sway in the Peach State. When "Big John" Connally, the former Texas governor, stumped explicitly for Gingrich in late October, the campaign did its best to roll out the red carpet for him. The mayor of Carrollton, Vince Cashem, even gave Big John a plaque, making him an honorary citizen.

Time was allocated for personal campaigning based on the population of the given county. In each, "total shaking hands" was calculated.[19]

In mid-October, the Association of Classroom Teachers met at Griffin High School for board business, but also to "Meet the District VI Congressional Candidates." Gingrich was in attendance, eager to meet his elder opponent in open combat. He had even prepared notes for his talk, unheard of for him. He wanted to address "corruption in Congress," the "Department of Education," and "revenue sharing to local schools." But Flynt was a no-show.[20]

Commercials were purchased during *The Sonny and Cher Show*, *The Bionic Woman*, *Charlie's Angels*, and the all-important college and professional football games. The campaign also bought less-expensive television spots during the Atlanta Flames hockey games and reruns of *Star Trek*.[21]

Fund-raising records were kept on paper, handwritten, listing each individual donor and how much and how recently he or she had given. Technologically speaking, it was all prehistoric, even by 1976 standards, but there was a passion and devotion to the candidate in Georgia's Sixth District that year that was not evident in most other races around the country. Gingrich simply inspired people, and hundreds contributed their hard-earned dollars in small amounts.

But once more, it was not to be.

Gingrich lost again to Flynt, this time by 5,132 votes. Gingrich had been stymied once again by national forces, reaching down to adversely affect the outcome of his race. Flynt had been carried—dragged—across the finish line by the favorite son of Georgia, Jimmy Carter.

While Carter won the national contest over Gerald Ford by the narrowest of margins in both the popular vote and the Electoral College, he took Georgia with over 65 percent of the popular vote.[22] In the Sixth District, Carter ran even stronger, and in so doing, brought in thousands of yellow-dog and straight-ticket Democratic voters.[23]

Gingrich had been at it for four years, day and night, morning 'til late. Twice he'd been offered tenure at West Georgia and twice he'd turned it down, not wanting to make a commitment he couldn't keep, and wanting to keep his political options open. In 1976, his political option had been thrown back in his face by the voters of the Sixth.

He still got a lot of feedback from supporters, such as this letter (which he has kept since the day after the '76 election):

> Dear Newt,
>
> I wish to express my appreciation for the hard, fair campaign you fought and lost. Although you may have lost yesterday, I believe the future will prove you right for standing up for your ideas. I'm sure your defeat was difficult to accept, but I still feel you did the right thing in taking on Jack Flynt again. God bless you, and the best wishes for whatever you may decide to do in the future.
>
> Sincerely,
> Pat A. Anders, M.D.[24]

But even knowing he had an eager constituency, after four hard years with nothing to show for it, a second eyelash defeat was enough to drive any man around the bend.

CHAPTER 3

THIRD-TIME CHARM OFFENSIVE

"Call me Newt."

1977–1978

After fighting off two furious efforts by Newt Gingrich to unseat him, Jack Flynt had had enough. Though still in his early sixties, the jowly Dixiecrat looked at least ten years older. Running twice against the much younger man had run him down and eventually out. In his twelve elections and twenty-four years serving in the US. House of Representatives, Flynt had often run unopposed. He was a card-carrying member of the old-boy network, with friends in Congress like Speaker Tip O'Neill to help him out here and associates in his district to look after his political affairs there.

"Congressmen are not bribed anymore. They simply have a lot of friends who are willing to help them out whenever they find it necessary," Gingrich said.[1]

But all that had come before had changed, gone with the wind. A second invasion of Yankees was taking place, and Georgia's politics was going through a reconstruction—so to speak. There'd been a dramatic influx of new voters into Georgia, especially suburban Atlanta, with different ideas and no connection to any new-boy network, much less an old one. Flynt's Jim Crow world had radically changed with the flood of carpetbaggers. Atlanta—and Georgia, along with the rest of the country—was changing.

The ways of Washington and Capitol Hill had also changed, and not to the liking of an old bull like Flynt. He had been made the chair of the House Ethics Committee, and in July 1977, his own Ethics Committee Counsel, Philip A. Lacovara, went public with his frustration over the slow pace of the committee's investigation into influence-peddling by South Korean lob-byists. In a memo "leaked" to the *New York Times,* Lacovara charged that "subpoenas, depositions and other testimony had been delayed."[2] Lacovara was no wet-behind-the-ears neophyte, having earned his spurs as a top Watergate investigator. He knew corruption when he saw it, and he saw it in Koreagate.

Flynt wasn't used to fighting with his own staff. Despite slow rolling even the investigation *into the investigation,* Flynt feared that Lacovara would resign in protest, bringing even more unwelcome attention on his somnolent committee. Lacovara resigned in July.

In August, a story appeared in which Flynt jetted off to Europe, osten-sibly to investigate Koreagate and interview that country's chief lobbyist, Tongsun Park, who was holed up in London. Though he was in London for eleven days, Flynt never laid eyes on Park. People saw the trip for what it was: a giant taxpayer-funded junket for a self-centered old man.

In August 1977, while Flynt was still ruminating about grappling again with Gingrich, the thirty-three-year-old gave a speech to the "newly formed Republican Luncheon Club," whose tongue-in-cheek theme was "Let's Quit Picking on Jack Flynt."[3] It was designed to tweak Flynt on ethics. Between the Gingrich assault at home and the changing culture of Washington, Flynt threw up his hands and quit.

Gingrich was also spearheading the efforts in Georgia to halt the Panama Canal Treaties, which would require the votes of the state's two senators, Sam Nunn and Herman Talmadge. The senators were being pulled in one direction by President Carter and in another by the citizens of their state. Grassroots resistance was strong, and Gingrich was using the issue to gear up for a third try at Congress.

He headed "Georgians Against the Proposed Panama Canal Treaties" and stumped the state in search of signers to a petition opposing them. At a press conference, Gingrich ripped into Carter's plan and called the docu-ments transferring Teddy Roosevelt's miracle "ill-conceived." Eventually, more than fifty thousand Georgians put their John Hancocks on the peti-tions, which were delivered to the state's congressional delegation.[4]

The drive gave Gingrich yet another platform from which to speak. He was invited to Fort McPherson by the American Defense Preparedness Association to speak to the membership about the treaties. The invitation, signed by one Henry Steadman, M.D., concluded brightly, "Dress for ladies is optional and for men business suits or military uniform. If you are married feel free to bring your wife—if not bring your lady friend."[5]

Newt was receiving fan mail from many people now, including an elderly woman, Martha Arnold, who effused over hearing him on a radio show with local personality Neal Boortz: "I am very proud to have my name on the petition to save our Panama Canal. I have supported Gov. Reagan all the way & am a reg. Republican."[6]

He also got more than his fair share of hate mail.

But it wasn't only Republicans opposed to the treaties. Numerous Democrats also stepped forward to support Gingrich's petition drive. In speech after speech, he lacerated the treaties and the process, saying it would "destroy public faith" and that the US State Department was "negotiating in secret and then leading us around in pageantry."[7]

In the spring of 1978, Jimmy Carter's long and hard work paid off, and the Panama Canal Treaties passed the Senate with the two-thirds approval required by the Constitution, albeit it by only two votes on one part and one vote on the other part. It was a politically costly victory, as a swath of Democratic senators—and some Republicans—would regret their decisions in 1978 and 1980. Many—including Carter himself—believed these losses were due in part to the hugely unpopular treaties.[8] Supporting the treaties would prove to be politically toxic, while opposing them—as did Ronald Reagan and Newt Gingrich—would be an elixir.

By the fall and winter of 1977, Republicans nationwide were beginning to feel their oats. Georgia's Republicans met in Macon to map out their 1978 offensive, but it would not be easy: Georgians still loved having their favorite son in the White House.[9] In contrast, freed from the burden of defending Richard Nixon and then Gerald Ford, national Republicans criticized Carter and the Democrats in Congress with abandon and relish, as appropriate to a party out of power, having neither responsibility nor authority. The two-party system the Founders had warned against flourished in America in 1977, as it had since the election of 1800, only thirteen years after they'd gathered in Philadelphia to create a Republic.

Even without an incumbent Flynt, Gingrich would have to fight again for the seat he'd coveted for more than four years. And this time, if he wanted to have the national impact he had so long desired, he would have to win. At one point, a National Republican Congressional Committee functionary, Wilma Goldstein, called the verbose man and told him in no uncertain terms, "You cannot send any more memos of national strategy until you win."[10]

On April 17, 1978, Newt Gingrich formally announced his third candidacy at the State Capitol at the curious hour of 2:30 in the afternoon. Letters went out to hundreds and he received good media coverage. A "Democrats for Gingrich" group was quickly assembled, headed by Kip Carter, a local party activist. He was no relation to the president, but nonetheless it was a great name among Georgia Democrats in 1978. Typewritten handbills were mass-produced and mass-distributed.[11]

Hoping to replace Flynt as the Democratic nominee was Virginia Shapard, a state senator in her early forties, a handsome if somewhat severe-looking woman, married to a successful businessman. With their four children, they lived in a nouveau riche, white-columned mansion in the Atlanta suburb of Griffin. One newspaper bitingly said of her, "If elected, she will be apparently leaving her four young children at home to be reared by the servants."[12]

Shapard was the only woman in the Georgia legislature—and its first female state senator—and cultivated the image as a crusading reformer. As such, she enjoyed highly favorable media coverage. Like so many others in the legislature, she was not a native Georgian, having been born on Long Island.[13]

The race for the Sixth had become one of the top House contests in the country, and money and endorsements rolled in for Gingrich. All the major contenders for the 1980 GOP nomination came in for the young hopeful. At one event, Gingrich introduced the ever-dependable "Big John" Connally, calling him a "top contender for the 1980 Republican Presidential nomination." Connally returned the praise, saying the young man had "depth and knowledge."[14] The event raised $7,000 for Newt's coffers.[15] The campaign's overall budget was projected to be around $225,000.

Gingrich started throwing elbows immediately. His campaign prepared and distributed a handbill, the top of which blared, "If you like welfare cheaters, you'll love Virginia Shapard."[16] The flyer assailed Shapard for a vote in the state senate against a bill that would have reduced corruption in the state's public assistance program. Shapard declaimed, "You understand the racial slur implications embodied in a flyer like this. It's just going out in the white community. That sort of campaigning is unconscionable."[17]

Federal and state welfare and food assistance programs had been widely known to be among the most poorly run and crime-ridden government programs around. Lurid stories filled the nation's newspapers about "Welfare Queens," including the one Ronald Reagan had been railing against for years, as documented by the *Washington Post*. With Americans' growing cynicism about government, the swelling popularity of tax cuts, and the deep wounds in the nation over the Panama Canal Treaties, the atmospherics were aiding candidates like Gingrich.

Also coming in to aid Gingrich was Carlyle Gregory, a young but battle-tested GOP operative from Virginia, where he'd already scored a number of GOP wins. Gingrich's two previous campaigns had been free-flowing affairs—not quite "Amateur Hour," but lacking the order needed for a first-rate congressional race. Gregory was tall, easygoing, and patient, with the understated sense of humor that he would need for the long days and nights of dealing with an undisciplined candidate who was bursting with nervous energy and ideas. The first thing Gregory did was change the colors of the campaign's posters from the environmental green to a patriotic blue.[18]

Senator Herman Talmadge had a full peach basket of problems in the last years of the 1970s. For years, he'd done politics in Georgia his own way and not always on the sunny side of the street. He was hammered over his votes in support of the Panama Canal Treaties, while also going through a very public, messy divorce from his wife, Betty, a true steel magnolia of the South. Betty Talmadge had first learned of her own divorce when her husband announced it on television.

The court ordered her to pay her husband $750,000 of the meat brokerage business she had nurtured into a multimillion-dollar company out of what was once a side family enterprise.[19] Understandably, this did not sit well with the soon-to-be-former Mrs. Herman Talmadge. From the front porch of the Talmadge family mansion, *Lovejoy*, situated on thirteen hundred acres, Betty dropped one ugly bomb after another on her estranged husband. She charged him with serial adultery and "habitual intoxication."[20]

It was pure soap opera, and the national media—especially the tabloids—ate it up; Betty Talmadge was great copy, as befitting any good Southern woman with a gracious exterior and faithless husband. In her spare time, she did needlepoint, including one pillow that read "Uppity Women Unite."[21] Still, Betty needed something else to do with her hands. She looked at the Sixth District, took the measure of Shapard and Gingrich, and plunged in, seeking the Democratic Party's nomination.

In the spring of '78, Gingrich latched on to the new tax cut proposal being offered by Congressman Jack Kemp of New York and Senator William Roth of Delaware.[22] While Gingrich, the two-time loser, could not compete with Kemp for national press attention, he was getting a healthy amount of his own coverage from the Washington scribes. In May, the nationally syndicated columnists Jack Germond and Jules Witcover devoted an entire piece to the Georgian, centered on his newfound love—as well as the Republicans'—for massive cuts in personal income taxes.

"It's the first time in my life that the Republicans have had a substantive issue on which they can outpromise the Democrats," he enthused to the columnists.[23]

Previously, Republicans had been the "eat your spinach" party of no fun. When they did support tax cuts, invariably these were focused on businesses, not individuals. The arcane world of balanced budgets and depreciation schedules and amortizations were what animated economic Republicans. Otherwise, Nixon had transformed the GOP's economic policy into a Keynesian one, once noxiously paraphrasing economist Milton Friedman's "We're all Keynesians now."[24]

Ronald Reagan, Kemp, and Gingrich begged to differ. Kemp's proposal—which he proposed as a "Jobs Creation Bill"—was first offered in Congress in the fall of 1976, but it went nowhere. After the defeat of Gerald Ford—in part because Carter had promised his own middle-class tax cut—Republicans, and especially Reagan, began taking a closer look at Kemp's seemingly wacky idea. Reagan embraced it during several radio broadcasts, and Kemp—along with *Wall Street Journal* columnist Jude Wanniski and the father of the idea, Dr. Arthur Laffer—expounded on it day after day.

The selling point to the plan was that it would not cost the government anything, as illustrated in Laffer's Curve, which essentially showed that at a certain point in the raising of taxes, government revenue fell because so much money was taken out of the private sector. Under the Laffer plan, when taxes were reduced to a certain point, economic expansion would produce more revenue for the government than what it had lost in the first place with the tax cuts.

But that was the inside aspect of selling the plan. For the rest of the country, what caught their eye was the simplicity of the notion: cutting taxes across the board by 33 percent for all Americans in all tax brackets.

Kemp was the GOP's Prometheus. He'd brought fire to Republican kind, but more importantly he represented a new breed of conservative, always on offense, never on defense—familiar territory for the old quarterback. A new conservative movement was in full flower, exploding with new ideas on economic, social, defensive, and foreign policies. In district after district, GOP candidates like Gingrich were "preaching Lafferism and fealty to the Kemp-Roth bill."[25] Kemp signed an endorsement letter for Gingrich, sending it to thousands.[26]

Gingrich was also making corruption in Washington a central piece of his reformist message. He held a press conference in East Point where he offered seven proposals to "clean up congress." Not only did he go after elected representatives, he also targeted for criticism the Clerk of the House. "The Clerk of the House secretly intervened in a grand jury investigation by seeking to block a subpoena for a suspected member's personnel files. In short, the Clerk of the House was trying to shield a Congressman from a criminal investigation," said Gingrich, righteously indignant.[27] It may have been the first time such a thing had ever been raised in a political campaign.

The GOP's party committees—the Republican National Committee, under the tutelage of Bill Brock, and the National Republican Congressional Committee, under the exuberant leadership of Congressman Guy Vander Jagt—had revolutionized their organizations in the post-Watergate years. Though only moderately conservative, both men reached out to conservatives like Gingrich and other aspirants in order to help them win in 1978 and beyond.

The Local Elections Division of the RNC took their show on the road, traveling to countless towns and cities to train managers, fund-raisers, and organizational men and women. In Georgia—at the Holiday Inn at the Atlanta Airport—young GOP operatives—including Ed Goeas, Ed Blakely, Dennis Whitfield—spent countless hours in their own smoke-filled rooms giving instructions on how to win Republican races. All in all, the schools and their young teachers were impressive. The cost to attend for the aspiring operatives and supplicants was ten dollars, just enough to cover the box lunch served during classes.[28]

Though becoming something of a political celebrity in Georgia, and earning more attention nationally, Gingrich was not going to be handed the 1978 Republican nomination. He drew two primary opponents, Mike Ester of Atlanta and Dave Barrow of Bowden. That he had primary opponents in 1978, unlike in 1974 and 1976, was indicative of the rising hopes and chances of the GOP. On the Democratic side of the ledger, Virginia Shapard and Betty Talmadge were not alone either. State senator Peter Banks jumped in, as did another Atlanta resident, Doug Steele, as well as a public school teacher from Concord named Jim Huffman.[29] Also, there was internal dissent at the NRCC, some arguing against backing Gingrich a third time. Gingrich offered his own view for this Washington opposition to his candidacy: "Because I was a troublemaker. Because I was not them," he said.[30]

Racial attitudes among Georgia voters were changing rapidly, as the declining political fortunes of one statewide Democratic candidate demonstrated. Under the protection of the Federal Communications Commission, politicians' speech was ruled "protected," which allowed Democratic gubernatorial contender J. B. Stoner to run TV ads asking for white votes to stop "the n----s."[31] He'd run in 1974 and received more than seventy thousand votes in Georgia, mortifying millions of others in the state.

Stoner was at it again, running in the Democratic primary for governor in 1978. "His percentage in this primary will be taken as an indicator of the extent of hard-core racist sentiment in the state," said the *New York Times*.[32]

Stoner was decimated, garnering only 5 percent of the vote.[33]

In direct contrast, in his 1978 congressional campaign, Gingrich was actively wooing blacks in Georgia and making impressive headway. From the beginning of his political career he'd always had terrific relations with the black-owned *Atlanta Daily World*. He named Gloria Lovett, a prominent African American in the district, as his "Assistant Campaign Director."[34]

Gingrich called for "bi-partisan townhall meetings" in which all the candidates would appear jointly, twenty-eight in all. He pointed out that since Georgia residents did not register to vote by party and could vote in any primary, it would "give the voters a chance to measure every candidate."[35] What the canny Gingrich did not say was that he was extremely comfortable in such settings; he would polish off all his opponents and scoop up more primary votes for himself. He had no takers on his seemingly magnanimous offer.

He also made frequent mention on the stump that his wife, Jackie, was a public schoolteacher and that he, Gingrich, had attended public schools his whole life and then taught at a state university. However, he did oppose tax credits for parents sending their children to private or parochial schools. He also told professional women's groups he opposed the Equal Rights Amendment, supporting instead the enforcement of laws already on the books. Before one such group, he was asked about the plight of "battered women," but was stumped on how the private sector could address this issue besides simply calling attention to it.[36]

The appeal of Kemp-Roth across the country and in Gingrich's Georgia should have come as little surprise. Tax revolt had been brewing for a while, and it finally exploded into the national media and the national consciousness.

In June 1978, with the landslide passage of Proposition 13, a massive cut in California's skyrocketing property taxes, shouts for tax-cutting initiatives echoed across the country. More than a dozen measures similar to "Prop. 13" sprang up. Gas taxes were cut by referendum in Missouri, and citizens groups everywhere pressured their legislators to cut taxes and hold the line on spending. Gingrich had wisely recognized the national mood and had positioned himself at the head of the mob—at least in Georgia. Just a few years earlier he had turned up his nose at tax cuts, like most Republicans, seeing them as irresponsible.

Ministers across the state urged their congregations to go out and vote, and in the August GOP primary, Gingrich easily waxed his two opponents. Because he received more than 50 percent of the primary field, he would not have to worry about a runoff. Things were a bit dicier for Virginia Shapard on the Democratic side. She finally won the nomination in a runoff, but only by the margin of 52–48, leaving her weakened for the fall match against the energetic college professor.

Gingrich was seizing the "jobs issue" for himself, long the domain of the Democratic Party. A newspaper ad that ran across the district read:

Newt Gingrich will fight for 1,200,000 jobs.

How? The same way President John F. Kennedy did: by a drastic cut in taxes. Newt supports the Kemp-Roth tax cut bill, which would cut personal income taxes by 30 percent. Norman Ture, an economist who helped design the Kennedy tax cut, estimates the Kemp-Roth bill would create 1,200,000 new jobs the year it's passed.[37]

Mindful of his still heavily Democratic state, the ad never mentioned Gingrich's Republican affiliation and indeed, across the bottom, made an open appeal to "Split your ticket—the difference is worth it."[38]

Shapard did manage to raise one issue that seemed to catch Gingrich off guard. The "Dorchester Fund" was a concept that had been put together the year before by a group of investors to help fund a novel Gingrich had been working on about the Soviets attacking Western Europe. Raising the issue of the fund's existence set off Gingrich, who angrily denied any impropriety, saying it was a "perfectly legal corporation." Some wondered why he responded so hotly if it was all on the up-and-up.[39]

But the "Dorchester Fund" was a rare issue in which Gingrich was on the defensive. In the much more important issue of "listening to the black community," Gingrich was on offense, while his opponent simply was not on the field. RNC chairman Bill Brock had obsessed for two years about recruiting more black Americans to the GOP. Gingrich was actively wooing the black community, while Senator Shapard missed several important forums organized in the district by the minority population.

"I think this shows how much Virginia Shapard really listens to the black community," Gingrich noted acidly at his opponent's no-show.[40] Not missing a trick, his campaign took out newspaper ads, scoring Shapard for missing meetings she'd agreed to attend with African Americans. The ad, which carried a photo of Newt talking with a middle-aged black woman, again did not mention his political affiliation. A columnist for the *Atlanta Constitution*, Lee May, took note of Gingrich's efforts with the African American community:

He is working black areas . . . like a certified Democrat. He goes to churches, talks at black gatherings, walks the streets . . . Gingrich, when he came by, looked the picture of new politics. Not like the typical

Republican at all. The "right" haircut, just the proper length. No white socks; his were black . . . [Shapard] doesn't even know her way to Marko's Lounge, a black nightclub on Cambellton Road. At least Gingrich has come that far.[41]

Newt's wardrobe had improved greatly since 1976. The used car salesman ties, shirts, and suits had been banished (hopefully burned), and the long sideburns had been eighty-sixed, along with the steel-rim glasses. He was now photographed in attire befitting a young politician on the go: red ties and solid blue, gray, or black suits. Gingrich had also lost weight—something he'd struggled with his whole life—and presented a more "light and lively" image. Still, years later he joshed, "One of the discouraging realities of life is that diet and exercise works."[42]

He was an evolving young man, and the media took notice. The *West Georgia News*, under the headline "A New Newt Gingrich Arises," opined, "We may have seen a new Newt Gingrich the other day. A Newt Gingrich not ranting about a canal . . . but addressing himself with skill to the issues that matter of most importance to the people . . . taxes, inflation and their pocketbooks."[43] Said his former colleague, Steve Hanser, "I think he was maturing. I think [he'd] become very good at what he did. He had a real knack with people."[44] Still, there was the occasional rumor about Newt and other women, including his campaign driver.[45]

Two days before the election, the *Washington Post* said Shapard "has fewer liabilities and is favored."[46] It would not be easy for Gingrich, as the district was still heavily Democratic, and Democrats—including Shapard—had won for years by simply running against the Republican Party, the party of William Tecumseh Sherman, the party of Reconstruction, the party of Lincoln.

Bad blood curdled between Gingrich and Shapard. In the few public forums at which she would agree to appear with him, Shapard sarcastically called him "Professor Gingrich," and he returned the fire, calling her "Student Shapard."[47]

By campaign's end, it had taken an especially ugly turn. In a joint appearance before the Chamber of Commerce, Shapard called Gingrich "duplicitous" and he called her a "liar." Her beef was with his television commercials, which accused her of being "soft on welfare cheaters"; his beef was that she had cancelled a joint television appearance at the last minute, claiming she wanted to reschedule it. She claimed *he* had wanted to reschedule it.

The repeated charge by Gingrich that she was ducking him was a bit of campaign theater; they had met in debate and town halls more than a dozen times.[48] In yet another joint appearance, Shapard walked into the lions' den by going to Carrollton, Newt's home turf. The crowd was loaded with Newt fans who pummeled the poor woman repeatedly over her husband's wealth.[49] Newt revealed his net worth as a paltry $10,000.[50] Shapard refused to reveal her and her husband's net worth. This also became a festering issue. When asked about the "negativism" of his campaign, Gingrich replied, "She started the negativism."[51]

His campaign issued release after release, blasting her over her opposition to tax cuts. She repeatedly called them a fraud, and Gingrich was only too delighted to have to defend them.

The Gingrich campaign was well run and disciplined—if a bit formulaic—but it was not without its moments. Newt gave a speech to a local College Republican group in which he leveled the standing GOP leadership and the makeup of the party, charging that the Republican Party had not had a "competent national leader in his lifetime." He said the GOP did not need "another generation of cautious, prudent, careful, bland, irrelevant, quasi-leaders."[52] The GOP chairman of the Sixth, Robert D. T. Simpkins, went public and lashed Gingrich for his intemperate remarks.

Though Simpkins threatened action, Gingrich was unimpressed and unrepentant. He issued a response, saying, "I am afraid my opponents don't understand the critical nature of this election."[53]

On November 5, the Republican-leaning *Atlanta Daily World* issued its final judgment and warmly endorsed Gingrich. The black-owned paper had endorsed him twice before, so this was expected. Still, in a long editorial, the paper said:

> Gingrich is a man who has worked closely with the people and he is a man of compassion and understanding of the needs and aspirations of the mass of people—blacks and whites . . . Irresponsible attempts are made to smear Gingrich with a racist charge. We have known this man many years and he is no more racist than the editor of this newspaper . . . Let's vote

for a candidate rather than a political party label on Tuesday. We endorse Newt for Congress and urge our readers to vote for him.[54]

After three campaigns, Newt had become a one-name celebrity, at least in the greater Atlanta area. His full-page newspaper ads were prevalent, each ad featuring a shopping cart, an economic symbol reminding voters of the spiraling cost of food. In one, bags full of groceries were seen shrinking from 1968 to 1978, creatively illustrating the cost of inflation and how consumers' purchasing power had shrunk dramatically. Many of the ads proclaimed, "Newt's family is like your family," and featured a beaming Gingrich along with his wife, Jackie, and their two pretty daughters, eleven-year-old Jackie Sue and fifteen-year-old Kathy.[55]

Jackie Battley of Columbus, Georgia, had been Newt's high school math teacher, seven years his senior. She had received an undergraduate degree in math from Auburn at a time when female mathematicians were rare. Gingrich had pursued her until she finally relented and married the much younger man. To all, she was the model of class and dignity, his best confidant and advisor, a tireless campaigner who by 1978 had battled serious health issues, weight problems, and rumors about the state of their marriage. But she was pleasant with a ready smile. She was an energetic campaigner who was Newt's greatest asset. She signed the ubiquitous "wife letters" that every campaign utilized in 1978.

With all the public appearances and media coverage she was receiving, Jackie had become something of a local personality herself. She was also a trusted advisor to Newt, according to campaign aide Chip Kahn.[56]

She took it all in stride. "I have Newt's schedule stuck to the refrigerator door at home," she shared. "I keep up with him that way." She only asked that when she was needed on the trail the campaign give her a little forewarning, "So that I can get the housekeeping done before I have to leave."[57]

On the weekend before the election, Newt appeared at the Atlanta International Raceway and was endorsed by Richard Petty, stock car racer and beloved son of the South. Shapard countered with Rosalynn Carter, who came in to campaign for the Democratic nominee at the Atlanta State Market, though some of the media and the locals were offended by the fifty-dollar-per-head charge to attend the event.[58] On the same day, Jackie Gingrich sent out invitations far and wide for voters to come to the Gingrich home for a "bring-your-own-peanut-butter-sandwich open house."[59]

He might not have shown it, but deep down Gingrich knew that if he failed on this, his third try for Congress, he would probably be through as a candidate. Everything was at stake and he threw himself into the campaign. He joked to a group of teachers in Fayetteville, "I probably have the biggest incentive to win. I need the job."[60]

Shapard's team was biting their nails. "I'm worried," said Mrs. Shapard's chief campaign advisor, Ray Abernarthy. "Anybody with any sense would be."[61]

Just a few days before the November election, a columnist for the *Clayton News-Daily* spied in Gingrich the strengths and weaknesses that had eluded most others:

> Gingrich is an unusual combination of political sophistication and unorthodoxy. An academic, he is fond of alluding to the political theory of Thomas Jefferson just seconds after he has told a calculated and corny "preacher" joke. He woos the support of blacks and conservationists while . . . calling loudly for tax cuts and budget trimming, two subjects which have generally been anathema to minority interests.
>
> More than Shapard, he seems to genuinely enjoy the chess aspect of campaigning, and nobody could deny he is a bold player . . .
>
> But if he wakes up a loser on Wednesday . . . [h]e will no longer have the sustenance of the media's attention, which he seems to thrive on. And he will face the almost insurmountable stigma of being a perennial loser, Georgia's own Harold Stassen.
>
> Either candidate could become a congressman of national prominence immediately, just because of who they are.[62]

On election night, November 7, the returns trickled in slowly with the Sixth bringing up the rear due to its heavily rural voting. A reporting error by the Associated Press mistakenly gave six thousand more votes to Shapard than she had won, and this added to the drama and nail-biting of the evening. The error was later corrected.

After a long night, Gingrich finally prevailed, winning 54.4 percent of the vote: 47,078 votes to Shapard's 39,451. The third time was the charm.

Just after 11:30, Gingrich said, "We're now claiming victory. We're running consistently ahead of our vote in '76." He was thirty-five years old.

Chip Kahn was going through a terrible time. His wife, Mary, had delivered a healthy baby just before the election who died a few days later of a rare infection. The night of the win, a grieving Kahn spoke to Newt from the hospital, who brusquely brushed aside his attempt at joshing him about a job in Washington. Kahn had loaned the campaign money, had devoted himself to the effort, and, while it was loud where Gingrich was and he may have misunderstood what Kahn said, he never forgave Gingrich. Later, the campaign took up a collection for Kahn to help with expenses, but he wasn't hired for Gingrich's congressional office.[63] After moving to Washington, Kahn and Gingrich would have dinner together, all friendly and nice, but he never went to work for Gingrich. They bumped into each other several years later and Gingrich was cordial but Kahn was thinking, "Forget you." Still, Kahn was later invited to Gingrich's wedding to his second wife, Marianne, in Ohio, and he attended. Kahn recalled the wedding was a modest affair.[64]

Around 11:45 p.m., Virginia Shapard conceded. "We have lost, but we haven't really lost because all of you people have worked so hard . . . We ran this campaign with dignity."[65] She was bitter, offering no congratulations to Gingrich, but instead attacked his campaign.

Fate had lent Newt a hand. On Election Day, it had rained for the first time in "49 days," as Shapard wryly noted. "All my polls showed I would do well with older voters, and they're not as likely to go out in bad weather." She was also saddled with a huge campaign debt—more than $100,000—which FEC law said her husband could not help her pay off.[66]

Gingrich, for his part, did not mention or congratulate Shapard in his victory comments. He was the only Republican congressional candidate to prevail in Georgia in 1978.

An eclectic party ensued at the Atlanta Airport Holiday Inn:

Eskimos were conspicuously absent, but just about every other minority and majority seemed to have a representative at Newt Gingrich's third biennial post-election party. Scattered about the room were blacks and whites, overdressed Republicans and underdressed Democrats, old people, little kids, an Oriental woman, a belly dancer and two men with broken feet.[67]

A shopping cart had been the symbol of the Gingrich campaign, and now one was wheeled in front of the stage from which he spoke. Jackie and daughters Kathy and Jackie Sue beamed, even if the swarm of people and media cameras overwhelmed them a bit. Behind them on stage, a large blackboard—a subtle reminder of Gingrich's now previous profession—spelled out the math; it all added up to a spectacular win for "Professor Gingrich" and a startling defeat for "Student Shapard." An acceptance speech had been prepared, but as usual Gingrich preferred to wing it: "We need you to be the same angry customer about government as you would any other business that didn't give you your money's worth."[68]

The belly dancer brought her own record player. Her presence became an issue as some Gingrich aides fretted over how to get the press to ignore an exotic and beautiful woman in a sultry harem outfit as she twirled around, making suggestive eye contact with a room full of middle-aged Baptist men. The media did not ignore the woman.

Talking to reporters after becoming the second Republican ever elected in the region, Gingrich emphasized his own family values. He said the first thing he was doing was going to Disney World with his wife and daughters.

The first thing he did the next day was go to the Atlanta Airport to shake hands with the morning shift at Eastern Airlines, thanking the voters who had voted for him. He did likewise at the Ford Motor plant in Hapesville and at Delta. He also "stood at the red light at the Arrowood Shopping Center in Jonesboro for two hours during rush hour traffic shaking hands."[69] Some of the Atlanta media were on hand. Gingrich, ebullient, told them it was "fun to be a celebrity," even as one of the workers called him "Senator."

"I am fairly unique," he held. "I am a strange guy named Newt Gingrich who was born in Pennsylvania and grew up everywhere [his father was in the military] . . . [I am] a college teacher who is a Republican who was willing to run three times and I think that makes me weird."[70]

A day after his big upset, the Atlanta Journal, which had endorsed Shapard over Gingrich, did a 180 and issued an editorial praising him: "So we believe that in choosing Gingrich . . . the voters . . . are sending to Congress a man who will serve them well and who offers a real hope for a new era of effective Republicanism in Georgia."[71] The *Constitution* was also conciliatory.[72]

At a post-election meeting with African American leaders from the Atlanta metropolitan area, Gingrich told them, "Call me Newt."[73] He held a press conference on Wednesday and proclaimed, "You have a whole generation of born-again tax cutters."[74]

Gingrich had won against all the headwinds of 1978 Georgia. President Carter was still hugely popular in the state. Of Georgia's ten congressional districts, five Democratic incumbents ran unopposed. In "four others, they won by margins of 82–18, 77–23, 76–24, and 67–33."[75]

The GOP had a good if not great off-year election. It picked up a handful of congressional seats, three senators—putting it at 41—enough that they could, at least in theory, mount a filibuster. Overlooked was the dramatic impact of the Panama Canal Treaties. Virtually every senator who had voted for the Panama Canal Treaties, regardless of party, lost their primary or reelection bid.

Post-election political prognosticators were all over the lot about the future of the GOP. A Washington insider, David Gergen, writing for the *Washington Post*, urged the Republican Party to embrace "restraint." He criticized Republicans like Gingrich who had campaigned heavily on Kemp-Roth and said, "Outside of a handful of purists, there is now almost universal agreement that the evangelical crusade Republicans launched this fall on behalf of a one-third cuts in federal taxes . . . was a political blunder of the first magnitude." The former Nixon aide recommended that the GOP "jettison" Kemp-Roth "altogether."[76]

It wasn't going to work out that way at all.

PART II

THE CONGRESSMAN

(1979–1989)

CHAPTER 4

THE FRESHMAN

*"I'm willing to be ineffective in the short run if it means
in the long run, we're able to build a majority."*

1979

Newt Gingrich hadn't even been sworn into his first term in Congress, but that didn't stop him from gaining a little national publicity. In December 1978, a month and change after winning the election, he called for the expulsion of Michigan congressman Charles Diggs, along with Pennsylvania congressman Daniel Flood, both mossy-backed Democrats. Government corruption was as old as the Republic, and a time-honored tradition in Congress, as witnessed in the recent ABSCAM probe by the FBI—using agents wearing burnooses, posing as Arab sheiks, and carrying briefcases full of cash—rooting out more corrupt members of Congress.

In one memorable videotaped scene, a Republican member of Congress, Richard Kelly of Florida, was seen stuffing the cash into his pockets and under his pants while another congressman, Mike Myers of Pennsylvania, got into a shoving match with his aide over who would take the bribe and how much.

Kelly was the only Republican snared in ABSCAM; all the others were Democrats, nearly all from either New Jersey or Pennsylvania. Congressman John Murtha of Pennsylvania almost took the cash, too, but balked at the last minute, though he kept the door open for future discussion by indicating that he wanted to "do business" with the sheiks in the future. When the charges were handed down, Murtha was listed as an "unindicted co-conspirator"—a term Americans had become familiar with during Watergate—and only saved his political hide when he turned stool pigeon for the state against two of his indicted colleagues.[1]

Capitol Hill also remained awash in "Koreagate" rumors, in which members of Congress were taking cash and gifts from a South Korean lobbyist to gain "influence."[2] Attention focused on Tongsun Park, lobbyist for the South Korean government, but investigators believed the Congress-buying spree went all the way to the president of South Korea.[3]

When it came to the corruption of the era, Flood and Diggs were no pikers. Flood was standing trial for accepting bribes totaling $100,000, and Diggs had already been convicted on twenty-nine counts of receiving kickbacks from his staff in the amount of $60,000.[4] Both Flood and Diggs had been reelected despite the stench around them. Both were Democrats. Congressman-elect Gingrich was taking on the majority party and the insular congressional establishment. He wasn't even in office yet.

"I've been in Washington and heard guys the last two weeks saying you've got to play along and that he [Diggs] isn't doing anything so bad, and he needed the money. That's insanity—how can you say guys who make the laws should be excused from felony counts," Gingrich said.[5]

Ironically, Jack Flynt, whom Gingrich had lost to twice and whom he would soon succeed, was still the lame-duck chair of the House Ethics Committee for another month. Since he was an ally of House Speaker Tip O'Neill, and since many of the House members charged with corruption were Democrats, clean government groups charged Flynt with sweeping most of his committee's investigations under the carpet.[6] No crusading reformer, Flynt understood a previous House Speaker's edict, "to get along, go along."

Of the initial Koreagate investigation beginning in 1977, Flynt dissembled to reporters, "I can't say anymore about it, because it's an element of an ongoing investigation."[7] Over the charge that dozens of members were on the take from the South Korean government, he simply said he'd "uncovered no evidence to support such figures."[8] Flynt, however, promised to issue subpoenas for "persons with Asian names."[9]

Flynt was also disinterested in looking deeper into the charges against Diggs and Flood. Diggs was black, which made the whole thing even touchier. The entire Congressional Black Caucus—all sixteen members—dug in their heels in defense of their friend.

Gingrich had a lot to learn about Washington.

His friends at the black-owned *Atlanta Daily World* gave him a warm sendoff, noting he was "the first Republican to represent the Sixth . . .

since the Reconstruction Period." Gingrich hosted a breakfast for around a hundred fellow Georgians, "mostly a cross section of Black leaders" that "were apparently impressed by this freshman congressman . . . This is an unprecedented breakfast. In our 50-year-history we do not remember any other Congressman or U.S. Senator coming . . . to host a meal . . . so soon after taking office."[10]

It was actually worse than the *Daily World* realized. In all the years Jack Flynt had been a part of Georgia's congressional delegation, he never once held a leadership breakfast, because he refused to sit at the same table with Andrew Young, the black congressman from Atlanta.[11]

Gingrich pledged his support for a holiday for the slain Dr. Martin Luther King Jr. and introduced his interracial staff to the breakfast meeting. The newspaper was filled with comments from constituents and community leaders praising the young former professor, though he did slip into a bit of pander-mode when he "lamented the lack of black pictures in Washington. 'There are 861 statues and paintings in the Capitol. There are zero black ones.'"[12]

Gingrich's '78 election was a major breakthrough for the GOP in Georgia, and yet a number of local Republicans were disquieted by his campaign. Some Republicans had been rumored to be miffed and quietly voted for Virginia Shapard. He ruffled a few more feathers by passing over both Carlyle Gregory and Chip Kahn for the top position in his congressional office, opting instead for a young man by the name of Bob Weed, who Gingrich told the *Newman Times-Herald* was the "most successful campaign manager in Virginia Republican history."[13]

Gingrich was also almost obsessive about his House taping machine, into which he recorded his thoughts and musings almost daily. Staff were carefully assigned to take care of the tapes and detailed memos were handed out to insure the taping machine operated smoothly.[14]

The tapings would eventually be used as briefing tapes on campaigns and campaign strategies that were widely distributed to GOP challengers. Part of his team at the time was an obscure pollster, Dick Morris, years before he became a close advisor to Bill Clinton. Gingrich was obsessed with many things, but most especially the politics of politics.[15]

He also authored a very detailed and comprehensive memo describing left-wing "smears," including those against Robert Bork, Ed Meese, and Ray

Donovan. Understanding how it worked and the mechanics behind such campaigns "will then help prove our point that a group of vicious, irresponsible, and morally corrupt power hungry left wingers are willing to say and do anything to retain their power against the will of the American people," Gingrich wrote.[16]

The 96th Congress, which arrived in January 1979, was impressive. Along with Gingrich, other newly minted congressmen included Richard B. Cheney of Wyoming, Geraldine Ferraro of New York, Phil Gramm of Texas, Don Albosta of Michigan, Tony Coelho of California, Olympia Snowe of Maine, Richard Shelby of Alabama, Jim Sensenbrenner of Wisconsin, Bill Nelson of Florida, Ron Paul of Texas, Kent Hance (who had defeated a young George W. Bush) also of Texas, and several others who would go on to political fame.[17]

The class of '78 also contained some real "Peter Principle" politicians, including Democrat Michael Barnes of Maryland and Republicans Jon Hinson of Mississippi, Dan Crane of Illinois, and Joel Deckard of Indiana.[18] All would go on to embarrass their constituents.

The section at the back of the House floor where the members from the South gathered was inelegantly referred to as "Redneck Row."[19] Newton Leroy Gingrich joined Redneck Row on January 3, 1979.[20] The overwhelming numbers of this informal group's members from below the Mason-Dixon line were still Democrats, but conservative in many regards.

Gingrich won appointment to the Committee on House Administration. There he found himself at an immediate political advantage: House Administration had supervision over the in-House budget. Putting Gingrich on this committee was akin to letting a fox loose in the henhouse.

The bureaucracy of Washington—including Capitol Hill—had grown exponentially over the previous decade. A chronic critic of wasteful government spending, the legendary Democrat Bill Proxmire, a senator from Wisconsin, "noted that over the past decade, the number of congressional aides had increased from 10,700 to 18,400 and the congressional payroll soared from $150 million to $550 million." Proxmire, who sponsored the monthly "Golden Fleece Award" for the most wasteful government program, said, "Senators and staff are stumbling over themselves."[21] Gingrich would follow Proxmire's lead in the House: "I'll use this committee to carry on my fight to clean up Congress and help lower fiscal spending."[22]

Gingrich settled into his duties, but was keeping up his relentless pursuit of Charles Diggs, a task made easier by his role as Ethics Committee chairman and the departure from Congress of his predecessor Jack Flynt. The new congressman from the Sixth District was the only member of the Georgia delegation supporting expulsion. Tip O'Neill and the Democratic House continued to drag their feet. In mid-January 1979, only days after being sworn in, Gingrich was circulating a letter asking "the House Ethics Committee to investigate whether there are grounds to expel Diggs from Congress."[23] Fourteen Republicans signed up; so, too, did Congressman Dick Gephardt of Missouri, an up-and-coming Democrat.[24]

In a moment of incredible audacity, he sent another letter directly to Diggs, threatening him with expulsion if he tried to cast a vote on the House floor. Gingrich had been in Congress for less than a month.

Days later, the upstart Georgian was published in the op-ed pages of the *Washington Post*, making his case against Diggs, pointing out that the Detroit congressman had already "been tried, convicted, and sentenced to three years in prison," yet was still roaming the halls of Congress and still voting. "Frankly, I don't think we can tolerate the idea of a convicted felon making law."[25]

In his original conviction, "a jury of 10 black women, one black man and a white man" convicted him "on 29 felony charges."[26] Opinion in the African American community was sharply divided. In Diggs's hometown of Detroit, the Reverend Charles Williams of the Saint Mark Baptist Church supported Diggs's expulsion and sent a group to Washington to meet with their congressman and call for him to step down. Conversely, the head of the National Postal Alliance, Robert L. White, supported Diggs. Some noted, "The only problem is that if Diggs serves time, then his constituents will not be represented during that time."[27]

Congressman Parrin Mitchell of Maryland, former head of the Black Caucus, had his own take on representation: "The will of the people—that's what the House is all about. If they want to elect Hitler or a Klansman, it's their right."[28]

In closing his piece in the *Post*, Gingrich quoted from a letter Jefferson had written to John Adams, extolling the new American Republic and saying that it would be "founded on principles of honesty." He also cautioned that "either force or corruption has been the principle of every modern government."[29] The short piece meandered off the topic of Diggs; clearly Gingrich was attempting to impress Washington's denizens with his grasp of history.

Capitol Hill was still paying only slight attention to Gingrich, but this would change quickly. In order to redress the inequity of the exemption congressmen enjoyed by not having to participate in the bankrupt Social Security system, Gingrich fulfilled a campaign promise and introduced his first bill, calling for an end to the preferential system.

"The first bill I'm introducing requires Congressmen to pay their fair share of the Social Security tax they passed."[30] The scheme Congress had come up with for itself was appalling, to say the least. Under their own privileged system, federal employees—including elected officials—paid in $26,000 over their lifetime and once they retired, would receive $22,000 per year for the rest of their lives. The crassly generous returns were not based on superior investments; instead, they were subsidized by the US taxpayer. "If they paid it themselves, they might understand the pain it causes hard-working families when they are hit by both inflation and Social Security tax increases."[31]

Leading by example, Gingrich opted out of the corrupt system even though, as a young man, he said it "might cost me from $130,000 to $300,000 if I'm reelected and live a long life."[32]

He introduced it on the House floor as H.R. 2339 and "was referred to the Committee on Ways and Means."[33] The bill covered only twenty-nine lines on the House document, but to the entrenched establishment it might as well have been a declaration of war.

He also co-sponsored H.R. 1598 at the end of January, "To provide for permanent tax rate reductions for individuals." The bill was sponsored by Jack Kemp and co-sponsored by several dozen of the best and brightest of the upcoming crop of young conservatives in the House, including Barry Goldwater Jr. of California.[34]

On the evening of Friday, January 26, 1979, two years after his unhappy and partial term as vice president ended, Nelson Aldrich Rockefeller was unexpectedly struck down by a heart attack.[35] He'd been governor of New York for four terms and had sought the GOP presidential nomination, sometimes desultorily, sometimes aggressively, in 1960, 1964, and 1968. His candidacies, except in 1964, were mostly a figment of the New York and Washington political establishment's imagination. He was, in fact, too liberal, too overbearing, too Eastern Establishment, too rich, too cosmopolitan, and too divorced. His second marriage in 1963 to Margaretta "Happy" Large Fitler Murphy—who had been betrothed to an old friend—and her early pregnancy had done nothing to improve his chances. Nor had it endeared him to the increasingly conservative GOP that loved Barry Goldwater.

The evening of his death, Rocky had dined with Happy, and returned—it was reported at the time—to his office at Rockefeller Center, ostensibly to work on an art book. Rumors swirled around Republican circles that Rocky was really working on his young assistant, with whom he had been having an affair. He had first met the young woman when she was hired on his press staff while he was serving as vice president to Gerald Ford.

Rocky had had a major coronary while *in flagrante delicto* with his young aide. She was much smaller than he and, for a time, she could not get out from under him. Finally she did, but called neither the police nor an ambulance. Instead, she called her girlfriend, Ponchitta Pierce, a New York television personality.[36] Reports at the time indicated that although he was first stricken at 10:15 p.m., the assistant did not call for an ambulance until 11:16.[37]

Rockefeller's limo driver had dropped him off at 25 West 54th Street around 10:00 p.m. Media reports initially said Rocky was at his office at Rockefeller Center that night, but in fact, the ambulance found the stricken man at 13 West 54th Street, next door to the woman's home at 25 West 54th Street. Rockefeller owned both buildings.[38]

A longtime Rockefeller aide, Hugh Morrow, appeared and tried to assemble what was left of the old man's dignity before the paramedics, the police, and the cream of the New York media showed up. However, by the time they arrived, he was dead.

Rocky was cremated eighteen hours after his death, the family refused an autopsy, and the young woman went into hiding.[39] At 4:00 a.m., reporters knocked on her door, but she would not speak to them except to confirm that Morrow was in her apartment, obviously trying to clean up the public relations mess left for him by his old boss.[40]

The twenty-five-year-old, who that night was seen wearing a "long black evening gown," melted into the ether of history. She was to receive $50,000 and a Manhattan townhouse in Rockefeller's will.[41]

A comedy of errors ensued as no one seemed to get the story right as to how and under what circumstances Rocky died. Both the young woman and Pierce were put under what amounted to house arrest by the family's many PR operatives, and neither was allowed to talk to the media. Outside of the hospital where Rocky had been taken, Morrow told a gaggle of snickering reporters, "He was having a wonderful time with the whole art enterprise. He was having a ball."[42]

Rockefeller's was a brand of Republicanism that was all but gone in the GOP. Internationalism and big government activism with a social conscience, a political philosophy that he embraced, was out. In his time as governor of New York, the state budget had gone from roughly $2 billion to almost $9 billion. Taxes had increased in that same time from $94 to $460 for every man, woman, and child in the state.

The cream of the East Coast elite turned out for the funeral of the über–East Coast elitist.

He was lauded by all, including President and Mrs. Carter, who attended the services with Vice President Mondale, former president Ford, and other dignitaries from the political, philanthropic, and international communities. Richard Nixon did not attend, but he did pay a sympathy call on Mrs. Rockefeller. In character, he said Rocky was a "tough guy."[43]

The embarrassing circumstances of Rockefeller's death added colorful symbolism to the corruption rampant in the old-style Republicanism the former vice president embodied. Gingrich's aggressive public relations campaign to present himself as the face of a new kind of Republicanism could not have been more timely. What a few days earlier had appeared impertinent and audacious, now began to seem almost cathartic. Gingrich slowly picked up more public support in his drive to oust Diggs. By the prerogative of the House he could force a vote, but he needed forty-three GOP representatives—10 percent of the House—to do so. There were plenty ready to support him, but Gingrich's initiative did not even come close to getting the support of all his fellow Republicans, a commentary on the insiderism of the era. Artfully, the House Democrats stalled for time on the resolution, which prevented Diggs himself from voting and bought themselves some breathing room to figure out how to handle the hot potato.

Ultimately, they handled it by standing with Diggs and telling Gingrich to stick it: they refused to stop the convicted congressman from voting in committee or on the floor while his appeal was under consideration. Gingrich raised the stakes by calling for Diggs's expulsion outright, but Diggs was defended passionately by Majority Leader Jim Wright, who said expulsion was "the most severe punishment the House can bestow."[44] Only three members had ever been expelled from the House, and all three expulsions took place during the Civil War, when the offending members had joined the Congress of the Confederacy.

On March 1, Gingrich introduced House Resolution 142, "To expel Charles C. Diggs, Jr., of Michigan."[45]

In early March, Gingrich's resolution was voted on. "The freshman Republican's resolution was referred to the Ethics Committee by a vote of 322–77, where it was tabled and subsequently died."[46] Bluster was one thing, but an on-the-record vote for a convict was another. Previously, the Democratic caucus voted to support Diggs—but on a voice vote that was not recorded. And of the 276 members of that Democratic caucus, only 82 showed up the day the vote of caucus support was scheduled to voice their opinions.[47]

The matter dragged on for three more months, until June, when Diggs finally admitted to his fellow members that he had taken $40,000 in kickbacks, promised to repay them, and reluctantly accepted a censure by the House, the first in sixty years. "In July 1979 the House voted unanimously to censure Mr. Diggs, who had remained free on appeal, after half an hour of floor discussion in which no one spoke in his defense."[48]

The plan was for Diggs to pay back the embezzled monies at the rate of $500 per month plus interest, which Tom Edsall of the Baltimore Sun noted "would take more than seven years."[49]

Diggs's court appeal failed. He served fourteen months of a three-year sentence.

Gingrich won plaudits for his tenaciousness and drive for reform, but he also created as many enemies on both sides of the aisle for embarrassing their beloved institution. One lifetime enemy he made then and there was Texan Jim Wright, House majority leader, who had a strong taste for destroying his political enemies. Gingrich had been in the House precisely six months and had already managed to tick off its most vindictive member. Of Wright, Bob Livingston, a member from New Orleans and friend of Gingrich's, said, "He was imperious . . . a sense of entitlement, of being in the majority forever and the Republicans were peons." Of Newt, he said, "He was fearless."[50]

In July, the young back-bencher and some fellow political climbers pushed Republican National Committee chairman Bill Brock on how to wage political war against Jimmy Carter. Meeting with Tory party officials in Washington, Gingrich learned how the British conservatives, tired of losing, undertook a fifteen-month effort to unseat Prime Minister James Callaghan and replace him with Margaret Thatcher. The economic conditions in Great Britain were atrocious, thus making the Tories' job easier, but Brock, Gingrich, and the GOP were impressed.

They began their own efforts, aimed at Carter, focused on their own budget proposal but centered on massive tax cuts for the individual. Out of the box, they labeled Carter's a "budget of despair" and theirs a "budget of hope."[51] Talking about hope was not something the Republicans had much experience with in the past. That had been the domain of the Democratic Party since FDR.

Brock's RNC, along with the NRCC and the GOP Senatorial Committee, had come a long way. All had risen from the ashes of the post-Watergate landscape, in which GOP donations had dried up and the so-called election reforms had chased big givers into submission. Freed of the yoke of Nixon and Ford, and with Carter to push against, the committees were reborn into impressive operations for recruitment, research, fund-raising, and morale.

They still had to fend off GOP members of Congress who tried to foist their ne'er-do-well children off on the committee. Various "Muffies" and "Buffies" and "Skips" and other offspring, including professional inheritors, took up time, space, and money at the RNC. It was this "preppie" deadwood that Brock was determined to clean out.

The Republicans were on offense and it felt good. Gingrich went so far as to publicly suggest a coalition government in the House, where the GOP would caucus with Southern conservative Democrats and overthrow House Speaker Tip O'Neill. It wasn't realistic, but it was a good indicator of the mood among the GOPers. Surprisingly, "a half-dozen or so conservative Democrats [took] Gingrich up on his invitation to join in a coalition."[52]

Worried about losing control of his own increasingly conservative conference, John Rhodes of Arizona, the House minority leader, scrambled to stay in the lead of the parade, though he scoffed at Gingrich's idea of a coalition-governed House. The fact that Rhodes went out of his way to criticize Gingrich's notion was a testament to the Georgian's increasing influence, as well as his uncanny abilities to command attention and get under people's skin.

Rhodes and O'Neill were both fighting off Gingrich, which was bizarre, as he had only been in office a few months. The Speaker and the minority leader had fifty-two years in office between them, having both arrived in Washington as part of the class of 1953.

The national media was paying more and more attention to Gingrich and his band of rebels. By late October 1979, the *New York Times* ran a major story on him and other back-benchers, which featured a photo of a newly light and lively Newt. Raising cain had obviously consumed a lot of calories:

> There was a time when freshmen Congressmen, like obedient children, were seen but never heard on Capitol Hill. However, the current class of Republican newcomers . . . is making a lot of noise and attracting a lot of attention. Many of them are also experts at the use of television, a medium that had helped erode party loyalty and aided the growth of the Republican Party in the Sun Belt. Lawmakers such as Newt Gingrich, the only Republican in the Georgia delegation, have the styled "blow dry" hair that distinguishes TV-age politicians of both parties.[53]

The old guard GOP could not figure out if Gingrich was an asset or just a pain in the neck.

In addition to their heavy use of blow dryers and hair spray—something appalling to the older members, who favored Brylcreem—the new Republicans were far more conservative than their older counterparts.

And the new Democrats were more liberal. The beginning of the polarization of the two parties—which had started with the 1964 Republican nomination of Barry Goldwater and the 1972 nomination of George McGovern by the Democrats—was accelerating.

The allure of Washington had not turned Gingrich's head. Yet. Mindful of his tenuous hold on his congressional district, he went back frequently to tend the home fires. There he met with small businesses, conducted town hall meetings, held political fund-raisers, and maintained a high profile in the African American community. According to Mel Steely, a friend and activist, Gingrich was dedicated to the district issues, even leasing a Winnebago to travel and handle constituent services. A young aide was apparently also interested in constituent services. He "was a former student that had become absolutely committed to Newt . . . one time we had people calling us and saying your van is here but we can't get anybody to answer it . . . it's bouncing up and down. He'd have his girlfriend in there and was having some recreation during his lunch period."[54] The youthful driver later offered some marijuana to a reporter and was finally let go. [55]

Only two members of the Georgia congressional delegation supported the Martin Luther King holiday, Congressman Wyche Fowler and Gingrich. He was frequently seen at black churches attending services.

Before the Fulton County Republicans, Gingrich ripped the established order in Washington. "We . . . are rapidly moving toward a system where there is one set of laws for the lawmakers . . . and another set for the people. There's a sense that Congress is a club, which makes different rules for itself." He scored his new colleagues on Capitol Hill for covering up for corrupt fellow members, for enriching themselves in bypassing Social Security, and for supporting a campaign finance scheme, paid for by the taxpayers, that even the *Washington Post* labeled a "politicians welfare bill."[56]

One week earlier, Ronald Reagan had paid a visit to the president's backyard and ripped him and the Democrats in Congress on all manner of things, both foreign and domestic. It was one of the rare appearances the Californian made in 1979, as his campaign operatives were holding him back, fearful that the Gipper might say something that would upset his front-runner status. Still, he signaled his case for a new GOP: "Republicans are the party of working people and those who believe in freedom, and we have faith in the marketplace."[57]

Gingrich ended his first year in Congress with an American Conservative Union rating of 89, considered good but not great by the stalwart organization founded in the ashes of the Goldwater campaign of '64. He ducked a couple of votes on abortion and parental consent for abortions for under-aged pregnant girls, and he also voted for the creation of a Department of Education, but on spending and tax-cut votes he was solid. He liked beer and loved ice cream but had no head for Scotch, the preferred drink of Southern gentlemen. When traveling, he would often take twenty-minute power naps and would wake up entirely refreshed and not groggy. As expected, he constantly read and had a near photographic memory. Unfortunately, not everything he memorized was worth remembering. The next year, his ACU rating dipped to 76, considered mediocre by Washington conservatives.[58]

Democrats had a stranglehold on Georgia's constitutional offices, as well as the legislature; and for the most part they regarded Gingrich as an interloper, a carpetbagger, and a hated Republican. He was the only GOP representative in Georgia's ten-member House delegation. With the census only one year away, Peach State Democrats began a plot to redistrict Gingrich out of existence after 1980.

Dr. Donald Fairchild, a "professor of political science at Georgia State," said to the United Press International that "state legislators may be tempted to 'gerrymander' the 6th District since that seat is now held by the newly-elected Rep. Newt Gingrich, the lone Republican in the Georgia delegation and a potential target for the heavily-Democratic General assembly."[59]

But Republicans were planning their own counteroffensive.

In 1979, members of Congress could earn outside income from speeches, book royalties, and businesses they may have owned before being elected. Disclosure was required but languidly enforced. Some members had done quite well in 1978. Minority Leader John Rhodes made as much as an additional $85,518 (only a range was required for reporting purposes), while Democrat Phil Gramm of Texas may have pulled in as much as $174,057 on top of his congressional salary.[60] With the concentration of high-priced lawyers, lobbyists, politicians, and pampered talking heads, it was hard to throw a dart in any direction in Washington and not hit a millionaire.

In 1978, Gingrich's household income to support himself, Jackie, and their two daughters had been $10,166, just about coolie wages.[61] Gingrich never worried much about money and was not allowed to handle the family finances; Jackie did that. As a public schoolteacher, she had brought home the bacon in that election year, yet they lived meagerly, even in rural Georgia; but Congressman Gingrich was now beginning to see opportunities— financial and political—in public speaking.

Still, he was a doting father, reading often with his daughters and taking canoe trips in the Okefenokee Swamp for a week at a time, camping amid the kudzu and the mosquitoes.[62] He went roller-skating with his daughters, and "I ended up . . . clumsy, not very good at it, clinging to the rail, hoping I won't fall and hurt myself. And this little four-year-old kid skates backwards past me, looks up and waves. I've always used that to remind myself that everybody is good at something."[63]

Gingrich was interested in the new ideas and energy emanating from the Washington GOP. He endorsed a proposal by fellow conservative Dan Quayle of Indiana to grant young, first-time homebuyers a 20 percent tax credit to assist them. "According to the National Association of Home Builders, the cost of buying a median priced new home has risen from $23,400 in 1970 to $67,000 this year."[64] Quayle's plan was complicated, but essentially it allowed homebuyers to save money—tax free—until they had enough for a down payment.

The name of the bill, the Young Families Homeownership Act,[65] helped to frame the debate to the Republicans' advantage. It was one more piece of evidence that the GOP, led by Jack Kemp and others, was emerging as the ideas factory in national politics. Kemp and Gingrich got on well, and the former quarterback journeyed to Atlanta to host a joint fund-raiser with Newt to raise money in advance for Gingrich's first reelection bid in 1980. Newt gushed, "I have no doubt that one day Kemp will be President of the United States."[66] More than four hundred attendees raised more than $20,000 to hear the two young congressmen speak.

Gingrich oddly said at one point in his talk that the choice between Reagan and Carter was "nonsense."[67] Later, as he came to understand the meaning of Reagan, he clearly saw the distinction between his fellow Georgian and the former movie star from California. Reagan, he said, "actually represents the beginning of a different order."[68] But, he said, "my model was actually Wellington because he wages the Pennisular campaign with a very small army."[69] Gingrich was coming to learn that a small motivated force could beat a large, unmotivated force.

Sometimes his zeal for publicity went too far, though. In late October 1979, he took to the floor of the House and called on the entire House leadership to resign. He also sponsored a bill earlier that would mandate that Congress stay in session during the entire August recess, embarrassing the House leadership on both sides while continuing to make enemies.[70] The August recess was sacred to Congress. It was simply an entitlement the self-enhancing members had enjoyed for years, despite their giggle-inducing pleas that these days away from Washington were for work in their respective districts.

He also strayed into foreign policy, as when he blasted Carter for not standing firm in supporting the beleaguered Shah of Iran, whose hold on his country was slipping.[71] He spun the charge into a patriotic message: Carter's presidency had done much to undermine America's prestige in the world.

A year before, nobody could spell his name. Now, Newt Gingrich was mingling with the national powers of politics and media. The year before Congressman-elect Gingrich had been cautious about the trappings of power: "Gradually, they tie up your good sense. They call you 'congressman.' They give you this special office. They take care of this; they take care of that. Pretty soon, you actually think you're important, and you're not. The job is important. Being the representative is important. The person who does it is just a person."[72]

But by the end of his first year, Congressman Gingrich's head was being turned.

CHAPTER 5

THE YEAR OF REAGAN

"Republicans are practicing . . . the same thing that
Abbie Hoffman practiced on the streets in 1968."

1980

Since landing in Washington in late 1978, Newt Gingrich had quickly gained a national reputation for his combative style and his leadership of the young, aggressive, conservative House Republicans. The *New York Times* put it this way:

> Mr. Gingrich, along with a band of young, conservative Republicans, turned their junior status to advantage and waged guerrilla warfare against the Democratic House leadership and even their own party's leaders. Under Mr. Gingrich's tutelage, about a dozen of the insurgents formed a group known as the Conservative Opportunity Society [COS] . . . Republicans, Mr. Gingrich maintains, have become so accustomed to their minority status that they need to be prodded to challenge the status quo.[1]

His fiery contempt for the Democratic establishment had not waned by 1980. A contested congressional race in Louisiana had been under investigation by both the Justice Department and the House Ethics Committee. The Democratic-controlled Ethics Committee determined that, while "58 votes were bought," it was not enough to continue the investigation since the Democrat, Claude Leach, had won by 266 votes. Congressman Bud Shuster of Pennsylvania was livid: "Apparently a 'little bit' of fraud is permissible with the Democrats. If there is $266 in a cash register at the supermarket and the cashier takes only $58, is this 'little bit' of robbery also permitted[?]"[2]

Gingrich darkly warned it would be "very dangerous for Congress to vote to cover up one more example of unethical behavior."[3]

Barely into his first term, Gingrich had already surpassed Republican congressman Phil Crane of Illinois to become one of the most influential conservatives in Congress, especially among the younger crowd of Reaganites. Crane, of course, had cut himself out of the herd with his quixotic (and some Reaganites felt mean-spirited) challenge to Reagan for the 1980 nomination. The *National Journal* called Gingrich "the intellectual leader of this younger group."[4] He'd also surpassed Congressman Bob Bauman of rural Maryland, who it was discovered was a closeted homosexual, despite a seemingly happy marriage and children. The AP reported on Bauman's "alcoholism and homosexual tendencies."[5]

Gingrich was still clinging to his belief that if the GOP had sizable gains in the November elections, then enough conservative Democrats could be convinced to cross over and support a coalition of conservatives to oust Speaker Tip O'Neill.[6]

Newt Gingrich announced his candidacy for reelection to the US House on May 28, 1980, in a breakfast meeting with 150 supporters at the Stadium Hotel in Atlanta. Afterward, he and some of the supporters walked to the State Capitol, where, armed with sufficient petitions, he filed his candidacy.

He spoke for only five minutes—which was surprising for the oft-verbose young man, who sometimes needed five minutes just to clear his throat.

While proud of his first year as a burr under the saddle of the powers that be, he also starkly outlined the stakes in 1980: "People are losing faith in their government and the institutions that make this a free country." He continued, "Unemployment, the high cost of energy and the ever-present threat of world-wide Russian domination are the perils confronting today's American democracy . . ."[7]

Being on offense and staying on offense came as naturally to the young congressman as breathing. It was simply a part of his makeup, hardwired into his psyche. He embraced Jack Kemp's radical Urban Jobs and

Enterprise Zone idea, which granted favorable tax rates to stricken areas such as the South Bronx. "The best way to economically energize an area is to create new, productive jobs. Economic growth will mean lower unemployment and more opportunities for Black Americans—the group hit hardest by high unemployment."[8] It was an intriguing idea, so intriguing that House Speaker Tip O'Neill had blocked a vote on it for years, fearing the credit that might flow to the GOP.[9]

The Veterans of Foreign Wars endorsed Gingrich in 1980, breaking a long history of nonalignment. They also endorsed Reagan and dozens of Republicans across the country. House Minority Leader John Rhodes, for whom Gingrich was sometimes an asset, sometimes a pain in the assets, went to Georgia to stump for the young man. Also coming in was Major General John K. Singlaub, USAF (ret.), a hero of World War II, Korea, and Vietnam. Gingrich and his featured guests levelled the Carter Administration for allegedly leaking Stealth technology to the Soviets.[10]

In the early 1980s, Gingrich launched a new weapon, taking advantage of a rule allowing House members to read items into the record after congressional sessions. He gave frequent speeches criticizing Democrats for their position on a wide range of issues, from communism to school prayer to Central America—speeches given before an empty House chamber, but broadcast nationwide on the recently established cable network C-SPAN. This tactic was also used by Gingrich's followers—a group of conservative Republicans elected mostly in the 1980s and labeled the party's "young Turks," in contrast to the GOP's less aggressive old guard. No holds were barred.[11]

His campaign in 1980 would have to be different from his previous efforts. Now he was an incumbent, having to defend himself even as he assaulted the very institution he was operating in. For the first time, a campaign chairman was selected, John Grunden, a pillar of the greater Atlanta business establishment. Grunden, a hugely successful entrepreneur, was on virtually every local business and civic board, and (as befitting the establishment) was a Methodist instead of a Baptist.

He told local reporters, "It will be interesting to see who has the courage to run against Newt Gingrich."[12] Gingrich mirthfully told the *Washington*

Post, "I represent the Atlanta Airport . . . sooner or later everybody is my constituent!"[13]

Gingrich delighted in taking on the political establishment in Washington, but there was also a joy to campaigning back home in Georgia's Sixth District. "One of the biggest things about politics is this sensation of being a celebrity—of having them know your face. It really helps," he told the *Carroll County Georgian.*[14] While stumping, he usually subsisted on barbecue chicken and Diet Coke, as befitting any good Southern politician.[15]

Gingrich and the Republican revolutionaries continued their assault on House Speaker Tip O'Neill. Over the previous year, no less than eighty-seven tax-cutting bills had been offered by the House GOP and every one of them was referred to various committees, controlled, of course, by the Democrats, never to see the light of day again.[16]

Gingrich wrote in the *Conservative Digest*:

> The Democratic Party is now controlled by a coalition of liberal activists, corrupt big city machines, labor union bosses and House incumbents who use gerrymandering, rigged election rules and a million dollars from taxpayers per election cycle to buy invulnerability. When Republicans have the courage to point out just how unrepresentative, and even weird, liberal values are, we gain votes . . . Fear and corruption now stalk the House of Representatives in a way we've never witnessed before in our history.[17]

Jack Kemp hit upon a new strategy: to offer one bill that would compel the leadership into bringing all the bills to the House floor by April 15, 1980, for open debate and up or down votes. Gingrich enthusiastically supported the Kemp spring offensive.[18]

The first termer also continued to push for his idea of "coalition politics" in the House between the GOP minority and the conservative Democrats. Ed Feulner, head of the small but influential Heritage Foundation, wrote a nationally syndicated monograph promoting the idea, pointing out that "four states—New Hampshire, Vermont, New Mexico and Texas—have had working coalitions in their state legislatures for some time." Feulner was prescient in his April 1980 piece: "If the Republicans pick up 35 to 40 seats, the possibility of putting together a conservative coalition would loom very real indeed."[19]

The economy continued to spiral downward while inflation spiraled upward, along with interest rates. The International Monetary Fund forecast a long period of worldwide recession.[20] The Republicans were championing their own budget, offered by Congressman Del Latta of Ohio, which reined in federal spending while cutting taxes across the board, but the establishment Republicans were still dubious of their younger and hard-charging colleagues and their poster boy, Ronald Reagan. They didn't give a whit about balancing the budget. Not now, when so many people were suffering. Gingrich took to the floor of the House in early February 1980 with a long speech on the problems with the Democrats' economic program and what the Republicans had to offer as an alternative.[21]

He also announced his intention to seek reelection running against congressional corruption and the economy. His speech cited chapter and verse of Washington wickedness, confirming Twain's contention that Congress was America's only native criminal class.[22]

During the campaign, his newspaper advertising was issue-based, filled with sharp copy. Some advertising contained helpful advice on how constituents could split their votes for Democrats lower down the ticket and Newt, higher up. Many ads had the big headline: "The politicians had their chance. Now you can have yours."[23]

As Gingrich was gearing up for his first defense of his long-sought congressional seat, a Democratic opponent was beginning to emerge, Atlanta lawyer Dock Davis. Davis immediately filed a complaint with the Congressional Franking Service about the content of the congressman's newsletter, but the committee (comprising two Republicans and two Democrats) swatted it away by a 4–0 margin.[24] Gingrich's campaign plan amounted to stressing two points, including "expressing the anger of working Georgians" and his plan to "offer hope."[25] He was also using his frank newsletter to maximum benefit, decrying tax increases and wasteful government spending.[26]

By June, Ronald Reagan had finally dispatched his last remaining rival for the GOP nomination, Ambassador George H. W. Bush. However, Reagan needed to come up with a running mate. For one reason or another, bridesmaids were rejected. Conservatives, however, especially Gingrich, were certain of their number one choice for Reagan's number two: Congressman Jack Kemp of Buffalo, New York. Gingrich, like many other conservatives, excitedly supported Kemp for vice president over the rest of the field, especially the moderate, country-club Bush.

Gingrich was less than hopeful for Reagan's chances against Carter, however. "It all depends on the economy two to three weeks before the election. In November the public will decide the one who frightens them most and vote against him."[27] Gingrich himself faced no primary opposition. As expected, the Democrats selected Dock Davis to run against him in the fall. But taking no precautions, Gingrich already challenged Davis and Davis's primary opponent, Jim Huff, to debate in every county in the district. Gingrich was already a Jedi Master when it came to the politics of permanent offense.

Elsewhere in Georgia, Senator Herman Talmadge was in the fight of his life. In a primary during early August 1980, he fought off five challengers, but failed to get more than 50 percent of the vote and would face Lt. Governor Zell Miller for the right to represent the Democratic Party in the November election. Talmadge had been denounced by his beloved Senate for "reprehensible conduct" for filing false expense claims to that body in excess of $40,000, along with campaign finance irregularities. Miller, a former US marine, was clean as a whistle and a near teetotaler, though he did earn the nickname "Zig Zag Zell" for his sometimes shifting positions on politics. His campaign slogan was "The best Senator money can't buy."[28]

On the Republican side of the Senate race, the former state chairman of the Georgia GOP, Mack Mattingly, won his party's nomination against token resistance, though few gave him a snowball's chance against either Talmadge or Miller, especially with Carter at the top of the ticket in the heavily Democratic state. Meanwhile, Carter was nominated for the Nobel Peace Prize.

By early September, knowledgeable Republicans (and some reporters) knew the Reagan campaign was an unadulterated mess. A meeting of surrogates and Reaganites was convened on Capitol Hill, ostensibly to hear from campaign chieftain Bill Casey and pollster Dick Wirthlin. What Gingrich and company got instead was a too-small room and a junior-varsity "briefing" from Rich Williamson, who had joined the Reagan campaign after guiding the Phil Crane candidacy onto the rocks of defeat.[29]

Oddly, Terry Dolan, head of the National Conservative Political Action Committee—which was running a multimillion-dollar independent expenditure on behalf of Reagan—was also present. Campaign laws at the time specifically prohibited any coordination between the official campaign and independent groups; and while Dolan's out-of-place appearance may not have broken the law, it certainly sent up red flags at the Federal Election Commission. The presentation was not what the Reagan surrogates wanted or needed, as Williamson and Dolan spent most of the time whining about how mean Carter was. Incensed at the meaninglessness of the meeting, Kemp stormed out.

Gingrich was further frustrated because he thought he had some salient insights into his fellow Georgian, Carter, whom he'd known for years, but found the Reagan campaign distinctly uninterested.[30]

A big photo-op was planned for the steps of the Capitol with Reagan, George Bush, Senator Paul Laxalt, the Reagan campaign chairman, and all the GOP-elected officials and aspirants. But what was the point, Gingrich complained. It would be pointless unless it conveyed a message. After repeated attempts, he finally got Bill Casey on the line and pleaded with him to make the event substantive.[31]

As part of the up-and-coming conservative movement's revolutionaries, sometimes derided as "The Crazies," the *Wall Street Journal* said, "A prime example . . . is Republican Rep. Newt Gingrich of Georgia, a precocious freshman who—not one to hide his light under a bushel—sees himself as the Vince Lombardi of the House Republican Party. 'One of my problems is the problem Vince Lombardi had when he took over the Green Bay Packers. We have a party here that's not very used to winning. It's not even used to fighting very well.'"[32]

The Crazies—Gingrich, Kemp, Bob Dornan of California (whose uncle played the Tin Man in *The Wizard of Oz*), Senator Paul Laxalt of Nevada,

Congressman Bob Walker of Pennsylvania, and Congressman Vin Weber of Minnesota—joyously upset both the Republican and the Democratic establishments on the Hill. Barber Conable, a moderate congressman from Rochester, New York, lamented that the Crazies had a "disproportionate influence . . . because they're so strident and uncompromising."[33]

Majority Leader Jim Wright, fighting to hold on to the House seat he'd had in Texas for more than two decades, complained, "Republicans are practicing, in a little more subtle form, the same thing that Abbie Hoffman practiced on the streets in 1968."[34] The GOP Crazies audaciously floated the rumor that a group of conservative and moderate Democrats were ready to cross over and vote for a Republican speaker. It was all smoke, of course, but it was one more way for the GOP to stay on permanent offense. "I know five Democrats in three states who have talked to Republicans and said they would consider voting for the more conservative candidate for Speaker," Gingrich told the National Journal.[35] Twisting the knife, he said he knew the Democratic leadership was already tormenting some of their more conservative members.[36] The Crazies, "an increasingly bloodthirsty group," had suddenly become media darlings, and the nation's newspapers were filled with lurid stories of how they were upsetting Washington.[37]

The Republican house was divided against itself: Reagan, his Crazies, and much of the muscular New Right on one side—the GOP establishment, moderate George H. W. Bush, and Minority Leader Bob Michel on the other. The Crazies—Gingrich and Walker—sent a scathing letter to their GOP colleagues, calling for support for an Ethics Committee investigation of no less than seventeen Democratic members. They said the House was experiencing a "crisis of corruption."[38] The letter repeatedly referred to "corrupt," "corruption," and "unethical."[39] Of the seventeen members, one was the incontestable Charlie Wilson of Texas, who a few years later would be under investigation for cutting the funding for two planes for the DIA because "it refused to let his girlfriend fly with him in a government plane in Pakistan in 1986."[40] Still, the vast majority of the bill of particulars against the Democrats was filled with serious and multiple examples of fraud, bribery, vote selling, racketeering, and "Tammany Hall." Twain was right. Congress was America's only native criminal class. Gingrich and Walker kept up the drumbeat for weeks.

Just one day before the November showdown between Reagan and Carter, most political writers were sticking to their prognostications of a "too close to call" election. Reagan, according to the wire services, was ahead in the Electoral College, barely ticking to the requisite 270. The story, which ran just three days before the first Tuesday after the first Monday, confidently predicted only modest gains in the House and Senate.[41]

Gingrich wrote the Reagan high command an unsolicited memo offering advice on the South: "The only way . . . [to] understand it is to go see a couple of Burt Reynolds movies to realize that Jody Powell and Hamilton engaged in a barroom brawl."[42]

Reagan blew out Carter by almost nine million votes and swamped him in the Electoral College.[43] Republicans took control of the Senate for the first time in more than thirty years and, with the addition of what would become known as "Boll Weevil" Democrats, operational control of the House. The GOP handsomely added governors and state legislators. It was a rout of historical proportions. Dazed Democrats promised Reagan a honeymoon of up to six months. A Democratic operative went so far as to say, "There's a lot of good feelings for Ronald Reagan on the Democratic side."[44] On the other hand, there were a lot of shots fired across the bow of the incoming Reaganites about not touching sacred cow social programs, but Newt was, as always, on offense, saying Reagan should not "nibble" at the federal budget but instead take "big chunks."[45] He also feared Reagan would be easily outmaneuvered by Tip O'Neill.

Gingrich won decisively, too, taking 59 percent in a district that would once have sooner voted for a yellow dog than for a Republican. He smashed Dock Davis, 96,071 to 66,606.[46] What made the win especially impressive was that Gingrich had not used the information that had come into his possession via Davis's first wife. She had shared with him that while Davis was serving in Vietnam during his navy years, when he came home, he brought his mistress with him. "He had . . . the ex-wife willing to testify about it."

But Gingrich said, "No, we're not going to use that kind of stuff. We're just not going to do it." Recalled Mel Steely, "When he criticized people, it wasn't on a personal level."[47]

"The period between a presidential election and the following January 20th is normally one of the calmest in Washington." So opined the *National Journal* in the latter half of 1980. "The winning candidates for the White House and Congress recuperate and begin to plan what they will do with their mandates. The losers quietly and quickly fade away. And the rest of the nation tunes out Washington to focus on football and the holidays."[48]

Gingrich, quoted in another article, simply said, "Some things I do really antagonize the Democrats."[49]

The black-owned *Atlanta Daily World* had endorsed both Gingrich and Reagan. While their support of Gingrich was no surprise, the Reagan endorsement was far from certain, given his campaign promises to cut the budget and a number of social programs.[50] After both won in landslides, the stage was set for fireworks in Washington.

Gingrich was more than prepared to really antagonize the Democrats now.

CHAPTER 6

CARTER DOWN, REAGAN UP

"Genuine Revolution."

1981

The old cliché on Capitol Hill was that a member could either be a show horse or a workhorse. Newt Gingrich was sometimes both. On his workhorse side, he convened a meeting of farmers and exporters of farm products to try to find a way for the marketplace to replace government while maximizing profits for both. It was called the "Congressional Farm Export Project."

"Farm exports are one of this country's greatest national assets," he said. "Every time we increase farm exports by $1 billion, we create 31,700 new jobs."[1]

On the show-horse side, Gingrich and Elliott Levitas, a Democratic congressman from Georgia, introduced a bill calling on the newly installed president to undo any deals Jimmy Carter had made with the Ayatollah Khomeini to secure the release of the fifty-two American hostages held captive for 444 days in Tehran. They were released minutes after Ronald Reagan was sworn in on January 20, 1981.[2]

The bill called for the US government to cease the release of any Iranian assets held in American banks, while also calling on Reagan to "apprehend, try, and punish" those Iranians who took part in the hostage crisis. It even called on the Iranian government to make reparations to the American hostages.[3] The bill was obviously a public relations stunt, as it was virtually unenforceable.

Gingrich also had to look over his shoulder in Georgia. The 1980 census had been completed, as prescribed by the Constitution, and congressional lines would be redrawn in the Peach State. There was nothing most Democrats—and a few Republicans—would have liked better than to gerrymander the young cage-rattler out of his seat and out of existence.

Meanwhile, he was called in by the leadership to give briefings to the newly elected crop of Republicans on how to hold on to their seats and navigate the new political universe:

> When I came in, we faced an obvious and simple playing field. We were the minority and it was our job to fight in opposition to the majority and the Democratic Administration. Now, however, new Republican Members don't know whether to play as angry members of the minority team or cooperative members of the government team, since their party controls the Senate and the White House.[4]

To Gingrich, it was permissible, even encouraged, to question liberal authority.

Ronald Reagan had brought a revolutionary force to Washington and the GOP, and many, including Gingrich, were positively giddy. By February 1981, Reagan had already introduced his new budget, which featured radical cuts in federal spending and "across the board" cuts in personal income taxes, the largest in history. Gingrich knew, though, that the plan had little chance of success inside Washington until and unless members of Congress got support from outside of Washington. "If they write, wire and call their congressmen, the Reagan program will pass; if they don't, it will fail," he said.[5]

Whatever doubts he had, Gingrich set them aside when he was asked to "head a task force to push Reagan's tax cut proposal through Congress."[6] It was heady stuff for the sophomore congressman, given there were so many more senior Republicans in line ahead of him. Gingrich was, however, more temperamentally suited to the task than some of his older, more moderate colleagues.

But Big Brother was everywhere in 1981. The Internal Revenue Service—insanely—planned to tax airline employees for free flights they might get from their carrier or a free meal a restaurant owner offered a down-on-her-luck waitress whose only income was derived from slinging hash in a greasy spoon. Only a moratorium imposed by Congress stopped the IRS from taxing these and other "fringe" benefits. The moratorium was due to expire in

May 1981, and a bill to make it permanent was now part of Gingrich's portfolio. "People have been taxed and taxed to death," he said.[7]

It was true. Tax-cutting fever was spreading across the land. Gingrich proposed an even larger tax cut for senior citizens than what was currently being debated for all taxpayers in Congress.[8] His proposal was a giant pander, true, but it also put the Democrats on the defensive over the issue, as they would be forced to argue for higher taxes for Granny.

The Cold War was raging, and the election of Reagan did anything but reduce tensions between the West and the East. Gingrich was even more hardline when it came to the Soviets than Reagan was. He wrote a thoughtful piece for the *Washington Post* on military policy, raising the new concern that the problem in the Cold War was not just matériel, but the superiority of the leadership of the Soviet officer corps over the West's.

"The danger is not merely that the Soviet Union has more men, spends more money or has more equipment than we do," said Gingrich. "The danger is that their officer corps has begun to be better trained intellectually, more deeply steeped in history, and is asking the right questions about war."[9] He wasn't for blindly throwing money at the Pentagon, however. "It doesn't matter how much money you spend if you spend it badly."[10]

His rhetoric could be grating, even unnerving. He had become involved in a small group of defense-interested representatives. As he said to the *Wall Street Journal*, "We are the war-winning military-reform group. It is our determination that if we have to go to war we will win." He also supported the development of the controversial neutron bomb, which could kill people but leave buildings intact.[11] In the aftermath of Vietnam, with the GOP already accused of being "warmongers," Gingrich's comments sent up red flags among many.

For him, though, the phrase "permanent offense" never had to be explained. Of the Democrats, he told the *Wall Street Journal*, "You are seeing the marriage of McGovern-type policies of redistribution for the poor and Hoover-type policies for the really wealthy, combined with the . . . machine political vision of keeping all power in the hands of the politicians by considering tax cuts only one year at a time."[12] The paper called him a "brash, cocky Georgian . . . "[13]

Reagan was already getting blowback from some elements of the conservative movement for not emphasizing social issues. The Reagan White House was focused on the ailing economy and America's Sad Sack national defense, not school prayer, busing, and abortion. The president was especially worried about Soviet incursions into the Caribbean and Central America, which he described as a "Red lake."[14]

The "Social Right," an important part of his winning coalition, was now feeling left out in the cold. Paul Weyrich, head of the Committee for the Survival of a Free Congress, blasted the White House for its "country club mentality."[15] Reagan liked and respected Weyrich, but these attacks by conservatives stung, as he later memorialized in his diaries. Many also attacked Chief of Staff James A. Baker III, especially given his history of working for Gerald Ford and George Bush. The attacks revealed that some conservatives thought Reagan could somehow be "controlled" by moderates within his White House.

Gingrich was conflicted, as he acknowledged how close Republicans came to losing against Democrats: "The economic issue and the national security issue between them brought us close to a majority. But it was the moral issue that carried us to victory."[16] He was also dubious about Baker.

On March 30, 1981, Ronald Reagan was nearly killed by an assassin's bullet. Only sixty-nine days into his presidency, Reagan had emerged from the Washington Hilton where he'd just given a poorly received speech to the AFL-CIO. As he emerged, John Hinckley Jr., a deranged young man who had been stalking actress Jodie Foster, fired six shots in Reagan's direction. The sixth bullet ricocheted off the presidential limousine and entered Reagan's left side, just below his armpit. It lodged in his chest just one inch from his heart.

At the George Washington Hospital, Reagan issued one deadpan line after another, often via a pen and pad of paper, demonstrating the "grace under pressure" of which President Kennedy often spoke. Before going under the knife, he told the gathered physicians, "I hope you people are all Republicans." Lead surgeon Dr. Joseph Giordano said, "Today we are all Republicans, Mr. President."[17]

Reagan had come as close to death as can be imagined, having lost half the blood in his body. Only his will, his physicality, the quick thinking of the Secret Service, the attending surgeons, and God's mercy kept him from passing through death's door.

By the end of his two terms, he would have beaten the twenty-year jinx on the presidency. Since 1840, every president elected during a "twentieth year" (1840, 1860, 1880, etc.) had died in office, from William Henry Harrison to Lincoln in 1860 all the way to JFK a hundred years later. This, combined with his courageous and sometimes joking manner, helped create a wellspring of affection for the Gipper that never diminished.

In July, Reagan was faced with the second biggest crisis of his young presidency. America's air traffic controllers were upset about wages and the hours they worked. Though under contract to the government, the fifteen-thousand-strong PATCO—Professional Air Traffic Controllers Organization—threatened a walkout unless they got a new contract that called for wages to be increased by $10,000—up to $59,000 per year—and an immediate reduction in their workweek from forty hours to thirty-two.[18]

Gingrich's district was heavily involved in the business of airlines because of the presence of the Atlanta Airport that employed tens of thousands, including maintenance workers, pilots, flight attendants, and, of course, air traffic controllers, many of whom lived in the Sixth District.

Complicating the matter was the fact that PATCO had been one of the very few unions to endorse Reagan in 1980.[19] This tidbit was included in virtually every story covering the threatened strike. Gingrich was as unsympathetic as Reagan to the demands of the controllers. He went for the jugular, saying, "You can say all you want to that it's a good cause. But the simple matter is, like any terrorist, you are holding the nation hostage for your own reasons."[20] If the controllers went on strike and broke their contract, they could be arrested and imprisoned. Meanwhile, millions of Americans would be stranded. The flying public angrily began making alternative arrangements to take buses, trains, or automobiles.

Reagan ordered the striking controllers to report back to work—or else.

"Or Else" Day came on August 5, and Reagan stunned the nation—and, as it later turned out, deeply impressed the Soviets—by firing the air traffic controllers who, as a bonus, were barred for life from ever working in their chosen profession.[21]

Gingrich had met with PATCO union members in Atlanta before the strike and he warned them not to walk, remembered longtime friend Mel

Steely. "Don't do this," Steely recalled Gingrich telling them. "If you go out on a strike, you're dealing with Ronald Reagan. You're not dealing with Jimmy Carter."[22]

The House had voted 238–195 for what started out as Kemp-Roth, then became Gramm-Latta, but was pretty much all Reagan. James A. Baker III, White House chief of staff and über-Washington power broker, agreed with Gingrich. "I happen to think that Ronald Reagan has changed the course and direction of Government more than any President since F.D.R."[23]

In August, Congress put its final seal of approval on Reagan's radical plan to cut personal income taxes across the board by more than 25 percent—less than the 30 percent he'd originally wanted but far more than the Democrats who ran the House wanted to give him. Gingrich had done a good job for Reagan rounding up votes. He was especially "proud of the Georgia delegation." Though he was still the only Republican among them, eight of the ten-man delegation from the Peach State had voted with Reagan for the radical tax cuts.[24]

Reagan was at Rancho de Cielo, high in California's Santa Ynez Mountains. On an oddly foggy morning he signed it, one of the most monumental pieces of tax legislation in American history. Gingrich accurately called the moment a "Genuine Revolution" and compared the era of Reagan and the change being wrought to that of FDR and his New Deal. "We've had 50 years of government growing larger and larger and thrusting its influence further and further into people's private lives. We're not going to do away with that overnight, but we've taken some big steps."[25]

Despite Reagan's historic legislative accomplishment, the media, and in particular the *Washington Post*, failed to give Reagan the credit he deserved for bringing it to fruition, just as they underplayed the tax cut's long-term economic and political significance.

Nancy Reagan had her own opinion about the *Washington Post*, which never seemed to give her husband the benefit of the doubt. At dinner parties, she told a joke at the expense of the paper and how it always played to type: "How would the *New York Times*, the *Wall Street Journal* and the *Washington Post* report on the world ending tomorrow? The headline of the *Times* would say, 'World Ends Tomorrow. See page a27 for details.' The headline of the

Journal would say, 'World Ends, Stock Market Plummets!' The *Washington Post*: 'World Ends Tomorrow; Poor and Minorities Hardest Hit!'"[26]

Despite the growing respect for him in Washington's political circles, Gingrich was not immune to silly public relations stunts. At one point, a harebrained idea was suggested—and seized upon—to spend a day in a wheelchair so he could better understand the needs of the handicapped.[27] A full media and speech schedule was implemented so everyone could see Newt on wheels.

On a more serious note, he was the prime mover behind a resolution to place a statue of Dr. Martin Luther King Jr. in the US Capitol. The Gingrich-inspired resolution passed the House 386–16 and went to the Senate for their approval as well.[28] Of all the 861 statues and busts in the US Capitol, as of 1981, there was not one depicting a black American.[29] As a Georgian and as a conservative facing reelection, it was a courageous decision, especially since his district was only around 20 percent African American. A considerable number of iconic conservatives opposed the memorial, including Senator Jesse Helms of North Carolina and Congressman John Ashbrook of Ohio.

Gingrich would not back down, however, saying, "The reality is that for black Americans . . . King is unequivocally the symbolic spokesman, the moment in history, the representation of the change from segregation to integration."[30]

Interestingly, he also introduced a bill to make marijuana legal for cancer patients. This was a more radical idea for a conservative in 1981, as the issue of marijuana use was laden with all sorts of cultural overtones, going back to the rise of the anti–Vietnam War movement and the growth of the drug culture. While some states allowed usage of the drug, the federal government had classified it as having no medical applications whatsoever.[31] In the culturally conservative Sixth Congressional District, residents looked askance at its use for any purpose at all. Gingrich's proposal was a risky but courageous one.

Gingrich's elevated status manifested itself in many ways, from heading White House lobbying efforts and chairing meetings on the future of the Republican Party, to appearing on important public policy shows. Such was the case of *Revitalizing America*, a sane discussion on national policy held between Congressmen Richard Cheney, Dick Gephardt, and Gingrich, which aired on PBS.[32]

Gingrich was also becoming a more frequent guest at the White House, even "accompanying the president back to Washington on Air Force One." Gingrich, along with several other members, "agreed that Reagan was the most effective presidential leader they had encountered, and that he had been especially impressive in winning the support of Congress."[33]

The American economy continued to falter. Beginning with Reagan's inaugural in January 1981, there had been a brief spurt upward over the spring, but it had petered out by the fall and unemployment continued its seemingly inexorable march upward. Increasing joblessness spread across the land and with it, renewed gloom. "We didn't expect as great a rise in unemployment as has occurred this fall," Gingrich told reporters.[34] He offered a bill to speed up the second phase of the Reagan tax cuts, which was scheduled to go into effect in July 1982. Newt proposed phasing it in seven months ahead of time. "Increasing take-home pay now will boost consumer spending and business investment and that means more jobs," he said.[35]

But Republican fortunes had sharply declined since the astonishing victory of the Californian and the new class of conservatives in November 1980. They had come in promising radical change and a revitalized economy; this they had not delivered. In a House special election in Mississippi, the Republicans lost a seat they'd held since 1972. After the 1980 census, the district had changed and black voters had been added. The Republican candidate had only fallen short by 1 percent, but even so the loss of the seat echoed down the halls of Congress and through the Republican drinking establishments.

Gingrich was analytical: "Reagan is currently winning the votes in the House but not the argument in the country. The intellectual and philosophical framework is not getting across nearly as much as the costs of his program and that reasserts the idea of the Democratic Party as the poor man's party."[36]

Reagan's election had swept in GOP control of the Senate for the first time since 1952, and though his party did not gain an outright majority, they had what Gingrich called "de facto parliamentary" control of the House.[37] Operationally it was in the hands of the Republicans and the Boll Weevil Democrats, mostly conservatives from rural Southern districts. Republicans had hopes of gaining outright control in 1982 or 1984, but the loss in Mississippi set them back and sent a chilling message to the Boll Weevils to stay put and not switch parties, as some Republicans had been pressuring them to do.

Still, talk of a "political realignment" was thick in political circles, and many political panels were being held in Washington to discuss the matter. The congressman from Georgia said, "Our basic theory is if we can sweep the lower middle-class precincts and get some black votes, we can be the majority party in the South in 10 to 20 years."[38]

By the fall of 1981, support for Reaganomics was beginning to lose steam. Inflation had fallen, in part because of his decontrol of the price of oil, one of his first actions upon becoming president in January, but also because of his tightening monetary policies. Interest rates were also slowly dropping, but not enough yet to spur new borrowing. They had come down a bit from the highs of the Carter years, when mortgages topped 21 percent, but not nearly enough to encourage economic growth. "Interest rates are so high they dominate everything," Newt bewailed. "I was told over and over again that we have until about December. If we can't bring it down by December, we're in big trouble."[39]

The tax cuts had not yet taken effect.

Reagan's approval numbers continued to track downward, dragging the fate of many GOP challengers—and a goodly number of incumbents, including Gingrich—along with them. In a bow to the changing nature of politics, however, two longtime Democratic congressmen, Gene Atkinson of Pennsylvania and Bob Stump of Arizona, abruptly changed parties to join the party of "Reagan Democrats" in the fall of 1981 (Stump would go on to win reelection handily in November 1982, while Atkinson would lose by 21 percent).

But even with the White House, the Senate, and "de facto parliamentary" control of the House, party denizens wanted outright control. As of October 1981, the Republican Party was tantalizingly close, down 241 to 193 with one vacancy. It was the most seats Republicans had held since 1956. Minority Leader Bob Michel, a moderate, was hankering to become Speaker, but Gingrich didn't care whether the Speaker was a Republican or a Democrat as long as conservatives had control of the House. "If we pick up as few as eight seats next year, the odds of electing a conservative Democrat speaker are enormously improved," he said.[40]

To make unprecedented gains in 1982, however, would require an unprecedented economic revival. As Ohio congressman Ralph Regula said in August 1981, "There were two weddings last week. Prince Charles married Lady Diana and the Republican Party married the economic issue. For better or worse, it's our economy now."[41]

The growing pains inside the new GOP were exacerbated by the growth of the conservative movement, aka the "New Right." Everywhere, print and electronic stories appeared about the "movement," as it was called by insiders. Insightfully, Leslie Lenkowsky of the Smith-Richardson Foundation said, "Without the New Right, the Republicans could not be elected. With it, they may not be able to govern."[42] Gingrich was simpatico with the New Right, yet he kept it at arm's length, saying, "The commando raids, the fierce fighting, if continued, will lead to the isolation of the right as a negative movement."[43]

Unemployment kept climbing throughout the year, crossing the 10 percent line of demarcation the Friday before the November elections. Gingrich could sense and hear the growing frustration from his constituents. "Reagan is going to have to move decisively this fall to cut further spending," he warned. "Most of my voters don't quite blame Reagan . . . but they say he better do something. He got all the praise, and he's the one who will hear the boos."[44]

Heading into 1982, the Republicans were in big trouble.

CHAPTER 7

OFF COURSE

"I think they're having one [huge] brawl."

1982

Newt Gingrich was furious.

White House chief of staff Jim Baker had gone on CBS's *Face the Nation* in early 1982 and said that the Reagan Administration hoped to hold GOP "losses under 38 seats" in the House elections later that year. Baker also elaborated that the White House had "given up hope of winning control of the House this year."[1]

No one knew if Baker was running a bluff by lowballing the GOP's prospects or just being downright pessimistic, but Gingrich didn't care. The Georgian fired off a too-hot-to-handle six-page letter blasting Baker, and released it to the media, where it was given top billing. The media loved it when politicians of the same party fought with each other out in the open. It was better than the Hatfields and McCoys.

"Your remark will cost the President votes in the House and Senate," Gingrich acidly wrote. He went further, saying Baker's comments would lead to "a shattering defeat for Ronald Reagan's dreams." He accused Baker of placing his "credibility" among the Washington press corps "ahead of the party."

> Having a senior White House official on national television saying that relative victory equals a 37-seat loss—which would reduce us, by the way, to 156 members—is a disaster; it spreads dismay and despair among your own troops. You seemed to be saying, "Vote with Ronald Reagan

and lose your seat. Or vote against Ronald Reagan and maybe you won't be one of the 37."[2]

Gingrich also said, "[F]reshman House Republicans described a recent meeting with Baker in terms such as 'outrage,' 'disaster,' 'despair,' 'infuriating,' and 'disillusioned.'"[3] He accused Baker of giving aid and comfort to the enemy. Just a little over a year earlier, the theme of the Republicans' confab in Detroit had been "Together . . . A New Beginning."[4] But as of early 1982, the GOP band had broken up. RNC chairman Dick Richards, a stalwart Reaganite from Utah, called for the resignation of Oregon's Bob Packwood from the Republican Senatorial Committee after the liberal senator said Reagan was "destroying the party's appeal to blacks, women, Jews and Hispanics."[5]

Baker was fit to be tied about Gingrich's letter, especially since it was given to the media and his conservative critics, many of whom regarded the tall and cool (some said calculating) Texan as a "'moderate' interloper."[6]

A day later, Gingrich wrote Baker a handwritten letter of apology, which the White House, of course, tit for tat, released to the national media. "Dear Jim: In looking at my recent letter, I realize that some parts are too strong and too personal, and I apologize." David Gergen, a Baker water carrier, told the New York Times—ominously—that "'nothing untoward' had been done by White House officials to convince Representative Gingrich that he ought to apologize. However, he said that Kenneth Duberstein, the White House director of Congressional relations, had talked with Mr. Gingrich to inform him of Mr. Baker's anger."[7]

But he'd only backed away from the personal comments, not the ideological content. Gingrich had simply reflected the attitude of most conservatives toward Reagan's chief of staff. Namely, they didn't trust him. In February 1982, Richard Viguerie, publisher of Conservative Digest, released a devastating portrayal of the Reagan Administration. On the cover, Reagan was depicted tied down Gulliver-style, accompanied by the story title "Has Ronald Reagan's Presidency Been Captured by Wall Street-Big Business-Corporate Executive Suite-Big New York/Houston Law Firm-Eastern Liberal-And/Or Establishment-Non-Reaganite Republicans? Do You Have To Ask?"[8] By July, it had gotten even worse. Conservative Digest wondered in another cover story, "Has Reagan Deserted the Conservatives?"[9]

Reagan was asked about Viguerie's charges in a live, nationally broadcast White House press conference, and while the Gipper tossed it off with a twinkly eyed joke, in private he fumed. In his diary, Reagan wrote, "Rcv'd. letter from Richard Viguerie with copy of *Conservative Digest*. He tried to write in sorrow, not anger about my betrayal of the conservative cause. He used crocodile tears for ink."[10]

Gingrich was in a gloomy mood. Several weeks later, he wrote a twelve-page letter to fellow Republicans, morbidly assessing their diminished standing. "Republicans tend to have blurred and unfocused opening statements, while Democrats tend to focus effectively and persuasively," he said. A reporter described the letter as "written with the sort of soul-searching that comes of watching and reviewing transcripts of Sunday interview shows on television."[11]

He wasn't the only American angry or depressed. New York straphangers were startled to see a near-empty Amtrak train with only Treasury Secretary Don Regan and a few aides on it, as the rest of the crowded and jostled passengers jammed into other cars in the late-morning rush hour. An early April snowstorm had closed the New York airports, which only added to the melee. A Treasury official sheepishly blamed the Secret Service. "A private car . . . at the cost of six ordinary tickets, $32 each, the same price paid by the people standing and glaring back at the club-car serenity for Mr. Regan." As Regan and his aides relaxed, an angry bystander complained, "There they were lounging in this car, and the man standing next to me is telling me about his heart trouble."[12]

Congress had to take up a vote in the spring of 1982 to raise the debt ceiling, which had for years stuck in the craw of conservatives. Gingrich said that he "would vote against the debt limit unless Congress seriously considered . . . 'dramatic' spending cuts . . . [He continued,] 'I am perfectly willing to have the government come to a halt this Spring for two, three, four weeks.'"[13]

Later, Gingrich circulated a letter signed by fifty-three of his fellow conservatives urging the rest of the House to go along with spending cuts. He was in a fighting mood now, blasting both the Hill Democrats and the staff surrounding Reagan. "The liberal Democrats are responsible for the overspending that has caused the government to reach the debt ceiling," he said at a Capitol Hill press conference. As UPI reported, "Gingrich said he believes President Reagan's advisers persuaded him he 'couldn't touch the liberal welfare state' and that is why Reagan has not proposed deep spending cuts in entitlement programs such as Social Security."[14]

The Hill conservatives demanded: (1) a constitutional amendment to balance the federal budget; (2) the preservation of the third year of the Reagan-Kemp-Roth-Gramm-Latta tax cuts to take effect in July 1983; and (3) huge spending cuts to reduce the 1983 deficit, projected to be around $100 billion. Gingrich bitingly said, "The effort to avoid angering liberals has gotten nowhere."[15]

The Reagan Administration had astonishingly proposed new tax increases in early 1982, and the conservatives were having heart palpitations. A House-Senate Conference, as part of the budget deal for 1982, proposed a $98.3 billion tax increase over three years. It raised taxes on gasoline, it raised taxes on dividend interest, it raised taxes on certain consumer goods, including a sixteen-cent tax on a pack of cigarettes . . . All in all it amounted to the biggest peacetime tax increase in history.[16]

Incredibly, Ronald Reagan embraced the bill. Two dozen conservatives— including former members of Reagan's own White House—signed a statement pledging to defeat it. To reach conservatives, Reagan had gone so far as to have a letter under his byline published in the new *Washington Times*, which had quickly established itself as the conservatives' morning paper of choice over the perceived-liberal *Washington Post*. To reach conservatives, the Reaganites now opposing Ronald Reagan sponsored an "urgent conference" on Capitol Hill.[17]

Newt Gingrich was at ground level of the in-house revolt against the revolutionary Reagan. So, too, was his comrade in arms, Jack Kemp. Both had been weaned on supply-side economics. But astonishingly, Lyn Nofziger, who had recently left the White House (and who had earned high praise for his handling of the media during the assassination attempt on Reagan), and Marty Anderson, a longtime policy advisor to the Gipper, joined in the counter-revolution. Their statement read, "In the present weak economic climate, and during a time in which the Congress refuses to support the spending cuts required by the budget resolution, we friends and supporters of Ronald Reagan oppose the tax increase now before the House-Senate conference. We believe that to restore the health of the economy and put

Americans back to work, America should follow a course against high taxes and Federal spending."[18]

House Speaker Tip O'Neill was exultant of the ideological fisticuffs inside the GOP. "I think they're having one [huge] brawl," he joyously exclaimed.[19]

Kemp later said that Reagan had berated him in a private meeting. "Now I know the woodshed is oval," he said. To which O'Neill quipped, "You ought to know. You've measured it often enough."[20]

Shortly, however, Nofziger was brought back into the Reagan fold and now supported the massive tax increases. He even went so far as to meet with the Cabinet and tell them not to campaign for any Republican who opposed the tax bill, which had become known as "TEFRA" for "Tax Equity and Fiscal Responsibility Act of 1982."[21]

Gingrich was slightly apoplectic. The out-in-the-open donnybrook was the "opening round of a fight over the soul and future of the Republican Party," he fumed.[22] Kemp, more measured, called TEFRA a "dramatic U-turn" in Reagan's policies. Reagan was angry himself, calling the criticisms of the conservatives opposing TEFRA "plain hogwash."[23] Reagan went so far as to hold a rally on the steps of the US Capitol in the summer of 1982, the audience mostly comprised of tourists and Republican Party staffers. In his televised address, Reagan backed away from the word *compromise*, but the young Georgian pointed out, "Now he's going on television to explain why he didn't mean it."[24] The *Wall Street Journal* weighed in, against Reagan.[25] Gingrich would rather die than agree with the corporate elitists at the *Journal*, but he did note that there was a feeling in '82 that something was not quite right at the Reagan White House.[26]

The RNC budgeted an unprecedented $350,000 in advertising to support the president's new economic plan. His on-again, off-again allies in the New Right were off the reservation again, and Richard Viguerie, a majordomo in the conservative movement, denounced the ad blitz as "unprincipled desperation."[27] The deficit had grown to nearly $200 billion—terrifying official Washington—and there was open talk in the conservative movement about a challenge to Reagan for the 1984 nomination, maybe by Kemp himself.[28] What Viguerie and Kemp did not understand but Gingrich acutely did was "Reagan was never going to be as conservative as the movement wanted him to be."[29] On the other hand, Gingrich always believed Reagan thought TEFRA was "horse---t" and "he'd been talked into a dumb thing by his staff."[30] In fact, Reagan said so himself, confiding to one businessman, "I wasn't elected to raise taxes, and I don't like doing it."[31]

A vote was scheduled for August on TEFRA, with the president working against many conservatives in Congress. Even the US Chamber of Commerce was in open revolt—against itself—as some in the leadership supported the tax increases while others opposed them.

An accusation going around Washington in conservative circles, which ended up in the influential Evans and Novak column, was that Jim Baker had essentially walled off Reagan, not allowing him to hear any dissenting opinions about the new tax increases. Even a Reagan favorite, Jack Kemp, could not get another meeting with the Gipper after the White House let it leak out that Reagan had dressed down his young acolyte.

Gingrich and Kemp emerged as the two ringleaders, working furiously to defeat Reagan's tax increase. At a GOP House leadership meeting in April, Gingrich and others "opposed the shape of the emerging compromise . . . producing cheers and applause."[32]

Reagan and O'Neill were working to gain House passage. The two Irishmen appeared together in a Rose Garden ceremony, calling for the tax increases as means of precipitating a drop in interest rates for the slowly growing stock market.

"The leaders of the opposition to the bill in the House are not Democrats, they are Reps. Jack Kemp of New York and Newt Gingrich of Georgia, conservative Republicans and avid believers in the supply-side economic theory that made Reagan so confident a year ago," reported the Associated Press.[33]

O'Neill, for whom the phrase "upper hand" never had to be explained, said, "The tax bill will not repeal Reaganomics, but it is at least a step in the right direction. It is a step away from 'trickle down' economics and a step toward common sense." O'Neill bashed the two young conservatives often, as did White House aides and the House leadership of both parties. Gingrich, in a flight of hot rhetoric, called the fight one between the "Washington political establishment" and the "long-anguished voice of the American people."[34] Meanwhile Bob Dole was listing other potential tax increases, including on businesses and retirement benefits, and introduced a bill "to enhance the Internal Revenue Service's enforcement capability," reported the

National Journal.[35] It was also reported that Reagan wasn't overly thrilled with Dole's proposals.[36]

American newspapers were having a field day. They could not believe their good fortune: Reagan being opposed by Reaganites. Who could resist? The *Washington Post* featured opposing viewpoints on the issue, by two Republicans. Bob Dole for TEFRA, Newt Gingrich against.[37]

The tally was not good for Reagan. Gingrich's office counted "only 138 firm votes for the bill, 205 opposed and 91 undecided."[38] Reagan was meeting extensively with members—one-on-one, in small groups, and over the phones—but the harder he pushed, the more resolute conservatives seemed to be becoming. It didn't help when he quoted Barry Goldwater's admonition years earlier for conservatives to "grow up."[39]

Reagan went on national television to ask the American people to weigh in. They did, but unfortunately for the president, they weighed in against the tax increase and they let both the White House and Capitol Hill know it. Americans were aghast that Reagan was pushing for something they believed he had opposed for years.

Not so subtly, the Republican National Committee made it clear in phone calls and conversations to GOP members of Congress not to expect campaign help in the fall if they did not help Reagan in the summer. It was right out of the Richard Nixon handbook, *How to Make Enemies and Lose Influence over People.*

Gingrich was dismayed but also philosophical about the temporary split with Reagan: "For the first time, they're beginning to realize to what degree events dominate the best-laid plans of mice and men."[40] The young Georgian appeared on PBS's *MacNeil/Lehrer Report,* a signal honor in Washington. There, he did not back down in his opposition to Reagan and the House Democrats. He lamented, "The only bizarre part of the whole thing is Ronald Reagan being for it."[41]

Deep into the typically long, hot, humid, and rank summer in Washington, the House finally voted in favor of TEFRA, 226–207. Reagan had successfully persuaded 103 Republicans—along with 123 Democrats—to vote for it. The Senate was just as tight, passing 52–47.[42]

Weary from the intra-party battle, the president headed to Phoenix for the funeral of his father-in-law, Dr. Loyal Davis, and from there retired to his ranch in Santa Barbara for the rest of August 1982. But, as the Reagan

White House predicted, interest rates began to drop sharply from 20 percent to 14 percent and the stock market went on a buying spree.

Gingrich opened up another front when he took on the status quo of the military establishment in a speech at West Point. It was right out of a Cold War novel. In front of a hundred military experts and top brass, the young congressman excoriated the existing conditions in the military. "Gingrich, a leader in the group of senators and congressmen known as the Reform Caucus which is demanding changes, said both in formal speeches and interviews that the military must figure out a way to win a war with the Soviets . . . 'The reality is that in a serious war with the Soviet Union . . . we lose.'"[43]

Gingrich was becoming a frequent participant in War College exercises, sometimes as the president, other times as a general.[44] During a break, a reporter asked those present if anyone disagreed with Gingrich's apocalyptic pronouncement, but he was met with stony silence.[45]

Back in January, Gingrich spoke to one thousand Solidarity Day demonstrators in Lafayette Park, just across from the White House. It was about the only enjoyable thing he'd been involved in for all of 1982. He shared the podium with Reagan's ambassador to the United Nations, Jeane Kirkpatrick, as they took up the cause of the Polish people against the oppressive Soviet-backed government.

Later that year, along with a small group of others on Capitol Hill, he signed onto a radical plan to shoot down incoming Soviet missiles. The plan was called "High Frontier."[46]

The Pentagon was skeptical of High Frontier, which in its early planning stages claimed to "function through the release of a barrage of small, high-speed rockets which would each release hundreds of steel cubes in order to destroy enemy missiles through high velocity impact."[47]

Gingrich also proposed tax credits for home computers, an idea he'd gotten from friend and futurist Alvin Toffler, as enthusiastically reported in *Computerworld* magazine.[48]

Rockets and computers brought out the nerdy side of the Georgian, but political pugilism brought out his rhetorical fisticuffs. At a press conference in Philadelphia, just after a jury in the District of Columbia reinvented jurisprudence by proclaiming Reagan assailant John Hinckley Jr. to be "innocent by reason of insanity,"[49] the Georgian hotly said the decision was "a logical result of the liberal welfare state approach."[50]

He blasted his own party for lacking "a governing strategy since August 1981. There are underlying contradictions in government that no one has been willing to confront because they require tough medicine that both parties prefer to avoid."[51]

He also ripped a congressional proposal to grant legal status to illegal immigrants: "Illegal immigrants don't deserve to get a free ride from the federal government. They shouldn't get amnesty just because they snuck into the US and have been here for a few years."[52]

In November 1982 the GOP lost 26 House seats.[53] Nonetheless, it could have been much, much worse. For once, the Republican Party's campaign committees worked effectively to marginalize the losses, but even Minority Leader Bob Michel of Illinois won with less than 52 percent.

Hostility over Gingrich's divorce and swift remarriage in 1981, along with the general frustration with Reagan and the recession, almost cost Gingrich his seat, but he won reelection in November 1982 with 55 percent against an underfunded state representative named Jim Wood.[54] Tony Coelho, a liberal congressman from California and head of the Democratic Congressional Campaign Committee, bemoaned the fact that his committee had not spent resources trying to defeat Newt. "Our biggest mistake was in not targeting . . . Gingrich."[55]

Newt was despondent, feeling his party had blown an historic opportunity to become the true majority governing party by picking up control of the House. "We have failed so far to hammer home that Tip O'Neill and Jimmy Carter brought the country so close to bankruptcy that it's hard to come back."[56]

He'd also gotten in a bit of hot water for touting a friend and expert on military matters, Mike Bressler, to some newspapers, recommending him as a columnist. Bressler was also employed by the Southwire Company, located in Carrollton, Georgia, and many in management there had been contributors to Gingrich's congressional races.[57]

In Massachusetts, a liberal Republican congresswoman of long-standing, Margaret Heckler, lost to Barney Frank, after being outspent by hundreds of thousands of dollars.[58] In Arkansas, a bright, if libidinously aggressive young politician named Bill Clinton staged a comeback at the tender age of thirty-six by winning back the governorship. Clinton had lost to banking executive Frank White in 1980 because of the Reagan upheaval, because he'd forgotten the "Bubbas" of his state, and because many saw his wife, Hillary Rodham—nicknamed "Hot Rodham" in the local newspapers—as being a bit of an ice queen.

Indeed, Republican forays into the South had mostly come to naught. Democrats regained the same seats they had lost two years before.

In one of the final acts of the 97th Congress, a full-time historian was named to organize the upcoming two hundredth anniversary of the people's house—in 1989. Surprisingly, the vote was not unanimous, 230–97. Gingrich, the historian and college professor, supported the initiative, and was appalled that so many of his colleagues opposed the creation of the office. "Gingrich cited opposition to the resolution as an indication of the members 'self-contempt, self-flagellation . . . And we wonder why nobody appreciates us.'"[59]

There was a swift answer to Gingrich's query. The final act of Congress was to vote itself a pay raise of $9,100, a healthy 15 percent increase at a time when more than 10 percent of the American workforce was staring down the barrel of a bleak and joyless Christmas. The bill, masquerading as a "continuing resolution," only made it through the House by a 204–200 margin.[60]

Gingrich voted against it, saying, "I just couldn't vote for a bill that contained any pay raise for Congress."[61]

CHAPTER 8

A DECADE OF GREAT DEBATES

"We must develop a missionary approach to politics . . ."

1983

The decade of the '80s was mostly a blur of activities, struggles, arguments, debates, victories, and defeats for conservatives, and Newt Gingrich was no exception. He had his fingers in more pies than could be counted and he was fighting the liberal establishment more and more. The *New York Times* published a profile of the Georgian that opened, "There were times . . . when the House of Representatives looked like the Newt Gingrich Show."[1]

Big issues dominated the 1980s, led by Ronald Reagan. Communism, the American economy, the military, space, spirituality, the environment, AIDS, freedom, privacy, the nuclear freeze, aid to the Nicaraguan Contras, Iran-Contra, the Middle East, Social Security, the Strategic Defense Initiative, the Supreme Court—all dominated the national arguments, and Gingrich was a part of many, if not most, of these contentious debates. January greeted Reagan with newspaper ads by big business attacking his economic policies! No wonder Reagan had been always skeptical of corporate America, especially banks, after they tried to eliminate federal income tax withholding on dividend and earned interest.

After his relatively close shave in November, Gingrich stepped up his attention to the Sixth District. Since the big win in 1980, he'd been spending less and less time in the Sixth, stretching his time out to visiting each of the eleven counties only once a year.[2] But in early 1983 he wrote, "Many Members regard this as a burden. I think they look at their trips back home in the wrong light."[3]

He initiated a weekly column titled "Notes on Self-Government," which was distributed and picked up widely in his district, especially with the smaller daily and weekly papers, including his old friends at the *Atlanta Daily World*. Indeed, one of his columns in March 1983 was titled "Coming Home: An Important Part of the Job." Others were titled "Why Deficits Are Important to Each of Us"[4] and "Liberal Democrats Continue Bad Medicine."[5] He also authored a column praising C-SPAN, as it was the citizens' way of closely watching their Congress.[6]

At a state party confab, Gingrich told the assembled Republicans of a "second new era of conservatism." In it, he stated, "We must develop a missionary approach to politic[s] and care about the people and talk in their language. Go out and preach a conservative posture for individual freedom and work for a strong, lean, vigorous non-bureaucratic government."[7] The audience ate it up. At the age of thirty-nine, he'd already become one of the most sought-after speakers in American politics.

A new sex scandal hit the US House of Representatives in July when it was revealed that Republican congressman Dan Crane of Illinois had had sexual relations with a seventeen-year-old female page; Democratic congressman Gerry Studds of Massachusetts, it was also revealed, had had sexual relations with a seventeen-year-old male page. Both indiscretions had taken place several years earlier, but the House voted to reprimand the two men.

Crane was censured by a vote of 289–136, while Studds was censured by a vote of 338–87.[8] Clearly, the Congress, though overwhelmingly Democratic, had stronger opinions about underage homosexual relations than underage heterosexual relations.

Gingrich, on the floor of the House, called for the ouster of both men: "This is not a question of sexual relations between consenting adults. This is a question of the powerful exploiting the powerless, of an adult preying upon schoolchildren."[9] He also told Brit Hume of ABC News, "This is not a question of the integrity of Studds and Crane, we already know about their integrity, this is a question about the integrity of the U.S. House of Representatives."[10]

Gingrich was praised by the nation's religious leaders, but he was ruthlessly denounced by his colleague, Congressman Dick Ottinger of New York, who called the critics of Crane and Studds men "who wear morality signs.

I saw you on television seeking to profit politically from the misfortunes of our colleagues, Studds and Crane, and I was thoroughly revolted, repulsed." The criticism came in the form of a handwritten letter to Gingrich, who showed it to a colleague, Tom Hartnett, who promptly made copies and sent them into Ottinger's district where there they got into the hands of the media. Then Ottinger really lost it.[11]

Congress was also wrestling with aid to the Nicaraguan Contras, the anti-communist guerrillas opposing the Soviet-backed regime in Managua that was headed by strongman Daniel Ortega.

Again, Gingrich was in the thick of the fight. It was a contentious issue, and many votes went along party lines, with Republicans supporting Reagan in wanting to arm the "Freedom Fighters," a move that Democrats opposed. Gingrich denounced his Democratic opponents, using the word *radical* continually. "Because they fail to understand the nature of evil, radical Democrats support policies at home that favor the criminal rather than the victim."[12]

The national media was again not outside the scope of his scorn. "Somehow, too many in the news media don't want to face the facts about world events," he said.[13] He also accused the media of being "used and exploited" by Latin American communists.[14] Only five years in Congress, Gingrich was accumulating a treasure trove of first-rate enemies.

After Reagan had given a nationally televised address outlining his policies in Central America, he met with a group of supporters at the White House, including Gingrich. It was one of the few times the president had been unable to rally big public support. Gingrich again blamed the national media. "A major problem in this country is the degree to which the news media, both because of bias and because of style, makes it very difficult to communicate the problem," he told journalists after the meeting.[15]

After yet another meeting between Reagan and Gingrich and some other GOP congressmen, the president noted, "Newt Gingrich has a proposal for freezing the budget at the 1983 level. It's a tempting idea except that it would cripple our defense program. And if we make an exception on that every special interest group will be asking for the same."[16]

The Congress publicly and loudly voted to end "covert" aid to the Nicaraguan Contras, 228–195.[17] The contentious issue would be voted on time and time again. Gingrich, after a meeting with Reagan, said that "he [Reagan] personally favors threatening Nicaragua with air and naval blockades."[18] Reagan may have favored a similar policy when it came to the national media.

Sometimes world events came home to America in frightening incidents. In the fall of 1983, a bomb was detonated near the Senate minority leader's office. No one was killed, fortunately, but much damage was done. Shortly thereafter, Gingrich was on the House floor when a man in the gallery got up and began yelling. Capitol police wrestled him to the ground and found a bomb strapped to him with enough explosives to destroy a goodly portion of the lower chamber and dozens of people, including Gingrich.[19]

In October 1983, Ronald Reagan was golfing at the Augusta National Golf Club—in Gingrich's backyard—when a deranged man, Charles R. Harris, drove a truck through an iron gate barricade and took several hostages, including two Reagan aides, holding them in the pro shop at the club. Reagan was on the links, and in an attempt to ameliorate the situation he called the disturbed man on the pro shop's phone line to talk to him. Harris refused, insisting he would only talk to Reagan in person and one-on-one. The crisis ended when Harris released the hostages and surrendered to authorities. No one was injured. The hostage-taker was distraught over losing his job and the death of his father.[20] President Reagan was never close enough to have been in any real danger, but the day's events did bring home the very genuine concerns of Mrs. Reagan regarding her husband's safety. After all, he'd already been shot once.

Days later, two truck drivers drove vehicles through a marine checkpoint in Lebanon and into a barracks. They detonated a bomb, killing 220 young marines and another 21 service personnel.[21] Several days after that, American military forces led a successful invasion of the island of Grenada, where Soviet-backed communists had overthrown the government—killing the prime minister there—with the intention of installing a pro-Moscow regime.[22] The island, while small, was strategically placed in the Caribbean, and would have been a significant Cold War advance for the Soviets had

Reagan not ordered the successful military incursion. American opinion was divided until a planeload of endangered American medical students attending school in Grenada returned to the States; some got out and kissed the ground, all recorded for the networks. Americans then realized the significance of the Soviets' invasion and Reagan's response. Still, the national media hammered Reagan over both Grenada and Lebanon.

Gingrich took it all in and said darkly, "Danger gets closer and closer to Americans every year. There is danger whether it's in downtown Atlanta late at night, in our own neighborhoods in the form of a robber, travelling abroad as an American medical student in Grenada or as a peacekeeper in Lebanon." He compared the Soviets' modus operandi in Grenada to their actions in Afghanistan in 1979. Again he blasted the national media: "They really want to believe that America is consistently wrong and the Soviets always have a reason for their actions. They are trying hard to make it look like the Americans invaded a poor, innocent country for no reason."[23]

Republicans—organized by Gingrich's newly formed Conservative Opportunity Society—met in Baltimore to review the year and make plans for 1984, a critical election year for Reagan, his party, and their ideas. Henry Hyde said succinctly, "We have to show people they can become Republicans and lightning won't hit them."[24]

David Hoppe, a young GOP House aide, said you could divide the conference into three sections and that a plurality thought Gingrich was "crazy," including those in the "old line country club."[25]

The GOP was getting pummeled in the pages of the daily newspapers. For Republicans living in New York, Boston, Washington, or Los Angeles, it got downright depressing to read the articles and columns. The *Washington Post* was no exception. On December 7, 1983, the newspaper launched a surprise attack on Republicans with a screaming headline, "To Blacks, GOP Offers Little."[26] It was part of a theme the newspaper was pushing under "The Politics of Fairness." In order to illustrate their point, the *Post* and ABC News polled African Americans, asking their response to statements such as "If blacks would try harder, they could be just as well off as whites." Fifty-five percent of blacks agreed in 1981 with this statement, but "by 1983 only 35 percent agreed with this."[27]

Gingrich said in the story that "it is in the interest of the Republican Party and Ronald Reagan to invent new black leaders, so to speak—people who have a belief in discipline, hard work and patriotism, the kind of people who applauded [Reagan's actions in] Grenada . . ."[28] He was accused of presumptuousness, especially when he said that America could not "define black leadership as either politicians or preachers."[29] But Gingrich's point was not lost on all. Indeed, on the matter of African Americans and the GOP, he knew more, frankly, than did most in his party.

He'd also surprisingly paid tribute to liberalism in America in the cause of civil rights. In March, during an extended debate over the Humphrey-Hawkins bill designed to achieve full employment, Gingrich said: "One of the great lessons of liberalism in the last 30 years has been its unstinting fight against racism, whether in the United States or overseas. Liberalism has done two other things. It has fought for compassion for the poor and disadvantaged, and it has fought against violence whether at home or abroad."[30]

Unsophisticated observers were stunned, but those who knew Gingrich understood he was at heart a classic liberal in the nineteenth-century meaning of the term, as he championed the individual and individual dignity over the state.

Concluding, the history professor pointed out the failures of both conservatism and liberalism in meeting the needs of black Americans.

While Reagan and the Republican resurgence of 1980 had been nothing short of historic, it would be rendered nearly meaningless if he and they lost the White House and more congressional seats in 1984. In some ways, the election of '84 would be more important than '80, as it would be a validation of the intervening four years. If Reagan won reelection, his place as a game-changing leader would be secure. If he lost, he would be regarded as a detour in history.

Gingrich continued his war against elements of the national media, especially the networks:

Sixty Minutes and other TV shows spend their time telling us what's wrong with the world. If Edison had invented the electrical light during the time of the Liberal Welfare State, CBS News wouldn't have reported it as a breakthrough. Their story probably would have begun, "The candle-making industry was threatened today." And Walter Mondale would have introduced a bill to protect candle factories.[31]

In late 1983, Mondale was the frontrunner for the 1984 Democratic nomination. With unemployment at more than 8 percent, he was ahead of Reagan in key national polls among all voters.

The GOP was still beset with problems late into 1983. Reagan's secretary of the interior, Jim Watt, had emerged as both a problem and an embarrassment as the man had both feet perpetually jammed in his mouth. Never one for the niceties of "diversity," which had emerged as an issue and a cause during the previous few years, in observing a commission to advise on coal usage, he said, "I have a black, I have a woman, two Jews and a cripple."[32] Washington society was aghast.

So was Gingrich when he was told the White House planned to weather the newest storm over the blunt-talking Coloradan. He said they were "deluding themselves" if they thought the controversy would go away.[33] He called Watt's comments a "slur on millions of Americans" and said that Watt was "incredibly destructive for the Republican Party and its president."[34]

Gingrich sent Reagan a letter calling for Watt's dismissal. A few days later, Reagan acted on it, "accepting Watt's resignation" in the lexicon of the town, which of course meant the person resigning had, in fact, been harshly sacked.[35] Reagan nominated his old friend Bill Clark, who had been National Security Advisor, to replace Watt.

By the fall of 1983, conservatives—especially those of the New Right—were divided over Reagan. Just a few months earlier, the Soviets had shot down KAL 007 as it flew from Anchorage to South Korea. All 269 passengers were killed as the defenseless civilian plane fell five miles out of the sky. One of Gingrich's colleagues, Congressman Larry McDonald of Georgia, had been on board. McDonald had been a member of long-standing of the John Birch Society and Gingrich noted the reputation of the group when he said, "[M]any in this house and in the national news media would have called him paranoid. Well, paranoia didn't kill Larry McDonald."[36]

Hardline anti-communists were deeply disappointed in the Administration's response. Reagan went on national television to eviscerate the Soviets; some diplomatic and trade punishment was enacted, but nothing like the Cold Warriors wanted. Gingrich criticized the Administration "for not imposing more stringent sanctions against the Russians."[37] Both houses of Congress passed resolutions harshly condemning the Soviets.

Appearing on *MacNeil/Lehrer*, Gingrich elaborated: "I think the first step for us is to begin to be honest about the nature of the dictatorship that we're dealing with . . . and to quit trying to appease a nation which is clearly a threat to civilization." Not pulling any punches, he called the Soviets "barbarians."[38]

But he wasn't about to break any more than that with Reagan. The president was earning the ire of the New Right, including Richard Viguerie and Howard Phillips, who were once again advocating a challenge to Reagan from the right in the 1984 primaries. "Reagan is just the sort of nice fellow I'd like to have as a neighbor," said Phillips. "But he defers too quickly to anyone in a three-piece suit."[39]

Gingrich aimed his criticism not at the president but at his staff. Reagan, he said, was "the only coherent revolutionary in an Administration of accommodationist advisers. The Administration has had no capacity to launch strategic offenses on behalf of Reagan's vision."[40]

Indeed, the *Washington Post* had previously reported that the White House staff was "at each other's throats."[41] Illustrating Gingrich's point, the paper continued in another report, "Overshadowing everything is the effort by members of the president's party, including White House aides and congressional leaders, to get the president to approve pragmatic budget revisions."[42]

A new phrase entered the conservative lexicon: "Let Reagan Be Reagan." Buttons and bumper stickers were manufactured, reflecting the ridiculous sentiment. The slogan and the thinking behind it were silly, frankly, as well as insulting. The Gipper knew exactly what he was doing, but the opinion bought in to the notion that he was some sort of easily manipulated puppet. Even a moderate Republican, Representative Barber Conable, saw this was nonsense, saying Reagan was "a more complex man" than many in Washington thought.

But the fact remained that conservatism, Republicanism, and Reaganism were very much in disarray at the end of 1983. "The principal cause of the

GOP malaise is President Reagan's coyness about seeking reelection," reported Eric Gelman from *Newsweek*.[43]

But while the media was busy mocking his disheveled party, Gingrich was keeping his eye on the coming election. "Our real goal is to pull away from the liberal Democrats. In the past what we have managed to do brilliantly is blur the issues," he said.[44]

The 1984 election would be different.

"There's no reason to waste our energies on an internal civil war," Gingrich would admit.[45]

CHAPTER 9

MORNING IN AMERICA

"They are using the guerrilla tactics of Jerry Rubin
to advance the causes of Jerry Falwell."

1984

Newt Gingrich began January 1984 with only $11,387 on hand in his campaign's bank account, far less than any other Georgian incumbent, not to mention most other incumbents around the country. He announced his candidacy for a fourth term on April 14 in a mailing to constituents signed by Newt and Marianne, his wife since 1981.[1] He was also targeted for defeat by the Council for a Livable World and "Freeze Voter '84," a so-called peace group. They planned on spending $3 million to defeat a handful of Republicans in 1984, Gingrich among them.[2]

The Republicans' wholesale efforts in the South kicked off in late January 1984 at the Southern Republican Leadership Conference at a hotel in the Buckhead section of Atlanta. A reception, with the theme "Solid South," started things off with speeches from President Reagan, Senator Paul Laxalt, RNC chairman Frank Fahrenkopf, and local hero Newt Gingrich. The overflow audience numbered more than twelve hundred.[3]

Gingrich was used to speaking to small audiences and classrooms. Speaking to a packed hall and sharing the platform with the president was heady stuff. Newt was also still repairing issues in his district from two years earlier. He continued the weekly columns in small dailies and weeklies in the Sixth in a perpetual effort to shore things up there.

On one particular day in February 1984, he met with Bill Bennett, the head of the National Endowment for the Humanities, discussing one of their favorite topics, America's heritage. A high point in March was receiving the "Golden Bulldog" award for his efforts to limit federal spending.[4]

Gingrich was again engaging his adversaries, this time over Nicaragua. He worked to organize a House resolution against ten of his fellow members who had audaciously sent a letter to Daniel Ortega, expressing their support for his communist regime and questioning US policy toward the Central American country. Gingrich was appalled, as were many Americans. The letter had opened, "Dear Comandante," and read, in part, "We have been, and remain, opposed to U.S. support for military action directed against the people or government of Nicaragua."[5] Gingrich called the letter an "unbelievable document."[6] This solicitous salutation in and of itself drove conservatives bonkers.

On the *MacNeil/Lehrer NewsHour*, Gingrich laid into the signees, as the letter asked the communist Nicaraguan government to help their supporters in America. He went toe-to-toe with one of them, Stephen Solarz of New York, and for all intents and purposes wiped the floor with him.[7] He was also looking into legislation that would prohibit members from contacting foreign powers with whom the United States was in conflict.

"I find it incredible that they would write a positive letter to a regime that is in every way a prototype moving toward being like Castro's Cuba. These guys live in cuckooland."[8]

The letter was signed by Gingrich's old nemesis Jim Wright. It was cosigned by Ed Boland of Massachusetts, Mike Barnes of Maryland, David Obey of Wisconsin, and Robert Torricelli of New Jersey, among others.[9] The letter violated the Logan Act—in spirit if not in black-letter law—which prohibited citizens from attempting to make or subvert the foreign policy of the United States. The Logan Act had been on the books since the days of John Adams. Gingrich said the letter "clearly violates the Constitutional separation of powers. It's at best unwise—at the worst illegal."[10] Relations between Gingrich and Wright hit rock bottom. They would not improve. Even Reagan, in his diaries, called Wright one of several "storm troopers."[11]

It was debates and fights like this that Gingrich relished. First, it was for the cause of anti-communism; second, it allowed him to display his knowledge of history, such as the Federalist Papers and the "Citizen Genêt case in 1790."[12] Third, it included passion, and Newt always loved a passionate fight. He often cited Madison, who wrote, "Knowledge will forever govern ignorance; and a people who mean to be their own governors must arm themselves with the power which knowledge gives."[13] However, the *Post* published a long editorial advising that if he pursued a legal course using the Logan Act, "Mr. Gingrich himself might end up behind bars, and in very large company."[14]

Several days later, Gingrich replied under the "Taking Exception" allotment, which the *Post* sometimes made available to parties who thought they'd been wronged by the paper. "It's true that nearly all of us have gotten into the sloppy habit of writing the Soviet Union and other countries, asking them to release political prisoners. Even there, I'd note . . . that such letters are not in opposition to U.S. policy . . ."[15] The piece was impressive in its grasp of American history.

Gingrich's vituperative actions against his House colleagues brought him into conflict time and again with another old archenemy, Speaker Tip O'Neill. They had already butted heads badly over the line-item veto. The day after the State of the Union address in January, Gingrich and a handful of cohorts issued a debate challenge to O'Neill and company, but they were dismissed, with the Speaker making derisive references to "crustiness" and "ruthlessness."[16]

Gingrich and his band were forming plans to make O'Neill's life miserable for all of 1984. They attempted to reserve six months of "Special Orders," four hours each night in which they would castigate the Democrats in the living rooms of sixteen million potential C-SPAN viewers.[17] The Georgian described it as "Chinese water torture."[18] Nothing doing, said the Democrats. In January, O'Neill attempted to muzzle the Crazies by only allowing those acknowledged by the "legitimate leadership" of their party to be recognized on the floor of the US House. Gingrich impertinently wanted to know what the Speaker meant by "legitimate leadership," and the response was those who had been elected to leadership posts on the various committees.[19] Since this was done by seniority, it meant the old guard of the GOP could be brought into league with O'Neill and the Democrats could effectively silence Gingrich, Kemp, and the Crazies. Gingrich was unflinching. He told the *Christian Science Monitor*, "You don't compromise with a dictator."[20]

For his part, Minority Leader Bob Michel said of his young, independent-minded sometime allies, "I have given them some fatherly advice . . . [to] be gentlemanly, and once you've made your point, get on with the business of governing." O'Neill, in speaking of the conservatives, said, "I don't think much of what that group has to say at any time. I think that about sums it up."[21]

During much of 1984, the conservatives on the House floor repeatedly declared "unanimous consent to bring up bills that would" score political points for the GOP and against the Democrats. "For the next 10 months, the country will see the Democratic leadership consistently block issues that have majority support in this country," Gingrich told the New York Times. The goal, he said, was to "systematically challenge the way the Democrats run the House." The paper described Gingrich's gang as a "hit squad."[22]

Meanwhile, the minority leader—often in name only—Michel, could only watch the young upstarts; they never consulted him or sought his approval on any of their initiatives or actions. O'Neill lamented that his golfing partner Michel could not control his own conference. "Poor Bob is running into problems," he said.[23]

Michel could only warn his Crazies that "you can only go so far, and then you're going to get it."

Gingrich was having none of it: "What the establishment wants, of course, is a muddled election with muddied results. This will allow them to get in the backroom with one more bipartisan commission of establishment figures, only to make up one more muddled set of proposals which will inevitably mean less defense, higher taxes for the American people and higher inflation."[24]

Gingrich and his ideological revolutionaries weren't going to take any guff from anybody, as they had shown time and again. On the other hand, sometimes they were referred to as "Reagan Robots,"[25] other times "Crazies," other times "Young Turk Republicans,"[26] and other times, at least by Michel and O'Neill, things that would never make it into a family newspaper.

Under the "Special Orders" of the House, the members of the Conservative Opportunity Society petitioned to give closing remarks each legislative day. By 5:00 p.m., most members were already bending elbows at the many gin mills that dotted Capitol Hill, including the Monocle, the Hawk n' Dove, or in their own private suites in the Capitol. But these younger members didn't mind speaking before a near-empty chamber, as the always-reliable C-SPAN was there to broadcast the five-minute remarks, reaching more than seventeen million of the thirty-four million homes that had cable television at the time.

O'Neill had unwittingly created the opportunity for Gingrich to bludgeon him with these "Special Orders" speeches broadcast over C-SPAN. Wary of the way the networks manipulated coverage of the proceedings in Congress, O'Neill had authorized the installation of live television cameras for gavel-to-gavel coverage in the House chambers that were controlled by the House, not the networks, in 1978 after a ninety-day test of such a system the previous year. Not even PBS, however, was willing to take the broadcast feed and distribute it.[27]

When Brian Lamb, who was still in the process of organizing C-SPAN, met with O'Neill in 1978, the Speaker endorsed Lamb's plan to distribute the live feed to participating cable operators when he learned that gavel-to-gavel coverage was a key element of the start-up's mission. C-SPAN began broadcasting live from the House chambers in March 1979 (and continues to do so more than three and a half decades later).[28]

"It gives us an enormous ability to reach out to the country and explain what's happening," Gingrich said of the "Special Orders" broadcast on C-SPAN.[29] The *Washington Post* noted that Gingrich, Bob Walker, Vin Weber, Connie Mack, and others, "while largely unknown in official Washington," were "developing a national following."[30] All were getting fan mail from across the country and not just their districts. Near paranoia, O'Neill thought the Reagan White House was orchestrating everything. While the insurgent Republican congressmen sometimes worked out of Walker's office, their daily dose of "Special Orders" was more freewheeling. "We would literally gather in the back of the chamber and look at our watches and say, well, geez, it's seven o'clock." They'd then pick a topic and be off. "We haven't talked about education for a while, why don't we talk about education?" said Walker.[31]

All were also viciously attacked by the Democrats—and some Republicans. Congressman Bill Alexander of Arkansas called them "ticks on a dog." Others simply called Walker, Gingrich et al., the "C-SPAN Boys."[32]

In the spring of 1984, Speaker O'Neill ordered the TV cameras to periodically pan the chamber to show that Gingrich was speaking to an empty House.

Republicans were furious and vowed revenge.

On May 15, the battle between Gingrich and O'Neill spilled out of the House, beyond C-SPAN and onto the network news, when the Speaker became furious, lost his temper, attacked Gingrich, and in the first time in nearly two hundred years—not since 1798 had the House of Representatives done this—had his remarks "taken down." He was ruled out of order, an old-style and hugely embarrassing reprimand of O'Neill. The rules of the House "preclude personal attacks and insults."[33] Joe Moakley of Massachusetts had to tell his old friend to address Gingrich "in a more proper manner."[34]

Under the "Special Orders," Gingrich, Bob Walker, and other Republicans had taken to the floor to assail Democrats—some by name— over their various foreign policy positions. Gingrich had asked his staff to research all the foreign policy mistakes and blunders made by Democrats during the past fifteen years, especially those showing them to be soft on communism and hard on America. Mocking the Democrats, Gingrich piled on the comments, telling the chamber and the sixteen million who got C-SPAN that "once a communist regime is in, these Democrats give it unlimited sway to get even with history . . . Every time a communist movement takes power, Democratic congressmen say it will be fair, progressive, enlightened . . . Trash America, indict the president and give the benefit of every doubt to Marxist regimes. That's the standard formula."[35]

He also named names, including Ted Kennedy, Walter Mondale, and Barbara Boxer. Both he and Bob Walker quoted directly from statements in which Democrats attacked the United States and praised communist governments.

Jim Wright, the majority leader, leapt to his feet and shouted, "Will the gentleman yield?" Gingrich refused. Then the Speaker dropped his gavel and stormed out of his chair high above the House floor: "Finally, O'Neill himself, a large, imposing, white-haired figure, came lumbering up the aisle to join the fray."[36]

"Will the gentleman yield?" O'Neill yelled at Gingrich. Gingrich yielded. Enraged and red-faced, O'Neill returned the fire. Shaking his finger at Gingrich, he roared, "You deliberately stood in that well before an empty House and challenged these people and you challenged their Americanism, and it is the lowest thing that I've ever seen in my thirty-two years in Congress!"[37] Gingrich asked for a point of personal privilege, "the formal term for a personal complaint against a colleague."[38] The rules called for him being recognized on this point.

Calling a member "un-American" or sympathetic to communism was not out of order, but calling a member "lowest" was considered out of order. The House parliamentarian, William Brown, advised the presiding officer that O'Neill was indeed out of order in his comments about Gingrich, and that the Speaker could have also been prevented from speaking on the floor for the rest of the day, but the Republicans, at Michel's request, did not press this. For a few nervous minutes, "Brown consulted a dictionary to see if the word *lowest* was a slur."[39]

Trent Lott asked for a ruling and ironically it was Joe Moakley, a hack Democrat from Massachusetts and longtime friend of O'Neill's, who indeed grudgingly ruled against the Speaker. *Newsweek* defined what it called Gingrich's Newtonian law: conflict equals exposure equals power. "If you're in the newspaper every day and on TV often enough then you must be important."[40]

As a smiling Gingrich walked up the aisle and back to his seat, his GOP colleagues gave him a standing ovation, some slapping him on the back and gathering around him. Even moderates like Hamilton Fish, "the personification of the responsible Republican moderate"—whose family had represented the same seat in Congress at intervals since John Tyler had been president—stood for Newt.[41] Bob Michel, however, did not applaud.[42]

Still, while Gingrich was proud of his victory over O'Neill, "Leaders from both parties say they are getting tired of Mr. Gingrich and his allies, who openly prefer public clashes to private compromises," the *New York Times* reported. Even one of Newt's allies, Trent Lott, expressed his concerns in the article. "A lot of people feel their integrity and motives have been impugned, on both sides of the aisle . . . There were hurt feelings and tempers involved here, and both sides have some legitimacy," the ambitious Mississippi congressman said.[43] But the Gray Lady noted, "At 40 years of age, Mr. Gingrich is serving his third term in the House, and he handled himself with even-tempered, if slightly cocky, coolness."[44]

O'Neill, for his part, put on a brave face and let the rebuke slide off, sharing that he did not say what he *really* thought of Gingrich and company.[45] Another ally of Gingrich's, Rep. Vin Weber of Minnesota, stuck to his guns: "Tip O'Neill is one of the cheapest, meanest politicians to occupy that office in this century." Even Michel, the quintessential calm negotiator, agreed with Weber.[46]

Off the floor, O'Neill referred to Weber, Walker, and Gingrich as the "Three Stooges." Gingrich retaliated by informing O'Neill that fifty Republicans were lined up to give future floor speeches and that he, the Speaker, might be mentioned in a few. "I have concluded it would be best if I were not on the floor," a dejected O'Neill told reporters.[47]

The *Wall Street Journal* advised Washingtonians not to "invite Tip O'Neill and Newt Gingrich to your next dinner party."[48]

Some columnists threw around the charge that Gingrich had engaged in "McCarthyite" tactics, an old chestnut in Washington. In fact, Gingrich had accused the Democrats of "McCarthyism of the Left" on ABC's *World News Tonight* just a few days earlier.[49] Congressman David Obey of Wisconsin, a Democrat who hated Gingrich and the Crazies, circulated a letter to all House members in which he wrote that Gingrich "may look prettier than Joe McCarthy, but it still looks like a duck to me."[50]

All the news shows covered the imbroglio extensively. The lead editorial, for example, in the *Wall Street Journal* titled it "The War on the Floor."[51] A number of articles retold stories of past brawls in Congress.

Gingrich was profiled in the *Journal* a week later, accompanied by the paper's trademark artist rendition of the Georgian, a signal honor.[52] A reporter asked O'Neill if he and Gingrich would "kiss and make up," but the Speaker demurred. On CBS's *Nightwatch*, Gingrich said, "Let me tell you, it feels pretty darn scary. I felt a little bit like [Gen. George Armstrong] Custer at the Little Bighorn."[53]

On the other side of the aisle, an enterprising individual took all the C-SPAN tapes of performances and lowlights involving O'Neill and called it "Tip's Greatest Hits," circulating it widely. "Tip's Greatest Hits" was a hit within the GOP as it displayed him "overruling, ignoring, insulting or denouncing assorted Republican members from his lofty perch at the front of the House chamber." Unwittingly, O'Neill had unified the diverse House GOP conference—all 166 of them—as they never would have been without his heavy-handed tactics. "He has molded the House Republicans, a farrago of conflicting philosophies and clashing ambitions, into a single unit held tightly together by mutual disdain for the Speaker," said the *Post*.[54]

At the annual White House correspondents dinner on April 13, 1984, the media and the Democrats commiserated over

the new Young Turk Republicans (some of them actually Middle-Aged Turks, plus a few Born-Again Turks) who've become overly zealous and dogmatic partly because they are emboldened by having one of their own in the White House . . . "These people are the crazies, the radicals, the movement conservatives," growled one Democrat. "They're using the guerrilla tactics of Jerry Rubin to advance the causes of Jerry Falwell. Unfortunately, they are incapable of embarrassment as a group."[55]

On *The McLaughlin Group*, a weekly public affairs show hosted by the supercilious John McLaughlin, "Issue One" was Newt Gingrich and his dustup with O'Neill.[56]

The war of words continued unabated throughout the spring and summer of 1984.

Hostilities were not only high on Capitol Hill; they were raging in Central America as well. While touring the area in a helicopter, two members of Congress, including Senator Pete Wilson of California, were shot at over El Salvador. Fortunately, all were unharmed.[57] President Reagan had just taken to the airwaves once again to outline his policies for combating the Soviet-backed communist regimes just a few hundred miles from the United States.[58] Later in the year, the House did vote emergency funds to aid El Salvador's fragile government in attempting to fight off communist guerillas. Gingrich—as did eight of the nine Democrats from Georgia—voted for the bill.[59]

The Democrats were completely stymied by the Republicans' superior use of television in 1984. House Democratic aide Steve Skardon whimpered, "How can we compete with the president's incredible magic on television?"[60] Of the use of C-SPAN, Gingrich knew all along what he was doing. "The key is not whether the House is empty but whether the speech is good. If we can break their back on this issue, we'll have gone a long way towards saving the West."[61]

Preparations were moving ahead for the Republican National Convention in Dallas in late August. Dallas was a controversial choice because of the assassination of John Kennedy there twenty-one years earlier. But it was also the capital of the New West, a popular television show was named after the city, and Reagan's campaign chair, Senator Paul Laxalt, wanted it there. He'd tried to have the 1980 convention in Dallas but was overruled by then party chieftain Bill Brock. Now the head of the Republican Party was Frank Fahrenkopf, Laxalt's friend and lawyer from Nevada.

"Dallas, with its location, affluence and political ambiance, illustrates the complete dominance in the Republican Party of Mr. Reagan and the Sun Belt conservatives," the New York Times reported.[62] For the first time ever, Gingrich would be a delegate to a national convention. It would also be the first convention he attended since supporting Nelson Rockefeller in Miami in 1968. But if you scratched the surface of the young Newt Gingrich that year, it was Richard Nixon, the eventual nominee, whom he admired. "My model . . . as a young person . . . was Nixon. He was very smart."[63]

By the middle of 1984, the economy had recovered and its expansion was accelerating. Employment was up, housing starts were up, the stock market was up, GNP was up, and in the adage of the time, "Everything that is supposed to be going up is going up and everything that is supposed to be going down is going down." And the third phase of Reagan's three-year tax cut had yet to kick in.

Back home in the Sixth District, Gingrich was renominated without opposition, while the Democratic field opposing him drew four opponents who would first have to carve each other up before getting the chance to take him on. He would also be running with Reagan at the head of the ticket. He formally launched his campaign on June 30.

In July, a fiscal issue for which Gingrich fought for years finally came to fruition when Reagan signed into law the Tax Reform Act of 1984, which protected employees' benefits from the long arm of the Internal Revenue Service. "If [the IRS] had its way with work incentives, workers could have ended up paying taxes on free parking, company picnics and even the traditional holiday ham and turkey. Georgians can now enjoy their work incentives without having to worry if the IRS is looking over their shoulders." His district was filled with tens of thousands of airline employees who benefited from these so-called fringe benefits, and the new law would protect them as long as they were made equally available, "except in the case of parking spaces."[64]

By a count of 378–29, the House also easily passed voluntary prayers in public schools. Again, it was an issue Gingrich had championed. He said any effort to prohibit a moment of silence would be tantamount to "thought control."[65] At a rally for school prayer, speakers included Redskins coach Joe Gibbs and NFL greats Rosey Grier and Lenny Moore.[66] Gingrich was the organizer of the rally and President Reagan publicly promoted both the event and Gingrich at a CPAC speech, telling his audience to try to be there.[67]

In late July, Congress went into recess, Washingtonians headed for the Delaware and Maryland beaches, and the Democrats made for San Francisco for their quadrennial confab. But some Republicans headed to the Bay Area, too, including the Right Reverend Jerry Falwell of Thomas Road Baptist Church, Liberty Baptist College (now Liberty University), and Ted Koppel's *Nightline*, on which he seemed to have a permanent seat. Falwell planned to hold a "Family Forum" conference in the gay capital of America. Residents took the bait and "traffic stopped as police tried to keep the crowd, mostly young men and women in hippie style and punk clothing, under control," reported Maureen Dowd for the *New York Times*. "Outside was a scene straight out of the early 1970s."[68]

Speakers at the Forum included Phyllis Schlafly and Gingrich. It was "designed to show the Democrats in town that a platform that is for abortion, against school prayer and for homosexual rights is out of touch with 'traditional family values.'"[69] Capitol Hill aide Chris Matthews called the Republicans "a posse of political peeping Toms."[70]

Police scuffled with gays—about a thousand protesters showed up—all for the benefit of the news media, who beamed images into the homes of millions of middle-class Americans. Gingrich, noting that Democratic presidential nominee Walter Mondale had just taken New York congresswoman Geraldine Ferraro as his running mate, "said that if Mr. Mondale 'could not stand up to' the National Organization for Women . . . 'how will he do with Chernenko?'"[71] Chernenko, by way of reminder, was one of a string of Soviet premiers between Leonid Brezhnev and Mikhail Gorbachev, the newest in a long line of what could be called the "Soviet Premier of the Month Club," as they kept dying off.

The Republican National Convention was held in Dallas in late August, and it offered a marked contrast to the Democrats gathering the prior month in San Francisco. Though the temperature would be over one hundred degrees each day, the convention center would be a frosty seventy-two degrees for the 2,235 delegates. One wag described the weeklong gathering as a "hug-a-thon."[72]

A highlight of the trip to Dallas was a reception at the Southfork Ranch, the setting for the television show *Dallas*. At another party featuring Texas barbecue thrown for Japanese businessmen and elected officials, one quipped, "If we Japanese ate barbecue like this every day, we'd be bigger."[73]

At the convention, Gingrich, the first-time delegate, was selected to co-chair a platform committee dealing with education, an issue close to the heart of the former college professor. Awkwardly, he proclaimed, "We're the first generation in American history not to educate our children as well as we were educated."[74]

The GOP's gathering was for the most part a coronation of Reagan. One hundred and six politicians and wonks worked on the final platform, and the document had Reagan's stamp of approval all over it. Indeed, the White House had drafted much of the document before shipping it off to Dallas. The exception was the categorical refutation of tax increases over the next four years. Gingrich said the White House was "antsy" over any no-new-tax pledge.[75]

Gingrich, Kemp, and others wanted language in the strongest possible terms—"ironclad," in Gingrich's words[76]—but the Reagan White House wanted to go only so far as to say the president would rule out any tax increase except "as a last resort." Gingrich acidly said Reagan should decide if he stood with Bob Dole and Walter Mondale, "or with foes of Mondale's higher taxes."[77] Vin Weber raised the notion of a floor fight in the convention against Reagan over the issue. Weber, Gingrich, and Kemp all testified before the platform hearings, urging that Reagan and the Republicans should not give up the no-new-taxes high ground to Mondale and GOP moderates.

The final platform "compromised" on the tax issue by inserting a strategic comma that strengthened the arguments of Kemp and Gingrich, and the committee issued a final document very much to Reagan and the conservatives' liking: "We therefore oppose any attempts to increase taxes, which would harm the recovery." Gingrich went on *MacNeil/Lehrer* to explain his strategic comma in terms only grammarians and supply-siders would understand: "It changes dramatically the meaning of the sentence. The sentence without the comma basically says we're against those taxes which might affect the economy. The sentence with the economy [sic] says we're against taxes because they would affect the economy, and I think there's a big difference in how the structure of the sentence means."[78]

With that, Team Gingrich declared victory, but Dole denounced the revolutionary document. The platform was certainly not to the liking of the few remaining moderates in the party. Looking at the wreckage of progressive Republicanism, Rep. Olympia Snowe of Maine, a member of the platform committee, whimpered, "It's just not the party I used to know."[79] Even Reagan's daughter, Maureen, voted against its final passage.[80]

Indeed, the Reagan White House had backed down a bit on the tax issue, after being warned by Gingrich of possible future political problems for Reagan if he was ambiguous on the matter. The Georgian crowed, "We have clearly set the long-term philosophical direction of the party."[81]

Gingrich was prescient in recognizing the political harm that backing away from a pledge to oppose new taxes could cause a sitting Republican president. But his claim of setting the "long-term philosophical direction of the party" ended up way off the mark, as George H. W. Bush's ill-fated flip-flop on his "read my lips, no new taxes" pledge just a few years later proved.

The *New York Times* called the forty-year-old congressman "a leading conservative theoretician."[82] The platform did not contain any language on the gold standard or a flat tax, two issues near and dear to the heart of Kemp, but which gave the Reagan White House a heart attack.

Kemp called the GOP document "the most pro-family, pro-American, pro-life platform in history." Gingrich piled it on, saying, "This week is the beginning of the end of the welfare-state Republican Party."[83] However, the Reaganite convention delegates were not entirely accommodating to those establishment types whom they perceived had deviated from conservatism:

> On the floor below, Barry Jackson, an alternate delegate from Iowa and the co-chairman of the party in Johnson County, sported a red, white and blue button that said, "Republican Mainstream Committee"—the insignia of the small organization of Republicans who identified themselves as "moderates." A trail of hissing followed him as he walked by other state

delegations. "Why don't you just get out of here?" "Go to the Democrats—that's where you belong!"[84]

Even as Reagan was on the eve of his coronation, there still existed a small band of liberal Republicans who opposed him.

Gingrich said Reagan was "symbolic of a national, long-term, conservative movement," but moderates like Jackson weren't so sure.[85]

It was only ten years since Richard Nixon had ignominiously left the White House, just a step ahead of impeachment by the House and a trial in the Senate. He'd left the GOP in a shambles because of his arrogance, corruption, and abandonment of conservatism. In ten years, everything had changed. Nixon and Nixonism had been soundly rejected by the Grand Old Party. He and his legacy, a walking ghost of a past Republicanism no one wanted haunting their party anymore, were nowhere in evidence in Dallas.

George Will wrote a long, thoughtful column on what had happened inside the two parties during the previous decade and cited a decade-old poll in which respondents, when asked what came to mind when they thought of the GOP, said "Hoover" and "Nixon."[86] That was then.

The Republicans left Dallas more unified than they'd been in years. Even in 1972, Nixon's coronation caused indigestion among anti-communists, as giant photos of Mao and Brezhnev had adorned the convention hall in Miami Beach that year.

The economy had begun to recover in 1983, and by 1984 it was roaring along with a phenomenal growth rate of more than 7 percent. It was creating jobs so fast that there were labor shortages in some parts of the country. High inflation and high interest rates had been eradicated. Reagan's ad-makers, the Tuesday Group, produced the highly effective "Morning in America" ads.

It was Reagan's convention, it was Reagan's platform, it was Reagan's party, and it was Reagan's world. In the words of Bob Hughes, GOP chairman of Cuyahoga County in Ohio, Reagan "so dominates the political scene, he's the colossus . . . Reagan is the only issue for the average voter."[87]

Gingrich, though, saw some problems with the party, saying it had been "klutzy" in dealing with women's issues and minority issues.[88] He did say, however, that male voters thought Mondale was a "jerk."[89]

Part of the backdrop of the convention—like any of them—were the smoldering ambitions of men who thought they, too, had what it took to ascend to the highest office in the land. Dole, Kemp, and of course Vice President Bush were all eyeing 1988. So, too, was outgoing Delaware governor Pierre "Pete" du Pont, who was one of the more interesting and thoughtful Republicans around at the time, even though critics said his first name reminded voters of a French waiter and his last name of a toxic-waste dump.

Several articles reviewed all the possible candidates for the 1988 GOP nomination, and Gingrich's name was mentioned, including one in the *Christian Science Monitor.*[90]

Maureen Dowd wrote a highly favorable piece in the *New York Times* on the Republicans' outreach to women, although moderate women complained about the conservative women in the party on deep philosophical grounds. "With their beehive hairdos and the hour-and-half makeup jobs in the morning—where did they find them? It's just unreal," said Mary Stanley.[91]

Maybe there was something in the water over at the *New York Times.* Maybe they, too, had caught the Reagan fever. Whatever. In their post-mortem editorial on the convention, the Gray Lady was jawdroppingly favorable to the GOP. After a couple of pokes over money ("If the left includes limousine liberals, it is now possible to speak also of chopper conservatives") the paper opined:

> It's a mistake to think of what's happening in Dallas as simply conspicuous conservatism or a hypocritical outreach to the left. There are energetic figures here, like Newt Gingrich of Georgia and Jack Kemp of New York and Vin Weber of Minnesota, who see outreach not in being conciliatory but in being firm on behalf of principles that are not necessarily partisan . . . In this view, the way that the Grand Old Party reaches out most effectively is precisely by standing up on issues . . . [92]

Virtually every story in 1983 and 1984 had Kemp and Gingrich joined at the hips, as examples of new-age conservatism. Sometimes Trent Lott's name would be thrown into the mix or Vin Weber's or Bob Walker's for leavening, but it was always Kemp and Gingrich or Gingrich and Kemp. They went together like peas and carrots. Except when they didn't. On at least one occasion, according to Kemp aide David Hoppe, they fought and had to be brought to the negotiating table to "kiss and make up."[93]

The day before the convention began, Gingrich had published an op-ed in the *Times* on the state and future of the Republican Party, impressive for a third-term congressman, and again, a sign of a new attitude at the paper. In his piece, he noted that the 1984 Republican and Democratic conventions would be the first that the networks did not cover "gavel to gavel."[94] He was getting a lot of media attention, including as the subject of a favorable Michael Barone column that reviewed his life and times and wrote about Gingrich, "He's smiling the smile of a man who thinks he just may have given birth to ideas that can change America and the world."[95]

Upon returning from the GOP lovefest in Dallas—where even one-time Reagan enemy Gerald Ford praised the Gipper—a rally was held for Gingrich in his district, "which will feature a live band, cloggers, free watermelon," the *Atlanta Daily World* proclaimed in advance.[96] At another event in the district, a luau fund-raiser was held, complete with grass skirts. The host, Dave Parrish, a successful businessman, was African American.[97]

Gingrich was busy "delivering at least two speeches a day, giving television and newspaper interviews by the dozens, and still finding time to sell his new book, 'Window of Opportunity.'" He was becoming more and more of a political celebrity, which he thought was "just swell." It was "'wild' . . . to observe reporters fighting one another on the convention floor each night for a private word with him, and to see delegate after delegate jockeying for an opportunity to shake his hand." However, "he acknowledges his new-found celebrity is something of a fad."[98]

So much had changed in so short a time. He'd left his first wife, Jackie, in a divorce and was remarried to Marianne. But his political stock was rising quickly. Ten years earlier, he had a hard time getting the weekly newspapers to pay attention to him in some of the backwaters of the Sixth District. Now he was a recognizable face, and everywhere he went, it was, "Hey, Newt!"

The primary to select a Democratic challenger in the Georgia Sixth was thrown into a runoff, as not one of the four candidates won an outright majority of the vote. Gingrich would have to wait and see who would be selected, State Rep. Gerald Johnson or Robert Watson.[99]

In September, Gingrich held his sixth annual "Forward America" fund-raiser, which was becoming a staple of Georgia GOP politics. Nearly nine hundred people attended the event at the Omni Hotel in Atlanta. The founder and president of Amway, Rich DeVos, was the featured speaker. Gingrich told the crowd, "We are at a moment . . . we can lead the entire world into freedom. This is the most decisive election in my life time: partly because Ronald Reagan is very good and Walter Mondale is very bad."[100]

He had lost weight again. Smiling broadly, he was photographed with President Reagan in the Oval Office, introducing the Gipper to Georgia's poster child for muscular dystrophy, Dawn Alford.[101] It was just days before Reagan's first debate with Walter Mondale and he looked serene.

Gingrich was more serene than Reagan (after the Gipper's disastrous first debate with Mondale), when he appeared in an HBO special entitled *Countdown to Looking Glass*, a fictionalized ninety-minute accounting of growing Cold War tensions in a Middle East superpower showdown. Also featured were Eric Sevareid, longtime radio and television commentator; Paul Warnke, great diplomat of the Cold War; and former senator and poet/philosopher Eugene McCarthy.[102] It was heady stuff for the young man, who was described in one news account as "one of the very least camera-shy members of the House."[103]

A political gift was dumped in Gingrich's lap when Joseph Lowery of the Southern Christian Leadership Conference invited Nicaraguan dictator Daniel Ortega to visit Atlanta. Gingrich, never one for missing an opportunity, slammed the visit.[104]

He received the warm endorsement for his reelection from the black-owned *Atlanta Daily World*, just as he had in every election for the previous ten years. "He has stood up to the Speaker of the House . . . He has addressed many Negro audiences and has stated some strong facts urging support for the people. He has been elected for three terms going into the fourth, and his record deserves his reelection. We are happy to endorse his reelection."[105]

His election effort was short on big ideas, and focused mostly on successful constituent efforts, wise for a young incumbent whom some felt had gotten a bit too big for his britches. The newspaper ads were simple and to the point, relaying one story after another of a Georgian who had been helped by Gingrich. Post offices saved. Surgery arranged for overseas military personnel. Disability payments made available. The ads had a simple message: "It's not always the big things that count. Newt Gingrich works hard to help people not only for the big things, but the things that are really important to them."[106] The ads were paid for by Friends of Newt Gingrich.

Just days before the November election was the one-year anniversary of the liberation of Grenada, a major foreign policy and military success for Reagan. A Soviet-backed regime had been ousted and Republican-affiliated organizations were pushing for rallies on one hundred campuses across the country to mark the occasion on October 24 and 25. Maurice Bishop, the Marxist head of Grenada, had said he wanted to create "a communist society on the Soviet model."[107]

Gingrich said, "On October 25, 1984, America will debate the difference between bondage and freedom . . . [I] invite . . . liberal Democrats to come and explain why they thought Iran was a more appropriate model than Grenada."[108] It was pure Gingrich.

The reelections of Ronald Reagan and Newt Gingrich were never really in doubt.

On Election Day, two networks—CBS and ABC—called Georgia for the Gipper only a few moments after polls had closed there. In all, Reagan took forty-nine of fifty states and might have taken Mondale's Minnesota if he'd campaigned there as his manager, Ed Rollins, wanted him to do the weekend before the November 7 election. Mondale won his home state by just over three thousand votes out of more than two million cast. It was Geraldine Ferraro's first national campaign and it showed. On her plane at the eleventh hour, she told her staff, "I don't want anyone on this airplane talking about losing. We're going to *win*."[109]

It was only the fourth time since Reconstruction that the formerly yellow-dog Georgia had gone Republican in a presidential election (the first time being for Barry Goldwater in 1964 and the second and third for Nixon). Evangelicals, whom Jimmy Carter had politicized back in 1975 and 1976, had by 1980 turned away from the "San Francisco Democrats" and to the "Religious Republicans," giving Reagan and his party their votes by a 3–1 margin. "For years born-again Christians and fundamentalist Christians voted Democratic, particularly in the South," said Democratic pollster William Hamilton.[110] Reagan helped change that.

Gingrich easily waxed his Democratic opponent Gerald Johnson, 69 percent to 31 percent. Johnson had tried to make Newt's national following an issue in the campaign. "He's lost touch with the folks back home . . .

Newt has become a right-wing reactionary, and he's found a place in the national media." Gingrich was unaffected, telling reporters it would be "the least difficult race I've had."[111] He was right.

The 1984 election had come and gone with very few surprises. As expected—by the late fall of 1984 anyway—Ronald Reagan thumped his hapless opponent, Walter Mondale, who fell before the conservative's juggernaut, just as Pat Brown had in California in 1966 and Jimmy Carter had in 1980. But his landslide win was a fairly lonely one, as few new Republicans had any national coattails to grab onto in November. The manner in which Reagan-Bush '84 was run was the subject of debate for years. Just a few months earlier, Republican strategists had dreamed of a second realigning election, to bookend the election of 1980, making the case for the end of the New Deal, the end of the Great Society, and the end of moderate Republicanism.

Gingrich authored yet another column, this one a post-mortem on the election results. It was filled with effusive thanks to the voters. He concluded, "I look forward to a serious effort to put aside narrow partisanship and to spend at least the next year working together with Democrats, Republicans, liberals and conservatives to solve our problems. We must implement the mandate of your vote."[112] Gingrich's deeds and words had up to this point been anything but conciliatory toward either the Republican or Democratic establishments. His new stance would be tested.

The tensions at the end of 1984 were no less than they'd been at the beginning, although the Democrats apparently surrendered in their attempts to block the "Special Orders." It was the final triumph of the year for the GOP. O'Neill's spokesman Chris Matthews harrumphed bitterly, "They cost money, these right-wing follies."[113]

Still, this did not stop the dire predictions by the national media that Reagan would have to succumb to the Democrats' domestic agenda. Some of the predictions also came from members of his own party, including the Ichabod Crane of Wyoming, Alan Simpson, who won reelection to the Senate by a margin of 78–22, proof that Lincoln was right; you could fool all the people some of the time. Gingrich simply said Reagan's legacy could be either like Taft, the anti-reformer, or Teddy Roosevelt, the crown prince of reform.[114]

As yet another testament to his growing influence, Gingrich was invited to Indianapolis to address the annual meeting of the National League of Cities. In no uncertain terms, he told them that Washington must get its fiscal house in order. He again proposed a freeze on nonmilitary defense and domestic spending, except for Medicare and Social Security. Lecturing the three thousand attendees, he stormed, "We should all of us be less selfish. Congress has to be less selfish. The Pentagon has to be less selfish. You have to be less selfish . . . The time has come for all of us to grow up."[115]

CHAPTER 10

FAMILY FEUD

"After Reagan it will be a big bloody battle."

November 1984–January 1985

R onald Reagan had won an historic landslide reelection—one of the largest electoral margins ever recorded in modern times as well as one of the largest in terms of the popular vote—but his party had only picked up 14 House seats and had a net loss of 2 Senate seats.[1] There was some bitterness in Republican circles over the belief that Reagan had run his campaign the same way Richard Nixon had run his in 1972, shunning down-ticket Republicans.

On the other hand, Reagan had run as an unabashed conservative, Walter Mondale as an unabashed liberal; the choice could not have been clearer between the two competing philosophies. Nonetheless, the *New York Times* only went so far as to call the pasting Reagan administered to Mondale a "setback" for the Democrats.[2]

Reagan's savvy campaign manager, Ed Rollins, said before the election, "By Inauguration Day the camps will be divided. There is no question that we are going to have a primary season in 1988 that will make the Democratic race in 1984 look tame. The whole direction of the party, post the Reagan era, is up for grabs."[3]

Reagan had created a new political party and governing coalition, but much of it was held together by disparate conservatives' devotion to him. The Gipper was the party's superglue. Bill Hamilton, a Democratic pollster, said the demographic of the Republicans began changing even before the 1980 election, when Mr. Reagan wooed Christian ministers who use television as their pulpit. They are a major part of the Jack Kemp-Newt Gingrich-Jesse Helms wing of the Republican Party . . . "This year they went almost three to one for Reagan, and two and a half to one for the Republican candidate for Congress."[4]

Of the looming split inside the GOP, Hamilton predicted "a mean fight."[5]

When you threw into this stew Reagan Democrats, neocons, theocons, libertarians, globalists, isolationists, Police State Republicans, Vichy Republicans, intellectualists, moralists, absolutionists, country club Republicans, bowling league Republicans, Ivy League Republicans, prairie league Republicans, sellout Republicans, access-selling Republicans, lapsed Republicans, pink elephant Republicans, teetotaling Republicans, preppy Republicans, blue-collar Republicans, K Street Republicans, Main Street Republicans, Wall Street Republicans, street-walking Republicans, Know Nothing Republicans, Sun Belt Republicans, Bible Belt Republicans, Rust Belt Republicans, Farm Belt Republicans, belt-tightening Republicans, bootstrap Republicans, lace curtain Republicans, Delta House Republicans, Omega House Republicans, Gypsy Moth Republicans, Gold standard Republicans, Welfare State Republicans, disestablishmentarianism Republicans, and statist Republicans, there was bound to be an opinion or two, not to mention more than a few disagreements.

Minutes after the Gipper had been reelected by the second-largest landslide in US history, *Time* magazine opined, "Many in Washington now regard him as a lame duck."[6]

Reagan himself was mirthful in his diaries. "Well 49 states, 59% of the vote and 525 electoral votes. The press is now trying to prove it wasn't a landslide."[7]

Before the November election, there had been some talk among the conservative Republicans in the House and the Boll Weevils that if the GOP picked up 30 seats or more, they could overthrow O'Neill and install a former representative, Joe Waggonner of Louisiana, as Speaker. By the rules, the Speaker of the House did not have to be a sitting member of Congress. But with the disappointing election results, that plan went up in smoke.[8]

O'Neill and the Democrats had only one option to weigh and that was to limit the Young Turks' use of the "Special Orders" they had engaged so effectively for all of 1984. Martin Frost, a partisan Democrat from Texas and chairman of the committee with oversight of the end-of-day proceedings, said with a straight face that the decision to limit "Special Orders" was because of money and not politics or policy. Eventually, the decision to give or not give one hour each day was proposed to be put in the hands of Minority Leader Bob Michel, who was as repelled by his own Young Turks as O'Neill and the Democrats were. Gingrich, knowing Michel would clamp down on him and his cohorts, called the decision "pure political bossism."[9]

Still, one unadulterated winner of 1984 had been Brian Lamb and his brainchild, C-SPAN. Though relatively small in reach as of 1984, it had an outsized influence over Washington, and the ongoing fights between Gingrich and the Democrats in the House had rained down millions of dollars' worth of notoriety. Now everywhere in America where cable television was, subscribers wanted to know how to get C-SPAN.

C-SPAN had been broadcasting House proceedings for several years by this point, but the Senate had pronounced that the cameras would never be allowed into their august presence. Bob Dole, the incoming majority leader, bitterly fought against cameras in the upper body.

Congressman Mickey Edwards, the nominal head of the American Conservative Union, came out of nowhere to blast Gingrich for his "confrontation[s]" with Tip O'Neill, saying they cost the GOP more seats. Edwards had not been a factor in any way, shape, or form for years, but his popping out of nowhere to offer an opinion was not ignored.[10]

The fight predicted inside the GOP wasn't off in the future. It had already begun. The media lapped it up. Reagan chortled to himself that the media was downplaying his landslide and that he no longer had a Congress to work with. He went to the ranch to savor his victory.[11]

Jack Kemp, Gingrich, and the Young Turks said the entire tax code needed to be scrapped, the slate wiped clean, and a whole new tax law enacted. The phrases "tax simplification" and "tax reform" were passed around conservative circles beginning in the early days of 1985. Of course, the establishment once again thought the Crazies were, well, crazy.

There was also a fight looming between the supply-siders and the budget-balancers. Gingrich was mortified when the politically hobbled David Stockman, who was still Reagan's budgetmeister as director of the Office of Management and Budget, spoke of a "grand compromise." In a long, long, long public letter printed in the editorial pages of the *Washington Post*, the Georgian told his old friend in no uncertain terms, "You're becoming the greatest obstacle to a successful revolution from the Liberal Welfare State to an Opportunity Society."[12] Frankly, Gingrich was punching down.

Gingrich loved the word *opportunity*. His new book was called *Window of Opportunity*, and he was gratified that Reagan frequently used the word on the stump. But he and his fellow House conservatives were disappointed that their old colleague, Stockman, had lost his mind, the pressure of the office having made him somewhat of a laughing stock.

Though the conservative movement since the time of Barry Goldwater had begun changing the face of American politics, especially in the South, it did not mean the new Republican Party was going to embrace the racial politics of that region—or of the Democrats who once dominated it at the presidential level and still dominated it at the local and congressional levels. There were racists in the GOP in 1985, just as there were in the Democratic Party, to be sure, but the Republicans at least had the history of Lincoln on their side.

This extended to the apartheid policies of South Africa. While an American ally in the fight against world communism, it was still a black-majority country being controlled by an oppressive white-minority regime.

Many anti-communists, especially of a previous generation, gave lip service to ending apartheid in the African country, but for younger conservatives, support for the existing government was simply morally wrong and anti-intellectual. If America had been founded on the principle of "one man, one vote" and if it worked in other countries, then it would also work in the South African government. The Reagan Administration had embraced a policy of "constructive engagement" with the idea of a peaceful transfer of power, but many in America saw it as foot-dragging, too slow, too plodding.[13]

Newt Gingrich fired a warning shot across the bow of his own party, saying that "South Africans could not count on support for their racial policies from the younger breed of American conservatives."[14]

Gingrich had emerged as the main spokesman for the Republican revolutionaries in all matters. "At the center of the conflict is . . . Gingrich . . . the insurgency's high priest, whose barbed rhetoric has set its tone," said the *Washington Post*.[15] He was again featured in a number of high-profile stories, assailing Stockman, Dole, and others whom he saw as threats to the Reagan revolution. He appeared on *This Week with David Brinkley* in early December to defend his combative style against growing criticism, although the topics also covered terrorism and apartheid. On the show, Gingrich was able to restate his opposition to apartheid and warned of sanctions against the white-minority government unless it moved toward democratic rule immediately. "The only alternative is absolute bloody violence on an unimaginable scale . . ."[16]

Meanwhile, *Conservative Digest* was touting him to become the chairman of the Republican National Committee.[17] The Moral Majority said he had the "credentials to compete with Bush for the support of religious-right voters" for the 1988 GOP nomination, along with Kemp, Senator Bill Armstrong, and Ambassador Jeane Kirkpatrick.[18]

More importantly on the world stage, however, was the emergence of a new Soviet premier, Mikhail Gorbachev. This one was different. Younger, more television savvy. Three Soviet premiers had died in the past four years, leaving Reagan no one to talk to in the Kremlin.

Gingrich piled up enemies. His battle with Dole continued, unabated. "People like Dole and [Pete] Domenici spend all their time running around trying to feed the liberal welfare state they inherited," he said. Dole sharply replied, "There are always people who have all the ideas—but no votes."[19]

Just a few months earlier, while Gingrich was in San Francisco during the Democratic Convention and to promote his new book *Window of Opportunity*, an aide to a House Republican told the *Wall Street Journal*, "Some of our group feel his presence is a bit too over-antagonistic, exploitative—too media oriented."[20]

No reasonable historian of Reagan has ever suggested for a moment that absent the Twenty-Second Amendment, he would have sought a third term at age seventy-seven, but the presence of the amendment also took a great deal of negotiating power away from a reelected president, just as it had with Eisenhower, Johnson, and Nixon. Now Reagan's ability to get things done in Congress was hamstrung, as attentions on both sides were focusing on who their next nominees would be. "After Reagan, it will be a big, bloody battle," said John Albertine, a conservative economist. Meanwhile Tony Coelho chortled, "There's a bloodletting coming that is going to be absolutely wonderful."[21]

Fights were also looming in the GOP House conference. Bob Michel's run as minority leader was winding down as of 1985. Time had simply passed him by and members were jockeying for his position. The most aggressive were Dick Cheney and Trent Lott.

Tom Downey, a very liberal member of the House from New York, assailed Gingrich on the *MacNeil/Lehrer Report*, saying, "Newt Gingrich represents a wing of his party that just doesn't believe that the government is a particularly good idea except for delivering mail and having a huge defense."[22] Downey was wrong. There were some conservatives who didn't think government should be in the business of delivering the mail.

On the same show was Bob Dole, who audaciously suggested he could forge a budget compromise that would satisfy both Downey and Gingrich, and reduce the deficit. Gingrich replied, "You'd be a miracle worker if you could do that."[23]

The Conservative Opportunity Society was continuing to meet each Wednesday morning, usually in the offices of its nominal chairman, Vin Weber, though everybody knew who was really in charge of the COS.[24] As always, Gingrich was focused like a searchlight on getting the upper hand over the Democrats and, in so doing, making the House Republicans the good guys.

In tandem with Gingrich's thinking was the National Conservative Political Action Committee, who had just spent $14 million supporting Reagan's reelection. The group's unofficial motto was "Elect conservatives and make life miserable for liberals."[25] Gingrich utterly agreed.

The situation in the House had always been bad, but its large-scale deterioration had been coming for a long time. A state of war had existed between the two parties since the 1980 election. Even Newt's close friends said his style of campaigning was sometimes "too personal."[26]

Reagan, in his first cabinet meeting after cleaning Walter Mondale's clock and after receiving a depressing report from David Stockman on the deficit, harrumphed that he was "not in a compromising mood."[27] It was music to the ears of the Young Turks.

Stockman projected the deficit to grow to more than $200 billion in 1985.[28] *Where* to cut now divided the Reagan Robots. Jack Kemp inveighed against any cut in social spending, favoring instead to stimulate the economy and create more revenue for the federal honeypot.[29] Gingrich, more wisely, said that Reagan "has a remarkable capacity to let all of his staff argue in public for weeks and weeks and weeks and then reach beyond them and do what makes sense."[30] Gingrich also revived his aging proposal to freeze federal spending across the board for two years, including defense.[31]

As his star rose, Gingrich had been the subject of more and more profiles, mostly favorable, from conservative and liberal publications and writers. That is until he ran into the George F. Will buzz saw. Will was beloved by many as a fearless articulator of conservatism, often defending Reagan while elegantly dismembering liberals and liberalism. But Will was also an anomaly. For one thing, he was no fan of Thomas Paine, who was one of Reagan's favorite philosophers. Reagan often cited Paine's famous "we have it in our power to begin the world over again," which, to a Burkean conservative like Will, sounded like the dirty fingernails of a steelworker dragging across an Ivy League blackboard.

Will despised the notion of "populism." Gingrich was fond of it. Not that Will had grown up the scion of wealth and privilege, although both his parents were educators. He called the Georgian a "cherub with a chip on his shoulder. Round-faced and boyish beneath a shock of graying hair, Gingrich, 41, radiates intelligence and impatience." He elaborated, "When Republican colleagues say he is an agent of chaos, he says: you're darn tootin' I am."

Will scored Gingrich for his devotion to populism. He saved his most acidulous ink for the last paragraph:

But the Republican right cannot have it both ways; it cannot have its critique of modern government and its populism, too. If this democracy is going downhill fast, the *demos*—the people—must bear a large portion of the blame. So "conservative populism" is contradictory. It is, of course, flattering to "the people" to be told that they are virtuous and that an elite is to blame for the nation's ills. But is such flattery what is needed? It certainly is not new.[32]

Years later, Gingrich said Will was intimidated by him because he'd read more books than the scholarly columnist.[33]

CHAPTER 11

REPUBLICAN VERSUS
REPUBLICAN VERSUS
DEMOCRAT

*"The biggest division in the Republican Party . . . is between
those who are serious about building a majority party and
those who are locked into the mentality of a minority party."*

1985

The inauguration was scheduled for January 20, 1985, as prescribed by the Constitution. The problem was that January 20 fell on a Sunday, so the fortieth president was sworn in privately that day and publicly a day later. But even that didn't go according to plan.

A cold snap had descended upon Washington on the twenty-first with a daytime high of only seven degrees. Instruments were freezing to the lips of performers. The parade was cancelled, as was the scheduled swearing in of the president on the west facade of the Capitol. It was moved indoors to the Rotunda. The indoor events were more or less a disaster. At one inaugural ball (there were nine of them that year) at the DC Convention Center, drinks were overpriced, the entertainment was underwhelming, the heating was inadequate, and the coat-checking system was an unmitigated disaster. Women's expensive fur coats were stolen; fistfights broke out while others waited in line for hours for coats that never appeared.

It was the fiftieth time a man had been inaugurated as president of the United States.

Reagan, though, was unfazed by the changes. He gave a well-received, if subdued, speech. Again, he borrowed a page from Newt Gingrich's book, using the phrase "American Opportunity Society." Echoing the Conservative Opportunity Society, Reagan spoke of "an American opportunity society in which all of us—white and black, rich and poor, young and old—will go forward together, arm in arm."[1] A *New York Times* columnist referred to the phrase as "Gingrich's trademark."[2]

Reagan also made reference to his favorite phrase from philosopher Thomas Paine, that Americans had it in their power to "start the world over again." Gingrich called the address "a teaching document for the next generation of Republicans."[3] He sometimes used professorial phrases such as "sociological coup" and "alienation of democracy" to get his point across, but in this instance, his analysis of the Reagan address was spot on.[4]

Later, Gingrich hosted a six-hour indoor barbecue for constituents and friends, at which he could presumably sit and rest after standing in the Capitol for so many hours. Gingrich declaimed on the culture, as an enraptured Miss National Teenager, Kimberley Norris, listened: "Today we are engaged in a great civil war, an intellectual civil war."[5]

In one of his columns, Gingrich—self-aware—wrote, "I'm occasionally accused of being different than the average Congressman."[6]

Newt Gingrich was going international. After Vice President Bush declined an invitation to debate US policy in Central America at Oxford University, Gingrich leapt at the chance and journeyed to England to take on Sergio Ramírez Mercado, the vice president of Nicaragua, in early February. The resolution to be debated was "American involvement in Nicaragua is an affront to western values."[7] Gingrich's job was to defend Reagan's policies in Central America. The resolution passed 240–130, but the president of the society, Rowland Rudd, was effusive, saying Gingrich's performance was superb. By the judgment of the wise scholars of Oxford, America was an affront to Nicaragua, even as Mercado spoke first and then departed, refusing even to listen to Gingrich.[8]

Gingrich, attired in black-tie in the tradition of the forum, stayed and took questions and received a standing ovation from the left-wing audience. "Ramirez got his [ovation] because of what he represented. Gingrich earned his by sheer brilliance," said Rudd.[9] Still, this did not stop the *Wall Street Journal* from smarmily pointing out that Gingrich "lost" by a vote of the leftist student body, who had once voted against fighting Hitler.[10] Oxford was hopelessly leftist, anti-West, pro-deconstruction, and even against awarding an honorary degree to one of its most distinguished alumna, Margaret Thatcher. Thatcher, as always, had the last word on the matter when she said, "If they do not wish to confer the honor, I am the last person who would wish to receive it."[11]

Aid to the "Contras"—the Nicaraguan Freedom Fighters—came up again in April 1985, as it had all through the Reagan years. Reagan went before religious leaders arguing that the Daniel Ortega regime suppressed faith in the war-torn country, as befitting any good atheistic communist.

Reagan wanted another $14 million in aid.

The issue was fraught with high drama and high stakes. The Contras and the CIA were hugely controversial, as the agency had secretly mined the harbors of the country, handing out assassination guide books to the Contras, who had themselves been accused of killing civilians. Carter's former CIA chief, Stansfield Turner, said Reagan's strategy was a "dead-end policy."[12] Still, some Democrats thought aiding the anti-communist guerillas was important, including the unassailable Senator Sam Nunn, whose intelligence was widely regarded and whose integrity was beyond question.[13]

On the other hand, Gingrich was mystified by some of his House Democratic colleagues, like Barney Frank of the Bay State, who said he feared Connecticut more than Nicaragua, and Congresswoman Pat Schroeder of Colorado, who made fun of the idea that a communist regime taking military aid from the Soviets could be any threat to the United States. Gingrich, despite his disagreements with the two, called Frank "bright, intelligent and personable" and Schroeder "very bright."[14]

Reagan, Gingrich, and the Contras were crushed in the House vote, 248–180. Gingrich called the defeat "dangerous" for the United States.[15]

Gingrich later went on the *MacNeil/Lehrer NewsHour* to debate Tom Foley, who was third in line in the House leadership, over the issue of aiding the Contras. One month later, the House voted for "humanitarian" aid, but no armaments. Many conservatives voted against the bill, seeing it as feckless. The House also passed the Boland Amendment, which was designed to tie the hands of Reagan in Central America. Gingrich sneered at the amendment, offered up by O'Neill's friend and roommate of thirty years, Congressman Eddie Boland: "A vote for the Boland Amendment is in fact a vote for unilateral disarmament of the side that favors freedom in Central America," Gingrich charged.[16]

Democrats, in response, began referring to Gingrich, Dick Cheney, Jack Kemp, and others who had not served in the military as "war wimps."[17]

In May, Congress took up the issue of the controversial MX missile. Reagan was scheduled to meet in Geneva with Mikhail Gorbachev, and he wanted to go in with a strong negotiating position. Gingrich cut to the chase when he told the *Christian Science Monitor*, "[Y]ou'll see the libs [liberals] make their good, hard charge but you'll see the leadership not pushing . . . Would you want Reagan on TV that night explaining that 'the Democrats destroyed my bargaining position?'"[18] It was quips like this that made "libs" want to string up Newt.

As one gained a higher profile in Washington, one was often subjected to the standard-issue acerbic profile in the Style section of the *Washington Post*, whose "style" was usually to slobber over liberals and rip the innards out of conservatives. Gingrich foolishly agreed to be profiled, and writer Lois Romano hit him right between the eyes, calling him "abrasive," a "brat," and worse. Gingrich tried to make light of his reputation, saying he'd taken his friends' advice to lighten up. Still, "there are scars I have made in the last two or three years that will be with me through the rest of my career."[19]

The so-called friends were in the story, stabbing Newt in the chest. Only New Right leader Paul Weyrich was quoted supporting Gingrich without reservation. Romano did give Gingrich credit for "taking control of the GOP platform in Dallas . . ." though much of the story was personal, not political. Romano interviewed Jackie Gingrich, Gingrich's first wife, extensively. Romano resurrected the *Mother Jones* story of November 1984, a complete thrashing of Gingrich. Jackie told Romano, "I didn't find much in it off the mark."[20] The *Jones* story was written with the help of a vengeful former employee of Gingrich's.

The Romano tale revealed how Representative Tony Coelho made 252 copies of the *Mother Jones* piece and thoughtfully sent them to every Democratic House member. Newt did tell Romano his divorce from Jackie "was not pleasant." Jackie had one recollection of the divorce, Gingrich, another. She tried to reconcile but he resisted.[21]

They'd been married for twenty years and by many accounts, including those of their daughters and of Newt and Jackie themselves, most had been happy. The picture that emerged was of a shy student and an equally shy teacher who had once been in love, had grown apart from his wife, but who still had at least wistful feelings about the dead marriage. No one outside of a marriage could ever really know the highs and lows of intimacy, but you couldn't tell the *Washington Post* or *Mother Jones* that, especially about conservatives. (Some twenty years later, Gingrich was still paying Jackie alimony and had agreed to do so for the rest of her life.[22])

The divorce, *Mother Jones*, the Nicaraguan Contras, Eddie Boland, and Tip O'Neill were all caught up in the same web involving Newt and the Democrats' desire to get him, however they could. O'Neill told Coehlo, "I want you to get him."[23] Gingrich later said he knew because columnist Bob Novak told him about the Speaker's icy order.

Newt got his new committee assignments, though he did not get new offices. He also joined the Aviation and Surface Transportation subcommittees, beneficial for Atlanta, with its sprawling roads and ever-expanding airport. He immediately secured $225 million out of the overall $7.2 billion in federal highway money for his state. When called upon, he could bring home the bacon as well as anyone.

But what really got conservative blood racing in early 1985 was the ham-handed—some said "corrupt"—way in which the majority Democrats handled the controversy and outcome of the Eighth Congressional District race in Indiana. Simply put, the national Democrats stole the race, fair and square, even as the Republican there, Rick McIntyre, had been certified the winner by the Indiana Board of Elections and the Indiana secretary of state. Twice. He'd won on Election Day in November by a margin of 34 votes. The state law stipulated a revote. McIntyre won that by 415 votes. That should have settled it, but at the urging of Tony Coelho, House majority leader Jim Wright refused to seat McIntyre and instead, the losing Democrat, Frank McCloskey, was awarded the seat.[24]

The Reagan White House needed a spokesman to make the GOP's case and they chose not the minority leader, Bob Michel, but Gingrich instead, according to columnists Evans and Novak.[25] The Reagan White House, and frankly everybody in the GOP, was sick of Michel's affection

for going down without swinging, more interested in golfing and socializ-
ing with Tip O'Neill than with doing what everybody on the right thought
was right.

Thanks to the Georgian, Washington went into an uproar that cul-
minated in a walkout of Congress by all the members of the House GOP
conference, embarrassing to the Democrats as the network reporters filmed
it all. Reagan got in on the act when he personally called McIntyre to offer
his condolences while calling the whole fiasco a "robbery."[26]

The Democrats in the House assembled a twelve-member kanga-
roo court to review the Indiana election and, shock and surprise, the vote
came down 12–0 against McIntyre and for McCloskey. Gingrich called it a
"totally phony, totally deceitful setup."[27] The rest of the Republican establishment called it the "Bloody Eighth."[28]

"The final recount was overseen by a House task force that split 2 to 1
along party lines over whether to count certain unnotarized, absentee ballots," reported the *Post*.[29] The Democrats rejected a Republican suggestion
for a special election to definitively decide the Indiana Eighth. McCloskey
was seated by a vote in the House of 236–190, with ten Democrats joining
the Republicans. Wright pooh-poohed the complaints and said how "sorry"
he felt for them, naming Jack Kemp and Bob Michel. Conspicuously absent
was any mention of Gingrich.[30] Gingrich, for his part, used words such as
"corrupt" and "thugs" in describing the Democrats.[31]

The incident was galvanizing. The minority Republicans now fully
embraced Gingrich's idea of guerrilla warfare, introducing resolutions, forcing paper ballots rather than electronic voting, denouncing the Democrats
from the well in the most acerbic terms allowed, all to the point that
House majority leader Jim Wright recessed the chamber. In response, the
Republicans en masse went to the steps of the US Capitol and ripped the
Democrats even more for the benefit of the national media.

Congressman Dick Cheney, incensed, said they "ought to go to war."[32]
Others talked up physical retaliation against the Democrats. It was a seminal
moment in the evolution of relations between Republicans and Democrats
in the US House. From there on out, many of the more moderate members,
who had recoiled at the antics of the Conservative Opportunity Society and
their constant challenges to the Democratic status quo, took a hard look
at their milquetoast leadership under Bob Michel and another at Gingrich

and the Crazies. Centrist Republicans were frankly appalled at the "Banana Democracy" of the House Democrats.

Gingrich's hand had been strengthened. "This deep well of bitterness extends to the entire Republican Party," he warned, darkly.[33] Even Olympia Snowe of Maine, a moderate, was appalled at the Democrats' high-handedness: "This McIntyre thing symbolizes frustrations that have been building up for years."[34]

The *Wall Street Journal* observed, "Rep. Gingrich's strategy not only looks justified to us, but inevitable."[35] The entire fiasco led to a nearly permanent rift between the parties. Never again would Republicans work with the Democrats without suspicion. The atmosphere in the House was downright poisonous. Words like "embittered," "outrage," "last straw," and "sour" echoed throughout the chamber. The Republicans refused to be anywhere near the House when McCloskey was sworn in, and the controversy lingered for days in the media.

Amid the smoke and acrimony of the "Bloody Eighth," Reagan's proposed $14 million in aid to the Contras went down by the achingly close margin of 215–213.

The Republicans vowed revenge.

Reagan's secretary of state, George Schulz, took the long view. He sat down with a group of Reagan's Revolutionaries, including Vin Weber, after they suggested the State Department lacked courage in how it had presented the case for the Contras. "Boys, in 1964, I was one of two professors at the University of Chicago that supported Barry Goldwater publically. I don't need any . . . lectures from you on political courage."[36]

Gingrich earned high marks and praise for rallying the Republicans around the Indiana House seat. Another moderate Republican, Lynn Martin of Illinois, said of her colleague's style, "Without that, you could always be in a minority."[37] Other Republicans fretted—on background to the *Washington Post*—over Newt's renewed strength. "Some Republicans fear that the Indiana episode vindicates Gingrich, who has long said the Democrats should not be trusted. And they are seeking to prevent him from dominating the strategy decisions that lie ahead . . . Gingrich's high profile and inflated rhetoric made some of his Republican colleagues nervous."[38]

He was unmoved by any nervousness. "Before I came here the Democrats and Republicans played golf, and the Democrats came off the course and beat [their] brains out. Now Republicans feel it is legitimate for them to do the same."[39] He and his cohorts contemplated more ways in which to disrupt the business of the House.

The Democrats retreated to mockery. Jim Wright, majority leader, sneered at the Republicans' tactics, saying, "When this is over, maybe they'll have a prom."[40]

Vice President George Bush journeyed to Atlanta as the featured guest at a state party event honoring Gingrich. Gingrich, GOP state chair Bob Bell noted, had led the way for the party in Georgia, breaking the "drought" there for the once-hated party of Lincoln.[41] Since his win in 1980, the party had added a US senator, Mack Mattingly, and another House member, Rep. Pat Swindall, as well as a handful of local officials.

Trade was another issue in which Gingrich went against his own national party, favoring the parochial interests of his state and the South. He railed against Japanese imports, as they threatened the region's burgeoning "high tech" industry.

Another trade issue important to Gingrich was textile imports. Textile manufacturers had held sway over much of the South since before the Civil War. In 1985, they came up with a doozy of a proposal, which Gingrich sponsored in legislation. It called for reducing "the growth rate of imported products so as not to exceed the long-term growth expectations of the U.S. market for such goods." The bill was pure protectionism, anti–free market, and a sop to the millionaires and billionaires who owned those mills in the South. The usual accusations of "sweat-shop standards" labor and "government subsidized products" were aimed at the countries that exported clothing to America.[42]

It was clear to anyone with even less-than-perfect vision that the GOP was bipolar. The House Republicans embraced the politics of revolution, the Senate Republicans embraced the politics of respect, and the Administration was divided, with Reagan more comfortable with the revolutionaries but his aides more comfortable with the "thank-you note" set. Said the *Economist*:

But many conservative Republicans share the basic concern of the pugnacious young congressmen: they want to ensure that Mr. Reagan's second term is more successful than his first term in translating a right-wing vision, enunciated at the Republican convention and indeed throughout the campaign, into specific right-wing programmes. Language and attitudes may have changed, they say, but the fundamentals are unaltered. Many of the president's admirers came to Washington, like Mr. Reagan himself, as anti-government rebels.[43]

The life of a congressman wasn't all peaches and cream. Under the klieg lights of national fame, it was downright hard to have any semblance of a personal life. House members often kept their bags at the door of the chamber late into the evening, hoping against hope that a late-night vote would take place at the scheduled time, allowing them a hasty retreat to National Airport. Gingrich calculated that if a vote took place at 8:00 p.m., he could be out the door and into a cab and still make a plane scheduled for departure at 8:23, going through security and all. This was 1985.

Having adjusted his thinking to be sure he didn't forget about the home folks, Gingrich was now going home most weekends. On Mondays, he would depart from the Atlanta Airport around 6:30 a.m. after leaving his home in Jonesboro around 5:45. On the flight back to Washington, he'd review mail, have breakfast, and usually be at his office on the Hill by 8:20. The day was filled with an intermingling of affairs as they pertained to Georgia, his district in particular, and broader affairs of state, the deficit in particular. He'd eat lunch at his desk while making phone calls, and the day wouldn't be over until well after 8:00 p.m.[44] Everything he had to do was on the busy itinerary, including getting his driver's license renewed, a haircut, and having his teeth cleaned.[45] Mostly, he met with constituents and gave luncheon and dinner speeches. Rarely did he have a day off.

Representatives also had to disclose their finances, and Gingrich was no exception. In May 1985, his "minimum earnings were $99,600 including $22,200 in honorariums ($500 of which went to charity) and $5,000 in a book royalties advance. [He] reported no holdings and minimum liabilities of $20,000."[46]

Gingrich was also receiving, on average, one thousand letters per week, far more than ones received by other members of Congress, and not all were from his district.[47] In at least one of his weekly columns, he issued a broad invitation to Georgians to visit Washington, take in the museums—including his particular favorite, the dinosaurs—and come visit him. "We're in 1005 Longworth, right across the street from your Capitol."[48]

A major controversy broke out when it was revealed that during a state visit to West Germany, at the request of the German government, Reagan was to visit a cemetery in Bitburg where some members of the Nazi SS had been buried. Gingrich and Vin Weber went to the White House to implore Pat Buchanan, Reagan's communications chief, to put a halt to the planned visit, but they were shot down. They called the visit "morally wrong." Reagan went ahead, as he'd made a commitment to Helmut Kohl, chancellor of West Germany.[49] Dozens of members of Congress signed a letter to Kohl asking he withdraw his invitation to Reagan. Gingrich was one of the signees.

It wasn't just Soviet advances that worried Americans, but the growing threat of terrorism as well. TWA flight 847 was hijacked in June 1985, and after seventeen tense days in which thirty-nine American passengers were held hostage, the Reagan Administration earned high praise for ending the crisis decisively, in part by bringing in the International Red Cross to help mediate the situation. Seven Americans were still being held hostage in Beirut, but on the plane from Damascus to Rhein-Main US air base, those thirty-nine Americans were freed.[50]

Reagan was knocked by several conservatives of the "New Right," and Gingrich was only cautiously supportive. The *Wall Street Journal* lambasted the president under an editorial titled "Jimmy Reagan."[51]

Within days, Gingrich cosponsored and helped pass the International Airport Security Act of 1985. Part of its initial responsibility was to survey all international airports and proclaim them safe or unsafe for Americans to fly in and out of. Shortly after the act was signed into law, the US government began to periodically announce the safety or lack thereof of certain airports. In the mid-1980s, the airport in Athens, Greece, was often proclaimed unsafe for traveling Americans.

Another bill he cosponsored—then curiously voted against—was the American Conservation Corps. By the time members got through larding the proposal up with pork, it was unrecognizable, and the Georgian voted against what many felt was a good stab at reducing the unemployment of young Americans.[52]

The Reagan Administration and the Democratic Congress moved ahead with comprehensive tax reform, a bill that if successful, would be the most fundamental change to the tax code since 1954. In June, Gingrich offered one of his periodic "New Age" ideas when he proposed the government create the "National Foresight Capability" office. Senator Al Gore had suggested his own, "Office of Critical Trends Analysis."[53] Congress, lacking vision, did not act on either suggestion. Gingrich was bashed by *Southern Partisan* magazine, as they awarded him with their "Scalawag Award" for voting for the 1985 Civil Rights Act.[54]

Meanwhile, the 1986 campaign year was already gearing up, and an unusual opponent to Gingrich was testing the waters: the son of former president Jimmy Carter, Chip Carter. Carter had been in Florida, raising money while telling people he expected a race with Newt to be a "bloodbath."[55] All took note.

The issue of AIDS, Acquired Immune Deficiency Syndrome, was gaining greater and greater attention, though it only directly affected a small part of the population. At first, it was thought Haitians, hemophiliacs, and homosexuals contracted the disease; but shortly thereafter, it was narrowed down to gays who engaged in unprotected sex and who, via blood transfusions or dirty needles, could pass it on to others. Gingrich went on a local public affairs show in Atlanta to discuss the matter. Suffice it to say, the highly charged issue brought out the best—and the worst—in Americans. Gingrich called for treating the disease, though he compared it to the "bubonic plague" and what "chicken pox did to the Iroquois nation."[56]

The *Atlanta Daily World* continued: "Gingrich, R-Ga., said . . . health officials should stop reassuring people that AIDS isn't a disaster and start making them face up to its dangers." Elaborating, Gingrich said that "in order to contain AIDS, you have to contain people's behavior. In order to contain people's behavior, you have to get their attention." While he called for doctors to report patients who had AIDS-positive blood, he also came out against quarantining its victims.[57]

The public health risk of AIDS was on everybody's mind because, frankly, everybody was scared, as they didn't know how it was carried or transmitted. Could a mosquito carry it and inject AIDS-positive blood into someone who had been negative? Could it be transmitted by casual contact, by perspiration on one's hand? No one knew for sure and a low-level panic set in, especially in urban America. In Flint, Michigan, "a 27-year-old AIDS carrier who allegedly spat in the face of two police officers attempting to arrest him was arraigned Saturday on a charge of assault with intent to murder."[58]

In September, the House defeated a Gingrich proposal that would have "required 75% of food-stamp recipients to participate in state employment and training programs."[59] The proposal went down 227–183.

Apartheid, Central America, tax reform, AIDS, nuclear war, the economy, terrorism, the line-item veto, Gramm-Rudman, the Geneva Summit, the MX missile—all these issues and more raged through 1985.

The party was in conflict, no doubt. Partially because of Reagan, a libertarian strain had been introduced into the GOP. Some of the Social Right worried that younger conservatives had become agnostic on issues such as abortion. It looked to them as though the GOP was becoming "a party of greed and sex."[60]

The civil war was also manifesting itself in the fight for the 1988 Republican Party nomination, one very much worth having, coming on the heels of Reagan's successful two-term legacy. Contenders, including Vice President George Bush, Congressman Jack Kemp, Senator Bob Dole, and a smattering of others, all promised to be the "Son of Reagan." Problem was, the president already had two sons.

Republicans were beginning to think about a post-Reagan party. Private confabs and conferences, white papers and the like littered the political landscape on the right. Conservatives saw Reagan as epochal, a game changer. Establishment Republicans saw him as a nice guy who was a political aberration and whose legacy would be short-lived, as all sophisticated people knew the liberal welfare state was here to stay, and it was about accepting this as a permanency in life and culture, so the best thing to do was to prove they, the Republicans, could manage it better than the Democrats. It was not a message to blow the wind up anyone's skirt. A group of Republicans—long dubious of Reagan—held a top-secret meeting, which was later leaked to the media, called "Reagan Revolution Stage 2." Moderates in attendance included Governor Lamar Alexander of Tennessee, John Sununu of New Hampshire, and Jim Martin of North Carolina. Gingrich was invited to give the meeting a little seasoning, a patina of conservative thinking.[61]

Gingrich was also reflecting on his own future, his stance in the party, with the Conservative Opportunity Society—even as Vin Weber was the actual chairman—and in national politics. The successes of the past several years had gone to his head, some thought, including some of his closest friends. In the words of the *Washington Post*:

> By the time of the 1984 Republican National Convention in Dallas, many of Gingrich's ideas had found their way into the Republican platform and President Reagan was referring to the GOP as the "Grand Opportunity Party." [On the other hand,] this has not been a good year for Gingrich . . . [who,] according to associates, alienated even many of his friends with an increasingly overbearing manner.[62]

Still, he was philosophical. "I've said over and over again that this is a long-term effort. I'm very comfortable in not having our group trying to dominate through the entire 24-month cycle of a Congress. I don't think it's possible."[63]

Weber was feistier. "The biggest division in the Republican Party is . . . between those who are serious about building a majority party and those who are locked into the mentality of a minority party."[64]

The Democrats finally wised up and organized their own band of baying politicians to go onto the floor of the House at the end of the day to declaim whatever was on their minds, defend government programs, and attack the GOP.

Meanwhile, House Republicans were knocking heads with the Administration over the long-planned tax reform package. On the first vote to allow debate, the old coalition of Republicans and Boll Weevil Democrats came together to shoot down the legislation, a rebuke of both Reagan and Dan Rostenkowski, chairman of Ways and Means.[65] Only 14 Republicans out of 182 sided with the White House. Trent Lott warned Reagan, "Mr. President, if you're going to lie down with the dogs, you're going to get fleas." According to Lott, Reagan laughed.[66]

Gingrich had organized a letter to Reagan, signed by thirty-eight House Republicans, telling him the bill was so bad that he ought to junk it and start over. A White House aide, John Roberts, said, "The risk we run is that the White House could lose control of the party."[67]

Within a matter of days, Reagan went directly to Capitol Hill to meet with the recalcitrant conservatives. He had also been working the phones hard, calling some forty Republicans to bring them into line.

The Reagan visit did the trick. He promised the House Republicans he'd veto the bill if it did not contain a two-thousand-dollar exemption for every taxpayer, reduce capital gains, and contain a "lower top tax rate for individuals . . ." Gingrich said the president was gracious and that no mention was made of past unpleasantries. At the end of the forty-minute meeting, Reagan said, "Let's keep in better touch in the future than we have in the past." When journalists queried him about the meeting, the president mirthfully said, "We were just having a Christmas party."[68]

Kemp signed on to the bill immediately after the Reagan appearance, which took the wind out of the sails of the renegade Republicans. The Tax Reform Bill of 1985 passed the House on a rare voice vote, with not one Republican or Democrat asking for a roll call vote. Tip O'Neill was astonished. "I can't believe it," Gingrich said. "We goofed."[69]

Some, Gingrich included, were furious with Kemp for jumping ship. But on his visit to the Hill, Reagan had surprisingly been accompanied by Bush, which many saw as a shot across Kemp's bow. Kemp was Reagan's ideological and temperamental heir. He was even Reagan's friend. But Bush was Reagan's loyal vice president. It was all about 1988.

The old ideological divide of the GOP, from the time of Taft and Eisenhower, Goldwater and Rockefeller, Nixon and Nixon, Reagan and Ford, Reagan and Bush, was going to play itself out again leading into 1988.

CHAPTER 12

PLAYING FOR KEEPS

"We must master the art of dominating the headlines."

1986

Newt Gingrich was first among equals when it came to media attention. He'd been the first to cultivate the political potential of C-SPAN beginning in March 1979, when the House first went live, utilizing the national cable system with practical political ramifications, as it had enabled the minority GOP to level its position with the grassroots. Seeing how formerly lowly House members had become household names, even the stodgy Senate now considered broadcasting its proceedings, debating whether to alter its own rules, so as to make itself more palatable for viewers.[1]

Eight years in Washington had not diminished Newt's appeal nor his appetite. He said yes to every request, it seemed, even appearing on a PBS show about AIDS, along with the surgeon general, C. Everett Koop, and the mayor of New York City, Ed Koch.[2]

Tom Bliley, representative from Virginia, noted that such pandering, while in and of itself was meaningless, could mean "the difference between 'active opposition and passive opposition' in the next election." Gingrich closed a meeting with the estimate, "Potentially everybody is in our tent."[3] That would take an awfully big tent, however. According to the *New York Times* from the previous year,

Some Republicans like Senator Laxalt and Representative Newt Gingrich of Georgia talk of actually making gains in 1986. But most senior Republicans would be content to do no worse than the 10-seat loss of

1926. Privately, some admit that losses much larger than that would be demoralizing after a laborious, 10-year effort to rebuild the party after Watergate.[4]

Talk of realignment had been in the air in GOP circles since 1980 and even before, when some were already talking headily about a "coming new GOP majority." A poll after the 1984 campaign by GOP numbers-cruncher Bob Teeter showed, for the first time since before the New Deal, that the GOP had a numerical advantage over the Democrats, 47 percent for the GOP to 41 for the Democrats.[5]

President Reagan met with a group of House Republicans at the Capitol Hill Club, a favored drinking, dining, drinking, smoking, and drinking establishment. There, the leader of the free world told the insecure Republicans they were good enough, smart enough, and doggone it, people liked them. Nursing unanimously bruised feelings, Gingrich noted that Reagan "was talking with the guys he now understands can cause a lot of trouble in the partnership."[6] The threat was duly noted at Reagan Central. More seriously, Reagan also told them he was going to mount a new public relations campaign to win congressional approval for arms for the Nicaraguan Contras. He expected the House Republicans to be there when he needed them.

Tip O'Neill was also gearing up his opposition and bluster machine. Aiding the Contras, he said, would bring "disaster and shame." The Speaker then warned that within a short period of time "the shame of that defeat [of the Contras] will bring American troops into Nicaragua."[7] As always, O'Neill was unmeasured in his rhetoric. Gingrich, on the other hand, was sometimes maddeningly contradictory in his. Most of the time he inveighed against government. But he also said that "people want government to solve problems," and warned the GOP against becoming the "antigovernment party."[8]

But when it came to the communist oligarchy running things in Nicaragua, one thing was for sure: Gingrich was against *that* government. And the one in Moscow. "We are convinced that we're engaged in a global contest with the Soviet empire."[9]

Gingrich went on the *MacNeil/Lehrer NewsHour* to debate the legislation with an odious cretin, Congressman Mike Barnes of Maryland, who, rumor held, was the single most unpopular man on and off Capitol Hill.

The debate descended within moments into insult hurling, each congressman interrupting the other.

"Oh, come on!"

"The Democrats will vote to vacate the battlefield and allow the Soviet empire to dominate!"

"This is kind of really irresponsible!"

"It's not irresponsible!"

"Reprehensible statement!"

"What's irresponsible about it? It's accurate!"

"It is absolute nonsense! That kind of talk!"

It went downhill from there. Judy Woodruff, a well-respected journalist, sat helpless, unable to contain the brawl. All she could say over and over was, "All right. All right. All right."[10]

Leon Daniel summarized the scuffle: "Rep. Michael Barnes . . . compared the administration's tactics in support of Contra aid to those of Joseph McCarthy. . . . [Gingrich] responded by branding Barnes a radical whose opposition to aid for the Nicaraguan rebels helps the Soviet Union."[11] As one Washington scribe wryly noted, "Trading gloomy scenarios over Nicaragua does not constitute informed debate."[12]

The Democrats were ramping up for 1988, excited at the prospects of ending the Reign of Reagan. One of the contenders was Senator Joe Biden of Delaware. The Reverend Pat Robertson was also eyeing a run for the GOP nomination, saying he was "prayerfully considering" taking the plunge and mixing it up with the sinners of politics.[13] Gingrich saw Robertson's potential to bring in new voters—and also drive away old voters.

But Gingrich was talking up Kemp, his friend and sometime co-combatant of nearly ten years. Both were students of history. Once they got into a debate over Napoleon at Westphalia. "Here I was," said Gingrich. "A Ph.D. in European history, arguing with this, this football player, being bludgeoned into submission."[14] Gingrich was anti-Bush through and through. A memo circulated among the conservatives making this clear while also deriding Bush as representing "the Rockefeller wing opposing Reagan" and saying that Bush had failed at the only two assignments handed him in eight years of the Reagan Administration, "stopping drugs and cutting red tape."[15]

Early polls from mid-1985 were beginning to trickle out, and George

H. W. Bush led far and away among Republicans, leading in a Gallup survey with 53 percent to 18 percent for Bob Dole and 10 percent for Kemp. Gingrich earned a score of 1 percent.[16] But all the old concerns about George Bush were coming to the surface again: he wasn't a real conservative; he wasn't tough enough; he was too preppy; he was too beholden to Arab oil interests; he wasn't a real Reaganite. Bush worked overtime and bent over backward to alleviate the right, but all he earned was the scorn of columnists such as George Will, who compared him to a "lap dog."[17]

"The early polls all show him far ahead of any other Republican. Rep. Newt Gingrich (R-Ga.) an ardent supporter of rival aspirant Jack Kemp (R-N.Y.) said the other day that, even at this early stage, the imperative for the other contenders is to figure out how to 'stop George Bush.'"[18]

Kemp had his own problems besides trailing Bush in GOP polls. For years, he'd given his district short shrift. The denizens of Buffalo were proud of their quarterback congressman, but they also liked to see him once in a while. Kemp hadn't spent much time in the district in years. His home and family were in Maryland. For the first time, he was facing what looked to be a serious opponent, James Keane, a local politician. The Democratic strategy was to keep him tied down. It worked.

Tempers were still running high over the Indiana Eighth mess, and Newt was still taking potshots at the Democrats, previously calling them a "leadership of thugs."[19] Reagan had his own take on terrorist leaders around the world. In a speech at the American Bar Association convention, he had said, "We're especially not going to tolerate these attacks from outlaw states run by the strangest collection of misfits, looney tunes and squalid criminals since the advent of the Third Reich."[20]

In February, the Reagan Administration began a new drive to aid the Nicaraguan Contras, this time with a 100-million-dollar package. The Ortega regime found a sympathetic voice in the form of Gingrich's sparring partner, Congressman Mike Barnes. It was easy to see that he and Gingrich would again come to blows, at least rhetorically. And they did.

As the *Washington Post* reported, "In a news conference billed 'Mike Barnes, McCarthyism and Nicaragua,'" congressmen Bob Walker and Duncan Hunter joined Gingrich in laying into Barnes, saying his attempted "smear" of Reagan would "make the job of the Soviet analyst or Soviet planner easier."[21]

Gingrich met with Jewish leaders in New York, Miami, and Chicago in an attempt to get them to pressure congressmen supportive of Israel to back aid to the Contras.[22] Simply put, a vote against the Contras was a vote against Israel. He hadn't forgotten that it was the Soviets who had backed the Arabs against Israel in the Yom Kippur War and reminded them of it.

The issue of aid to Nicaragua heated up and the debate was white hot on both sides, dominating the media for days. All the Sunday talk shows were devoted to the issue.

In late June, Reagan and the conservatives won a huge victory in the House with the passage of the 100-million-dollar aid package to the Contras, 221–209. No one in Washington was prepared for it. Reagan had gone on national television to make an appeal, but the ratings for the viewership were low, despite it being a superb address, one of his best on the issue.

Dozens of Democrats—perhaps cajoled by the thought that voting against the Contras would be seen as a vote against America's interests— voted for the package. One reliable anti-communist Democrat was Charlie Wilson of Texas, who supported Reagan. Every Democrat in the Georgia delegation except one voted with Reagan. What saved Reagan's bacon was that he again hit the phones—hard—and rounded up enough wavering Republicans and Democrats to put the bill over the top.

Again, Evans and Novak had the inside dope, and again, Gingrich was the straw stirring the drink.

Three days before the confused White House argument over tactics, an insightful Republican analysis was written by Rep. Newt Gingrich of Georgia. Contending that Harry Truman "accomplished vastly more in foreign policy" than Reagan by projecting a vision to the country, Gingrich said: "Trying to win tactically in a House dominated by left-wing ideologues is a formula for frustration and defeat at the vision level."[23]

Meanwhile, Gingrich was participating in a press conference to endorse legislation regulating the smokestack industry, long thought by some to contribute to acid rain. "It's clear there is a relationship between burning fossil fuels and acid rain. We do know enough to do some things," Gingrich said.[24]

Conservatives had known for years that Gingrich was a closet tree hugger, since his days teaching environmental science at West Georgia.

As a longtime favorite of the National Federation of Republican Women, he journeyed to Phoenix to speak to fourteen hundred conference attendants.[25] There, he advised them to "stop being nervous about the news media" and use them. "We must master the art of dominating the headlines."[26]

Congress moved—clumsily but well-intentioned—to close public bathhouses in America. Some civil libertarians in the Republican Party were conflicted, including Gingrich. Frankly, the issue was well on its way to being politicized, with the left using AIDS as a pry bar for more money in research, and the right using it to limit the activities of gays, long the scourge of the Christian Right. Congressman Henry Waxman of California said closing bathhouses was not necessary.[27]

Very few in Congress agreed with Waxman. The vote to empower the surgeon general to shut down public bathhouses passed 417–8. Movie star Rock Hudson, a closeted homosexual, died just before the voting.[28]

Gingrich's own conservatism was constantly evolving, and one news report labeled him a "New Wave" man of the right, one who was not averse to using the national government to affect private behavior:

> As Gingrich has articulated the conservative credo, the federal government shouldn't become impotent or inactive. Instead it should redirect its activity away from unproductive social services and income maintenance, and toward growth-oriented, investment spending—like space stations, scientific research and infrastructure. Add Gingrich and his colleagues to activist liberals and to centrists of both parties, and you have an overwhelming consensus in Congress for an active, discretionary, problem-solving role for the federal government.[29]

Other conservatives saw in Newt a guy who just could not resist tinkering, the same charge they lodged against liberals. Even in the face of advocating national solutions to national problems, Gingrich saw himself as a populist, "carry[ing] the populist banner for Reagan and the Republicans, saying theirs is the party that has tapped into widespread frustration with the status quo."[30]

A number of conservatives were as frustrated with Reagan as they were with Gingrich. One Associated Press report at the time noted that conservatives were sometimes called "the orphans of the Reagan political revolution."[31]

Debates continued about the future of the two parties and which had the better claim to populism. At a forum in Washington, two unlikely allies were chosen to make the case for the GOP: Newt Gingrich and Dick Darman. Darman, the son of a textile mill owner and a Harvard Business School graduate who leveraged his education, intelligence, and family connections to important positions in the Reagan and Bush Administrations, was the working definition of *elitist*, but he better explained the concept and why it was a philosophy of the anti-elites, rivaling Gingrich:

> Darman described populism as an ill-defined movement that included people with high but frustrated expectations and individualists with class resentments whose dominant concern is for . . . opposition to elitism and the concentration of power . . . "It's a corrective force, not an ideology, and it has both negative and positive aspects," he said. "Negativism is a reactive resentment of abuses, positivism is creative programs to correct them. Populism today is a negative reaction to government and the positive creation of this administration of a society of opportunity."[32]

Gingrich was no slacker, however. Populism was "a special effort by individuals or regions to get access to the American dream that they've been deprived of." Populism, he said, would triumph over trendy elitism because "traditional life styles always defeat radical life styles . . ."[33]

Gingrich announced his candidacy for reelection on the last day of May in 1986. In front of his Clayton County headquarters, he formed "Newt's Co-filers." To file his intention of candidacy required a fee of $2,253, so his campaign cleverly came up with 2,253 individuals who would each put up one dollar and sign a petition supporting Newt. "My filing doesn't represent the candidacy of one person—but the commitment of 2,253 friends and neighbors because of honest, aggressive representation."[34]

Impressively—and aggressively, as promised—he challenged whomever the Democrats nominated to twelve debates in the twelve counties of the Sixth District.[35]

In his announcement, he said—again, aggressively—"I am proud of angry machine politicians who oppose me. This coalition of old-time machine politicians and leftwing radicals are right to oppose me and to contribute to my opponents. We are on different sides and we do have a different vision of America's future." He urged Georgians to "join that effort and endorse that crusade for an opportunity society by voting for him in November."[36]

Overall, the statement was defiant and defensive. Only in passing did he mention the voters themselves and what he would do for them if reelected. Having won reelection two years earlier with a skyscraping 69 percent of the vote, Newt was confident of another easy ride. He was again endorsed by the influential *Atlanta Daily World*.[37] Visitors to his office were plied with free Cokes and Georgia peanuts.[38]

The conservative and liberal ratings were issued for 1985 by the *National Journal*. Gingrich wasn't nearly as conservative as many thought and more liberal than many believed. His overall conservative rating was good but certainly not in Jesse Helms country. On social issues, he went up a bit higher to an 82, on the economy he got a 77, and on foreign policy a 79.[39] He foresaw no particular problems in seeking his fifth term of office.

Next door, in the Fifth District, Portia Scott, a businesswoman, was running for the Republican nomination. Portia was black, a woman, a conservative, and running in Georgia, one of the toughest states in terms of race in all of the South.[40] The party had come a long way in Georgia, due in no small part to Gingrich.

By the mid-1980s drugs and the importation of drugs from south of the border had emerged as a major issue in America. Gingrich supported a bill that was tough on drug dealers. "I am proud to have voted for a bill that will start a war on cocaine and heroin dealers and users." He urged prompt action by President Reagan.[41] "Just Say No" had also become a cherished cause of Mrs. Reagan's, aimed at America's children, and the public service campaign was deemed highly effective.

Gingrich had no primary opponent in 1986, so he took deep pride—and interest—in the victory of his friend Portia Scott, who had won decisively in her GOP primary race. In the fall, she would face Democrat John Lewis, a longtime veteran of civil rights causes in the South. It was the longest of long shots, even for Scott, the daughter of the publisher of the *Atlanta Daily World*, which referred to the GOP primary in the overwhelmingly Democratic district as the "redheaded stepchild of Georgia politics."[42]

Another flashpoint in the Cold War came when Moscow picked up and held Nicholas Daniloff, an American journalist, charging him with being a spy. The Kremlin had done so in a petty response to the Reagan Administration apprehending one of their real spies, operating in the United States. When the Soviets picked up Daniloff, Reagan responded by releasing the names of more than two dozen "Soviet United Nations employees" it was suggested could be recalled. Reagan had outed twenty-five KGB operatives.[43]

In the end, the Soviet Union blinked, Daniloff was released, along with Soviet dissident Yuri Orlov, and Reagan won the day.[44] Orlov had been arrested and imprisoned by Moscow for calling attention to human rights abuses inside the Iron Curtain.

Gingrich often seemed to have his own brand of foreign policy. He called for a US invasion and occupation of Libya if it did not cease its terrorist activities. He also said Gaddafi should be deposed.[45] The Reagan Administration had initiated a top airstrike against Tripoli as a response to Gaddafi's state-sponsored terrorism, but news of the hit leaked out to the media. Gingrich and others called for an aggressive investigation into the offices of Senators Robert Byrd of West Virginia and Claiborne Pell of Rhode Island, who were suspected of the leaks.

The strike on Libya took place at 7:00 p.m. Eastern time on April 14, but Pell had talked to the press at around 6:00 p.m., after a briefing at the White House.[46] The call for the investigation went nowhere, as everybody knew Capitol Hill was infected with a raging case of logorrhea.

After a long year of fighting with Treasury Secretary Jim Baker, Gingrich had finally come over and announced his support for Reagan's tax reform package, which had made significant changes since 1985, when it appeared to all that the House Ways and Means Committee had written the entire thing. The bill now had significant improvements: one in individual deductions, which would double, and another involving tax rates, replacing the previous fourteen brackets with only two—15 percent and 28 percent.[47]

Gingrich publicly came to Baker's defense, which was considered heresy in some conservative quarters:

> What little defense there was for Baker came from an unusual source: Rep. Newt Gingrich of Georgia, a leader of the back-bench right-wingers who call themselves the Conservative Opportunity Society. Last year Gingrich lambasted his ally Kemp for supporting the House Democratic tax bill so it could get to the Senate . . . But the former history professor, with a longer view toward building a Republican Party that is more than a mere agent for petty lobbies, changed his mind. Gingrich commended Baker for improving the House bill more than he had dreamed possible. He urged his colleagues to compare that product not with an impossible ideal but with present law.[48]

Jaws dropped all over Washington.

Actually, Gingrich was often both more subtle and more courageous than many gave him credit for. Jimmy Swaggart was a giant voice and power in evangelical circles and religious politics, including Georgia's. Gingrich had allowed his name to be used on the masthead of Swaggart's publication, *The Evangelist*, until he found out that Swaggart held anti-Catholic views. Being anti-Catholic was not considered such a bad thing in much of the South, even in the 1980s, but no matter. Gingrich demanded that Swaggart take his name off the masthead.[49]

The economy continued to boom along, gas prices were low—in some places seventy-nine cents a gallon—jobs and wages were up, inflation was running at less than 2 percent, and the Soviets were being kept at bay. The GOP was feeling chipper about not only keeping control of the Senate, but picking up seats in the House as well. Reagan hit the road for one more roundup to help Republican senators over the top, including Mack Mattingly of Georgia. Mattingly was a good friend of Gingrich's, and Newt had done a lot to help Mattingly win in 1980 by a razor-thin margin. Reagan came in to a huge rally of fifteen thousand fans in Atlanta and praised the senator and Gingrich.[50] He raised thousands of dollars for the GOP re-election drive.

Heading toward the November elections, the Republicans were feeling good.

It wouldn't last.

CHAPTER 13

END OF THE TRAIL

*"In my judgment, for Republicans, this
is a muddling-through election."*

1986

Economist James Buchanan of George Mason University won the 1986
Nobel Prize when he demonstrated a straight-line correlation between
government spending and political behavior, between money and elections.
In simpler terms, when mixed together, politicians and money became an
enchanting, addictive, toxic, corrupting elixir. Bribery and politicians went
together like peas and carrots. They were made for each other.

Buchanan named his theory "Public Choice."[1]

Because of the long coattails of Ronald Reagan in 1980, 12 Republican senators came into office that year. In 1986, of the 34 Senate races, 22 were
being defended by members of the GOP. But there was no unifying theme
to this campaign, as there had been in '80, '82, and '84; there was nothing to
give Republicans a framework from which to run. Gingrich fretted, "In my
judgment, for Republicans this is a muddling-through election."[2]

Some consultants said run on "Star Wars," some said run on the economy, and some said run on nothing.

Many ran on nothing.

Indeed, the Republicans were wiped out in the November off-year elections, even with Reagan hugely popular.

In Arizona, Representative John McCain was more successful than his
colleagues, winning his Senate race, replacing Barry Goldwater. McCain

151

was brash, hot-tempered, and a joyous member of the "Tip-baiter" club of Gingrich and company.[3] But in the process he rejected Reagan, telling the *National Journal* several years earlier that he hadn't run on "Reaganomics" but on "moderation" and that no one could call him a "Reagan Robot."

The Democrats had chosen Crandle Bray to face off against Newt. Gingrich won easily, garnering 60 percent to Bray's 40.[4] But he was one of the few bright stories in an otherwise dark election for the GOP. They were decimated in the US Senate, losing just about every seat they'd gained in 1980, thus forfeiting control of the body they'd held since January 1981. On election night, one could feel the power draining away from Bob Dole as, in a few short hours, he went from majority leader to minority leader. His features that night were dark, drawn, and furious.[5]

Most everybody in Republican circles had reason to be downcast. The economy was in great shape, Ronald Reagan was hugely popular, gasoline was cheap and plentiful, the Soviets had been brought to heel, and in gratitude the voters were throwing Republican senators out on their ears. No one on either side of the aisle saw it coming.

Like all men, Gingrich had good days and bad days. The difference with Gingrich was if he was having a bad day, he used his bullhorn to let the world know it: "Our message does not get through at the Reagan White House, as also was the case with Carter and Nixon and other Presidents, because Congress is seen . . . as a peculiar body with mere politicians who are grubby and demeaning and do not understand very much," he groused.[6]

It would get worse still for Ronald Reagan and the Republicans.

Just days after the election, it came to light that a rogue operation inside the White House was running an "arms for hostages deal," exactly the sort of thing Reagan had denounced for years. He went on national television and promised "to get to the bottom of the matter."

Gingrich, like most Republicans, called for "a prompt full disclosure at once so the government can continue to act with [out] any doubt in the administration."[7] Three investigations got promptly underway. The scandal became known as "Iran-Contra."

Hundreds of GOP staffers had lost their Hill jobs, but the startling revelation of the "arms for hostages deal" only deepened the GOP gloom. It had been cooked up in the basement of the White House by Lt. Col. Oliver North, US Marine Corps, running a rogue element inside the Reagan Administration. North, for a time, tried to hang it on Reagan, saying he'd briefed the president at Camp David, but Reagan, in his diaries, was furious with North for lying about his knowledge of the deal.[8]

The scheme involved selling arms to renegade countries in the Middle East, then using the money to purchase arms for the Nicaraguan Contras fighting the communist Sandinista regime. It was all hugely illegal under dozens of laws. Under the Boland Amendment, it was illegal for the US government to come to the aid of the anti-communist Nicaraguan Contras. The scheme also involved the possibility that American hostages being held in Iran would be released.

The scandal occupied Washington—including Congress, the media, and the insular establishment—from the end of 1986 well into 1987. The establishment smelled blood. Br'er Reagan had escaped the traps set for him time after time by the establishment, and now the Georgetown crowd was salivating at the notion of Ronald Reagan being led out of the White House in leg irons and an orange jumpsuit. The *Washington Post*, *National Journal*, *New York Times*, CBS, and *Newsweek*, in particular, despised Ronald Reagan.

North was oddly lauded by conservatives even as he tried to finger Reagan rather than taking a bullet for his commander in chief, as befitting previous military and civilian aides to the president. The rule always was, "When you become more of a hindrance than a help to the president . . ." North was a huge hindrance.

Along the way, Vice President George Bush was pulled into the fray, and for a time it looked as though Iran-Contra might drag down his bid for the 1988 GOP nomination.

Reagan first denied the matter, but seeing the political damage, he took responsibility and gave a speech in which he told the nation "mistakes were made." The Reagan White House saw a precipitous drop in the president's approval ratings, from the high 60s to the mid-40s. Gingrich was contemptuous of the White House's handling of the matter, saying "the President's first reaction was that if he blustered and was stubborn it would go away."

Senator Daniel Patrick Moynihan was even more blunt, saying the Reagan Revolution was "dead in the water."[9]

For a time, the Reagan White House was paralyzed, much of the problems manifesting from the arrogant Don Regan, Reagan's chief of staff. Washingtonians were mentioning Regan in the same breath as Nixon's John Ehrlichman and H. R. Haldeman, always a danger sign. The death knell came when, behind his back, Washingtonians were referring to Regan as the "Prime Minister." The *Post* put it best: "Regan, it is believed, acted as though 'Hail to the Chief' referred to the chief of staff."[10]

But hanging a president out to dry with a hyphenated scandal just didn't fill the bill.

The issue of aid to the Nicaraguan Contras had dominated the national debate for several years now. It was not an obscure issue as it was another important flash point in the Cold War. The Soviets wanted to pierce the Monroe Doctrine and set up a puppet regime less than five hundred miles from the United States. The Reagan Administration and conservatives like Gingrich wanted to oust the communist regime in Managua in part by funding the pro-American, if controversial, Contra rebels. The Sunday-morning talk shows often featured heated debates on the topic.

Conservatives pined for the days of Jim Baker, with whom they had publicly feuded, but with whom they could at least get an appointment or a phone call returned. Not so with Regan, who most believed was too impressed with himself. Washington had seen his kind come and go before. With a lot of backstage pushing and cajoling and phone calls by Nancy Reagan, plus public leaks and finger-pointing, the situation became untenable. Regan was finally thrown over the side after tendering his resignation. He was replaced by Tennessee senator Howard Baker.

Secretly, a lot of conservatives were pleased that someone as down-to-earth as Howard Baker, who knew how to get things done in Washington, had come in to bring order to a White House that frankly was spinning out of control. Gingrich told the *New York Times*, "I would give him very high marks for attempting to be Ronald Reagan's chief of staff, rather than . . . an alternative president."[11]

Baker's timely aid to Reagan could not be ignored or overstated. Also, it was a big sacrifice for the former senator, as it meant he'd have to give up his planned campaign for the GOP nomination in 1988. Baker was a true class act, a gentleman in a town where gentlemen were in short supply.

With all the bad news for the Republicans, the House side escaped basically unscathed, losing only a handful of seats in the November 1986 election. It was the first time in the century that fewer losses were sustained by one party in the lower house than in the upper house.[12]

In late November, Newt Gingrich unveiled a radical plan to make Social Security private. His diagram was based on the knowledge that the ratio of payers to payees would become unsustainable. "We know that the Democrats will smear and lie about us whatever we do. There is no sense in us trying to hide Social Security in the closet. They kick the door in." The Georgian's proposal would eliminate the FICA payroll taxes "and force workers under age 40 to set up Individual Retirement Accounts. It also would establish a value-added tax—basically a national sales tax—to pay the benefits of all current retirees and to ensure that no present or future retiree falls below the poverty level."[13]

Earlier in the year, Dole had nursed a freeze on cost-of-living increases for retirees through the Senate. Reagan was all for it as a means of bringing the outlays in line. He'd already reduced Social Security benefits in 1982 and he didn't want to go through that again. The bill barely passed the Senate and was headed to the House when Jack Kemp interceded, going to Reagan to make the case that it was politically disastrous. Reagan pulled the plug, the bill never got to the House, and Republican senators were left holding the bag, with nothing to show for their work except a vote that could be used against them in the fall elections.[14]

It was.

Bob Dole was fit to be tied. He never forgave Kemp.

The system was a mess, completely out of whack from where it had started in 1935. More and more people were getting benefits and not just seniors, but college students, the disabled, widows, and many others. It was also unfair as the more you paid in, the less you got. Washington liked to pick winners and losers in the marketplace, but the politicians constantly punished the winners to the benefit of the losers.

Some of those losers lived under the bridges and on the grates of the cities of America for no reason whatsoever other than they were mentally unbalanced. The issue of the "homeless" became a potent weapon disguised as an issue in the 1980s, blaming Reagan, conservatives, supply-side economics, the supposed budget cuts for these people being on the streets when the real culprit was the ACLU, which had gone to the courts earlier, claiming that institutionalizing the deranged and mentally unbalanced was a violation of due process, that they were being incarcerated for no reason whatsoever. The whole issue was a ridiculous waste of the national debate. There already existed thousands of homeless shelters across America, complete with hot food, a warm bed, and medical attention.

They were called mental institutions.

Washingtonians fretted or cheered the coming end of the Reagan Administration, even though it was still two years off. Stories abounded of the lameduckness of Reagan and his Administration, how the Iran-Contra scandal threatened to bring him low, and some rabid political enemies even whispered the word *impeachment*.[15] But his approval rating as of January 1987 was at 70 percent, like Ike at the same time in his Administration.[16]

One problem looming just over the horizon was the controversy over former Reagan White House aides leaving after the first term to go to K Street and cash in on their contacts while the gettin' was good. Attention focused on Mike Deaver, the closest aide to the Reagans for many years. Deaver—who went into business and signed up lucrative clients worth millions of dollars left and right, against the advice of Mrs. Reagan—was photographed for the cover of *Time* magazine in the back of a limousine on a phone, the Capitol dome behind him.[17]

Deaver was leading with his left chin. Over the years he had dived deeper and deeper into the bottle and had made more than his fair share of enemies in a town where the motto was "you know your best friend because he's the one who stabs you in the chest."

Another favorite joke that went around Washington was that no one should ever take friendship personally. Gingrich had little use for Reagan's peripheral aides, saying the failure of the Reagan White House to focus more on spending and budget issues was a "failure . . . the fault of the White House staff."[18]

Deaver meanwhile was heading straight for a fall.

Terrorism continued across the globe, but did not touch Americans often, except when a plane was hijacked or a few hostages were taken. No home-grown terrorist acts had taken place on American soil. In 1986, citizens had nearly free run of federal buildings, including the US Capitol. The steps on the western side were open; women, men, and children from all walks of life walked in and out of the Rotunda freely; and the police presence was light, to say the least.

Most drivers' licenses were slips of paper with no photo identification, and almost anyone could walk onto an airplane with no ID. Though passengers had to go through a metal detector, the machines were routinely set on low; men with pocketknives or women with nail files did not have them confiscated.

The Library of Congress was open to all, just like any other library in America, even as the Librarian was proposing to cut the use of the public reading rooms. Gingrich, the bibliophile, freaked over the idea, agreeing with a group of protesters—sponsored by Books Not Bombs—who staged a sit-in to oppose the curtailment of reading-room access.[19]

The paranoid librarian, Daniel Boorstin, spluttered that the Library of Congress was, well, not a library. Not a public library anyway. He suggested that if people wanted to read books in a library, they ought to go elsewhere, such as a public library, and leave him to his fiefdom and his strawberries.[20]

CHAPTER 14

JUST SAY NO

"We could survive the Soviets, but we might
not survive our own politicians."

1987

Newt Gingrich's long guerrilla war against James Claude "Jim" Wright Jr. began in 1987. It started as a one-man crusade that few in Washington took seriously. Before Gingrich was through, however, everyone would be watching in awe. He even used the *Congressional Record* in his full-scale war against Wright.[1] He'd become obsessed with getting Wright and generated a veritable blizzard of papers documenting widespread malfeasance. Gas leases, strange business deals involving his wife, Betty Wright, bizarre real estate deals, free Cadillac usage, shadowy bank schemes, a veritable cornucopia of corruption. There was also the charge that Wright made more than $340,000 off an investment of $9,000 in an oil exploration deal.[2]

Ethics was very much on the mind of Gingrich and the culture. Wall Street had had its share of new scandals and Washington's lobbying community was facing fresh scrutiny. Gingrich called for a general, all-purpose, special committee to investigate "questionable congressional ethics." In justifying the new government entity, he invoked the Founders and the bicentennial of the Constitution and said, bluntly, "The system is not working."[3] Already, the chairman of the House banking committee, Fernand St. Germain, a Democrat from Rhode Island, was in Gingrich's line of sight, having been accused of suspicious gift-taking from banks that came before his committee.

A fourteen-hundred-page Ethics Committee report "cleared" St. Germain.[4]

159

Gingrich and others squawked: the fix was in and they knew it. A Newt-inspired resolution calling for reopening the St. Germain investigation went down to a "narrow" defeat, 292–111. Even the reliably liberal *Washington Post*, who saw corruption and mayhem in the twinkle of every Republican's eye, had to guffaw over the cover-up the House Democrats had afforded their old friend "Ferdie."[5]

Gingrich was regularly making enemies on both sides of the aisle. Over cigars and cocktails, more and more members were blowing off steam in smoke-filled rooms, complaining about Newt. He knew he was making adversaries, and the old adage in Washington was "friends come and go, but enemies are forever."[6]

"You now have a House where it is more dangerous to be aggressive about honesty than it is to be mildly corrupt," he said.[7]

Speaker Tip O'Neill had finally retired from Congress after a decade as Speaker of the House. Sixty-three-year-old Jim Wright was elected as his successor in December 1986. He had barely settled into the Speaker's chair before Gingrich was all over him. Most of Wright's thirty-plus years in the House had been often as a firebrand, highly partisan, and often a rude and borderline bigot. The *New Republic* several years earlier said Wright "will never be taken for an Atari Democrat."[8] The *New York Times* inaccurately trilled, "An eloquent speaker, generally considered the most persuasive debater in the House, Wright is a courteous man, and invariably cordial."[9]

The Texan did not like Ronald Reagan, however, and made his low opinion of the Gipper and his approach to governance clear. Wright, aston-ishingly, had harbored White House ambitions for years, despite his many peccadillos.

Wright was so blinded by partisanship that he falsely accused Reagan of not taking responsibility for the murder of American marines in Beirut. Wright even went so far as to accuse Reagan of engaging in an "unforgivable placing of blame on others." And he said, "Mr. Reagan just somehow doesn't seem to have the grace ever to accept any blame upon himself."[10]

Curiously, Wright was popular with Congressman Dick Cheney of

Wyoming. Another member, Democrat Mary Rose Oakar, submissively said of the incoming Speaker, "He'll discipline us. We need it."[11] Wright was certainly disciplined when it came to his personal wealth, which had grown tremendously since becoming a public servant due to his many deals and investments in gas and stockyards. Wright got rich the old-fashioned way. He dealt himself into government grants and leases.

As Wright took the gavel from O'Neill, Gingrich observed, enviously, "The rules of the House are designed for a speaker with a strong personality and an agenda."[12]

As a sign he was moving up in seniority, Gingrich got better offices on Capitol Hill.[13] He was still trumpeting his plan to privatize Social Security "by establishing mandatory individual savings accounts." He also informed his constituents he was headed to New York for a speech and "a chance to talk about big solutions of the airplane magnitude."[14] One of those big ideas was to oppose what conservatives called "socialized medicine," but he wasn't alone in opposing a state-based mandate—though he had yet to explain the contradiction in supporting mandates to replace Social Security. Jack Kemp understood the radioactive politics of Social Security and said anyone who advocated a major overhaul to the system was a candidate for a "prefrontal lobotomy."[15]

Gingrich also took the traditional conservative position in opposing a lapse of the so-called Fairness Doctrine, which for years had mandated that radio and television commentary represent both sides. Reagan, ever the individualist, knew better and let it lapse, despite the pressure from many faint-hearted conservatives who thought that their philosophy could only succeed if it was jammed down the throats of American listeners and viewers. No one at the time ever imagined that conservative talk show hosts could succeed in the marketplace by simply talking about issues.

To his credit, Newt refused a 15.6 percent increase in his congressional salary the Hill had voted for itself, up to $89,500 from $77,400, which was scheduled to take effect on April 1.[16]

The coming presidential campaign was already heating up. On the Republican side, the prohibitive front-runner was the vice president, George Herbert

Walker Bush, who had developed a previously unknown taste for Reaganism, pork rinds, and country music. Conservatives, especially Gingrich, were dubious of Bush, even after an eight-year association with the Gipper. Gingrich was still championing the candidacy of his friend, fellow "Reagan Robot" and conservative revolutionary, Jack Kemp.

In the running for the Democratic nomination were the Reverend Jesse Jackson, Senator Al Gore, Congressman Dick Gephardt, Senator Paul Simon, former Arizona governor Bruce Babbitt, Senator Joe Biden, and Governor Michael Dukakis. The media dismissed them as "The Seven Dwarfs."[17] Gingrich had his own strong opinion on the field of Democratic aspirants, saying they were "by southern standards . . . close to European socialists."[18]

The House finally took up the proposal by Gingrich to create an office to investigate what he called a "pattern of corruption" in Congress. It was voted down, 297–77. These foxes preferred to guard their own henhouse. Gingrich had produced a list of ten members suspected of being dirty, all Democrats, which explained both the lopsidedness of the vote and the Democrats' fresh antipathy for the Georgian.[19] As always, he was not reticent about saying what was really on his mind, telling reporters that the existing investigation committee was ineffectual, "a paper tiger standing guard, protecting the members' rights to be mildly corrupt."[20]

As on nearly all Sundays, Gingrich appeared on a network talk show, this time *Face the Nation* in August.[21] He admitted he had not always said no, having once tried marijuana in college. Reagan's nominee for the Supreme Court, Douglas Ginsburg, had been derailed because he'd once taken a toke off a doobie, but suddenly it was cool for a politician to admit he'd once been a pothead. Dozens, including the young Al Gore and the old Claiborne Pell, all stepped forward to admit they had just said yes. Pell, the über-patriarch, sniffed that "I didn't like it and never tried it again." Among his class, dry martinis were the preferred means of getting bombed. Gore said his use in college was "infrequent and rare," but that's what all students said.[22]

On the advice of his campaign honcho, Lee Atwater, Bush had been popping up at one conservative event after another, trying to lock up the support of dubious Reaganites for the coming campaign. It was demeaning for Bush and earned him a blast from George F. Will for desperate, peripatetic courting of conservatives.

Frankly, a lot of people in GOP politics did not like Bush. The problems between Bush and Reagan in the 1970s had been well documented. His other political adversaries included many others such as Gingrich, Paul Laxalt, Kemp, Will, and the man from Kansas, Bob Dole. The popular and acerbic Kansan was gearing up for yet another presidential run.

In March 1987, Gingrich conceived the idea for Republicans to meet in Federal Hall in the Big Apple, the site of the very first meeting of the very first Congress. The event was tailor-made for the Georgian, given his taste for history and drama. But it also made sense, as 1987 was the bicentennial year of the Constitution. "At the site of the first Congress, Republicans will focus on ideas for the future and a reaffirmation of the hopes and dreams of our founding fathers," he said.[23]

Terrorism was becoming more and more of a reality for America, especially those flying in the Mediterranean or for Americans in the military. Gingrich took note of the various dangerous affairs in that region of the world. "The war between Iraq and Iran has now been going on for seven years . . ."[24] By all means, the Reagan Doctrine said, America should respond to aggressors. But invade? That was quite another matter. Iran and Iraq were two spiders trapped in a bottle, consumed by their ancient hatred. All who understood *realpolitik* understood that it was best to leave them in the bottle together, so they could not devote their attention and hate toward anyone else.

That summer was also marked by a renewed vote on aid to the Nicaraguan Contras, and the package passed the House, surprisingly, 214–201.[25] The debate was heated, to say the least, with both sides throwing brickbats.

What was especially remarkable was that the bill passed in the midst of the congressional investigation into Iran-Contra and the unremitting testimony on Capitol Hill, including the appearance of Lt. Col. Oliver North, in full military regalia. A gap-toothed, handsome, young, highly decorated Marine in front of a national television audience easily routed the potbellied bureaucrats in the battle of Capitol Hill. Ironically, the Democrats, who had once been licking their chops at the prospect of bringing down Reagan amid a scandal, could not hold the Contra tiger by the tail. North's testimony and the broad support of the American people for him helped push the Contra aid package through Congress. Of the mess of people and money and ideologies and hidden agendas, Gingrich, searching for *le mot juste*, said, "We could survive the Soviets, but we might not survive our own politicians."[26]

Still, the damage from Iran-Contra was severe. The report of the "blue ribbon commission," headed by former senator John Tower, exonerated Reagan, but still roughed him up and blamed him for not monitoring the events and people in his Administration more closely. The report reinforced an image of Reagan as detached and unaware of the inner workings of Washington. The media used phrases such as "blistering" and "national catastrophe" and "embarrassment."

Since coming to Washington in 1981, Reagan had floated above the town, untouched by the Democrats or the media. His strength came from without, from the American people. This was the first time his political enemies had laid a glove on him, though all agreed he should have been more attuned to the workings of his White House. Democrats lambasted him and stories in the media happily speculated that it was the end of Reagan, of Reaganism, of the GOP, and the chances for the Republicans in 1988.

"Many Republicans said that by not charging the President himself with lying or taking part in a coverup, the report left him at least some room to restore his own popularity and that of his party," chortled E. J. Dionne in the *New York Times*. Surprisingly, a compassionate Democrat, Senator Joe Biden of Delaware, offered words of support for Reagan. "'I think his action was one from the heart. I think he bled for those hostages,' he added, alluding to the effort to sell arms to Iran in exchange for the release of hostages held in Lebanon."[27]

Gingrich ripped Reagan in no uncertain terms, though, saying, "Americans came to believe he was larger than life. He isn't. He's a human being. He blew it."[28] Of the three-hundred-page report, Gingrich did say it was "sobering," though not "scandalous."[29] The Georgian's critical comments about Reagan were picked up everywhere. Congressman Dick Cheney was more charitable and took the long view. Reagan could recover.[30]

Reagan was being whipsawed in the pages of morning newspapers of the right and left alike. Apoplectic phrases were used liberally. From the right, George Will leveled the president over the debacle the new American embassy in Moscow had become. Russian contractors were used, and it was discovered that they had impregnated the building with literally hundreds of bugs and secret spying devices. Unless the new structure was torn down, it would be uninhabitable. Will, on the Soviets, quoted from the *Economist*: "The folly of 1970s détente was the belief that Western pliancy would help Soviet reformers. It doesn't. It helps Soviet opportunists."[31]

Reagan had a response for his detractors, early in the investigation process. At an event, he was asked about Iran-Contra and said, "Well, I'm not supposed to answer. But I'd like to ask one question of everybody. Everybody that can remember what they were doing on August 8 of 1985, raise your hand." No one raised their hands. He was winning the discussion until he said, "'It's possible to forget' approving the shipment of weapons to Iran."[32]

He also came down hard on the Soviets and the embassy, saying it would not be occupied and, therefore, the Soviets would not be allowed to occupy the new embassy that was being built in Washington. Charles Krauthammer, a liberal *Post* columnist and former speechwriter for Walter Mondale, oddly wrote that the Jim and Tammy Faye Bakker scandal signaled the end of the Reagan era.[33]

Still, Reagan's appeal to the better angels of Washington's nature brought forth defenders, especially Bob Dole, who had always had little use for the self-inflating White House staff. He knew Reagan had been poorly served. "If you don't protect the president, if you don't serve the president well, then you ought to move on."[34]

Gingrich also dialed it back. "What we have here is a mistake, not a scandal."[35]

Less understood was the so-called failed summit in Iceland. Reagan was roundly denounced by the media for refusing to give up his cherished missile defense system to Gorbachev. In fact, it was the turning point in the Cold War.

Reagan had more important things on his mind than the ranting of a handful of dyspeptic liberals. The market plunged five hundred points on October 19, 1987—called "Bloody Monday"—and despite enormous pressure from the Chicken Littles of Washington, Reagan kept his head and his cool and did nothing, confident that his hands-off approach would be the best thing to do. He recalled Harry Truman's old maxim: "A president's job is to say 'yes' and 'no' but mostly 'no.'"

In the fall of 1987, Gingrich once again set his sights on Jim Wright, this time excoriating the new Speaker over an unreported meeting he'd had with Daniel Ortega, the head of the communist government in Nicaragua.

"Mr. Speaker," said Gingrich, winding up, "your secret meeting with the Communist dictator on Veterans' Day was the most destructive undermining of U.S. foreign policy in our country's history."[36]

The Reagan Administration was putting pressure on Managua via their paymasters in Moscow to release nine thousand "political" prisoners rotting in Nicaraguan jails. By engaging in a clandestine meeting with the communist gangster, Wright had undermined Reagan's efforts. If it was deliberate, Wright would have been guilty of violating the Logan Act. "Under the U.S. Constitution, you have clearly interfered in the President's responsibility to execute foreign policy, and you risk crippling the United States," Gingrich concluded in his hot letter to Wright.[37]

Around the same time, seventy-five House members signed a letter opposing allowing Soviet general secretary Gorbachev to address Congress, as was planned for early December. Gorbachev was heading for the nation's capital for a summit with Reagan. Gingrich pulled no punches: "We should ask ourselves, 'If this were 1938, and Adolf Hitler were asked to address the British Parliament, what would Winston Churchill have done?'"[38]

The Pentagon decided in 1987 to take the bull by the horns and come up with rules to replace guidelines on sex in the ranks. "Sexual misconduct" now included "adultery, orgies, sodomy and sexual harassment," and would become a basis to grant or withhold security clearances. "By forbidding a variety of heterosexual and homosexual acts, the new regulation . . . weed[s] out individuals who might be susceptible to blackmail by espionage agents."[39]

The comments and rule books coming out of the Department of Defense might have been written by Mickey Spillane or Jacqueline Susann. Specifically, military personnel were prohibited from "acts performed with a minor or with animals, prostitution, pandering, sexual harassment, self-mutilation, spouse-swapping and participation in orgies." Sexual violence was also prohibited, as was "adultery that is recent, frequent and likely to continue, transexualism, transvestism, exhibitionism, incest, voyeurism and sodomy." Gay groups protested that hostile powers did not use sex for blackmail purposes but for money.[40]

Gingrich's war against Wright was gaining steam. In attempting to tie up the House to prevent the huge $12,100 pay raise the lawmakers had voted themselves, he also stopped a personal bill that Wright was trying to sneak through that granted a "$4 million tax break for a family in Fort Worth."[41]

A survey of most congressional offices reported by the *Washington Post* showed that most members said they would not take the raise, including Gingrich.[42] Most did, including Gingrich. It is listed throughout '88 and '89 that he was making $89,500, which includes a $12,100 increase.[43] Populist outrage had washed across the land. A radio talk-show host in Detroit urged his listeners to send tea bags to Congress in protest. The idea caught on and Capitol Hill was buried under tea bags.[44]

Gingrich, like others in the South, flunked out of "Trade School" and voted for the protectionist legislation being pushed by the dwindling textile mills and their unions that dotted the South. The bill was strenuously debated, but Reagan opposed it, despising any gaming of the system, and certainly was against the government picking winners and losers in the marketplace. Gingrich and the other sunshine free traders hid behind an obscure phrase from Adam Smith's *Wealth of Nations*, "mutual trade," as justification for their vote. Everybody knew it was about politics.

Strife on the floor of the House continued unabated. Gone were the days when members brandished pistols or beat each other senseless with walking canes, but make no mistake about it, partisan hatred was a cherished and time-honored tradition. By October 1987, a bill that raised taxes by more than $12 billion to ostensibly reduce the deficit passed the House 206–205, but only after Speaker Wright held the vote open past the fifteen-minute time limit. "As Speaker Jim Wright held the roll-call vote on final passage open . . . Republicans shouted, booed and demanded an end to the vote in one of the unruliest displays in recent House history."[45]

Only one Republican, Congressman Jim Jeffords of Vermont, crossed the aisle to support the tax increase. Another Republican, Connie Mack of Florida, said, "I have absolutely no respect for Jim Wright." The bill was "creative" in its proposed new taxes, including a tax "intended to discourage hostile corporate takeovers."[46] Gingrich had been organizing conservatives against the bill, and though he lost to the machinations by the Speaker, it came down as a Gingrich victory. He lambasted Wright for "railroading this tax increase over the wishes of Republicans and conservative Democrats alike."[47] The victory would prove to be Pyrrhic at best for Wright.

By the end of 1987, relations between Gingrich and Wright had reached a nadir, mostly because of the Georgian's incessant public campaign against the Speaker. Gingrich sent a "Dear Colleague" letter, complete with newspaper articles questioning some of Wright's deals.[48] Gingrich was not alone. Congressman Dick Cheney of Wyoming, for whom the word *prudence* was invented, now also had Wright in his sights. "I feel the speaker is playing fast and loose with the powers of his office," Cheney offered.[49]

Going even further, Gingrich used the *c* word with reporters. He accused Wright of "corrupt and blatantly unethical behavior" surrounding book contracts and their sizable royalties, Wright's work for troubled savings and loan banks in Texas, and a stockyard that was getting money from Washington. All in all, it was a target-rich environment for Gingrich.[50]

Gingrich's campaign against Jim Wright intensified as 1987 came to a close. He told the *Wall Street Journal*, "We currently have the least ethical speaker in the 20th century."[51] Considering some of the drunks and bums who'd held the gavel of second in line to the presidency, it was quite a charge.

As the year wound down, Washington and the country had slipped into full Christmas mode. The city-state was in a mad, impatient Christmas rush, same as most years. Impatient shoppers rushed to and fro; impatient drivers honked their way through the city, unwisely abandoning their cars on major thoroughfares at the first sign of snow; partygoers raucously demanded cocktails and canapés; and Congress rushed to get out of town with only one word on their minds in this, the most joyous and giving of all holiday seasons: *adjournment.*

Only in Washington could Christmas cards be seen through a political prism. The *Washington Post* devoted a long story in their infamous Style section in which writer Marjorie Williams invited Washingtonians to dump all over one another's cards. Williams made bipartisan sport of Senator Gary

Hart's card, Congresswoman Pat Schroeder's card, Newt Gingrich's card, Dan Quayle's card, Jack Kemp's card, and this: "the GOP consulting firm Keene, Shirley & Associates, whose card is a painting that depicts a pair of hunters blasting geese out of the sky."[52]

CHAPTER 15

TRUST BUT VERIFY

*"The House of Representatives has evolved into an
essentially corrupt left-wing machine whose ethics committee's
essential job is to run a sequence of whitewashes."*

1988

The seat of the national government was located in a putrid, malarial, fetid swamp that reeked in the summer as the denizens nearly drowned in their own perspiration. So when it came time to choose their national conventions, the Democrats selected Atlanta, which was even hotter than Washington, and the Republicans opted for New Orleans, which was even more humid.

The Big Easy was below sea level, which is where most people thought politicians belonged anyway. In Atlanta, street vendors sold an especially popular bumper sticker at the Democratic confab: "Die Yuppie Scum."[1]

In New Orleans, Republicans gathered to say good-bye to an old friend and hello to a new nominee. But it would not be the last time Ronald Reagan was a factor at a GOP Convention. He was going out on a wave of affection and adoration that exceeded any previous Republican president. As the years passed, his shadow extended and lengthened over the party.

Bush, not understanding the hold the man who saved his political chestnuts had over the Republicans, accepted the nomination with a clear denunciation of the previous eight years, calling for a "kinder and gentler" brand of Republicanism.[2]

Though both Bob Dole and Jack Kemp made more sense as Bush's running mate, he opted instead for the forty-one-year-old senator from Indiana, J. Danforth Quayle, scion of a wealthy publishing family. When asked at a press conference if Bush had taken Quayle because he could not pick one of his sons, Jim Baker simply shrugged his shoulders and smiled. The *Washington Post* observed that "as they stepped out . . . Quayle, eager and boyish, and Bush, obviously proud of his new running mate, looked like a father-and-son team."[3]

Bob Dole, the stand-up comic of the GOP, said he'd tried to call Quayle to congratulate him, but the young Hoosier was shaving. "First time," Dole quipped.[4]

Gingrich and many, if not most, of the Republican leadership and 1988 aspirants had signed the "Taxpayer Protection Pledge," which locked them into opposing any increase in marginal tax rates for citizens, and also a "Taxpayers' Bill of Rights," which was designed to clamp down on IRS abuses.

While Gingrich aligned with the party on most economic issues, on one important issue he remained on the cutting edge, beckoning his colleagues to follow. At the beginning of 1988, Gingrich was one of the few Republicans to attend the twentieth-anniversary memorial services for Dr. Martin Luther King Jr. at Ebenezer Baptist Church in Atlanta, the civil rights leader's home pulpit. Also in attendance was RNC chieftain Frank Fahrenkopf. It was sometimes hard to remember how young King was when he was assassinated. Had he lived, King would have been 59 in January 1988.[5]

The fact of the matter was that relations between Ronald Reagan and the conservative movement had not always been a match made in heaven. Newt Gingrich could be right in there throwing barbs at the Reagan White House too.

Again, a spat of stories emerged from the previous years saying the steam was out of the Reagan Revolution. Gingrich let himself be used, as when he told Gerald Seib of the *Wall Street Journal* in late 1987 that Reagan was "in some danger of becoming another Jimmy Carter."[6] Democrats and liberal Republicans had joined in earlier that year, pronounced the Reagan Revolution dead, and "Conservatives, increasingly in this winter of their discontent, have written off—and, in some cases, shown unmasked contempt for—the Reagan White House," chortled the *National Journal.*[7]

Some conservatives were harsh in their judgment of the man in charge of their revolution, saying that for much of his second term, he'd been governing from a "bunker." In a long piece in the New York Times, E. J. Dionne practically danced on the grave of Reagan's last term. "In brighter days, the challenge of the final years was to institutionalize the Reagan agenda. As Edwin J. Feulner Jr., president of the Heritage Foundation, warned in 1985, if that fails, 'it is unlikely that the Reagan era will prove to be the historic change in the direction of America that we have sought.'"[8]

"Analysis" pieces about Reagan and his revolution were using words such as *stale* and *confusion*. Yet another New York Times piece entitled "At a Crossroads," this one by R. W. "Johnny" Apple Jr., opined, "The erosion has been severe. It appears unlikely . . . that anything Mr. Reagan does now will repair all of the damage." The story went even deeper, darker. "Mr. Reagan's accomplishments, students of his Presidency say, have been to restore the confidence of the American people in themselves, their country and its leadership, and, initially at least, to take the initiative against the Soviet Union. These accomplishments now seem imperiled."[9]

Gingrich understood the first rule of Washington was not to take friendships personally. Oddly meanly, he said of the Gipper, "He will never again be the Reagan that he was before he blew it. He is not going to regain our trust and our faith easily."[10] But then he seemed to reverse his field, saying on the MacNeil/Lehrer NewsHour, Reagan can "regain our trust and our faith. I think the country wants Ronald Reagan to go back to being Ronald Reagan."[11]

Drift was an oft-used word in describing the Reagan Administration. In October 1986, just one month before the sordid tale of Iran-Contra broke, Reagan had stood at 64 percent approval; by March 1987, it was down to 40 percent.[12]

Reagan, for his part, confided in his secret diaries what he thought of his political enemies, which was not much. Yet, he was through the thicket and clearly relieved to be rid of the Iran-Contra mess and the men who had created it. Even Newsweek took notice: "He was confident, disarming and plausible, the Great Communicator once more." The president, they wrote, "was able to deflect sticky questions about the Iran-Contra affair while asserting the rightness and sincerity of his policies." He also made it clear he had no idea Oliver North had organized a "gun-running operation" out of his White House.[13]

But then Gingrich noted, "Support for Reagan is deep and emotional among precisely those Republicans who vote in primaries and caucuses . . . it's been a 23-year-long marriage, and it's not going to break up."[14]

Maureen Dowd, in a profile piece on Jack Kemp, wrote that after "years of Reaganism, they are feeling betrayed, arguing that true conservatism has not been tried."[15] In fact, while Ronald Reagan always knew what he stood for, more and more people in the GOP were interpreting Reaganism to mean whatever suited their own agendas. A headline in the *Wall Street Journal* summed it up: "Expanded Republican Party Finds Divisiveness May Be Its Biggest Political Headache in 1988." Gingrich saw the problem. "Sure, we're fighting each other, but if you're going to become the party of ideas, you're doing well if you move the arguments into your tent,"[16] which was a fancy way of saying what LBJ had said years earlier: "It's probably better to have him inside the tent p--sing out, than outside the tent p--sing in."[17]

Gingrich and Kemp, however, did spy something that had eluded nearly all except Reagan, and that was the growing power and importance of Hispanic voters.[18] Hispanics, they rightly saw, could or should be Republicans, because of the importance of the family, a strong Catholic culture, and entrepreneurship. Reagan had once said that "Latinos are Republican. They just don't know it yet."[19]

Kevin Phillips, one of the more acute if also out-of-the-ordinary political observers, said of the post-Reagan GOP, "There's no Republican who can hold the Reagan coalition together. But the Democrats are doing silly things that take people's minds off jobs, the economy and foreign competition. With their lack of talent and their fratricide, the Democrats are holding the Republicans together."[20]

Newton Leroy Gingrich and George Herbert Walker Bush had a far more tortured relationship than did Reagan and the rowdy conservatives. At the end of the day, the conservatives still loved Reagan and he still adored them, at least many of them.

But Gingrich and Bush did not go well together. Gingrich was fried chicken and Bush was filet mignon. Gingrich was country and Bush was country club. Gingrich was fried squash and Bush was fried oysters. Gingrich read books and Bush used them to decorate his homes.

They had nothing in common culturally, philosophically, ideologically, intellectually, and, most important, temperamentally. "Poppy" Bush wanted everybody to like him, especially the enemies of Republicanism. Newt, on the other hand, saw politics as warfare by other means, without the diplomacy. He counted his enemies as a mark of his accomplishments. To wit, he said of the Congress's refusal to create a new, independent committee to investigate the House, "The House of Representatives has evolved into an essentially corrupt left-wing machine whose ethics committee's essential job is to run a sequence of whitewashes."[21]

Gingrich appeared to have been proven right when the House Ethics Committee appointed Richard J. Phelan of Chicago to investigate the charges against new House Speaker Jim Wright. Phelan had raised money for Democrats much of his adult life, and Gingrich aide Karen Van Brocklin stormed, "It's going to be an absolute whitewash; he's a Democratic activist."[22] Simply put, the choice did not pass the giggle test. The Ethics Committee released a letter defending Phelan, a sure sign that his appointment was a problem. It was also announced that his contract was for $300,000. His previous big case was defending a grocery food chain against "salmonella poisoning." With all the well-poisoning going on in Washington, Phelan would fit right in. Gingrich dismissed him as a "partisan Democrat . . . non-investigative, corporate lawyer."[23]

Wright's cause was not helped when it was revealed that his attorneys were being paid with contributions to the Wright campaign fund. Nor when one of his aides told the committee that he had been assigned, at taxpayer expense, to work full-time on Wright's book. "I'm not going to deny it. I was assigned to do it. I did it as part of my job," said former Wright aide Matthew Cossolotto. It was also revealed that a corporation in Texas bought one thousand copies of Wright's book, as did the Teamsters.[24]

Conservatives went around the bend when Wright was reported to have said of the president, "Here is a charming person but a person with whom you simply can't really discuss serious problems." Gingrich returned the fire, calling Wright "ruthless, corrupt . . . suffering from megalomania. That makes him the most dangerous man ever to be Speaker."[25]

Of the five charges filed with the Ethics Committee against Wright, four were brought by Gingrich and the fifth by Common Cause.[26] The fact that a respected liberal lobbying group was also going after Wright was taken seriously by the media, who might have otherwise dismissed Gingrich as a gadfly. The participation of Common Cause gave the investigation a bipartisan, respectable veneer.

Kemp, meanwhile, had to fight off all the old stupid rumors again about homosexuality, which some thought were being pushed by Bush supporters.

To counter the false rumors, some Kemp geniuses came up with the bright idea of planting their own counter rumors about Kemp being a womanizer.

Gingrich allies were forming up from unexpected quarters. Evans and Novak did an uncomfortable profile of Speaker Wright, specifically citing his unheard-of 55 percent royalties of his book sales. A Washington-centric magazine, *Regardie's*, printed a story headlined "The Speaker and the Sleaze."[27]

Other publications, including the *New Republic*, the *Wall Street Journal*, and a number of Texas publications also ran roughshod over Wright. The Speaker had testified in September and afterward told reporters he did so with "total, absolute candor." Reporters giggled.

When his own books were thrown in his face, Gingrich snappily replied, "The Wright book was not written to discuss public policy. It was written to make money." Gingrich's books were heavy on policy and light on profit. On the other hand, he said his campaign against Wright was "to preserve the integrity of the House." Reporters giggled again.[28]

Since joining the Democratic leadership in the House, Wright's personal wealth had grown tremendously, nearly a million dollars by 1981. Suffice to say, Gingrich had a lot to work with when it came to the new House Speaker, and he knew that in Washington it was better to be on offense than defense, better to be respected than loved.

Even Dick Cheney, the taciturn representative from Wyoming, "never a member of the Newt Gingrich fan club" according to columnists Evans and Novak, now saw the tactical brilliance in Gingrich's incessant ethics crusade against Wright.[29] Cheney called Wright a "heavy-handed SOB."[30] Wright's defenders had their own choice phrases for Gingrich. The Democratic majority in the House intended to leave open the Iran-Contra special committee, all staff intact and all files open, as a means of maintaining a drip-drip-drip water torture on Ronald Reagan, even though the matter had been largely closed, taken out of the hands of Congress and placed into the hands of the Justice Department. The Tower Commission report had cleared Reagan of any responsibility, though it was obvious he'd been irresponsible in trusting some of his staff.

While few in the Republican conference—including the "Reagan Robots," who called Newt a friend and ally—thought much of his one-man band at the outset, it had picked up steam throughout the year, and when the Democrats stupidly threatened to go after Cheney and Minority Leader Bob Michel, one of the least offensive (and least effective) men in Washington, the Doubting Republicans suddenly saw the usefulness of Gingrich's offensive maneuver. Suddenly, Michel was firmly in the Gingrich camp, delighted to watch the young man tear into Wright daily.

As the *Post* put it, "Facing another year of torment from the Democratic majority, they perceive Gingrich's assault on the speaker as a way out."[31] They began to openly bargain with the Democratic leadership: We won't get off of Wright's back until you get off Reagan's back. In the inner sanctum of the Democratic Party, there was no debate over the portly young man. They hated him with white-hot hatred.

Most of the time, the Reagan White House wanted to kiss Gingrich. At some other times, they wanted to slug him, as when he'd issued harsh judgment of the Gipper's last years in office. Gingrich had sometimes gone off the reservation in his criticisms of Reagan and his Administration, but when the rubber met the road, he was a loyalist to the Gipper. "We're going to be central to protecting the Reagan legacy," he'd said some months earlier.[32]

The political arm of House Democrats, the Democratic Congressional Campaign Committee (DCCC), began a campaign against the "Gang of Four," which included Gingrich, Kemp, Vin Weber of Minnesota, and Bob Dornan of California. Dornan, for his part, was an unrelenting, over-the-top ideological warrior who some thought needed clinical assistance. The *Los Angeles Times* charitably said Dornan was "feisty, eccentric . . ."[33]

The head of the "DeeTripleCee" was Tony Coelho, a representative from the Golden State for whom synonyms for "fiercely partisan" had not yet been invented. He detested—detested!—Reagan and nearly all other Republicans with a passion. Coelho's committee produced commercials comparing Reagan with Richard Nixon and Iran-Contra with Watergate.[34] The best the Republicans could do was to distribute talking points defending Reagan and the legality of Iran-Contra.[35] There were lots of talking points on the economy, on the fight for Nicaragua, on the summit between Reagan and Gorbachev, and on forthcoming issues such as the deficit, health care and trade, financial security and campaign finance reform. Some things never changed.

Interestingly, the coverage of the *Washington Post* sometimes figured into the talking points, but only as a reverse barometer. If the *Post* was praising, then the Reaganites were doing something wrong. If the *Post* was criticizing (as it mostly did) the Reaganites were doing things right. If the *Post* was grousing, then the Reaganites were really doing things right.

All good Reaganites knew the *Post* was hopelessly, blindly, slavishly left wing, to the point of sometimes committing journalistic malpractice. To wit, the *Post* mostly took the side of the Soviets in any dispute with Reagan. The *Post* always took the side of the communist thugs running rough-shod over Nicaragua, rather than the pro–Freedom Fighting Contras. The *Post* routinely mocked the Reagan Doctrine. Thinking conservatives regarded the *Post* as a bad joke and nothing more. They much preferred the *Washington Times* as it contained straightforward reporting and excellent editorials and op-eds.

There was one particularly satisfying talking point, and that was Jimmy Carter's "Misery Index"—a combination of inflation and un-employment. It was well over 20 percent in Carter's last year. In Reagan's last year, it had been slashed to less than half. The *Post* ignored the sig-nificance as it was favorable to Reagan and they rarely printed anything favorable to the Gipper.

By the end of 1988, the talking points about Reagan's eight years were all good. As one wag said at the time, everything that was supposed to be going up was going up and everything that was supposed to be going down was going down.

Tony Coelho and the "DeeTripleCee" had some high-profile help in launch-ing political attacks on the "Gang of Four." Jim Wright got in some shots at Gingrich and his cohorts, saying they "remind you of gnats. A gnat can't do you any real harm, but the worst he can do is irritate you by flying around in your ear."[36] Famous last words.

Later, at the Democratic Convention in Atlanta, hundreds of party members wore buttons that "feature[d] a silhouette of a green salamander with a red slash mark through it . . . the 'Newtbuster' symbol has become familiar in a city awash with catchy political emblems."[37]

Gingrich, though, had his admirers on both sides of the aisle. A for-mer aide to Tip O'Neill, Kirk O'Donnell, said, "He's smart, he's shrewd, he's articulate, he's highly committed, and he's very ambitious. He's been a speaker-baiter since he's been in Congress, and furthermore, he's good at it."[38] To O'Donnell's point, Gingrich had in the past called Tip O'Neill a "thug" and compared Wright to Mussolini. Bob Livingston said, "I remember O'Neill was just about ready to come down and punch the guy."[39]

Wright wasn't the only House member embroiled in controversy. As of June 1988, fifteen members of Congress found themselves caught up in some sort of scandal. The House had devolved into a "Crook of the Week Club." Always the strategic planner, Gingrich anticipated he would soon become a target of Democrats trying to tag him with anything that could be painted in the press as an impropriety. He sent a letter to an outside legal firm, Topping and Swillinger, asking them to monitor and audit his office to head off any appearance of corruption "because of my commitment to ethics and because of the intense focus of my activities the Jim Wright-Tony Coelho ethics problem may incur."[40]

The Ethics Committee recommended to the full House the expulsion of New York congressman Mario Biaggi on the charges of taking bribes and then obstructing the investigation.

Gingrich's sole Republican colleague from Georgia, Pat Swindall, was now also fighting off accusations of fraud and abuse, including a "scheme to launder possible drug money." The amount in question was $850,000. Gingrich did not flinch and stated flatly that the Ethics Committee should also investigate Swindall.[41] Pat insisted the pronunciation of his name was "swinndaal," but some thought it more appropriate the other way.

Another scandal, revolving around Maryland Democratic congressman Roy Dyson, included the suicide of a staffer, who'd jumped to his death after the *Washington Post* disclosed that Dyson's hiring practices focused on "young, single men." Along with stories of excessive partying and drinking, Dyson's administrative assistant once drunkenly told a young staffer to do a "strip tease" for the rest of the staff. Campaign money was also misappropriated by Dyson amid rumors of other shenanigans.[42]

Gingrich was making more and more enemies. A former staffer whom he'd fired was on a jihad against him, and Gingrich "faced a resurrection of earlier unfavorable publicity about himself, including articles describing his bitter divorce in 1981 from his first wife, accounts of extramarital affairs and contentions that he had approached his wife in a hospital while she was recovering from cancer surgery to discuss details of their divorce."[43]

Languidly, Gingrich simply said, "I'm not a saint."[44]

In fact, his wife had already recovered from cancer by the time he asked for the divorce. Filing of the legal papers came after that.[45]

A complaint was filed with the Postal Service by the DCCC charging Gingrich's political action committee, Conservatives for Hope and Opportunity, with breaking regulations. The Post Office threw out the complaint. The *Washington Post* felled a small forest of trees to report on the filing, which charged that the group had spent more than $200,000 on fund-raising but had donated only $300,000 to GOP candidates. The article described Gingrich as "a thorn in the side of the Democratic leadership."[46] The DCCC petitioned the Post Office to prevent Gingrich's organization from donating any of its remaining money to Republican candidates.[47]

The Democrats ginned up mail and advertising in Gingrich's district in an attempt to defeat him at the polls in '88.

A steady drumbeat of questions and attacks against Wright, orchestrated by Gingrich, was widening, though much was against the backdrop of the presidential contest, with the nominations of both parties being fiercely fought over. The thoroughness of the Gingrich assault later came to light when it was revealed he'd been in contact with people in Texas trying to dig up more on Wright, as in the case of a letter from an attorney in Huntsville, referencing "the ethical nature of Rep. Wright's conduct."[48] The letter snarkily noted that the wife Wright was defending in 1989 was not the wife he was defending in 1963.[49]

Gingrich's growing list of political enemies dug up some material from early in his career concerning the "Dorchester Fund," a project in which a group of admirers pooled their money for him to write a novel. The total was $13,000, which was not an inconsiderable amount for 1977. When the first three chapters were presented to a book agent, he advised Gingrich his future was as a politician and not a novelist.[50] The money had gone for research and for supporting Newt and his family, but there was nothing untoward or illegal, especially since it had all taken place while he was still a private citizen. Virginia Shapard had tried to sink him with that back in 1978.

Gingrich may have drawn one of the weirder opponents for the campaign. The Democrats nominated David Worley, who refused nearly all chances to debate the incumbent, Gingrich. "Worley has declined all debate invitations so far . . . ," reported the *Atlanta Daily World*.[51] Worley said he would debate, but only under the following conditions: not on Friday or Saturday night, not in rural counties, not before audiences of less than 220, not during the World Series or the Olympics or during any of the presidential debates.[52]

By the middle of 1988, the House Ethics Committee had seen and heard enough; it was initiating its own investigation of the Speaker of the House, Jim Wright. They met well into the evening of June 10 before finally making their decision. The committee was made up of six Democrats and six Republicans, but had a Democratic chairman, Julian Dixon of California, known for his rectitude. The committee voted 12–0 for an investigation to go forward.[53]

Part of the allegations was that the man who'd paid Wright the extraordinary book royalties, Carlos Moore, had been paid the astronomical sum of $600,000 by Wright's campaign committees.[54] On top of everything else, Moore was a felon, having been convicted of tax evasion of nearly $150,000.[55]

In a previous incarnation, Moore had once headed the political action committee of the Teamsters under the watchful eye of James Riddle "Jimmy" Hoffa Jr. The conviction of tax evasion against Moore was over cash withdrawals from the Teamsters' political fund and then not accounting for the whereabouts of the money. Moore "denied that he pocketed the money but refuses to say which politicians received the cash."[56] All in all, Moore was a pretty shady character for the Speaker of the House to be hanging around with, but Wright steadfastly maintained his innocence, calling the charges "flimsy."[57] He stood his ground as Speaker and as convention chairman.

Moore called Gingrich, asking for a meeting. He also offered him the same publishing deal of 55 percent royalties that he had given Wright, but Newt wisely demurred on both offers. Reputable publishers were aghast at the huge royalties Wright was getting from his old friend.[58]

While Gingrich was delighted that the Ethics Committee had finally replied in the affirmative to the complaint he'd filed, he once again showed his mastery of the art of political attack, calling for the committee to hire an outside investigator and not rely upon their staff investigators, the clear implication being that they were conflicted.

Seventy-two Republicans of varying stripes signed Gingrich's letter to the Ethics Committee, including every member of the leadership, except Bob Michel. Even the risk-averse George H. W. Bush jumped in, calling for an investigation of Wright's finances, contributors, book deals, and the like. By now, Gingrich was *numero uno* on Wright's hate list. He said his regard for the Georgian was "similar to those of a fire hydrant toward a dog."[59] The *Washington Post* editorially supported the investigation of Wright but still saved a big backhand for Gingrich and the Reagan White House over their motives.[60]

Wright went on all the Sunday shows, *de rigueur* for Washington men under fire.

Gingrich was focused on national issues surrounding the 1988 presidential campaign and his quest to bring down Speaker Wright, but he also had to pay attention to his own reelection campaign. The opposition party back in the Sixth District, however, seemed eager to make his life easier this election cycle.

Gingrich's reelection campaign back home now looked to be a laugher. Nationally, the campaign of 1988 was shaping up to be one of the more inconsequential contests in recent memory. Bush campaigned in American flag factories and supported an amendment to the US Constitution banning flag burning. He also attacked Dukakis's support for the ACLU.

Meanwhile, Congress debated funding for "latchkey" children and money for combating drug use.

A young undergraduate at Emory University was, however, more articulate than many in the GOP on the issues of concern to them. "We believe in the pledge of allegiance and we don't want homosexuals to adopt children."[61]

The election of 1988 also featured the introduction of "Willie Horton" to the political universe. The Bush campaign had dug up and used the issue of weekend furloughs granted by Michael Dukakis while governor of

Massachusetts. Among those given furloughs was Willie Horton, who had murdered a young boy, and whose name would become eternally linked with the twin issues of race and politics.

After his sentencing for the murder, Horton, the not-quite-model citizen, was granted a weekend furlough by Governor Dukakis. He promptly skipped town and headed for Maryland, where he savagely beat a man and then brutally and repeatedly raped his wife. Horton had a rap sheet that made Al Capone look like a Boy Scout, but all the furlough-bestowing ruling class had cared about was his race. As a result, the 1988 contest was one of the most racially polarized in American history. Bush received a lesser percentage of the black vote than even Barry Goldwater in 1964.

The downward spiraling of presidential politics in 1988 was an omen of more bad things to come.

Ronald Reagan, who did think and talk and write about the past and the future and war and peace, was going out on a wave of wistful affection, with historically high approval ratings from the American people, though the hoity-toity of the academy and the media continued to hate him, mock him, and insult him. The Burkean columnist George Will sometimes had his doubts about Reagan, the devotee of Thomas Paine. In their day, Burke and Paine despised each other.

Speaking of the match between Bush and Dukakis, Will wrote, "This contest, which is too close to call, features two eminently arguable approaches to the future that the Reagan years—economic vigor, budgetary vandalism— have prepared."[62]

George Bush, former resident of Massachusetts, won a gentleman's landslide over Mike Dukakis, former governor of Massachusetts, 53.4 percent to 45.6 percent, though more handsomely in the Electoral College, 426–111.[63] But it was not a mandate for governance; Bush had stumped on such small-bore issues as to be ridiculously inconsequential. How really would or should a president control flag burning, mandate the pledge of allegiance, or regulate the American Civil Liberties Union?

His campaign was a cynical appeal to "working-class and lower-middle-class voters who might vote for either party . . . [but] Mr. Bush is at one with their values," wrote E. J. Dionne.[64] It was also noted that "Mr. Dukakis did not seem to gain from the support of Gov. Bill Clinton, who nominated him at the convention in a speech remembered largely for its length and dryness."[65] Clinton, a young politician eminently known in his home state as "Slick Willie," was booed from the floor by the delegates and cheered when he said, "I want to say, in closing . . ." The young man had confused a convention speech with a bull session at Yale.

In his own acceptance speech, thinking he had to separate himself from Ronald Reagan, Bush told the assembled in New Orleans, "I do not hate government," the clear implication being that Reagan did.[66] The subtle digs at Reagan riled some Reaganites, including chief number one Reaganite, Nancy Davis Reagan. The Bush speech had been written by Peggy Noonan, a pretty wordsmith who had worked a short time in the Reagan White House before decamping for her native New York.

Tony Coelho's attempts to unseat Gingrich in the election of 1988 were to no avail. After years of tormenting the Democrats, from Charles Diggs to Tip O'Neill to Jim Wright, Gingrich finally received some of his own medicine, but it was a weak witch's brew. The DCCC ran extensive radio and television ads against him in Georgia, but they had little impact. Gingrich won easily over his bizarro Democratic opponent, David Worley (with whom he finally debated after much pleading on Gingrich's part).

Pat Swindall, Gingrich's scandal-plagued Republican colleague from the Georgia Fourth, lost to actor Ben Jones. Pithily, the *Atlanta Daily World* wrote, "An indictment for perjury no doubt contributed to his defeat."[67]

Conservatives had previously worried that Bush "lack[ed] Ronald Reagan's sense of how to use the power of the presidency."[68] That group included Newt Gingrich. On the other hand, some saw Gingrich as a valuable intellectual ally on Capitol Hill. The *Wall Street Journal* said, "[Bush's] most important lieutenants will be idea-mongers like Mr. Gingrich."[69] And he was forever thinking about the GOP and the then-harebrained notion of taking control of the House. "Beyond reforming Congress, Mr. Gingrich's larger ambition is to remake the GOP into a party that 'thinks and acts like a majority.'"[70]

He used phrases such as "empowerment-orientated opportunity society,"[71] and this type of thinking just drove Bush up a wall. Bush wasn't interested a whit in ideas and certainly not in ideology, despite having said otherwise sometimes during the campaign. He was a man of the status quo and was only interested in what worked, according to the status quo.

Gingrich, the idea monger, was interested in "tenant management of public housing, choice in medicare . . . reforms . . . flexible freeze."[72] Or "the negative synergism of the welfare state."[73] Men like Bush rolled their eyes, regarding this as so much drivel. Another reform idea making the rounds was to introduce to America's public schools the teaching of free market economics.[74] Even Albert Shanker, head of the American Federation of Teachers, supported this nuclear option.

Days after the election, Gingrich was already advancing the radical idea for Bush to push a four-year federal budget, rather than the one-year budget each president fought with Congress about. The rationale was sharp and compelling: the same energy would be devoted to passing a four-year budget as a one-year budget. Gingrich's proposal fell on deaf ears at the Bush transition office.

Bush would come to kick himself for not taking the Georgian's advice.

CHAPTER 16

WRIGHT AND WRONG

*"The corridors are full of the sound of
long knives being sharpened."*

1989

Newt Gingrich's national publicity by this point was supercharged. "Guerrilla Gingrich," blared one headline in the *Wall Street Journal*. Nary a day went by that he was not in the national press or on network television. He was such compellingly good copy. To wit, a columnist quoted him saying, "Republicans are stupid. No other word is strong enough." The column, by Paul Gigot, favorably compared Ronald Reagan and Gingrich. He used the phrase "intellectual insurgency" and said the younger man was afflicted with "peripatetic optimism."[1]

Bush was beginning to assemble a mostly well-behaved and mannerly cabinet, including Dr. Louis Sullivan as Secretary of Health and Human Services. Gingrich was thrilled with the choice of his fellow Georgian. "He's southern, black, a national-class medical figure and he's solid on conservative issues."[2] Pro-lifers were frankly suspicious of Sullivan and wondered if Gingrich's passion to reach out to African Americans had trumped his pro-life position.

Gingrich easily spotted the trend lines in Washington and on Capitol Hill. Along with the election of Bush came a more aggressive and self-confident GOP, and the Democrats who had ruled the roost for the better part of fifty years were not pleased. Early in 1989, he told the *New York Times*, "I would be very surprised ninety days from now if anyone's convinced of serious bipartisanship."[3] The Democrats were hopeful, however, of working with the compassionate Bush and gleeful at the departure of the tough guy Reagan.

The new president's State of the Union address was unlike anything the Gipper gave, who spoke of vision and limitless horizons and heroes and the goodness of the American people and the future. While a generous amount of policy proposals were always mixed in, it was Reagan's soaring rhetoric that gained lasting fame. Bush's address was, according to Gingrich, similar to those given by governors: "turgid and dull." The *New York Times* also noted the difference between the fortieth president and the forty-first, saying, "The speech Mr. Bush delivered tonight was anything but an attack on the power of the state." Instead, he promised new programs for "drugs, homelessness and education . . ."[4]

Gingrich threw gasoline on the raging Jim Wright fire when he linked Speaker Wright with the star-crossed mayor of Washington, Marion Barry, who had been under constant FBI surveillance for drug use and a year later was set up in a sting operation by the Justice Department using an old girlfriend, Rasheeda Moore, and crack cocaine as the inducement. "I think Jim Wright and Marion Barry are perfect symbols for a corrupt Democratic Party," he said acidly.[5]

In the memorable words of *Washington Post* writers Tom Kenworthy and Don Phillips, "The corridors are full of the sound of long knives being sharpened."[6] A bizarre chain of events led to a game-changing coup for Gingrich in March 1989. It began when newly inaugurated President George Bush nominated former Texas senator John Tower for secretary of defense.[7]

Tower had more IOUs than could be counted. He'd been a minor hero to conservatives beginning in 1961 when he amazingly won Lyndon Johnson's Senate seat after Johnson became vice president. Though married, rumors of wine, women, and song had followed the diminutive Tower for years. His knowledge of defense matters was unparalleled, beginning with his naval service in the Pacific in World War II. Tower had divorced in 1976 from his wife of many years and had retired from the Senate in 1984.

Tower's confirmation hearings were rough from the start, but reached bottom when conservative activist Paul Weyrich was allowed to testify against him. Weyrich brought out discussion of Tower's rumored drinking and womanizing. The rumors were treated as facts; they made all the papers and networks. No women stepped forward, nor did any of Tower's bartenders, but the allegations were enough to sink the Texan's nomination 53–47, an unprecedented rejection of a former Senate colleague and an astonishing rebuke of Bush, who'd worked little to help Tower win confirmation. In a jaw-dropping move, the president sent a handwritten "bygones be bygones" letter to Weyrich. The letter was promptly copied and faxed all over Washington.

Panicked, Bush turned to forty-eight-year-old congressman Dick Cheney of Wyoming to fill the slot at Defense. Cheney, a longtime Washington insider about whom there were no rumors of women, booze, or excessive smiling, was confirmed easily.

Cheney's departure for the Pentagon opened up the minority whip position.[8]

"Within minutes of Bush's announcement, Rep. Newt Gingrich (R-Ga.) was on the telephone to seek his colleagues' support for the post of House minority whip."[9] But his candidacy frankly rubbed some the wrong way—and downright terrified other establishmentarians. The unseen hand of the Bush White House was at work, organizing opposition to the Georgian. Gingrich's ascension to Whip was not a foregone conclusion by any means. He hadn't started out as the front-runner; indeed, maybe four others were thought to be ahead of him.

As with most other fights in his life, he was going against the odds; and the establishment, who favored Congressman Ed Madigan of Illinois, a nondescript, non-confrontational, non-ideological, go-along kind of guy. Other candidates briefly thought of making the race, but only Gingrich and Madigan plunged in, one the young, ideological firebrand, and the other the establishment moderate. The vote would be secret.

Gingrich immediately won the endorsement of Bill Buckley and *National Review,* which he circulated widely. Moderates like Olympia Snowe of Maine and Bill Frenzel of Minnesota stunned their colleagues by supporting Gingrich. The Republican Conference had 174 members, so the winner needed 88 votes at a minimum for an outright win if all showed up. Madigan claimed he had enough votes to win.[10]

Gingrich's candidacy was seen superficially as a brash and premature grab for personal power as well as an ideological challenge to the establishment, but it was far more. It was also cultural, generational, and, given his eventual amount of moderate support, an expression on the part of the younger members against the "Old Bulls." Gingrich, Olympia Snowe of Maine, Nancy Johnson of Connecticut, Steve Gunderson of Wisconsin, Bill Frenzel of

Minnesota, and others in the party rejected the idea of permanent minority status for the GOP. Madigan should have expected the support of other moderates, but even moderates get sick of being pistol-whipped by Democrats. Frankly, they were sick and tired of being rolled by the Democratic majority and Michel's flaccid leadership.

"Gingrich . . . expresses all the frustration of a minority that has been out of power for 35 years," said the *Post*.[11] All saw it as "a referendum on the future of the party . . ."[12]

Gingrich's previous book deals came under renewed scrutiny. At one point, Gunderson led a delegation of nearly twenty Republicans into Michel's office to confront him over the underhanded tactics he and his office were using in an attempt to thwart Gingrich.[13] The confrontation ended up in a nationally syndicated Evans and Novak column. The smart money was on Madigan; Gingrich would be given some consolation prize where he could be controlled, or at least watched, by Michel and his boys.

The old guard did not want Gingrich as he wasn't housebroken in their view, but to a diverse array of GOP members, he at least represented a fighting spirit that Bob Michel and the old guard regarded as silly and puerile. Moderates like Snowe and Frenzel stunned their colleagues by supporting Gingrich. Bob Walker was immediately on the phone to Newt and then began calling others to round up support.[14]

The Bush White House was pushing hard for Madigan. As it turned out, both Bush and Michel were prophetic in their concerns about the conservative from Georgia. But he had an odd coalition of supporters, though it did not include Tom DeLay, a thin-skinned Texan with a taste for red wine, hot tubs, and women. DeLay was Madigan's campaign manager.

Stunningly, in March 1989, in the midst of his war with Wright, Gingrich's Republican colleagues elected him to the post of minority whip by a narrow 87–85 margin. In only his fifth term in office, and frankly not very popular, though greatly respected (and feared) inside of Washington, forty-five-year-old Newt Gingrich stunned the political world with his astonishing election to the number two position in the House Republican Conference and a very senior position in the GOP's hierarchy.

In the end, Gingrich prevailed with one member of the GOP caucus not voting and one ballot spoiled according to a Gingrich aide, Dan Meyer, who was in charge of the counting.[15] A Madigan supporter, Jim Courter of New Jersey, was running for governor and refused to come back to Capitol Hill, even when Michel offered to send a private plane. Another, Lawrence Coughlin of Pennsylvania, had been thought to be a Madigan supporter, but announced his support for Newt the day of the vote.[16]

Gingrich's rise to number two in the House Republican Conference surprised the political world and dominated talk in Washington for days. All the Sunday shows discussed the meaning of the vote and unanimously interpreted it as a rebuke of the GOP establishment and Heap Big Chief Establishmentarian George Herbert Walker Bush.

Bush held his nose and congratulated Gingrich and they had their picture taken together. "Hold your enemies closer . . . ," Don Bush knew. So did Godfather Gingrich. But the rumor around Washington was Bush was so upset he refused to speak to his White House political director, Ron Kaufman, for a long time.[17] Madigan was later rewarded with the agriculture cabinet post. Michel was clearly unhappy, but Jim Wright sent Gingrich a copy of *Reflections of a Public Man*, complete with a long inscription and drawing of Newt by Wright. Dazed at his astonishing win, Gingrich said, "You have to see this as a long evolution of growing up."[18]

Not everyone was pleased with Gingrich's upset victory. George Will wrote yet another column eviscerating Gingrich, comparing him to Robespierre.[19] But congratulatory letters poured into Gingrich's office from across the country.

After the bloody battle for the Indiana Eighth Congressional District, in which the House Democrats crassly and arrogantly refused to seat the Republican who'd won narrowly, the Republican minority had fumed at both the House Democratic leadership and their own leadership, especially Michel. "For all the partisan infighting in the House, there is a chummy collegiality and a loyalty to the institution that transcends party lines. Mr. Gingrich is not a member of that club . . ."[20]

Gingrich instead formed his own club, which was called the "92 Group." This was the name his odd coalition was called because they envisioned being in the majority in the House by 1992.[21] A new House member from

California, Chris Cox, said that Newt had taken the first-term GOP representatives' secret votes, 13–3.[22]

"Gingrich's promotion from back-bench bomb thrower to Minority
Whip was an expression of seething impatience among House Republicans
with their seemingly minority status."[23] Gingrich's supporters pointed to his
energy, communication skills, and commitment to capturing a majority of
House seats. "A year ago, no one would have predicted that this enfant terrible
of the Republican Party could mount a credible bid for the leadership—let
alone snag its No. 2 slot," the Congressional Quarterly said. "But Republicans
became particularly frustrated with their decade-old minority status in the
House when the Reagan era came to an end: Even the eight-year reign of
a president as popular as Reagan couldn't deliver them from their plight.
Gingrich's call for radical change fell on responsive ears."[24]

Still, Gingrich understood as few did how revolutionary the Era of Reagan
had been. It radically changed how citizens viewed their world and their
government. He wrote several pieces paying tribute to Reagan's presidency.[25]

Gingrich's new, high-profile role put his personal moral standards in the
spotlight. His opponents resurrected the contradictions between Gingrich's
ethics-and-traditional-values stand and his messy divorce from his first wife,
Jackie, who had been battling cancer at the time. With both guns blazing,
Newsweek pointed out "his management of a political-action committee that
raised $200,000—and gave only $900 to candidates."[26]

Two days before Gingrich was elected minority whip, the Washington
Post reported that he had persuaded twenty-one supporters to contribute
$105,000 to promote Window of Opportunity: A Blueprint for the Future,
which he had coauthored in 1984 with his second wife, Marianne, and science fiction writer David Drake. The book retailed for $14.95 and was 272
pages. The book sold only twelve thousand hardcover copies; the investors
reaped tax benefits and Gingrich and his wife made about $30,000, accord-
ing to reports.[27]

Marianne and Newt held a press conference to try to explain their deal.
Marianne was visibly uncomfortable. Gingrich acknowledged that their book
deal was "as weird as Jim Wright's," but was legitimate because "we wrote a real
book for a real [publisher] that was sold in real bookstores."[28] The book deal
remained a question and a sore spot, leading to calls for a Wright-like ethics
investigation.

Marianne's uncomfortable participation in the book-deal press conference with Gingrich was a harbinger of rough waters ahead for the couple. Everybody knew the marriage was in trouble. "I think as he began to look at a new phase of his life, he just needed—in his own mind—more support, not somebody constantly arguing with him," recalled his friend and biographer Mel Steely.[29]

Mirthfully, Gingrich reminded everybody that he got about 3 percent in royalties, while Wright got 55 percent.

He also hinted darkly that Wright was laundering money through his campaign committee, via friends and people who had business before Congress, and then pocketing it.[30]

From the looks of everything, Wright had used his book to blow a hole clean through the rule that prohibited gifts of more than one hundred dollars in value from people who had something they wanted from Capitol Hill.[31] In case after case, from Texas oil and gas concerns to a board member of the National Education Association to all manner of people and businesses, all these "novel" bibliophiles somehow mysteriously discovered a powerful desire to purchase dozens and dozens of copies of Wright's *Reflections of a Public Man.*

Dr. John Silber, president of Boston University, for whom Wright had arranged millions in federal grants, also found himself overwhelmed with a strange compulsion to purchase lots and lots of copies of Wright's thin book. By 1988, it was revealed Wright had made more than $61,000 in royalties, some of it previously undisclosed to the House oversight committees.[32] Suffice it to say, thousands of struggling writers had never come close to earning that kind of bread for their books.

But Wright's headaches were not limited to questionable book deals. More serious charges relating to oil and banking interests and excessive monies paid to his wife, Betty, also hung over his head through the spring of 1989. It was alleged that the company Betty worked for was a scam, through which a friend of Wright's, George Mallick, was lining the House Speaker's pockets with more than $145,000 in cash and gifts, and that Wright was casting votes that had a direct bearing on Mallick's business concerns.[33] Wright for a time hid behind his wife's skirts, falsely accusing Gingrich and company of attacking her.

The word *kickback* had appeared in more and more articles as 1988 moved into 1989, and the weight of evidence and leaks began to crush the hopes of Speaker of the House James Claude Wright Jr. of Texas. Still, as of early spring 1989, the only publication that catalogued all the charges against him was *Newsday*.[34]

Wright's colleagues were still defending him, if more nervously now. Vin Weber, a Gingrich ally, said, "Right now they're going through a tribal loyalty dance."[35] Tony Coelho, the rabidly ferocious liberal from California, was unwavering in his public defense of the Speaker, even as his own ethical clouds gathered.

Minority Whip Gingrich beat the war drums, and by summer the newspapers and networks were following his lead, taking a different angle almost daily on the now besieged Speaker. Even the *New York Times* supported it.[36] As much as a year earlier, E. J. Dionne of the Gray Lady had written of "speculation about whether Mr. Wright should step down has grown more audible . . ." Even when former Speaker Tip O'Neill rallied to Wright's defense, the attacks and rumors did not abate. Wright's defenders continued their derision toward Gingrich as nothing more than a "backbencher," but this did nothing to head off the circle closing around Wright.[37]

Stories were also being written about the tactics being used to go after Wright, a new wrinkle in newspaper coverage. Formerly, the rule was "just the facts, ma'am," but now political journalists were drifting more and more into "analysis," which allowed them to stretch their legs and delve deep into conspiracies, stratagems, and personalities.

A new story emerged that a staffer in Wright's office had spent hundreds of hours writing and editing the book in question. Even when it was found out that Gingrich and his staffer, Frank Gregorsky, had done much the same, the coverage of Wright was far more extensive.

Gregorsky had his hands full. He also organized the audacious "Majority Task Force" meetings where Newt and company spitballed about how to take over.[38] Gregorsky noted that most members were late to the meeting, some missing it entirely. Those attending seemed to only swap war stories. Off-the-wall ideas were also commonplace, as one member suggested the South could be flipped across the region to vote Republican.[39] Ed Derwinski, an irreverent conservative from Chicago, quipped, "Well, Newt, if you'll just plan the way, we'll bite our tongue until we see exactly where you're taking us."[40] Newt replied that part of the problem with Republicans was that "our guys are too nice."[41]

Gingrich wrote a personal letter on congressional stationary to former secretary of state Henry Kissinger where as an aside, he asked Kissinger to meet with his high-dollar fund-raisers in Atlanta. It was not a violation of House rules, but it skirted close to the line.[42]

Wright was the highest-ranking Democrat in America, and with that honor came a permanent bull's-eye painted on his back. That was the way the Washington pecking order worked. The fact of the matter was that congressional staffers were often treated like the hired help by members, and even the spouses of members, who used staff to take dogs for walks, pick up dry cleaning, house-sit, chauffeur, clean up their houses after raucous parties, pick them up from the gutter when they got roaring drunk, and bed with them, if they could be so convinced. It was an open secret in Washington that congressional staffers were little more than personal valets, drivers, and flunkies. Working on a book was a level of respect rarely afforded these congressional hod carriers.

In truth, part of the reason for Newt's elevation had been his willingness to take on Wright. Vin Weber, a Gingrich comrade in arms, said, "The dislike of Speaker Wright is different. Republicans think he is basically . . . a mean-spirited person, ruthless in the truest sense of the word."[43]

Buttons began appearing on Capitol Hill that read "Foley for Speaker," a reference to Tom Foley, the majority leader from Washington State.[44] Most thought it was a prank cooked up by Republicans as a way of embarrassing both men, but in point of fact it was the Democrats who were paralyzed: fearful that if Wright survived and they had spoken out against him, they would not survive . . . and that if he did not survive and they had *not* spoken out against him, they would not survive the media's second-guessing game. Still, the Emersonian rule of not striking at the king unless you intend to kill him was safer, and thus preferable to disappointing the nation's media.

Republicans were not so hidebound. They went after Wright with glee. Ed Rollins, head of the Republicans' congressional campaign operation, said the Speaker was his "No. 1 Target."[45] Gingrich was ruthlessly on the offensive. His dramatic contentions won him necessary congressional allies and his rhetorical skills made him eminently quotable, thus a media darling. "I'm so deeply frightened by the nature of the corrupt left-wing machine in the House that it would have been worse to do nothing," he was quoted as saying in the *New York Times*. "Jim Wright has reached a point psychologically, in his ego, where there are no boundaries left."[46]

A year earlier, a fire had started in Wright's Capitol Hill office. The running joke was that "the police were checking Newt Gingrich's whereabouts."[47]

It was only in the few days before the report was released that Democrats began to speculate on a political world that did not include Jim Wright. A clandestine, top-secret, hush-hush, invitation-only, covert meeting of top Democrats in Washington was heavily reported by the media. "The Democrats gathered thinking that their meeting, like others they have held, would be kept in confidence." Phrases such as "survive" and "last-ditch" and "defections" littered news reportage. Reporters even saw the Democrats leaving the meeting.[48]

Following the investigation, the Ethics Committee said it had reason to believe Wright had violated House rules sixty-nine times. Washington was frankly stunned over how harsh and extensive the Ethics Committee final report was on Wright. The investigation went far beyond its original mission; it was rediscovered that Wright's political opponent in 1948 had been murdered. Wright was not accused in any fashion, but it was just more grist for the mill.

Other tawdry and embarrassing things from Wright's past were dredged up, including the nastiness of Texas elections in an earlier era. Wright had lost a race because he'd been accused of being "soft on communism" and favoring interracial marriages.

On June 6, 1989, Wright resigned from the Speakership, the first time in history a Speaker had left due to scandal. Gingrich had been spotted earlier in the hall, whistling to himself, unaware that the whale he'd been hunting was about to surface and surrender, full of harpoons.

The lights and photographers usually only associated with the appearance of a president were in the House chamber. With a half hour to go, at 3:30 p.m., the rumor of the Speaker's imminent resignation had become a hard fact, as the floor and galleries were nearly full of people wanting to see history in the making. Dick Cheney, already installed as chief of the

Pentagon, was spotted at the back of the floor, waiting for the public execution. Wright did not call Bob Michel to tell him, their relationship had so soured. The GOP Whip meeting, scheduled for 4:00 p.m., was canceled for that afternoon.[49]

At the end of his wits and sanity and arguments, Wright took to the floor of the institution he'd come to love and profit from for a one-hour speech that was "tearful . . . angry, cantankerous. He waved his arms and pointed to documents as he defended himself."[50] It was a Nixonian performance, part "Checkers" speech, part "you won't have Nixon to kick around," part "I am not an educated man" resignation speech of 1974, which made anyone watching cringe in embarrassment.

Washington stopped for that hour as Wright spoke from the well, dressed in a black suit. His voice quavered, his wife, Betty, watched, and several times his eyes welled with tears. He occasionally held up his book. His departure had been preordained when the Ethics Committee comprised of six Republicans and six Democrats voted the previous April and issued a "statement of alleged violations" leveled at the Texan.[51]

In his bitter remarks, Wright spoke of "self-appointed vigilantes carrying out vendettas" but did not mention Gingrich by name.[52] He received a standing ovation from his fellow Democrats when he attacked the "mindless cannibalism" of his opponents.[53] But that was like charging someone with contempt of Congress. All sane Americans were contemptuous of Congress. It simply went without saying.

Gingrich watched, silent, sitting then standing, alternately putting his hands behind his back and in his pockets.

No one could look away from the self-immolation of a public man. It was irresistible. Wright could have fought the charges and prolonged the process, but he opted to simply resign from the Speaker's chair and, by the end of the month, from Congress. He had served as a congressman for thirty-four years; he had been Speaker for two years and five months exactly.

The day after Wright's fall from grace, Gingrich was unrelenting, saying the now-departed Speaker's remarks were "an insult to the ethics committee and an insult to institutional decency." He said he had to wait a day ducking reporters before commenting, so incensed was he over Wright's speech. When he walked into the meeting of the House Republican Conference, he received a standing ovation.[54]

Jim Wright left Washington, never to be heard from again. He moved back to Texas to teach, consult, and stew over Gingrich, against whom he harbored an understandable lifetime grudge. Years later, he returned to Washington for the unveiling of his portrait in the Capitol, but otherwise kept the town he'd loved at a distance for the rest of his life.

The Democrats were further stunned at the abrupt resignation of Tony Coelho, nine days after that of Wright's, due to his own ethical problems. He'd been linked to the disgraced Wall Street firm Drexel-Burnham and the phrase "junk bond," two things no politician should be associated with. The Democrats had been planning a counteroffensive against Gingrich—indeed, Common Cause now called for an ethics investigation against Gingrich over his own book deal—but the Democrats were sidetracked by the new and doubly depressing loss of Coelho, another member of their crumbling House leadership.

The last words spoken over the political remains of Speaker Jim Wright came from Gingrich. "As a human, I've always felt sympathy for him. I can feel sympathy for Willie Horton being in jail for the rest of his life."[55] As far as Newt was concerned, a so-called friend said, "The important thing you have to understand about Newt Gingrich is that he is amoral. There isn't any right or wrong, there isn't any conservative or liberal. There is only what will work best for Newt Gingrich."[56]

If possible, even more profiles and stories and columns were popping up about Gingrich and his campaign against corruption. Not one left out the terms "fire-breather," "guerrilla," "outrageous," "brash," "reckless," "cockiness," and "self-promotion."[57]

The stories also described him as "chief agitprop specialist" of the GOP. They also reminded readers that he'd once called Bob Dole the "tax collector for the welfare state." However, there was this backhanded compliment: "His ideas . . . spill out of his fertile mind like items from Fibber McGee's closet."[58]

Later in the year, Gingrich hosted a press conference on the grounds of the US Capitol "bashing" a "new Catastrophic Health Care Law," calling for its repeal. The bill was in essence an assets redistribution act, taking money from more wealthy seniors and giving it to less wealthy seniors.[59] That year, Congress also approved an increase in the minimum wage, from $3.35 an hour to $4.25, after Bush had vetoed an earlier effort to raise it up even higher.

Even so, only months into the new presidency, Washingtonians and journalists were already describing the new president's administration "adrift," and it became a top item for discussion on the popular show *The McLaughlin Group*, which had become required viewing for all in the city-state throughout the 1980s and well into the '90s.

The bloom was quickly coming off the rose for Bush. A Washington insider blurted out what everybody already knew: "They don't have an agenda." The new defense secretary, Dick Cheney, agreed: "Bush didn't come to town with [a] long list of 45 things to do."[60]

PART III

THE WHIP

(1989–1993)

CHAPTER 17

TWO IN THE BUSH

"The conservative movement . . . has never
regarded George Bush as one of its own . . ."

1989

Polling in mid-1989 showed that unregistered voters preferred the Republican Party in greater numbers than registered voters, so the party of Federalism began pushing a big government bill to make it easier for unregistered voters to register. The party that had once squawked against federal voting rights legislation and opposed the eighteen-year-old vote was now fully in support of federal voting rights legislation, including for young voters, led by Newt Gingrich.

After all, flexibility was the real mother of invention, at least in Washington.

"While some Republicans continue to oppose the bill as unwarranted Federal interference in local affairs, Mr. Gingrich said Republicans now have a political interest in easing voter registration because one of the largest groups of nonvoters, the young, are inclined to support the Republicans."[1]

Public surveys, including those by CBS News, showed that among voters under thirty, fully 34 percent said they were Republican while only 23 percent claimed to be supportive of the Democrats.[2] It was an astonishing development, due of course to the appeal of the oldest president in US history.

Early in 1989, Gingrich published a letter in the *Washington Post* proclaiming a "Bush realignment,"[3] but which was based on cultural issues. The Bushies were still skittish about Gingrich's election as Whip, though he'd shown no cause for concern—yet. Dick Cheney, newly installed at the Pentagon, spoke up for his old colleague. Gingrich's election, he said, "shows . . . the enormous desire . . . not to accept the status quo . . . There's nothing wrong with having strong partisan battles up there."[4]

Bush and his people understood flexibility and the need to "schmooze." In fact, with few legislative goals, it seemed the Bush White House schmoozed just to do so, and not really to accomplish anything. "We're dependent on the kindness of strangers," said one movie fan cum Bush White House aide.[5] Bush himself allowed his own flexibility to extend to nonsense, as he mused that maybe one day he would become another Teddy Roosevelt.[6]

Conservatives had many reasons to celebrate, and one way of expressing their joy was to produce pin-up calendars with each month dedicated to a different "playmate of the month." But rather than flouncy women dressed in risqué clothing and lingerie that Vargas and others made popular in every garage in America, these featured photos of Bill Bennett, Pat Buchanan, Ronald Reagan, Newt Gingrich, and other right-wingers who made conservatives' hearts go pitter-patter. Fortunately, none were dressed in skimpy clothing or showing gams that would have forced all viewers to avert their eyes. Conservatives sometimes still had trouble telling the difference between the body and the *body politic*. Actors Tom Selleck and Charlton Heston wisely demurred, but tellingly, Bush was not included.[7]

The rap on Newt Gingrich was that he saw the world in moral absolutes: the Republicans walked on water and the Democrats could not swim, his critics charged. The black-and-white world of Gingrich was how outsiders and the unschooled of the media saw it. Gingrich actually had spent a considerable part of his career fighting the GOP establishment, often with more vigor and venom than the Democrats. Offstage, he was quite friendly with a good number of Democrats, who, while deeply opposing his ideology, respected his tenacity and toughness. And, according to former aide Chip Kahn, he'd developed into a "phenomenal speaker," noting that he was better without a prepared text.[8]

"The Republicans, under the take-no-prisoners leadership of Representative Newt Gingrich of Georgia, the minority whip . . . having tasted the blood of a speaker, seems likely to broaden [their] assault on the Democratic leadership . . ."[9] Some on the other side of the aisle still wanted to get him and dredged up an old story about yet another weird book deal, in which investors lost money, but it was also in 1977, fully a year before he won a seat in the House.

Friend and colleague Nancy Johnson took up Newt's defense. "Questions were raised about Newt only after Newt raised questions about people in power."[10] As Gingrich's criticisms of Bush began to intensify, the president's inner circle increasingly kept him at more than arm's length. Hence, his relation with Bush was nearly nonexistent. Bush basically saw Gingrich as a "right wing gadfly."[11]

The Democrats were licking their wounds, having lost two top leaders, Jim Wright and Tony Coelho, inside of two weeks. They now spent most of their time griping about conspiracies. Rumors of secret Republican conference calls to coordinate "stink tank"[12] campaigns against top Democrats went through Washington. The word *plot* was bandied about Capitol Hill by the Democrats.[13]

Gingrich had them that spooked.

While Washington continued its petty arguing over personal freedoms and liberties, around the globe, in Tiananmen Square in Beijing, students were literally standing up to the communist thugs and their tanks. It was all being televised live on CNN, but also frequently on the three major networks. Many died in China, rather than continue living under the repressive communist regime. "Among the more dramatic moments on CBS was a recording of a denunciation of the Chinese Government by an English-language announcer on Radio Beijing and an appeal to the world to do something about the 'barbarous' actions," reported the *New York Times*.[14]

In Eastern Europe and the Baltics, tiny freedom movements of solidarity and revolutions made of velvet, led by bad poets and good electricians, were beginning to push back against the creaking corruption of communism. It was an astonishing moment in human history. Even liberals in America, who had been sympathetic to Moscow over the years, cheered the freedom-fighting civilians, garbed only in words and principles. On a Sunday show, Jesse Helms "found himself in agreement with, of all people, Representative Stephen J. Solarz, the Brooklyn liberal, that Washington could not tolerate such behavior."[15]

It was a wonderful, dangerous, and thrilling moment in world history.

Within a short time of becoming Whip, Gingrich produced his "manifesto," as called by the *Washington Post*. He poked some fun at himself, making references to "grenades in the halls, bombs in the Rotunda," but also made one thing abundantly clear: he was utterly convinced the GOP would shortly gain control of Congress, saying his election meant that the down-on-their-heels Republicans wanted "an aggressive effort to build a GOP majority in the House."

The article was also shot through with personal and possessive pronouns as well as a slightly messianic tinge: "We Republicans can launch a crusade to save our children and our future."[16] Newt's lifetime weakness was making bad decisions when he was on top. Everybody knew he was often at his best when things were worst and at his worst when things were best.

The piece went out of its way to mention many members of Congress, including his closest friends and allies, but one of his closest friends, Vin Weber, was not mentioned. For a number of years, Newt and Vin had been inseparable—eating and drinking together, plotting together, voting together. But after Newt was elected Whip, the tightly woven friendship began to fray. Indeed, Weber had advised Gingrich not to seek the post, but when the headstrong man from Georgia decided otherwise, Weber was there for his pal. However, it was clear the Whip's race began to put a strain on their friendship. Still, Weber, the loyalist, helped assemble the new Whip's office, including allowing his top aide, Dan Meyer, to move over to the new Gingrich shop. Meyer was low key, self-effacing, widely respected, and detail-oriented; in short, Meyer was everything Newt was not.

In the background, editorialists and liberals continued their call for an investigation against Newt, but everybody else was wondering what was up with President Bush and his iron-clad, rock-solid, strong-as-steel pledge to never raise taxes. Taxes and the Ethics Wars were all that Washington seemed interested in.

For many, it seemed as if the politics and the press were out of control, engaged in a scorched-earth strategy: "They see a press that is too quick to rush to print or broadcast what are merely allegations or rumors. They see politicians who are too eager to use ethics as a weapon for partisan advantage, as Representative Newt Gingrich . . . has long advocated as a means of regaining Republican control of the House."[17]

Liberal columnists denounced him in the harshest of terms.

Still, Gingrich's elevation to Whip, one of the consequences of his public flogging of Jim Wright, moved him permanently into the big leagues. During the 1980s, he'd bounced between Triple A politics and major league politics, but with the head of Wright on a pike, the Sunday shows recognized a new talent. No greater example existed of having arrived than going on *Meet the Press* or *Face the Nation* or *This Week with David Brinkley*. The agnostics and atheists and lapsed and fallen of Washington religiously and faithfully watched these shows. Presidential candidates and presidential biographers, first-tier cabinet secretaries and senators like Bob Dole, and syndicated columnists like Bob Novak and George Will, all part of the "PRC"—the Permanent Ruling Class—appeared frequently. Less frequently did House members appear, unless they were in the majority or a pet favorite of the hosts. So for Newt, occupying the number two leadership position in the House minority was indeed a big deal. But Newt was also great for copy and ratings, so the Sunday shows were delighted to book him.

For years, he'd had a love-hate relationship with the national press corps. Columnists alternatively gushed over him and groused about him, often in the same piece. One piece in the *Post* compared him to Dr. Jekyll and Mr. Hyde and complained that he was "adopting the language of moderation" so as to cover his true intentions "to associate his liberal opponents with pessimism and cultural despair."[18]

But then again, the same article said, "To the degree that the GOP became the 'party of ideas' in Ronald Reagan's heyday, Gingrich and his cohorts deserve a lot of the credit."[19]

The trial of former Reagan White House aide Lt. Col. Oliver North had come to a conclusion with North found guilty on three counts. The atmosphere in Washington was pure poison and "the current mood in Congress . . . has roots in increasingly bitter partisanship. A city that once prided itself on generally amiable competition was transformed into an arena in which enemies, divided by ideology as well as party, were willing to fight to the political death."[20]

Gingrich warned that other ethically challenged Democrats besides Wright and Coelho could end up in the soup. Around the salons of Washington, politicos were saying, "Gingrich is convinced that the only way for Republicans to regain the House is to destroy the Democrats one by one."[21]

In response, a Democratic member of Congress vowed to columnists Evans and Novak, "We're going to destroy Gingrich if it's the last thing we do."[22]

The Democrats weren't the only ones in Washington with ethical problems. Fifty-eight-year-old Republican congressman Donald E. "Buz" Lukens of Ohio, a minor hero to conservatives over the years in part for his exemplar moral standards, was convicted of having sex with an underage prostitute while also "contributing to the delinquency and unruliness of a minor."[23] The sixteen-year-old girl was black, which was widely reported, and this added to so many different interpretations that they were impossible to categorize or explain.

Gingrich called for the Ethics Committee to investigate his friend and colleague.[24] Lukens was convicted of the crime but appealed, losing the appeal as well. Buz quickly became a national joke and a disgrace to his constituents, having been further accused of "fondling" a female elevator operator in the Capitol. He served nine days in jail for that and was ordered to be tested for venereal diseases. Lukens was also involved in a House banking scandal and was accused of taking bribes. Still, he refused to resign. In 1990, he lost the GOP congressional primary to an obscure businessman by the name of John Boehner.

Other Republicans were also known to have lives that could not bear close scrutiny. Gus Savage, a congressman from Chicago, found himself under investigation for sexual misconduct, accused of sexually assaulting a Peace Corps volunteer while on an official visit to Zaire in 1988. Savage had a unique defense, saying he'd been set up by the Reagan State Department. "You know I have been No. 1 on the Reagan Republican hit list."[25]

It was the two-hundredth anniversary of George Washington's inauguration; the economy of the country was riding high, wide, and handsome; but the culture and politics were rapidly descending into a cesspool. Both sides hunkered down into what Congressman Leon Panetta called "trench warfare. The guy who leads the first charge gets the first hit."[26]

Tom Foley of Washington, a kindhearted, gentle, and ethical man from Washington State, moved up to become Speaker of the House after Wright. Behind him, another man of good judgment and character, Dick Gephardt of Missouri, became the majority leader. Gephardt was a leader in the pro-life movement, a stable and staunch ally who hosted many meetings and spoke at many pro-life rallies. Nary had a breath of scandal or controversy touched either man. Since the Democrats controlled the House by a 260–175 margin, their elections were assured.

By installing ethical, uncontroversial men in positions of leadership, it signaled what was hoped to be an armistice in the beginning of the end of the Ethics Wars. Foley offered a peace pipe and called for the need to "restore a sense of comity, mutual respect and cooperation."[27]

It would not work out that way.

Following Foley's plea, astonishingly, leading Democrats seemingly and suddenly called off their plans against Gingrich. One said, "Simply because if Gingrich is chopped up . . . it's the institution's reputation that suffers. I don't think it's in the institutional interest of the House . . . to try to be looking for something that's wrong with Gingrich." Respected congressman Les AuCoin of Oregon also counseled peace and that the Democrats should drop their "get-Gingrich sentiment. Do we really want a political killing field here?"[28] The head of the Democratic National Committee, Ron Brown, also signaled his intention to sue for peace in the Ethics Wars.[29]

The Georgian warily stood down for the moment.

But Lee Atwater, the slight, snarling boss of the Republican National Committee, the architect of the Willie Horton controversy, wasn't about to take the high road.

Atwater did not believe in keeping marital vows, promises, or campaign rules. He played to win, used any means to do so, and wisely put underlings in the position of ordering hits and strikes; if there was blowback, it would be directed at them. "He always manages to throw the gun in the river," said DNC spokesman Mike McCurry.[30] Secretary of State Jim Baker was also rumored to be disdainful of Atwater, having once been his boss in the Reagan White House.

A memo was generated at the Republican National Committee implying that Tom Foley was gay. The memo was titled "Tom Foley: Out of the Liberal

Closet," a highly charged phrase in 1989.[31] The memo then put Foley's voting record side by side with that of Congressman Barney Frank, "an acknowledged homosexual."[32] Atwater in the past had played the race card and the Jewish card and, close to running out of cultural stereotypes, he now played the gay card. An Atwater lieutenant who also torched his way across the scorched earth of South Carolina politics, Mark Goodin, was fingered as the person of interest regarding the shameful memo.

Atwater ordered the RNC's publicist, Leslie Goodman, "to contain the mess," and she immediately imposed a gag rule on the entire Republican Party apparatus, one that the publicity-hungry Atwater broke himself, though he only called a *Wall Street Journal* reporter back after he received a message.[33]

The poor folks in the RNC mail shop were blamed for sending the memo out, but they blamed the poor people in the graphics shop, who blamed the political shop, headed by Mary Matalin. She blamed Goodin in the publicity shop for drafting the thing in the first place. Goodin denied that he knew the implications of the phrase "out of the closet" and the use of Congressman Frank's name. "If I had recognized it for what it was, do you think I would have cleared it and sent it out? I'm not stupid."[34]

Bush "good cop–bad cop-ed" the issue and denounced the memo as "disgusting,"[35] as did Baker.[36] Atwater was not fired. People like Bush needed people like Atwater. People like Atwater needed people like Goodin. So Goodin took the bullet; he picked himself up by the scruff of his own neck and threw himself under the bus. Atwater reportedly kept him on salary for a year at the RNC until the heat blew over. Gingrich, like others, denounced the faux memo.[37]

Gingrich's office also had a hand in the sordid mess. A woman on his staff, Karen Van Brocklin, began calling reporters to see what they were digging up about Foley. One Gingrich aide told a reporter, "We hear it's little boys."[38] Gingrich took some heat for Van Brocklin's behavior; he put her under house arrest and prohibited her from talking to reporters.[39]

Foley had to go so far as to proclaim to his own conference that he was a "heterosexual."[40] In Washington, rumors and lies would be circulated and recirculated before the truth even got out of bed in the morning. It was no different for Foley. Everybody was passing the rumor along, adding innuendo and suggestion. It eventually burned itself out.

The matter faded with everyone's attention on Atwater, just where he liked it. He said the calls for his resignation were "flattering" as "'it suggests . . . I am responsible for everything bad that happens' to Democrats.'"[41] Like Bob Dole and others, however, Gingrich stood by Atwater.[42]

Foley simply waited for the truth to come out, which it did. He was just the calming presence Capitol Hill needed.

Within a few months, Atwater was ailing with brain cancer. He publicly apologized to Michael Dukakis for introducing Willie Horton into the 1988 campaign.[43] While in New York for treatment, with a close friend at his side, Atwater received a phone call from the Reverend Jesse Jackson, who wanted to pay his respects. Atwater demurred, citing weakness from treatment. After hanging up the phone, he said to his friend, "I'll be d--med if I give a photo op to that guy on my deathbed."[44]

Gingrich decided to get back to basics, to ideas and reforms that really got him hot and bothered. That and standing up to the Old Order of the GOP. He teased Foley to work in a bi-partisan fashion, saying the Speaker had to choose between "appeasing his left wing" of the Democratic Party or moving legislation through.[45] They did pass strict legislation essentially reregulating the savings and loan industry. George Bailey 1, Mr. Potter 0. That was how it appeared to the legislation's champions in the media and American consumerism, until they read the fine print, in which the criminality of the banking class was being underwritten by the American taxpayer to the tune of $157 billion.[46] The reputation of Congress to the American people had always been lower than a snake's belly in a wagon-wheel rut, but this was even a new low for Capitol Hill.

A debate took place on Buckley's PBS show *Firing Line*, postulating the prompt: "Resolved: The Cold War Is Not Coming to an End."[47] On Buckley's side was Gingrich, who, like the founder of *National Review*, said it was not coming to an end anytime soon.

In this debate, both sides were guilty of myopia, a disease common among elites of both liberal and conservative strains. Both sides agreed the Soviet Union was a permanent part of the world's existence. They only disagreed on whether relations would warm up between Moscow and Washington or remain cold. Neither side contemplated that within less than two years, the Berlin Wall would come down.

Buckley and Gingrich were at fault for the conventional thinking that it was a static world and there were certain things that must be accepted as a permanent part of the world, such as walls dividing cities or the inevitability of the Kremlin's enduring existence.

President Bush entered the second half of his first year in office by proposing a constitutional amendment to ban flag burning. The Supreme Court had recently ruled that burning the American flag was a constitutionally protected right under the speech provision of the First Amendment. The decision was controversial but entirely defensible. Yet that did not stop the lightweights around the Bush White House from smelling a cheap political opportunity to exploit. It was a true "through the looking glass" moment for Washington. The patriots were the ones arguing for amending the Constitution, while the defenders of the document and the First Amendment were derided as pointy-headed, granola-crunching, Chardonnay-sipping, vegetarian liberals who couldn't park a bicycle straight.

It took the Reverend Jesse Jackson to explain to the president and Attorney General Richard Thornburgh that the flag was only a symbol, and it was more important to protect the rights that flag represented than to protect the flag itself.

Gingrich, like other Republicans, fell in line behind the Bush Administration's proposed amendment and the politics behind it. He speculated that it "would be hard to explain" for Democrats to vote against the amendment.[48]

Flag fever inflamed the nation and the nation's capital. The sale of flags shot up, as did flag hats, flag shorts, flag shirts, flag cabanas, flag umbrellas, flag bumper stickers, flag motorcycle helmets, flag drinking glasses, and flag underwear, all patriotically respectful treatments of Old Glory.

The House passed a heated resolution expressing "profound concern" over the court ruling on flag burning, 411–5.[49] For Washington's shallow GOP politicos, the cheap political theater of amending one of the greatest documents in human history to gain a momentary political advantage gladdened their little partisan hearts as little else did. Senators and congressmen issued statements declaring their fealty to the flag, sounding like half John Wayne, half Audie Murphy, and half Rambo, even as many of them had received deferments from serving in Vietnam, including Gingrich, Dick Cheney, and others.

Bush was a bona fide war hero who had nearly died on one occasion, and had come close to being captured by the Japanese—which most likely would have led to his death—so his feelings about the flag were defensible, but even more so should have been his feelings about the near sacredness of the United States Constitution. But this was political war, and strategist Lee Atwater understood this, acutely. "The only people who will make it a partisan issue are Democrats if they choose not to support an amendment," he said.[50]

While the motives of Atwater and others were tawdry at best, the motives of some Democrats to oppose it were not completely altruistic. Yes, one element siding with the ACLU did see it as a free-speech issue, but a large part also was repulsed by patriotism, by expressions of love of America, that people who professed their love of their country were certified yahoos who needed to be marched off to reeducation camps and taught there was no such thing as American Exceptionalism. Vietnam, Nixon, and the rise of the counterculture all helped to institutionalize a form of anti-Americanism inside of the country's liberal café society. Sophisticated people simply knew that cynicism was fashionable and patriotism was tacky.

Good judgment, taste, or scholarship did not stop the House from passing a bill in mid-September, in essence rewriting the Supreme Court ruling and making it a federal crime to burn an American flag. Gingrich lead the parade. The irony was lost on many that for years, the prescribed way of disposing of an old American flag was to burn it. Apparently legislators wanted to govern what was in the hearts and minds of aspiring flag burners.

The Flag Amendment—to cowed constitutionalists and historians— was just as offensive as the Sedition Acts, which during another period of madness had astonishingly prevented Americans from speaking out against their government. Flag burning, civil libertarians knew, was less dangerous and just as protected. Ironically, all this insanity over regulating speech was taking place as the two-hundredth anniversary of the Constitution was being celebrated.

The Senate did vote and, by the margin of 97–3, it, too, voted to prohibit flag burning, with only Ted Kennedy, Howard Metzenbaum, and, surprisingly to some, Gordon Humphrey of New Hampshire—an erratic but thoughtful libertarian conservative—voting against. Bob Dole groused about the unlikely three, "If they don't like our flag, they ought to go find one they do like."[51]

After months of being questioned about his sexuality, Tom Foley did not much like his party being questioned about its patriotism either: "Anybody who suggests that there is a party difference in respect for the American flag is . . . twisting . . . manipulating . . . base . . . crass . . . reprehensible . . . disgusting." Jack Brooks of Texas, a decorated navy vet of World War II, went after Gingrich, personally, about both his manhood and his courage, sarcastically calling him "that big strapping [S.O.B.]."[52]

The eyes of Washington swung back again to sex, this time centering on Congressman Barney Frank and yet another Ethics Committee investigation. The openly homosexual Frank "acknowledged employing a male prostitute as a personal assistant."[53] Frank told the committee he had paid the young man for sex, but did not know his assistant was using Frank's apartment for male prostitution liaisons. Frank said he fired the young man when this was discovered.[54] If Frank had violated the policy of the House, he risked a range of punishments, from a simple letter of rebuke to censure to being expelled. Gingrich urged the Ethics Committee to proceed carefully and not prejudge Frank.[55]

Between Lukens, Savage, Frank, and others in Congress, it was little wonder that Americans wanted to avert their eyes.

Gingrich was not out of the woods in the ethics matter either. Richard Phelan, who had done such an extensive job on Jim Wright, was floating the trial balloon of going after more big game. The book deal was still there, still causing comments, and it left Gingrich twisting in the wind. Phelan was in the process of lining up a Republican investigator to look into Gingrich's affairs, just as Phelan, a Democrat, had indiscriminately gone after Jim Wright's affairs.[56]

The House Ethics Committee was also investigating the accusation that members of Gingrich's congressional staff had gone off salary only to go back on salary—at a much lower amount—and then back on to his congressional payroll at a higher temporary amount than when they'd been on the Hill before. If it was essentially a way to subsidize campaign work, then the maneuver was clearly a violation of the House rules. If the temporary raises were simply bonuses, then it was an infraction of other House rules. In the end it was widely ignored, as many congressmen did likewise for their staffs.[57]

Curiously, the four Gingrich staffers in question were all women. The mother of all leftist publications, *Mother Jones*, once again went after Gingrich, this time digging up an additional two women who said campaigns were planned in the district offices. Rich Galen, Gingrich's press aide, said if anything was awry, they were "mistakes of a clerical nature."[58] The publication had dug up two low-level disgruntled former employees whose allegations against Newt were pretty small-bore stuff. It was indicative of the lengths to which his enemies would go to try to stop him, slow him down, or bring him down.

His friends certainly did not want him to slow down. Bill Buckley invited Gingrich back on to *Firing Line* for a classic debate pitting the two of them, along with Jack Kemp and Jeane Kirkpatrick, against George McGovern, Gary Hart, John Kenneth Galbraith, and Pat Schroeder: "Resolved: Free Market Competitiveness Is Best for America."[59] The intellectual firepower of these eight distinguished Americans was awesome.

Some thought the Ethics Committee was proceeding too slowly in its look into Gingrich's book *Window of Opportunity* and its unusual financing arrangement. An outside law firm had been retained for $150,000 to investigate, far more than the amount involved in the book itself.[60] Shortly thereafter, the committee quietly shut down its investigation. Gingrich quipped, "If you have a picnic, flies come to the watermelon."[61]

The matter was closed and that was that.

Newt was going through a period of adjustment. He'd been on the outside, throwing political Molotov cocktails, for the better part of ten years. He now faced the conundrum of being a part of the establishment as his party's Whip, while also being the leading anti-establishment figure in the GOP. It had only been weeks since his election as Whip, and numerous leaks from Republicans—not Democrats—were ending up in the nation's newspapers, criticizing Gingrich.

The self-aware Gingrich noted, "I was off the reservation and it's fair to say I'm on the reservation now."[62]

CHAPTER 18

A NEW ORDER GOES UP,
A WALL FALLS DOWN

"It's hard for a politician to vote against a tax cut."

1989

The annual gathering of the Conservative Political Action Conference came and went in 1989 with the new president a no-show. He'd attended a couple of times as vice president, but only to either accompany President Reagan or look over his shoulder at Jack Kemp challenging him for the 1988 nomination. Indeed, for the four years of his presidency, Bush never accepted the invitation of CPAC.[1] This would be to his everlasting regret, as it turned out.

By contrast, Ronald Reagan attended every CPAC from 1974 until 1988, as a governor, as a private citizen, as a presidential candidate, and as a president, excepting only 1976 and 1980 when he was fiercely competing in the New Hampshire primary. Even then, he sent recorded messages and emissaries to the important annual gathering.

The 1990 CPAC featured Senator Jesse Helms, Jack Kemp, and, of course, Newt Gingrich, who by the last year of the decade had become firmly installed as a national conservative leader with a popular following all his own. His speeches always filled the CPAC hall. Gingrich had become so popular that between 1983 and 1987 he pocketed more than $111,000 in honoraria, ranking him high among his fellow House members.[2]

In many and varied ways, conservatives were finding more and more reason to fight with and openly criticize George Bush and his Administration. The Reagan White House always reached out to conservatives to listen to their complaints but to also brief them on policy and initiatives. Reagan often participated in these meetings. The Bush White House was doing no such thing and regarded most conservatives as a royal pain in the arse. They disagreed on "Hate Crimes," the "Americans with Disabilities Act," and various other appointments, presidential decisions, and legislation initiatives.

It was also known that Bush was dubious of Reagan's cherished SDI—the Strategic Defense Initiative—which also was cause for concern among conservatives.[3] David Broder, the much-esteemed dean of the Washington press corps, noted, "So Bush has set forth a minimalist program and has made it clear, by word and by deed, that he is ready to compromise on many points in return for Democratic cooperation in its passage."[4] The presidency was—as many had feared—simply another line item on Bush's résumé. He had no intention of shaking the very establishment to which he'd belonged his whole life.

It was the conservatives who would have to take the initiative. It leaked out that Jim Baker, Bush's secretary of state, had joked to Hill Democrats, "Let's hurry and cut this deal so we don't have to deal with Gingrich," before Gingrich had actually assumed his new duties as minority whip.[5]

Many were watching closely the election in Nicaragua between communist dictator Daniel Ortega and newspaper publisher Violeta Barrios de Chamorro, the publisher of La Prensa. She'd taken the paper over in 1978 after her husband had reportedly been killed by supporters of then-dictator Anastasio Somoza, who was pro-American.

The issue of democratic elections in Nicaragua had been forced by a young conservative activist in Washington who first mounted a campaign for Chamorro to run for president of Nicaragua, which no one had considered previously. He urged McLaughlin Group panelist Fred Barnes to make the seemingly off-the-wall prediction that Chamorro would run. That set the town and conservatives buzzing.

A bipartisan task force called "The Commission on Free and Fair Elections in Nicaragua" was formed that included former US senator Gaylord Nelson, a much respected liberal. Testimony was taken by the commission and a report produced and given to President Bush personally. They issued a report that became the basis for an acceptable democratic election in Nicaragua, notwithstanding the abuses by the ruling Sandinistas or the money pouring in via the US Embassy by the Bush Administration. Chamorro won, surprisingly, and the communists just as surprisingly surrendered power peacefully. Chamorro ruled Nicaragua wisely for almost seven years, instituting many reforms.

Meanwhile, House fights continued. House Speaker Tom Foley was given his own jet to use, just as the president and vice president. But Jack Kemp, now the HUD secretary, stopped an attempt to use almost $7 million in taxpayer funding for "a rock-n'-roll museum in Cleveland."[6]

The best the *Wall Street Journal* could say was that Ronald Reagan was in "sunny exile" as conservatives wrestled with their meaning. The laymen at the venerable broadsheet did not understand the "church and state" thing. The editorial page was reliably conservative, if a bit too supportive of big financial institutions for the populist American conservative movement, but the front section was wholly liberal, routinely bashing Reagan, Gingrich, et al. On the other hand, Gingrich deserved to be cuffed around a bit when he told the paper that post-Reagan, the party needed "a caring, humanitarian, reform Republican Party . . ."[7] Gingrich took to inviting reporters for power walks along the Mall in front of the Capitol at 6:00 a.m.[8]

Conservatism was under increasing assault on the college campuses. Ironically, at the very time when anti-intellectual collectivism was failing around the globe, it was on the rise in the academy. The study of George Washington or Thomas Jefferson—except to note that they were slaveholders—was verboten. Dead White Males were out and obscure African writers were in. Chants of "Hey, hey, ho, ho. West Civ has got to go!" were heard from Berkeley to Oberlin. Oppression studies had become the topic du jour. The only dead white male celebrated on the campuses was Karl Marx.

The great Russian dissident and writer Andrei Sakharov died, in the winter as all lions should. It was Robert Frost who said, "All animals are smothered in their lairs."[9] Not true for Sakharov. For many years, the Soviet system had tried to smother him, but he'd broken out and died, just as his handiwork and that of Solzhenitsyn and others was beginning to be felt in Chekhov's fabled cold Russian winter.

In late September 1989, President Bush went on ABC's *Prime Time Live* to make it clear yet again that the Democrats in Congress would only raise taxes over his dead body.[10] And, as a bonus, he was going to fight for a big cut in capital gains. Conservatives had always had their doubts about Bush, but he'd won their respect, if not affection, for holding the line on additional money going to Washington. To him, it was simply politics, but for thinking conservatives it was part of a larger construct: Where did power belong? Did it belong with the citizenry as the Founders intended, or did it belong with Washington? Liberals wanted a weak citizenry dependent upon government, while conservatives favored a strong citizenry dependent upon themselves. Democrats on the Hill were fighting for an increase in the marginal rates, and the class warfare argument once again raised its head in Washington.

Newt Gingrich clarified the matter when he said he was surprised that the Democrats had learned "so little" from the elections of 1984 and 1988: "It is clear that a tax-increase liberal Democratic Party will remain a minority . . ."[11]

Several days later, a large number of Democrats, heeding Gingrich's advice, crossed over to join the Republicans in passing a big cut in capital gains taxes, from 33 percent down to 19.6 percent.[12] The proposed lower capital gains rate, however, came with a distinctively Bush twist. The House vote was a victory, yes, but it was also the beginning of the end of the revolutionary Tax Reform Act of 1986, which Ronald Reagan had fought so hard for. The 1986 Act reduced the marginal rates for individuals to 28 and 15 percent while eliminating dozens of loopholes and setting the capital gains tax at 33 percent. Reagan was not all that fond of a capital gains tax, but given the choice between low taxes for the individual who earned a wage versus low taxes for property that increased in value, he opted for the individual every time.

The new rate applied to "stocks, bonds, real estate and some raw materials. Income from sales of works of art, coins, and other collectibles would continue to be taxed as ordinary income."[13] As brokers and bankers, for whom Reagan always had little regard, were welcomed in through the front door of the Bush White House, it was obvious why they and not coin collectors got the favored tax treatment. Bush's buddies at Yale and Phillips Exeter had all gone to Wall Street to become bankers and brokers.

News reports said Bush had devoted considerable energies to getting the bill through the House. Gingrich summarized the moment succinctly: "It's hard for a politician to vote against a tax cut."[14]

The proposed cuts in capital gains rates did not make it through the Senate. By the time President Bush signed the Omnibus Budget Reconciliation Act of 1989 in December,[15] it contained no reduction in the capital gains rates.[16]

Congressman David Obey of Wisconsin told the *Christian Science Monitor* that the ethics on Capitol Hill were on the rise, but the Ethics Wars were not over. Instead, a new front was opened in the Senate.[17] Five senators of more or less sterling reputation were caught red-handed "improperly intervening" for a California savings and loan operator, Charles Keating Jr.[18] For the Republicans, the Ethics Wars had taken a turn for the worse; the advent of the "Keating Five" was the unveiling of the clay feet of the once "holier than thou" John McCain.[19]

Since the early days of 1989, Gingrich and other GOP leaders had made plans to put the Democrats permanently on the defensive over ethics and corruption. They began meeting to plot strategy on how to convey a "corrupt, worn-out liberalism that is contributing to the deterioration of American life." Attending these top-secret meetings—which were immediately leaked to Tom Edsall at the *Washington Post*—were White House aides such as Jim Pinkerton; "Bush speech writer Peggy Noonan"; staff from the RNC, including Mary Matalin;[20] the other party committees, including Ed Rollins; consultants Eddie Mahe and Joe Gaylord;[21] lobbyists such as Charlie Black; and "black conservatives Robert Woodson and Keith Butler." The word *wedge* was on everybody's lips.[22]

Gingrich told the group, "Now we have a way of dividing America . . ." Education reform. "We [Republicans] stand for children who want to go to school. They [Democrats and unions] stand for a value system in which children have less value than other things."[23]

Still, the Republicans' goal of a more moral America was only effective if everybody on their team was above suspicion, and if the voters were fat and happy and ready to think of things other than their own well-being. The meeting closed on a downer when Matalin and Pinkerton told the group that Bush was not into revolution but simply into governing. Upon hearing

Matalin's presentation, one conservative passed a note to another that said, "All is lost." The headline of the Evans and Novak column blared, "No Bush Revolution."[24]

Profiles of Gingrich were commonplace now and uniformly harsh. One went so far as to go back and interview high school teachers, one of whom said he was not a "pariah," though he "was not the most popular boy on campus."[25] Clearly, the Style section of the *Washington Post* was out for maximum embarrassment as they opened every closet and rattled the bones of every skeleton. They dragged up every old (and new) inflammatory quote by Newt, tracked down every former friend who'd become an enemy, and got hold of Vin Weber, a friend who was evolving into a former friend.

No doubt the story was well researched and written by one of the best at the *Post*, Myra MacPherson, who had a unique talent for pulling the hide off the rich and famous. She reminded readers that Newt had not served in Vietnam and that he'd given several reasons why not, but it also uncovered new, heretofore unknown nuggets. The story pointed out his "pudginess" several times, and got him on record admitting he cried during his divorce from his first wife, Jackie. He further revealed that he and his second wife, Marianne, were separated. At the time Gingrich gave the marriage a "53–47" chance for survival. They got Jackie on record as well as Marianne, both of whom said that "personal relations" were not Newt's "long suit."[26]

Insensitivity notwithstanding, it was explosive and set the town's tongues to wagging and gums to flapping for days, even as Newt sometimes expressed his regret for not serving in Vietnam.

At a party function shortly thereafter, the Republicans were at a fever pitch, vowing to roll over every Democratic candidate by any means necessary. One functionary said, "There was spontaneous combustion here," and a resolution denouncing House Minority Leader Bob Michel—one of their own—was seriously debated. Michel, they agreed, had been too tepid in dealing with the Democrats on the Hill. The resolution against Michel was tabled, not because they did not think he deserved it, but because they thought it might backfire on Lee Atwater and Gingrich.[27]

Gingrich apparently had the Washington establishment so cockeyed with paranoia, one columnist compared him to Charles Boyer in the movie

Gaslight, in which a husband drives his young wife, Ingrid Bergman, crazy with bogus ploys. The liberal *Washington Post* had a different take, as they were mostly tone deaf and always blindly liberal: "The House Democrats looked back longingly to the time of Tip O'Neill, when joviality was king and Newt Gingrich was an after-hours pest on the floor," said the left-wing tabloid.[28] Democratic Party operative Bob Beckel recalled O'Neill complaining often about Gingrich.[29] O'Neill, in his book *Man of the House*, had nothing good to say about the Georgian, even going so far as to say that he "undermine[d] the dignity of the House."[30] He also once again called Gingrich and company "Reagan Robots."[31]

The new head of the DCCC, Beryl Anthony of Arkansas, a singular Gingrich hater, was unrelenting, referring in a fund-raising letter to "the unscrupulous tactics of Newt Gingrich."[32] The Democratic machine vowed each year to "get" Gingrich in Georgia, but this time the threat was not a hollow one.

Around this time, Gingrich received a chipper and cheerful letter thanking him profusely for his "support . . . to strengthen human rights conditions . . . for China in 1991." The letter closed by saying, "I appreciate your support and look forward to working with you in the future. Sincerely, Nancy Pelosi," although the letter was just signed collegially "Nancy."[33]

Newspaper stories of Gingrich's problematic forthcoming reelection drive began to closely track the Democrats' threats. Gingrich had problems in the Georgia Sixth, no doubt about it. One of the biggest was the hangover of the long-term strike by Eastern employees against odious owner Frank Lorenzo, who couldn't learn charm from a snake. Initially, Gingrich appeared to take the side of management, but then he seemed to switch over to the side of labor, including the popular pilots.

Still, Mike Flynn, the head of the local machinists' union that was leading the strike against Eastern, knew that Newt was tough, powerful, and thorough and had assembled an impressive political machine in the state, which held the IOUs of thousands of not just Republicans but Democrats and independents as well. "What's going to beat Gingrich is Gingrich," Flynn said.[34]

To that point, "Gingrich quit his position on a key transportation committee in the House, hampering his ability to represent his home district . . . where thousands hold airline jobs."[35]

Gingrich wasn't worried. His opponent for 1990 looked once again to be David Worley, the squirrelly non-debater from Jonesboro who hadn't changed much in the time since Gingrich had beaten him 59–41 percent.[36]

Newt's egotism sometimes got in the way of a good or important message, though. Shortly before becoming Whip, he held a press conference in which he proclaimed, "Other than Jack Kemp, I have been the most energetic Republican of my generation."[37]

CHAPTER 19

TROUBLE IN PARADISE

"Go to h—, Newt Gingrich."

1989

It hadn't taken long for buttons to appear in the nation's capital proclaiming, "Go to h—, Newt Gingrich." Turgid opinions were part of the city, especially when it came to politics and the Redskins. The city's mayor, Marion Barry, was on trial, and "Dump Barry" buttons were also plentiful.[1]

The new Whip warned that the politics in Washington were going to get even rougher. The establishment media began taking him more seriously, even as they increased the bashing. After all, he'd correctly predicted that Jim Wright would be gone as Speaker by June 1989. Wright had resigned on May 31.[2]

Gingrich's obsession with a Republican-controlled House necessitated permanent offense against the establishment, against the Democrats, and even against Republicans when the circumstances called for it. "Newt has said the only way for Republicans to get control is to destroy the institution, tear it down and then rebuild it," said the *Los Angeles Times*.[3]

He understood that his ascension changed the equation for both parties. Half the GOP said Gingrich was "driving the party."[4] Fittingly, his rise to power came just as C-SPAN was celebrating its ten-year anniversary.

Newt gave long odds that the GOP would capture control of Congress by 1992, but said "even money" when asked about 1996, though curiously did not give odds for 1994.[5]

He was cunning in his approach. He appointed as his deputies Bob Walker of Pennsylvania, who was a master parliamentarian even more loathed by Democrats than Gingrich himself—and thus a lightning rod—and Steve Gunderson of Wisconsin, a generally liked and well-regarded moderate. They printed buttons with the number 92 in the middle; around the edge they read, "Moderates make a difference."[6] Gingrich understood how to make deposits and withdrawals from the favor bank.

He also understood that controversy sold papers and pushed agendas. "If you're not in the *Washington Post* every day, you might as well not exist," he told *Newsweek*.[7] He wasn't just in the *Post* or *Newsweek*, though. There wasn't a day that went by that Gingrich wasn't in hundreds of newspapers across the country. More and more Democrats were coming forward to proclaim that they now knew Gingrich's formerly secret agenda: to tear apart the House in order for the Republicans to seize power.

However, the scorn heaped upon him began taking its toll. "I am the victim of a hypocritical, one-sided morality," he said. "I've been the whistleblower, because I helped bring a man (Wright) who was a scoundrel to justice, and now I'm being punished for this. I'm tired of being smeared. I'm tired of Democrats bashing me around."[8] Democrats merely smiled at Newt's whining and planned on inflicting as much pain as possible, as revenge for Jim Wright, Charlie Diggs, Tip O'Neill, and other Democrats with whom Newt had feuded and won.

With all the attention, however, Newt's signature on direct-mail fundraising pieces had become gold, and GOPAC was raising thousands of dollars more as a result.[9] The letters all spoke of taking control of Congress.

Hidden agendas were everywhere in Washington. Secretary of State Baker had been secretly cheering on Gingrich's campaign against Jim Wright—the two Texans despised each other over some Lone Star sword-crossing years earlier.

At their first meeting after his election as Whip, President Bush told Gingrich he was looking forward to working with him.[10] When it came to manners, Bush was nonpareil, but like all politicians he also had personal agendas and opinions. The White House later let it leak out that they had received assurances from Gingrich that he would be a "team player," but he did not elaborate which team he was intending to play for.[11]

Ethics were never far from the national debate. Often they were central. The Senate Ethics Committee was investigating Senator Alfonse D'Amato of New York, but this was nothing new.[12] D'Amato was always under a large bank of ethics clouds. Representative Jim Bates was thrown into the mix for sexual harassment of his own female staffers. Bates denied it but also apologized for being misunderstood. The embarrassing revelations of Gary Hart's peccadilloes while monkeying around with another woman, or Senator Joe Biden's monkeying around with his college transcripts and campaign remarks and plagiarizing other items were never far from anyone's mind. Both men became cautionary stories for how public officials should not behave.

Gingrich had a refined and sensible position on the matter: "I've always said you have to distinguish between sin, which is private conduct, and being a scoundrel, which is public conduct."[13]

In a previous time, he'd argued for expelling two congressmen found to have had sex with minors. "There is no high school or college in America where exploiting, seducing or sleeping with students, boy or girl, would be punished with a reprimand. The teacher would be fired."[14] Yet he said Buz Lukens should not be barred from voting in the House because his crime of having sex with an underage prostitute was a misdemeanor.[15]

Gingrich had already taken heat from some conservatives for urging caution in going after Barney Frank, an openly homosexual congressman. Yet another rumor going around was that Frank was "blackmailing" the Democratic leadership and that if they forced him out of his seat, he would "take a number of fellow congressmen with him by exposing their personal indiscretions," according to a tale Gingrich told the *Washington Times*.[16]

An authoritative report from the Center for Media and Public Affairs came out and the coverage of ethics by the newspapers was off the scale. According to the report, Frank received good coverage when it came to his wit or intelligence, but when it came to his "personal integrity," the rating was "91 percent negative." Gingrich received very little fair and balanced coverage from across the spectrum, according to the study, but this applied to Republicans broadly. Democrats received far more favorable coverage than did Republicans, especially at the *Washington Post*, where the broadsheet favored the Democrats over the Republicans by a 3–1 margin.[17]

Reporters claimed they did not like to wallow in the personal lives of politicians, but that was all hooey. They slurped up the rumors and innuendo and gossip.

Gingrich's ascension to Whip meant goodies, such as a new office in the Capitol, extra staff, and being invited to have cocktails with President

Bush and Chief of Staff John Sununu.[18] It also meant thinking in even bigger terms than before, as the office of Whip afforded him the luxury to do so: "Former Speaker . . . Thomas P. O'Neill Jr., an old Gingrich foe, always counseled that all politics is local. Gingrich and company are on the opposite track, contending that the House can be won back on the strength of national Republican issues."[19]

He also went into the Den of Iniquity, the Fourth Estate, as luncheon speaker to the National Press Club, where he appeared to poke fun at his own district, saying he was the congressman "who represents the Atlanta airport." He got a chuckle when he told the scribes it was "good to be back on C-SPAN." The remarks were punctuated with far too many personal pronouns and pandering. He got another laugh when he pointed out the modern realities of voting in America and the power of incumbency: ". . . to recognize that for the first time in history, you were 16 times more likely to be defeated this year if you were a Soviet Communist provincial leader . . ."[20]

All in all, Gingrich acquitted himself well, but there was just one small problem: not a single individual in the room was a voter in the Sixth Congressional District of Georgia.

Gingrich did not realize—or was unwilling to admit—that the intelligentsia of the Georgetown cocktail circuit would never accept him. He grew up an army brat, attended the wrong schools, taught at a public university, and, as far as they were concerned, was a bohemian.

Gingrich was also not out of the ethics forest. A previously raised charge was raised again. Some of his aides, including longtime advisor Sheila Ward, appeared to get bonuses in the form of an increase in their government salaries after performing duties on Newt's political campaigns. The Ethics Committee said they would investigate. With all the messes circulating, the AP published a headline for the ages: "Gingrich Complaint, Sex Cases Before Ethics Panel."[21] The media also noted the irony that Rep. Fred Grandy of Iowa, the skirt-chasing "Gopher" on the hit TV show *The Love Boat*, was now on the Ethics Committee investigating skirt chasers.[22]

The open-and-shut-and-open investigation into Newt's two book deals was finally shut as the outside counsel hired by the Ethics Committee said the matter lacked sufficient evidence to go forward. Much of what had been charged against Gingrich was fiction. A Democratic campaign committee immediately filed another complaint against him over the unusual rise in congressional salaries paid to former campaign workers. The supporting documentation was nearly seven hundred pages detailing the various charges against Gingrich. Some of the itemized charges were specious at best, as one charged that a Florida travel agency had solicited business using Gingrich's official letterhead. Another was for cosigning a mortgage for his daughter.[23] In a surprise to absolutely no one, the Congress voted for more money for the Ethics Committee because of all the investigations it was undertaking.[24]

The conservative movement had seen better days. Frankly, some thought it was the victim of its own success. At least that's what a lot of conservatives were telling themselves. The election of Bush was not a halcyon moment for the movement, but if the right could defeat the left when both had such lousy candidates, that meant conservatism was the better idea, the better way forward, they reasoned. They were celebratory enough, though, to host a "Salute to Newt Gingrich" night at the den of Republicanism, the Capitol Hill Club.[25]

Ironically, while the conservative movement was wandering in the wilderness, so, too, were the national Democrats, still licking their wounds after a third loss in a row for the White House. The young governor of Arkansas, Bill Clinton, who was already a Jedi Master at politics, went searching for the "New Democrat," who would lead the old Democrats to the promised land of subsidized milk and redistributed honey.

The *Post* spelled it out in September. For the old-line Democrats, "this has been the year of malaise . . . Democratic congressmen feel George Bush has pre-empted their favorite issues: détente, education, the environment, drugs. Feeding the gloom is acknowledgement by Democrats that they cannot regain the presidency relying on minority and special interest groups."[26]

The Democrats, who controlled both houses of Congress, were making no major plans, no grand ideas, no New Deal schemes or Great Society designs. Most of what they proposed or sponsored was small-potato stuff, a little there for labor, a little here taken away from business. After the fires of ideological passion of the 1980s, they'd been banked greatly, and men like George Bush, who did not enunciate great ideas, were in charge of the most important city in a world in which less powerful men and women were enunciating great ideas of power, people, and the perspective of history.

It sometimes seemed as if the word *bipartisan* had been tattooed on George Bush's forehead. It was in reality a part of his DNA. For Gingrich and company, bipartisanship was simply a four-letter word with prefixes and suffixes.

It all began coming to a head in a widely read column by Evans and Novak, titled "Trouble in Paradise." The famed and feared duo recounted in detail an ugly meeting between the White House and the House Republicans, with Bush and his chief of staff, the personality-challenged John Sununu, on one side and Gingrich, Bob Michel, and House Republicans on the other. The congressmen weathered a withering assault from the abrasive Lebanese Sununu.

"The meeting began with . . . Sununu hectoring the legislative leaders for demonstrating insufficient vigor in pressing White House programs." Bushism had come to include legislation to restrict guns and "mandated health benefits." Bush and Sununu played good cop–bad cop, with Sununu clearly enjoying his role as the bad cop. Michel was described as "red-faced."[27] Words like *harangue* and *excessive* and *complaintitis* peppered the must-read column. Clearly, the Hill Republicans were breaking away from Bushism.

Slowly, inexorably, the Hill Republicans—especially the conservatives—were separating from the Bush White House. This became even more evident in a subsequent story, in which Gingrich warned his fellow Republicans that if the United States bombed terrorist locations in Lebanon, they risked the transfer of terrorist anger from Israel to one directed at "US cities." Bush was no fan of Israel, that much was certain, but Hezbollah had murdered an American hostage, Lt. Col. William Higgins, USMC, and a military response was under consideration.[28] The new Whip was in the Evans and Novak column so often he was invited onto their CNN show.[29]

Still, it was noted he'd been taking a softer approach, as if he was dialing it back a bit. He and Marianne were trying to repair their marriage as well. Also, the ferocity of the press and the Democrats had taken him aback. For Gingrich, who sometimes had trouble seeing the other fellow's point of view, he had difficulty understanding how the Democrats could be bitter after years of withering under his assault, or how the media saw him as a target to be taken down a peg or three. Consequently, even Newt for a time became infected with the bipartisan bug. He seemed to be taking a more long-term approach to things. "Termites are as effective as dynamite in bringing down a house," he said. "They just take longer."[30]

In late 1989, the Republicans were given a gift. The House Democrats decided to undo the tax reform of 1986, of which they'd been such a large part, and push for new taxes on upper-income Americans, along with a new raise in capital gains. Gingrich could scarcely believe his good fortune, especially since so many Democrats were opposed. Part of the Republican strategy became threatening Democrats with campaigns in their districts, attacking them for supporting higher taxes.[31] In Maryland alone, three of its six Democrats voted for the Republican plan to cut capital gains.[32]

Like many modern conservatives, Gingrich had a refined sense of human rights and fair play, flag burning notwithstanding. In late 1989, a promise of Ronald Reagan's from the year before to pay off a debt was coming due. During World War II, Franklin Roosevelt, with Earl Warren's eager help, without due process, had incarcerated tens of thousands of Japanese, including American citizens, simply because they looked different. Stripped of their property, possessions, rights, and dignity, they were sent to dozens of "internment camps" that dotted the sparse terrain of the American West. Before all was said and done, more than one hundred thousand Japanese were "relocated."[33]

Some German nationals and Italian nationals had also been imprisoned, but not in the numbers or with the harshness directed at the Japanese. It was one of the darkest moments in American history. There remained approximately sixty-two thousand formerly relocated Japanese Americans still alive forty-four years later, and Reagan had both apologized on the part of the American government and promised recompense totaling about $1.25 billion, around $20,000 to each individual. Incredibly, some callous bean counters in the GOP Conference began an effort to stop the payments until Gingrich brought them to heel and to their senses. The national media was, to be sure, frugal in their praise of Gingrich.[34]

New York, the insular and self-absorbed town, loved nothing better than talking about itself. New Yorkers looked down their noses at Washingtonians, but most were oblivious. They hadn't come to DC for dining or shows or art or

music but for the politics: the dirtier, the grimier, the more salacious, the better. Money was good but media was better. It was the coin of the realm. Part
of the measurement of one's importance in the town was media, especially
appearances on television talk shows. Publications such as the *Washington
Times* charted the "upness" and "downness" of the town's politicos. In the
summer of 1989, Judge Robert Bork was "up" because of his availability,
but "by contrast, Peggy Noonan is way down on the charts . . . Ms. Noonan
enjoyed a brief period in the limelight and now is nowhere to be seen."[35]

The Hill and the Bush Administration were headed to yet another budget
impasse. Gingrich said, "If we can't get a good budget-reconciliation bill,
sequestration isn't the worst thing in the world."[36] The Congress did pass a
bill that tied a pay raise to outside compensation, yet another attempt to curb
the influence of lobbyists, access-sellers, and bottom-feeders. Honoraria,
travel, and gifts—along with women and alcohol—had once been an inte-
gral part of life of the Hill, along with golf, poker, and the occasional debate
or piece of legislation, but that was all part of another day, another time. It
was being slowly trimmed away. Gingrich voted for the measure.[37] The conservative media roundly denounced him.

The first session of the 101st Congress was coming to a close, and many
in the media decried how little the members had done, which had never
been heard before. The new minority whip joined the editorial writers of the
Washington Post to break bread and pontificate, two things Gingrich was
skilled at. "We are in fact at a crossroads, and I don't think anyone knows
which way it goes," he told the scribes.[38] As always, control of Congress was
on his mind.

Only two days later, he was part of an intraparty spat, with him on one
side and consultants, Bushies, and Ed Rollins, head of the GOP congressional
campaign, on the other, opposed to his "grand vision" nostrums about GOP
dominance.[39] Could the party compete with the Democrats at the nuts-and-
bolts level or would a Reaganesque big picture do more for the party's future?

Meanwhile, Newt continued to complain to anyone who would listen
that he was under attack by his political enemies, but the fault, they knew,
was not in the stars or themselves, but in the congressman. And the Ethics
Committee was still investigating him and the sexual escapades of three

other members. Being lumped in with accused child molesters and sexual harassers was not helpful. Yet, because he'd pulled back on the usual severe attacks on Democrats, Gingrich was convinced he was somehow moderating his image.

It was in late August when Gingrich ran into the buzz saw of an angry Eastern Airline employees strike. The mechanics still had not come to any settlement, and Gingrich showed his insensitive side when he blithely commented on the Neal Boortz radio show that the airline could be "non-union" in a matter of months, certainly not what the workers wanted to hear. One angrily stormed, "He's done in this district."[40]

Gingrich seemed convinced that his high-wire act in Washington was pleasing to the people of Georgia. It wasn't. There were more and more rumblings coming from Georgia about Newt's growing national presence and diminishing state presence. "He's in the national spotlight, and he's forgetting the folks back home," said one disgruntled constituent.[41] "I'd be more enthusiastic about Newt if he'd get as much impact on the environment and our rivers as he did on Jim Wright," said another.[42]

Some down in Georgia thought Newt was getting too big for his britches, that he'd forgotten the home folks and spent too much time worshiping at the altar of the Sunday shows rather than hitting his knees in church.

At the worst possible time, a shocking profile of Gingrich was published in *Mother Jones*. Charitably, it was devastating. Disgruntled former staffers wanting to grind an ax, including Chip Kahn and Kip Carter, were interviewed. The writer clearly took to heart the advice to write like someone who doesn't have a mother except, of course, the magazine. To top it off, the *Los Angeles Times* got a quote out of Newt's ex-wife, Jackie, about the article: "All I can say is *Mother Jones* scooped the world on Newt Gingrich."[43]

Also, it was revealed that Gingrich had sent a mailer to thousands of donors, asking them to help defray his considerable legal costs, estimated to be more than $125,000. There was nothing wrong in doing so, and indeed many politicians did likewise, but it became just one more thing to complain about Newt back home.[44]

His political organization there had been allowed to fall into disrepair, was making embarrassing mistakes, and was running out of excuses why he was everywhere, it seemed, except there. A political organization in the state under his control was sending letters to Republicans, by mistake, asking them for their help in finding Republicans to run against other Republicans.[45] The gaff was widely reported.

He was here, there, everywhere, but not seen in Georgia. He was in Washington brawling over spending and taxes, sequestration and ethics, but never seemed to be fighting for the Sixth.

The trendy magazine *M* had advanced the idea of "The New Sissy," and cited Phil Donahue, Geraldo Rivera, and, oddly, Newt as evidence of the new wimpiness of the American male. The article detailed how men were gradually becoming the soft losers of American life, while women were lifting "their wings" and taking flight.[46]

Gingrich was not the only one with impending campaign problems. The GOP had lost the governorship in the Commonwealth of Virginia, a race that everybody thought would be a walk in the park for the Republicans, as the Democrats had nominated L. Douglas Wilder, the lieutenant governor from Richmond—successful, handsome, tall, articulate, charming, and black. Astonishingly, a black man had won in the capital of the Old Confederacy. He'd defeated Marshall Coleman, a successful, handsome, tall, articulate, charming white man. It was a new day in the South.

Another African American, David Dinkins, won as mayor of New York City, defeating Republican Rudy Giuliani. "Led by Dinkins, blacks also succeeded white mayors in Seattle, Cleveland, New Haven, Conn., and Durham, N.C." Gingrich did take a moment to get outside of party politics to note the remarkable change in American politics when black candidates could compete anywhere and not just in minority-majority districts.[47]

The problem was, all these African American candidates were Democrats.

All in all, Election Day 1989 was lousy for the Republicans and great for the Democrats. "It's a very tough day for Republicans," sighed Gingrich. "Wait 'til next year," said President Bush.[48]

CHAPTER 20

BEATING THE BUSH

"On Right . . . Discontent with Bush."

1990

As late as January 1989—when Ronald and Nancy Reagan headed back to Rancho de Cielo—the Republicans had a political party with a coherent governing philosophy. Reagan knew that politics was about persuasion, success, patience, and permanent offense. He almost never retreated. Also, an intellectual basis for conservative governance was an underreported birthright the Gipper had bequeathed the Republicans. To the chagrin of many, George Bush and his followers simply didn't understand any of this, and what they did comprehend they eschewed or, worse, scoffed at. To them, Reaganism just wasn't sophisticated. The GOP had been poised in the last year of the next-to-last decade of the twentieth century to become the permanent majority party in America. Had been.

As soon as he was elected Whip, Newt Gingrich told journalists that "he wouldn't necessarily always support Mr. Bush's positions. He said he is whip for House Republicans, not the president."[1] No doubt Gingrich had a softer spot for Reagan than he did for Bush. Gingrich liked to tell people that on a plane with Reagan, the Gipper once looked out the window and quipped to a group of like-minded conservatives, "How tempting it would be to bomb the Capitol."[2]

Of course, the usual radioactive stories also still appeared. Typical of these attacks was one that unflatteringly characterized the new minority whip: "Newt Gingrich of Georgia, a man who believes Congress is a vipers nest of Commie sympathizers and check kiters."[3]

He acidly noted that in the context of the forthcoming congressional elections, "Republicans cannot rely on George Bush's popularity."[4] He also said the party would need to reexamine what it was and what it stood for if it was to be competitive in the off-year elections.

Some in the GOP said abortion was key and the party had better get with the program and come out unequivocally for abortion on demand, or they would be doomed to a minority status. Some strategists blamed Bush's pro-life stance for their ailing party. Senator Bob Packwood of Oregon, a sometimes-sober liberal Republican and enthusiastic supporter of abortion, who was also widely known, at the time, to be utterly respectful of women, told Bush the GOP would get clobbered in 1990 unless they rejected the pro-life position.[5]

Lee Atwater was ducking all the blame for the disaster of the city and state elections in 1989, and pointing fingers at the Republican candidates who lost. At the party's annual confab, even more pressure was applied to the GOP by the media and the left to get it to switch on abortion, using the inducements of "younger voters, women independents." Gingrich stood firm on the pro-life position, but Atwater just wanted to get past it.

The Democrats, fresh off their big wins the previous year, started 1990 on offense, as Senator Daniel Patrick Moynihan made what looked to be a serious proposal to rescind several previous increases in Social Security taxes, which had resulted in a $62 billion surplus. They dangled the bait in the hopes that Republicans would go for it.[6] Gingrich did, saying he'd be delighted to be the point man in defending Social Security, but that would put the GOP through the looking glass by opposing tax cuts and supporting a government-run welfare program they had opposed since its inception. He was talked out of it.[7]

The Republicans briefly regained the offensive, when they proposed—yet again—to privatize Social Security; the proposal was gaining favor in some quarters. Gingrich eagerly jumped on board. It earned him an invitation to *This Week with David Brinkley*. Up against Bob Dole, Fritz Hollings, and Richard Darman, who also appeared, Gingrich was the sole tax cutter in the crowd.[8] Like Nixon, Gingrich relished fighting odds as the sole man in the arena. Indeed, the old president made a courtesy call on the House Republicans to give them a pep talk. It was the first time in years the "Trickster" had been seen on Capitol Hill.[9]

Even with the slowing economy and his hands-off approach to governance, President George Bush enjoyed a 76 percent approval rating the first
year into his term of office. Surprisingly, only 13 percent disapproved of the
job he was doing. Indeed, all new presidents had high ratings at comparable
periods, except Ronald Reagan, Jimmy Carter, and Gerald Ford. The Bush
White House took the obvious conclusion and brushed off any criticism as
ill-informed or mistaken.

Gingrich didn't let Bush's high number stop him from routinely criti-
cizing, calling the Administration "incremental." Elaborating, he said that
Bush "nibbles around the edges rather than throwing ideological bombs."[10]
The folks at the Bush White House heartily agreed.

Gingrich, it seemed, was spoiling for a fight with Bush. "I cannot for the
life of me understand what their strategy is." Full throated, the Georgian
stormed, "The country doesn't understand what he's doing. The Congress
doesn't understand what he's doing."[11]

The Bush White House decided the Whip needed stroking, so Gingrich
was invited to join the president on a trip to Florida.

Still, the GOP was headed for a showdown between Bush and Gingrich
over the issue of anti-communism, which most thought had been settled
years earlier. The debate was moving from "Who Lost China?" to "Who Lost
the GOP?"

The debate only sharpened at the annual Conservative Political Action
Conference, at which Gingrich was a fixture. Again, Bush was a no-show.
There was a lot of grumbling heard in the halls of the Omni Shoreham Hotel,
where the annual confab took place amid the crumbling glory of the once-
great facility, over Bush and his men and their policies. Bush was a champion
of the status quo, any status quo. Though not by name, Gingrich called the
president out in his address.

When the Berlin Wall fell in late 1989, the Bush Administration had been
silent while Reagan was exultant. Bush hated challenges to the status quo,
and Reagan was the very personification of the notion.

It was clear that events and decisions were forcing a showdown inside
the GOP, pitting Bush against the Reaganites. Since he'd taken office one
year earlier, Reagan men and women had been unceremoniously forced out

of the new Administration. Many conservatives looking for jobs in the nascent Bush Administration could not even get their phone calls returned. It would also leak out from time to time what the Bushies thought of Reagan, which was not much.

As expected, the Ethics Wars that had paralyzed the House for the past year began to spread into the Senate. The "Keating Five" that included John McCain had already done their fair share to despoil the reputation of the Upper House. Now Senator Alfonse D'Amato, who had all the charm of a snake, was under investigation for improperly pressuring HUD officials into giving contracts to "relatives and political friends."[12]

Politicos and others bemoaned the lack of civility on Capitol Hill. Walter Mondale, a gentleman and a gut fighter, said, "We've got a kind of politics of irrelevance, of obscurantism, that is more prevalent than in any time I can recall." Even Mike Oreskes of the *New York Times* gagged on the mythology: "This unhappiness about modern politics is more than mere nostalgia for some idyllic past that never was." Lee Atwater had his own sophisticated take on the state of politics: "Bull permeates everything."[13]

A new front in the civil conflict between Bush and Gingrich was opened over a Voting Rights Bill. For several years, many Democrats (and a few Republicans) had labored to make voter registration easier—by making it possible to register when obtaining a driver's license, or in any federal building in the United States, for example. It would eventually become known as "Motor Voter." The populists favored it; the elites hated it. The Bush White House raised objections about fraud and costs, the usual stonewalls thrown up by obstructionists. In reality, the conventional wisdom in Republican solons was that more casual citizens tended to vote Democratic. This was the real reason for their GOP obstruction, with the notable exception of Gingrich.[14] He was a cosponsor and used recent polling data to buttress his point, that if more Americans had been registered to vote in the 1984 and 1988 elections, Ronald Reagan and George Bush would have increased their margins, as marginal voters preferred the Republicans.[15] Gingrich eventually convinced sixty-one of his fellow House Republicans to support Motor Voter and it passed.[16] Interestingly, no one ever objected to the anti-federalism aspects of the bill.

The Supreme Court once again demonstrated why the adult supervision it provided Washington was so important when it finally ruled that the Flag Protection Act was unconstitutional.[17]

And the Ethics Committee finally closed its investigation of Gingrich. He was cleared of everything but given an informal rap on the knuckles for not disclosing that he'd cosigned a mortgage for his daughter and thus had an interest in the house.[18]

Just beneath the surface, the tax issue was bubbling, beginning to come to a rolling boil. Bush had hated the "no new taxes" pledge he'd made in 1988. It was simply one of the things one did to get elected, telling the voters one thing and then doing something else once in office. Now, egged on by Chief of Staff John Sununu and Budget Director Richard Darman, Bush was about to initiate a civil war within the Republican Party. Gingrich said of Bush and company that "they were tone deaf" when it came to taxes.[19]

Bob Novak and Rowly Evans noted the problem: "The price paid for this by Bush has been a further mudding of what he really stands for."[20] Washingtonians liked to obfuscate the issue to real Americans, but the essence was that the budget needed to be cut by Congress or "sequestration" would take effect and automatic across-the-board cuts in spending would go forth, according to law. Or Congress and the president could raise taxes. By the spring of 1990, Bush had not come out directly for tax increases (though his aides were dropping broad hints). Gingrich, as House minority whip, had a minimal duty to party fealty and so said little on the matter.

Gingrich had to tend to the home fires anyway; he scored a nice hit when he convinced the US Postal Service to issue a stamp commemorating *Gone with the Wind*. Much of the Margaret Mitchell classic was set in his district.[21] As of May 1990, he'd raised and spent $617,220 on his reelection, an amazing amount even for a minority whip.[22] But then he wandered off the reservation when he gave a speech in Colorado and blamed the AIDS epidemic on "liberals who advocated free sex."[23]

Slowly but surely, the Republican Party was beginning to unravel over the inherent contradictions between Reaganism and Bushism. They also fell to fighting among themselves over the matter of Israel. Bob Dole, the Senate Republican leader, took on the matter of Israel and with it, Gingrich. They fell into an ugly public spat over recognition of Jerusalem as the true capital of the Jewish State. Dole had initially voted for a resolution supporting

the Israeli position on Jerusalem but then backed away from his vote, causing consternation. A handful of House Republicans, including Gingrich,
called Dole on the carpet for this, which he did not appreciate.[24] "Normally,
if I disagree with a fellow Republican I speak to them privately about any
problems instead of holding a press conference," the Kansan responded
testily.[25] Though other Republicans were involved, Dole's ire was aimed at
Gingrich, to whom he was becoming increasingly disdainful. Their relationship would get worse before it got much worse.

The separating of the Bush White House's uneasy relationship with the
right was slowly beginning to make it into newspaper articles and columns.
More and more meetings of disgruntled conservatives were taking place in
Washington and around the country, and the good manners of the Bushies
were beginning to wear thin.

The Bushies warmed themselves by the fire of high approval numbers,
and many openly dismissed the conservatives as just a bunch of professional
cranks who never really liked Bush in the first place. The new budget from
the White House called for additional spending, but because it had to
comply with Gramm-Rudman and keep the deficit at a certain level, new
revenues would have to come from somewhere.

And then, on May 8, 1990, an ominous headline appeared in the
Washington Post: "Bush Opens Door to Tax-Hike Talks." The president
himself was quoted as saying he wanted to talk to the Democrats "unfettered with conclusions about positions taken in the past."[26]

In August 1988, he had told the American people, "Read my lips! No
new taxes!"[27] Bush was now not only slamming the door shut on the Reagan
Revolution but crushing the centerpiece of his own 1988 win: his character.
Bush was breaking his word to the American people. He wasn't the first politician to do so, but he was the GOP's nominee after Reagan, and that meant
he had a certain burden to carry, especially after eight years as the Gipper's
veep. His win in the 1988 primary had come about because of his exalted
position and because of the weakness of the campaigns of Bob Dole and Jack
Kemp, not because he had developed any signature issue.

The phrase "only Nixon could go to China" had its roots in a *Star Trek*
movie, but everybody immediately grasped the concept as it applied to
increased taxes. Nixon had spent a lifetime bashing the Kremlin and Peking
and the "cowardly college of communist containment," so when he surprised

the world with his trip to China and deals with Brezhnev, he did so secure in the knowledge that his bedrock of conservative support would not become an earthquake of opposition. So, too, with Reagan—when he raised taxes or cut deals with Moscow, it was with the awareness that he, too, having spent a lifetime building up credibility with American conservatives, could occasionally move to the left. Indeed, if he did so and institutional conservatives attacked him, it made his policies that much more palatable to the centrists in his party.

Bush did not understand this, but he had never understood power or its uses. He did not understand that he had no wellspring of conservative support to drink from. He'd beaten Michael Dukakis in 1988 because the economy was sound as the dollar, because Reagan was hugely popular, and because Dukakis ran one of the worst general election campaigns in American history. Also, because he became identified with one signature issue, the one time he made a promise to all the American people. The one promise he was now breaking.

Reaganite Ed Rollins, who was operating behind enemy lines as head of the National Congressional Campaign Committee, went public immediately with his unadulterated observations: "The biggest difference between Republicans and Democrats in the public perception is that Republicans don't want to raise taxes. Obviously, this makes that go right out the door."[28] Rollins, a former boxer, street-wise operator, and protégé of Lyn Nofziger, patron saint of tough Reaganites, was about as familiar with Bush niceties as Bush would have been with a Roller Derby match.

The Bush White House let Rollins know of their displeasure with his comments, but he told them to get lost. What were they going to do, fire him over suggesting Bush keep a promise? Before 1990 was out, a lot of Republicans would be telling other Republicans the same.

Rollins was a Reagan pilgrim in an unholy land of Bushism. "He represented the establishment that we had fought . . . we win the game in 1980 and we hand the sword back to the other side." Rollins never had any respect for Bush, calling him a "lap dog" and "get along, go along." Elaborating, of Reagan's years, he said, "They undercut . . . [Richard] Darman, [David] Gergen . . . Reagan every day. Tore up poor Ed Meese, who was the ideological soul mate of the President and did everything they could to dump [him]. They got very indignant when you talked about the 'third Reagan term.'"[29]

Haley Barbour, later the chairman of the Republican National Committee, agreed with Rollins. "Republicans who were high on Reagan . . . expected Bush to be more like Reagan. They believed the 'Read my lips, no new taxes.'"[30]

White House spokesman Marlin Fitzwater did his best soft-shoe on the matter. He said a reporter's question "is not helpful, not useful, does not further the progress of the talks in any way." Gingrich did his best to square it, urging Bush to find other revenue sources than from individuals or businesses. He specifically urged that personal income taxes be ruled out.[31]

The Administration was engaged in a full-throated panic. Fitzwater indulged in the silly word games that were so popular in Washington, but which disgusted the rest of the nation. "No preconditions means . . . the table is clean."[32] Some of Bush's defenders were raising the idea of taxes on alcohol or cigarettes or maybe even a national sales tax. When Bush made his pledge, everybody had interpreted it to mean any kind of tax. Now the White House was scrambling, alarmed, trying to shift the debate or even back off a bit. The *Wall Street Journal* called their statements "equivocations."[33]

But it was too late.

The Democrats could scarcely believe it. They just had to figure out how to sell tickets to this out-in-the-street blood brawl. A headline in the *Wall Street Journal* politely screamed, "Confusion Creates Disarray in GOP, Hurts Strategy to Win Pact on Deficit."[34]

Bob Dole and a couple of other Republicans in the Senate said Bush was ready to talk turkey on taxes. But Senator Bill Roth of Delaware, famed member of the Kemp-Roth historic pledge Reagan had signed in 1981—which had kicked off a multiyear boom that created millions of jobs—said, "I have a message for the president. Read my lips. Keep the campaign pledge."[35]

The long-ignored vice president, Dan Quayle, told CNN, "The American people know this president doesn't want to raise taxes, period."[36] His comments, off the reservation as usual, were either ignored or derided.

It was the beginning of the end of the Reagan Revolution.

CHAPTER 21

THE "T" WORD

"The White House has caved in too quickly on tax increases."

1990

P aul Gigot, a gently traditional columnist for the *Wall Street Journal*, had always been a favorite in the Court of St. Bush. It was easy to see why:

> To believe a Bush "sellout" on taxes you have to believe that he, Chief of Staff John Sununu and Treasury Secretary Nick Brady are stupid enough to give up their country's best political issue without solving the budget problem. Only the White House press corps could really believe this . . . The old Reagan-era partisan divisions don't always prevail anymore. What Democrats would never concede to the Great Communicator, they just might to their fellow insider.[1]

Gigot was the last of the Bush White House's worries. Other conservatives were tearing their hair out, though. Dick Armey's aide Kerry Knott recalled Armey boldly telling George Bush in the White House if he broke his pledge on taxes, "I'm convinced you'll be a one-term president."[2]

As Bush moved more and more toward a restoration of moderate Republican governance, more and more conservatives spoke out and relations were becoming increasingly strained. Also, more and more comparisons were being made to Ronald Reagan, and Bush was coming off more and more as the loser in any contrast with the Gipper.

People all over Washington were mocking Bush. When it was reported that he was about to veto some piece of legislation, the sarcastic response was, "Yeah, read his lips."[3] There was some idle discussion on the right about a challenge to Bush in the 1992 primaries, but the only natural choice was Jack Kemp and he was in Bush's cabinet. Kemp had been a daring quarterback on the gridiron, but in the political game he was maddeningly cautious.

The situation was getting out of hand and the Bush White House tried to roll things back, claiming they were back to a "no new taxes" position and were—wink, wink—only trying to set up the Democrats to come out in support of the plan and then pull a bait and switch. Another ploy was to say that the White House was only floating the idea in the name of "good government."[4] No one was buying it.

A group of GOP senators outside the negotiations sent Bush a letter pleading with him not to break his pledge. Along with Newt Gingrich and Senator Phil Gramm, the rest of the congressional leadership of both parties, including Senator Bob Dole and Missouri's congressman Dick Gephardt, were part of the negotiations. Curiously, virtually none of the congressional negotiators was on good personal terms with Bush. The animosity between Dole and Bush was well known, as was that between Bush and Gingrich (and between Gingrich and Dole); but Gramm and Bush also did not get along . . . and it leaked out that Bush and Gephardt did not care for each other. Sometimes Washington resembled a gossipy junior high school more than a city of deliberation and thought.

The Sunday shows from *Inside Washington* to *Face the Nation* were all dominated by talk of Bush's teetering toward breaking his tax pledge. Ironically, of all the congressional leadership, with the notable exception of Bob Michel, Gingrich was at the time on the best terms with the Bush White House. He was there frequently in the spring of 1990, meeting with Bush. But this wouldn't last.

Criticism from the right was accelerating. *New York Times* columnist William Safire leveled Bush, accusing him of supporting "Big-Gov" republicanism.[5]

By mid-May 1990, the fight was out in the streets. A headline in the *New York Times* screamed, "New Political Realities Create Conservative Identity Crisis." The long story contained quote after quote from leading conservatives wringing their hands over the state of their movement and the loss of Ronald Reagan as their leader. Gingrich was in the story extensively, and stood out, along with Jim Pinkerton, as the only two conservatives who were thinking about "a new paradigm," as Pinkerton said.[6] In other words, if it worked, keep it; but if it didn't work, replace it. The concept of "New Paradigms" at least opened new debates and discussions, which in and of themselves were useful except to anti-intellectuals like Dick Darman, who went around scoffing, "Brother can you paradigm?"[7]

A biting quote by Kevin Phillips, an erratic former Nixon tactician, summed up his take on the problems of the movement: "It's a rare conservative power broker who sits and exalts in the position or acumen of Dan Quayle."[8] But most conservatives had long ago dismissed Phillips as habitually dyspeptic. While another, Paul Weyrich, submitted the notion that conservatism had to keep evolving or it would wither and die.[9] Others warned that Bushism was not conservatism, and at some point, men and women on the right would be forced to choose between the two.

One thing was becoming clearer, however, and that was George Bush had given up the ghost on holding the line on taxes, but, like so many things in his Administration, the matter was not settled quickly and quietly and cleanly. It was debated out in the open for weeks, allowing people to take potshots, to reflect, to change their minds, to strike at the king.

One month later, in June 1990, George Will, never enamored of Bush, struck at the king. In the early days of the conservative movement, Will had sometimes been dismissive of Ronald Reagan and favorable toward Nelson Rockefeller and George Bush, but into the late 1970s and with the revolutionary election of Reagan in 1980, Will had turned more toward the right, becoming a kind of elitist populist (or populist elitist), if there was such an animal. Will was marinated in the very Washington culture he often excoriated. By the late 1980s, he was already often excoriating Bush. When Bush broke his tax pledge, Will tore him apart, under the heading "He Moved His Lips and Said Nothing": "But for many Democrats, Heaven on Earth is watching George Bush eat his words to the sound of snickering . . . Bush can neither speak effectively nor keep silent with dignity . . . John Sununu, Bush's Doberman, who flaunts his cynicism so that his employer's will be less noticeable . . ." Will also took a shot at Gingrich because he'd gamely tried to defend Bush, parsing the meaning and intent of "new revenue."[10]

Even when it was apparent to all that Bush either had been rolled or had caved—take your pick—his White House was still claiming he had not broken his campaign pledge.

As of late June, Bush was telling the Associated Press that tax increases were needed.[11] A day later, on June 27, Bush gave up the charade and held a nationally televised press conference explaining to the American people why he'd stopped reading the lips of conservatives and started reading the lips of establishmentarians. He claimed that the savings and loan "crisis" was worse than forecast, as was the federal deficit. All that was true, but the fact of the matter was he'd broken his word. Politically, "He said he did not believe his credibility would be damaged 'in the long run.'"[12]

The nation's newspapers thought otherwise. In headlines across the country, Bush was pilloried. The *New York Post* screamed, "Read His Forked Tongue: New Taxes!"[13] The *Wall Street Journal* cried, "Flip Flop."[14]

The Senate majority leader, Democrat George Mitchell of Maine, triumphantly said, "The president has concluded that tax increases are necessary. We share the president's view."[15] They hoped to settle the matter before the August recess.

Conservatives across the spectrum were livid, especially Gingrich. Gingrich was at first disgusted over the way it had been handled, but when it sunk in that Bush was really breaking his pledge, he lost it. In an ugly phone call with Sununu, Gingrich slammed the receiver down, hanging up on the White House chief of staff when told about the big switcheroo by President Bush. Despite being in the leadership, he hadn't been invited to the meeting at the White House where Bush told the gathered he was going to raise taxes after all.[16] Still, Gingrich said nothing publicly. Yet.

The Democrats meanwhile were having a dandy time, dancing in the streets, clinking beer steins, toasting the discomfort of the GOP. It was a glorious time to be a Democrat. Bush's defeated rival, Governor Mike Dukakis, piled it on. "I told the truth, and I paid the price. Mr. Bush did not tell the truth, and now we must all pay the price."[17]

As of yet, it was not clear what form the tax increase would take, but everybody knew that to make up the budget shortfall, raising personal income taxes had to be in the mix. When Gingrich did speak, he was ultra-cautious, giving Bush the benefit of the doubt: increasing revenues did not *necessarily* translate into higher personal or business taxes. Representative Walker was not ultra-cautious. "I think we backed into something horribly stupid," he said.[18]

One day later, the revolt had spread across Republicanland. A White House official now embraced the horror and said, "We're trying to contain the firestorm."[19] A press conference at the National Press Club was called by leading conservative groups, who lambasted Bush with relish.[20] The Bush White House was paralyzed.

As public reaction to Bush's broken tax pledge spiraled out of control, the nation's attention turned briefly to the matter of personal misconduct by a nationally known Democrat. The House voted 408–18 in late July 1990 to reprimand Congressman Barney Frank of Massachusetts for "ethical breaches involving his relationship with a male prostitute . . . The drama reached a peak when Mr. Frank rose from his seat and apologized . . . about his mistakes and about his homosexuality, which he publically acknowledged three years ago." Gingrich had pushed for censure, a stiffer judgment, but the House voted this down, 287–141.[21]

With Frank's personal humiliation now dealt with, Congress and the nation returned to the matter of tax increases. The actual Bush plan was unfocused, which made the whole thing doubly worse. The plan called for raising taxes, but it did not say how. Bandied about were suggestions of beer, wine, cigarettes, gas, and limiting the deductibility of state taxes on federal returns. When reporters caught up with Gingrich and asked him about the Bush plan, he simply smiled and said, "It doesn't exist."[22] Every once in a while, he was capable of an apothegm.

Without specifics, the media and interest groups and members of Congress all jumped to conclusions, except in their denunciation of Bush and his White House. It went like this—back and forth—over the summer of 1990. Congress went into recess with no agreement in place on a budget, but with battle lines set and the issue and tempers broiling in the steam closet that passed for the nation's capital.

As George Bush was in the process of dismantling Reaganism, it escaped everyone's attention that the new normal was low unemployment, high growth with low inflation, and low interest rates. The economy since the end of the Carter Recession in 1982 had been bubbling along, with none of the "boom and bust" that had marked the economy of the post-1945 America. If politicians could just be convinced to keep their mitts off of the economy, it would take care of itself, just as all free marketers believed, including the architects of the new normal from the Reagan Administration.

Gingrich had been laying low for much of 1990, at least as far as leading any new lost causes. He was now a member of the leadership and had to act "leaderly." The legend of Gingrich was that he was in the mold of Sam Adams, the fiery revolutionary, but in fact he was sometimes more like the conciliatory John Adams. Gingrich was fiercely partisan, though not always fiercely ideological. "I'm a pragmatic free-enterpriser," he once proclaimed.[23] Like all members, he had home state concerns and he had to surrender to the realities of modern politics, such as supports for agriculture subsidies and protectionism for textile manufacturers.

But the attempted seduction of Gingrich by the Bush White House was under way. Sometimes he spoke publicly like a Bush supporter, vociferously defending the Bush country club, into which he'd been invited. It was something he'd wanted his whole life—to be accepted by his betters. In this way, he was much like them.

At least Gingrich put his money where his mouth was. Members were only allowed to keep a certain portion of their lecture fees, so Gingrich donated his overage to the Atlanta schools. Gingrich proposed to pay third graders in five poor Georgia communities $2.00 for every book they read over the summer,[24] which he would cover with his speaking fees. He also gave nearly $30,000 to the Atlanta zoo.[25]

Later in the year, Gingrich produced the now-famous GOPAC memo for House Republicans on words to use and words not to use—at least in a public political context. "Call your opponent a 'sick, pathetic, liberal, incompetent, tax-spending traitor'" was the way to go in describing the Democrats. For the sweet and gentle Republicans, calling themselves "humane, visionary, confident, candid, hard-working reformer" was recommended. In politics, sticks and stones could break bones but names could also hurt, and Gingrich had come up with 133 nasty idioms to hurl at the illiterate, vile, and disgusting Democrats.[26]

For a time, Gingrich's personal and professional ambitions converged. He always wanted to be coveted by the establishment and he always wanted to be the architect of a GOP takeover of Congress. Some thought Gingrich saw a path to power through the Bush Administration, overlooking that the victory of 1988 had been without content and that the GOP had actually lost down-ticket races. Even the *Wall Street Journal*, in a surprisingly favorable story on Gingrich, said he'd "been struggling for more than a year to give new direction to conservatism . . ."[27] That the *Journal* was now being nice to Gingrich was a sure sign that some thought he was becoming a Bushie, an establishmentarian to their liking.

To be sure, the White House had exerted great pressure on Gingrich to keep him in line. Budget Director Darman "begged" Gingrich "not to 'trash' Bush" at an early White House meeting.[28] For a moment Gingrich agreed and stayed silent, but his doubts were on the rise.

May 15 was set as the first day of negotiations between Congress and the Administration over how to raise taxes on the American people. Gingrich issued a statement saying how "honored" he was at his selection to the negotiating team by Minority Leader Bob Michel.[29] Michel, of course, did not say "boo" without the Bush White House's approval, and they saw Gingrich and Phil Gramm as just the conservative cover they needed.

The *Wall Street Journal* summed up the White House sentiment to Gingrich's presence: though Gingrich was doing little to stop the negotiations from going forward, the same could not be said of the Bush White House, especially Darman, when it came to the House minority whip. "Mr. Darman acknowledges that some people were concerned that the fiery Mr. Gingrich might not play by the rules of budget summitry, 'which essentially require that you be relatively temperate.' So far, he says, Mr. Gingrich has 'favorably surprised some people.'"[30] The elites could be so patronizingly polite.

Gingrich began edging away. Acidly, he said the meetings were like "watching the Republicans punch themselves in the face."[31] Foolishly, the Bush White House was comforting itself with the silly notion that the Democrats would get blamed for any tax increase; the Democrats were comforting themselves with the more realistic possibility that the Republicans would engage in a bloody civil war over the matter.

Increasing conservatives' angst was a forthcoming summit between Bush and Mikhail Gorbachev. They were deeply worried that Bush would not aggressively stand up for Lithuania or the emerging democratic movements in the Warsaw Pact countries and within the Soviet Union itself. The belief was prevalent on the right that Bush and Secretary of State Jim Baker had already given away too much to Moscow while asking for little in return. House Speaker Tom Foley was not making any plans to be in Washington when the

Soviets arrived, according to the *New Republic*. "His office informed [reporters] that the Speaker would not be leaving the beach in Barbados where he was tanning during recess."[32]

In mid-June, all the antagonistic elements of the GOP gathered for a fund-raiser at the Washington Convention Center to celebrate the sixty-sixth birthday of President Bush. Dixie Carter of *Designing Women* fame belted out the national anthem and Whitney Houston sang "One Song," written for the event by Marvin Hamlisch. "Miss Houston, draped in floor-length fur, swept out of the room immediately after performing."[33]

The Democrats were wrestling with their own skeletons. Since 1988, the party had been haunted by the specter of Mike Dukakis and his furlough program that let rapists and murderers out for weekends.

Gingrich had signed a peace accord with Bush, but he was still at war with the Democrats. Dick Cheney, the secretary of defense, was locked in a vinegary fight with the Democrats over military salaries, and Gingrich was in there with the rest of the Republicans, throwing hand grenades at the other party.[34] He said that men and women in uniform were being held "hostage" over a pay-raise issue.

On August 2, 1990, Saddam Hussein invaded Kuwait, starting another kind of war, throwing a new monkey wrench into all arguments for a moment. There was no doubt that US forces could evict him from Kuwait, but some thought the corrupt Kuwaitis were barely worth defending. They were submissive and hedonistic to the point of being denounced by other Gulf countries as "the Lotus Eaters of the Gulf." The small nation was incredibly rich with oil and was ruled by the Al-Sabah family, who mainly kept the wealth and the material goods to themselves. If it was clear that Saddam was not planning to use Kuwait as a base from which to strike Saudi Arabia, and thereby control a great deal of the world's oil, then it was possible the world and the United States would have let him be. The nations of the Middle East had been attacking each other and seizing property for thousands of years. This was no different, really. Except for the presence of oil, America never would have gotten involved.

But Bush and the neocons around him saw this as a moment for presidential leadership, not diplomacy. The only communication with Saddam was to get out of Kuwait. Bush even used the phrase "line in the sand."[35] Most everybody in the Republican Party was on board with taking action against Saddam, including Gingrich.

Bob Dornan, "B-1 Bob," the contentious, flamboyant, ribald, staunch conservative congressman from California, said, "Speak softly and carry a big B-2."[36] He was also on board but he pretty much favored invading anybody, anytime. Bush froze Iraq's financial assets in the United States.

Gingrich expanded on his previous budget proposal. This one was mostly individual tax cuts and cuts in capital gains to stimulate growth in the economy, as many felt it was slowing. It featured other bells and whistles such as special tax breaks for families with dependent children, deferred taxes on investment income, and the like. The Bush White House did not snap it up. By the late summer of 1990, Gingrich was clearly out of favor at the Bush White House, so openly critical was he of the tax increases. He mirthfully compared Bush's plan to "New Coke," a biting reference to the product the Coca-Cola Company wished they had never heard of.[37]

He also made a quick swing thorough Georgia, just long enough to attend a fund-raiser for his reelection that featured famed novelist Tom Clancy, to which tickets were going for fifty dollars apiece.[38]

The Andrews Air Force Base budget negotiations resumed in September after stalling over the summer, and a framework was developing, even as the Bushies treated Gingrich like "the uncle that you didn't want to have at Thanksgiving," said one observer.[39]

Most of what congressional Republicans were offering was in the form of tax credits and breaks. Neither side was pushing for real cuts in federal spending, except for Gingrich, who, later in the month, came up with a bill to allow the president to exempt necessary defense and social programs from the automatic cuts heading their way under Gramm-Rudman.

CHAPTER 22

NERVOUS BREAKDOWN

"Read My Lips—I Lied!"

1990

The American presidency carries with it the personal legacy of each man who has occupied the office. Some legacies are tiny, like that of one-month president William Henry Harrison, who became a trivia question. Others are tragic, like James Buchanan, the most qualified man ever to seek the office and yet one of its most miserable and disappointing failures. Others, such as Washington, Jefferson, Monroe, Lincoln, FDR, and Reagan, left legacies of greatness.

But no man seeks the presidency in order to carry out all the policies of the previous occupant of the Oval Office, even if they are of the same political party. Harry Truman was more aggressive on repairing race relations than FDR and more suspicious of the Soviets. LBJ went much further with government social programs than the more conventional JFK. Certainly Teddy Roosevelt embraced progressivism more assertively than William McKinley ever contemplated. Indeed, presidents who succeeded men of their own party tend to pursue more assertive social and economic policies. A notable exception was Calvin Coolidge, who was more conservative than Warren G. Harding in all aspects, in all pursuits, including fidelity.

George Bush followed the rule rather than the exception in breaking from Ronald Reagan. He rejected Reaganism and all that it stood for. Bush was going to chart his own course. Unfortunately, this set him apart from the optimistic populist conservatism that Reagan had bestowed upon the GOP in January 1989. For many years, the Republicans lacked a coherent governing philosophy, which, for a political party, is like a thoroughbred running the Belmont Stakes without a jockey.

But Bush got into office and jerked the reins of the racing conservative thoroughbred, pulling the confused horse to a halt and then attempting to make it run clockwise. Indeed, in the actual world of racing, confusing and abusing horses in such a fashion can cause them mental anguish, even nervous breakdowns, sometimes leading to their destruction.

Bush caused the conservative GOP to have a nervous breakdown.

He ran an anti-intellectual campaign in 1988, denounced Reaganism with his "kinder and gentler" soggy observations at the convention, and then pursued mostly anti-intellectual programs such as the Flag Burning Amendment, which forced an unnecessary argument between patriotic conservatives and constitutional conservatives. After hundreds of thousands of professional hours, it passed the House 254–177,[1] not nearly the two-thirds required to change the Constitution. Mercifully, the issue died. But the damage had been done.

And then Bush broke his tax pledge, about the one and only deal he'd made with the right and the only measurement of his character in the public arena. Everyone knew he was a good father and husband, but these were measurements of private character, not public. He'd been a war hero, but that was it. As far as they were concerned—both the conservatives and the American public—Bush was of bad character because he'd broken his word. The *New York Post*, never a shrinking violet when it came to summing up a national crisis, printed an issue with the headline "Read My Lips—I Lied!"[2]

The outcry from conservatives was even louder, more explicit, and more earthy. Reagan's former political aide Lyn Nofziger spoke for all: "There's no question the damage is done and he's already confused voters as to whether the Republican party stands for or against tax increases."[3] Nofziger advised candidates running that year to run as fast as possible from Bush.

Pat Buchanan, one of the most popular conservative commentators in the country, wrote a long essay entitled "The End of the Reagan Revolution."[4] He cited an earlier quote by Jack Kemp who said, "If Mr. Bush were nominated, the Reagan Revolution would be over."[5]

Lee Atwater, the still-ailing chairman of the RNC, made a surprise visit to HQ to discuss strategy. In spite of the brain tumor, he was sharp in a meeting with Ed Rollins and Newt Gingrich. The consensus was that Bush would be okay as long as he didn't raise personal rates.[6] They were kidding themselves and Gingrich knew it.

Atwater later issued a statement about the RNC meetings in Chicago—which he did not attend—that he was still watching things, that he was putting GOP operatives Charlie Black and Mary Matalin in temporary charge of the RNC and that "the Doctors tell me that my tumor has stopped growing and is dying."[7] Those who knew him, knew Atwater was spinning his own imminent death.

American conservatism never recovered from the spring, summer, fall, and winter of their discontent with George Bush in 1990. The expansionist government policies of Bush were more akin to those of Richard Nixon—minus the corruption—than they were to Reagan's. Bob Livingston hated the whole ordeal and said, "That was the vote that I regret the most in my 22 years. I got sucked in . . . I drank the Kool-Aid . . ."[8] Livingston succumbed only after heavy and unrelenting pressure by the Bush White House.[9]

There had been a brief interval in which it appeared Gingrich was supporting Bush, and indeed some news reports indicated as much, but his resolve hardened quickly within days of Bush's reversal. He was already on record telling columnists Bob Novak and Rowly Evans that Bush breaking his pledge was "the biggest single mistake" of his presidency.[10] But then, in late July, he bizarrely told the press, "I am prepared to sponsor and support raising taxes."[11] Nobody could figure it out. Had the long days taken their toll? Was Gingrich misquoted? Had he jumped the shark? Gone over to the Dark Side?

The comment threw everything into a state of confusion for several days. Some denounced him, others scratched their heads, and others thought he was deliberating floating a trial balloon just to see how many would shoot at it (many did), but within a few days, after some tap dancing, Gingrich was back on the anti-tax reservation. At the time, he was often in the White House and, on at least one occasion, wrote a handful of notes to allies—all on White House stationary! It included one to Congressman Guy Vander Jagt apologizing for "losing my temper"[12] and another to a member congratulating him for his efforts in the annual congressional baseball game. He was not afraid of name-dropping.[13]

Now he was back to his original position, only harder.

Eccentric economic theorist Jude Wanniski, through his newsletter *Polyconomics, Inc.*, said, "We have House Minority Leader Newt Gingrich to thank for pulling the nation back from the brink of disaster. The best news for us . . . is the emergence of Newt Gingrich as a world-class leader."[14] Wanniski was always exuberant and often ahead of others, but this time he was prophetic. Or seemed to be. A couple of months later, he sent Newt a letter taking much of his praise back, saying that Congressman Joe Kennedy got the best of Gingrich on a CNN discussion because Newt used the word *taxes* rather than *growth*.[15] In short order, Gingrich wrote back with his tongue firmly planted in his cheek, "Dear Jude, You're right. I failed. I'll keep studying."[16]

By August, Gingrich was in open revolt, and the Andrews Air Force Base budget negotiations had all but collapsed. Bush lashed out at the Democrats for not offering any plan, and so did most of the Republicans, including Gingrich, but the Democrats had a pat hand, perfectly willing to let the GOP guess how many aces they were holding. Bush issued an ultimatum to the Democrats. They ignored the bluff, simply saying they were not going to offer any new taxes until they saw the White House's cards.

Letters poured into Gingrich's office, 100 percent in support of him holding the line against the Bush tax increases.

House Budget chairman Leon Panetta, Democratic congressman from California, was clearly enjoying the president's predicament. "We didn't pledge that every time the Republicans slit their wrists that we would slit ours."[17] Bush urged Hill Republicans to get tough on the Democrats, but few took up the call.

At a private dinner of top Republican "wise men" held at the Mayflower Hotel in Washington, John Sununu and Ed Rollins began screaming at each other over the Bush tax increase and Gingrich's opposition to Bush.[18] Word of the formerly private dinner spread quickly throughout Washington.

Gingrich took the bull by the horns and gave a new economic speech, containing some of the items he'd raised before the Committee for a Sound Economy, but this time he ratcheted up the debate even higher, calling for tax *cuts*.[19] "Breaking again with President Bush and other budget negotiators . . .

Gingrich called . . . for big tax cuts instead of tax increases to stimulate the economy and avoid a recession," reported UPI.[20] The speech got a lot of play in the media, and headlines such as "Gingrich Breaks with Bush on Taxes" were common in newspapers around the country.[21]

Gingrich had also signed a direct mail fund-raising piece for his campaign in which he proclaimed, "I strongly believe that increasing taxes on working people will NOT solve our country's massive budget problems! Clearly, cutting wasteful federal spending is the way to balance the federal budget."[22] Rollins also had the first of several tussles with Dick Darman over the tax increases. The conservative Rollins could not understand how it was that the Bush White House was so in love with the collectivist state.[23] And the fund-raising at Rollins's NRCC absolutely dried up, vanished, so upset conservatives were with Bush over the tax increases. Bush told Rollins he would sign no more fund-raising letters for the NRCC, but since his signature was going over like a lead balloon with donors, Rollins heaved a quiet sigh of relief. Rollins's bigger headache was that previously safe incumbents were now surprisingly vulnerable.[24]

Gingrich was earning more favorable profiles from the mainstream media. The Georgian was in the news every day, feeding reporters fresh quotes, so much so that it was a wonder he got anything done. One story in the *Washington Times* by respected journalist Don Lambro called him "the party's chief strategy setter in Congress . . ."[25]

Gingrich had already received phone calls from Administration officials, including Jack Kemp, Dick Cheney, and Dan Quayle, ostensibly to lobby him to support the Bush tax increases, but in fact, in confidence, they each told him in effect to follow his own instincts and oppose them.[26]

It was becoming clear now that the inclusion of Gingrich and Phil Gramm at the Andrews Air Force Base budget summit had been mere window dressing, political cover. The *Wall Street Journal* said as much: "Republican congressional staffers say that Sen. Gramm and Rep. Gingrich were named to the summit negotiating team by Republican leaders who figured they would be more likely to help see any resulting compromise if they participated in reaching it."[27] In other words, the goal was to make these two conservatives into establishment co-conspirators.

Naively, Gramm said, "I can't envision a circumstance where the White House would sign off on a budget agreement if I objected."[28] But it was already out among conservatives that Gramm would do whatever the Administration wanted him to do, while Gingrich was going to oppose higher taxes if it finally came to that.

Over at the conservative Heritage Foundation, Dan Mitchell said of Gingrich, "He realizes that falling on his sword for the White House isn't exactly a great thing to do for his political career."[29] He'd appeared to waver on the matter several times over the spring and summer, but after his newest speech proposing cuts, Gingrich's name was stricken from the Bush Frat House. At the summit meetings, he attempted to cajole fellow Republicans into support of his tax cuts rather than Bush's increases. The once-respectful relationship between him and Budget Director Dick Darman was souring badly.

By September 19, 1990, the Budget Summiteers had less than two weeks to come up with a solution, which was essentially a choice between automatic cuts under Gramm-Rudman, targeted cuts by the Congress and the Administration, or tax increases. An agreement to raise taxes by more than $100 billion was in place, along with concurrent spending cuts over five years. The new federal rates would be on beer, cigarettes, and gasoline—basically the fuel for your average Reagan Democrat. Scheduled for additional federal taxes were "luxury" items such as electronics, boats, planes, cars, and jewelry. The elites' wine was also scheduled for a tax increase. Unsettled was whether to cut capital gains, for which the Bush White House was pushing especially hard. The framework was in its sixth iteration.[30]

Gingrich was now being "excluded" from the budget meetings for having "particularly inveterate views."[31] There was another factor motivating Gingrich in his headlong rush toward tax cuts and away from Bush: his opponent in Georgia, David Worley, was "drooling at the thought" that Newt was "being forced to back President Bush's tax increase."[32] Bush's broken pledge was playing just as badly in Georgia as it was everyplace else.

Worley had won the Democratic nomination to take on Gingrich again. He was still a bit of an oddball and had run a poor campaign in 1988, but had gained a lot of experience and was running a tighter, more focused machine in '90, smartly positioning himself as the populist Democrat and attacking Gingrich as an out-of-touch Washingtonian. When the Congress had voted itself a pay raise in '87, an agreement had been made by both parties not to politicize it. Fat chance. Worley was hanging the raise around Gingrich's neck like a string of garlic.

The irony was Gingrich was seen in Washington as too much of an outsider, but in Georgia, too much of an insider, a curious position for a man who called the bailout of the savings and loan industry "the largest white-collar crime in American history."[33]

Washington was hurtling toward the possibility of a government shutdown. Back in 1981, the federal government had closed for several days, but essential functions continued operating, like air traffic controls and the Social Security Administration, based on a previous legal opinion by President Carter's attorney general, Benjamin Civiletti.[34] Some now said essential services such as food inspection would be shut down or curtailed. Some saw a partial government shutdown as no big thing, not anything most Americans would notice. "But Washingtonians sense that the horrors of sequester are not yet widely appreciated."[35]

The budget summit members met yet again. "Come Monday, Oct. 1, the bulldozer of automatic budget cuts plows into the debt-ridden house of the federal government," prophesied the *Christian Science Monitor*.[36] The chairman of the Federal Reserve, Alan Greenspan, dangled an inducement: if an agreement was made, he'd lower interest rates.

But, if a deal was made, it still had to pass Congress. Asking members to vote for tax increases just weeks before an election was akin to asking them to stick their heads in a guillotine. "Some congressmen resent a Republican president who protects himself at the expense of House Republicans," continued the *CSM* report.[37] Amateur Machiavellians were all over the media. Would the House Republicans win by causing Bush to lose? Did they have a hidden agenda to prefer Gramm-Rudman as a means to shrink government? Stories and columns were rife with speculation.

As events were spinning out of control, new ideas were being floated, including raising the top marginal rates, something that had once been hands-off, and also a "surcharge" on those making more than $500,000 per year. The Bush White House had avoided changing the tax code Reagan had negotiated with Congress just a few years earlier, bringing the top marginal rate down to 28 percent.[38] They wanted the fig leaf of preserving the historic deal so Bush could at least say he had not increased personal income taxes.

All of a sudden Bush, who was once thought to be invincible, was drawing a land rush of attention from major Democrats looking to take him on, including New York governor Mario Cuomo, who had electrified his party with his speech at the Democratic National Convention in San Francisco in 1984.[39]

With a looming crisis in the Middle East, a slowing economy, a budget crisis, and a thousand other problems to attend to, Bush headed off to Kennebunkport for the rest of the summer. Congress did what they liked to do best in August. They took the month off.[40]

Nothing much occurred over the rest of the month if one overlooked a war over taxes and an actual war. *Roll Call* published a list of the undergraduate, advanced, and doctoral degrees of all the members of Congress, as if this meant anything. For the populists out there, far, far, far too many members had "J.D." after their names.[41] A month later, the same publication did a yearbook-like review of the members of Congress—Best Hair went to Congressman Gary Condit of California, Best Smile went to Senator Joe Biden of Delaware, Congressman Charlie Wilson was the Biggest Flirt, and Gingrich and Bob Dole won for Best Sound Bites.[42]

For this August recess, Dr. Gingrich and his sound bites were heading down to Georgia.

CHAPTER 23

THE WHIP WHO WENT
OUT INTO THE COLD

*"He has reasserted himself as the natural
leader of the conservative movement."*

1990

During the August recess, Newt Gingrich met his opponent, David Worley, in a freewheeling one-hour radio debate in Atlanta. There, Worley repeatedly brought up the congressional pay raise while, according to count, the word *liberal* was issued by Gingrich "at least two dozen times."[1] Gingrich claimed the pay increase actually cost him money since outside income had also been severely restricted. To the workers in Georgia making $17,000 a year, the argument engendered no sympathy. Gingrich pulled down more than ten times as much as they did.

Worley had come loaded for bear and had learned a lot about politics since his last go-around with Newt. Gingrich had more irons in the fire than could be counted, including chairing a GOP group called "Republican Action for the '90s," but as his race was shaping up in Georgia, some were betting that he wouldn't be around for the 1990s. Not as a member of Congress anyway. Worley had come up with a simple but effective slogan: "Boot Newt." It was catching on in Georgia.

For his work over the summer in pushing back against the Bush Administration's proposal to raise taxes, Gingrich was earning high praise from some in his conference. Typical were the comments of Tom DeLay of Texas who said, "Many of us in the House are so proud of Newt's leadership on this issue . . ."[2]

Gingrich was asked his opinion in early September of the odds of hammering out a budget deal. He said there was a one-in-three chance.[3]

Some members were frankly sick and tired of the whole summit process and looking for alternatives. "We've gotten nowhere," lamented Dick Armey.[4] There was discussion over a short-term solution rather than the five-year plan the summiteers hoped to achieve.

Dick Gephardt defended the process, saying, "The talks are not collapsed. We're just moving them to a different stage."[5] Both sides were in general agreement on luxury taxes on cars, boats, "small private aircraft, expensive electronics, jewelry and furs."[6] They also agreed to increase taxes on cigarettes, alcohol, life insurance, and airline tickets. They basically planned to get taxpayers coming and going.

And yet, the Democrats wanted even more. They wanted additional taxes of 20 percent on incomes of $125,000 or more, and higher taxes on gasoline than what was being proposed.[7] Most of what congressional Republicans were offering was in the form of tax credits and breaks. Neither side was pushing for real cuts in federal spending, except for Gingrich, who came up with a bill to allow the president to exempt necessary defense and social programs from the automatic cuts heading their way under Gramm-Rudman.

Washington was traveling along two tracks: Iraq and taxes. As the Mideast crisis grew, Bush's job approval ratings continued to climb again, but even then, more than 60 percent of the American people thought the economy had slipped into a recession, the first one in eight years.[8]

Acidly, Gingrich said of Bush, "The Congress and Saddam Hussein are the two groups he doesn't seem able to work with."[9] Bob Dole was also grouchy, which was about the only thing he and Gingrich shared.

Iraq and taxes changed everyone's plans, especially the two political parties. The plan for the Democrats had been to go after the Republicans on the economy and abortion, and the plan for the Republicans had been to run a national anti-incumbent campaign. All that went out the window.

The stressful situation in Washington was showing. Gingrich let loose with a string of invectives against the Democrats over the budget, calling them in a memo "sick, pathetic, liberal, incompetent, tax-spending traitors,"[10] familiar language to GOP partisans who had been following him closely. Dole upbraided him for the language, happy to have a chance to embarrass his younger House colleague.

Stress was also manifesting itself on national television.

Senator Fritz Hollings of South Carolina and Sam Donaldson of ABC mixed it up over textiles, among other things. "Senator, you're from the great textile-producing state of South Carolina. Is it true you have a Korean tailor?" To which Hollings shot back, "Well, I tell you the truth, I think I got that suit right down the street where . . . you got that wig, uh, Sam."[11]

The *Post* Style section ran a snarky profile of Senator John Warner of Virginia, not commonly thought to be a member of Mensa, yet married twice to beautiful and wealthy women: first to Catherine "Bunny" Mellon, from whom he divorced but got a fabulous country estate and a lot of money, and then famed movie star Elizabeth Taylor, from whom he got a seat in the US Senate. Along the way he had also been secretary of the navy. The headline for the report said, "If John Warner Is So Dumb, Why Is His Life So Good?"[12]

The two sides were far apart on almost everything, but counting the proposal by Gingrich, there were actually three sides. Of the suggestion advanced by some to raise taxes, Gingrich sniped, "Don't punish the country because you hate the rich."[13] Adding further to the budget dilemma, Bush had given up the ghost on cutting capital gains taxes, leaving his party hanging out to dry. Some had hoped to keep the measure in and trade with the Democrats for a raise in the top marginal rate.

At the last moment, the Bush White House and the Democrats came up with an agreement to raise taxes by more than $130 billion on cigarettes, gasoline, and alcohol, while unspecified cuts in spending were established as well.[14] The Bush plan also called for those who had lost their jobs to wait two weeks before filing for unemployment and an increase in Medicare taxes.

Gingrich was skeptical to say the least, though he did not attack it right away. Cigarette taxes would go up by 50 percent, the beer tax would double, and the appallingly high $12.50 tax on a gallon of hard liquor would increase by $1.20.[15] Gasoline would go up by 5 cents per gallon in 1990 and another 5 cents in 1991. And yet the proposal featured a third, hidden 2-cents-per-gallon tax on gasoline. There were so-called luxury taxes right off the board game Monopoly, but it was window dressing: the boat tax did not kick in until purchases over $100,000.[16] Only people like the Bushes had yachts worth that much. George Will sniffed that smokers and beer drinkers could handle the additional federal taxes, though he did warn liberals to "stay away from yacht dealers."[17]

Deductions for high earners would fall, thereby effectively increasing their taxes, and Medicare payments made by the elderly would go up. The *New York Times* called it a "major increase in taxes . . ."[18] On the last day of September, Bush and the congressional negotiators gathered in the Rose Garden to meet the press and announce the deal. One member of Congress was missing, however. "The political strain that the negotiations have engendered was illustrated by the absence from the Rose Garden meeting of . . . Newt Gingrich . . . ," observed the *New York Times*.[19]

Before the Rose Garden ceremony, Bush met in the Cabinet Room with the summit negotiators and went around the room, demanding fealty from each. Each pledged yes to the president, except Gingrich, who told Bush, "I feel it is my duty to tell you it won't pass the House."[20] Gingrich later described Bush as "p--sed off."[21] Later, at a party fund-raiser, Bush gave Gingrich the cold shoulder, except to say, "You are killing us."[22] No matter. He and his conservative revolutionaries were going to the mattresses. "If they want a war, we will give them a war . . . ," Gingrich vowed.[23] Plus, they wanted respect, which they weren't getting from the Bush White House. "We need to be dealt with respectfully, or we will prove to them that we're an independent center of power."[24]

All in all, there was something for everyone to oppose, something for everyone to get angry over. The deal was not overly complicated and neither were the politics. The Republican Party had split into two organisms and a showdown between the two was looming. There was debate over whether this was the largest tax increase in American history . . . or just the second-largest tax increase in American history.

The politics were atrocious for the GOP. Bush had given up his tax pledge, he'd given up on cutting capital gains, federal spending would increase, and all entitlements (except Medicare) were spared. Most of the anticipated savings would come out of Defense. Surpluses were projected several years down the road. John Sununu groused on CNN and to other media about Gingrich balking at the last minute.[25]

Bush spoke to the press and said, "I will do everything I can to lay aside partisanship here and to take the case for this deal to the American people in every way I can." Tom Foley, Speaker of the House, was equal to the task: "We pledge our efforts with yours to convince our colleagues . . ."[26] Senators Phil Gramm and Bob Dole were there, also promising support and passage, attacking those who opposed it. Liberals were already signaling their opposition, just as conservatives were. The *New York Times* took note with a headline, "Deficit Pact Blurs Party Boundaries."[27] Outside the party boundaries, inside the conservative movement, the proletariat was massing, unwilling to grab their forelocks in deference to their betters. After his falling out with Bush, Gingrich phoned his friend and colleague Bob Walker and said, "I think I just declared war." Shortly thereafter, the two, joined by others, began "lining up folks against the president."[28]

Within hours, the civil war in the GOP was being reported in the nation's media. Gingrich by this point had come out ferociously against the plan and was buttonholing fellow Republicans to oppose the bill based on the higher gasoline taxes. Rumors were going around that Gingrich was gunning for Michel's job. Capitol Hill was knee-deep in bad blood. Things were especially bad between their respective staffs, according to Congressman Bob Walker.[29]

Dan Quayle was deployed to Capitol Hill to quell the insurrection, but it was to no avail. He spoke like an insider to a bunch of outsiders and left the field of battle badly defeated. Call it a bar brawl, call it a family feud, call it a donnybrook, but whatever it was called, it was a full-scale revolution inside the Republican Party.

Gingrich went public, saying the plan would "lose jobs, raise taxes and deepen the recession."[30] Gingrich went on CBS's *America Tonight* with Leslie Stahl to explain how he as the Whip could take on his own president.[31] White House officials were described as "very upset" with Gingrich.[32] A Newt ally, Vin Weber, said Gingrich "is not dumb enough to pick a fight with the president of the United States . . . to advance his own interests."[33] Some weren't so sure.

Gingrich fought back, trying to make it understood he was not George Bush's Whip, but the Whip for the House Republicans. The White House and their allies were making it about loyalty to Bush; the conservatives were making it about loyalty to principles. Bush aides, including Dick Darman and John Sununu, were deployed to help quell the war, but bringing these two into the fight was akin to pouring napalm on an inferno. Sununu appeared before the House GOP conference, but it ended up an ugly mess. At one point, Bob Walker told Sununu that the Bush White House had no vision, to which the chief of staff replied, "Our vision is to be the problem solving administration." Gingrich and Walker went slack jawed. When Walker pushed back, Sununu replied, "Walker, you're full of s--t."[34]

The media was already beginning to tear apart the deal, examining the inequities of the treatment of a two-income household and how, with the proposed limitation on deductions for higher incomes, it effectively pushed those houses into paying higher taxes just as if the marginal rates had been increased. There were even more convoluted tax proposals, and this only served to make people madder, as if someone was trying to pull the wool over their eyes.

In an attempt to quell the growing outrage, Bush gave a nationally broadcast speech from the Oval Office, making the case for higher taxes. It flopped. The message was that the new taxes were "needed to keep the economy out of recession . . ." He further "appeal[ed] to voters not to punish politicians who support it."[35] Curiously, Bush's strongest argument was that the new revenue was for funding the troops in the Middle East, but he did not delve deeply into this point. It was only two months earlier that Saddam Hussein had invaded Kuwait.

Leading a band of conservative renegades, Gingrich announced he would organize and lead a fight against the Bush tax increases on the floor of the House. In fact, most of the fight would be carried out in the media and political circles. "Mr. Bush's task is complicated by the public defiance of Representative Newt Gingrich . . . who should be rallying the troops on Capitol Hill but instead has broken with the bipartisan budget agreement," noted the *New York Times*.[36]

The word *revolt* appeared in every news article about the Bush-versus-Gingrich budget fight. The Bush White House fought back with Dan Quayle, their liaison to the conservative movement. He went on *Nightline* and was pummeled by Ted Koppel, with Jeff Greenfield throwing in a few kicks for good measure, calling him "much maligned . . . Quayle is still grappling with the ghost of 1988, the image of a man out of his depth, the butt of a thousand punch lines . . ."[37]

From the standpoint of constitutional government and traditionalism, the budget process was also frowned upon because it put the power of the budget in the hands of the White House and a few members of Congress, as opposed to the tried-and-true system, which had used the committee process and testimony to hammer out a federal budget. "It's not the way congress is supposed to work," said Thomas Mann of the Brookings Institute. "This is an extraordinarily centralized and expedited process . . ."[38]

Indeed it was probably unconstitutional, as it clearly violated the separation of powers. The argument in favor of the new process said the old process inevitably led to disaster. All knew what was going on, though; the Washington Buddy System had falsely used the "crisis" of the automatic budget cuts to scare people into accepting higher taxes and more government. But when Alan Greenspan put his "Good Housekeeping" stamp of approval on the budget deal, all of inside Washington breathed a sigh of relief. As chairman of the Federal Reserve, his word and opinion were final. Bush had already gone on national television to make an appeal to the American people to put pressure on their congressmen to vote to raise their taxes. He called the deficit a "cancer." He called on the American people to "bear a small burden" and implored that it was "our last, best chance to get the federal deficit under control."[39] In the "rebuttal," Senate Majority Leader George Mitchell followed Bush and endorsed the president's plan for tax increases.[40]

But according to congressional sources, "calls and mail . . . were . . . running heavily against the plan."[41] Gingrich went on *MacNeil/Lehrer* to report that 83 percent of calls to his office were running against Bush. He said that on Capitol Hill among congressmen he'd spoken to, phone calls were 3–1 opposed to the tax increases. He was firm in his opposition, but was also polite and even kind in his references to Bush, disappointing his red-meat supporters.[42]

The vote was coming up quickly, just hours away, and no one seemed to know whether it would pass. John Cochran of NBC News reported that Gingrich observed that the speech by Bush "failed to win over the nation . . ."[43] Both sides thought the vote would be close. Worrisome for Bush, Congressman Dan Rostenkowski came out against the plan at the last moment, steamed that he as the chairman of the Ways and Means Committee had been ignored in the process.

As the clock struck 1:00 a.m. on October 5, 1990, Newt Gingrich became the official leader of the opposition within his own party. He led 105 fellow Republicans in voting against the Bush tax increase. He did not rise to speak out against the bill, preferring to let others do that. There was some nervousness among his troops, but as soon as they counted the Democrats, they knew the increase was about to go down in flames. Gingrich's friend and lieutenant Bob Walker was so confident, he watched a Pittsburg Pirates game in the cloakroom.

Democrats voted in higher numbers against the budget than for it, but that did not matter. All the attention was on the House Republicans and Gingrich. The White House summoned up every resource to pressure them, but it was for naught. House Speaker Tom Foley made an impassioned plea for the budget deal, but it was no soap. In the time before the vote, one of his own, Democrat James Traficant of Ohio, alluding to the suspected criminality of Congress, rose on the floor and said, "Tonight, we'll find out if the death penalty really is a deterrent."[44]

Another Democrat, eighty-one-year-old George Crockett, had wearied of the deliberations, so he went to his office to take a snooze. When his alarm sounded, despite his two hearing aids, he did not rise from his slumber and missed the vote.[45]

The vote wasn't even close. Bush's budget went down 254–179. Many Democrats joined in with Gingrich's Rebellious Republicans. Why should they take the heat for a tax increase when Bush's own party refused to?

It was a signal moment in the history of Republicanism and conservatism. Republican presidents usually got their way, even when members of their own party had differing notions. Richard Nixon got much from Congress, as had Ronald Reagan, but they had a hold over conservatives that Bush did not possess. Indeed, as of this vote, Gingrich now had a greater hold over American conservatism than any elected official in America. Reagan was still *numero uno* and would always be, but he was happily retired in California, riding horses, spending time alone with Nancy.

Overnight, Gingrich became the most important elected conservative in America. His defiance and disregard for the presidential endorsement angered Senate Minority Leader Bob Dole, who was quoted in *Newsweek* as saying, "You pay a price for leadership. If you don't want to pay the penalty, maybe you ought to find another line of work."[46]

Washington and the nation were thunderstruck.

In stark terms, the *Washington Post* reported, "The bipartisan budget agreement failed its first legislative test early today in a sharp embarrassment to President Bush . . . Three-fifths of the House Republicans followed House Minority Whip Newt Gingrich (R-Ga.) who opposed the deal, rather than their president . . ."[47]

Others, however, were jubilant. A Democratic congressman walked into a post-vote leadership meeting and quipped, "Where's President Gingrich?"[48] More seriously, Stephen Hess of the Brookings Institute and one of the reliable "wise men of Washington" said, "If we were a parliamentary form of government, the government would have fallen last night and the Queen would have called in Newt Gingrich and asked him if he could form a new government."[49] Bush's entire suit of armor had been shucked. Shortly, much of the government began to shut down.

Gingrich said the American people had "defeated the package" and not himself.[50] He called it a "tidal wave of anger."[51]

The reaction of the Bush White House was not to pick up the pieces or change the negotiating process or back off on raising taxes: the reaction was to instigate a whisper campaign to unseat Gingrich as minority whip.[52]

No doubt some House Republicans were angry with Newt, but since more than half had joined him in opposing Bush, all it did was prove once again that the Bush White House was very poor at counting.

Still, it was tricky ground. Bush was still the commander in chief, and thousands of US troops had been deployed to Saudi Arabia as a staging ground for a possible invasion of Kuwait with the goal of evicting Saddam Hussein. If not handled adroitly, attacking Bush could be interpreted as being unpatriotic, which was just fine with the Bush White House.

John Sununu and Dick Darman now came in for some very harsh press. The *New York Times* described their retinue as "bad-cop, bad-cop."[53] Washingtonians chortled; schadenfreude was one of the city's favorite dishes. A Republican member of Congress, Ralph Regula of Ohio, had voted against the tax increase and in retaliation the Bush White House demanded the return of tickets to the president's box at the Kennedy Center.[54] Regula took his constituents to a movie instead.

Tom Edsall, a well-regarded scribe for the *Post*, did his own analysis of the vote. He quoted a GOP consultant as saying, "We may have seen a Republican House whip 'Carterize' his own president." Deep into the story, Edsall nailed the phenomenon: "The Republican Party, in turn, has split into a governing party led by George Bush and a revolutionary wing, led by Gingrich and allies in both the House and in the conservative movement, determined to take over Congress for the GOP."[55] He saw that Gingrich had a larger and longer purpose to refashion both parties with the Democrats as the organizer of big government and the GOP as the instrument of less government and less taxes, in line with the Reagan model.[56] It was, as Edsall saw it, a "realignment strategy."[57]

At an emergency cabinet meeting, officials openly criticized Sununu and Darman, "fretting that the two men were too eager for revenge against Representative Newt Gingrich."[58]

The Administration attempted to restart the negotiations, not with their own party but with the loyal opposition, which only served to harden Pharaoh Gingrich's heart.

Meanwhile, Washington was awash with anecdotes and minutia about the closing of the Washington Monument and national parks. "The Smithsonian Institution [and the] Washington Monument" and other popular sites were closed, among them the gallery in the House, which was often filled with tourists watching the sausage being made.[59] All the tiny, bite-sized innuendo circulating were designed to get men and women of principle to break their principles and embrace the politically expedient.

"Mindful of public perceptions and of constituents in town who were locked out of the capital's tourist attractions, members talked more about the shuttered museums than about the real devastation that could be wrought by a closed Government," said the *New York Times*.[60] Saner people knew that if federal workers were cut back by one day, the earth would not stop spinning on its axis.

The Democrats poured it on, playing the "warm heart–cold heart" card. "We're dealing with real human beings, and their families, and their hopes and fears and concerns," wailed Senator George Mitchell of Maine.[61] A game of chicken went on in Washington for a couple of days about stopgap spending measures and the like, while behind the scenes an even worse bill was being constructed, if Gingrich and company were to be believed.

Republicans were taking pot shots at the Bushies, and on the record and for attribution, too, a sure sign of executive weakness.

Several agonizing days passed for George Bush. He was so invested in his own plan to raise taxes, the shadings and half meanings and qualified phrases were thrown to the wind. He was bound and determined to raise taxes rather than allow the automatic spending cuts to kick in. The top rate on income taxes was still at 28 percent, but several days later, Bush signaled that he'd be receptive to raising this to 31 percent.[62] Bob Livingston of New Orleans was dismissive. He voted against the new bill. So did Gingrich and 134 other Republicans, even more than had voted against the first one. It was astonishing and a giant rebuke to George Herbert Walker Bush. He'd unified the party—against himself.

Finally, a new budget passed 250–164.[63] Conservative Republicans gagged. Only 32 Republicans voted for it, along with 218 Democrats. The bill passed at two o'clock in the morning on Columbus Day, the anniversary of the day on which America was discovered.[64] If anything, Gingrich's influence over the GOP Conference had grown significantly in just a few days. It was certainly more than Bush had as of October 1990.

The new bill had more new taxes, all up front. The spending cuts were amorphous and loaded at the back end, in subsequent years, which meant they were almost certain not to be made. Vague references were made to cuts of $100 billion all the way up to $500 billion, but no one and everyone knew it was all a fraud anyway.

Even in the Senate, with Bob Dole carrying Bush's water overtime, 24 Republicans voted for the bill and 20 voted against. It passed 66–33. Dole was a war hero, a stand-up guy, a man of enormous character, but also someone who so desperately wanted to be a part of the "game," as he called it, that he sometimes let this color his judgment.[65] He pleaded with the press that his job was to be responsible and that his name was not "Newt Dole."[66]

Still, Gingrich came down as the big winner, and not just in the conservative media (such as it was), but also with Bill Safire, columnist for the *New York Times*: "Newt rightly put loyalty to the party's principles ahead of Presidential discipline . . ."[67]

Bush came down as the big loser and a permanently damaged political leader. No longer did conservatives take him at his word, flimsy as that was even before breaking the no-tax pledge: "The White House has been just floating, without any strong ties to causes or issues or philosophy," waxed the *Times*. "George Bush doesn't understand people who really believe and are really committed and who don't want to compromise on principles in the budget process, because he is the ultimate pragmatist who just wants to make government work."[68]

Richard Viguerie, godfather of the New Right, went even further: "George Bush has destroyed his base, he will never put Humpty Dumpty back together again. The only core base he pays attention to is the Yale Alumni Association."[69]

CHAPTER 24

FALLOUT

*"We're really getting slaughtered, because the president
looks indecisive and the Administration looks rudderless."*

1990

President George Bush went for a jog. A phalanx of reporters were at
the ready with note pads and cameramen, film and videotape whirring.
When he was asked what he would do to clean up the White House mess,
the president smirked and pointed to either side of his torso as he ran by
and remarked, "Read my hips."[1] He was mocking the "read my lips" solemn
promise he'd made to the American people a little over two years earlier. In
this gesture, he revealed that the tax pledge was just a cynical campaign ploy.
No one would ever truly trust George Herbert Walker Bush again.

A Bush aide dejectedly told *Newsweek*, "The public is not laughing."[2]

George Will weighed in again. His judgments were almost always
heeded. In a column dripping with contempt, he ripped George Bush, his
policies, and his staff:

> What has been described as Bush's modesty is actually arrogance. He is
> governing less by continuous acts of public consent than by a small elites'
> entitlement, the right of the political class to take care of business cozily.
> By his capital-gains obsession, Bush is dissipating the principal Reagan
> effect on the Republican Party, the appeal to those blue-collar Democrats
> for a while stopped seeing Republicans as "the rich."[3]

In just a few months, Bush's poll numbers had plummeted, despite
the growing potential for war in the Middle East. The dragged-out budget

273

negotiations, plus the fact that Bush had broken his pledge and now found himself defending the rich, had caused his approval rating to rocket downward from 76 percent approval and 16 percent disapproval in early September 1990 to 49 percent approval and 30 percent disapproval as of the first week of November.[4] It was an astonishing 41 percent turnaround, demonstrating what little hold Bush had on the American people.

Newt Gingrich went on NBC's *Today* with Deborah Norville. She asked him if he was aware of things that Bush was not aware of to justify his opposition of higher taxes. Gingrich replied, "Well, maybe we have a slightly different perspective."[5] The subtlety of class warfare within the GOP was lost on no one. The *Independent*, a London paper, said, "In its next phase, over the coming week, the budget impasse may turn into a simple, brutal battle between the parties. But so far it has been more illuminating to see it as a Republican-Republican quarrel: Bushism versus Gingrichism; George against Newt."[6] Of Gingrich's ambitions, the paper expanded, proclaiming, "His many enemies say his ambitions are far-fetched: to become the first Republican Speaker since 1955 and to reclaim the Reagan legacy, as President Gingrich, by the end of the century."[7]

Gingrich was soaring among his people in Washington, but his campaign in Georgia was in sick shape. Because of the protracted negotiations, he was still in Washington, still debating the budget as of the last week in October like most everybody else. Few times had Congress stayed in session this late, this close to the elections.

Two years earlier, the Democrats' congressional elections unit had given David Worley the maximum amount, $50,000, but this time, figuring he was a lamb before the slaughter once again, they only gave him $5,000. It was a poor decision. While Gingrich was fighting Bush and the White House over taxes on the average American, Worley was running hard-hitting radio ads attacking Gingrich for voting for a pay raise and for riding around Washington in a taxpayer-funded limousine, which was all true.

At a particularly bad time, while Americans were shelling out as much as $1.65 for a gallon of gasoline, it became known that an unmarked little shack on Capitol Hill was where members of the congressional leadership— including Gingrich—could fill up their gas tanks for free. The perk was supposedly for their government limos, but it was an open secret that they also filled the tanks of their personal cars.[8]

The final-final-final budget deal had been voted on, and again the majority of House Republicans—including Gingrich, of course—voted against it. Even with the advantage of time and motion, the Bush White House had brought only a few Republicans over to their way of seeing things. Forty-seven GOPers sided with Bush and 126 sided with Gingrich. Nonetheless, it passed. The final vote on the Bill With No Name was a squeaker, 228–220, again, another major embarrassment for Bush, despite the outcome.

Hatred for Gingrich and the conservatives was now widespread in Bushland. The Democrats were enchanted that all the debate over the new taxes was on the right side of the spectrum and inside the GOP.

"It's a crazy time and a lot of people are irritable," said Ed Rollins. "They [the Bushes] can only hate one of us at a time. One week it was Saddam Hussein, one week it was Newt Gingrich, and me today."[9] Rollins had been audaciously telling GOP House candidates to *run against* the Bush White House.

Bush personally tried to fire Rollins from his post at the NRCC but could only wish that he could fire Newt from his in Congress. There was some idle speculation that Gingrich might challenge Bush in the 1992 party primaries. The phrase "civil war" was used over and over to describe the ugly split in the GOP. It was even reported that Bush had refused to shake Gingrich's hand.[10]

Newsweek's Eleanor Clift, Tom DeFrank, and others leveled Bush: "He made incomprehensible jokes. He was strangely eager to please even those who were fighting him, and powerless to punish defectors. As in the bad old days, he looked goofy. In the resulting chaos in Washington . . . a Bush League of stumblebums . . ."[11] John Cochran of ABC said, brutally, "[Bush] got his head handed to him."[12] Washington columnist and funnyman Mark Shields was telling a joke around town: "George Bush is in a room with Saddam Hussein, Moamar Kaddafi and Newt Gingrich and he's got a gun with two bullets. What does he do? He shoots Newt Gingrich twice."[13]

Again, rumors cropped up that the Bush White House was attempting to oust Gingrich as Whip. But Democratic congressman Jim Cooper of Tennessee said that Gingrich's maneuvers had been so complete, "he has become de facto speaker of the House."[14]

With the budget deal over, members rushed back to their districts to pick through the rubble of many of their campaigns. Weighing on the Republicans was Bush's standing, with one frank GOP operative speculating, "If the Nov. 6 results are as bad as they appear, the consensus will be that George Bush blew it."[15] The *Los Angeles Times* reported that GOP consultants were in "near-panic."[16]

Evans and Novak called the whole mess, "The most humiliating defeat in Congress by any Republican president in recent history."[17] Of Gingrich, Novak said on CNN that he was "much stronger now . . . A major figure in this town, not to be trifled with."[18]

The Republican Party was broken in two, more badly broken than at any time in the past, save the 1976 primary campaign between Gerald Ford and Ronald Reagan. The previous cultural differences between the populist conservatives and the insular moderates had gone mostly undiscussed. The fights had been more about ideology and issues. Now it was about everything. And, to top it all off, absolutely no one thought the budget deal would bring down the deficit. The real by-product was the rising anti-incumbent tide at work in the land. The only thing holding it back was the situation in the Middle East, and the growing prospects for war. The very same people who wanted to throw the bums out were also deeply patriotic citizens who supported their president in a time of national crisis.

Gingrich high-tailed it back to his district, like nearly every other House member, to squeeze out a few days of campaigning. Gingrich hadn't been back to the Sixth in a month. Frankly, the situation had deteriorated badly, as Worley and the *Atlanta Constitution* had been pounding him daily. "Even before his election as minority whip, Mr. Gingrich seemed more interested in flighty ideology than in the problems of his district . . ."[19]

Gingrich's campaign had been running radio commercials claiming that Worley had not paid any income taxes for three years, but Worley labeled them false and demanded their withdrawal and an apology. Worley produced his tax returns, proving he had indeed paid his federal income taxes, although he'd been campaigning full-time for the past three years. He charged that Gingrich was "drunk with power."[20] It was all eerily reminiscent of several years earlier, when a hard-charging young candidate was making the very same accusations against Jack Flynn that Worley was now making against Newt.

Still, no one outside of Worley's campaign, and certainly nobody in Washington, thought he had a chance of beating Gingrich.

Gingrich also had other headaches, including a legal tab of more than

$145,000 from the various complaints filed against him. He used his campaign funds to pay the lawyers, but that did not look good to the public or the contributors.[21] Like most other campaigns, consultants were pulling in more and more of the money raised, and entertainment for these interlopers was often more costly than entertainment for constituents. It was reported that as of October 1990, more than $36 million had been spent on consultants just on House races.[22] Millions more were being spent on these marginally talented political commissars by Senate, gubernatorial, and local contests. The average House campaign spent $130,968 on consultants in 1990; so far Gingrich had spent $265,874.[23]

Following the months-long debacle in DC, a GOP operative quipped, "When Newt Gingrich beats the White House and the entire congressional leadership you've got a problem."[24] Nationally, Gingrich's reputation was enhanced. Rollins took note, saying yes, "the guy is tedious, he's also the hardest working guy in the world . . . he can be charming."[25] Rollins and Gingrich had an excellent working relationship, seeing the world in approximately the same way. They could argue and grouse, but rarely raised their voices to each other.[26]

It seemed to all that Gingrich would cruise to another solid win in Georgia's Sixth. Worley's campaign manager, Kate Head, was focused, however. "Gingrich spends more time on TV than he does in the district."[27]

In an odd way, Gingrich's campaign against the president had undercut him. Combating Bush had not helped him with loyal Republicans, but the worsening domestic and world situations were also not helping him. He was getting blamed for taking on Bush, but he was also getting blamed for the current state of the country—for which he'd taken on Bush in the first place. He was getting little credit for challenging the tax increases because, in the end, they'd gone through. Marginal voters would take it out on incumbents. A giant majority wanted the Congress replaced. The term *free fall* was bandied about when it came to GOP candidates. Contributions to the national Republican committees had dried up. Rollins was forced to borrow $5 million just to keep the doors open at the NRCC.[28]

Worley hammered Gingrich over voting for the congressional pay raise, over voting against an increase in the minimum wage, how the Sixth ranked at the back of the pack in terms of federal boodle, and, of course, the strike by Eastern Airlines employees, where Gingrich seemed to side with management over labor. Worley employed a lot of good sound bites, a big improvement over two years earlier. "Maybe he can push the President of the United States around, but he can't push us."[29] It was good cleavage; it cut Gingrich off from his base *and* from loyal Bush supporters.

Gingrich also got inferentially dragged into the "Keating Five" scandal, which had nearly sunk a number of US senators, including John McCain. A letter had surfaced that Gingrich had signed, asking a government regulatory board if it was going too far in pursuing its investigation of suspected savings and loan banks. Gingrich had not taken any money from Charles Keating, the figure at the center of Lincoln Savings and Loan, as had McCain, but the timing of the letter caused more damage to his reelection chances. Another signer of the letter was Dick Cheney.

Worley didn't miss a trick. He called on Gingrich to "come home, apologize and explain his role in helping jailed S&L operator Charles Keating. This is just further proof that Newt is part of the problem in Washington."[30] Worried, Gingrich's campaign unveiled a number of hard-hitting radio commercials as the days dwindled down toward the election. Worley was getting to Gingrich's right on populism, on being against any form of gun control, eliminating franked mail, and repealing the $35,000 congressional pay raise.[31]

On Election Day, Republican challengers were wiped out. Prior, some GOP Pollyanna-types had talked of defeating Senator John Kerry in Massachusetts. But any hopes of off-year gains had been decimated by the policies of the national GOP and the Bush Administration. Republican incumbents held on as best they could. The media were banned from their Washington "victory" celebration.

In North Carolina, Jesse Helms—aided by a controversial ad that depicted a white man being passed over for a job because of quotas and awarded to a black man—won reelection over Harvey Gantt, the black mayor of Charlotte. He chortled to the crowd, "I've been at home watching the grieving face of Dan Rather . . . The mighty, ultra-liberal establishment has struck out again."[32]

Ann Richards won in Texas for governor, thereby guaranteeing her a national platform from which to torment George Bush, whom she loathed, and who, in return, was loathed by all the Bushes. Democrats also took the governorship of Florida. In Vermont, the Socialist candidate for Congress, Bernie Sanders, defeated the incumbent Republican, Peter Smith, who had voted for the Bush tax increase.[33]

Across America, Republican incumbents lost. The Democrats won five million more votes than did their minority counterparts. An exception was the victory in a Pennsylvania congressional race of an unknown, Rick Santorum, who beat a seven-term incumbent by running as a populist outsider.

The national election was widely seen as a vote of "no confidence" in George Herbert Walker Bush, who had over the year appeared at more than one hundred GOP fund-raisers.

As for the Georgia Sixth, it was close. It was astonishingly close. It was unbelievably close. It was "shorter than pie crust," as they say in the rural South. Gingrich—by a nose and an eyelash—defeated David Worley after the recount of a recount, which was only completed two weeks after the November 1990 elections. The final margin after the final recount was even tighter than it had been on Election Day. Gingrich won by less than one-half of 1 percent. Gingrich was finally declared the winner by 972 votes out of 156,740 cast.[34]

No one saw it coming, least of all the national media, all of whom had predicted an easy reelection for him. His own polling showed a cakewalk. Just days before the election, the Washington Post reported, "Gingrich appears to be in no serious jeopardy . . ."[35] Plus, Gingrich was outspending his opponent better than 4–1, more than $1 million to around a quarter of a million.[36] In articles published after the outcome had been decided, voters made clear they hoped Newt had gotten the message that he had become too full of himself.

The situation in Washington would be no better for Gingrich. The Bushies were still gunning for him and his colleagues in the House were making noises about taking him out of the number two position. The Democrats, having missed the chance to go all in for Worley, were vowing not to make that mistake in 1992.

As 1990 wound down, the National Council of Teachers of English awarded their annual "Doublespeak Award" to George Bush for "grossly deceptive, evasive, euphemistic, confusing or self-contradictory" statements for reversing his position on taxes. Third place went to Newt Gingrich, also for reversing his position on taxes.[37]

The war inside the GOP was not over; far from it, it had actually widened. In fact, it had stretched to all fronts, as far as the eye could see. Burton Yale Pines of the Heritage Foundation grouched, "It took Richard Nixon six years to destroy the Republican Party. Bush has done it in two."[38]

Gingrich, despite his scare in the election, did not back off at all on the matter of taxes or the philosophical makeup of the GOP. Some thought he'd pull back and keep a low profile. Instead, he was expanding his interests to the whole party, seeing from the perspective of the past two years how things had gone so badly off the rails for the Republicans. "What we need is not hard choices, it's hard thinking," he said.[39]

To make his point on what was wrong with the Bush White House and the sad state of the party, Gingrich called for the resignation of Richard Darman as Bush's budget-meister. In a speech to the American Legislative Exchange Council, Gingrich compared Darman to Michael Dukakis, which was basically an assault on Darman's manhood. He also called Darman a "technocrat," which was another broadside; he was on a roll. "Ideological battles matter," he said.[40] This was tantamount to a declaration of permanent war against the Bushies. He also played the populist card: "I'm not as smart as the director of the budget—I didn't go to the Kennedy School."[41]

Darman refused to address Gingrich's charges but there was nothing that would quell the mêlée inside the GOP. A profile of Gingrich said his "political passions are in a state of permanent arousal . . ."[42]

Gingrich also urged Bush to adopt a veto stratagem against the Democrats, but no one at the White House was interested in anything he had to say. There was a war on, and it was cultural and it was ideological and it was personal. Numerous stories were devoted to the problems plaguing the GOP—again—and everybody in Washington knew John Sununu was gunning for Gingrich and others he deemed insufficiently supportive of Bush. To call the GOP a "soap opera" was an insult to daytime programming. The Bush White House was described as in a "meltdown" and in "disarray."[43]

Vice President Dan Quayle had better political judgment than many gave him credit for, but when he was off, he was awful. As the Gulf War loomed, he made a nasty crack about the "McGovern-Buchanan axis . . . There is a strain of isolationist sentiment in our party."[44] He went even further, calling it "populist demagoguery."[45] The comments appeared in the country's newspapers, ironically, on the eleventh day of the eleventh month, reminding everyone of the foolhardiness and stupidity of the First World War. Quayle would have been well served to have read *All Quiet on the Western Front*. While legitimate debate was going on inside the Democratic Party about the wisdom of sending young Americans to die in the sands of the Middle East—for the Kuwaitis?—little debate was countenanced inside the Republican Party, without one being branded an isolationist or a pacifist or a coward. A New Order, to be sure.

The post-election infighting continued, with everybody in the party now sitting with their backs to the wall, holding their cards close. Eddie Mahe, a hard-boiled GOP operative, said frankly, "Bush will be opposed for renomination and the challenge will be serious enough that he won't be able to ignore it."[46]

Humorist David Barry summed up the national sentiment toward the culture of the Bush White House: "Wealthy WASPS have less fun in their entire lifetimes than members of other ethnic groups have at a single wedding reception."[47] Senator Howell Heflin of Alabama, a down-home good ole boy cracker country lawyer who saw everything from the bottom up, agreed. He called the GOP the "Grey Poupon crowd, the Gucci-poochie-coochie shoe-wearing, Mercedes-driving, polo-playing, Jacuzzi-soaking, Perrier-drinking, Aspen-skiing, ritzy rich, high-society Republicans who eat broccoli."[48]

Meanwhile, a rising voice for conservatism was just beginning to extend his influence: "A large new noise echoes across the invisible cacophony that is talk radio, rising above the interviewers, sports yakkers, religion rappers, money doctors, put-down artists, psyche soothers, morning-zoo shock jocks and all purpose schmoozers. The name is Rush Limbaugh . . . "[49] A huge profile ran in the December *New York Times Magazine*, which sometimes derided Limbaugh. It was hard proof of his effectiveness, his conservatism, and how much of a threat the left perceived him to be. Among conservatives, it was a prized badge of honor, to be hit by the *New York Times*.

The GOP House leadership was reelected across the board and, dismayingly for the Bush White House and its friends, no one stepped forward to challenge Gingrich for minority whip. Having been chastened at home, however, Gingrich told a Washington reporter that he needed to pay closer attention to the Sixth District.[50] He said from now on he would be home every weekend. When he'd traveled earlier in 1990, it was not back home but to other parts of the country for speaking engagements or to help incumbents and challengers. He'd made forty-two trips to locales other than Georgia.

In the end, Gingrich had been preserved from gerrymandering in Georgia, not because the Democrats in the legislature didn't want to hurt him, but because they wanted to help their buddy Ben Jones more. Jones was a loyal Democrat, running for a House seat at the time.

Demographics, not Democrats, are what really saved Newt. The suburbs around Atlanta were growing quickly and prosperously and Republicanly. The old yellow-dog Democrat South was dying, being replaced by doggone Republicans.

Bush's men didn't wait around. Within weeks of the off-year elections, they began sketching the outlines of his reelection effort. Nearly all the same players—except for Lee Atwater—were slated to reprise their roles in the Bush campaign. There was little mention of Dan Quayle at this point, because frankly a lot of people around Bush wanted him to dump the young, star-crossed veep. A new poll by NBC/*Wall Street Journal* said that when asked, "69 percent said the thought of Quayle as president made them 'uncomfortable.'"[51]

CHAPTER 25

THE MOTHER OF ALL

*"The spectacle of Washington . . . resembles nothing
more than the sight of a relapsed drunk . . . still
grasping his bottle, even as he retches into a toilet."*

1991

White House officials soothed themselves that George Bush was in good shape for 1992, especially in the South and especially in states like California. In fact, the GOP had gone backward in the Sunbelt. But, as the editor of a magazine by, for, and about political consultants sniffed, "They are spin doctors who write their own prescriptions."[1]

Talk was rampant among some in the media that New York governor Mario Cuomo would finally take on Bush. The New York media loved Cuomo but there were quiet rumors in political circles that either he or his wife, Matilda Raffa Cuomo, were "mobbed up." These same rumors had circulated earlier about Geraldine Ferraro's husband, John Zacarro, a New York real estate developer. Outside of New York, most Democrats knew that Cuomo was a nonstarter, not just because he was smug and sanctimonious, but because his ethnicity and liberalism just wouldn't play well with Democrats below the Mason-Dixon Line.

Virtually no one was talking about the governor of Arkansas, Bill Clinton, although he was a proven vote-getter in Arkansas. When his name did come up, Democratic insiders made derisive comments about him not being able to keep his zipper up.

Conservative groups and individuals were beginning to realize how important Newt Gingrich's fight with Bush was to their cause. Many began agitating for some formal recognition of Newt at the annual Conservative

Political Action Conference, where he spoke every year and always packed them in. They were also agitating more openly for a conservative challenger to Bush in the 1992 primaries. A group was formed, "Conservatives for a Winning Ticket," which was pushing for Jack Kemp, or commentator Pat Buchanan, or Pete DuPont (who was regarded as even more of an elitist than Bush, if that was possible), or Colorado senator Bill Armstrong, or any other number of potentials—including former New Hampshire senator Gordon Humphrey, who, while voting the rightist line for twelve years, was also regarded as being one of the oddest men ever to serve in Congress.

The feeling among the political classes was that though George Bush had been heavily damaged over the budget fight, the looming war and its antici-pated success along with the discord inside the Democratic Party would ensure his reelection. It was simply a Republican era, at the presidential level. The GOP had won five of the previous six elections, and even in 1976, when former Georgia governor Jimmy Carter had defeated unelected incumbent Gerald Ford, it was seen as an anomaly because of the Watergate scandal.

Ed Rollins, appearing on ABC, was cocky, despite his dead relations with Bush and the White House. He asserted, "Obviously if any one of their three frontrunners, Mario Cuomo, Jesse Jackson, or Michael Dukakis, is nominated, George Bush will win easily."[2]

Others weren't so sure. In response, a Democratic operative crowed, "Bush isn't the Gipper. These guys have no fear of him and they're all free-lancers."[3] He was referring to Rollins, Newt Gingrich, and others who did not have any trepidation about Bush. He was right.

Paul Weyrich, head of the Free Congress Foundation, speculated that the Republicans were "moving back to a pre-Reagan party."[4] He also wrote a piece on how the GOP was in fact two parties, but everybody knew that already. There was the *Wall Street Journal* elitist Republican and the *Farm Journal* populist Republican. One was Bush, the other Reagan. With one, you covered your wallet. With the other, you gave the shirt off your back.

Other Democratic consultants and observers thought that Bush in 1988 and Jesse Helms in 1990 had unleashed a new type of political warfare based on "cultural and racial issues that are battlegrounds for the next 10 years."[5]

In early January, the House Republican leadership held a subdued press conference featuring Gingrich, Michel, Lewis, and Jerry Solomon of New York. The body language was the most interesting thing given the various animosities. As usual, Michel glossed everything over with happy talk, but no one was buying it. Michel later announced that he would run for another term, at the behest of Bush, who feared Gingrich as minority leader.[6]

No one in their right minds thought that the Iraqi army could stand up to the American fighting man, but no one thought the American military would go through the Iraqi military like no one's business either. The war was over in a matter of hours, with Saddam's elite forces begging for mercy, wandering the desert, trying to find anything that was white so they could surrender to the nearest American. No one thought the Gulf War would take years, but some thought months or weeks . . . but hours?

Indeed, in order to manage expectations, the Bush White House had briefed congressional leaders and then told the American people to expect a many-months-long war. Gingrich had a long and thoughtful prediction: Saddam, he said, was "going to get his butt kicked."[7]

The war resolution had barely passed the Senate 52–47, and while the House margin was bigger, it was not overwhelming, 250–183. Gingrich and most Republicans voted for it. But public support for the war and the American fighting man was overwhelming.

America was briefly unified, because that is what Americans always did at the first blush of a foreign crisis. Like the Flag Amendment, ridding Kuwait of Saddam became another faux expression of patriotism. No doubt the American GIs deserved the respect of the American people and got it, but they also deserved the respect of the civilian leadership of the US government. The hundred-hour war cost the American taxpayer untold billions of dollars. Few Americans were killed by Saddam's army because Saddam's soldiers were too busy turning tail and running back to Baghdad, but they did rape and loot the country, acting more like stoned juvenile delinquents than professional fighting men. They set fire to oil rigs, tore down buildings, spray-painted graffiti, and generally trashed the little country.

In gratitude for the great fighting force committing so many resources to liberate their country, the Al-Sabah family did not arrange for cheaper oil to be sold to America and gave most of the billions in rebuilding contracts to the Germans, the Japanese, the French, indeed, pretty much every other country with a pick and a shovel. The whole thing was a farce.

Gingrich was a gung-ho supporter of the Gulf War, as was most everybody in America, although the issue was far more divided on Capitol Hill. But he was talking up 1992, just like everyone else in the GOP who had failed to study recent history. They were expecting the American people, in an outpouring of gratitude, to sweep Bush back into office because he'd hurled Saddam out of Kuwait and back to Baghdad. They'd forgotten that in 1945, the British people, in an unprecedented show of gratitude, threw Winston Churchill out on his bum just weeks after defeating the country that had nearly destroyed the British Empire.

For a few months, every drop of American ink in the nation's newspapers and every second of airtime were devoted to the Gulf War. Bush's approval ratings climbed into the low 90s, something not thought possible by pollsters and political scientists. Giddily, David Gergen wrote for *U.S. News & World Report* that not only could Bush win in a landslide, he could also sweep out "large numbers of congressional Democrats."[8] Longtime Republican consultant David Keene, agreeing with Gergen, said that Bush would be "unbeatable" as long as he avoided "kinder and gentler affairs with Democrats over taxes ..."[9] Keene and Gergen had worked together on Bush's 1980 presidential campaign and often saw things the same way. No one was calling Bush a "wimp" now, the unfortunate and inaccurate slur hung on Bush by his political enemies.

But over the course of 1991, quickly and relentlessly, Bush's poll numbers slipped down.

The ice had broken somewhat between Gingrich and the White House. There had been some phone conversations with various officials and, for a time, both sides signed flimsy neutrality acts. Gingrich swore off a race for the Senate in 1992, preferring to stay in the House. In February he said explicitly, "I would like to be speaker of the House."[10]

As with everything now, the Gulf War became politicized. Gingrich was talking up how veterans would be recruited to run for office in the future, and pollsters and consultants said the war would be a "realigning" issue and that it could lead to a new order of Republicanism. Democrats who'd voted against the war resolution tiptoed around, hoping it would not be effectively used against them in '92. Everybody now assumed it to be a foregone conclusion that Bush would be reelected, possibly in a landslide. Democrats meanwhile were discussing finding a Gulf War vet to run against Gingrich, who as they pointed out, had never served in the military.

Gingrich wrote a very confidential memo to Dick Cheney, now installed at the Pentagon, in which he expressed deep frustration with the state of America's military, referring to "Pentagon rice bowls." He also told the defense chief the leadership meeting with Bush was "very disheartening."[11] Another letter to Bush's chief of staff, John Sununu, made the Pentagon memo look like a Valentine's Day card. The letter began, "Dear John." It went quickly downhill, citing Newt's "deepest anger," adding that Sununu was "insufferably arrogant and offensive" and "losing your touch" and "suffering hubris" and trying to "bully us" and was "cynical, arrogant, destructive." The hot letter was ostensibly over the budget negotiations but it was also over turf and the two smartest kids in the class.[12]

By comparison, Gingrich was known around Washington to be brash, yet also most knew he had a tender heart. Sununu was known around Washington by many as someone whose timely demise could not come soon enough.

Gingrich was also receiving a lot of mail supporting him in holding firm on the budget, including a letter from Nobel Prize–winning economist Milton Friedman. "I write to congratulate you on the stand you have taken about the so-called budget agreement."[13] Gingrich treasured the letter. He also got a form letter from President Bush imploring him to vote for the budget resolution.[14] This letter, he treasured less. He also received a form letter from Lee Atwater, imploring him to vote for higher taxes.[15]

The hated phrases "chicken hawk" and "draft dodging" were hurled more than once against Gingrich, Cheney, Bill Bennett, and others who had not served in Vietnam—even by celebrated conservative writer Deborah Orin of the New York Post.[16] Gingrich, meanwhile, hauled out the heavy artillery by playing the UN card against the Democrats. A spokesman for the Democrats, Laura Nichols, had a nice rejoinder when she said, "Gingrich continues to assume that we had 500,000 Republicans fighting in the Gulf rather than 500,000 Americans."[17]

Gingrich openly speculated that some liberals in Congress would be suspected of leaking confidential intelligence information, and that the entire Democratic Party institution needed to rethink its position on the military and warfare, especially since the war in the Gulf was going so swimmingly.

Everybody in the political establishment and across the spectrum was proclaiming the war, when it was successfully concluded, to be a smashing political success. From neocons like Charles Krauthammer to Democrats and establishment Republicans, nearly all exclaimed that life in American politics had changed permanently, and that Bushism had supplanted Reaganism as the inspirational philosophy of the future GOP. Conservatives disagreed, but few were listening to them in the time of the Gulf War.

Above it all loomed James A. Baker III, the secretary of state. Baker had left politics behind and though he'd been good at it, both the infighting and the broken-field running, his distaste for the game had grown, along with his taste for statecraft. He observed with bemusement while the hacks fought over the political spoils of war.

Like so many things that politicians got their hands on, the Gulf War, in which surely both registered Republicans and registered Democrats fought, became highly charged.

Gingrich's politicization of the war was considered unseemly by many. "The very same Democratic leaders who . . . would have stopped the President in the Persian Gulf are effectively stopping the President here in Capitol Hill," he said. "If Gen. [H. Norman] Schwarzkopf had to report to the Democratic Congress, we'd still be unloading the first five tanks and debating over which way they should point."[18]

Bush spoke to a joint session of Congress, and the Republicans conspired to hand out little American flags that only they would wave on the floor of the House. Some Democrats went to Gingrich to ask for their own flags. Gingrich relented, and American flags were seen on both sides of the aisle.[19] But the Republicans also wore little yellow buttons that read "I voted with the president."[20]

Bush received eleven standing ovations during his short speech to the Congress. John Sununu said the war would not be used for partisan advantages. There was nonetheless open talk in Republican circles about how the Gulf War would lead not only to a Bush reelection, but to the actual takeover of the House and Senate. As of 1991, the Democrats had a 12-vote margin in the Senate and a staggering 101-vote margin in the House. "I think we are right on the verge of taking them to the cleaners," Gingrich crowed.[21] Indeed, a headline in an Associated Press story read, "GOP Trying to Capitalize on Gulf War Victory."[22] Even Iraqi soldiers, when surrendering, were chanting Bush's name, according to Dick Cheney.[23]

The "bloody shirt" had been waved before by the Republicans, but not since the post–Civil War era when the Republicans dominated national politics for years, mostly because they'd been the party of the North, the party that had won the war (they claimed), and the party of Abraham Lincoln. Republicans reasoned the bloody shirt had worked once before, so why wouldn't it work again? Republicans, who had once been skeptical about congressional races in 1992, were now talking openly about taking control of Congress.

But there was still a year to go before the 1992 elections. When asked about the divisions in the GOP, Gingrich crassly told the Associated Press, "Saddam came along and saved all of us."[24]

CHAPTER 26

SHADOW OF THE FAT MAN

*"America is not going to elect a draft
dodging, pot smoking, womanizer."*

1991

If you are a Democrat with a compulsion to run for president, this would be a good time to find a detox program for the ambition-addicted. President Bush's popularity is at Founding Father levels."[1] So wrote one of the leading lights of the Washington press corps, Howard Fineman, in early 1991, when the conventional wisdom was that the Gulf War had salved all wounds in the GOP and wiped out any chance the Democrats had for winning the White House in 1992. Newt Gingrich agreed with Fineman, saying, "The Democrats are becoming an aberrant party."[2]

George Will had written near the end of the Gulf War that, as things looked then, George Bush was a lead-pipe cinch for reelection, which meant the country would suffer from not having the "clarifying conversation of a serious presidential contest."[3] Will said the Democratic Party, like Iraq, was a "twisted pile of blasted hopes."[4]

In the middle of 1991, a *Times Mirror* poll showed the Republicans opening up a sizable lead over the Democrats for 1992. Hypothetical polling a year and a half before an election is as worthless as teats on a bull, but you couldn't tell the rejoicing Republicans or the despondent Democrats that. An obscure Democratic operative from Chicago, David Axelrod, said *his* party was in the middle of a "nervous breakdown."[5] In a hypothetical matchup, Bush was beating New York governor Mario Cuomo 77–16! Other Democratic operatives worried, according to Tom Edsall of the *Washington Post*, that quotas and other "racial issues" would be used effectively against their party by the Republicans.[6]

There was a huge parade in Washington in June to thank the troops and celebrate the end of the Gulf War. For a time, patriotism bordering on nationalism was out of control. Opponents of the war were harassed, including actress Margot Kidder, who "was branded a Baghdad Betty."[7]

But by the fall of 1991, the wheels, the rims, the axle, and the lug nuts were coming off the Bush Administration, and, by extension, the Republican Party. Unemployment was rising, as were Americans' fears about the economy. Stock prices were falling, consumer confidence was falling, and interest rates were rising. At a press conference in October 1991, Bush cryptically told the press corps, "All is not well."[8] His staff said he had the "jitters."[9]

It all came to a head at a fiery White House meeting between Capitol Hill conservatives and Bush. In a special election to fill the Pennsylvania Senate seat of John Heinz (who'd died tragically in a midair collision earlier in the year), the presumed favorite was former governor Dick Thornburgh, running against an old Kennedy retread, Harris Wofford, who was supposed to be the sacrificial lamb. But the lamb came from 44 percentage points behind and slew the lion, without so much as a jawbone of an ass, although he did have James Carville as his chief consultant. It was seen as a referendum on Bush. The Republican establishment was shaken to the core. To help get Thornburgh across the finish line, GOP ad man Roger Ailes had been asked to pitch in, but it was to no avail.[10]

Gingrich and other conservatives demanded Bush take action with an immediate economic growth package, but Bush was described by columnists Evans and Novak as "weak and confused."[11] Party leaders from around the country also pleaded with Bush. A story went around Washington that a group of county GOP leaders were telling the president of the plight of people in their regions and giving him political advice; Bush allegedly cut them off by saying, "If you're so smart, how come you're not president?"[12] The story was apocryphal, but to those who knew Bush and had seen his arrogance up close and personal, it had the ring of truth to it.

Gingrich and a group of conservatives eventually offered their own tax-cut package, but without White House support, the party was divided once again and the package sank without debate. Speaker Foley, whose party had offered their own tax cuts, denounced the GOP plan as a "cynical political maneuver."[13] The Gingrich plan had called for cutting taxes for those earning less than $50,000 per year.

John Sununu was fired in mid-December by Bush's eldest son, George W., as the chief of staff had rubbed just about everybody the wrong way. Sununu's removal had been rumored for days. Everybody was in on the deathwatch, a ritual that imbued Washington with a truly breathtaking mania. For Washingtonians, it was always a great time to drink and gossip and watch someone's world end. In the end, no one mourned Sununu but everyone was glad to bury him.

Gingrich was in hot water himself. In the annual *Washingtonian* poll, he was voted "worst House member" by the readership, although they tilted to the left: they also voted Jesse Helms as "worst Senator."[14] Had the poll been of Capitol Hill staffers, the results most certainly would have been different. Gingrich had his detractors but he also had a lot of fans there. Helms, while controversial, was beloved on the Hill by many, including his friend Senator Joe Biden, the staunchly liberal Delaware Democrat.

Newt Gingrich wasn't looking forward to 1992 any more than Bush was. Bush was in an open war again with conservatives, and Gingrich had gotten a new district in Georgia after all, one much less to his liking.

After months of meetings and commentary and testing the waters, Patrick J. "Pat" Buchanan, conservative syndicated columnist, announced in late 1991 he would challenge Bush for the GOP presidential nomination.

To call the Buchanan campaign audacious was an understatement, but he showed astonishing strength in the New Hampshire primary, winning more than 40 percent and exposing the ideological and cultural fissures in the GOP. Buchanan had the aggressive backing of the *Manchester Union Leader* and most of the new talk-radio phenomenon. He also received the support of the venerable American Conservative Union, whose board voted 14–2 to endorse Buchanan.

His candidacy was scaring the daylights out of the Bush White House.

The economy had dropped into a recession, and Bush, once thought to be weak, then strong, was now weak again, at the worst possible moment.

The media had a new infatuation, Governor Bill Clinton of Arkansas. His personal record of fidelity was spotty, but with the economy in worsening shape, many voters weren't bothered by his avoidance of military service, or the emergence of other women with whom he'd had relations even though he was married, or his mediocre record as governor of Arkansas. Bob Livingston deadpanned, "Berlusconi was a piker when it came to Clinton" and women. The Italian prime minister was notorious for having a libido the size of Sicily.[15]

In fact, Clinton was seen as a bit of a policy wonk, having advanced the label of "New Democrat" and working with left-of-center think tanks, including the Progressive Policy Institute. He'd been publicly supportive of the Gulf War, so Republicans would have a hard time hanging the "peacenik" label on him, though he'd been precisely that in the '60s.

As the GOP became the party of Luddites, Newt Gingrich also seemed less and less focused on ideas as he found less receptivity for them. These were the dark times for American conservatism. Along with the end of the Soviet threat, George Bush had driven passion and ideas out of the GOP marketplace. Whereas Gingrich had been pounding out ideas both crazed and considered since the late 1970s, he, too, seemed to have hit the end of the trail, falling back into a defensive posture, lashing out at the left rather than trumping it with vision. The GOP was staking its ground on opposing quotas and minority preference programs. They had become the aginners again.

Even Democrats noticed that the winds seemed to have gone out of Newt's sails. At one point, he joked to reporters, "And you guys thought I was a revolutionary."[16] Though the comment related to the congressional workweek, it was apropos of his new demeanor. He was not in the good graces of the Bush White House, but at least lines of communication were open and he was saying nice things about Bush in the press. He was decidedly low profile, like many of his GOP colleagues, even the conservatives. War will do that. Gingrich, it seemed to all, had given up his notions of a "national conservative crusade," as reported by the *Wall Street Journal*.[17] His enemies within the GOP conference, like Mickey Edwards, were snickering.

The Republicans had swallowed the anchor, given up on the thrill of intellectual exploration, and settled for the calm port of Bushism where there was no risk, no reward, and no victory, just a sort of biding time rather than changing the future. Gingrich had turned forty-nine in June 1990, and all of a sudden he was no longer the brash young man in the room. He was middle aged, like most men in Congress, blending in, like most men in Congress.

He hadn't given up on his conservatism, though. A Republican congressman from Washington State, Rod Chandler, was pushing an idea for Washington to help Americans purchase health insurance. Gingrich was wary. "We have to, at some point, offer a convincing solution that is market-oriented and decentralized or we will get eroded into bureaucratically rationed health care," he said.[18]

He was spending an inordinate amount of time on fighting federal funding for the widening of Tara Boulevard in his district because of the impact it would have on local businesses. He'd done a U-turn after initially supporting the widening of the road. He was also hosting a "Rhino Walk" in Atlanta to raise awareness of the endangered status of the black rhinoceros in Kenya.[19]

At his first town hall meeting of 1991, in Jonesboro, more than two hundred constituents would give him what for, venting and complaining about all manner of things related to his failings. He wryly noted that some people would forgive him but others were "going to carry that anger the rest of their lives." He was all over the district, glad-handing, announcing federal boodle, doing what any good politician who'd nearly lost would do: making amends.

He was back once a week, had hired a chief of staff just for the Sixth, held local hearings on local matters, and was known to drop his gs on occasion. Gingrich was also raising money hand over fist for the 1992 elections. Sometimes he was accompanied by his wife, Marianne, who often sat silent.

When the subject of gay rights came up, Gingrich reflected the view of his Baptist district. "There is a very broad community in my district which would be opposed to homosexuality and which would be vehemently opposed to establishing a legal right based on sexual behavior," he told the *Atlanta Journal and Constitution*.[20] But on a C-SPAN broadcast of a meeting with the *New Republic*, he also signaled that he did not oppose gays in the military. "With C-SPAN cameras rolling to catch his fire-and-brimstone response, Mr. Gingrich said he didn't see any argument for dismissal in matters regarding the private lives of military personnel."[21]

He did remain deeply interested, however, in his "Earning by Learning" program in which the government would pay children to read books. Some of the money Gingrich had donated to charity went to inner-city programs in Atlanta to pay poor children to read books. He introduced a bill to promote literacy in American prisons and was pushing for Atlanta to get a future Olympic Games. It was clear that all the frenetic energy aimed at his district had knocked off a considerable amount of weight; his suits looked downright baggy on him.

The bad news for Gingrich was the Sixth District had been nearly completely redrawn right underneath his feet. He would have to run in a virtually new Sixth District, mostly suburban, north of Atlanta. His old district had been an odd conglomeration of urban and rural. The portions of the old Sixth that had heavy African American populations (and where Gingrich had always had good relations) were put into another district to create favorable conditions for black candidates.

The Speaker of the Georgia house, Thomas Murphy, had what everybody knew was a "vendetta" for Gingrich, whom he hated.[22] To make Newt's district as tough as possible, he was willing to risk the futures of three, maybe four, Democratic congressmen by making their districts far more Republican. A political observer in Georgia said, "They are interested in crucifying Newt Gingrich, but [he] is the type of man you shoot here and then he pops back over there."[23] Eventually, Gingrich moved from an apartment in Jonesboro to the north Atlanta suburbs, into his new district.

At a particularly bad time, it came to light that dozens of members of Congress, including Gingrich, had bounced thousands of checks at the House Bank. The bank covered the overdrafts indefinitely and none of the members were charged fees. It looked to all Americans like another insider privilege afforded to Congress but not them. Across the country, people raged against the House Bank and the members, including Newt.

Tom Foley, Speaker of the House, ordered the bank closed after all accounts were settled. But the matter would not go away, as more and more members announced they'd bounced checks. Gingrich claimed that he had bounced only three checks and had covered them quickly—others had bounced dozens of checks for thousands of dollars—but the bouncers were all lumped together. He was the only member of the Georgia delegation who had bounced checks.[24]

All told, 134 members had bounced checks at the House Bank, but never for the meal check, as yet another embarrassing revelation showed that members of Congress routinely stiffed the House restaurant, totaling hundreds of thousands of dollars in unpaid bills. The media tried out "Kitegate" and "Rubbergate," but neither of them flew durably. The *Wall Street Journal* had still not given up its animus toward Gingrich; he was the only Republican singled out in an editorial on the whole check business, including him with a number of Democrats.[25]

The notion of term limits for members of Congress was gaining more and more currency with the American people. Stories also emerged about the drivers provided for the congressional leadership, including Newt's, Detective George Awkward, a Capitol Hill police officer who was being paid around $60,000 per year to chauffeur the Georgian around.[26]

In October, an elderly tourist tottered down the steps of the Capitol and lay bleeding with a broken wrist, but the nearby ambulance would not help her because it was reserved for members of Congress only.[27] When people heard, they were outraged.

The great civil rights attorney and leader Judge Thurgood Marshall, an African American, resigned from the Supreme Court, where he'd been since LBJ had nominated him in 1967. A debate was kicked off in Washington about the "black seat" on the court. Gingrich went right to the politics of the matter, saying it was "an opportunity for the president now to decisively swing the balance of power towards a stricter interpretation, a more historically based court."[28] Ever since the fearsome fight over Robert Bork's nomination by Reagan in 1987, the process had become completely politicized. Gingrich was simply expressing the views of the conservative side.

Within days, Bush nominated Clarence Thomas, an African American, who had been head of the Equal Employment Opportunity Commission under Reagan. Just as quickly, Thomas was under attack for both his conservative views and his relationship with an employee at the commission, Anita Hill. Gingrich jumped into the fray with both feet, attacking Thomas's attackers, saying they were attacking Thomas because he "doesn't think like a black."[29]

By the time Thomas was confirmed—barely—it had turned into one of the ugliest, most heinous and despicable fights in the history of Senate confirmations. It was the worst kind of "he said, she said." Newsrooms exploded between men and women, dinner tables exploded between men and women, classrooms exploded between men and women, and even at finer restaurants in Washington, the luncheon conversation often got loud and ugly between men and women over the dispute between Thomas and Hill, whether she was a kook or a spurned lover, and whether he was a sexual harasser or a victim of an out-of-control liberal witch hunt that could simply not tolerate a black conservative male. Joe Klein, a liberal writer with *New York Magazine*, called Bush's nomination of Thomas "cynical and corrupt."[30] Ted Kennedy and Arlen Specter got into an ugly argument on the floor of the Senate. Commentators wrung their hands and lamented that civility was dead in Washington. Then they took turns trading verbal fisticuffs.

As always, the GOP political class politicized a very serious matter involving the American workplace. "Even before we say a word or do a thing, they [the Democrats] have to face a severe straining in the feminist-black coalition. We won our nominee. We hurt the Democrats. Everything beyond that is pure gravy,"[31] said one fixture among Washington Republican insiders.

Newt had his own opinion of the consultants who figured so prominently within the Washington "Inside the Beltway" GOP crowd. "Consultants, in my opinion, are stupid. The least idea-oriented, most mindless campaign of simplistic slogans is a mindless idea."[32]

About the only person left in Washington with a sense of humor was columnist Mark Shields, who quipped, "There are only two places left to go and see white guys fight—a hockey game and the Senate Judiciary Committee."[33]

In case anybody doubted the world had changed radically and perhaps forever, it was announced by the KGB that they were selling their top-secret files "from the Stalin-era" to the highest bidder. To sweeten the sale, the super-secret Soviet spy agency offered to throw in a sit-down with a top KGB official.[34] The Soviets needed to sell what assets they could because their Central Bank had run out of money.

In the United States, Gingrich and others were pushing for the release of private phone calls between Democratic members of Congress and the Sandinista government of Nicaragua.[35] The unspoken allegation was not without foundation. A *New York Times* story detailed how a Communist official from Managua "collaborated" with three Democratic members of Congress, including former Speaker Jim Wright, to block aid to the Nicaraguan Contras.[36]

Clinton, after overcoming his own problems and a weak field, raced toward the Democratic nomination, aided by people from all walks of life, including Burt Reynolds, who chipped in $1,000 for the campaign.[37]

Though Bush was not much interested in sloughing through yet another messy primary, the "hacks and flacks" of Washington could not wait. The *Washington Post* quipped, quoting Bob Beckel, "This administration is making the Haitian government look organized."[38]

The old divisions that the war had masked over were opened again, with Reaganites on one side and the Bushies on the other. Ed Feulner, head of the much-lauded Heritage Foundation, proclaimed, "[Bush] has been a disappointment . . . He had the opportunity to carry the Reagan revolution forward, and he didn't."[39]

Bush finally offered up a $300 rebate for every American as a means of getting the economy going, but even his own HUD secretary, Kemp, made fun of it, calling it "Jimmy Carteresque."[40] Bush meanwhile had sunk well below 50 percent approval.

A story in the *Wall Street Journal*, menacingly titled "Malaise, 92," by two of the paper's most respected journalists at the time, Michel McQueen and John Harwood, read:

> A year after an impressive foreign-policy victory, the president looks like
> an ineffectual leader, saddled with a weak economy, dropping like a stone
> in public-opinion polls and suffering from a debilitating ideological chal-
> lenge within his own party. Jimmy Carter in 1980—or George Bush in
> 1992? The two are beginning to look alike.[41]

CHAPTER 27

ALPHA AND OMEGA

"Listen, if I had to do that over, I wouldn't do it. Look at all the flack it's taking."

1992

The bad patch for George Bush lasted from the fall of 1991 into 1992 with no letup in sight. He was star-crossed, and in January traveled to Japan, where after a strenuous tennis match and fighting off a flu virus, he threw up in front of the Japanese prime minister and the assembled guests, all captured on film and repeatedly (some thought joyously) broadcast by the American networks. Frankly, the video of the president was downright scary, as he went white and fainted and looked as if he were dying. Bush recovered but his campaign never got on its feet.

News reports described his Administration in terms like "free fall" and "shell-shocked" and worse. His first four years in office had been spent globe-trotting; this became an issue to an electorate scared about the economy.

At campaign rallies, supporters unenthusiastically chanted "Four More Years!" But no one really wanted another four years like the previous four years. Newt Gingrich urged Bush to do a mea culpa, to say he'd tried to work with the Democrats and then to run an anti-establishment campaign, but this was just not a part of Bush's DNA. Gingrich told him, "You should say we can't have a cocaine-selling, check-bouncing, extravagant-spending Congress raising taxes." To which Bush replied, "You said it, I didn't."[1]

Bush eventually proposed health insurance plans and tax cut plans, but they were dismissed as election-year gimmicks. He was getting zero benefit of the doubt from the national media now, and so his campaign tried to run against the national media rather than Bill Clinton.

The *National Review*, like many on the right, spanked Bush hard, but could not bring itself to endorse the wholly unqualified Pat Buchanan. Gingrich campaigned with Bush in the all-important Georgia primary, including celebrating Martin Luther King Jr. Day in Atlanta, where speaker after speaker rubbed Bush's nose in it, including King's own daughter, the Rev. Bernice King. Bush placed a wreath at King's burial site, but since 1988 and his campaign's use of the "Willie Horton" issue, plus his refusal to sign new civil rights legislation over "quotas," Bush's relationship with Black America was awful.

In keeping with a trend that had begun in 1976, the national media began a love affair with Clinton's strategist James Carville and Bush's strategist Mary Matalin, especially when it was discovered they were seeing each other. It made the tale all the more delectable. Their story turned everything conventional on its head: they were from different parties, and *she* was the Republican and *he* was the Democrat. The power had moved from the politicians to the consultants and now, because the consultants controlled the narrative, if the candidate won, it was because the consultant was a genius who was able to take "that idiot" in hand and guide him (or her) to the win. If they lost, it was the candidate's own fault for (a) being a lousy candidate, (b) not raising enough money, (c) not listening to the consultant, or (d) all of the above.

The matter of Newt Gingrich's new congressional district was still not settled by January 1992, and certainly not who would represent it. The Justice Department struck down the new lines in Georgia because they did not go far enough in creating districts in which African Americans could win outright or at least be competitive.

For the first time in years, Newt drew a significant primary challenger for the GOP nomination in the Sixth Congressional District, former state representative Herman Clark. Plus, because of the eventual new makeup of the Sixth of Georgia, nearly one out of four voters there had never seen Newt's name on a ballot before. This in itself was a problem as they'd never made a psychic investment in Gingrich, and most of the news they were hearing about the beleaguered congressman was not good. It would quickly get worse.

Clark was running an aggressive campaign but was also trying something unique: he was running commercials at movie theaters around the new congressional district. He hired John McLaughlin and Tony Fabrizio as his consultants. They had apprenticed under the black belt Arthur Finkelstein, who had won many more GOP primaries and general elections than nearly anybody else in the business. Finkelstein had masterminded—in part—Ronald Reagan's remarkable comeback in the 1976 primaries against Gerald Ford. He and his "kids"—as his apprentices were known—had changed the face of primary politics in the 1970s and '80s.

Gingrich was showing up on more and more "vulnerable" and "target" lists. The phrase "Newt basher" was showing up often in the press. Also, as House minority whip, his only committee assignment was the House Administration Committee, and there was no patronage to distribute from the committee that oversaw paperclips and office furnishings. However, as an incumbent, albeit a damaged one, he did hold a significant fund-raising lead over Clark as of early 1992.

These were bad times for Gingrich. He was getting routinely bashed in the media, in columns by George Will over his bounced checks, for his Town Car and $60,000-per-year driver courtesy of the American taxpayer, for his hubris in general. Given that dozens of other members had bounced hundreds of checks, his piddling little twenty-two bounced checks over three years—more than the three he had claimed originally, but all of them eventually covered—seemed to be somewhat of a tempest in a teapot.

House Republicans were uneasy about Newt, and rumors went around GOP circles that someone—maybe Tom DeLay—would challenge him for the Whip position. Gingrich's adult daughter, Kathy, went public to tell the world she disagreed with her father on abortion. She was pro-choice. He was putting on weight again.

Newt's marriage to Marianne was never good and he was even going through a lot of staff. Enemies seemed to be everywhere—in Georgia, on Capitol Hill, in the Bush White House, and in the national media. A reporter tracked down his first wife, Jackie, who'd been mostly silent for years. Not this time: "He's the father of my children and I don't ever see him. They have to contend with the fact that he's their father."[2]

An aide to Bob Michel told *Time* magazine, "Maybe the Democrats can't get Clinton elected, but at least they should be able to get rid of Newt. It would make our lives up here so much easier."[3] The national Democrats were running ads in his district, attacking him over the bounced checks. The ads featured Herman Clark, strumming the tune of "Old MacDonald Had a Farm" and singing, "With a bounced check there and a pay raise there. Here a check. There a check. Everywhere a bounced check."[4] Even the *Washington Post* reprinted a portion of the ditty.[5] Clark resurrected the phrase "Boot Newt." Gingrich's campaign retaliated with "Newter Rooters." Liberal columnists retaliated with "Neuter Gingrich."

Liberal activist Ralph Nader set up a special committee, in concert with the trial lawyers, to spend thousands to defeat Gingrich. They all agreed that a "scorched earth" strategy was needed to rid them of the nettlesome Newt. The Sierra Club weighed in and endorsed Clark. So did the National Education Association and other left-wing groups. The *Atlanta Journal and Constitution*, Newt's *bete noire* for years, published front-page articles day after day excoriating him. The headline to one story read, "The Whip Becomes a Whipping Boy."[6] The editorials were even worse.[7] One churlishly claimed, "Gingrich plays politics with welfare-reform proposals."[8]

The left was smelling blood.

Gingrich replied with ads that attacked both Clark *and* the local media. He apologized repeatedly to his constituents. "I occasionally make mistakes . . . It's true, I'm a human being."[9] The phrase "acid test" did not come close to summarizing Gingrich's 1992. About the only silver lining was that Hill staffers in *Washingtonian* magazine voted Gingrich "best leader" along with Dick Gephardt.[10] And, "as they say in Georgia, Gingrich . . . has some big dogs under his porch."[11]

Sacrifice was everywhere in Washington, though. The secretary of state, Jim Baker, who'd been mostly watching the antics of the town with bemusement, told his staff to book him on commercial flights when he was traveling for purely personal reasons.

The voters of 1988 had never really made an intuitive investment in George Bush. By March 1992, his approval rating was down to 40 percent, and the all-critical "handling of the economy" response was at a deathbed, Jimmy Carter–like 18 percent. Bush's spring was just as bad as Gingrich's. He'd gone to South America, which was a disaster. His environmental policy was ripped by both the tree huggers *and* the tree cutters. According to a *Wall Street Journal* poll, fully 51 percent of all voters had "serious doubts" about voting for Bush because he'd broken his pledge not to raise taxes.[12] His campaign stumbled along, and when he threw out the first pitch at the new Orioles ball park in Baltimore, he was booed. There was the economy, the breakup of Yugoslavia, rumors of a Ross Perot–Jack Kemp ticket or a Kemp-Perot ticket, Clinton's barbs, a leaky White House, infighting in the Administration, infighting among the campaign staff; it was definitely the spring of Bush's discontent.

This, however, did not stop Gingrich from gushing over Bush's term of office and the man himself. He called Bush "the best all around politician I've ever seen," and goofily compared him to Abraham Lincoln and Andrew Jackson.[13] Ralph Hallow of the *Washington Times* acidly wrote that Gingrich was now Bush's "water boy."[14]

Gingrich had endorsed Bush's renomination over Pat Buchanan, stumping for the president in New Hampshire, loudly saying that Buchanan was unqualified to be president. Gingrich also attacked Buchanan in personal terms, comparing him to the racist David Duke.[15] Gingrich and Buchanan had had a falling out months earlier over who was "the rightful heir to the Reagan Revolution," according to muckraking journalist Jack Anderson.[16] He wasn't alone, though. Neoconservative Bill Bennett said Buchanan was "flirting with fascism" and was "antisemitic [sic] in his heart."[17] Neocon columnist Charles Krauthammer also ripped him.

Concern over the Buchanan challenge manifested itself in many ways, and Gingrich sometimes huddled with the Bushies to plot strategy. The Bush campaign was divided over how to handle Buchanan. Helping Bush, though, was a fierce and bloody fight inside the Buchanan campaign. Buchanan's campaign manager (and younger sister), Angela "Bay" Buchanan, wanted her brother to focus on social issues. Chief pollster and strategist Tony Fabrizio, the same Arthur Finkelstein protégé helping Herman Clark in his GOP primary against Gingrich, wanted Buchanan to focus on economic issues. The fight spilled out into the media. Fabrizio lost. He left the campaign, and Buchanan lost the Georgia primary, 64 percent to 36 percent. The Buchanan offensive had been blunted.

Fabrizio had already called his friend John McLaughlin on Christmas Day of 1991, telling him he was quitting the Buchanan campaign because "Buchanan issued a statement today saying all the homeless should be locked up!" McLaughlin roared with laughter.[18]

Bush, who'd been glacier-like in recognizing the independence of the Baltic States, now nearly tripped over himself in recognizing the independence of the Ukraine from the Soviet Union in December 1991.

Even as Gingrich was now slow rolling his opposition to George Bush, a member in good standing of the Establishment, Bob Beckel, called him "the low-life from the low lands."[19] Gingrich had managed to anger both Buchanan's supporters and Bush's supporters, including many in his new congressional district in Georgia. Gingrich wrote a blunt memo to Bush with a prescription for winning that somehow ended up in the pages of the *Washington Post*.[20] The memo told Bush to recast the debate and promise a bold and new way forward. He warned that the Perot threat was real and said that the American people were scared. He also recounted all the shortcomings of the past four years. The memo was discussed widely in the media.

Bush was once again not happy with Gingrich, nor was his White House. In a meeting with congressional leaders, the president blamed the Georgian for his poor political standing in the country, as reported by Evans and Novak.[21] The feared columnists also reported that anyone around Bush who warned of an election problem was dismissed, cut out, and isolated. All the Bushies wanted to hear was happy talk. The truth was heresy.

Some conservatives openly speculated that a win by Bill Clinton or one of the other Democrats would be best for their cause. Dave Keene of the American Conservative Union said, "A lot of conservatives believe it would be in the interests of the movement and the party for Bush to lose."[22] But Bill Kristol, Dan Quayle's chief of staff, painted a dire picture of the fall of Western civilization with liberals running amuck in Washington. An old Florida Reaganite, Tommy Thomas, took out a full-page ad in the *Washington Post* costing tens of thousands of dollars calling on Quayle to step aside.[23]

Meanwhile the Bush White House—in the form of Quayle—attacked Pat Buchanan as not a real conservative, which some saw as foolish on a number of levels. First, it tended to legitimize Buchanan, it angered his supporters, and it caused those conservatives supporting Bush to shake their heads and publicly defend their old friend Buchanan.

People were mad at Congress. According to a *Washington Post* poll, the approval rating for Capitol Hill had sunk to 22 percent, the "lowest ever."[24] Across the board, polls demonstrated sourness throughout the land. Articles about the Congress used phrases such as "body count" and "life among the ruins" in describing the situation. Legislation ground to a halt. As of early 1992, fifty members had announced their retirement, many beating a hasty retreat to a more profitable and less stressful sinecure at some cushy K Street lobbying or law firm.

The House banking scandal was still around, still spreading ill will. By March 1992, 355 current and former members had admitted to having written bad checks.[25] Estimates on the total amount of bounced checks reached into the millions. A comprehensive list was handed out in the House press gallery and dozens of eager reporters grabbed for them, anxious to find out who had bounced how many for how much. The list included Gingrich, Nancy Pelosi, Tom Foley, Susan Molinari, Ed Markey . . . indeed, it seemed as if more members had bounced checks than had not.

The matter exploded when the Justice Department announced a probe to see if any laws had been broken by members. Previously, Gingrich had said he'd bounced three checks, but that increased to "about 20," and finally plateaued at twenty-two.[26] Gingrich apologized to his constituents, but it remained to be seen if he would survive the primary. He'd been sloppy and he knew it, giving his political enemies an opening.[27] He tried to get ahead by releasing the amount of each check. Some were as small as $20.95, but one was for $9,463.00.[28]

Gingrich was a piker, though, compared to Tommy Robinson of Arkansas, who had bounced an appalling 996 checks. Robinson had recently switched parties from Democrat to Republican. Close behind Robinson was Democratic member Bob Mrazek of New York with 972 bounced checks. The scandal was bipartisan and bicoastal. California's Barbara Boxer, a liberal, bounced 87 checks; her colleague, Duncan Hunter, a conservative, bounced 407.

A spokesman for Gingrich "revised" the number of checks his boss had bounced, now "upward to 30."[29] He rationalized it by saying it had happened over a thirty-month period. It was also revealed that Secretary of Defense Dick Cheney had also bounced checks while a member of Congress. Gingrich, in an attempt to stay ahead of the story, went hard after Speaker Tom Foley over the management of the House Bank. He said, "This is a Democratic machine political scandal," overlooking the fact that many of the check-kiters were Republicans, including himself.[30] Despite the giggling, Gingrich said with a straight face, "We Republicans had no choice, no control and no oversight."[31] With an audacity that left opponents and friends shaking their heads, Gingrich proclaimed, "There's a difference between being embarrassed and being a scandal."[32]

In an appearance on *This Week with David Brinkley*, Gingrich said that Speaker Foley is "totally mismanaging the corruption of the House."[33] Foley, appearing in a separate segment, took the bait and ownership of the scandal, saying defensively that he was capable and confident he could clean up the mess.[34] Brinkley asked him about his own bounced checks and Gingrich alluded to "a technical problem" as if some of the rubber checks were not his fault, but that of the Democrats who ran the House bank.[35]

The stratagem to nationalize the House banking scandal made sense simply because there were more Democrats in Congress than Republicans. If it meant sacrificing a few of their own to defeat more Democrats, well, such were the fortunes of war.

Foley was not pleased, nor was Gingrich's Georgia colleague John Lewis, who compared Newt to Joe McCarthy.[36] Everybody was mad at Gingrich, but he had not stumbled into his position. The GOP House leadership met and decided that the best defense was a good offense. Though they, too, had bounced checks, they decided to heap as much blame on the Democrats as possible. Newt was back in the saddle, lobbing rhetorical bombs, where he was most comfortable. All the usual attacks and labels were brought out and dusted off in news reports about Gingrich, including "a bomb thrower, a pit bull . . . guerrilla."[37]

Gingrich also hooked up with a group of freshmen conservatives who unimaginatively called themselves the "Gang of Seven," which included Rick Santorum and John Boehner. Gingrich took them under his wing and convinced them to offer a bill to permanently close the House bank, a legislative flourish that Speaker Foley's action soon made unnecessary. He also introduced a bill to radically reform welfare. With only a few months to go before his own primary, Gingrich had decided that passively waiting around was not going to work. He got his partisan mojo going.

Then the Justice Department announced an investigation of the House post office, where allegations of "stamps for cash" had been floating around for years—along with drug trafficking, specifically cocaine, and embezzlement by employees. Congressional offices were given an allotment of first-class stamps, but members and staffers were taking these to the House post office to exchange for cash and then pocketing the money.

The postmaster resigned in short order. Then the House sergeant at arms resigned. The House announced they would investigate the charges of corruption at their own post office, but nobody trusted them anyway. Gingrich went hard after the Democrats on the bank and the post office.

Even Foley's wife, Heather, who had served as his unpaid chief of staff, was rumored to be implicated in the post office scandal. Fingers were being pointed everywhere. Gingrich charged Foley with covering up the drug dealing in the House post office and Foley, furious, spluttered out his response, repeatedly calling the accusation and Gingrich "outrageous . . . outrageous." But again, he was on the defensive. Gingrich's spring offensive had been ballsy and it worked. Sam Donaldson played right into Gingrich's hands, asking if he thought Foley had engaged in a "criminal cover-up" of the drug-trafficking matter.[38] Gingrich never flinched: "There is no question that Tom Foley's office sat on that information for 10 months . . ."[39]

The choice for conservatives between Bush and Buchanan was at best a Morton's Fork (both sides were unacceptable). Neither was appealing and both were deeply flawed, each with his own interpretation of American conservatism. Bush finally won the nomination because he was the incumbent and because the candidacy of Buchanan was just a bridge too far for most conservatives.

Despite being hit with everything, including the kitchen sink, Bill Clinton emerged from the New Hampshire primary just a few points behind the hometown favorite, former Bay State senator Paul Tsongas, who had apparently beaten cancer but not expectations. Having gone through a sex and drugs and draft card Mixmaster, Clinton rock-and-rolled into the Southern primaries, where the regional favorite made semi-quick work of the Yankee Tsongas as well as Jerry Brown and Senator/war hero Bob Kerry of Nebraska, who despised Clinton as a physical and moral coward. Brown and Clinton also hated each other. People hadn't even learned how to pronounce Tsongas's name properly before Clinton waxed him, and, with only token opposition left, Clinton headed for the Democratic nomination, with most everybody in politics convinced he was a dead duck in the general election.

The conventional wisdom was there was no way Americans would vote for a "draft-dodging, pot-smoking womanizer" as president of the United States. The contrast between the war hero Bush, a charter member of the "Greatest Generation," and Clinton, a charter member of the "60s Generation," could not have been greater.

Enter Ross Perot.

Perot was impossible to categorize. He was a Texas billionaire, and was becoming popular on cable television for his common sense approach to issues that mattered. As a Texan and a hugely successful businessman, some thought he was a conservative, but as a Bush basher, some thought he leaned Democratic. He scored strongly in the polls and everyone assumed he was taking votes away from Bush. In the spring of 1992, Bush was weakly in first, with Perot right behind and Clinton pulling up the rear. Some idle columnists speculated about the House deciding the outcome, in true populist fashion.

An attractive and fiery young beat reporter for the *New York Times*, Maureen Dowd, spotted the growing populist wave before anyone else. Dowd said, "[The voters] are fed up with pampering, preening and prodigal behavior among the Washington aristocracy . . ."[40] One of the goodest and oldest of the good old boys, Congressman Jack Brooks of Texas, lamented, "There is a move afoot to destroy the Congress as we know it."[41] Another revealed his true concern when he told Dowd, "They've already taken the sex and drinking out of politics."[42]

Washington newbies and back-benchers, including John Boehner, a freshman congressman; Mike McCurry, a Democratic consultant; and Mitch Daniels, a Republican consultant, all said they thought the jig was up and Washington was about to experience a tidal wave of reform, washing out the old and corrupt politicians.

Contempt of Congress reached rock bottom when it was revealed that a secret sanctuary at the posh Greenbrier resort in West Virginia had been constructed as an emergency shelter for representatives and their staff. Assuming a nuclear war destroyed the rest of the country, members could still meet and argue over parking privileges.

The populist moment Gingrich had been working for looked as if it was arriving, but the problem was, the focus of most populist angst was aimed at the Republican White House and a Republican president whose bearing and background and breeding bespoke a life in the lap of luxury, his days in the Pacific as a daring navy pilot in World War II and as a Texas oilman notwithstanding. The goal of a Republican takeover of Congress was fading quickly for 1992.

Gingrich saw the situation all too clearly. In a speech in Indiana, he told the audience that Bush could lose in the fall—heresy for a top Republican—if he did not get right with the American people over the economy.[43] Clinton was also aiming up from a populist position, charging Bush with presiding over the worst economy since Herbert Hoover.

The Bush campaign was promoting "family values" as a way to wage war against Clinton rather than win the hearts and minds of the American voter. Of course, the Democratic Party wasn't about to roll over and play dead. They meant to keep what was theirs, plus take some of the Republicans' toys. They were all too eager to throw "Are you better off than you were four years ago?" back in Bush's face.

Part of the unraveling of the Buchanan campaign was due to his tendency toward bombastic statements, plus lingering suspicions about his views on Israel and minorities. At one point he said it "would be easier to settle a million Englishmen in Virginia than a million Zulus."[44] While Buchanan's point may have been well taken, the statement also made some people cringe.

Bush was nearly out of the woods for the 1992 nomination.

The country was a mess, and the election was no better. Bush, Clinton, and Perot were as flawed a group of presidential candidates as had ever been put forward for the American people to judge and consider to be their next president. It was not an awe-inspiring group, as far as the vast majority of Americans were concerned. Mary Matalin, a senior strategist with the Bush campaign, was not worried about Perot, telling the *Washington Post* that "people don't do a protest vote for president."[45]

Gingrich beat back the primary challenge of Herman Clark on July 21 by a nose and an eyelash, an uncomfortable repetition of his close call less than two years earlier in the 1990 general election. It was the anniversary of the first walk on the moon. Out of more than seventy thousand votes cast, he prevailed by less than one thousand, about the same margin he'd won by in

November 1990. To win, Gingrich had to spend more than $1 million to Clark's $160,000. It was ticklish too. For most of the evening, Clark led in the balloting until after 1:00 a.m., when Newt finally pulled ahead.

This was getting to be old hat for Newt. He kept winning, but the victories were increasingly becoming nail-biters. Even outraising and outspending Clark, he still had to borrow $100,000 in the closing weeks for more television advertising. Gingrich hadn't officially announced his candidacy until just two months before the primary. He'd only recently moved into his new district, renting a condo. The district was so heavily Republican, the GOP nominee was a sure bet to win in the fall.

Gingrich had been pounded by the media, by the establishment Republicans, and by liberal Democrats. Given all the baggage he was carrying, his political survival was nothing short of remarkable.

With the local primaries settled, attention now turned to the national campaign. In August, despite any misgivings he may have had, Ronald Reagan did go to the Republican convention in Houston and gave one of the best speeches of his career in an attempt to shore up the campaign of his former vice president. In the process, he reminded everybody watching how much they missed him and what a decent, honorable, and principled man he was. He could still wage political battle, even at the age of eighty-one. His Monday-night speech was the highlight of an otherwise bleak GOP gathering and many wept, thinking this was the last time they would see the Gipper. Reagan had been aided in his speech by Landon Parvin, one of a coterie of speechwriters that included Ken Khachigian, who were favored because they were such excellent writers and because they kept low profiles.

But, because doubts remained about Reagan's enthusiasm for Bush, he had to go out of his way to say that he "warmly endorsed" Bush for reelection.

Unfortunately Pat Buchanan had spoken ahead of Reagan, declared a "Culture War," attacked Hillary Clinton, attacked the left, and went overtime pushing Reagan out of prime time. Reagan, the old theatrical trouper, could clearly be seen looking impatiently at his wristwatch.

The Bush campaign operation was feckless from beginning to end. It didn't leak; it gushed. Bush put out the word that anyone caught leaking would be fired.[46] This new directive was leaked to reporters. The campaign was rife with factionalism and indecision. When it became known that the campaign was paying for limousines for senior staff, this also took a toll on morale. Both stories were promptly leaked. In national polls, Barbara Bush was more than twice as popular as her husband. The campaign thought they might be able to hide behind her skirts.

They assumed the solution was for Bush to do more interviews and to target "older white voters, particularly men."[47] When they did go after Clinton, the former governor easily parried the attack. The Republicans attacked Hillary, they attacked the state of Arkansas, and they attacked New York City, where the Democrats held their very successful convention under the quasi-biblical theme "A New Covenant."

Oddly, the Bush campaign had been cocky all through the summer of 1992 until a poll came out of California with Clinton crushing—destroying—Bush 60–28! When this was released, the mood and the psychology of the race changed dramatically. Republicans had owned California since Ike. An inevitable sense of losing overtook the national GOP. Morale was a zero and contributions to the GOP dried to a trickle. By the fall, Clinton was maintaining a 20-point national lead over Bush.

Bush said God was not present at the Democratic Convention. Clinton accused the Republicans of intolerance. Mary Matalin accused Clinton of dying his hair. Bush yelled at protesters in New Jersey, calling them "draft dodgers." Clinton's campaign staff followed behind their man with a dustpan, cleaning up his messes.

It got really juvenile when Gingrich tried to graft Woody Allen, who'd left his wife, Mia Farrow, for a younger stepdaughter, onto the Clinton campaign. Gingrich's remarks on le affaire Woody backfired a bit. It was all too tawdry, or at least it seemed so until Clinton went on MTV and joked to an audience of young people about smoking marijuana. Gingrich ripped him. "He has a deep psychological need to pander to the worst instincts of whatever group he is in front of . . . a sick thing," said Gingrich.[48] Clinton wisely did not respond.

During the campaign, a rumor swept Washington circles that a network had inadvertently caught Clinton and a male aide on tape sitting on the sofa of a hotel lobby when an attractive, unknown woman entered the room. The aide nudged Clinton and said, "There's one, Bill," to which Clinton replied, "Naww, she's not my type—but Hillary might go for her."[49]

Newt Gingrich had barely escaped the July primary. His opponent, Herman Clark, ran the type of race that Newt used to run, charging the incumbent with corruption and insiderism, running as an outsider and reformer, hitting Newt hard over the bounced checks. Even as Gingrich had the pleasure of campaigning side by side in Georgia with Reagan that fall; even as the Justice Department cleared him and a handful of other congressmen in the House banking scandal; even though he ended up beating Clark; even though Rush Limbaugh came in for a fund-raiser for Newt; everybody could see his mood was low. He talked openly about quitting politics even as he was surprisingly endorsed for reelection by his old nemesis, the *Atlanta Journal-Constitution*. He won back his seat by a better-than-expected margin, 57–42, but who knew going in?

Turnout was very high in the Sixth District, reassuring to Gingrich. Plus, Clinton was campaigning hard for the state, eventually winning it, although Georgia added three other GOP congressmen, John Linder, Jack Kingston, and Mac Collins. Newt was no longer the sole target of the Bulldog Democrats.

Bush lost California, the first time (excepting the Johnson landslide of 1964) since 1952 that the Republicans lost there. The election of '92 was driven by consultants and personality politics. High points included Clinton going on the *Arsenio Hall Show* and playing the saxophone. He spoke in vague terms about tax increases as "premiums" and "contributions," and used the word games of politics better than anyone since Nixon. When Clinton spoke about welfare assistance, he used a double entendre, sounding as if he were both for and against reforming the corrupt-ridden federal program, cagily saying his plan was to "end welfare as we know it."

A persistent rumor going around conservative circles and California political classes was that Ronald Reagan had voted for Clinton and not George Bush in the November election. "Mr. Reagan reportedly disliked Mr. Bush's reelection campaign, and there have been persistent reports that he was no fan of Mr. Bush."[50] Cathy Goldberg, Reagan's media representative, refused to knock down the rumor, simply saying, "I wasn't in the voting booth with him." She declined to ask the Gipper about his vote.[51] Had Reagan voted for Clinton, it would have been consistent with many conservatives who had gone from guarded support to lingering doubt to open hostility toward George Herbert Walker Bush.

Nancy Reagan's sometime lunch companion, columnist George F. Will said, ". . . when the dust settled . . . the party had lost the presidency; it held 18 governorships, five fewer than in 1981; . . . it had 176 House seats, 16 fewer than in 1981; it controlled 29 state legislative bodies, six fewer than in 1981."[52]

For establishment Republicans, even more demoralizing than the loss of the White House was the fear of the Clinton gang, aka Woodstock Nation, now blowing into town in January 1993. During the heat of the primaries, as another of her libidinous husband's infidelities spilled out into the public square for all to click or wag their tongues at—this time about Gennifer Flowers, a lounge singer in Little Rock—Hillary called her "the daughter of Willie Horton."[53] No one quite knew what Hillary meant by this. The rumor going around Republican circles was there'd been a Faustian bargain made between Bill and Hillary Clinton: she'd look the other way if he agreed to share power.

Yet as even the Bush campaign and Dan Quayle talked about the "cultural elite" and "family values," and made expansive allusions to the rumors about Clinton's drug use and more than rumors about womanizing, a great swath of the American people seemed not to care.

The Perot candidacy had thrown off the storyline of the election, but not the outcome. Bitter Bushies blamed Ross Perot (when not blaming Pat Buchanan, evangelicals, whomever) for costing their man reelection, but post-election polling showed the little Texas business executive taking proportionally from each candidate.[54]

It cannot be underestimated that with the demise of the Soviet Union, for the first time since 1948 the American people did not have to consider who they wanted to sit across the table from a Soviet premier. This was the real "Peace Dividend" and it was paying off for Clinton. In any Cold War context, Clinton would have come up short against Bush, but foreign policy was off the table as an issue in 1992.

The Bush people were gone, driven from office and, on top of it all, humiliated at the last, as the president of the United States was photographed dissolving in a self-pitying crying jag, as Bob Dole tried to console him at a private dinner with GOP lawmakers. Bush was a man's man and this sad spectacle made it even harder for his supporters.

Conservatives had mixed feelings, frankly, about Bush's departure and the arrival of the "Man from Hope." Bob Novak gave the Bush eulogy on his CNN show *Crossfire*:

> The legacy of George Bush is a failed presidency, another Herbert Hoover presidency. It started bad, it went downhill. He won a war. He did a brilliant job of winning the war, but that has . . . a low retention value. I think he has left the Republican party in worse shape than it's been in any time since . . . I think since the '30s, because it is out of gas, and it's out of steam ideologically, and George Bush has to bear a lot of the burden.[55]

But Bill Clinton was, to many conservatives, a man-child at best; a spoiled and immature adolescent trying desperately to measure up to the masculine men who'd occupied the Oval Office before him. Rumors were already seeping into political circles of his frequent temper tantrums and outbursts and "purple faced rages" and one could only imagine him holding his breath until he got his way.

Conservatives had complained for years about media bias, and the documentation of voting and ideological preferences and financial giving backed up their complaints, but the 1992 election was the first in which the media became an active surrogate program for the Democratic candidate. It was a dangerous development, antithetical to the intentions of the Framers.

Gingrich would have to face new fights with the new Administration without his old friend and ideological soul mate, Vin Weber of Minnesota. Weber had gone to Washington as part of the Reagan Revolution, but he was burned out by 1992. He'd also been singed by the House banking scandal, having bounced 125 checks; this factored into his decision to quit, knowing it would be thrown in his face repeatedly during the campaign. He left Congress but not Washington, becoming a well-regarded K Street lobbyist.

Rumors also swept GOP circles that Minority Leader Bob Michel was on the verge of hanging up his pistols. For a lot of impatient conservatives—including Gingrich—Michel's sidearms had been water pistols at best. They were anticipating a more confrontational leader, even one who was downright trigger-happy. Speculating, Gingrich later said Michel probably thought he was a "bomb thrower . . . unpredictable . . . unreliable."[56]

Gingrich, unopposed, was reelected Whip, but he made it clear he would run for minority leader in 1994 if Michel retired. A liberal Republican, Jim Leach of Iowa, enthused, "There has never been . . . a generator of ideas as Newt Gingrich."[57]

Joining the House leadership was Dick Armey, a Texas congressman and former economist who resembled and talked like a longshoreman. If possible, he was full of more whiz and vinegar than anyone else in Washington. He won with Newt's backing over an old foe, Jerry Lewis of California. With the exception of Michel, the entire House GOP leadership was now comprised of movement conservatives—including Bill McCollum of Florida, Henry Hyde of Illinois, Bill Paxon of New York, and Duncan Hunter of California. Some moderate members of the conference were decidedly unhappy, including Steve Gunderson of Wisconsin, who resigned as deputy whip in protest. Fred Upton, another moderate from Michigan, also took himself out of Gingrich's sphere of influence. The national media made much of both departures as indictments of "right wing militancy."[58]

Gingrich approached Armey, Bob Walker, and Bill Paxon about coordinating more closely. All except Armey jumped at the idea. Armey said that "he'd never flown in formation before," but he later agreed to try.[59]

At the time, someone tried to hang the moniker "Prince of Gridlock" on Gingrich but it didn't stick. And because of all the new conservatives in the leadership, it was a double-edged sword for Newt. While having ideological allies, it also meant ideological critics; he would have to play his hand with his back to the wall.

With Bush gone and the GOP without a national leader, the party was speaking with many voices, including that of the more and more dominant Rush Limbaugh, whose national radio show really took off after Bush went back to Houston. Millions listened and laughed at Limbaugh's witticisms and snarky put-down of liberals. He was the populist cousin to the erudite William F. Buckley.

Gingrich's voice was also rising. He was setting his sights on a lifelong dream: control of the US House of Representatives. Of course, some in the GOP counseled him to make nice with and accommodate the Clintons and accept that the era of Reagan was over. Bob Novak thought otherwise. "If there's any chance for the Republicans to take over the House it's because of what Gingrich is doing and what the flame throwers are doing."[60]

The GOP and the conservatives had become liberated with the departure of Bush. It was refreshing for many, as if a great weight had been lifted. The official rejection of Bush had begun at the Houston convention, where the platform specifically rebuked the tax increase of 1990. Previously, George Will in his column had taken the audacious step of calling on Bush to step down as the GOP's nominee. In a later column, Will called the Bush campaign an "intellectual slum."[61] Disgusted with the status quo, Will had written a well-received book entitled *Restoration*, making a case for congressional term limits, which the columnist described as a "bad idea whose time has come."[62]

For the first time in twelve years, Newt was presented with a clean slate. No Republicans in the White House and now he was in the leadership, free to pursue his agenda. It was back-to-fundamentals time. "We have 6,000 years of written historical experience in the Judeo-Christian tradition. We know the rules that work. We know that learning, study, work, saving and commitment are vital."[63] He also saw how impressive Clinton's campaign really was and said so: "The best of any Democrat's since 1960."[64]

CHAPTER 28

BLOODY NOSES AND CRACK'D CROWNS

"I walk down the hall knowing that a significant number of Democrats dislike me intensely because I represent a force that will end their careers."

1993

By the early part of 1993, Newt Gingrich had surpassed Bob Dole as the principal spokesman for the GOP. A schism between outsiders and insiders sometimes emerged, but neither man really wanted this; they were unified in their opposition to Bill Clinton. Truth be told, Gingrich sometimes wanted to be an insider—and Dole was more outsider than many comprehended. Dole tolerated the establishment, but he was still a rural Kansan with a deep disregard for the elites.

At the first meeting between Clinton and the GOP leadership following the election, Dole was there, but Gingrich was on vacation. Conservatives like Grover Norquist had settled on Newt as their spokesman, and he wrote a long piece for the *American Spectator* laying out the case for full-scale guerrilla operations against the Clintons.[1]

The annual Conservative Political Action Conference was meeting under the theme "Back to the Future," which all knew meant good-bye to Bushism. The conference was organized by Zorine Bhappu Shirley and was one of the most successful in years.

The battered GOP members of Congress retreated to New Jersey to lick and anesthetize their wounds, but even in defeat there was controversy, this time surrounding the retreat itself being underwritten by corporate lobbyists.

A Hill staffer observed quite frankly that if the GOP agreed to take the lobbyists' money for a meeting, but did not allow the lobbyists to attend, then the lobbyists were "not going to give us the money."[2]

Other new conservative groups were springing forth, reminiscent of the 1970s, though these were less intellectual and more political, more interested in directly taking on Bill Clinton rather than simply advancing the ideas of conservatism. One of those new political groups was Empower America, headed by Bill Bennett, Jack Kemp, and Jeane Kirkpatrick. On the surface, each represented the social, economic, and foreign policy groupings of the GOP, respectively. But truth be told, both Bennett and Kemp were big-government conservatives and Kirkpatrick was traveling an ideological road, from Humphrey Democrat to Reagan Republican.

At yet another conservative summit, this one sponsored by the National Review Institute, Gingrich spoke. "Clinton's failures are not opportunities. Clinton's failures are a distraction," he said. "They are secondary to the real problem—it is much more important for us to develop a positive vision."[3] This was January 1993, just a couple of days after Clinton had been sworn in, and already Gingrich was on offense.

New groups were emerging and old groups were staging comebacks. The listenership for Rush Limbaugh and other conservative talkers in the "New Media," which was already high, jumped up even higher. The *American Spectator* began advertising on Limbaugh's show; within days, their subscribing readership exploded tenfold. The National Rifle Association, similarly undone by the burden of George H. W. Bush, was also gaining new members at an impressive clip.

At the Super Bowl in Atlanta between the Cowboys and the Bills, Republicans held fund-raising events, including one that featured special guest O. J. Simpson, who was a close friend of fellow NFLer Jack Kemp.[4]

Since 1987, when Reagan had refused to re-sign the so-called Fairness Doctrine, AM radio had gone through a huge rebirth. It had been wilting in the shadow of FM until free opinion was allowed to flourish on talk radio without the government mandate of "equal time." Now the marketplace governed the AM dial and, led by the must-listen-to Rush Limbaugh, the Prince of Amplitude Modulation, and others, talk radio grew steadily from a handful to dozens to hundreds upon hundreds of local and regional "Baby Limbaughs." They wielded enormous influence. Even liberals like James Fallows were forced to sheepishly concede, "Limbaugh is a first-class satirist whose intelligence the chattering classes underestimate . . ."[5] Fallows, as a card-carrying liberal, could not resist a shot at Limbaugh, though, saying "his grasp of public policy is spotty."[6]

ABC's *Nightline* devoted an entire show in early 1993 to the talk radio phenomenon, focusing on Limbaugh.[7] His following stretched into the millions who delighted in his withering put-down of liberals, feminists, environmentalists, Clintons, and others generally on the left. He was truly unique, with a gift for humor that eluded many conservative leaders and, while not urbane and suave like William F. Buckley, Limbaugh followed him as one of the most important and influential conservatives of the twentieth century. Gingrich and Limbaugh were becoming friends quickly, and spoke often as 1993 progressed.

Gingrich was also smitten with a young pollster and rhetoric therapist, Frank Luntz, a once-shy young man who'd come up in New Right politics but as years went by had eschewed conservatism for opportunism. In Luntz's defense, he was not alone. He recalled the first time he had a serious meeting with Gingrich, begging off on continuing the conversation over lunch. "I can't. I'm doing a testing for New Line Cinema for a film, *Corrina, Corrina*. He looked at me . . . it was one of those classic Newt looks."[8]

Luntz was later brought into Newt's inner circle after passing the muster of two trusted confidants, Jeff Eisenach, the quintessential policy wonk, and Gay Hart Gaines, a striking and talented Palm Beach socialite who doubled as a smart and tough political operative. Gaines had taken over GOPAC for Gingrich, cleaning away the cobwebs and stale old mission and transformed it into a model of policy and political action. The organization she took over was riddled with debt, but she soon eliminated that and turned GOPAC into a profitable operation. At the first staff meeting, she said, "Look left and look right because in three months, half of you will be here." An important part of Gaines's game plan was the mass producing of Gingrich's lectures on tape. They were hugely popular.[9] Gaines convened private dinners in her home with power brokers and high rollers and the rule was total Omerta. Bill Kristol violated the rule. Gaines said, "The next morning, in the *New York Times*, was everything about my dinner." She burned a phone line to

Kristol and told him, "I know it was you and you're never, ever going to be invited back!"[10]

At the time, Arianna Huffington, the Greek-born, Cambridge University–educated wife of Republican congressman Michael Huffington, was also trying to enter close orbit with Gingrich but he resisted, seeing her as a social climber and nothing more. "He didn't like her. He saw through her. He just saw her as an opportunist and not a real believer," said one source close to the Georgian.[11]

GOPAC rivaled the RNC as far as reach and credibility because of Gaines. She and Newt and a couple of others in NewtWorld spoke a language that few understood. Another member of Newt's inner sanctum was Joe Gaylord, who, while talented, also was turf conscious in the extreme. He was sometimes obsessive over who could come close to Newt and he especially despised Luntz. He did everything he could to undermine and otherwise ward off the brash young man. But Newt needed Gaylord.

Gingrich once told Luntz, "I have two people in my life who are essential, my wife and Joe Gaylord. I'm not always sure which one is more essential."[12] Gaylord seemed not interested in ideas one whit, just power and his own conspicuous consumption. At one point, according to Luntz, Gaylord actually attempted to pay the young man to get him away from Gingrich. Luntz was appalled.[13] Still, Gaylord had a reputation for organization.

For years, while Congressman Guy Vander Jagt was nominally in charge of the NRCC, everybody in Washington knew Gaylord treated the committee as his own personal fiefdom before going into business for himself. Vander Jagt knew the party needed Gingrich's leadership, but he told his former second-in-command Gaylord that his new boss's intellect might need harnessing. "I know that he's got a thousand ideas, I know that he's really smart, but half the time, I don't understand what he's saying," he told Gaylord.[14]

Gingrich's past came back for a time to haunt him when his first wife, Jackie, sued him for nonpayment of $1,300 per month in alimony, and for failure to pay the premiums on her life insurance policy. She was demanding "jail time" for her ex-husband. Gingrich denied the charges and said he was current with both payments. The dispute was resolved, and when a spokesman

BLOODY NOSES AND CRACK'D CROWNS | 323

for Gingrich, Allan Lipsett, was asked if things would be more "amicable" between the two now, he simply replied, "Let's just say it's settled."[15]

The incident brought up bad memories of the divorce that had been finalized more than a decade earlier. At the time, several staffers had been extremely dismayed over the divorce and sometime thereafter left Gingrich's office. Jackie was vocal with some of the staff back then, telling them her side of the story about the dissolution of the marriage. Contrary to popular belief, the divorce hit Gingrich hard, in spite of his instigation. Revisiting the issue now did little to improve his mood about his personal life.[16]

Because the Clintons had run essentially a personality campaign, they had opened their personalities to mockery, in which late-night television hosts, Republicans, conservatives, and radio talk show hosts indulged with relish. No less a figure than the happily polysyllabic Bill Buckley wrote that Clinton was a "fornicator" and a "liar."[17]

George Stephanopoulos, a Clinton spokesman (and for a time a diminutive sex symbol and favored Hollywood role model), went on CNN and got nailed by Bob Novak for having no plan for governance.[18] In a joint appearance with Stephanopoulos and another Clinton aide, Paul Begala, on ABC's *Nightline*, Gingrich ripped the Clinton White House staff, calling them "inadequate" and saying that Clinton was being "ill-served."[19]

As a consequence, the Clinton cabinet-clearing and nomination process was one of the messiest in modern history. One potential nominee after another had to be withdrawn for ethics reasons, for tax reasons, for other reasons, as with both Zoe Baird and Kimba Wood, two very attractive if underwhelming nominees for attorney general, who both had "nanny problems." Gingrich quipped, "You can't have a person who ought to be prosecuted serving in the Cabinet."[20] He was one of the first to call for Baird's nomination to be withdrawn and hammered away for several days on the issue. To add insult to injury, Baird and her husband paid a $2,900 fine to the INS for employing illegal immigrants at their house.

Clinton kept insisting he wanted a cabinet that looked like America. He ended up with a cabinet of millionaire lawyers. Inside of Washington, one could throw a dart in any direction and hit a millionaire lawyer, but outside of Washington they were few and far between. As a consequence, Clinton never got the "honeymoon" from the national media that other presidents had enjoyed. Across the board, from the left to the right, they set upon the Clinton White House and rarely really let up. Only months into his presidency, *Time* magazine did a cover story of an extremely small Clinton with the headline "The Incredible Shrinking President."[21]

And then there was Al Gore. The actual fortunate son of a US senator, Gore did—in his defense—go to Vietnam and serve in the US Army, though he saw no action except perhaps an occasional paper cut from writing press releases. Still, he did what nearly no one else from his Harvard class cared to do and that was serve his country. Many of them spent their time protesting and chanting, "Ho, Ho, Ho Chi Minh, NLF is going to win."

The Congress and the Pentagon were far less ambivalent about gays in uniform, a top priority of the Clintons. Some of the most virulent opponents to gays in the military were members of Clinton's own party, including Senator Sam Nunn of Georgia. Gingrich opposed it on the grounds that it represented "social engineering" and would "weaken morale" inside the military.[22] Another vocal opponent was General Colin Powell. Fighting with Nunn and Powell was "foolish" according to Gingrich.[23] He later upped it, calling Clinton's behavior on the matter "bizarre."[24] Gingrich himself had to do some tap dancing; he had seemed to support gays in the military just a year before in an interview with the *New Republic*.[25] His spokesman, Tony Blankley, denied that Newt had changed his position.

There was a real fear inside the Republican Party that Clinton might actually turn out to be a "New Democrat," pursuing centrist policies that would banish the GOP to minority status for another generation. It was to the fortunes of the GOP that Clinton pursued the marginal issue of gays in the military—settling after months of negotiations for "Don't Ask, Don't Tell," which is what the unspoken policy had been all along—and the more central issue of Hillarycare, which the more people learned about it, the more it scared the bejeepers out of them. The latter would become an excellent weapon in the hands of the Republicans.

Still, the GOP had no plan of its own. E. J. Dionne wrote a column for the *Post* saying that they needed one.[26] The *New York Times* warned Gingrich against "mindless obstructionism."[27] The media was full of unsolicited advice.

Gingrich, however, was the first in the GOP to take on Hillarycare. In a widely discussed newspaper piece, he warned Clinton not to go it alone: "If Clinton brushes aside the offers of help from Republicans and decides to lead a partisan rush to comprehensive reform, it will blow up in his face, and in the ashes of that explosion will be buried the chances of genuine health care reform for another generation."[28]

Clinton was pursuing a big "stimulus" package to get the economy moving, along with tax increases and spending cuts to try to close the monstrous deficit left behind by Bush, projected at $319 billion.[29] He was also toying with the idea of a new gasoline tax and had abandoned the middle-class tax cut he'd hinted at during the campaign.

Gingrich was right there, hammering Clinton.

The Democrats were united, but the fissures Clinton hoped to exploit in the GOP were widening. Bob Dole said he could potentially support the higher taxes on higher wage earners, but Gingrich drew a line in the sand, saying that Dole's acquiescence was "an enormous mistake."[30] Gingrich also fretted that Dole's position would make it harder for the GOP to get back on its feet. Neocon Bill Kristol saw things the way Gingrich did, especially in light of the Bush tax increases. "It's not so easy to reclaim your virginity," he quipped.[31]

Gingrich—the Georgia Bulldog—was already thinking offense, and was ready to go to battle with Clinton over "class warfare" and anything else he could dig up.[32]

Case in point, Gingrich was one of the first to raise the idea of an independent counsel to investigate the financial improprieties associated with an Arkansas land development corporation in which the Clintons had been involved. The company was called Whitewater. It would become one of the first original scandal names since Watergate and gave headline writers all sorts of opportunities to get creative.

One young back-bencher appreciated Gingrich's style. He'd won his seat in Ohio by questioning the ethics of an older Republican and once in Washington, thumped his chest and announced, "I came as a reformer. But when people in charge don't want to reform—the only way—is revolution." Thus said John Boehner to the *Cleveland Plain Dealer*, in January 1993.[33]

An editorial in the *Washington Times* on the new GOP offensive encapsulated the thinking of most: "In the view of many House veterans, and in the view of many freshmen, the GOP had little but defeat to show for its Bush-era accomodationism."[34]

When the Democratic majority in the House tried to convey full voting rights on the delegates from the American territories that would have added five to their already handsome vote total, the GOP threatened a suit on the constitutionality—Article One, Section Two—and the power grab was beaten back.[35]

During a rules debate on the House floor in January, Don Edwards, an acidic Democrat from California, was in the Speaker's chair. When Gingrich's time was up, Edwards gaveled and said, "The gentleman from Georgia has expired."[36] One side of the aisle chuckled and applauded at the incredibly tasteless joke, but the Republicans sat in stony silence. By attacking Newt personally, they were making him a figure of sympathy, and thus more popular within his own conference. They were inexorably becoming the architects of their own undoing.

Gingrich and company also won a big fight when they matched a request by the majority to make one-hour speeches from the floor of the House under Special Rules. Democratic congressman David Bonior had made the request for the majority to the House Parliamentarian, but Gingrich moved to have it extended to the minority. When granted, it guaranteed the Republicans a full year of unfettered access to C-SPAN, which they'd been much more effective in using than had the Democrats. It also guaranteed them the right to go first every evening.[37]

Gingrich once told Bob Walker, "How much would you give to be able to make a speech before 100,000 people in a stadium? Well, you reach five times that many at the minimum every time you go on C-SPAN."[38] Walker was a happy warrior, having a ball tormenting the opposition, like many of the so-called Reagan Robots.

Gingrich, as usual, was a regular on the Sunday talk shows. It was also a time when a president of the United States could call a press conference and all three networks would broadcast it, but this, too, was fading into history.

The battle lines were being drawn, even as some old allies turned into Clinton stooges, as in the case of the US Chamber of Commerce, which sided with the White House and against the GOP on a number of bills, including tax increases and Hillarycare, understanding that her plan would shift the cost away from corporations to government, in essence, a federal subsidy for the private sector.

Gingrich and others were furious with the Chamber, essentially black-balling them from the GOP Conference. Clinton did this to people. He brought out the worst in Washington and the opposition, but the fights to come would be bloody and gruesome. They would make anything that had gone on before look like a folk dance.

CHAPTER 29

THE TEMPEST

*"He's . . . going to end up like the French Socialists, just
being so far out of whack that the country repudiates
him, or he could easily end up like Jimmy Carter . . ."*

1993

B ill Clinton was itching to get the United States involved in the civil
war in the former Yugoslavia, if only to prove he had the "right stuff"
as president. He met with an unenthusiastic congressional leadership, but
only Newt Gingrich "expressed outright dissent to the president against
military intervention."[1] Western Europe showed little interest in getting
involved in a fight in their own backyard, but Clinton claimed he did not
need UN support to act unilaterally and plunge America into a conflict no
one in America understood or cared about. Comparisons to Vietnam were
bandied about. Senator John McCain opposed any action on the basis that
American air strikes would not "beneficially affect that tragic situation."[2]
He also compared the situation to Vietnam, as in *quagmire.*

Ironically, as the issue developed, it was doves like Clinton and George
McGovern, now head of the Middle East Policy Council, who had the
itchy trigger fingers, while hawks like Gingrich, McCain, Barry Goldwater,
and others saw intervention as pointless and probably counterproductive.
Political correctness began driving the debate when the issue of Serbian
abuse of women cropped up.

Another foreign-policy dilemma was the rumor of a planned assassination of then-president Bush by Saddam Hussein. The plot had been
uncovered by the Kuwaitis. Both sides of the aisle agreed that if found to

be true, Baghdad should be bombed into the Stone Age. Gingrich was the most hawkish, calling for Saddam's ouster via US military forces.[3]

Midyear, Clinton ordered Tomahawk missiles to hit Saddam's intelligence headquarters. "It was essential that a youthful president—widely viewed as indecisive and at odds with his own military—demonstrate to Saddam Hussein and the world that he will not be pushed around," wrote one of the most influential foreign policy columnists around, Marianne Means of Hearst Newspapers.[4] Gingrich cheered on the attack.

The partisan skirmishes between the Clinton Administration and the Republicans in Congress, supported more and more by the New Media, were multiplying and accelerating. A Clinton stimulus went down in defeat. Fights over nominees. Fights over spending. Fights over government. The situation between Clinton and the Republicans, never good, had become near poisonous, and he'd been in office less than six months. Clinton was only a nine-to-five ideologue, but he was fiercely partisan, a "yellow-dog" Democrat; hating Republicans was as natural to him as eating quarter pounders with cheese. Clinton charged that the Republicans had not offered any spending cuts, and they jumped right back in his face, accusing him of an "outrageous lie."[5]

Leading the New Media was, of course, Rush Limbaugh. He had already coined a phrase for the Clinton Agenda: "Raw Deal." Each day he opened up his show by saying, "America Held Hostage, Day . . . " a riff on Walter Cronkite's Iranian hostage count up in 1979 and 1980. Limbaugh had become a fast-moving cultural icon. Restaurants had "Rush Rooms"; he had a book out, *The Way Things Ought to Be*, which became the fastest-selling hardcover in publishing history; and there were T-shirts, bumper stickers, a TV show in the works, a syndicated column, a newsletter, and a national lecture tour. Limbaugh was filling a heretofore unrequited need for American conservatives to laugh and feel witty all at the same time. Limbaugh really was something new under the sun. At least for three hours a day.

One scandal after another was bubbling up, including one involving the White House Travel Office and charges of its politicization, as well as the politicization of the IRS. The dustup over the Travel Office was indicative of larger battles to come. Gingrich, smelling blood, expanded the argument against his opponents, saying, "This is about corrupt one-party rule for four decades."[6]

When the head of the House post office fingered Congressman Dan Rostenkowski in a plea bargain deal, it was clear his days were numbered. But he was not alone. Other members, mostly Democrats, had been a part of the stamps-for-cash laundering operation. Even better from Newt's perspective. He pounded the Democrats for days. House Speaker Tom Foley said Rostenkowski was an "honest man." Gingrich pounced, keeping the issue alive even longer.[7] Bill Clinton jumped in with both feet, declaring, "I need Rostenkowski." The Democrats, in embracing their old friend so tightly, were foolishly taking ownership of congressional corruption.

At the worst possible time, questions were raised involving Foley and insider trading and $100,000 profits off of initial public offerings. Foley denied it but closed his trading account anyway after it was revealed he'd turned a profit off forty of forty-two stocks he'd picked, leaving one to question why he wasn't trading full-time on Wall Street.[8] Gingrich slammed Foley again.

A new *Wall Street Journal* poll showed congressional approval at an all-time low of 23 percent.[9] One of the most unpopular members of Congress, Michael Barnes of Maryland, said that the Democrats respected Gingrich "for his intellect but he is sometimes hated for his tactics."[10]

As the GOP was accelerating away from Bushism and re-embracing Reaganism, they still weren't sure where they stood on everything. Some Republicans (and a few conservatives) were embracing Hillarycare, as it shifted the burden from businesses to the government (taxpayers) to pay for health insurance, more to the bottom line for corporate executives.

The new Clinton budget featured tax increases across the board on individuals and, as a result, was shunned by conservatives. Gingrich and company denounced the corporatists in unprintable language. Comparisons were made to the Canadian system of socialized medicine; Hillarycare proponents snorted how superior their system was to a free-market-based system.

The Heritage Foundation, which also supported mandates to the individual to purchase insurance, found itself locked out by their friends in the GOP. Initially, Gingrich and other conservatives had supported the Heritage national health plan because it had the imprimatur of the conservative think tank, but most had dropped away by the spring of 1993, including Gingrich. The Georgian expressed his skepticism often and loudly. Clinton hammered away day after day that the American health care system was "broken." Nowhere in the Clintons' proposed reforms, however, was found any restrictions or reforms of trial lawyers, whose frivolous lawsuits had driven up costs across the board, for insurance companies, for doctors, and for patients. Never in the history of America had so many done so little for so much.

On the other side and considered just as sacred were the insurance companies and health care companies, including hospitals, and they were showering millions down on both parties, much of it to Republicans, to stop Hillarycare. Even though they were in the minority in the House and the Senate, the three biggest recipients of insurance and medical contributions were all Republicans, with Arlen Specter of Pennsylvania leading the way. Gingrich was one of the biggest recipients in the House, getting $169,559 from these interests as of the end of 1992.[11]

John Boehner went to war with the Chamber of Commerce, urging Republicans to boycott an awards ceremony.[12] Gingrich agreed and also called for a boycott. Of the 100 Republicans invited, only 32 showed up. Main Street conservatives had just beaten up Wall Street Republicans by a score of 68–32.[13] It was not even close and another indication that the GOP was tipping away from Bushism toward Reaganism.

But not everybody was on board with the renewed embrace of conservatism or the new favorite indoor sport of Clinton-bashing. GOP minority leader Bob Michel, still minority leader, kneaded his fingers and worried that he'd never seen the Republicans so "conservative and antagonistic." He fretted that many in his own conference were "not very cooperative" and that many were just "hardliners."[14] On the other hand, some conservatives were worried that Gingrich was holding back at just the point when he should have been heaving Molotov cocktails. Bob Novak said Gingrich was the one Republican "most capable of sketching a vision and lifting the party's spirits . . ."[15]

Another bone of contention inside the GOP was term limits. Most libertarian conservatives were opposed, but Gingrich was for them albeit reluctantly, as he told columnist Bob Novak.[16] The public mood was overwhelmingly in favor of term limits by a better than 7–1 ratio.

The Perot vote in the 1992 presidential election was seen as anti-Bush, and it was; but in a larger sense, it was anti-Washington, anti-elites, and anti-establishment. It was conservative but not overly religious; it was libertarian but not libertine. The question was always which party could channel this populist, Jacksonian, contrarian voter. Bush had suffered because he was the establishment, but now Bill Clinton was very much the establishment. A group of House Republicans, including Gingrich, joined, with much ballyhoo, Perot's new political organization, United We Stand America, and posed for photos with the wily Texan.

The "Perot vote," as it came to be known, intrigued and eventually obsessed Gingrich. In September, he began meeting with the young, impulsive pollster and wordmeister Frank Luntz. Luntz was in bad odor with some Republican Party insiders for consulting for a time on Ross Perot's presidential campaign before he left in frustration. Gingrich, however, was fascinated with the young man and his knowledge of the "Perotistas," as they were known in some quarters. One-fifth of the electorate should have held the attention of any reasonable politician, but only Gingrich, aided by Luntz, studied it and strove to develop pitches and programs to bring them back into the conservative fold, if not necessarily the Republican fold.[17]

Perot was making noises about a third party and possibly recruiting candidates for Congress in 1994. No doubt Clinton was doing his best with Hillarycare and tax increases to drive away the suspicious-of-Washington populist Perot voters; but the GOP, after four years of Bush, was no option either, unless things changed quickly in the party.

The Clinton White House was also reaching out to Perot, even as Bushies continued to foolishly attack him.[18] The debate over how to handle Perot continued throughout 1993 and into 1994, unabated.

Gingrich's GOPAC was extending its reach and influence as the former college professor took to lecturing again, using Kennesaw State College in

334 | CITIZEN NEWT

Georgia as a base of operations, and teaching via satellite to students at more than one hundred colleges and universities around the country, including Harvard. Liberal opponents charged partisanship, but even the *New York Times* wrote, "The critics acknowledge that there is nothing illegal about the arrangement . . ."[19] The twenty-hour course was named "Renewing American Civilization" and included top professors and academics. Gingrich and company got ticked off at the hypocrisy of campus liberals complaining about indoctrination—it struck some as a tad ironic that an associate communications professor at Kennesaw, Peter Chiaramonte, criticized the academic credentials of Gingrich, who had an undergraduate degree from Emory, a graduate degree and a PhD from Tulane, and many years of experience teaching college at West Georgia.[20]

Opponents also questioned the funding, as wealthy supporters gave tax-exempt contributions to GOPAC to cover the costs associated with the class. Gingrich was not compensated; that was the only difference between how higher education typically operated and the GOPAC-sponsored class at Kennesaw. The president of Kennesaw, Dr. Betty Siegel, came out and publicly defended Gingrich and the class before the tempest finally began to settle down.

After all the clamor and showboating and bravado, the course began. More than one hundred undergraduates showed up for a lecture on American history on a Saturday morning.

A couple of minor dustups occurred in the press, usually involving Gingrich, GOPAC, and travel costs, but nothing came of them as he shrugged off the allegations. The only other dark cloud was Gingrich's old nemesis Herman Clark, who claimed he was preparing to run again against Gingrich. But Newt had already amassed $364,664 for 1994, making him one of the most endowed incumbents in the House.[21]

The Christian Right was reengaging after more or less taking a pass on Bush in '92, though many in both the GOP and the conservative movement held them at arm's length. At the head of Pat Robertson's Christian Coalition was thirty-two-year-old Ralph Reed, who looked and acted younger than even twenty-two. He had been quoted over the years claiming he'd put his political opponents in "body bags" and comparing his tactics to "guerrilla warfare" and the Viet Cong.[22] As a College Republican, he'd once paraded up and down Pennsylvania Avenue with a bull horn, repeatedly chanting,

"Wake Up, Ronnie!" to Reagan in the White House in the aftermath of the Soviet shootdown of KAL 007. Reed's sentence structure was shot through with first-person pronouns and made clear that ideology was not as important to him as winning at any cost, to the glory of his own publicity. Reed was at the vanguard of the new breed of GOP celebrity consultants.

Off-year gubernatorial elections in New Jersey and Virginia were underway, but the GOP was not thought to be in a position to win either. Still, both Dole and Gingrich campaigned in the Commonwealth for George Allen, the GOP nominee and former member of Congress, who was a tobacco-chewing, avuncular, and charming conservative, the son of a former Redskins coach. Both he and the GOP nominee in the Garden State, Christie Todd Whitman, were lagging far behind in the polls.

The first outcropping of anti-Democratic establishment activity came in mid-1993, when GOPer Bret Schundler was elected mayor of Jersey City, where Republicans were about as popular as a case of herpes. Only 6 percent of voters in the corrupt and burnt-out shell of a metropolis were Republicans. The previous mayor, a Democrat, had gone to jail for corruption, as had fourteen of his brother mayors in the Prison Guard State. Schundler was a pure child of Kempism, the first generation.

"New Jersey City is headed in a new direction, one that points to deregulation, privatization, school vouchers, enterprise zones and fiscal restraint," said the *Washington Post*.[23]

But Gingrich was enthralled, too, seeing the basket case of a city as a laboratory for change and an opportunity to refute the liberal nostrums that local conservatism only worked in rural and suburban areas. Schundler, who was white, had won a special election by a whisker, but six months later, running for his own term, he gathered an amazing 69 percent of the vote in a city that was overwhelmingly black, Hispanic, and Asian.

As evidenced in the Jersey City vote, crime was emerging as a big issue for 1993 and 1994. The left was focusing on gun control, while the right was going after tougher sentencing, tougher judges, bigger prisons, and a new "Three Strikes" idea. The legislation provided for automatic sentencing if an individual was convicted of three state crimes. It was arbitrary, it was terrifying, and it was politically devastating for those who opposed it.

There were some efforts by the GOP in even the most liberal states to mount serious Senate and House races in 1994 against Democrats always considered unbeatable. The Bay State was a fine kettle of fish, with Ted Kennedy so popular. "The GOP search for someone has been disappointing although Willard 'Mitt' Romney . . . is a possibility."[24] But a local GOP operative described the state of his campaign as a "disaster."

Clinton tried to catch up to the anti-Washington populist wave, cutting back on limousines for White House staff, but he got little credit for his actions. The anti-Clinton sentiment sometimes got downright fevered. The president's counsel, Vince Foster, a deeply troubled and unhappy man, missed Arkansas terribly and hated the Washington shooting gallery in which he'd found himself. Rather than quitting and going home, he committed suicide one evening at an obscure park in Virginia, raising the paranoia of some on the right to embarrassing levels, who produced volumes and white papers on tawdry and unfounded rumors about Foster, Clinton, Hillary, and friends. Foster's own suicide note was memorable for the line about Washington, "Here ruining people is considered sport."[25]

Unbounded, having neither responsibility nor authority, conservatism was winning the national debate with liberals over all manner of things. Not *Republicanism*, mind you, but *conservatism*. Liberalism hadn't had anyone good on television in a generation, but with Clinton now in the White House, he wasn't about to go on every Sunday talk show (though he would have if his staff had let him), so the defense of liberalism fell to people unequal to the task.

The Clintons helped to unify conservatives as much as anyone. President Clinton's budget passed the House 219–213, with 38 Democrats defying their president and crossing over to vote with the Republicans, who all voted nay. Same thing in the Senate, where Bob Dole led all the Republican senators against the Clinton tax increases. Dole had said to an astonished world, "We will oppose any new taxes."[26] Washington was struck dumb. In both chambers, not one Republican voted for the Clinton plan. Gingrich had successfully "whipped" and Dole had just terrified the Senate Republicans. Gingrich said afterward, "These votes only last 15 minutes; the taxes can last a lifetime."[27]

Reagan's 1984 manager, Ed Rollins, understood what few did, and that was GOP opposition to George Bush's tax increase in 1990 unified and redefined the party.[28]

While all the Republicans were jubilant about defying the president, many Democrats ran for the tall grass, knowing they were badly on the wrong side of the tax and spending issue. David Gergen, a recent hire of Clinton's who'd worked for Nixon, Ford, Reagan, and Bush—and whose presence was considered somewhat of a coup inside of Washington—was sent out to spin the vote for the Clinton White House.

Around this time, Gingrich became one of the first congressmen in history to have an e-mail address.[29]

The fights over Clinton's nominees continued unabated. When Roberta Achtenberg, an out-of-the-closet lesbian, was nominated to the Department of Housing and Urban Development, social conservatives including Senator Jesse Helms of North Carolina pitched a fit. "She has been a militant activist demanding that society accept as normal . . . a lifestyle that most of the world's religions consider immoral, and which the average American voter instinctively finds repulsive."[30] Gingrich was usually reticent to get involved in these type of social issues, but when it was learned that Achtenberg advocated including gays in the Boy Scouts, he responded, "Defending the Boy Scouts' right to remain a heterosexual organization strikes me as a legitimate non-demagogic public policy position."[31]

The fight over the gay lifestyle extended even into the Deep South, into Gingrich's Georgia and Cobb County, where the county commissioners voted to defund any art that celebrated homosexuality. CNN was all over the story and reported the opening of a commissioners meeting with a prayer: "We declare, Lord God, this city shall not be famous for perversion."[32] Gingrich did not duck it, and supported defunding gay art, even as Atlanta was set to sponsor the "Gay Games" in 1998.

The eternally youthful Gingrich turned fifty in June. His campaign turned Metamucil into lemonade and held fund-raisers around Georgia to raise campaign cash at $500 per head. The invitation noted that it was also the fiftieth anniversary of the famous meeting in Morocco between FDR and Churchill.

As a "birthday gift," he received a huge increase in funds for the Whip's Office, a jump of $114,000, over 15 percent, far more than nearly everybody else in the leadership. Overall, the Congress cut funding for its own operations by nearly 6 percent in real costs.[33] This was serious business to members and their staffs. While they might quibble about a $600 toilet seat here and there at the Pentagon, the "Imperial Congress" demanded the best for themselves, and cut only with broken hearts and political pressure. Two members from North Carolina, a Democrat and a Republican, got into a spraying match over cuts in franking privileges, with one accusing the other of being the "biggest franker in North Carolina."[34]

Gingrich remained indifferent to personal wealth. New disclosure reports showed him to be, along with Cynthia McKinney, one of the two poorest members of the Georgia delegation. His savings and checking accounts were under $15,000, and book royalties were less than $2,500.[35] Like everybody else in the House, he had to abide by new rules that prevented him from taking any money for outside speeches. Previously, members had made tens and even hundreds of thousands speechifying, but that era was gone. Any money derived from public remarks had to be donated to charity. Gingrich used $7,500 to purchase two Komodo dragons from the National Zoo and donated the lizards to Zoo Atlanta.[36] He personally escorted them south.

Rumors began circulating that House Minority Leader Bob Michel was getting ready to retire in 1994. It leaked out that he had approached two Chicago corporations about joining their boards. Bob Novak called Michel "peevish" and proclaimed Gingrich to be the natural leader of the Republican Party.

For the rest of 1993, Michel was nonexistent. Gingrich held the party meetings; Gingrich was doing the press conferences with Bob Dole; Gingrich was representing the House Republicans in meetings with Clinton and doing the "press avails" outside the White House. Michel was nowhere to be seen, and most felt Newt would replace him if he stepped down. Gingrich certainly wanted to.

A rash of Democrats had retired in 1992, and it looked as if another large group was getting ready to hang it up in 1994 as well. The Democrats still had a stranglehold on Capitol Hill, but things had changed radically since the old days when it was a combination of *Animal House*, *High Noon*, and *Viva Las Vegas*. In the old days of the New Deal and into the Great Society, a member could drink, chase skirts, get cash from lobbyists, and generally run amuck without fear of it all showing up in the newspapers. Slowly, with the reforms beginning in the 1970s, being in Congress just wasn't as much fun. They expected you to work.

A real fear about 1994 was gripping some quarters of the Democratic Party. The word *bloodbath* popped up occasionally. If Clinton's poll numbers did not perk up and the economy did not come around, the elections could be worse than the typical off-year campaigns in a president's first term.

The Bush family was gone but they'd not been forgotten. The former president was reportedly not handling his forced retirement well, nor was the rest of the family, especially Jeb and George W., who were making plans to run for the governorships of Florida and Texas, respectively. The early money favored Jeb, and the Washington press corps also liked Jeb more than they liked George. It colored their reporting and many thought Jeb would win in 1994 but that George W. was, at best, a sacrificial lamb to the incumbent, Ann Richards, whom the family, especially Barbara Bush, really hated for her rough depiction of Bush at the 1988 Democratic Convention. Indeed, the Bush political operation often seemed more about settling scores than advancing ideas.

In late 1993, Gingrich journeyed to Bosnia for two weeks to observe the civil war there more closely. Upon his return, though he'd softened on the whole matter, he was still resolute that no American GIs be deployed under the current circumstances.

At the close of the year, for the first time in print, someone raised the notion that the GOP could take control of Congress for the first time since 1954. The party had been wandering in the desert for forty years. Still, sensible people didn't say such foolish things in public. Hard-liners accused Gingrich of softening his image in anticipation of moving up, possibly to replace Bob Michel, while soft-liners accused him of throwing red meat to the lions, in anticipation of a full-scale revolution in 1994. He oddly said, unsettlingly, "People like me are what stand between us and Auschwitz."[37] No one knew what he meant.

At one joint press conference, Michel introduced Gingrich as "our distinguished whip" so all of Washington really knew how bitter he was that the revolution had passed him by.[38] Some were already throwing elbows for Whip if Gingrich succeeded to minority leader.

Within a matter of days, in December 1993, Michel made it official and said he would retire in 1994. He was a good man but left no memorable legacy except of a fine singing voice and a reputation for good manners. The notion of GOP control of the House was not only beyond his ken, it probably terrified him. Liberal columnists mourned his departure in advance. Another resident of the Land of Lincoln, Michael Jordan, also announced his retirement, but it was safe to say his impact on the NBA was far more permanent than Bob Michel's was on national politics.

Three days after Michel's announcement, Gingrich announced his intention to seek the position of minority leader. He claimed to already have the support of 105 of the 175 members of the conference, including youngsters like John Boehner and Rick Santorum. And why not? He'd been helping and mentoring many for years. Many had listened to his lectures on tapes sent out by GOPAC. As a show of strength, he held a press conference surrounded by 60 of his GOP colleagues.

At that press conference, he told reporters he was not a "bomb thrower" but a "truth thrower and in this town, the truth is a bomb."[39] To Gingrich's point, he had a lot of scalps on his wall, including Charlie Diggs's, Tip O'Neill's, Jim Wright's, and Tony Coelho's. Now the GOP had to pivot. In the days of Reagan, they had a man and a program to defend. With Bush, they wanted to defend neither. Now they had a president to oppose, unencumbered from within their party, but they also needed to unveil pro-growth policies, something to pitch to the American people about Republican governance. Gingrich knew it wasn't enough to simply oppose Clinton any longer. The GOP had to make a case.

The GOP was getting off the defense, having swept away the last remnants of Bushism. A new age of Enlightenment was slowly taking over the Republican Party since the rise of Reagan. They were offering competing ideas to Hillarycare, including medical savings accounts, though a divergence between the GOP House plans and the GOP Senate plans had emerged. While the House GOP version did not mandate that citizens purchase insurance, the Senate GOP version did.

Gingrich was not backing away from criticizing Clinton. He smashed Clinton over Haiti and he bashed him over Somalia. *Pathetic* was the word he used to describe Clinton's efforts to get NAFTA passed.[40]

Pat Buchanan, Jesse Jackson, Ralph Nader, and Ross Perot were working hard to stop NAFTA. Gingrich, Clinton, Al Gore, Rush Limbaugh, Ronald Reagan, and Henry Kissinger were working hard to pass it. The fight produced some of the oddest coalitions in history. Free-trade Democrats and Republicans working together against blue-collar Republicans and labor-backed Democrats. But cats and dogs fell from the sky when Gingrich praised Clinton, Gore, and the free-trade Democrats in their efforts to pass the legislation.

Meanwhile Clinton jabbed his sometime allies in organized labor as "Neanderthals."[41] Gingrich scored impressively when NAFTA did in fact pass the House, 234–200. He had delivered 132 Republicans (after promising 118) to vote for the divisive trade bill. He'd once been a vocal opponent of free trade, but the Georgia economy and his outlook had changed since the 1970s, as had the entire GOP. The days of Smoot-Hawley were behind them. Gingrich had actually rounded up more Republicans than Clinton did Democrats.

Still, the pressures of office might have been getting to Clinton. In an interview with *Rolling Stone* magazine, he accused the "knee jerk liberal press" of never giving him credit for anything and for allowing "the right wingers [to] always win."[42]

Clinton may have had a point because the Republicans had swept the quinella of the Virginia and New Jersey statehouses and Gracie Mansion in New York City and the mayor's office in Los Angeles. Republicans thought there was an outside shot of winning the Senate back in 1994, and as many as 25 House seats to boot, though some Republican senators were under ethical clouds, making it a long shot—better than 10–1 odds—of winning. The GOP had not settled on a plan to confront Hillarycare.

One side, led by Bill Kristol, argued that the existing health care system was fine and did not need any massive overhaul. The other side was led by Frank Luntz, who was telling Gingrich his polling showed that people thought the health care system was *not* fine and that something needed to be done.[43] Both men were considered to be shrewd operatives and both made compelling arguments. Former defense secretary Dick Cheney weighed in on

Kristol's side, saying it was a "manufactured crisis" by the Clintons.[44] Gingrich appeared before a breakfast with Washington journalists and also appeared to be siding with Kristol.[45] He savaged Hillarycare as "socialism now or later," saying it was about seizing "control of the health care system and centraliz[ing] power in Washington."[46]

Luntz wasn't about to give up, however. Gingrich and the Republicans eventually pursued a hybrid: undermine the credibility first of Hillarycare and then come back with their own plan. "Harry and Louise," the husband-wife duo, began appearing in Health Insurance Association of America commercials fretting at their kitchen table about the Clinton health care proposal. The commercials were devastating in their effect on Hillarycare. The White House set up a "War Room" to mount a counteroffensive.

Clinton spoke to the nation via a speech to Congress, extolling Hillarycare, but opposition was growing almost as fast as indifference. Gingrich sliced and diced it. "It was a great description of the problem and a poor description of the solution," he said.[47] A short time later, the Administration sent their legislation to Congress. It specified the complete overhaul of a semi-private system to an entirely government-owned-and-operated health care system.

Senator Arlen Specter, a liberal Republican from Pennsylvania, was nonetheless a fierce opponent of Hillarycare. He directed his staff to devise an organizational chart of the new government program named for the First Lady. The resulting schematic was so convoluted and complex it was impossible for *USA Today* to publish it. The *Washington Times* was more successful and devoted their entire editorial page to the diagram. It terrified people as it laid out, in black and white, dozens of agencies and commissions, bureaus, departments . . . It frankly resembled a diagram of the Stalinist system of government. Lines went everywhere and it was clear that going to the emergency room with a simple sprain or injury would result in paperwork, time, and bureaucrats. But not actual medical attention. The *r* word—*rationing*—was unspoken by the Clintons but understood by everybody else. It was the very definition of socialism: the sharing of scarcity. The *t* word was also on everybody's lips. *Taxes.* As in taxes on everything to pay for Hillarycare, including cigarettes, income, cigars, smokeless tobacco, booze, medicine, and so on and so on and so on.

Gingrich was primed. He called Hillarycare a "bureaucratic monstrosity . . . German socialism and Italian corporatism."[48] Some accused him of being an obstructionist. He didn't mind. Over the years Gingrich had picked up every name imaginable from the Fourth Estate, but he did write a letter to the *Wall Street Journal* in October 1993, objecting strongly to being called "nihilistic."[49]

In December, in a signal honor, Gingrich was a clue in the *New York Times* crossword puzzle. Twice in two weeks. Number 57 across on the eighth[50] and again, 43 across on the thirteenth.[51]

Gingrich was on a roll.

PART IV

THE SPEAKER

(1994)

CHAPTER 30

WAR OF THE REBELLION

*"Here is a Clinton nightmare: more than 200
House Republicans led by Newt Gingrich."*

Winter 1994

On January 5, 1994, an old adversary of Republicans cast his last roll call vote as Thomas P. "Tip" O'Neill Jr. passed away at the age of eighty-two. He was the quintessential Boston "pol," a garrulous, backslapping bear of a man, a through and through Democrat, who could not fathom what anybody would see in Republicanism. He'd been born to Boston machine politics, elected to the House in 1952, replacing JFK when he moved on to the US Senate. While people may have disagreed with O'Neill, they could not disagree with his patriotism, his faith, his love of his wife and children, or his ethics. Never in his life was there even a whiff of scandal. This was ultimately a very good man.

It was a myth, though, that he and Ronald Reagan were great friends. They weren't. But if it was true O'Neill had little regard for Reagan, it was also true he had little regard for Jimmy Carter. Nonetheless, both Carter and Gerald Ford attended the funeral in Boston; neither President Clinton nor Reagan did. "He was the last of the great Irish big city politicians," said Newt Gingrich. "He loved life and politics and represented the best of America. I'll remember him as tough but very human."[1]

As of January 1994, the Republicans *still* hadn't settled on a definitive plan for how to handle Hillarycare, but the conservative movement took their lead from Bill Kristol's many faxed memos—via his Project for the Republican Future—which said the Clinton plan would create far more problems than it solved. Gingrich still fretted, however, that if the Republicans did not come up with an alternative, they would look "like George Bush, really out of touch."[2] He elaborated, "I will say to folks who say we can be against everything; that is nuts."[3] Texas Republican Tom DeLay had a different take, saying, "The Republicans' strategy" is to destroy the Clinton plan.[4]

It was a chance to have a national debate about power and where it should reside. In fact, Gingrich challenged House Democratic leader Dick Gephardt to do just that, debate on the floor whether Hillarycare was socialism.[5] The Missourian showed Gingrich his stuff, and the House moved to allow for more televised "Oxford-style" debates, at the urging of Gingrich and others. An added feature was they took phone calls from viewers. "It offers some possibility for a more policy-orientated House dialogue . . ."[6] The debates were broadcast on C-SPAN, which by 1994 had a potential audience of sixty million viewers in the many local cable networks around the country that carried it as part of their "basic cable" package for customers.[7] The ensuing contest of ideas was a boon to America as it lifted the discourse.

The nation's governors met in Washington at the end of January 1994 and, like most everybody else in politics, were talking about health care. The Clintonistas had succeeded to that degree, getting everybody to talk about a subject believed to be favorable to Democrats. At the meeting, Governor Howard Dean of Vermont offered hope that Clinton would "run a compromise on health care that will appeal to the majority of Congress."[8] To Dean's point, both parties had organized task forces to examine how to make compromises on national health insurance.

The Democrats were not entirely on the defensive. They began airing an ad that concluded, "The Republicans. First, they said there was no recession. Now they say there is no health care crisis. They just don't get it."[9] The story in the *Washington Times* went on to say that a majority of Americans believed there was a health care crisis.[10]

At the end of 1993, the conventional thinking was, as expressed by Paul Gigot of the *Wall Street Journal*, that the GOP could pick up around 16 seats in November 1994, which would put them back at the high-water mark of 192 that they had under Reagan in 1981. However, Gigot noted, it was not inconceivable that they could get to 201, which the party had under Ike in 1956.[11] Another familiar Washington writer, Morton Kondrake, agreed with Gigot: "Rep. Newt Gingrich probably won't be speaker in 1995 but how about . . . Colin Powell?"[12] He speculated that the GOP might pick up enough—14 seats—to form a coalition government with conservative Democrats.[13] It was 1980 all over again.

But even Gingrich for a time was accepting conventional wisdom: the GOP would pick up seats in 1994, but not come close enough to control until 1996. "If we get back to 192 this year we'll be poised to take over the House in 1996," he said.[14] But a week later, on Mary Matalin's gab show on CNBC, he speculated that it would be possible in 1994 to "elect a Republican speaker."[15] Lee Edwards, in his landmark book *The Power of Ideas*, said, "Newt Gingrich was amusing pundits and Democrats with his detailed plans for a Republican takeover of congress."[16]

Across the aisle, the Democrats knew their fate was tied to the Arkansan, and this made many of them uncomfortable, to say the least. They knew how undisciplined he was, despite his immense gifts. They also knew the quality of the Clinton White House staff was not up to snuff. "He's going to be out there fighting for us . . . ," said one Democratic congressman, but it sounded more like a warning than a rallying cry.

More disheartening was the ongoing investigation of Democratic congressman Dan Rostenkowski for his alleged corruption involving the House post office. As a sign of good faith, he paid back $82,000 in questionable expenses, but that only made him seem even guiltier.[17] Something was terribly amiss, though. He had an upcoming primary in March, but $460,000 from his campaign coffers had gone to pay his lawyers while only $100,000 went to the actual campaign.[18] Gingrich, seeing the hanging fastball, smashed it out of the park.

As the new year began, the media and the country were taking a closer look at "Whitewater," a failed development in Arkansas in which the Clintons were involved and some investors lost their shirts. Bob Dole, Gingrich, and the Republicans, who had previously opposed the Independent Counsel Law, now altered course 180 degrees and supported the naming of an independent investigator into the Clintons' involvement in Whitewater and a failed savings and loan, Madison Guaranty. It was all a complicated mess but blessedly for the Republicans, the scandal had a memorable name, similar to Watergate without needing the suffix *gate* attached to it.

It was then revealed that in the growing Whitewater matter, some $50,000 was taken from Madison Guaranty and given to Clinton in 1984 to pay him back for a personal debt. It was getting messier and messier; people were learning how business was done in Little Rock, which for years had been a "cooling off" town for New York mafiosi who were on the lam. Madison Guaranty had made a lot of money in the 1980s and then lost a lot of money. In the S&L crisis, the taxpayers shelled out millions to pay Madison depositors. The Clintons never got hurt in the collapse of Madison or Whitewater, though they claimed to have lost $69,000. There were no documents to prove it.[19]

It was also all tied up in the investigation of the suicide of White House counsel Vince Foster, as he had many of the Whitewater/Clinton files. It was alleged that these were removed from his office after his death on the orders of Hillary Clinton. The whole mess would get worse, much worse, before it got better, and with the way the Clintons were behaving, many thought they certainly had something to hide. Between the characters at the center of this squalid mess, Jim and Susan McDougal, the suicide of Foster, the shifting stories of the Clintons, and the fact that it had all taken place in Arkansas, the whole thing felt seedy.

Hillarycare suffered a huge reversal when the Congressional Budget Office released a study that said by 2004, fully 23 percent of the federal budget would be devoted to funding the program. This was not what the Clintons had been telling taxpayers, although it was hard to comprehend how insurance for every malady could be provided for every American and not cost the government and the taxpayers more money. Gingrich, over the top, declaimed, "With this analysis, the Clinton plan is indeed dead."[20]

Gingrich was appearing almost weekly on the Sunday shows. His stock continued to rise. Some in the GOP thought he should be chairman of the 1996 Republican Convention.[21]

The budget Clinton sent Congress allowed for heavy federal outlays in nearly all departments and all agencies, and increased taxes, though the deficit also grew. Gingrich rolled out the old cliché and said it was "dead on arrival."[22] In fact, the Clinton budget was not DOA. It passed the House,

223–175, almost exclusively along party lines. A GOP alternative budget with lower spending and tax cuts went down 243–165. The Clinton budget did not include the middle class tax cut on which he'd campaigned in '92.[23]

The economy continued to fumble along. It grew, but more slowly than it had in the last two years of the Bush presidency.

As of early 1994, an old Gingrich adversary, former congressman Ben Jones—"Cooter" from *The Dukes of Hazzard*—was making noises about running for the Georgia Sixth in November. The trouble for Jones was that the novelty of a low-level comedic TV actor, recovering alcoholic, and serial husband had worn off in Georgia. He made some snarky comments about Gingrich, but few took Cooter seriously anymore.[24] He went after Gingrich hammer and tong, attacking him in the most vicious possible terms and then saying Newt was responsible for the venom in American politics. Gingrich said that Jones was "a very fine spokesman for liberalism."[25]

Several low-level Republicans in the Sixth District also made noises about taking on Gingrich in the primary, but the bet was on Gingrich. One potential challenger held a press conference on the steps of the US Capitol until the police told him to move along.[26]

While Gingrich was displaying temporary restraint when it came to the Clintons, CNBC's Roger Ailes was doing anything but. He appeared on the Don Imus radio program and cracked that Clinton was heading to New York because skater Nancy Kerrigan was going on *Saturday Night Live* and "She's the only one he hasn't hit on."[27] He noted that of Hillary's three lawyers, one was dead and a second was under investigation. "I wouldn't stand too close to her."[28] Ailes had them rolling in the aisles when he quipped of Mary Matalin and Jane Wallace, the cohosts of *Equal Time* on his cable network, "These are girls who if you went into a bar around 7, you wouldn't pay a lot of attention, but [they] get to be 10s around closing time."[29]

At the heart of the debate over Hillarycare was Senator Daniel Patrick Moynihan, the much-esteemed intellectual from Hell's Kitchen in New York. He had sweated and labored and thought his way out of poverty to become one of the leading thinkers in national politics. Moynihan noted that the last public bill-signing ceremony by President Kennedy was to create community mental health care centers. The object, Moynihan said, was to close the giant factories that had been built for warehousing the mentally ill and to "treat people locally. We emptied out our institutions . . . But we didn't build the community health centers. And 30 years later we have a problem of homelessness," said the great man wistfully. "It never would have happened if we hadn't set out to improve things," he said.[30]

The Whitewater scandal cascaded along. Gingrich was enjoying it all, saying Clinton "has a very big problem engaging reality."[31] In an attempt to clean up the mess, the president held a press conference where he revealed that their losses on Whitewater were far less—$22,000 less—than what they had claimed previously.[32] The scandal was not put to bed, though, especially since the Clintons had always refused to release their income taxes for the years in question, including the year of a highly suspicious $100,000 paid to Hillary in a single afternoon that concerned cattle futures. It also bade badly that she had legally represented the failed S&L, Madison Guaranty, before a state bankruptcy board while her husband was the governor and they both had a fiduciary interest in the bank. Clinton acquitted himself well in the press conference and won the day with the press, but the issue was far from over. Gingrich and the Republicans did all they could to keep the pot boiling, but they didn't need to do much: the media was hot on the trail and a grand jury had already been convened.

Still, Gingrich made broad hints about the extent of the charges against Clinton and said that Whitewater could potentially paralyze the White House, just as Watergate did to Nixon. He even cranked it up higher, saying, "This is more than Watergate."[33]

"The president was furious," reported Rita Braver of CBS, when she asked him about Gingrich's remarks.[34]

The off-year elections were shaping up to be an ideological showdown, nothing less, and as the fortunes of the GOP were brightening, those of Bill Clinton were darkening. The heady days of the new young presidency had passed. They had come in full of promise and full of themselves. They were going to show the town how things were done. They were going to rise above it all. They were different, they told themselves. The town said otherwise. A new reality had set in for the Clintons, and it included their past catching up with them.

Two events from Clinton's first term were animating a conservative populist uprising against the Clintons: the 1992 Ruby Ridge massacre in Idaho, and the 1993 Branch Davidians debacle in Waco, Texas. Neither Clinton nor Attorney General Janet Reno had offered any words of comfort or apologies for the men, women, and children murdered by the US government at Waco. As far as conservatives were concerned, the government had acted as if private citizens were in fact wards of the state, and the state had the choice to dispose of anyone as they saw fit.

These incidents and others added to a surreal feeling in the countryside. For the first time anyone could remember, Americans feared and hated their own government. Patriotism, for many, was defined as being for the country and for the Constitution, but against the government. Many hated Clinton in the same way liberals hated Nixon and Reagan.

Few liberals were sticking with the Clintons. Richard Cohen of the *Washington Post* ripped them, "If anyone has threatened the Clintons's [sic] 'political agenda,' it is the Clintons themselves. For some reason—arrogance, a sense of victimization, the need to hide something—they have refused to look the public in the eye and give candid responses to certain questions."[35] The Clintons had pitched themselves as "two for the price of one" in the election, and the chickens were coming home to roost.

Also part of that new reality was that Clinton was the butt of jokes every night on the talk shows.

Gingrich joined Dole in the call for an independent counsel to be appointed by the attorney general to investigate the Clintons and Whitewater. For his troubles, he was bashed yet again by conservative writer George F. Will, who said that the Georgian's "enthusiasm . . . dethroned his judgment."[36] Will was a strict constructionist, but Gingrich and Dole had seen what the Iran-Contra investigation had done to some good Republicans during the Reagan years and, as partisans, they felt it was sauce-for-the-goose time. Will explained that the appointment of an independent counsel was akin to the creation of a fourth branch of government, unaccountable to the other three. He was right, but this was politics, and politics was, paraphrasing Clausewitz, simply war disguised.

By 1994, Gingrich was one of the longest-serving teachers of the Joint Officer War Fighting Course of the Air University. He taught officers from all the services as a distinguished visiting scholar and professor of the National Defense University. He began in 1983 and never stopped.[37]

Giving political cover to Dole and Gingrich was Congressman Jim Leach of Iowa, a moderate Republican who had spent most of his career getting under the skin of conservatives. The Washington establishment loved Leach, and when he called for an independent investigator, they listened. "What the documents do indicate is that a savings and loan was allowed to have a prolonged existence, utilizing taxpayer insured deposits and operate as what appears to be a private piggy bank for Arkansas insiders and the political establishment," Leach said on CNN on January 4.[38] He said it raised "very serious ethical questions" about Clinton.[39] Leach's harsh assessment took the scandal to a much higher level.

Then the New York Times weighed in and supported the appointment of a special prosecutor.[40] The White House vowed to protect the Clintons' privacy, but even the Times pointed out that both had revealed deeply personal things about their lives when it suited them politically.[41] Reno agreed with Dole and Gingrich and shortly thereafter appointed an independent counsel, Robert Fiske, to investigate the Clintons.

Henry Gonzalez, the fanatic Democratic chairman of the House Banking Committee, refused under pain of death to investigate the Clintons and Whitewater. Gonzalez compared the American Pledge of Allegiance to "Sieg Heil," so one was excused if they thought he was certifiable.

Gingrich saw the political opportunity. He held, "If we have to go to the country and talk about a cover-up Democrat Congress, we can do that, but we'd rather not."[42]

Clinton's rapacious sexual appetite had become a running joke. It sometimes seemed that there was not a woman in Washington who hadn't fended off a pass from "Slick Willie," and the matter was easy fodder for the late-night comics. Jay Leno took special delight in tormenting Bubba. On a school in Arkansas named after Clinton, Leno joshed, "They've already set a record for handing out condoms."[43] Everybody knew somebody who had a story about Clinton grabbing or groping a woman. The astonishing thing was not just that he got away with it, repeatedly, without being sued, but that Hillary put up with it, as did the American people. But Clinton had been perfecting the talent of "getting away with it" since his childhood. He could, as they say, charm the pants off you. Or her.

But with the publication of the *American Spectator*'s exclusive, long, and sordid story about Clinton's days as governor—in which he spent days plotting to sleep with women and nights sleeping with them, sneaking them into the governor's mansion past a snoring Hillary, or cruising Little Rock's night-clubs on an all-night trim hunt—it all seemed to get a little more serious, a little more dark, a little more "stalker-like." State troopers Larry Patterson and Roger Perry had allegedly acted essentially as pimps for Clinton, trying to score girls for the governor. *Time* magazine called him a "reckless, obsessive womanizer."[44] If Hillary was awakened in the wee hours by her glandular husband, according to *Time*'s report, she would greet him with a "mouthful of four-letter words."[45]

Criticism rained down on Clinton from all sides now, including on his foreign policy. Somehow the United States had gotten stuck with the mess in the former Yugoslavia, even as other European countries turned their heads. From the standpoint of some European leaders, the United States had picked the wrong enemy. During World War II, the Serbian people had valiantly and victoriously fought the Nazis while the Croats and the Muslims sat on their hands. The United States bombed the Serbs for bombing Muslims, their ancient enemy. Gingrich quipped that the Clinton foreign policy in Bosnia was "worthy of Finland."[46]

China, too, was kicking sand in Clinton's face, as was North Korea.

Also from the right came the outrage over US troops being sublimated to the UN, replacing the dark green helmet the American fighting man had worn since World War II with the pasty blue helmet of the United Nations. Gingrich, speaking for all conservatives, said the UN was not worth an American dying for. Politicians from the left and the middle also ripped Clinton on foreign policy, especially Senator Moynihan.

The Clinton White House, via beleaguered aide Dee Dee Myers, attacked Gingrich for his criticisms on Bosnia, but the Georgian sneered, "I'm willing to debate anyone in the administration who know something about foreign policy, but I'm not about to debate Dee Dee Myers."[47]

CHAPTER 31

THE "GET CLINTON CONSPIRACY" MEETING COMES TO ORDER

"It was not Republicans who delivered subpoenas to the White House . . . That was an independent counsel."

Spring 1994

In a sit-down interview with Richard Cohen of the *Washington Post*, Bill Clinton moaned that there was an organized conspiracy to get him and Hillary, and that their enemies had a million dollars squirreled away to fund the scheme. Some Americans laughed at their paranoid president, but the Clintons really believed, courtesy of the apple-polishing writer Sydney Blumenthal—nicknamed "G.K." by the Clinton staff (for "Grassy Knoll")— that there really was an ongoing "vast right-wing conspiracy" out there to destroy Bill and Hillary.

The First Lady was even more paranoid, telling *Elle* magazine there was "a well-organized, well-financed attempt to undermine my husband, and by extension, myself, by people who have a different political agenda or have another personal and financial reason for attacking us."[1]

To some pathologists, Hillary bore a great similarity to Richard Nixon in their common belief that no one who opposed them could have legitimate reasons for doing so. If they were opposed, then those in opposition must be corrupt and therefore destroyed.

By 1994, everybody in America could do a reasonable Bill Clinton impression, often with sexual innuendo mixed in. All this only emboldened conservatives and Republicans to use the Clintons as punch lines and punching bags. Newt Gingrich was at the front lines of the Clinton Wars. On a daily basis, he was raising the ante on the ongoing Whitewater controversy, spotlighting each new revelation, talking up each new discrepancy between what the Clintons said and what the record showed. "The Clintons have a number of relationships that have to be looked at in a very serious way," he told the Washington Times in March.[2]

A preliminary crime bill finally passed the House easily, 285–141, with most of the funding going for more cops, more prisons, and tougher federal guidelines for sentencing. The federal death penalty was expanded from two forms of crime to sixty-five! A tricky provision calling for "racial justice" essentially established quotas for the death penalty nationwide, regardless of the race of the inmates on death row. Statistics at the time showed young black males committed violent crimes out of proportion to their percentages, but the Black Caucus wanted to slow the rate of their executions. Gingrich objected, as did most Republicans, calling it "quotas for death penalties."[3] They voted against the bill based on this objection, but hoped it would be changed in the conference committee.

The plan by House leaders was to have the bill finished and to Clinton by Memorial Day, and certainly no later than June. The White House wanted a big bill-signing ceremony on the South Lawn to send Democrats off on a high note to campaign for reelection. By fall, the crime bill would become the keystone for GOP destruction of the Clinton agenda.

As of April, however, the opposition had not yet congealed.

Gingrich was again a clue in a crossword puzzle, this time the Washington Post.[4] As busy as he was, he wasn't too busy to take a large role in a conference on African American entrepreneurship, sponsored by the state of Maryland. He was the only white man mentioned in the material, a testament to the good relations he'd had with the black community.

Being on offense was fun for the Republicans. Because they controlled nothing—not the House, the Senate, or the White House—they had neither responsibility nor authority. As of the spring of 1994, unemployment was at 6.5 percent and the deficit was forecast to be somewhere around $220 billion. To make a political point about Clinton's tax raise, Tea Party reenactments were organized in cities around the country, including Boston, natch, but also Atlanta and Washington.

Gingrich conceded the tax issue of 1994 didn't have the potency it did in the late 1970s, but it was still a good idea to cleanse the party of the Bush tax increase. "The once solid Republican advantage on the tax-cutting issue has been significantly diminished . . . largely as a result of Bush's 1990 decision to . . . raise taxes."[5] It was time to get back to basics.

Gingrich called again for congressional investigations into Whitewater, citing "the public's right to know," a page right out of Watergate.[6] On March 5, White House counsel Bernard Nussbaum resigned, in part over the president's decision to appoint an independent counsel to investigate Whitewater. Nussbaum was eventually replaced by Lloyd Cutler, a seventy-six-year-old utility infield attorney for the professional Democratic establishment in Washington.

Gingrich couldn't resist reminding listeners that Hillary Clinton had been on the House Watergate staff: "I'm sure she could explain to her husband what procedures are in the House of Representatives."[7] Hillary was by no means off-limits; in full political mode, Gingrich "announced . . . it would be chauvinistic not to attack the first lady."[8]

He also scored a direct hit with his quip, "That a group that couldn't manage a development as small as Whitewater, probably can't run health care for an entire country."[9]

Part of the funding for Hillarycare would come from cigarette taxes— again—proposed as high as $2.00 per pack. As of 1994, a pack of smokes was retailing for around $1.84. Smokers were being herded more and more into financial, rhetorical, and physical ghettos.

Gingrich got into trouble when he appeared on *Meet the Press* and claimed his monthly insurance health care cost was $400 per month, when it was in fact just a little more than $100 per month. As a federal employee, he participated in a private pool and, like many other federal employees, opted for Blue Cross. The taxpayers picked up the other $300 per month, just as they did with the nine million other federal employees. Democrats revealed their low monthly premiums in the taxpayer-subsidized program as a means of embarrassing Gingrich.

He also nearly got nailed—as did broadcaster John McLaughlin—for trafficking in unfounded rumors about the voting habits of a member of the Congressional Black Caucus. The matter blew over, but Gingrich had gone too close to the line. Walking him back and taking bullets when he had to was Gingrich's very able press secretary, Tony Blankley.

When there was real news over Whitewater, such as the resignation of Associate Attorney General Webster Hubbell, a Clinton crony who was mixed up in Whitewater, the town and the media exploded. The day of the Hubbell resignation, Gingrich and Bob Dole held a joint press briefing, as they frequently did now, though it was mostly about legislation and not the growing scandal. Dole couldn't resist ribbing "Newtie," as he sometimes called his House colleague.[10] "Be sure you get a good shot of Newt there," he joshed to the media. They laughed. Gingrich took the Dole kidding well—most of the time, anyway. Dole was hugely respected with some reporters, even beloved, so when the Kansan compared Whitewater to Watergate, that took it up yet another notch.[11] At the time, Dole was the most popular Republican in the country, and Gingrich took care never to cross the elder statesman.

On March 8, 1994, the stock market closed at 3,851, down four and a half points.[12] But at that moment, Gingrich was nationalizing Whitewater and attempting to drag in the whole Democratic Party. He accused the Democrats of stonewalling, an old Washington standby, and also supported a House resolution calling for investigations, an even older Washington standby. But the standbys helped to keep the story alive.

At about the same time, several newspapers, including the *Boston Globe*, began profiling Gingrich and writing that he had mellowed and was no longer tossing rhetorical hand grenades.[13] Knowing a good thing when he saw it, he played along for a time, telling the paper, "We've laid out what we think is a mature, responsible path."[14] He gave a long, extemporaneous speech in Washington to the National League of Cities and outlined in detail what the conservative position was on health care: federalizing the issue and issuing mandates to the citizenry was just as offensive as Washington telling the cities what to do and how to do it.

He described Hillarycare as a "large, monstrous national bureaucracy" and said that if it passed, lobbyists and lawyers and consultants would spend their time pushing for loopholes and exemptions anyway, which would make the proposed new system of government even worse. He also dropped in several references to failed national health care systems in other countries and later, in a Q&A session, scored impressively by making the point that rationing health care was the same as rationing elderly people.[15]

The speech did not receive the media attention it would have had it been about Whitewater. Appearing on CNN, Gingrich pointed out, "It was not Republicans who delivered subpoenas to the White House and to the Treasury. That was an independent counsel."[16] By this time, three Clinton lawyers had resigned from the government over Whitewater. One columnist noted the atmospherics: "Talk radio, call-in TV shows, panel discussions: after the questions about Whitewater and Hillary Clinton, an ubiquitous topic was the role of the press, and whether reporters who had never gotten over not meeting Deep Throat in a dimly lit parking garage were in a feeding frenzy."[17]

Columnist Anna Quindlen took it to Gingrich, saying he "could make the Lord's Prayer sound like an accusation."[18] Yet another liberal, Congressman Mike Synar of Oklahoma, called Gingrich a "legislative terrorist."[19] A writer for *Newsday*, Pete Hogness, made the ugly insinuation that Gingrich was a racist because he analyzed Hillarycare and pointed out that the suburbs would subsidize much of the inner city under the plan. "If your skin is black or brown, it'll sting from the lash of Gingrich's racial insinuations," said Hogness.[20] Another writer called Gingrich "the Charles Barkley of American politics."[21]

A minor story in the *Atlanta Journal-Constitution* reported on a private meeting Gingrich had with some fellow Republicans, in which he outlined a plan for their party to get on permanent offense, not simply by attacking the Clinton proposals, but by offering fresh, new market-based ideas. A big portion of the early sketches involved rooting out forty years of corruption on Capitol Hill. Early iterations referred to it as a "mission statement" and "vision," which he presented at yet another GOP retreat, as reported in *Roll Call*:[22]

> The draft statement that Gingrich presented last week expresses the Conference "mission" this way: "As House Republicans we will work together to offer representative governance, and to communicate our vision of America, through clearly defined themes, programs and legislative initiatives to earn us the honor of becoming the majority party in January 1995."[23]

Clinton's firewall of Democratic support, never strong, was weakening as some members of his party, including Indiana congressman Lee Hamilton, began floating trial balloons in support of a congressional investigation into Whitewater. It was the first breach but it was a significant one; Hamilton had been in Congress since 1965 and was widely respected.

The centerfold for corruption, Illinois Democrat Dan Rostenkowski, was still serving in the House, even as he was negotiating with federal prosecutors to lower his jail time if he gave up his chairmanship. Rostenkowski had been charged with all manner of corruption and abuses of power. The government's chief prosecutor against Rosty was Eric Holder, a big-time Democratic activist whom Clinton had appointed in 1993. Republicans, including Gingrich, were watching for favoritism. A Democrat was being investigated by a Democrat who had been appointed by a Democrat. It got even better. Rostenkowski's attorney was Robert Bennett, also Clinton's attorney and brother of neoconservative spokesman Bill Bennett.

Thousands of documents had already been surrendered to the Office of the Independent Counsel by Susan and Jim McDougal, close friends of the Clintons, and the proprietors of Whitewater and Madison Guaranty. The content of some of the documents leaked out to the media, and they painted a less-than-pretty picture of the president and the First Lady, including improper tax deductions and a forgotten $20,000 loan to Clinton's mother.

Gingrich was hammering away. At a fund-raiser in Oklahoma, he said, "There's something very wrong . . . It gets to be a core question of whether or not the president of the United States is going to be honest with the American people."[24] He was in the Sooner State to raise money for a special election in May to replace the incumbent Democrat, Glenn English, who'd resigned to take a job as a lobbyist.

The Democrats had had pretty much a stranglehold on the district since statehood. Attendees plunked down a symbolic $19.94 for the chance to listen to Newt. He donated $1,000 to their effort from his own campaign, plus another $1,600 raised in Georgia, to help out their fellow Republicans in Oklahoma.[25] He told them the May special would have special implications for 1994.

Meanwhile another Clinton counsel, William Kennedy III, hit the bricks because of discrepancies in his federal tax returns. Gingrich had already called for his resignation. Le affaire Kennedy revealed all, including a very messy and sad divorce. Kennedy was also a veteran of the mysterious Rose Law Firm of Little Rock, whence Hillary, Vince Foster, and Webster Hubbell also hailed.

Two issues were animating a conservative populist uprising against the Clintons. In Idaho, the FBI and the BATF (Bureau of Alcohol, Tobacco, and Firearms) mercilessly gunned down the family of Randy Weaver, falsely thinking they were plotting against the government. Weaver had moved to a bucolic portion of Idaho known as Ruby Ridge to raise his family away from a corrupt society. In short order, the US government began spying on and harassing Weaver and his family based on false information, culminating in a siege in which FBI and BATF marksmen from long distance shot off the face of Vicki Weaver, killing her, and shot a teenage boy, Sammy Weaver, in the back, killing him. Randy Weaver was also shot but he survived. At the subsequent trial, convictions were brought against the US government and millions were paid out in settlements to the remaining Weaver family.

Then in Waco, Texas, a religious sect, the Branch Davidians, had set up a private compound in a rural area where several hundred families of husbands, wives, and children created a commune to worship as they saw fit. Unfounded rumors swirled about guns and child molestation, but there was no proof and no witnesses. No one could figure out how and why the federal government had jurisdiction or interest anyway.

Again, the FBI and the BATF laid siege on the compound and, after days, moved in, complete with tanks and guns and gas. Eighty-two innocent Americans were murdered by their own government. Attorney General Janet Reno later claimed the government had to kill the children in order to save the children.

Public attitudes toward the federal government began shifting dramatically. In a land built on the premise that every citizen was entitled to due process and was innocent until proven guilty, the lame rationalization of the Clinton Administration's top justice official that rumors of lawbreaking justified the murder of civilians did not sit well.

The political world stopped on April 22, 1994, when the death of Richard Milhous Nixon was announced. It was scarcely believable. So many had wished for his death for fifty years—and not just liberals and Democrats either; over the years, he had been vilified by Republicans, conservatives, and anti-communists.

Republicans from across the country, including Newt Gingrich, Jack Kemp, and Jesse Helms, went to the Nixon funeral. All five living presidents and their wives went to California for the funeral, at which Bob Dole gave a heartfelt and touching eulogy. President Clinton, too, was impressive in his remarks. Nixon had been a part of the national political debate from the late '40s right up until his death. His damaged psyche made him one of the most fascinating and studied men in the history of the presidency. The funeral of Richard Milhous Nixon cost the American taxpayer $311,039, a bargain when considering his years of service and entertainment to the American people.[26]

There was something deeply significant about the demise of Nixon—the internationalist, the New Deal Republican, the corrupt politician—coinciding with the rise of Newt Gingrich's new GOP, which was suspicious of international adventurism, deeply opposed to activist government, and ran explicitly against the criminality of Washington and the welfare state. Another GOP president had eclipsed Nixon in the imagination of the Republican Party. They now hung the sun, moon, and stars on the Gipper.

There was whispered buzz at the Nixon funeral about "Ronnie."

"Is he okay?"

"He doesn't seem himself . . ."

Yet no one suspected or could imagine the bomb about Reagan that was to be unleashed later in the year.

But that was months down the road. The last time President Ronald Reagan ever appeared at a public event was at the funeral of Richard Milhous Nixon.

CHAPTER 32

PANIC IN LAFAYETTE PARK

*"The Democratic Party is decaying and decrepit and scandal-
ridden. That to me is a very exciting thing to campaign on."*

Early Summer 1994

On May 6, a young Arkansas woman named Paula Jones came forward
with specific and lurid charges against Bill Clinton from the time he
was governor, claiming he'd sexually harassed her when she was a state
employee. The Clinton machine went into full combat mode, attempting
to destroy Jones and her story. Jones was not a part of the "vast right-wing
conspiracy," but rather a simple and down-to-earth young woman who had a
sordid story to tell about Clinton. But this did not stop Clinton zealots like
James Carville from smearing the poor woman, impugning her upbringing
and her sexual appetites. Another Clinton aide, George Stephanopoulos,
went on CNN and confidently predicted, "Paula Jones is not going to succeed with this suit."[1]

Newt Gingrich should have left well enough alone, but chose instead to
wade into the swamp. "We have become a very weird and, in some ways, sick
culture," he pronounced. He said Jones's charges were "serious and should be
litigated."[2] The "glass houses" charge would later be leveled at Gingrich, when
he insisted that society paid too much attention to "prurient interest[s]."[3]

The national media was no slacker in the Clinton Wars either, as Jeff
Greenfield of ABC pointed out: "And then there's the always voracious
appetite of the press for the taste of high-ranking blood in the water."[4]

Jokes even made the rounds about impeachment, and there always
seemed to be fresh stories of discord in the White House. Hillary Clinton
threw a lamp at Bill. Hillary threw an ashtray at Bill. Hillary threw

obscenities at Bill. Hillary was hosting séances to talk to Eleanor Roosevelt. An unknown half brother was discovered. An unknown half sister was discovered. Staff were hired and fired willy-nilly. White House counsel Bernie Nussbaum was forced out in part because he had the tact and manners of a bloodthirsty grave robber.

In late May it came to light that a high-level White House aide, David Watkins, had commandeered the Marine One helicopter for a golf outing in Maryland. The photo of a US marine in dress blues saluting a golf bag raced across the country, earning more guffaws and shaking heads. Watkins was fired and the government reimbursed, but more damage was done.

By the end of May, more and more people in Republican circles were talking about their still-developing pledge to the American people if they gained control of Congress. Most knew it was a lot of hooey since no rational person thought the GOP could win control of Capitol Hill in 1994, but it was a nice thing to speak and dream about, and it positioned the Republicans to be able to talk about what they were for and how they would help the American people. Basically, that they weren't just about Clinton-bashing.

One of the items being bandied about in the Republicans' plan was a decree that would make any laws passed by Congress the law for everybody—including Congress. For years, populists had gagged on the fact that in case after case, Congress had imposed one after another tax or bill or regulation or mandate on the American people, only to exempt themselves from the same laws. From workplace rules to participating in Social Security and Medicare, the government arrogantly proclaimed to the people who paid their salaries, "Do as we say, not as we do." It was sickening to voters and, under the Equal Protection Clause of the Fourteenth Amendment, unconstitutional. No wonder millions of Americans held Congress in contempt.

Appearing on CNN's *Capital Gang*, former congressman and Gingrich sidekick Vin Weber was positively giddy about a GOP pledge. "The House Republicans have a whole strategy, by the way, which they're going to kick off on September 28, led by Newt Gingrich on the steps of the Capitol, there's a whole three-week offensive aimed at nationalizing all the House elections this fall, and I think it's going to be successful."[5] The paragons of political knowledge on the set—Mark Shields, Margaret Carlson, Al Hunt, and Robert Novak—were dubious.

In fact, Carlson made it clear she thought the GOP would nominate a bunch of "far right . . . Christian" candidates who could not possibly win in the general election.[6] Meanwhile her liberal colleague, Al Hunt of the *Wall Street Journal*, took issue with a column by Novak, in which the feared writer forecast difficult times ahead for Bill Clinton.[7]

On the other hand, one of the most popular and respected columnists in the country, Cal Thomas, saw the potential for a resurgent GOP and the chance for history. "The Republican Party has its greatest opportunity in 40 years to transform the political landscape for perhaps as many as the next 40 years, but it will require unity and something dramatic to capture enough people's attention and allegiance."[8] He compared Gingrich and the party to Martin Luther, seeking knowledge and independence from the status quo. Still, Margaret Carlson was right to the extent that all the Republican nominees in 1994 would not be unspoiled superheroes.

Very few were looking ahead to the presidential race of 1996; at least no one was talking about it much. Everybody was sure Bob Dole would make one last grasp for the brass ring, and both Jim Baker and Colin Powell were taking samples. So was Dick Cheney. Moderate GOP commentator David Frum speculated that Dole would "fizzle early" in the 1996 primaries. The smart money was on Cheney.[9] Otherwise, Frum spent the entire column trashing the GOP.

In the Oklahoma special election, Frank Lucas became the first Republican to win the seat. Ever. Everybody saw it as a referendum on Clinton. Republicans were ebullient, Democrats guarded.

The South was considered a "target rich environment" for the Republicans, and they were recruiting candidates everywhere, some good. They had high hopes for Jeb Bush, running for governor in Florida; less so for his brother, George, running in Texas against the popular incumbent, Ann Richards.

It was going to be a big year, with 28 open Democratic seats due to retirement or higher office. Compounding things was the observation of political scientist Merle Black: "Clinton is not an asset in most Southern congressional districts."[10] When a Kentucky district that had been held by the Democrats for 129 years went Republican in another special election in May 1994, it sent shockwaves through the political system. A TV commercial that had aided the Republican candidate was of the Democratic candidate dissolving into Bill Clinton. Gingrich quipped, "I wouldn't be too surprised to see that ad in 200 districts in October."[11]

The banter continued back and forth. Both sides said if Clinton could straighten up and fly right, then all bets were off. If he continued his downward plunge, anything could happen. However, few in either party were feeling very secure about the elections five months out. It was true that voters were more upset with the Democrats than the Republicans, but just a year and a half earlier it had been the Republicans with whom they were angry. It would turn around again. Nothing was for sure.

As far as Gingrich's own prospects for reelection, they were brightening considerably. His new district was more suburban, more upscale, and more Republican. As a result, they asked for less and less time to be devoted to constituent services. The Democrats looked as though they might nominate retread Ben Jones to run against Gingrich, but the incumbent had already raised $100,000 and all the old slights and fights and bad feelings toward Gingrich seemed to have faded away. He had a token primary opponent and was unworried.

Gingrich pounded the Democrats, saying that "morale and momentum" were going for the GOP and that the Democrats were running away from Clinton and for the tall grass.[12] Clinton raged and told his fellow Democrats to fight back. A Clinton advisor, Paul Begala, told columnist Bob Novak that the Democrats would "beat the Republicans like a bad piece of meat."[13] No one quite knew what that meant.

Years of smarminess by liberals, plus the growth of a vibrant, non-subsidized economy and the changing nature of the country made the South a potential battleground for the GOP, even as a vast majority of state legislators, congressmen, and governors in the region were Democrats. In 1994, there were "50 Democratic House members and 34 Republicans from the eight Southeastern states."[14]

Washington was descending into the hot, sticky, humid summer for which it was infamous.

Of more importance to Republicans than the feelings of the Clintons was, how far was too far? For some conservatives, lobbing rhetoric shells at the Clintons was fun, but many went overboard, sometimes with nasty and unfair comments about the Clintons' daughter, Chelsea. How far could they go in attacking Hillarycare or the other proposals emanating from the White House without it backfiring? Should they simply fight Hillarycare, or should they come up with their own plan? How far could they run down the Clinton legislative agenda without offering their own competing legislative proposals? Being in the opposition was harder than it looked.

Some argued for a watered-down version of Hillarycare, but that came mostly from the "Amen" corner of K Street, more concerned with their corporate clients than with the finer philosophical points of the allocation of power. A headline in the *New York Times* spelled it out: "Lawmakers Sow Health Bills and Reap Donations."[15] According to the accompanying story, $19 million had already been donated to incumbents from the insurance and health care lobbies. Gingrich alone received $81,000, but that was small potatoes compared to Jim Cooper, a Democrat from Tennessee, who'd been the beneficiary of $359,000 of corporate largess.[16]

Anxious to come up with a plan, the GOP went to their favorite retreat in Maryland to develop some sort of consensus on health care. The consensus coming out of the meeting was there was no consensus. Gingrich was still hopeful for a bipartisan approach, and Bob Dole agreed this was the best way. However, both men were on record as being opposed to mandates and universal coverage. Gingrich said, "There's a general sense that we want to ensure universal access. And we want to see if there's some noncoercive way to ensure universal coverage."[17]

Gingrich made a huge tactical error in late June when he pushed for GOP votes against Hillarycare and Democratic amendments to the bill. Despite the misgivings many on the left had about the behemoth piece of legislation, their animosity toward the Georgian trumped their concerns about nationalizing the private health care industry. Gingrich did not have the numbers for victory, but his politicizing put the Democrats on record multiple times for Hillarycare. It was not a part of Gingrich's plan, but it did work to his and the GOP's benefit. Of course, he then went on a Sunday show and said the GOP was "eager" for a bipartisan solution to the American health care system. It was comments like this that sometimes drove his supporters and allies up the wall.[18]

Gingrich plunged into the no-win scenario of predicting the future. In front of a group of Washington reporters, he predicted the GOP would pick up somewhere between 15 and 70 congressional seats.[19] The attending scribes giggled behind their notepads. Even with the two special election victories, Republicans needed to take 40 seats for outright control of the House, and absolutely no one thought that was possible in May 1994. Saner observers such as Charlie Cook of the famed *Cook Political Report* were predicting a pickup of between "15 and 20 seats" for the Repubs.[20]

By mid-1994, the House Democrats had agreed to some type of hearings on the matter of Whitewater. They weren't happy about it, but the public and media pressure was such that they could no longer ignore the burgeoning concern. In June, along a party-line vote, the Senate endorsed a resolution by Majority Leader George Mitchell that would prohibit any questions on Madison Guaranty or Whitewater.[21]

Support for the White House plan on health care was waning, including among Democrats. Gingrich noted that when the vote came up in a subcommittee of Ways and Means, "the vote was zero in favor, four against and seven abstained, including the four Democrats who cosponsored the Clinton plan."[22] The market-based Republican version of health care reform, he noted, had more cosponsors than did Hillarycare.[23]

The GOP race in Massachusetts against Ted Kennedy was generating a lot of interest, not just because Republicans loathed Teddy but because the candidate, Mitt Romney, was a wealthy scion of Detroit and the son of the moderate governor of Michigan, George Romney. Mitt was running as a big-government, pro-choice Republican who had rejected Reaganism as a governing philosophy. Romney was in some ways a throwback to Rockefeller, but some in the GOP saw Mitt as a vanguard of a future brand of Republicanism.

The first time it appeared in print that the GOP was contemplating a national campaign to win control of the Congress was in the *National Journal* in a story by longtime reporter Richard E. Cohen.[24] He reported that the GOP was making plans for an "extravaganza" at the US Capitol where hundreds of Republicans would unveil "the top 10 bills that they would bring to a vote on the House floor within 100 days if they controlled the House next year."[25]

It was to be called a "contract with the American people."[26]

Wags on Capitol Hill were referring to the drip-drip-drip waiting game to see what punishment Dan Rostenkowski would eventually receive as a "death watch."[27] Setting aside partisanship, Gingrich said, "You hate to see any human being go through this kind of agony."[28]

The Republicans were just as giddy about picking up seats in the state legislatures and governorships, including Florida, Texas, and New York, and holding California for the GOP.

Reporters kicked over the embers of GOPAC again, reporting on what it raised and what it spent. Fortunately for Gingrich and the GOP, Lisa Britton Nelson was recently hired to work with candidates on the presentations. Nelson had solid credentials, having worked for Bill Buckley at the *National Review* and the magazine's think tank, known in conservative circles as simply "NRI." What some reporters refused to understand was that the very mission of GOPAC was to recruit and train candidates. When Newt asked Gay Gaines to leave as chairman of the NRI to take over GOPAC, he told her, "I believe we can win the House in 1996, and if we do everything right, we could win in '94!"[29] As chairman of GOPAC, she wrote a letter to the *Washington Post* explaining how the organization worked and how Gingrich had traversed the country, raising more than $1 million for a variety of candidates, with none of the money raised going to either Gingrich or GOPAC, though the group did pay for Newt's travels.[30]

Still, the Federal Election Commission filed suit against GOPAC, alleging that five years earlier, it had failed to report political activities. Nelson and Gingrich both vowed to fight the suit.

Gaines was described in a *Palm Beach Post* profile as a "dynamo," and no one doubted it for a moment. She was society, but she was also unafraid to get her hands dirty or stick to her conservative principles. She and her husband, Stanley, numbered among their dinner companions Bill Buckley, Gingrich, and Margaret Thatcher.[31]

By now, the Clinton White House was completely defensive over Whitewater, and the president could not welcome a foreign dignitary or give a speech without the media ragging after him about it.

The health insurance industry to date had spent $10 million on the "Harry and Louise" ads. By June 1994, support for Hillarycare (aka "Clintoncare") had fallen to 44 percent.[32]

Still, some Democrats were hopeful about November, including Majority Leader Dick Gephardt, who told reporters, "If Republicans continue to make the problem of creating gridlock then we will pick up more seats than anybody imagines."[33] Democrats reasoned that JFK had picked up seats in 1962, and the economy of 1994, while no great shakes, was making a slow comeback. Sure, Clinton was unpopular, but he wasn't hated by a large swath of people like Nixon was.

The development of a legislative plan of action was indeed going to be an important step for the GOP. Not since the Reagan years had the party embraced a platform of positive action designed to move power away from Washington and back to the American people. One of the keener minds on the American right, Jeff Bell, warned at conference, "There is going to be an enormous temptation to run as 'not Clinton' and to not flesh out anything of our vision of what this country could look like."[34]

The charges and counter charges only accelerated between the two parties. Vic Fazio, head of the Democrats campaign committee, rolled out the old chestnut and claimed the religious right was taking over the GOP. Gingrich responded that the Democrats had an "antireligious bigotry" and then he dropped the big one and said, "Any value or lifestyle is acceptable to the Democratic leadership, unless it involved going to church."[35] Fazio cited as his evidence that the religious right "claim . . . a major role in electing eight members of Congress."[36]

For nearly sixteen years, the bulk of the national media had eviscerated Gingrich in print, sometimes with truly over-the-top comments and allegories, so it was unexpected when *USA Today*'s Leslie Phillips called him "brainy, articulate, charming, in-your-face, sharp-tongued and, as he says, 'manically persistent.'"[37] So, too, did the legendary David Broder, who also was taking a closer and more respectful look at the congressman from Georgia. Broder was cognizant that Gingrich was "an accident of history," when John Tower nosedived and George Bush plucked Dick Cheney out of the House leadership for the job at Defense. This elevated Newt to Whip and then the minority leader. But the respected columnist also said Gingrich's rise was inevitable because of the changing ideology, nature, and geography of the GOP. The party was more conservative, was more Southern, and had more attitude.[38]

With all the attention—even more than normal for Gingrich—and his sometimes enigmatic statements to the media, he was becoming a target yet again, especially regarding his personal life. His divorce fourteen years earlier from his first wife, Jackie, and subsequent marriage to Marianne curiously showed up again in the gossip columns, including *Parade Magazine*.[39] He also got whacked once again by Jeff Birnbaum of the *Washington Post* over disclosures by GOPAC.[40]

Toward the end of June, Gingrich sent down the word to oppose all attempts to fix Hillarycare. The two sides were just too far apart, he said. The battle lines were drawn. Speaking for the GOP, he said:

> We'll have everybody in America who wants terms limits and is mad at Congress join everyone in America who's afraid of "big government" health care on one synthesis . . . like nitroglycerin. We're going to invite every talk show host in the country to come to Washington to spend a week broadcasting from the center of disaster: "This is your life behind closed doors."[41]

Some moderate Republicans like Fred Grandy of Iowa were attempting to push Gingrich into making a deal, but he'd become resolute, especially after the special elections the GOP won in May; both were by and large referendums on Clinton. The mainstream media flayed Gingrich for it, including the *Hartford Courant*, which questioned his sanity.[42] They also bashed him over previously misstating how much his health insurance cost and who paid for it. He was becoming a bigger and bigger target for the Democrats.

At a Democratic retreat in San Francisco, Representative Jim Brady of

Louisiana said the problem with the White House and the party was they had not gotten the message out, the typical lament of every political party that was losing the argument. It never occurred to those losers like Richard Nixon—who made the same lamentation—that maybe the American people heard them loud and clear—but just didn't like what they were saying.

As soon as Brady said they weren't talking enough about accomplishments, he previewed a commercial bashing Gingrich over his misstatement on his health insurance.[43] Clinton's pollster, Stanley Greenberg, was also in attendance and said presciently, "We are in the battle of a lifetime here. I believe it will turn elections."[44] The participants also engaged in the usual bashing of the GOP for being taken over by Christians. James Carville noted, "There are some hard, hard-core Clinton haters. This guy gins up more feelings and pulls them from greater extremes than any politician I know."[45]

The Clintons were thinking about the upcoming off-year elections, but they were also thinking about 1996. So, too, were the Republicans. Bob Dole won an early Iowa straw poll, handily beating Lamar Alexander, Bill Bennett, and others. Bringing up the rear was Colin Powell with only 13 votes. Gingrich got less than 10 votes. Alan Simpson was also on the ballot, but out of 1,349 votes, he did not receive one.[46]

Clinton and the Republicans agreed on nothing now. Even at the death of the thug dictator of North Korea, Kim Il-Sung, Dole and Gingrich lambasted Clinton for offering his "condolences to the people of North Korea" for their loss.[47] Dole called Sung a "brutal dictator" and Gingrich said acidly, "I don't think we sent any condolences when Mao Zedong died."[48] Gingrich was wrong but should have been right. As the New York Times noted, Gerald Ford "fell all over" himself "with praise for Mao . . ."[49]

The war of words continued. Tom Foley said the Republicans were "putting politics above the interests of the people," and Dole shot back that the Democrats were "looking for enemies instead of solutions."[50] Dole was often the model of civility, but everybody could see his partisan and competitive juices rising in the summer of 1994.

The handbill of the East Coast Establishment, the New York Times, said that Gingrich had "unified the House GOP as no one has in 50 years." The story floated the idea that opposition to Hillarycare could lead to a

Republican takeover of the Congress, something that had not been expressed in the national media before. The story did note that Gingrich "was not a modest man. He calls himself a revolutionary and . . . compares [himself to] . . . Vaclav Havel, Lech Walesa and Boris N. Yeltsin."[51]

The appointment of a new special prosecutor, Kenneth Starr, gave a strong patina of seriousness to the investigation into Whitewater. Rumors swept Washington of imminent indictments related to Whitewater, while other rumors that Vince Foster had been murdered by Clinton associates were also hot fodder in the town. Fingered by the Democrats for rumor-mongering were Al D'Amato, Roger Ailes, and naturally Newt Gingrich.[52]

In mid-July, along with House Speaker Tom Foley, Senate majority leader George Mitchell, who'd been almost invisible for the previous several years, panicked and withdrew Hillarycare. Later in the month, Mitchell reissued it as a bill with his and House majority leader Dick Gephardt's names on it. The Clintons had become so radioactive that Mitchell, Foley, and company knew it would be used as a club against the entire party in the fall of 1994.

Gingrich already knew this. "Any candidate who votes for the Clinton health plan in any of its various forms has got an enormous burden to carry back home," he said.[53]

It was noted by all reporters covering the announcement by the genial congressman from Missouri that "the most striking feature of the rhetoric surrounding the House Democrats' introduction of their bill was their insistence that the measure 'is not the Clinton bill' as Majority Whip David E. Bonior (D-Mich.) put it."[54] In the handout material, it noted the "key differences from the Clinton plan."[55] The *Chicago Tribune* devastatingly led with a story, "The Clinton health-care plan is dead. Congressional Democratic leaders decided they had to kill President Clinton's health care bill to save it."[56] Support for the Clinton plan had crashed through the floor, down to 40 percent.[57]

The ploy did not work, as Gingrich noted "he did not know a single Republican who would support the plan."[58] He called it a "warmed-over version of the Clinton plan." Gingrich then touched the raw nerve saying, "They are desperate to avoid" putting Clinton's name on any new bill. "We're told by pollsters you lose 20 to 30 points automatically if you put Clinton's name in front of the term 'plan.' So they want to hide it. But the fact is, this is the bill the President would be eager to sign."[59]

The political situation was getting worse and worse for Clinton and the Democrats, even as the media now referred to the national health care proposal as the Mitchell Plan or the Mitchell-Gephardt Plan. Outside the urban areas, it was not selling.

Money was pouring into the Republican National Committee in Washington—but never so fast that they didn't know what to do with it. It was coming mostly from small donors via the mail and telemarketers who endlessly pounded the mailboxes and phones of John and Jane Q. Citizen. The money was coming in not for anything the GOP stood for, but for what it stood against: the Clintons. The party's chieftain, Haley Barbour, a drawling good ol' boy from Yazoo City, Mississippi, was no yahoo. His easygoing, hard-drinking, cigar-chomping demeanor belied a good tactical mind, especially at seizing opportunities for political gain. Appropriately using gambling metaphors, he advised GOP givers on the sidelines, "When the dice are hot, it's time to bet the ranch."[60] From January to June 1994, the national party had raised around $25 million, but expected this to accelerate in the weeks and days leading up to Election Day, especially with so many competitive races being talked up.

The heady Republicans met in Los Angeles to plot strategy and stroke fat cats. Bob Dole, usually the most cautious man in the room, told the gathered to focus on the number "47"; a pickup of 40 in the House would make Gingrich Speaker and 7 in the Senate would make Dole majority leader. Oddly, Dole was ahead of most everybody else in the party in seeing the chance to make history in November.[61]

In late July, a column by Michael Barone speculated openly that the GOP could take the House of Representatives. Using anecdotal information from a few Democratic districts, Barone pointed out that if these incumbents were behind this far from the election, then there could be a national trend at work in favor of the GOP. When Barone spoke, people listened. "There is evidence . . . of a national mood swing against Democrats—and Bill Clinton," he wrote.[62]

Gingrich himself was sticking to his prediction that his party would pick up somewhere between 20 and 70 seats, which was not a prediction as much as it was both an excuse and a safeguard.

Gingrich was everywhere at all times, and the strain sometimes got to him. He and Congressman Charlie Rangel got into a nasty spat on CNN over sending troops into Haiti, which had been a political and economic mess for years.

"Well, I'm certain that Newt Gingrich supported President Reagan . . . when he sent in the marines to rescue eighteen white kids in Grenada."

"Charlie, that's just plain baloney. That is racism on your part, and it's ridiculous."

The back and forth went on, but Gingrich would not back down.

"I'm tired of racism. There weren't eighteen white kids. There were about three hundred Americans of all nationalities."[63] As usual, Gingrich had the last word.

Gingrich continued at a frenetic pace through the summer.

Much of the stuff going around political circles about Bill Clinton had been true, especially when it came to women, but Jerry Falwell went over the top and around the bend when he distributed a videotape that implicated Clinton in a murder. Both Bob Dole and Gingrich begged off, claiming they hadn't seen the tape so could not comment. Other Republicans ran for cover, fearing to incur Falwell's wrath, but a few like Jack Kemp and Bill Bennett denounced the video and Falwell with it.[64] Some in the media pounded the issue and others pounded the whole "religion and politics" thing, but it mostly went ignored.

Since the beginning of time, first ladies had received high approval numbers. Until Hillary Clinton. A midsummer poll by Gallup for CNN and USA Today had her approval at 48 percent and her disapproval at 46 percent, astonishingly bad for a first lady. No one, not even Rosalyn Carter in her husband's worst days, had poll numbers this bad.[65] No one was without an opinion about Hillary Clinton.

Clinton had become a punch line. The late-night comics all mocked him and Hillary with impunity. Comical buttons and stuffed animals and board games were flying off the shelves, mocking the Clintons. Books, too, including the newly released On the Make: The Rise of Bill Clinton, published by Regnery and authored by respected Arkansas journalist Meredith Oakley. It was well-received, as Oakley herself was a liberal who had known and covered the Clintons for years.

Regnery also published another book, Guns, Crime, and Freedom, authored by NRA chieftain Wayne LaPierre with a foreword by famed novelist Tom Clancy. It astonished the elites as it quickly shot to the top of the

New York Times bestsellers list and stayed there for weeks. LaPierre went on a book tour and drew thousands not only in Houston and Oklahoma City but also in Boston and Los Angeles. The book, the tour, and the foreword by Clancy had all been conceived by Brad O'Leary, an eccentric bon vivant—if also often brilliant GOP operative—and a young conservative marketing executive.

Just for sport, the Republicans questioned the attorney general about the legality of the legal defense fund the Clintons had set up. They even threatened hearings to determine if it violated the gift ban. Janet Reno refused to look into the matter, and this simply added to the atmosphere of doubt. Shortly thereafter, the Clinton White House abandoned the plan to get high-dollar contributions for the fund and instead attempted to rely on direct mail to raise the money to pay their defense lawyers.

A newly elected Republican state representative in Georgia, Mitchell Kaye, quipped, "Every year they release two liberal Democrats in the wild here so they don't become an endangered species."[66] Kaye's district, the prosperous Cobb County, was noted for, the reporter from the *New York Times* said, "Chevrolet Suburbans bearing Christian fish symbols and 'Rush is Right' bumper stickers."[67] The *Times* reporter also noted the "New South" was where "people wear shoes."[68] The national media spent a lot of time in 1994 putting the South under a microscope, examining it like a one-cell amoeba or strange life-form they could not comprehend but could narrowly categorize.

Gingrich felt compelled to write a letter of complaint about the portrayal of his beloved Georgia in the *Times*. The missive concluded, "Could it be that poverty, racism, crime and violence have been solved in New York City, and you can share your wisdom with the rest of the country?"[69]

CHAPTER 33

THE REPUBLICANS
TALK CONTRACT

"This was the week that liberal health care died."

Late Summer 1994

In an absolute shocker to everyone, the Clinton Crime Bill went down in a stunning defeat in the House of Representatives in August 1994. For months, the Administration and the Democrats had counted on the crime bill as their fallback to tout in the fall campaign if Hillarycare faltered. Crime was the number one issue in the country, and voters wanted to know that Washington was doing something about it. It was a procedural vote that was expected to pass easily, which made the loss that much more stunning.

Indeed, the morning of the vote, the White House was predicting the bill's passage in the House. Congressman Chuck Schumer, a liberal Democrat from New York City, also predicted its passage, although he thought it would be close.

Inside Washington, few were calling it the "Clinton Crime Bill," but outside Washington, everybody in conservative circles and who listened to their radio was calling it by that appellation. For weeks, the National Rifle Association had been softening up the bill via talk radio. They had retained an outside conservative public relations firm to stir up opposition. Rush Limbaugh was popular but so, too, were dozens—even hundreds—of other national and regional talk radio shows, and virtually all were conservative. When Ronald Reagan, toward the end of his term, refused to extend the "Fairness Doctrine," it threw AM radio into the free market, without government quotas for political speech, and conservative talk quickly flourished. Try as they might, liberal talk radio could never gain a toehold, as radio stations and Republicans "shared a personal sense of exclusion" compared to television broadcasts. "The average Republican had as good a chance of being abducted by aliens as appearing on one of the Sunday morning television interview shows like . . . *Face the Nation*."[1]

The day that Clintoncare was withdrawn and replaced with the Mitchell-Gephardt bill, a conservative PR guy was at his friend Frank Donatelli's home for an after-work drink. As they watched the news about the health care name swap, Donatelli turned to his friend and said, "What do you think this means?" The immediate reply was, "They've realized the name Clinton is a burden on the bill and that's why they are dropping it."[2] With that, the PR man dashed back to his office and began typing memos on an IBM Selectric II typewriter. He faxed them out to all points, advising everybody to always call the crime bill the "Clinton Crime Bill." Within a short period of time, the bill had been indelibly stamped, which was like putting a millstone around its neck.

For weeks before the vote, faxes went out day and night to radio talk show hosts with talking points and anecdotes about the widespread problems with the Clinton Crime Bill. Packages were sent to Capitol Hill and the media with a comical police officer on the outside and titled "Clinton Crime Busters Action Kit." Inside were an assortment of children's games and toys and crayons and coloring books to make the point that the Clinton Crime Bill was about everything but fighting crime. The NRA sent postcards to their members urging them to call and write their congressmen to vote against the bill.

After weeks of assault aimed at the outside, the vote came up and all the insiders figured it would pass. It went down 225–210. For a moment, the city was aghast and no one had anything to say.[3] This was huge. According to a Gallup poll at the beginning of the year, half of the American people said crime was the number one problem facing the country.[4]

Dick Gephardt hadn't even bothered to "whip" the vote. His office never did a preliminary count. Fifty-eight Democrats, including members of the Black Caucus, crossed over to vote against the legislation. "Democrats were so stunned at their loss that they could hardly explain their gross miscalculation," said the *New York Times*.[5] The White House said that they'd been lied to by some members who said they would vote for the bill and then voted against it. Charlie Wilson of Texas said that voting for the Clinton Crime Bill would have been "just like putting a gun in your mouth in rural Texas."[6]

The *New York Times* ran a devastating headline, "A President Staggering," and devoted long column inches to the fall of the House of Clinton.[7] The downward spiral seemed to accelerate by the day now. Clinton was truly reeling. News reports described him as "visibly shaken."[8] Then he got mad. Then he convened a four-hour meeting in the White House. Then he denounced the NRA. Then he left town. Then he went to church and crucified the Republicans.

At the end of the vote, Dick Armey rubbed it in. Armey told House Democrats, "Your president is just not that important to us."[9] Angry Democrats shouted, "Our president!" When Newt Gingrich tried to speak, the Democrats loudly shouted him down. As for Gephardt, he was reported to have looked like "he'd just been slapped across the face 50 times," according to the Associated Press.[10] He suspended the work of the House for the rest of the day.

In Minnesota, Clinton gave a speech denouncing the National Rifle Association. CNN's Bernard Shaw caught up with Gingrich. "Bernie, it's very difficult for me to sit through a speech and watch the president of the United States being deliberat[ely] misleading," he said.[11] Clinton was calling the Crime Bill vote a "procedural trick."[12] Accusations were also raised that the NRA made "threats" to some GOP House members.[13] What Clinton was talking about was that the vote was actually a vote on whether to vote on the bill, but in fact these procedural votes in Congress were nearly as old as the institution itself. Clinton refused to talk to the GOP leadership. For four days.[14]

The GOP could not believe its luck but took full credit for the defeat, even though they had mostly just sat on their hands in the weeks leading up to the vote, other than sending out the mailer. The genuine credit belonged to the NRA, and Clinton knew it. The real architect of the underground campaign to defeat the bill was Tanya Metaksa, who was the head of the political arm of the organization. Metaksa was smart, tough, and sometimes anti-social.

Gingrich held a press conference and taunted Clinton, saying if he wanted to get things done, he'd better start working with the Republicans. But Clinton did not hear the Georgian, as he was heading for Camp David on Marine One, having blown off a meeting with Hill Republicans. Gingrich intimated some sort of compromise with the Clinton White House and promptly got his hand slapped back by conservatives. Had they known he called Leon Panetta, White House chief of staff, to try to make a deal, conservatives would have gone through the roof. Thankfully, Panetta—fuming—had rebuffed Gingrich's entreaty.[15]

Clinton exhorted congressional Democrats to get their act together.

Days passed and Congress could not come to an agreement on the Clinton Crime Bill. The allotted time for their recess was dwindling as well. The debate over health care fell completely off the map. It was all crime, all the time. By now, the mainstream media was calling it the Clinton Crime Bill, as the Sunday show *This Week with David Brinkley* referred to it.[16] Gingrich was the principal guest, natch. There, he ripped Clinton. "The President says whatever he thinks will work . . . He ought to tell the truth."[17] On CBS, Gingrich said Clinton was on a "Kamikaze mission . . . partisan . . . shrill . . . intense" to jam the bill down the throats of Congress.[18] He also had a strong opinion about the main goal of Hillarycare, which was universal coverage: "You cannot get to universal coverage without a police state."[19]

The impasse went on for nearly two weeks. A rump group of Republicans and Democrats came up with their own crime bill without any ban on semi-automatics. It didn't go anywhere but again, it delayed a vote on the Clinton version. The Republicans' war of attrition was working. Not only were they delaying any vote on Hillarycare, they were also draining any remaining political advantage out of whatever crime bill might eventually get passed.

Gingrich said, "I don't think you have to have winners and losers here," but that was puffery.[20] Politics was always about winners and losers. The NRA finally came out of the jungle and began airing commercials featuring Charlton Heston. Moses intoned, "What you don't know about the crime bill is a crime."[21]

Ancient and not-so-ancient hatred rose to the surface. Gingrich had made it abundantly clear that he had little use for much of the White House staff, but in this he was far from alone. He singled out Clinton aide George Stephanopoulos, saying he "was physically uncomfortable being in the room" with Republicans.[22]

Gingrich was getting points from nearly all quarters for his tactical achievements, though the right could not hold indefinitely. Clinton met at the White House with the unholy eleven Republicans who had voted for the crime bill, but Gingrich and Henry Hyde were also present, to make sure nothing went awry and the advantage was not surrendered.

The White House was organizing counteroffensive campaigns in targeted GOP districts, trying to push them into supporting Clinton. Also, a handful of black members announced they were going to vote for the bill if and when it came up again. Both sides floated phony numbers, trying to gain a psychological advantage, but it was clear the inside deal-making was working to effect for Clinton.

Polling showed as high as 78 percent of the American people supported the "gun ban."[23]

There was just too much pressure from all sides on forty-some moderate-to-liberal Republicans, and by late August, the Clinton Crime Bill finally passed the House, 235–188. Adding to the surrealness of the fight was that the final bill passed on a Sunday. It was still stuffed with largess and graft. However, the pork had been reduced substantially, from $1.2 billion to $380 million; the overall cost had been cut by more than $3 billion. The gun ban survived.

As to Clinton's weakness, the president could not bring over enough of his own Democrats to pass the bill, but instead had to pressure and make deals with establishment Republicans. This, however, also spoke to Gingrich's own weakness. By now, Clinton despised his House nemesis, but the conservatives in the GOP despised the moderates even more. Lyn Nofziger, Reagan political operative since the 1960s, said with no hesitation, "The long-term aim should have been to win a Republican majority in the House, and you don't do that sucking up to President Clinton."[24]

The same thing happened in the Senate, although Dole had been even more steadfast than Gingrich. Nonetheless, in the end the moderates in the GOP got panicky and broke the Kansan's pick.

Allegories to warfare and battles in Washington in 1994 were frequent. As the vote was proceeding, the conservative PR guy who had orchestrated the grassroots campaign against the Clinton Crime Bill on behalf of the NRA called Tanya Metaksa and said, "I feel like it's the Alamo. We lost the battle but we did enough damage that we're going to win the war."[25] The authors of *Storming the Gates*, Dan Balz of the *Washington Post* and Ron Brownstein of the *Los Angeles Times*, compared the August hostilities to the Tet Offensive from the Vietnam War.

Clinton finally got his bill and signed it in mid-September on the South Lawn, but the political advantage had been shot down. Clinton was photographed hugging Senator Joe Biden of Delaware. One of the few Republicans who did attend the bill-signing ceremony was Mayor Rudy Giuliani. Other Republicans just mailed in their regrets. Indeed, the Clinton Crime Bill would prove to be a hindrance for anyone who voted for it in the fall elections.

Clinton's poll numbers continued to sink beneath the waves. George Will recalled what Oliver Wendell Holmes once said of Calvin Coolidge, inviting a comparison to the current occupant of the Oval Office: "While I don't expect anything very astonishing from him, I don't want anything very astonishing."[26] The "Comeback Kid" was on the ropes. His approval rating according to CNN/USAToday/Gallup was 39 percent, while his disapproval was at 52 percent. The ABC poll was just as bad.[27] It was Clinton's forty-eighth birthday.

Both sides knew that the fight that reduced the Clinton Crime Bill to a millstone had left Hillarycare for all intents and purposes DOA.

As Gingrich stood over the corpse with the chalk outline that was once a grand scheme to turn over one-sixth of the American free economy to government control while making millions dependent upon that government, he gave an autopsy report to reporters:

"This was the week that liberal health care died."[28]

Newt Gingrich sat down with a group of reporters in August 1994 and pronounced, unprompted, "I feel *great*" in Tony the Tiger style.[29] The *Miami Herald* editorial praised the Georgian, calling him the "generalissimo of bare knuckles partisanship . . ."[30]

The estimable and respected political analyst Michael Barone penned a feature calling Gingrich "The Happy Warrior," an appellation usually reserved for men like Al Smith, Hubert Humphrey, and Ronald Reagan.[31] "Once considered an impractical intellectual and political bomb thrower, Gingrich is now setting the course for a Republican Party that could take effective control of the House next session."[32] Another scribe called him an "ebullient Republican phrase-making machine . . ."[33]

The rise of Gingrich was part of a larger story, and that was the rise of Republicanism in the South, something no self-respecting yellow-dog Democrat could have imagined just ten years earlier. The South and the border states were becoming increasingly Republican, and not just in presidential years. Meanwhile New England and the mid-Atlantic states had seen a prodigious drop-off in GOP representatives. "In 1960, only one in every 14 Republicans in the House was a Southerner; today, it is one of every three," reported David Broder.[34] The party itself had been reconstructed.

But the region was also changing. There were fewer and fewer references to the Civil War, including the display of the Confederate battle flag, fewer references to Robert E. Lee, and more references to the Grand Ole Opry and Elvis Presley.

Gingrich's GOPAC was hauling in the money; many individuals were making six-figure donations.[35] Again, Gingrich was bashed over GOPAC and the influx of cash. He shrugged his shoulders and declaimed, "I try to do what I think is right. People who like it can send money. People who don't, don't send money."[36] One who "liked" was Donald Engel, former aide to disgraced junk bond magnate Michael Milken. Engel was also the prime mover behind the disgraced Wall Street bash, known as the "Predators Ball."[37]

In a letter to the *New York Times*, Chairman Gay Hart Gaines explained GOPAC's mission: "We have trained thousands of people—activists and candidates—to become more enlightened and effective . . ."[38] Gaines had righted the ship there and it, too, was firing on all pistons.

The GOP was moving ahead with plans for a fall offensive, a continuation of their spring offensive that had bled into the summer offensive. So far it had all gone according to luck, not planning. The spring had been dominated by the twin Clinton scandals of Whitewater and Paula Jones, the summer by the debacle over the crime bill and the eventual death of Hillarycare, and, having softened up the president, the Republicans were now preparing to unveil their "Contract with America," known more popularly as the "Republican Reform agenda."[39]

The timely death of the Clinton health plan was matched by the timely death of the Mitchell-Gephardt alternative plan. In the Senate, Republicans essentially talked and amended the Mitchell bill to death.

Vice President Al Gore had led a rally on Capitol Hill to revive health care, but it was over. There would still be some twitches, but the patient was lifeless as far as everybody was concerned, which opened up a lot of time for finger pointing and backbiting among the Democrats. Gingrich occasionally floated the idea of the GOP coming up with its own health care plan, but at this late date, he reckoned everything would become a target; the better part of valor was to give lip service to the notion without coming up with something substantive. He and the GOP had the political offensive, and there was no sense in diverting attention.[40] He argued against his own argument by saying the Republicans should stop being "the bookkeepers of the welfare state."[41]

The dead embers of Hillarycare were kicked around and no doubt it had collapsed because of its own weight (it was fourteen hundred pages), but it also fell apart because of the unrelenting GOP assault on it, some of it factual, some less so. A Republican senator from Idaho, Larry Craig, took a wide stance and said the Democratic bill authorized a "medical Gestapo" that could go into private homes and review the medical records of private citizens.[42]

Indeed, the summer and fall of 1994 could best be described as a nightmare for the Democrats. They were running like scalded dogs from Clinton, hoping to save their own hides. Congressman Jim Moran, an unsavory hack from northern Virginia, said publicly that he did not want Clinton coming in and tainting his reelection chances.[43] The word *abandoning* was cropping up more and more in news articles. Democratic columnist Mark Shields called Clinton "the Rodney Dangerfield of American politics."[44]

The DNC was being unfavorably compared to the RNC in press accounts, and the chairman, David Wilhelm, was being hung out to dry for the messy state of his party even though all the problems had emanated from Bill and Hillary Clinton. But that was how Washington worked. Wilhelm clearly missed the peace and stability of Chicago, where he had cut his political teeth.

Incredibly, in a poll by the GOP firm American Viewpoint, Republicans held an edge, 44 to 42 percent, when they asked voters what their preference was in the fall.[45] It wasn't just that the Clinton White House was dysfunctional, but the economy was also limping along. The conservatives frankly hadn't been this giddy since 1980.

In Palm Springs, Sonny Bono was running for Congress. In the panhandle of Florida, a long-shot, wet-behind-the-ears country lawyer named Joe

Scarborough, deeply conservative, had won the GOP primary over opposition from the Republican establishment. Still, he would face an entrenched Democrat in the fall, a tall order. In Pennsylvania, conservative congressman Rick Santorum, who could teach a porcupine a thing or two about being prickly, was running for the Senate. In Massachusetts, businessman Mitt Romney was making a race of it against longtime incumbent Ted Kennedy for the Senate seat there, which had been in Democratic hands since 1953.

Barbara "Bar" Bush released a thick memoir, and it wasn't anything if it wasn't memorable. Brahmins used to only have their names in the newspapers when they were born, graduated from an Ivy League school, married, or laid to rest. Mrs. Bush threw that old formula out the window with her denunciation of Pat Buchanan for sending a "racist message," her support for abortion and gun control, and her detailing how she was an emotional basket case in the 1970s, for which she blamed "the hormonal changes of menopause."[46] She also ripped Gingrich "for wrecking negotiations with Democrats in 1990" over the budget deal in which her husband broke his pledge not to raise taxes.[47] In case there was any doubt, Barbara Bush was letting the world see her Rockefeller elitist slip.

Meanwhile, the Democrats had to contend with candidates like incumbent Joe Kennedy, whose maid accused him of keeping a "duffel bag" full of marijuana in his closet.[48] In New York, a Republican candidate was having a hard time explaining to voters the "protection" order his wife had obtained against him.[49] In North Carolina, Republican candidate David Funderburk was battling charges about a past history with the John Birch Society. Candidates from both parties ran the gamut from impressive to imbecilic in 1994.

Gingrich's general election opponent, Ben Jones, was running goofy ads against him, but to seemingly little effect. Jones offered Gingrich $4,000 to debate him, but Newt brushed him off.[50] He'd already handily defeated a nuisance primary challenger in July, taking 77 percent. Just two years earlier, he'd nearly lost his primary and, with that, his political career. He'd gone from the precipice to near the mountaintop in less than two years. Gingrich was occasionally pinged in the media for collecting hundreds of thousands of campaign dollars from health care interests, but it was by and large relegated to the back pages of the nation's newspapers.

The Democrats, meanwhile, were eating their own young. The chairman of the DNC, David Wilhelm, had angered so many in his party with his behavior and ineffectiveness that they demanded he resign, but the young politico hung on to the job by a fingernail.

By September, it was clear that the Republicans had a real chance to defeat some of their worst tormentors. Gingrich had become devastatingly subtle in how he dealt with them. During the raging debates over the Clinton Crime Bill, Gingrich appointed backbench Republicans to negotiate with frontbench Democrats. This served two purposes. First, it made the junior members even more loyal to him. Second, it really miffed the opposition.

It had already leaked out to Bob Novak that Gingrich's staff was busy with plans for his elevation to minority leader, but they also reported on super-secret organizing for the long, long, long-shot possibility that he could become Speaker.[51] Employing the tired cliché, a Gingrich aide told Novak, "We're not measuring drapes but some planning is necessary."[52] Still, the number "40" danced in Republicans' heads, as that was the magical threshold needed to cross over to the Holy Land of Majority.

Dole was "all-in" on this campaign. He loathed the Clintons and said right up front that he would "obstruct" what he felt needed to be obstructed. He also had a long memory, referring to the "Spanish Inquisition" that Reagan and Bush nominees were treated to. "Remember Robert Bork? Remember John Tower? Remember Ed Meese?"[53] It was clear he was also still miffed at the GOP senators who had cut and run on the crime bill.

It had been a dream of Gingrich's for years to do a big, unifying event with everybody present, in front of the world. He had succeeded fourteen years earlier in persuading the Reagan campaign to do a big photo-policy event on the steps of the Capitol with lots of GOP candidates, but then the entire focus was on Reagan.

Now plans were moving forward for the Republicans' "Contract with America" event on September 27 on the steps of the US Capitol. The party was going to defy every rule of politics and run a national campaign with no national candidate. It was unprecedented. The Contract contained ten specific promises that hundreds of Republican candidates would sign and vow to enact in their first one hundred days if they gained control of Capitol Hill. The breathtaking audacity was such that few really mocked it. The ten-point plan had been poll-tested, sure, but the points also conformed to GOP dogma, although the promises to go after corruption were relatively new issues for the Republicans.

Frank Luntz had polled all ten points of the Contract and knew they were popular. It was important not to call it a "Republican Contract" as it would make it appear too partisan.[54] Gingrich aide David Hoppe confirmed this, saying that Bob Dole "felt that the divisions among the Senate Republicans . . . were much deeper than they were among the House Republicans."[55]

The eventual Contract included reforms of Capitol Hill from top to bottom, balanced budgets, a major reform of federal welfare, tax benefits for the working poor and senior citizens, the funding and deployment of Reagan's cherished Strategic Defense Initiative, term limits for members of Congress and committee chairmen—and a major overhaul of the newly passed Clinton Crime Bill. For the energized Republicans, 1994 wasn't just about philosophy or ideology; it was also about good old-fashioned score settling.

CHAPTER 34

YOU SAY YOU WANT
A REVOLUTION?

*"Today, on these steps, we offer this Contract as a first
step towards renewing American civilization."*

Fall 1994

Contract Day finally arrived, September 27, 1994. On the day of its unveiling, the *Post* ran a large headline: "Democrats Pull the Plug on Health Care Reform."[1]

More than three hundred Republican challengers and incumbents from all fifty states and the territories assembled on the steps of the US Capitol at 11:00 a.m. A large map of the United States adorned the back of the stage with the caption "Contract with America." This had been Newt Gingrich's dream for years. The day was magnificent. Blue skies, light wind, and a photo op for the ages. There were hundreds of reporters and cameras there to cover the unveiling. Flags flew; bands played; photographers snapped.

Gingrich told reporters that each of the Contract's ten points had at least 60 percent support among the citizenry. According to the preamble, the Contract was an attempt to "restore the bonds of trust between the people and their elected representatives."[2] It used the phrase "national renewal," which Ronald Reagan had also used in his 1981 inaugural to describe the theme of his new Administration.

Gingrich spoke, calling the day "an historic event," and proclaiming—a bit over the top—that, "Today, on these steps, we offer this contract as a first step towards renewing American civilization." As always, Gingrich spoke without a text. But he'd been preparing himself for this moment since he was a professor at a dusty school in rural Georgia. Dick Armey also spoke, saying, "Today, we Republicans are signing a 'Contract with America.' We pledge ourselves, in writing, to a new agenda of reform, respect and renewal."[3] Both men emphasized the Contract's key selling point: "We explicitly state, if you give us control and we don't do what we say, throw us out. We mean it."[4] There had been some unfounded rumors that Gingrich was having second thoughts about locking in his party, but as it was, he never betrayed his feelings.

Later, candidates came forward, four by four, to sign the Contract, pledging to support ten specific items for reform and Republican governance. Provided they won, of course. Of the 157 House Republicans vying for reelection, 5 did not sign the Contract . . . but 185 GOP challengers did.[5] Armey's aide Kerry Knott was impressed with the entire operation and Gingrich's ability to organize things when he was focused.[6] The staffs worked so closely together, they also often socialized with each other. "I think we all realized when Newt and Dick were together, it was a pretty strong team," Newt's inability to execute "his ideas very well" notwithstanding.[7]

Predictably, some in the national media were dubious about the whole thing. "Led by the minority whip, Newt Gingrich, this group of Republicans would balance the budget while adding to defense spending and cutting taxes on capital gains . . . They would also ease the tax burden on non-poor families with children, corporate investment, retirement savings . . . ," declaimed the *New York Times*.[8] With all the alliteration they could muster, the Gray Lady called the Contract a "politically preposterous prospect" and "duplicitous propaganda."[9]

Washington Post columnist E. J. Dionne, an unreconstructed leftist, hated the whole affair. "Why don't they just . . . stop pretending that small government is just around the corner?"[10] The *Christian Science Monitor* was just as skeptical, saying "the contract fails to serve the political interests of the signatories."[11] The point the *Monitor* was making was that all elections are local, especially off-year elections. But that missed the point. Gingrich and the Republicans were attempting to nationalize and harmonize an off-year election, something that had never been done before.

A moderate Republican from Iowa, Fred Grandy, who was not running for reelection, said that if he were a Democrat, he'd "be in church right now giving thanks" for the specificity and promises of the Contract.[12] Armey—never, ever, ever at a loss for words—replied, "I've never known [Grandy] not to be critical of any idea that wasn't his own."[13] Grandy had reason to doubt—he had already claimed he'd been told by Gingrich not to offer any legislation that might "attract bipartisan support."[14]

The day after the unveiling, the *Post* ran another large headline, which read "GOP Offers a 'Contract' to Revive Reagan Years."[15] Gingrich and his band of merry conservatives could not have been more thrilled.[16]

Most issues were in fact working in the GOP's favor, as "gun control, abortion, term limits, and immigration are fueling activity among moderate-to-conservative voters."[17] But even a "strategist" for the House Republicans expected that by the time the election rolled around, the Democrats would get their act together and raise enough money to maintain their majority.[18] Most everybody held fast to the idea of "22–30 seats" going Republican in November. Almost no one could embrace the harebrained notion of a complete takeover by the GOP. The way of the world had been Democratic control for forty years and it was expected to continue. Some of the "wise men" of Washington weighed in with their thoughts. "There's no question but that a significant loss of seats could be a plus for Clinton and not a minus," intoned one of those wise men, Norman Ornstein of the American Enterprise Institute.[19]

It wasn't only liberal editorialists who were dubious. So was George Will, who doubted the entire event and said the odds were so long against the Republicans taking control as to be far-fetched.[20]

The season of proposing or passing legislation was nearly over; Washington was hurtling toward the electoral selection of new representatives by the American people. It was by their decision that the fortunes of many in the corrupt city-state could be made or broken. The denizens of the town could now do what they did best, which was to eat, drink, and gossip about politics. It was politics, politics, politics all the time.

The march of Democratic candidates away from Bill Clinton was turning into a stampede.

"Psychologically, he is on every ballot," Gingrich said of President

Clinton.[21] The beleaguered Arkansan held a press conference to defend his Administration and his record to date, but he mostly accused the Republicans of trying to "stop it, slow it, kill it, or just talk it to death."[22] The media pressed him on his inability to get legislation through a Democratic Congress, and he vowed to bring back health care in the 104th. He also singled out Newt's beloved Contract for harsh criticism, saying it would take "us back to the Reagan-Bush years" and that it would "[divide] our citizens."[23]

Gingrich, responding, went for the throat, mocking Clinton. "I'm going to bring in all of my left-wing, counterculture friends to design a bunch of programs that are bound to fail, and you're an obstructionist if you don't agree."[24] Gingrich was off message at this point, and he was drawing unwanted attention. The unflinching remarks were picked up everywhere. It was clear that he really did not like his fellow boomer, the president.

According to Bob Novak, in another unguarded moment Gingrich said that he might run for president in 1996.[25] With Novak—who had been a longtime friend and trumpeter for Jack Kemp for president—it was the wrong thing for Gingrich to say. Even more wrong was pollster Frank Luntz gushing over a Gingrich presidency, saying, "Gingrich is a great communicator. He is Ronald Reagan, only smarter."[26] A Democrat pushed back, saying, "This is a man who married his high school math teacher!"[27]

Secretly, a small group of Gingrich staffers were quietly making phone calls and asking questions about how a transition to the Speakership would transpire if it came to pass. As the *Washington Times* reported, "Mr. Gingrich's chief of staff, Dan Meyer, has been collecting data about the tasks the majority oversees—from dining halls to telephone systems—to help the Georgia Republican and others prepare for a smooth transition."[28] Historians and experts were sought out, but there were few people around who remembered the last time Republicans controlled Congress. Democrats publicly pooh-poohed any talk of GOP governance, while Gingrich's office got into the "measuring drapes" syndrome, leaking to columnist Bob Novak that if the Republicans took control of Congress—the elections were still a month away—"that the Democrats will be given the same number of staffers and offices—not one person more and not one square inch more—as has been provided Republicans."[29]

One thing was for sure, everything Gingrich was doing and saying and all his political operations were coming under increased scrutiny. GOPAC was far ahead of the other leadership PACs in terms of fund-raising, at $2,919,946 as of the fall of 1994.[30] Gay Gaines ran a tight and effective ship. There was some scrutiny over cross-pollenization between the various entities in NewtWorld—as the staff often called it—but so far, his enemies and the media had not come up with anything concrete. Jeff Eisenach, the executive director of GOPAC from 1991 to 1993, was also one of the cofounders of the Progress and Freedom Foundation, a think tank organized in 1993 with fund-raising help from Gingrich.[31] Now serving as the president of PFF, Eisenach had to tap-dance for the media, saying, "There are also a lot of people here who have never had much of anything to do with Newt."[32]

Gingrich was also signing direct-mail letters for the party committees. Checks cascaded into the organizations. In late September, the staff of the Federal Election Commission announced they were fining Gingrich $3,800 for late reports on some contributions to his 1992 congressional campaign. The announcement came two years after the infraction and only weeks before the '94 elections . . . but only a cynic would suggest that bureaucrats at the FEC had violated election laws by attempting to affect the outcome of the elections through an abuse of power.[33]

Gingrich was also accused of touting the companies that had given money to PFF, which the New York Times reported "underwrites his weekly call-in program on National Empowerment Television and raises money for his college course, 'Renewing American Civilization,' which is televised to more than 130 classrooms across the country."[34]

Not everything was sweetness and light on the right either. A handful of conservatives were being ornery. They griped that Gingrich had been too helpful to Bill Clinton on passing NAFTA, that he should not have allowed moderate Republicans to negotiate directly with Clinton on the crime bill, and that the Contract did not call for a reduction in the tax increases of 1993. Gingrich was Reaganesque, saying, "I don't spend enough time communicating to them."[35]

His race in the Sixth looked good. Despite the regular thrashing he'd received over the years from the editorial writers at the Atlanta Journal-Constitution and his close electoral calls of the past couple of years, Gingrich was stomping challenger Ben Jones in a party poll, 62–25 percent.[36]

Then, the floodgates opened against the Contract. The Democratic establishment hit it high and low, from the White House to the courthouse, saying the Contract belonged in the outhouse. Falsehoods were spread about it, as in the case of Congresswoman Louise Slaughter of Rochester, New York, who said the GOP was threatening to withhold financial support from GOPers who did not support the document.[37] Slaughter was regarded on both sides of the aisle as a woman of high drama and low intellect.

Yet even some Republicans who had participated in the Contact ceremonies dismissed it as a "PR stunt" that would have little bearing on the next Congress. Mitt Romney, running in Massachusetts, ran away from the Contract, rejecting it as a representation of Gingrich and Reagan. Romney was an elitist Rockefeller Republican through and through and had little use for those not born to the manor.

Gingrich went hither and yon defending his beloved Contract. He and former representative Tony Coelho went toe-to-toe on CNN, with Judy Woodruff acting more as a referee than as a moderator.[38] He went on CBS and *Today* and PBS and dozens of other channels and shows. Clinton, visiting Ted Kennedy's family estate in the exclusive section of Hyannis Port on the somewhat exclusive Cape Cod, said, "They want to stick it to ordinary Americans. They want to go back to the way they did it before."[39]

When White House chief of staff Leon Panetta was asked how he reacted to the phrases "Majority Leader Bob Dole" and "Speaker of the House Newt Gingrich," he laughed and said, "Pretty frightening words."[40] Not frightening, but surprising, was that Gingrich and Dole were campaigning together. Dole went to Atlanta for a huge fund-raiser for the party and for his younger colleague. In public they were respectful, and Dole was almost playful.

Another benefit of the Contract was that it dominated the national and local news for days, giving challengers something positive to talk about, leaving their opponents on the defensive. Political scribe and commentator Charlie Cook called the Contract the "defining" moment of the fall political season.[41]

Many were not leaving it all to the Contract, though; just to be on the safe side, they were also running commercials of their Democratic opponents "morphing" into Bill Clinton. By late October, dozens of Democratic candidates across the country were all turning into Clinton. It was called "the Coattail Curse."[42] This, too, was more evidence of Gingrich's goal to nationalize the elections. GOP candidates all across the country said explicitly that they were running against Bill Clinton.

It was clear there was a real joy in Clinton-bashing among many Republicans and all conservatives. They found him to be a fatuous, self-absorbed draft dodger. Of course, across the aisle, many thought the same about Gingrich.

The "enemies of the state" were clearly delineated now to Washington society: they were Newt, talk radio hosts, and the Reverend Pat Robertson. But "ever since Ronald Reagan's breed of conservatism rode out of the West to dominate the GOP, the party's moderates have been denounced, derided and shoved aside."[43] Columnists wrung their hands about the new nastiness of the right: how it used to be principled and how it used to be about issues and how the conservatives were now just out for blood. They had also written this in 1980, 1964, and 1952 . . .

Unknown to all was a secret list in Gingrich's possession of more than a dozen conservative Democrats he felt might be convinced to switch to the GOP if the election was close and he could offer them a better deal than the Dems. That list included Gary Condit of California, Sonny Montgomery of Alabama, and Billy Tauzin of Louisiana. With the exception of Condit, every last one of the members on the target list was from the South, and all their districts had gone for Bush over Clinton in '92. Many expressed their admiration for Gingrich.[44] Just to unnerve his "friends" on the other side of the aisle, Gingrich predicted that as many as eight would switch to the GOP. Most assumed this would be the only way for the GOP to gain outright control.

Still, a growing trickle of writers and scribes and columnists were daring to think the unthinkable and write the unwritable. One even went so far as to refer to "the impending Gingrich era."[45] A financial analyst for Salomon Brothers went on CNN and predicted that Gingrich would become Speaker because 10 Democrats would cross the aisle and join 30 new Republicans to elect him.

The GOP was targeting 96 seats nationwide, with most in the Midwest and the South.[46]

Gingrich hit the road, campaigning in district after district, almost exclusively for challengers and often for long shots. Most of the events he attended were fairly low cost, but drew in hundreds of people, all wanting to meet the leader of the revolution. Wherever he stumped, he promised change, change, change. He promised a "complete reversal of political direction" if the Republicans were victorious.[47]

If there was any doubt about the Republicans' opposition to the Clinton Crime Bill, they were allayed in a Harris poll when 54 percent agreed that the bill "contains too much unnecessary spending and crime will not be reduced."[48] The decision by the NRA to go after the bill by citing the pork turned out to be one of the most important developments of 1994. Crime was not only taken away from the Democrats as an issue, but their image as wasteful spenders was reinforced as well. Even more insulting to Clinton, fully 60 percent said the ban on assault weapons would do nothing to stop crime. Suddenly, a Gallup poll said Americans trusted Republicans more than Democrats on the crime issue by a 43–39 margin.

Other pieces of Democratic legislation never saw the light of day because of GOP efforts to delay them. Among these was a bill on lobbying reform, obstructed ostensibly because it limited grassroots lobbying. Another was a bill on Superfund reform.[49] A trade agreement was also delayed. The Republicans didn't want the Democrats to get any credit before the election. Finally, a *Post* headline proclaimed, "GOP Taking Joy in Obstructionism."[50] The story noted that the GOP had learned much from opposing the Clinton Crime Bill—political capital could be gained in opposing new legislation if the case was made first that it was bad legislation. The phrase "principled obstructionism"—coined by Bill Kristol—entered the Washington vernacular.[51]

The situation got so frustrating, John Breaux, an easygoing senator from Louisiana, quipped, "I've come to the conclusion we can't get 60 votes . . . to break a filibuster for the Ten Commandments."[52] From late September to early October, the GOP used nearly a half-dozen filibusters in the Senate to stop legislation.[53] The 103rd Congress ended with neither a bang nor a whimper but with a lot of question marks and the Republicans backslapping each other over all the legislation they had gummed up in committee or on the floor.

"Defeating this president's health care plan was the most positive thing that this congress did," crowed Senator Phil Gramm of Texas.[54] Another,

Mitch McConnell, said "gridlock" could have "a good name."[55] Congressional disapproval was at an all-time high, according to GOP pollster Bill McInturff, but he reasoned since Congress was dominated by the Democrats, this would accrue to the Republicans' benefit.[56]

Incumbents took wing and headed home, with Republicans looking forward to the election and Democrats dreading it. According to the *Rothenberg Political Report*, there were 123 competitive House seats, with Democrats holding 80 of them. For the GOP to win control, they would have to keep all of their own and take 50 percent of the Democratic seats. A tall order, especially since the average off-year elections only saw a turnover of 26 seats.[57] The difference was, with the rash of retirements, there were 52 *open* seats this year.

The 103rd Congress adjourned October 8 and sailed into the murk of irrelevant history. The *Washington Post* decried it as "just about the worst Congress in 50 years," criticizing both parties.[58] Conservative and middle-of-the-road Democrats were bewailing the lost opportunities of the past year. Senator Bob Kerrey of Nebraska, a widely respected centrist Democrat and wounded hero of Vietnam, said, "We all look like jerks."[59] Gingrich had a different take, saying, "We can be proud of this session."[60]

Obituaries for the mostly forgettable two-year legislative session popped up all over. Major Garrett of the *Washington Times* penned, "The 103rd Congress neared its end yesterday amid the smoking ruins of no less than six significant Clinton initiatives either dead, talked to death or abandoned for reasons of political expediency."[61]

Democratic consultants were giving their clients a lot of bad news, saying it "has become increasingly bleak in the last several days."[62] At one time, they'd been hopeful about Senate pickups in Wyoming and Ohio, as well as keeping Tennessee, but while they were putting up a brave face, it was becoming clear that the Democrats were in the bunker, hoping to mount a "Battle of the Bulge" counteroffensive against the GOP before the snows of November. Democratic consultant Mark McKinnon told the *New York Times*, "We feel that the Republicans have been finger-painting all over us for months, and it's high time we threw some paint back in their faces."[63]

In a late primary, Speaker of the House Tom Foley of Washington State received an astonishingly low vote total. Term-limit referenda were appearing all over the country, including in the Evergreen State. Foley, for whatever reason, had foolishly participated in a lawsuit to block term limits there.

All around the nation, little and not-so-little signs were erupting, appearing, signaling that something was coming. The Republicans were dripping with confidence and the Democrats were oozing stark fear.

Clinton went out for more or less a month of stumping across the country for candidates who welcomed him with open arms—or at arm's length. Many times he showed up in a city or locale only to find none of the candidates on the dais. A headline in the *New York Times* said, "Clinton Tours Connecticut with Willing Democratic Nominee."[64] Desperately, the president exclaimed, "I am not at issue here."[65] In fact, he was.

Many of the Clinton cabinet were also out stumping for Democratic candidates, trying to shore up the party's fortunes. So were some of the White House staff, including George Stephanopoulos, who went to Cleveland and said before a partisan audience that Gingrich was "being corrupted by power he doesn't even have yet."[66]

It was a strange coincidence that Democratic candidates across the country were "in another part of the district/state" the day the president was there to ostensibly campaign for them. Jim Moran of Virginia hid in the drinking establishments of Alexandria any time Clinton could be detected upwind. Clinton went to Michigan, usually reliable stomping grounds for a Democratic president and, again, local Democrats took wing. Not one Democratic politician would appear on the dais with the leader of the Democratic Party.

A new *Times-Mirror* poll came out in early October and the results were astonishing. In September, the American people had been evenly split over who they would vote for in November, but just weeks after unveiling the Contract and opposing Hillarycare and the Clinton Crime Bill, the Republicans had moved Americans to say they would vote GOP by a margin of 52–40.[67]

The GOP was rolling in money now, much of it as a result of the conservative groups doing the dirty work. After a recent three-day weekend, 134,000 fund-raising response mailers arrived, a record, according to the RNC.[68] They claimed they were raising $400,000 per day. For the year, the parent GOP organization said it had raised $41 million and announced it would raise a grand total of $60 million by the election, a record for an off year.[69] The finance chairman of the DNC, Terry McAuliffe, announced his haul was running far behind; the Democrats would raise nearly $20 million less than the GOP.[70]

In mid-October, Gingrich spoke to a small group of lobbyists where no press was allowed, but where extensive notes were taken and leaked to the media anyway. Present at the private briefing were access sellers for GTE, Bell South, and a host of other communications and technology companies.[71] The mere fact that the weak sisters of America—corporate executives and lobbyists—were meeting with Gingrich was telling about the state of politics in the fall of 1994.

Gingrich was unrelenting. He said the election was a chance to "get even for the Clinton tax increase."[72] He used words like "Stalinist" and "punitive."[73] He characterized the "Clinton Democrats" as "the enemy of normal Americans."[74] But Gingrich did not stop there. He said the GOP would use subpoenas to go after their political enemies if he and the Republicans gained control of Congress. Alarm bells went off inside the salons of both parties.

Gingrich did not back away from the leaked rhetoric. In fact, he continued to take the same stance in public. Chillingly—for Democrats, anyway—Gingrich told ABC, "The amount of investigating that would go on, if you had a Republican House and a Republican Senate can't possibly be helpful to this administration."[75]

Gingrich went back to Georgia for a campaign swing. Some of his supporters wore buttons that read "Newt-er Cooter," which had been Ben Jones's name on the TV show *The Dukes of Hazard*. Jones was practically stalking Gingrich, even following him to Wisconsin in an attempt to confront his opponent.[76]

In Washington State, where Tom Foley had fallen badly off the pace against GOP nominee George Nethercutt, the race was a dead heat.[77]

Still the Democrats, having departed Washington, seemed to be getting their second wind; the Republicans, with Gingrich at the helm, seemed to be faltering.

Two days later, the White House decided to engage in their own nationalization by announcing an "anti-Gingrich campaign."[78] Leon Panetta spoke to reporters and blasted the Georgian for all manner of things. It was silly, frankly, as it only elevated Gingrich. Tony Blankley, Gingrich's effective spokesman—who was British and had grown up in the shadow of Winston

Churchill, as his father was Churchill's financial advisor—had some fun with the Clintonites. "[They seem] to be going . . . weak at the knees at the mere mention of the words 'Newt Gingrich.' They ought to have a scotch and get a good night's sleep."[79]

National reporters were beginning to trail Gingrich, as he stumped for House candidates across the country, a sure sign of possible new powers. Already, he'd gone to 125 congressional districts, according to Katharine Q. Seelye, political reporter for the *New York Times*.[80] Dan Balz, a longtime scribe for the *Washington Post*, also picked up the scent and trailed Gingrich to Connecticut to do the "Could he become Speaker and if he does what will he do and will Washington be the same?" story.[81] He called Gingrich a "bomb throwing backbencher." He also quoted Gingrich as ill-advisedly saying, "I think I am a transformational figure."[82] Some thought so, including Tom Brokaw of NBC, who was planning to follow the Georgian around for the last day and a half of the campaign for a long piece about the leader of the Republican Revolution.[83]

The election had yet to be held, but one of the most perspicacious journalists around, Karen Tumulty of the *Los Angeles Times*, wrote that "in many ways, the Gingrich Era has already dawned."[84]

CHAPTER 35

EVE OF DESTRUCTION

"If we don't do well then throw us out for another 42 years."

November 1994

As Newt Gingrich moved potentially closer to power, more and more psychobabble pieces popped up, a sure sign that Washington's drinking and writing classes were drinking a lot and writing a lot. There was also a lot of increased speculation about party-switching Democrats. One real politicist, conservative Democrat Ralph Hall of Texas, said, "Talk to me [November] 9th."[1] But the Republicans were playing hardball, threatening fringe Democrats with future primary challenges and strong general election challenges if they did not switch parties. As Bill Paxon of the NRCC said, "There's one way to avoid being targeted by the Republican Party, and that's to join it."[2]

Gingrich told the *Los Angeles Times*'s Karen Tumulty that if the GOP took control of Congress, it was because "I've spent much of my career reporting accurately on a Congress that's worthy of being despised."[3] He wasn't kidding for one second.

The "let's keep expectations under control" stratagem was now out the window. Republicans from Gingrich on down were talking openly about GOP control or at least "operational control," meaning they would take enough seats to unofficially coalition with conservative Democrats in the House to push through their legislative program. "We'll be either the strongest Republican minority since 1954 or we're going to be the majority. Our working assumption is that we'll be a majority," said Gingrich.[4] This was not just bluster on Gingrich and the Republicans' part. The election was less than two weeks away and millions were cascading into the GOP at all levels. Now was the time to press the bet and Gingrich did so, even giving odds. He went on *Rush Limbaugh* and predicted "the odds are at least 2–1 we'll be the majority."[5] The *New York Times*'s Katharine Seelye called him a "one man intifada."[6]

On the other hand, speaking for much of the Fourth Estate, Bill Schneider of CNN wrote skeptically in the *National Journal*, "The GOP has met with striking success as an opposition party. For some reason, however, Republicans this autumn seem intent on reminding voters of the party's failures as a governing party."[7]

Profiles of Gingrich were everywhere on television and in print. Most of his quotes were good, tight, and interesting, though some were inevitably cringe inducing. He was getting big and receptive crowds according to Barry Hutchinson, his full-time traveling assistant.[8]

The American economy in the fall of 1994 wasn't all that bad; it just wasn't all that good either. The growth rate was around 3.5 percent and unemployment was at 6 percent. But the sense among the American people was uneasy. The Democrats had tried to strengthen their campaign against the Republicans and their Contract by raising the specter of Reaganomics and the Gipper himself. "The problem is that Ronald Reagan's name is not exactly mud with American voters. Polls show him to be the best-regarded president of the last two decades, with Clinton near the bottom," noted the *Christian Science Monitor.*[9]

The Democrats made a commercial mocking the Contract, with footage of Newt Gingrich approaching a podium in slow motion as the voiceover intoned: "Huge tax cuts for the wealthy, billions in defense increases, a trillion dollars in promises . . . devastating cuts in Medicare."[10] The initial budget was $2 million for the near national buy attacking the 1980s and the Reagan Era.

Speaker Tom Foley was still struggling in his campaign. He complained that local talk radio was "abusive and slanderous," but also that all his press coverage had "become overwhelmingly negative."[11] The seat he'd held with ease for thirty years was now in danger of slipping away. If he lost, he'd be "the first speaker since William Pennington of New Jersey in 1860 to be voted out of office."[12] The NRA was pummeling Foley with TV ads featuring their president, Charlton Heston. Just to torment Bill Clinton, they were also distributing millions of bumper stickers that proclaimed, "My President Is Charlton Heston."

In Pennsylvania, endangered Democrat Paul McHale was trying to stave off his own political funeral by producing a "Declaration of Independence," in which he spelled out his differences with Bill Clinton. He flailed desperately as his opponent, James Yeager, ran commercials of McHale "morphing" into Clinton.[13]

In the South and especially Gingrich's Georgia, Republicans had long ago shed the "Reconstruction" millstone and were on course for sizable pickups. It was especially galling for the son of the South, Clinton, and the summer son of the South, Al Gore.

The GOP and Gingrich were especially proud that they had recruited more than two dozen black candidates to run for Congress. One such man was J. C. Watts, a GOP candidate in Oklahoma. Watts was running in a district that was only 7 percent black and was 2–1 Democratic. Nonetheless, he was running as a strict devotee of Gingrich's Contract, totally supportive of the agenda of social conservatives. It didn't hurt that Watts was the former starting quarterback for a nationally ranked Oklahoma Sooners football team. Gingrich took special interest in Watts because his victory would be a huge breakthrough in the African American community.[14] He went in to campaign for Watts twice, despite the difficulty in getting to the rural Oklahoma district.[15] "The old order wouldn't accept him." When asked why, Gingrich said, "Because he's black."[16] Gingrich understood the nature of the revolution he was leading. "The reason the old order doesn't have to be articulate is they're not trying to teach it."[17]

Adding to the esprit de corps of the Republicans, Congressman John Boehner, who was unopposed, donated $50,000 to the NRCC and then sent $70,000 in checks to 55 GOP challengers out of his own campaign kitty.[18]

In other states, consultants and campaigns resorted to gimmicks and slurs in the final days. Ben Jones was continuing to stalk Gingrich across the country, showing up in places like Connecticut, where the House Minority Whip was stumping for GOP challengers. Candidates' manhood or womanhood was questioned; aides wearing stuffed-animal costumes were sent out to trail candidates by their opponents. Harassing phone calls were arranged when candidates appeared on local radio shows.

Jim Wright emerged from self-imposed seclusion to rip Gingrich once more. "What Gingrich did to me, he's trying now on the Congress itself."[19]

The 1994 election was shaping up as a referendum on Reagan versus Clinton. The Contract in fact had Dutch Reagan's fingerprints all over it, while the Democrats' agenda had the Clintons' fingerprints all over it. Gingrich taunted them, saying, "If the Democrats want to go home and attack Reagan and defend Clinton, I think that is a dead loser for them."[20]

Clinton took wing for the Middle East. At least in the Middle East, there was occasional talk of peace accords. Al Gore, on the stump, fired a huge salvo at the GOP, saying they appealed "to the worst in people, to anger, frustration and fear."[21] A Republican candidate in California said of his opponent, incumbent Lynn Schenk, "We're going to wrap [Clinton] around her neck like a millstone and toss them into the San Diego Bay."[22]

The stories of conservative Democratic congressmen switching after the election popped up again, a sure sign that there was something in the air. It was just days before the election and these presumed happily ensconced members should have been looking forward to another two years in the majority. But they weren't; these Southern boys were as nervous as a cat on a hot tin roof.

Just one day before the elections, the *Wall Street Journal* and NBC released a national survey that confirmed what everybody thought they knew: there was widespread disgust with the status quo, and the Democrats were paying a heavy price.[23] Fully 46 percent of likely voters were going to pull the straight line level for Republicans, and only 35 percent were going to vote for the Democrats. The margin had in fact widened since the last survey three weeks earlier. A plurality said they planned on voting for their own incumbent, but even that was only marginal good news with so many open Democratic seats. On the issues of taxes and crime, the GOP was cleaning up.[24]

Anecdotal evidence was springing up all over the country of unusually competitive races in traditional Democratic strongholds, as well as enormously more activity at the grassroots level for the GOP than for their counterparts. As a topic, health care had fallen off the map. The economy, crime, taxes, and corruption were on the minds of American voters. Hillary Clinton, however, was still a big negative for many Americans.

On the stump, Clinton was shameless. He told senior citizens that if the Republicans won and the Contract was enacted, it would mean a cut of $2,000 per month in benefits. "There were audible gasps in the audience of 400 senior citizens at the Portuguese Social Club" in Rhode Island.[25] Gingrich and Bob Dole had said repeatedly that Social Security was untouchable. But that did not stop Clinton from making the false charge repeatedly. He also claimed—without evidence—the Contract would cost a trillion dollars. He warned the voters there and in other parts of the country not to fall for "a bunch of cheap political promises by con people."[26] He said the Republicans were going to "sucker punch" the American people.[27]

Bob Dole, party chairman Haley Barbour, and other GOP leaders jumped right back at Clinton over the charges. They called it "The Big Lie" and Dole, who never needed a doctor to find the jugular vein, said the Democrats "will say almost anything to keep control of Congress, no matter how desperate, false or hypocritical their scare tactics are."[28]

Three scenarios had emerged: One was the GOP picking up 40 House seats, which would give them marginal control. It would be seismic. The second scenario had the GOP gaining 66 seats. The third, more outlandish, forecast a possible pickup of 88 House seats. Nothing had been seen like that since the 1930s with the Democratic firestorms of the New Deal, which swept away hundreds of Republican House members in 1930, 1932, 1934, and 1936. To put it in perspective, FDR's Democrats lost more than 70 seats in the off-year elections of 1938 and *still* retained control of the House!

Gingrich and his folks were utterly convinced that in less than a week, he would become the Republican Speaker of the House and third in line for the presidency. Bob Novak's column five days before the national elections called him "the Speaker Presumptive."[29] From here on out, there would be none of that "sneaking up" nonsense. The Big One was coming.

With all the attention focusing on Gingrich and the House, it was easy to overlook the hundreds of other races going on, including in the all-important US Senate, where the Democrats were defending 22 incumbents and the Republicans only 13. Of those, 9 seats were open.[30]

Abruptly, Gingrich canceled the last days of stumping and returned home to Georgia for his own campaign. For a moment, Democrats chortled and gloated that the revolution had faltered and that Gingrich was in trouble again in his own district. After all, his opponent, Ben Jones, had produced a poll showing a tight race, with Gingrich down to a lead of only 6 percent. Gingrich's own polling showed him ahead of Cooter by more than thirty points.

Gingrich spokesman Allan Lipsett quipped, "We understand President Clinton is out campaigning and he's doing such a good job for Republican candidates that it wasn't necessary for Newt to travel around the country."[31] It was a snarky comment befitting James Carville or Paul Begala, if the shoe had been on the other foot.

As of the weekend before the election, the nation's newspapers were filled with hand-wringing stories about the state and cynicism of American politics. Horror of horrors, "going negative" was en vogue. The *Washington Post*, in a lengthy Style section piece, laid much of the blame at the feet of the right generally, and of Dole and Gingrich specifically. The article said Dole had a "reputation for meanness" and called Gingrich "famously confrontational."[32] One liberal quoted in the piece was allowed—without challenge or evidence—to compare Dole and Gingrich to the racist David Duke and the bigoted Father Coughlin.[33]

Much more interesting was the continuing upheaval going on in House Speaker Tom Foley's district. George Nethercutt had the Speaker on the ropes. Foley's campaign was desperately trying to regain the initiative, going after his opponent rather than defending his own record or the record of President Clinton. "If this fails here, it will fail elsewhere, and Republicans will take control of the House," intoned Bob Novak ominously.[34]

Polls released the weekend before the election showed for the first time the Republicans more popular than the Democrats. This fact was noted in the *Washington Post*. "A batch of weekend polls that measured the electorate's party identification all held good news for Republicans—most finding that for the first time since the 1950s, more Americans prefer Republicans to Democrats."[35]

The bellwether races were going to be in Indiana and Kentucky, where polls closed at 6:00 p.m. Polls closed later in Vermont, Maine, Georgia, Florida, South Carolina, Connecticut, and several other states, each of which had hotly contested races for governor, the Senate, and obviously the House.[36]

Gingrich was looking at an entire country that was, for Republicans in 1994, a target-rich environment. The total firepower of the GOP—allies in the Christian Right, the term-limits movement, gun owners—was trained squarely at obliterating vulnerable Democrats and protecting incumbent

Republicans. Without a national candidate to act as the catalyst, the synergy was remarkable. Gingrich was the closest the Republicans had in 1994 to a presidential nominee. He was certainly the national leader of the GOP, having overshadowed Bob Dole.

The Clinton White House kept pushing the line that the election was not a referendum on their man, but their man kept talking as though it was. He blamed the "messes" on Reagan and Bush—"12 years of Republican administrations"—and wondered aloud why voters would give Congress back to the people who nearly "wrecked" the country in the 1980s.[37] Behind the scenes, Clinton operative Paul Begala said they were "shell shocked."[38] But the White House had only itself to blame for allowing Republicans to create an unfavorable image of Clinton that was never refuted.

A *Post* reporter, Guy Gugliotta, summarized the way he saw Republicans waging political warfare in their campaign: "It looks easy. All you need is a lot of money, a hatred of government and a few attack ads depicting your opponent as 'soft on crime,' 'part of the problem,' and a 'big spender' with the sexual mores of a warthog."[39] Check, check, and check.

Finally, Election Day arrived and not a moment too soon. At last, the voters would be heard from rather than the Knights of the Keyboard.

CHAPTER 36

REALIGNMENT

"The Gingrich Era."

November 8, 1994—Election Day

Newt Gingrich cast his paper ballot at an elementary school in Marietta, surrounded by a throng of cameras. He was in a dark suit and paisley tie, his hair still wet from a morning shower. The plan was to keep a low profile for the day, take phone calls from friends and pollsters, and get ready for what all in Republicanland hoped—and all in Clintonville feared: a big Republican night. His opponent, Ben Jones, also voted that morning, and some people thought that he and Newt looked a little bit alike. Jones was also chunky with a thick mass of salt-and-pepper hair. But there the similarities ended.

Even as late as the morning of the election, some newspaper reporters were arguing that the Contract had given more energy to the Democrats than to the Republicans because it was a diversion from Clinton's problems. RNC chairman Haley Barbour begged to differ. He was the picture of calm and cool; his staff, however, was anything but serene. An RNC press aide, Leigh Ann Metzger, was seen "gobbling Mylanta" in vain hopes of calming a jumpy tummy.[1]

Don Fierce, Barbour's political consigliore, was seen in the halls of the RNC, bouncing off the walls. "His eyes were wild with apprehension, notwithstanding that he claimed he was in a great mood."[2] When asked directly, he blurted, "Of course I'm nervous!"[3] A lot of GOP operatives went golfing on Election Day, knowing there was nothing else to be done from DC unless you were an election lawyer, in which case you stayed behind the transparency with the sign "Break Glass in Case of Emergency." In this case, both sides were on the lookout for rumored or actual voting fraud going on in the states. The most honest and rational of all the RNC staffers was probably Paula Nowakowski, who frankly said, "We really have nothing to do. There's nothing to do but pace."[4]

The weekend before the elections, President Ronald Reagan released the bravest and saddest letter he'd ever written, announcing to the world he was suffering from Alzheimer's disease.

It was a blow to the party that loved him and that he loved, but all agreed the best way to move forward was to win the impending election for his sake, as Gingrich had made it a referendum on Reaganism.

Hundreds of Republican election-night parties across the country took on a similar form. All were in rented hotel ballrooms, nearly all in suburban America. The audiences were overwhelmingly white, middle class, and middle-aged. Men were clean shaven, dressed in suits and ties. Each room was decorated in red, white, and blue bunting. Women wore dresses or business suits, their hair in place and makeup on properly.

Two bars were arranged at either end of the rooms, serving beer and wine. Ubiquitous bowls of stale pretzels or greasy nuts sat on the tables, which were covered with yellow or white tablecloths. In many hotels, two risers had been assembled: one for the candidate and one for the media.

Somewhere in the hotels, each candidate was holed up in a suite with his manager, press secretary, finance- and fund-raisers, the campaign's lawyer, other key staff, family members, and close friends. The manager was most often a young and high-strung male, thin, with eyeglasses, sometimes prematurely balding, obsessive about either smoking or jogging, it made no difference which . . . it was something to do while thinking and plotting.

There were platters of sandwiches and cold cuts, cheese and vegetables, and bowls of crackers. No one would be doing any heavy drinking at this time—that was for later, win or lose. Before heading down to the hall to claim victory, the candidate was drinking coffee or soda pop. There was plenty of smoke in the air.

A number of private lines had been installed in the suite, and the numbers given to a precious few. As precincts closed around the country at alternatively 6:00, 7:00, and even 8:00 p.m., partisan ballot-watchers would be there as the machines were opened or paper ballots counted under vigilant eyes. Most campaigns had identified their "bellwether" precincts. Waiting for the tabulations at hundreds of precincts might take hours, but having watchers at anywhere between ten and thirty of them would, once phoned in to the hotel suite with the nervous candidates and perspiring staff, give a good indication as to the outcome of the race.

Throughout the night, the precincts would trickle into the election offices and in turn be reported by the local TV stations, breaking into network programming. The suites were thick with tension as candidates and their teams watched the three TVs in the room, each alternating between local and national news. Gingrich and company would gather at the ultra-modern Cobb Galleria in Atlanta. Later, Gingrich's wife Marianne was spotted off in a corner, smoking, seemingly indifferent to the history being made that night.

Dan Rather of CBS forecast a "possible Republican hurricane."[5] Results began coming in at 6:00 p.m. Eastern Time. Within hours, the writing was on the wall.

It was an utter and complete decimation of the Democratic Party. They lost the House, badly; they lost the Senate, badly; they lost gubernatorial races; they lost state houses all across America, badly; they lost hundreds of state legislative seats. Badly. The word *realignment* was on everybody's lips. So, too, was the name Newt Gingrich. "Newt is dangerous because he's smart, he's articulate and he is in control of his party," declaimed a bitter Democratic congressman, Mike Synar.[6] Synar, a liberal from Oklahoma, had already lost his primary to a retired high school principal, Virgil Cooper. In the general election, Cooper, in turn, lost to the GOP nominee, Tom Coburn.[7]

The embattled Chicagoan Dan Rostenkowski, an eighteen-term veteran and holder of one of the most Democratic districts in the country, lost to the longest of long shots, Republican challenger Michael Patrick Flanagan, even after heavily outspending his GOP opponent. No one, including Rostenkowski, saw it coming. Rostenkowski harrumphed, "I'm going to Washington to clear out my desk."[8]

The Speaker of the House, Tom Foley, lost in Washington State, the first incumbent Speaker to be defeated in more than one hundred years.[9]

Republicans picked up House seats north and south, east and west. In Texas, the longtime chairman of the Judiciary Committee, Jack Brooks, fell before Hurricane Gingrich. In Kansas, the chairman of the Intelligence Committee, Dan Glickman, also swooned. A first-termer, liberal Marjorie Margolies-Mezvinsky, lost in suburban Philadelphia in large part because of her tie-breaking vote for the Clinton tax increases of 1993.

The Republicans won four seats apiece in Ohio and North Carolina and three in Georgia. In Ohio, Ted Strickland, a smug liberal, lost after just one House term. In Oklahoma, J. C. Watts won against all racial and political odds.

CBS won the network rating wars that night, with Rather calling it for the Republicans at 10:37 p.m., declaring they had won outright control of Congress.

Gingrich and the Republicans had blown the doors off the 40 seats needed to win a majority in the House. By the time all the results were in, they had picked up 52 seats. With 230 Republican seats in the House, and only 204 Democrats and one independent, it was the first time since 1954 the Republicans controlled the House.[10]

Bill Paxon declared a new era of GOP control and dominance. "Yes! Yes! Yes!" he hollered. "When you've waited this long that's all you can say."[11]

The mood in the Clinton bunker was abject bitterness. As one after another after another became a handful, and then a group and, by night's end, a massacre of Democrats, there was no grayness to interpret. The results were right there in black and white. It was a complete refutation of Clintonism and a complete embrace of Reaganism. The election of 1992 had been clouded by the presence of George Bush on the ballot, and many Reaganites had, in fact, chosen the third way in the form of Ross Perot. But the contest between celebrity collectivism and character conservatism had not really taken place until this night in 1994. It was a contest between the idealism of Reagan and the idolatry of Clinton.

Clinton aide George Stephanopoulos was not magnanimous, telling reporters only that the Republicans would now have to accept "responsibility for governing."[12] Clinton watched the returns at the White House but did not emerge to talk to reporters. He issued no statements.[13] When it was clear that Republicans would take control of everything, President Clinton made a congratulatory phone call to Gingrich, but the Speaker-elect oddly ducked it, claiming they were still "sorting things out." He later admitted that was a mistake: protocol dictated that the president always took precedent. An hour later, he returned the call and Clinton took it, congratulating his fellow Southerner. Gingrich recalled the call as "cordial . . . professional."[14] Clinton could be excused for not being warmer, as he and his party had just had their rears kicked from one end of the country to the other.

Over in Texas, Senator Phil Gramm was in no gentler or kinder mood, going hard after Clinton. Around the country, many victorious Republicans were in a feisty mood, and why not? They had the Clintonites beat. Bob Dole thundered, "We're going to change America. We're going to give America back to the people!"[15]

In Atlanta, late into the evening, Gingrich appeared before a throng of cheering conservatives and hundreds of reporters and cameras. It was clear that his lifetime plan for Republican control of the House and the Senate was coming true. He would finally become Speaker of the House.

Despite the atmosphere of historic joy, Gingrich aide Joe Gaylord still could not get past his loathing of Frank Luntz. Luntz casually walked into the big hall and Gaylord barked over and over, "Get the f--- out of here! This is my room! Get the f--- out of here!"[16] It really was inexplicable. Luntz was shy and gentle and utterly obsessed with politics and polling and not turf. Late in the evening when Newt addressed the senior staff on the historic occasion, he asked three individuals to also comment, including longtime Reaganite Grover Norquist and conservative writer John Fund. The third was Luntz. He took personal satisfaction that Gaylord was not asked to speak.[17] Gaylord was also extremely jealous of Gaines and her close relationship with Gingrich. "He didn't treat me very nicely a lot of the time," Gay Gaines said later.[18]

All the networks cut in live for his remarks. Gingrich was remarkably restrained, even humble for a revolutionary, saying the election was not a victory for Republicans or Democrats, but was "about the American people making a set of choices."[19] It was, he said quietly, a "very serious and solemn obligation."[20]

Just as Reagan had been magnanimous toward Jimmy Carter on Election Night in 1980, Gingrich was the same toward Clinton. He made the case that elements of the Contract could be supported by Clinton and the Democrats. Going further, he said, "Every day we fail to act, children are at risk. Every day we fail to change things, people literally die. There will be a presidential campaign in 1996 but let's postpone that. Let's spend 10 to 11 months actually trying to do good things for the children of America."[21]

Gingrich knew what he was doing. Men voted for the Republicans by a 12-point margin, but women voted Democratic by an 8-point margin.[22] The men's vote had been firmly in control of the GOP, but the women's vote had moved left. By invoking children and by using a softer tone, his goal was to get women to look more closely at the Republicans. This was a critical part of the plan for permanent realignment.

One-third of the electorate claimed they were supporters of the National Rifle Association, and they voted overwhelmingly for the Republicans. One-third of all voters said they were voting Republican because of their opposition to Clinton. Whites had abandoned the Democrats, but blacks had stayed loyal. The all-important "Perot voter" went 65 percent for the Republicans.[23] Born-again voters—one-quarter of the electorate—went by a 3–2 margin for the GOP.[24] In districts with retiring Republicans, they stayed Republican, but in districts with retiring Democrats, they went hugely for the GOP. Only half of those voting expressed confidence in the government's ability to solve problems. In California, Prop. 187, which essentially outlawed social services to illegal immigrants, passed by a margin of 2–1, apparently not so controversial after all.

Gingrich had a lot going on that historic night, but he still found time to call White House chief of staff Leon Panetta to offer an olive branch.[25] Letting reporters in on this was part of the cuddly approach. Dole, in Washington, also blew wet kisses to Clinton and the Democrats: "We intend to work with the president. We only have one president and that's President Clinton and we're going to do the best we can."[26] Dole may have been the first one to publically utter the phrase "Speaker Gingrich" in addressing the crowd.[27] He was holding court in the aptly named Renaissance Hotel. The paroxysmal crowd chanted, "Dole! Dole! Dole!" and "Ninety-six! Ninety-six!"[28]

In the narrative of the Republican Party, there have only been a handful of elections that were truly meaningful or that demonstrated a shift in American political history. Without a doubt, the election of 1994 was one of those consequential elections. Soon, even a liberal president would be telling Congress and the nation, "The era of big government is over."[29]

To understand the dramatic shifting nature of the election of '94, it must be noted that *not one* incumbent Republican candidate for the House or the Senate or a governorship lost that night. Out of 435 House races and 35 Senate races, many of them involving Republican incumbents, nary a Republican of any stripe lost. The GOP picked up a net of 11 governorships, giving them the bulk for the first time since 1970. When the dust settled, the House went from 176 Republicans at the beginning of the 103rd Congress to 230 at the start of the 104th Congress; the Democrats went from 258 to 204. The Senate Republicans in that period gained 10 seats, totaling 53 in 1995.

As any student of the Constitution knew, if you control the House, you control much of the nation, because the House controls the money and taxes and regulations. With no filibuster to contend with—and therefore no need for a "super majority"—the Speaker of the House is one of the most powerful men in the world. The GOP won back the Senate after losing it in '88, but they hadn't had the House for *forty years*.

On the afternoon of the election, Gingrich was taking a nap, preparing for the long night, when he was gently shaken by Frank Luntz telling him, "Congratulations, Mr. Speaker." Luntz had gotten the projections from the Associated Press, even though polling places would still be open across the country for hours.[30] Bob Walker later called Gingrich and repeated similarly.[31]

Also in Atlanta that night were Gaines and a popular local radio talk-show host, Sean Hannity. Gaines said, "It was the most raucous, exciting night of my life."[32] Meanwhile, Hannity noted, "It was witnessing history . . . It was transformational."[33] Hannity was acting as the emcee of the festivities that evening, making announcement after announcement about Republicans winning and Democrats losing. As a result, he was on stage all night.[34] The place was packed with people, TV cameras, and journalists. Finally, Hannity got to introduce Gingrich as "Our next Speaker!" The roar of the crowd was off the charts.

Hannity recalled the first time he met Gingrich, when Hannity was getting his start with a small radio show in Huntsville, Alabama, and Gingrich was in town but still made time for the young man.[35] And when the young conservative radio host asked the incoming Speaker if he would appear on his show the next day, Gingrich unhesitatingly said yes. Sure enough, the next day, when he was in demand by everybody, he still found the time to appear on Hannity's Atlanta radio show.[36]

"GOP Captures Congress," screamed large headlines in many papers around the country on the morning of November 9.[37] The *Washington Post* described Clinton's legislative program as "shredded."[38] His aides, the "472 Club," drowned themselves in their sorrows, the arms of lovers, and booze. One wailed, "Think relaunch. Think relaunching this presidency."[39] On November 9, 1994, that was like imagining the relaunch of the *Titanic*.

Most stories ascribed the crushing defeat to the failures and doubts about Bill Clinton and the Democratic Party; few embraced the notion that the nation had swung to the right and was positively embracing conservative governance.

Members of the Administration consoled themselves, saying it was better to face the next two years without control of Congress than without Democratic control of the White House. There was also loose talk about Clinton not worrying about a legislative program for the next two years, but rather redefining himself as the opponent of the Republican Congress. There was also loose talk about a one-term presidency. White House chief of staff Leon Panetta was spinning like a top, trying to make the case that the upheaval of November 8, 1994, was akin to the election of 1992. "There's no question the voters are sending the same message they sent two years ago . . . ," he said.[40]

The reality was, outside of his tax increase of 1993, the failure of Hillarycare, the months devoted to gays in the military, and the smoking hole of the Clinton Crime Bill, the Administration had nothing to show for their first two years in Washington. The Clintonites would sit up for hours convincing themselves they were working hard by talking. Like many on the left, they thought talking was motion and effort.

David Broder, the eternal truth teller, saw the election results as a con-tinuing embrace of Reaganism, noting that hundreds of GOP candidates had unabashedly campaigned as conservatives, many even further to the right than the Gipper himself. "The exit polls suggested that ideology was more of a force in voters' decisions than the anti-incumbency that echoed so loudly on the talk-shows for the last year," asserted Broder.[41]

George Will, commenting on ABC, agreed with Broder, saying the election was yet another victory for Reagan.[42] Dick Wirthlin, Reagan's old pollster, called it a "rolling realignment" that had begun with Reagan in 1980, faltered in 1992, and was reasserting itself again in 1994.[43] Even the Washington Post had to acknowledge that "the huge Republican gains also marked a clear shift to the right in the country, as attacks on big government and taxes and calls for a return to family values resonated for GOP candidates in races at all levels."[44]

The three men most responsible for the upheaval of 1994 were Bill Clinton, Ronald Reagan, and Newt Gingrich. Clinton because he'd failed the promise of 1992 to be a "New Democrat," and Reagan for his own revolution of 1980. That revolution had been cast aside in 1988, only to be rekindled in 1993 by Gingrich.

Clinton's behavior helped the GOP, but it also made it easier for Gingrich to make his argument against government, against centralized authority. As people soured on the same old, same old of George Bush and then Clinton, they turned to Reaganism once again and Gingrich presented it in the form of the "Contract with America." He knew Washington bureaucracies were the real enemy of freedom and innovation.[45]

He knew what needed to be done. He just had to make the argument.

As the sage of the original American Revolution, Thomas Paine, said, "I love the man who can smile in trouble, that can gather strength from fatigue . . ." It was a uniquely American concept to struggle, to have hope, and to conquer. In America, no one was royalty and no one had special rights granted them by illicit governance. All were equal before the eyes of the government. At least, that had been the plan.

Newt Gingrich was just as average and just as unique as anyone else. Like his fellow Americans, he believed in the Jeffersonian concept that a person could rise to the highest level of achievement without heavy-handed government or nobility. He believed in the privacy and the dignity of the individual, and that true American conservatism found itself in the private person.

In the wake of the revolution of '94, the way forward for the GOP was not entirely clear and it was murky at best for the Democrats. One of the most incisive observers among the corps of moderate Democrats, Al From, of the Democratic Leadership Council, said, "The battle for the soul of the Democratic Party is far from over." Then, unexpectedly, he continued: "But the battle in the Republican Party is just beginning."[46]

Curiously, From was not alone. Voices inside the GOP—mostly moderate Republicans—also raised concerns about the coming struggle for the soul of their party.

Gingrich, though, had no doubts, at least none he showed outwardly that evening and as the historic 104th Congress convened and the gavel would soon be handed over to him. In the ultimate scene of the movie *The Candidate*, Robert Redford's character turns to his manager and says, "What do we do now?"

Gingrich and his band of revolutionary conservatives knew exactly what they were going to do. They were going to remake government and, hopefully, remake America by remaking conservatism. They were going to, as Reagan quoting Paine said, "Make the world over again."

EPILOGUE

"He is . . . the most corrupt speaker ever . . .
Gingrich is downsizing government . . . Gingrich
should be serving a term in prison."

The unbalanced statement of a street-theater Newt Gingrich hater? A crazed blogger on the Internet? One of the myriad left-wing columnists or reporters for the left-wing *Huffington Post* or the left-winger *New York Times*? No, these were the words of a small academic work (some would say screed) entitled *Newt Gingrich: Capitol Crimes and Misdemeanors* by an obscure academic, John K. Wilson, who, after a cursory survey of his career, was shown to be littered with ultra-leftist causes and fads. In a little more than two hundred pages of this book, published by a very minor house in Maine, no real evidence is offered of capital crimes or misdemeanors. In fact, according to Wilson, Gingrich is really guilty of the "destruction of the principles of social responsibility."[1] Loosely translated, this means Gingrich opposed collectivism.

That book and others are symptomatic of Gingrich Derangement Syndrome, a mental disorder of the left that even surpassed their hatred of Ronald Reagan, in part, I suspect, because Gingrich had fun beating the left and he let them know he was having fun beating them, which infuriated them. "Now, part of the reasoning for . . . the left hated me . . . is that I actually asserted a countervailing [force] and . . . I was actually quite cheerful about taking them on."[2]

Of Washington, Gingrich said, "There are two games in this country. One is played by the 5,000 insiders in Washington who write the laws and tell the lies and the other by the rest of us, who pay the price. That's what we can't tolerate."[3] In this simple statement made more than four decades ago,

Gingrich concisely described the political realities of our country. He has spent his ensuing career fighting the political wars arising from this national split personality. But as Clausewitz said, "The problem with wars is that everything is simple, but the simple is very hard."[4]

Newt Gingrich remains one of the four most important conservative leaders of the twentieth and twenty-first centuries, following Barry Goldwater, Bill Buckley, and Ronald Reagan. How many national figures have had as long effect on the national debate as Gingrich? Richard Nixon and Reagan for sure, but they were both presidents who had a profound impact on the national political debate for a long time. Abraham Lincoln was only a part of the national debate for seven years.

One is hard-pressed to think of someone who was not elected chief executive having as much influence for as long as Newt Gingrich. From the 1970s right up until the second decade of the twenty-first century, Gingrich's opinions and actions interested many. Possibly only Henry Clay and William Jennings Bryan had as much sway on the national debate for as long as Newt has.

Gingrich was also a Happy Warrior, although sometimes a moody one. Certainly a combative one. Gingrich accumulated enemies like he was eating breakfast. After all, he said, "It is impossible to maintain civilization with 12-year-olds having babies, 15-year-olds killing each other, 17-year-olds dying of AIDS, and 18-year-olds getting diplomas they can't even read. Yet that is precisely where three generations of Washington-dominated, centralized government, welfare-state policies have carried us," as reported in one of the few objective books on the Georgian, Newt!, written by respected columnist Dick Williams.[5] "For some, his references seemed loony—from envisioning space colonies to praising the invention of the restaurant salad bar," Williams wrote.[6]

In 1995 and 1996, Gingrich was second only to Clinton in the number of death threats received. Maybe because he said, "Liberalism is dead. What you have is a secular socialist model, which has nothing to do with liberalism. The secular socialist model is about power so it's never exhausted."[7]

Radio talk show host Sean Hannity once did a roast of Gingrich, following football great Lou Holtz. It was a fund-raiser for Boy's Town. "Don't ever follow Lou Holtz" was Hannity's sage counsel. Hannity was impressed with Newt's grasp of history and his speech-making abilities. At events Hannity emceed, he said that "every time, [Newt would] ask for a pen. Then, he'd take a napkin and he'd write down a few thoughts and then he'd give a forty-five-minute speech that would bring the house down . . . He always has something new. Whatever he's learning at that point in his life: If it's about lightbulbs, he'll use a lightbulb analogy."[8] Hannity said, "Newt is one of the most misunderstood people. The false narrative is he's the Gingrich that stole Christmas . . . He is a deep thinker, a serious intellectual, solutions-orientated."[9]

Newt was invited to the Obama White House but never in eight years to the Bush 43 White House. To this day, Gingrich and the Bushes and Bushies, such as Karl Rove, can barely be in the same room with one another. The family of long memories could never forgive Gingrich for taking on President Bush over his broken pledge on taxes in 1990. Gingrich bluntly said that "neither Bush nor Rove was a conservative."[10] He later elaborated, "I have a PhD in history. I've written twenty-three books and made six movies and I helped engineer the rise of the modern Republican Party. You would think at some point those credentials would get you somewhere."[11]

Gingrich accumulated ideas and this, too, angered many, as his ideas were often an indictment of the established order, a clash of the conservative freedom versus the liberal justice. Gingrich also understood the American Revolution was a political upheaval not an economic one. One of the seminal founders, Benjamin Rush, wrote to Thomas Paine, "The war is over but the revolution goes on." On the other hand, Newt's continued revolution had chaotic elements, as Frank Luntz observed. "Half of his ideas are brilliant. You should follow them to the letter. The other half are insane and you should ignore them."[12]

Ed Rollins agreed. "They used to tease about having a bottom drawer in one of the files, which is all Newt's . . . ideas."[13] Another chronic Gingrich critic, Steve Largent, NFL Hall of Famer turned GOP congressman from Oklahoma, thought Newt was long on ideas and short on humility. Retorting, Bob Livingston said of Largent: "Not only did he talk to God but God talked back."[14]

Vin Weber, Gingrich's constant ally early in his career, said his meteoric rise was unexpected. "I don't think that they ever thought that Newt Gingrich would rise to any position of substantial leadership in the House, much less be the Speaker of the House of Representatives. They thought he was brilliant but he was consigned to forever be a gadfly."[15]

Two words were found frequently in Gingrich's lectures and interviews: *individualism* and *populism*. To Gingrich, they were the underlying principles of American conservatism.

A quick survey of available books on Newt Gingrich shows most are invariably written by liberals, overly harsh, and often factually thin. They focus on embittered former staffers, allegations of infidelity, anything they can find and hurl at Gingrich.

In another book that fits this category, *The Broken Branch*, the authors Norm Ornstein and Thomas Mann of the Brookings Institution and two card-carrying members of the Washington establishment, by and large trashed Gingrich, largely because they didn't understand him. They'd been tracking Gingrich since he first appeared on the scene and seemed amazed that he never joined the establishment. Yet another book, titled *From George Wallace to Newt Gingrich*, is again another left-wing slam. And in yet another book written by a liberal on the history of the conservative movement, *To Make Men Free*, Heather Cox Richardson penned, ". . . [Bill] Buckley's new political magazine *National Review*, resurrected the traditional Republican link between federal aid to African Americans and communism."[16] She also ridiculously claimed that Republicans wanted wealth to concentrate at the top, "just as the defense of antebellum slavery had been." She charged: "like their Southern predecessors in the 1850s"![17] Richardson is not alone in being a historically illiterate liberal with a political agenda. Yet another, *Glass Houses*, chose to focus on his grandfather. His biological father was a navy man, who left home after Newt was born and later allowed him to be adopted by his stepfather in exchange for not having to pay child support. Gingrich's mother was said to be manic-depressive, and Newt's half sister is an openly lesbian writer. The first question is, of course, is any of this really relevant?

One of the few books that took an honest look at Gingrich's legacy was *Kings of the Hill* by Lynne and Dick Cheney. In it, the famed couple claimed that Gingrich altered the course of American history. And he did. If nothing, he was known to be blunt, as when in private he called Hillary Clinton a "b--ch" as related in *The Clinton Tapes* by Taylor Branch.[18] Branch did not hold back, relating how Clinton had once fallen asleep in the White House barber's chair and could not be roused.

Many books quoted former disgruntled staffers who all too happily unloaded on Gingrich, disappointed that he wasn't always warm and fuzzy, like so many in politics. Incredibly, they charged no unethical or dishonest behavior, just that he often moved on from them to other staffers.

Chip Kahn saw similarities between Gingrich and Clinton and Gingrich and Barack Obama. Newt is "extremely charismatic" and is also a "user."[19] But he said, "I've never felt the same way about anybody since then."[20] Kahn's wife, Mary, despised Gingrich, telling Nigel Hamilton, "Newt uses people and then discards them as useless."[21] Lee Howell, another former staffer, was found frequently eviscerating his old boss in books. But dozens of other aides had warm stories about Gingrich.

Part of the reason I chose to write this political biography is because much of what has been written by leftists about Gingrich is false, exaggerated, or irrelevant and also because I've come to the conclusion that conservatives cannot allow most liberals to write our history. Most modern liberals cannot be trusted to record conservative history accurately anymore, they are too interested in rewriting history to fit their sequence of events, much like Big Brother in *1984*.

Conservatives need to be concerned about protecting their true history, which means simply reporting accurately on the facts of significant and relevant events to the issue or individual under examination, something liberal outlets increasingly avoid. Case in point: the unctuous and liberal *New York Times*, in one of the first stories concerning Nancy Reagan's death, devoted the first three paragraphs to Iran-Contra.[22]

Gingrich's reputation and legacy continue to rise and not just because of the tawdry conviction and prison sentence of former Speaker Denny Hastert, the ignoble departure of former Speaker John Boehner, forced out by conservatives, and the underwhelming and unsound tenure of Speaker Paul Ryan. Gingrich's reputation is rising because he got things done, because the Republican Party since the time of Reagan had been mostly marked by failures and reversals, marked by George H. W. Bush and George W. Bush.

They called it the "Gingrich Revolution" just as they called it the "Reagan Revolution"; and while it was certainly ideological, it was personal too. Most revolutions are also personal crusades, from the American Revolution to the French Revolution. So it was with the Gingrich Revolution.

Curiously, the media never describes American left-wing upheavals as "revolutions," as if the liberal status quo was the accepted governing method. Although, Major Garrett argued in his book *The Enduring Revolution* that Gingrich was given too much credit for 1994. "The truth is, Gingrich was neither the general nor the beguiling mystical leader of the Republican Revolution."[23] Bob Livingston took a longer view, saying, "We had forty years of history against us. I mean, nobody could bet on it."[24]

When the Republicans took over Congress in November 1994, for the first time in forty years, they joyously told the self-congratulatory, creepy, and supercilious Harvard to go screw itself. It was one of the fringe benefits to winning. The pompous poofs of Boston had arrogantly held orientation sessions in the liberal enclave to presumably indoctrinate new members as to how they really needed to vote, despite telling their constituents something else. Gingrich and the incoming Republican class jubilantly gave the middle finger to the ultra-leftists and organized their own orientation session instead, in conjunction with the Heritage Foundation in Baltimore, in the wake of 1994.

Conservatism was becoming sexy again, in some cases literally. Comely conservatives such as Laura Ingraham and Ann Coulter, both seen frequently on cable television, were emerging as fetching articulators of the right. Ingraham was photographed for a national magazine in an appealing leopard-print mini skirt, demonstrating how far conservatism had come culturally, from the "little old ladies in tennis shoes" who nominated Barry Goldwater in 1964.

As of late November 1994, Gingrich wasn't letting any grass grow under his feet. He was already at work on yet another book. *To Renew America* reviewed in stark terms the problems of America and his bold solutions. Ten years earlier, he'd written another explosive book, *Window of Opportunity*, and it also had set Washington to talking, as he took it directly to the bureaucracies that hindered progress in America. He also suggested to the incoming class of freshmen Republicans to read a number of things, including how Napoleon lost at Waterloo to the Duke of Wellington, as a lesson in how a motivated, smaller force can win over an unmotivated, larger force.

He also circulated helpful tips from Field Marshal Bernard Montgomery's orders of the day: "Honesty in everything about the campaign; Co-sharing in power, information, etc.; We go slow now in order to go rapidly later; Keep everything simple, stick to fundamentals; Keep trying, openly admit mistakes, learn from each other; Have some fun along the way."[25] Sometimes Gingrich was accused of engaging in "'GobbledyNewt'—his philosophical mix of futurism, high technology, free enterprise and space."[26]

Trent Lott once told Gingrich aide David Hoppe: "I would have not done the things Newt did, and we would not have been the majority."[27] True enough. Lott was the quintessential get-along, go-along type. So was Bob Dole, who said, "Newt is a brilliant guy. He's articulate and knowledgeable, all the good things you would want in a leader . . . I always thought, he's a great man in his own opinion . . . He lacks something that give[s] people that confidence . . . now whether it's his personal life, or . . . it all started way back when he referred to me as a tax collector for the welfare state, which I didn't appreciate. We ran the Senate like adults."[28]

Part of the reason Newt Gingrich has been an important voice on the national scene for so long, in addition to his brilliance, is pure persistence. "Newt Gingrich had survived two disheartening election defeats in the 1970s. He had hung onto his congressional seat twice by fewer than 1,000 votes. He has contested the senior leadership of his party and rebuked a popular Republican president. Yet here he was, the King of the Hill in one national magazine, the Man with a Vision in another. He was leader of a new American revolution."[29]

Henry Clay in the first half of the nineteenth century. William Jennings Bryan in the latter nineteenth century and early twentieth century. Richard Nixon in the middle of the twentieth century. Ronald Reagan in the last quarter of the twentieth century and early decades of the twenty-first.

We can add Newt Gingrich's name to that select list of individuals who had an effect on the national debate for more than three decades.

That, in and of itself, makes him an interesting figure, a subject worthy of an honest accounting of his rise to power and subsequent accomplishments.

ACKNOWLEDGMENTS

Citizen Newt now constitutes my sixth book, with hopefully still many more to come, the Lord willing and the Devil doesn't interfere. One would think I would write with more confidence now and I do, but I still remain terrified of this portion of the book, the acknowledgments, for fear of leaving someone out or, a somewhat even greater fear, that I will include a person or persons not worthy in later retrospection. In the past, I've erred on the side of caution and included many. Not this time, as I've pared it down to just those people who I believe I am truly in their debt.

None of this would be possible without my dear and beloved soul mate and spouse, Zorine. It's now been thirty-five years of splendid life together, and often I wonder where the time has gone. Zorine has made my life so pleasurable and so enjoyable, I find myself with an inexcusable lack of vocabulary to express the joy and happiness Zorine has given me and that we've shared. Thank you, my darling Reggie.

Thank you, Mother—Barbara Shirley Eckert—as well. You've been a loving rock for my many years, stoic and strong and yet also tender, faithful, and joyful. Thank you to our children—Matthew, Andrew, Taylor, and Mitchell—for your love and support and patience. Thank you to my longtime friend and business partner, Diana Banister, who each day spells out the meaning of integrity and loyalty.

Scott Mauer is a scholar and my special champion. He came along in the nick of time to take over the all-important editing and fact checking of

Citizen Newt, working tirelessly and to perfection, without missing a beat or skipping a fact. Thank you, Scott.

Thanks also to Michael Patrick Leahy, a terrific writer and editor and friend, who also helped immeasurably with this effort. Again my thanks. Thanks to my team at HarperCollins Christian Publishers: to Brian Hampton, publisher, Nelson Books; Webster Younce, my editor and advisor; Janene MacIvor, also my tender and tough editor; Tiffany Sawyer, publicity; and Stephanie Tresner, marketing.

A special thanks to Newt's two daughters, Kathy Gingrich Lubbers and Jackie Gingrich Cushman.

Thank you to Bridget Matzie, a great agent and a great friend.

Thank you to Callista Gingrich for allowing Newt to spend so much time with me, as I queried him endlessly about all manner of things, for hours on end. Gingrich and I often met early Sunday mornings at the Basilica in Washington over coffee or breakfast while Callista performed in the Sunday choir. Our time together was invaluable, as I came to slowly understand his perspective and outlook.

Thank you all.

Craig Shirley
Ben Lomond, VA

NOTES

PROLOGUE
1. "Republicans Prepare for Florida Debate," *The Situation Room*, CNN, January 26, 2012.

INTRODUCTION
1. Bob Livingston, in discussion with the author, February 17, 2011.
2. Associated Press, "Rep. Gingrich Says He Smoked Marijuana Once," November 6, 1987.
3. Chip Kahn, in discussion with the author, November 9, 2010.
4. "Gingrich Challenges John Flynt," *Atlanta Daily World*, November 3, 1974, 2.
5. Newt Gingrich, in discussion with the author.
6. Steve Hanser, in discussion with the author, October 21, 2010.
7. Newt Gingrich, in discussion with the author, February 9, 2016.
8. Ibid., September 23, 2010.
9. Wayne King, "Divided G.O.P. in Georgia Facing a Rout on Tuesday," *New York Times*, November 2, 1974, 12.
10. David S. Broder, "Bright Lights on the GOP Front," *Washington Post*, June 30, 1974, C6.
11. Chip Kahn, in discussion with the author, November 9, 2010.
12. Ibid.
13. Ibid.
14. Jimmy Carter, "Bridging the Gap," *New York Times*, August 12, 1974, 23.
15. Mel Steely, in discussion with the author, November 22, 2010.
16. Zell Miller, in discussion with the author, November 19, 2010.
17. David S. Broder, "Governors Feeling Feisty," *Washington Post*, June 9, 1974, A1.
18. Mike Feinsilber, "Ford Calls Inflation 'Public Enemy No. 1,'" *Atlanta Daily World*, August 15, 1974, 1.

19. Richard L. Lyons, "Rockefeller Becomes Vice President," *Washington Post*, December 20, 1974, A1.

20. "Ford: 'To Heal the Nation . . . Was the Top Priority,'" *Washington Post*, September 17, 1974, A14.

21. Wayne King, "Divided G.O.P. in Georgia Facing a Rout on Tuesday," *New York Times*, November 2, 1974, 12.

22. *Statistics of the Presidential and Congressional Election of November 7, 1972* (Washington, DC, US Government Printing Office, 1973), 10.

23. David S. Broder, "Bright Lights on the GOP Front," *Washington Post*, June 30, 1974, C6.

24. Newt Gingrich, in discussion with the author, October 31, 2010.

25. Alan Sverdlik, "*Atlanta Daily World*," *New Georgia Encyclopedia*, December 12, 2009, http://www.georgiaencyclopedia.org/articles/arts-culture/atlanta-daily -world.

26. Bob Gingrich, in discussion with Peter Boyer, PBS, http://www.pbs.org/wgbh /pages/frontline/newt/newtintwshtml/bgingrich.html.

27. Newt Gingrich, in discussion with the author, September 23, 2010.

28. Ibid.

CHAPTER 1: PROFESSOR GINGRICH

1. Roy Reed, "New South Rising Crop of '76 Prospects," *New York Times*, September 27, 1974, 37.

2. Ira Kantor, "Remembering Harry Chapin: Three Decades Later, Looking Back at a Singer with a Cause," *New York Daily News*, July 10, 2011, http://www .nydailynews.com/entertainment/music-arts/remembering-harry-chapin -decades-back-singer-article-1.156726.

3. "Kennedy, Mondale Ask Early Tax Cut," *Washington Post*, April 21, 1974, 2.

4. Hobart Rowen, "Tax Cut: The Policy Debate," *Washington Post*, March 24, 1974, A4.

5. "Recession and Inflation," *Washington Post*, July 25, 1974, A24.

6. Newt Gingrich, in discussion with the author, September 23, 2010.

7. "Gingrich Runs for Congress in District 6," *Atlanta Daily World*, April 7, 1974, 3.

8. "Gingrich Accuses of Incompetency and Indifference," *Atlanta Daily World*, April 18, 1974, 11.

9. Ibid.

10. *Atlanta Journal*, March 1974.

11. Brochure by the Gingrich for Congress Committee, "The Politicians Had Their Chance. Now You Can Have Yours," Private Archives Collections of Carlyle Gregory.

12. Chip Kahn, in discussion with the author, November 9, 2010.

13. "GA District 6," *Our Campaigns*, http://www.ourcampaigns.com/RaceDetail .html?RaceID=149436.

14. Newt Gingrich, in discussion with the author, October 31, 2010.

15. "PTA News," *Atlanta Daily World*, April 7, 1974, 3.

16. "Big Easter Show," *Atlanta Daily World*, April 7, 1974, 3.

17. "The 6th District Needs Newt," *Atlanta Daily World*, November 3, 1974, 11.
18. "Gingrich Challenges John Flynt," *Atlanta Daily World*, November 3, 1974, 2.
19. Ibid.
20. "We Support Gingrich Too," *Atlanta Daily World*, November 5, 1974, 5.
21. Paul West, "Reagan Here to Boost Gingrich," *Atlanta Constitution*, October 25, 1974, 6A.
22. Ibid.
23. Ibid.
24. Newt Gingrich, in discussion with the author, October 31, 2010.
25. John Huey, "Gingrich Says Flynt Farm a Tax 'Ripoff,'" *Atlanta Constitution*, October 26, 1974, 5A.
26. Ibid.
27. Cliff Green, "Gingrich Is Tough One for Rep. Flynt," *Atlanta Constitution*, November 3, 1974, 15B.
28. *Atlanta Constitution*, September 21, 1974.
29. John Huey, "Gingrich Says Flynt Farm a Tax 'Ripoff,'" *Atlanta Constitution*, October 26, 1974, 5A.
30. *Atlanta Constitution*, September 21, 1974.
31. Chip Kahn, in discussion with the author, November 9, 2010.
32. "Gingrich Plan Would Attack 'Exploitation,'" *Atlanta Constitution*, October 27, 1974, 6A.
33. Reg Murphy, "Jack Flynt May Be Losing His Race," *Atlanta Constitution*, October 30, 1974, 4A.
34. Ibid.
35. Newt Gingrich, in discussion with the author.
36. "Gingrich Cites Need for Reform," *Atlanta Constitution*, October 31, 1974, 3A.
37. Cliff Green, "Gingrich Is Tough One for Rep. Flynt," *Atlanta Constitution*, November 3, 1974, 15B.
38. "We Support Gingrich Too," *Atlanta Daily World*, November 5, 1974, 5.
39. Mel Steely, in discussion with the author, September 23, 2010.
40. David Nordan, "Races Hot, But Not in Top Spots," *Atlanta Constitution*, November 3, 1974, 7A.
41. "Sixth District," *Atlanta Journal-Constitution*, October 30, 1974, 26A.
42. Cliff Green, "Gingrich Is Tough One for Rep. Flynt," *Atlanta Constitution*, November 3, 1974, 15B.
43. "Gingrich Predicts Win Tuesday," *Atlanta Constitution*, November 4, 1974, 3A.
44. Bob Beckel, in discussion with the author, October 22, 2010.
45. Chip Kahn, in discussion with the author, November 9, 2010.
46. "GA District 6," *Our Campaigns*, http://www.ourcampaigns.com/RaceDetail .html?RaceID=31926.
47. Bill King, "GOP's Gingrich Trailing in 6th," *Atlanta Constitution*, November 6, 1974, 14A.
48. Ibid., 1A.
49. James M. Naughton, "Democrats View Their Victory as Spur to Legislative Moves; Ford Asks Responsible Action," *New York Times*, November 7, 1974, 1.

50. Mary Russell, "Democrats Put Halt to Republican Momentum in South," *Washington Post*, November 6, 1974, A7.

51. Roy Reed, "The South: G.O.P. Is Set Back in Region as the Democrats Stress Economic Issues," *New York Times*, November 7, 1974, 32.

52. Christopher Lydon, "G.O.P. Suffers Setbacks in the State Legislatures," *New York Times*, November 8, 1974, 18.

53. Ibid., 31.

54. Wayne King, "Georgia's Gov. Carter Enters Democratic Race for President," *New York Times*, December 13, 1974, 93.

55. "Politics: Carter: Entering the Lists," *Time*, December 23, 1974, http://www .time.com/time/magazine/article/0,9171,911584,00.html.

56. "Harris Will Announce," *New York Times*, December 13, 1974, 18.

57. R. W. Apple Jr., "Watergate Panel to Expire Today," *New York Times*, June 30, 1974, 28.

58. John Dillin, "South: How Can Republicans Make a Comeback?," *Christian Science Monitor*, November 7, 1974, 5.

59. U.S. Inflation Calculator, "Historical Inflation Rates: 1914–2013," http://www .usinflationcalculator.com/inflation/historical-inflation-rates/.

60. James Reston, "Ford's First 3 Months," *New York Times*, November 3, 1974, C19.

CHAPTER 2: AGAIN UNTO THE BREACH

1. Newt Gingrich, "Letter to the Editor," *Atlanta Daily World*, May 8, 1975, 4.

2. "State GOP Convention Begins Today," *Atlanta Daily World*, May 30, 1975, 1.

3. Newt Gingrich, "Warnings to Ford from a Southern Republican," *Baltimore Sun*, June 29, 1975, K3.

4. Craig Shirley, *Reagan's Revolution: The Untold Story of the Campaign That Started It All* (Nashville: Thomas Nelson, Inc., 2005), 20.

5. "Ga. Republicans Lash Demos for Income, Crimes Problems," *Atlanta Daily World*, July 13, 1975, 2.

6. Newt Gingrich, "Warnings to Ford from a Southern Republican," *Baltimore Sun*, June 29, 1975, K3.

7. Newt Gingrich, in discussion with the author.

8. "Three Men in a Tub," *Wall Street Journal*, December 2, 1975, 26.

9. "Gingrich Urges Veto of Solons' Pay Hikes," *Atlanta Daily World*, August 12, 1975, 3.

10. Lou Cannon and George Lardner Jr., "Wallace, Reagan Desperate for Success in N. Carolina," *Washington Post*, March 23, 1976, A2.

11. David S. Broder, "Callaway: Reagan Has Lead in South," *Washington Post*, July 24, 1975, A1.

12. Rowland Evans and Robert Novak, "Ford's Campaign Strategy," *Washington Post*, June 21, 1975, A13.

13. "Sen. Brock Boosts Gingrich Campaign," *Atlanta Daily World*, July 18, 1976.

14. *West Georgian News*, October 15, 1976.

15. Newt Gingrich papers, box #3, University of West Georgia Archives.

16. Ibid.
17. Newt Gingrich papers, box #6, University of West Georgia Archives.
18. Newt Gingrich papers, box #9, University of West Georgia Archives.
19. Newt Gingrich papers, box #11, University of West Georgia Archives.
20. Newt Gingrich papers, box #12, University of West Georgia Archives.
21. Newt Gingrich papers, box #13, University of West Georgia Archives.
22. Dave Leip's Atlas of U.S. Presidential Elections, "1976 Presidential General Election Results—Georgia," http://uselectionatlas.org/RESULTS/state .php?year=1976&fips=13&f=0&off=0&elect=.
23. *Statistics of the Presidential and Congressional Election of November 2, 1976*, comp. Benjamin J. Guthrie, (Washington, DC: US Government Printing Office, 1977), 10.
24. Newt Gingrich papers, box #2, University of West Georgia Archives.

CHAPTER 3: THIRD-TIME CHARM OFFENSIVE

1. Myra MacPherson, "The Book Brouhaha," *Washington Post*, June 12, 1989, C8.
2. Bernard Weinraub, "Controversy Grows Over Carter's Move to Sell Iran Planes," *New York Times*, July 12, 1977, 1.
3. *Times Free Press*, November 23, 1977.
4. "'Georgians Against Panama' Seeking 50,000 Signatures," *Atlanta Daily World*, October 25, 1977, 5.
5. Newt Gingrich papers, box #4, University of West Georgia Archives.
6. Newt Gingrich papers, box #5, University of West Georgia Archives.
7. "'Georgians Against Panama' Seeking 50,000 Signatures," *Atlanta Daily World*, October 25, 1977, 5.
8. Jimmy Carter, in discussion with the author, July 11, 2006.
9. "State GOP Leaders Set Macon Meet," *Atlanta Daily World*, December 2, 1977, 2.
10. Newt Gingrich, in discussion with the author, December 5, 2010.
11. Newt Gingrich papers, box # 14, University of West Georgia Archives.
12. "Nation: Woman's Work," *Time*, November 20, 1978.
13. Margaret Shannon, "Senator Without Frills," *Atlanta Journal-Constitution*, October 10, 1976, 30.
14. Joseph Atkinson, "Connally Blames Congress for Many of Nation's Ills," *Atlanta Daily World*, September 24, 1978, 1.
15. Newt Gingrich papers, University of West Georgia Archives.
16. Ibid.
17. "Shapard Hits Campaign Flyer as 'Racial,'" *Atlanta Daily World*, November 5, 1978, 2.
18. Carlyle Gregory, in discussion with the author, October 12, 2010.
19. Karen De Witt, "Senator's Ex-Wife Goes It Alone," *New York Times*, May 24, 1978, C1.
20. Myra MacPherson, "The Metamorphosis of Betty Talmadge," *Washington Post*, April 5, 1978, B1.
21. Karen De Witt, "Senator's Ex-Wife Goes It Alone," *New York Times*, May 24, 1978, C1.

22. "Gingrich Launches Tabloid, Asks for 33% Cut in Taxes," *Atlanta Daily World*, April 11, 1978, 3.

23. Jack Germond and Jules Witcover, "Following Laffer's Curve," *Chicago Tribune*, May 24, 1978, B4.

24. "Nixon's Program—I Am Now a Keynesian," *New York Times*, January 10, 1971, 1.

25. Jack Germond and Jules Witcover, "Following Laffer's Curve," *Chicago Tribune*, May 24, 1978, B4.

26. Letter to "Fellow Conservatives" by Jack Kemp, Private Archives Collections of Carlyle Gregory.

27. *Atlanta Daily World*, February 28, 1978.

28. "GOP Holds Candidates School," *Atlanta Daily World*, June 6, 1978, 6.

29. "4 Congressmen Qualify; Two Are Challenged," *Atlanta Daily World*, June 8, 1978, 2.

30. Newt Gingrich, in discussion with the author, December 5, 2010.

31. Wayne King, "Georgia to Pick Candidates Today; Incumbents Regarded as Favorites," *New York Times*, August 8, 1978, A10.

32. Ibid.

33. Wayne King, "Busbee and Nunn Easily Capture Nominations in Georgia Primary," *New York Times*, August 9, 1978, A16.

34. "Newt Gingrich Appoints Asst. Campaign Director," *Atlanta Daily World*, August 29, 1978, 3.

35. "Gingrich Calls for Bi-Partisan Townhall Meetings This Summer," *Atlanta Daily World*, June 8, 1978, 5.

36. Ibid.

37. "Newt Gingrich Will Fight for 1,200,000 Jobs" (paid political announcement), *Atlanta Daily World*, September 17, 1978, 2.

38. Ibid.

39. *Carroll County Georgian*, October 19, 1978, Newt Gingrich papers, box # 33, University of West Georgia Archives.

40. "Black Unemployment Concerns Gingrich," *Atlanta Daily World*, October 22, 1978, 5.

41. Lee May, "See Gingrich Run," *Atlanta Constitution*, October 31, 1978.

42. Kathie Obradovich, "Gingrich in '12? He's Beyond Book Tour," *Des Moines Register*, September 14, 2010, http://blogs.desmoinesregister.com/dmr/index.php/2010/09/14/column-gingrich-in-12-hes-beyond-book-tour.

43. *West Georgian News*, March 8, 1978, Newt Gingrich papers, University of West Georgia Archives.

44. Steve Hanser, in discussion with the author, October 21, 2010.

45. Chip Kahn, in discussion with the author, November 23, 2010.

46. "A Survey of the Races in All 50 States," *Washington Post*, November 5, 1978, D4.

47. *Griffin Daily News*, September 28, 1978, Newt Gingrich papers, box #24, University of West Georgia Archives.

48. Newt Gingrich papers, box #35, University of West Georgia Archives.

49. *Atlanta Journal-Constitution*, October 18, 1978, Newt Gingrich papers, box #36, University of West Georgia Archives.

50. Newt Gingrich papers, box #37, University of West Georgia Archives.
51. *West Georgian News*, Newt Gingrich papers, box #34, University of West Georgia Archives.
52. *Southside Sun*, July 20, 1978, Newt Gingrich papers, box #18, University of West Georgia Archives.
53. Ibid.
54. "We Must Help Send Gingrich to Congress," *Atlanta Daily World*, November 5, 1978, 4.
55. Newt Gingrich papers, University of West Georgia Archives.
56. Chip Kahn, in discussion with the author, November 9, 2010.
57. Newt Gingrich papers, box #1, University of West Georgia Archives.
58. "6th Dist. Congressional Race Appears Tightest as GA. Polls Open Today," *Atlanta Daily World*, November 7, 1978, 1.
59. *Southside Sun*, November 2, 1978, Newt Gingrich papers, box #37, University of West Georgia Archives.
60. *Atlanta Constitution*, September 22, 1978, Newt Gingrich papers, box #32, University of West Georgia Archives.
61. *Atlanta Constitution*, November 5, 1978, Newt Gingrich papers, box #43, University of West Georgia Archives.
62. *Clayton News-Daily*, November 3, 1978, Newt Gingrich papers, box #40, University of West Georgia Archives.
63. Chip Kahn, in discussion with the author, November 9, 2010.
64. Chip Kahn, in discussion with the author, November 23, 2010.
65. *Atlanta Constitution*, November 8, 1978.
66. Newt Gingrich papers, box #66, University of West Georgia Archives.
67. Georgia newspaper account.
68. *Newman Times-Herald*, November 9, 1978, Newt Gingrich papers, box #50, University of West Georgia Archives.
69. *Newman Times-Herald*, November 22, 1978, Newt Gingrich papers, box #62, University of West Georgia Archives.
70. *Atlanta Constitution*, September 9, 1978, Newt Gingrich papers, University of West Georgia Archives.
71. *Atlanta Journal-Constitution*, November 8, 1978, Newt Gingrich papers, box #56, University of West Georgia Archives.
72. Newt Gingrich papers, box #61, University of West Georgia Archives.
73. "A Congressman of the People," *Atlanta Daily World*, January 28, 1979, 4.
74. *Columbus Ledger-Enquirer*, November 9, 1978, Newt Gingrich papers, box #55, University of West Georgia Archives.
75. Jack W. Germond and Jules Witcover, "Campaign Spending: Reform in the House," *Baltimore Sun*, November 17, 1978, A17.
76. David Gergen, "Wanted: A GOP Program," *Washington Post*, November 19, 1978, C8.

CHAPTER 4: THE FRESHMAN

1. Doug Harbrecht, "Abscam Tape Will Exonerate Me, Murtha Says," *Pittsburgh Press*, September 8, 1980, A1.

2. "Leon Jaworski Hired to Probe New Scandal," *Atlanta Daily World*, July 24, 1977, 2.

3. Scott Armstrong, "Information from Habib Led to Probe of Korean Influence," *Washington Post*, June 17, 1977, A3.

4. William Cotterell, "Gingrich Vows to Lead Drive to Expel Diggs," *Atlanta Daily World*, December 21, 1978, 1.

5. Ibid., 4

6. Carlyle Gregory, in discussion with the author, October 12, 2010.

7. Charles R. Babcock, "Korea Seen as Aiding in House Probe," *Washington Post*, February 9, 1977, C2.

8. Ibid.

9. Richard Pyle, Associated Press, December 16, 1977.

10. "A Congressman of the People," *Atlanta Daily World*, January 28, 1979, 4.

11. Newt Gingrich, in discussion with the author.

12. George M. Coleman, "Rep. Gingrich Pledges Support for Nat'l King Holiday, Jobs," *Atlanta Daily World*, January 28, 1979, 1.

13. *Newman Times-Herald*, November 22, 1978, Newt Gingrich papers, box #62, University of West Georgia Archives.

14. Letter to Newt Gingrich from Greg, March 7, 1986, Newt Gingrich papers, University of West Georgia Archives.

15. Letter to Newt Gingrich from Dick Morris, January 26, 1988, Newt Gingrich papers, University of West Georgia Archives.

16. Letter to Ed Fulner, Burt Pines, and Paul Weyrich from Newt Gingrich, June 6, 1988, Newt Gingrich papers, University of West Georgia Archives.

17. "The Class of '78 in the U.S. House," *National Journal*, November 11, 1978, 1816.

18. Ibid.

19. Richard E. Cohen, "The New Breed of Southern Members Is Not Much Different from the Old," *National Journal*, July 1, 1978, 1040.

20. Andrew R. Dodge and Betty K. Koed, eds., *Biographical Directory of the United States Congress, 1774—2005* (Washington, D.C.: Library of Congress Cataloging-in-Publishing Data, 2005), 1124.

21. Robert Parry, Associated Press, February 10, 1980.

22. "Cong. Gingrich Named to Two Key House Committees," *Atlanta Daily World*, January 25, 1979, 2.

23. David Espo, Associated Press, January 17, 1979.

24. "15 Ask House Panel to Act in Diggs Case," *Los Angeles Times*, February 2, 1979, A1.

25. Newt Gingrich, "A Precedent for Charles Diggs," *Washington Post*, February 21, 1979, A15.

26. "Congress Showdown Looms over Diggs' Fate," *Atlanta Daily World*, January 18, 1979, 1.

27. Ibid.

28. "Congress Evades Issue," *Atlanta Daily World*, March 8, 1979, 4.

29. Newt Gingrich, "A Precedent for Charles Diggs," *Washington Post*, February 21, 1979, A15.

30. "Rep. Gingrich to Introduce Social Security Tax Bill," *Atlanta Daily World*, February 8, 1979, 2.

31. Ibid.
32. Ibid.
33. "H.R.2339-A Bill to Provide Mandatory Social Security Coverage for Members of Congress," Congress.gov, https://www.congress.gov/bill/96th-congress/house-bill/2339.
34. "H.R.1598-Tax Rate Reduction and Indexing Act of 1979," Congress.gov, https://www.congress.gov/bill/96th-congress/house-bill/1598.
35. Eileen Putman, Associated Press, February 9, 1979.
36. David M. Alpern, "Rocky's Final Hour," Newsweek, February 19, 1979, 35.
37. Robert D. McFadden, "Rockefeller Aide Did Not Make Call to 911," New York Times, February 9, 1979, B3.
38. David M. Alpern, "Rocky's Final Hour," Newsweek, February 19, 1979, 35.
39. Peter Kihss, "Rockefeller's Family Gathers for Services," New York Times, January 29, 1979, A1.
40. Robert D. McFadden, "Call to 911 for Stricken Rockefeller Did Not Identify Him, Tape Shows," New York Times, January 30, 1979, A13.
41. Alex Cockburn, "Press Clips on a Famous Death," Washington Post, February 4, 1979, A1.
42. Robert D. McFadden, "Rockefeller Is Dead at 70," New York Times, January 27, 1979, A1.
43. Peter Kihss, "Rockefeller Left a Last Political Comment," New York Times, February 1, 1979, B3.
44. Mark Russell, "House Strongly Rejects Move to Expel Rep. Diggs," Washington Post, March 2, 1979, A2.
45. "H.Res.142-A Resolution to Expel Charles C. Diggs, Jr., of Michigan," Congress.gov, https://www.congress.gov/bill/96th-congress/house-resolution/142.
46. George Derek Musgrove, Rumor, Repression, and Racial Politics (Athens, Georgia: University of Georgia Press, 2012), 101.
47. "House Shifts Bid to Expel Diggs to Ethics Panel," Atlanta Daily World, March 4, 1979, 1.
48. Irvin Molotsky, "Charles Diggs, 75, Congressman Censured over Kickbacks," New York Times, August 26, 1998, http://www.nytimes.com/1998/08/26/us/charles-diggs-75-congressman-censured-over-kickbacks.html.
49. Thomas B. Edsall, "Diggs Bows to Censure by House," Baltimore Sun, June 30, 1979, A1.
50. Bob Livingston, in discussion with the author, February 17, 2011.
51. David S. Broder, "House GOP Sees Deep Tax Cut as Election Issue," Washington Post, July 23, 1979, A1.
52. Mary Russell, "O'Neill Rebounds from Setbacks in Party and on Floor," Washington Post, November 22, 1979, A3.
53. Steven V. Roberts, "House G.O.P. Freshmen Are Speaking upon Party Issues," New York Times, October 29, 1979, A16.
54. Mel Steely, in discussion with the author, November 22, 2010.
55. Ibid.

56. "Gingrich Hits Public Financing of Candidates and Corruption," *Atlanta Daily World*, March 27, 1979, 1.

57. "Reagan, Gingrich Say Hope in GOP," *Atlanta Daily World*, May 22, 1979, 3.

58. "Federal Legislative Ratings," *American Conservative Union*, http://acuratings. conservative.org/acu-federal-legislative-ratings/?year1=1980.

59. Rhonda Cook, "5th Dist. Among Several in State Facing Changes," *Atlanta Daily World*, April 29, 1979, 1.

60. Associated Press, May 16, 1979.

61. Ibid.

62. Newt Gingrich, in discussion with the author, October 31, 2010.

63. Ibid.

64. "Gingrich Favors Tax Cuts for the Young Home Buyer," *Atlanta Daily World*, May 6, 1979, 6.

65. Ibid.

66. "Kemp to Speak at Gingrich Fundraiser," *Atlanta Daily World*, October 9, 1979, 3.

67. Tom Barton, "Election Termed 'Nonsense' by Congressman Gingrich," *Savannah Morning News*, September 19, 1980, 8C, Newt Gingrich papers, University of West Georgia Archives.

68. Newt Gingrich, in discussion with the author, May 7, 2010.

69. Ibid.

70. "House Leadership Asked to Resign by Gingrich," *Atlanta Daily World*, October 26, 1979, 2.

71. "Gingrich Hits Carter for Encouraging Shah to Step Down in Iran," *Atlanta Daily World*, November 22, 1979, 7.

72. Beau Cutts, "For Newton Gingrich, After Twice Coming in 2nd, How Sweet It Is!," *Atlanta Constitution*, November 9, 1978, 1A.

CHAPTER 5: THE YEAR OF REAGAN

1. Susan F. Rasky, "Washington Talk: Working Profile: Representative Newt Gingrich; From Political Guerrilla to Republican Folk Hero," *New York Times*, June 15, 1988, A24.

2. Jay Perkins, "Republicans Accuse House Democrats of Trying to Cover Up Vote Buying," Associated Press, March 3, 1980.

3. Ibid.

4. "The New Guard," *National Journal*, July 12, 1980, 1145.

5. Associated Press, "Bauman Charge Reported 'Accident' in Probe," October 16, 1980.

6. Richard E. Cohen, "A Republican Plot?," *National Journal*, August 23, 1980, 1410.

7. Deric Gilliard, "Balanced Budget, Restoring Faith in Congress Top Goals," *Atlanta Daily World*, June 1, 1980, 1.

8. "Gingrich Backs Plan to Create More Jobs in Major U.S. Cities," *Atlanta Daily World*, May 27, 1980, 1.

9. Jane Seaberry, "Reagan Faces Tough Choices on Deficit, Taxes," *Washington Post*, November 11, 1984, G1; *Miami Herald*, "Candidates Trade Views on Issues," October 12, 1984, A1.

10. Tyrone D. Terry, "Plane Secret Leak Angers Gingrich," *Atlanta Constitution*, February 12, 1980, A1.
11. Robert Byrd, "Conservative Rising Star Feeling Secure These Days," Associated Press, September 21, 1984.
12. "Grunden to Head Gingrich Campaign," *Atlanta Daily World*, February 14, 1980, 5.
13. Maryon Allen, "Maryon Allen's Washington," *Washington Post*, July 27, 1980, H2.
14. Bob Bolding, "Incumbent Gingrich: More Sophisticated, but Glad to Be Home," *Carroll County Georgian*, October 30, 1980, 6A.
15. Newt Gingrich, in discussion with the author, October 31, 2010.
16. "Rep. Kemp to Campaign for M. Mattingly," *Atlanta Daily World*, February 22, 1980, 2.
17. Suzanne Michele Bourgoin and Paula Kay Byers, eds., *Encyclopedia of World Biography: Ford–Grillparzer*, 2nd ed. (Detroit: Gale, 1998), 330.
18. "Rep. Kemp to Campaign for M. Mattingly," *Atlanta Daily World*, February 22, 1980, 2.
19. Edwin Feulner, "Conservative Coalition Seen," *Atlanta Daily World*, April 13, 1980, 7.
20. "Short-Term Economic Picture Is Grim for World, Study Says," *Atlanta Journal*, June 25, 1980, 12A.
21. "House of Representatives," *Congressional Record*, February 12, 1980, Newt Gingrich papers, University of West Georgia Archives.
22. "Statement of Congressman Newt Gingrich," Newt Gingrich papers, University of West Georgia Archives.
23. Newt Gingrich advertisement, Newt Gingrich papers, University of West Georgia Archives.
24. "Gingrich Newsletter Upheld," *Atlanta Daily World*, July 3, 1980, 3.
25. "1980 Themes for Newt Gingrich Campaign," Newt Gingrich papers, University of West Georgia Archives.
26. Newt Gingrich advertisement, Newt Gingrich papers, University of West Georgia Archives.
27. Maryon Allen, "Mary on Allen's Washington," *Washington Post*, July 27, 1980, H2.
28. Robert E. Taylor, "Despite Difficulties, Sen. Talmadge Leads Pack for Reelection," *Wall Street Journal*, August 4, 1980, 1.
29. Rowland Evans and Robert Novak, "Fiasco in Room EF100," *Washington Post*, September 3, 1980, A19.
30. Newt Gingrich, in discussion with the author.
31. Newt Gingrich, in discussion with the author, May 21, 2006.
32. Dennis Farney, "'New Right' Adherents in Congress Now Play Mainly Defensive Role," *Wall Street Journal*, September 16, 1980, 27.
33. Ibid.
34. Dennis Farney, "Democratic Chiefs Are GOP's Prime Targets in Congressional Races," *Wall Street Journal*, October 22, 1980, 1.
35. Richard E. Cohen, "A Republican Plot?," *National Journal*, August 23, 1980, 1410.

36. Ibid.
37. Dennis Farney, "Oilcan and Sword: House GOP to Pick Between 2 Weapons," *Wall Street Journal*, November 28, 1980, 1.
38. Letter from Newt Gingrich and Robert Walker, September 2, 1988, Newt Gingrich papers, University of West Georgia Archives.
39. Ibid.
40. Ibid.
41. Clay F. Richards, "50-State Survey Shows Election a Tossup," United Press International, November 1, 1980.
42. Greg McDonald, "Gingrich Offers Reagan Lesson in Georgia Politics," *Atlanta Journal-Constitution*, September 11, 1980, 1A.
43. Bill Gold, "43 to 35 Loss Is No Disgrace," *Washington Post*, November 10, 1980, D14.
44. Jay Perkins, "House Democrats Hold Key to Extent of U.S. Conservatism," Associated Press, November 8, 1980.
45. Ibid.
46. "GA District 6," *Our Campaigns*, http://www.ourcampaigns.com/RaceDetail .html?RaceID=49082.
47. Mel Steely, in discussion with the author, November 22, 2010.
48. Richard E. Cohen, "A Republican Plot?" *National Journal*, August 23, 1980, 1410.
49. Richard E. Cohen, "House GOP May Surface If Party Gains in Fall Elections," *National Journal*, July 12, 1980, 1142.
50. *Atlanta Daily World*, November 2, 1980, Newt Gingrich papers, University of West Georgia Archives.

CHAPTER 6: CARTER DOWN, REAGAN UP

1. "Gingrich Seeks New Ways to Aid Farmers," *Atlanta Daily World*, January 1, 1981, 2.
2. Steven R. Weisman, "Reagan Takes Oath as 40th President; Promises an 'Era of National Renewal' Minutes Later, 52 U.S. Hostages in Iran Fly to Freedom After 444-Day Ordeal," *New York Times*, January 21, 1981, A1.
3. "Gingrich Says Repudiate U.S. and Iranian Agreement," *Atlanta Daily World*, January 29, 1981, 6.
4. William J. Lanouette, "House Freshmen Get the Message—Pay Attention to the Folks Back Home," *National Journal*, January 31, 1981, 177.
5. "Georgia Political, Business Leaders Favorable to President's Proposals," *Atlanta Daily World*, February 22, 1981, 1.
6. "Georgia GOP Lawmakers Invited to White House," *Atlanta Daily World*, April 24, 1981, 1.
7. "Gingrich Hits Taxing of Fringe Benefits," *Atlanta Daily World*, May 24, 1981, 2.
8. "Gingrich Co Sponsors Elderly Tax Cut Bill," *Atlanta Daily World*, May 28, 1981, 1.
9. Newt Gingrich, "Washing Report," *Atlanta Daily World*, May 22, 1981, 6.
10. Brad Knickerbocker, "Defense Reform Group in Congress Tries to Reorder Pentagon Priorities," *Christian Science Monitor*, December 16, 1981, 1.

11. David M. Alpern and John J. Lindsay, "Fighting to Win the War," *Newsweek*, September 14, 1981, 27.

12. "Rostenkowski's Relief Plan," *Wall Street Journal*, March 27, 1980, 28.

13. Dennis Farney, "Republicans Reflect on What They've Wrought," *Wall Street Journal*, August 6, 1981, 22.

14. Ronald Reagan, *The Reagan Diaries*, ed. Douglas Brinkley (New York: HarperCollins, 2007), 1.

15. Dick Kirschten, "Putting the Social Issues on Hold: Can Reagan Get Away with It?," *National Journal*, October 10, 1981, 1810.

16. Ibid.

17. Pierre-Marie Lozeau, *Nancy Reagan in Perspective* (New York: Nova History Publications, 2005), 84–85.

18. H. Josef Hebert, "Air Traffic Leader Says Controllers Willing to Risk Jail to Strike," Associated Press, June 19, 1981.

19. Associated Press, "Air Controllers Endorse Reagan," October 23, 1980.

20. Patricia Koza, United Press International, June 19, 1981.

21. Joseph A. McCartin, "The Strike That Busted Unions," *New York Times*, August 3, 2011, A25.

22. Mel Steely, in discussion with the author, November 22, 2010.

23. Adam Clymer, "A Political Realignment Just May Be Under Way," *New York Times*, August 2, 1981, 1.

24. "'Genuine Revolution' Is Seen by Gingrich," *Atlanta Daily World*, August 7, 1981, 3.

25. Ibid.

26. Craig Shirley, *Last Act: The Final Years and Emerging Legacy of Ronald Reagan* (Nashville, TN: Nelson Books, 2015), 318.

27. "Gingrich to Spend 2 Days in Wheelchair," *Atlanta Daily World*, August 20, 1981, 6.

28. "House, 386–16, Votes Memorial to Dr. King," *New York Times*, September 16, 1981, A16.

29. George M. Coleman, "Rep. Gingrich Pledges Support for Nat'l King Holiday, Jobs," *Atlanta Daily World*, January 28, 1979, 1.

30. Peggy Andersen, "House Votes to Honor Slain Civil Rights Leader," Associated Press, September 15, 1981.

31. "Gingrich Bill Seeks to Legalize Marijuana for Use of Cancer Patients," *Atlanta Daily World*, October 4, 1981, 10.

32. "Public Policy Forum: Revitalizing America," *Washington Post*, February 28, 1981, 4.

33. Lou Cannon, "The Master Politician Has His Day," *Washington Post*, August 2, 1981, A8.

34. "Speed Up Tax Cuts Says Rep. Gingrich," *Atlanta Daily World*, November 29, 1981, 2.

35. Ibid.

36. Adam Clymer, "Mississippi Loss: 2 Warnings for G.O.P.," *New York Times*, July 9, 1981, A21.

37. Dennis Farney, "Republicans Reflect on What They've Wrought," *Wall Street Journal*, August 6, 1981, 22.

38. Richard E. Cohen, "In the Conservative Politics of the '80s, the South Is Rising Once Again," *National Journal*, February 28, 1981, 350.

39. Associated Press, "Congressmen Say Interest Rates No. 1 Voter Concern," September 10, 1981.

40. Dennis Farney, "Conversion of 2 Democrats Revives Plan for a GOP Takeover of House Next Year," *Wall Street Journal*, October 15, 1981, 27.

41. Ibid., 22.

42. George E. Jones, K. M. Chrysler, and Carey W. English, "The Conservative Network," *U.S. News & World Report*, July 20, 1981, 46.

43. Ibid.

44. David S. Broder, "Action on Economy Is Seen as Essential," *Washington Post*, September 10, 1981, A7.

CHAPTER 7: OFF COURSE

1. Howell Raines, "G.O.P. Figure Irked by House Forecast," *New York Times*, March 6, 1982, A8.

2. Ibid.

3. James R. Dickenson, Bill Peterson, and Paul Taylor, "Ever Feeling Cold, Republicans Are Warring with One Another," *Washington Post*, March 7, 1982, A8.

4. David Fox, "Ford, but Not Nixon, to Address GOP," Associated Press, June 25, 1980.

5. James R. Dickenson, Bill Peterson, and Paul Taylor, "Ever Feeling Cold, Republicans Are Warring with One Another," *Washington Post*, March 7, 1982, A8.

6. Howell Raines, "G.O.P. Figure Irked by House Forecast," *New York Times*, March 6, 1982, 8.

7. "Reagan Aide Gets an Apology," *New York Times*, March 7, 1982, 25.

8. Francis X. Clines and Bernard Weinraub, "Briefing," *New York Times*, February 18, 1982, D19.

9. Lou Cannon, Maralee Schwartz, and David Hoffman, "Reagan's Humpty-Dumpty Coalition," *Washington Post*, August 15, 1982, A5.

10. Ronald Reagan, *The Reagan Diaries*, ed. Douglas Brinkley (New York: HarperCollins, 2007), 97.

11. Francis X. Clines and Warren Weaver Jr., "Briefing," *New York Times*, April 7, 1982, A14.

12. Ibid.

13. Peter Grier, "Washington Warms Up to Balanced Budget Law," *Christian Science Monitor*, March 24, 1982, 1.

14. Robert Mackay, United Press International, April 2, 1982.

15. Jay Perkins, "GOP Group in House Threatens Government Shutdown," Associated Press, April 2, 1982.

16. Robert W. Merry, "Congress Votes $98.3 Billion Tax Boost over 3 Years,

Bowing to Pressure from Reagan and Budget Deficit," *Wall Street Journal*, August 20, 1982, 3.

17. David Hoffman and Thomas B. Edsall, "Reaganauts Scramble on Tax Rise," *Washington Post*, August 5, 1982, A1.

18. Steven V. Roberts, "Tax Rise Opposition Increases," *New York Times*, August 6, 1982, D1.

19. Ibid., D2.

20. Mary McGrory, "It's Not the Persecuted with the Tax Bill Credibility Problem," *Washington Post*, August 12, 1982, A3.

21. Howell Raines, "Reagan Runs a Reverse, Collides with Right Wing," *New York Times*, August 15, 1982, D4.

22. Steven V. Roberts, "Tax Rise Opposition Increases," *New York Times*, August 6, 1982, D2.

23. Howell Raines, "Reagan Runs a Reverse, Collides with Right Wing," *New York Times*, August 15, 1982, D4.

24. Howell Raines, "Leadership Image Risked," *New York Times*, August 17, 1982, A1.

25. "Turn Back, Mr. President," *Wall Street Journal*, August 13, 1982, 16.

26. Newt Gingrich, in discussion with the author, January 9, 2011.

27. Howell Raines, "Reagan Runs a Reverse, Collides with Right Wing," *New York Times*, August 15, 1982, D4.

28. Ibid.

29. Newt Gingrich, in discussion with the author, January 9, 2011.

30. Ibid.

31. "$100-Billion Tax Bill Agonizing to House Republicans," *Washington Post*, August 8, 1982, G1.

32. Rowland Evans and Robert Novak, "The Turning of the President," *Washington Post*, April 23, 1982, A29.

33. Donald M. Rothberg, "Washington Dateline," Associated Press, August 17, 1982.

34. Jim Luther, "Reagan Gets Tax Hike After Narrow Approval by House, Senate," Associated Press, August 20, 1982.

35. Timothy B. Clark, "Flat-Rate Income Tax Debate May Spur Attacks on Some Tax Breaks," *National Journal*, November 13, 1982, 1928.

36. Ibid.

37. Bob Dole, "I Am Not a Liberal . . . or a Lemming," *Washington Post*, August 8, 1982, C8; Newt Gingrich, "The Tax Bill Is a Turkey," *Washington Post*, August 8, 1982, C8.

38. Hedrick Smith, "Reagan Tax Plea Joined by O'Neill," *New York Times*, August 19, 1982, D6.

39. Ibid.

40. Herbert H. Denton, "Reagan Faces Problem of Balancing Theory with the Intrusion of Reality," *Washington Post*, August 10, 1982, A4.

41. "Republican Tax Revolt," *MacNeil/Lehrer Report*, PBS, August 10, 1982.

42. Robert W. Merry, "Congress Votes $98.3 Billion Tax Boost over 3 Years, Bowing to Pressure From Reagan and Budget Deficit," *Wall Street Journal*, August 20, 1982, 3.

43. George C. Wilson, "Military Pessimism Aired," *Washington Post*, June 6, 1982, A7.
44. Newt Gingrich, in discussion with the author, January 9, 2011.
45. George C. Wilson, "Military Pessimism Aired," *Washington Post*, June 6, 1982, A7.
46. Howard Benedict, "Today's Topic: A Defense System to Destroy Enemy Missiles," Associated Press, September 28, 1982.
47. "Absence of Space on Capitol Hill," *National Security Record*, June 1982, no. 46, 4.
48. "Bill Pushes Home Units," *Computerworld*, June 14, 1982, 38.
49. Laura A. Kiernan, "Hinckley Is Committed to Indefinite Stay at St. Elizabeths," *Washington Post*, August 10, 1982, A1.
50. United Press International, June 26, 1982.
51. Richard E. Cohen, "Reagan Picks His Spots but Do They Want His Help?," *National Journal*, October 16, 1982, 14, 1745.
52. "Gingrich Opposes Amnesty for Illegal Immigrants," *Atlanta Daily World*, September 23, 1982, 2.
53. Howell Raines, "Reagan Facing Demands for Compromise on Economy After 26-Seat Loss in House," *New York Times*, November 4, 1982, A1.
54. Newt Gingrich, in discussion with the author, January 9, 2011.
55. Albert R. Hunt, "The Prospect of a Reagan-O'Neill Compromise," *Wall Street Journal*, December 6, 1982, 26.
56. Richard E. Cohen, "Reagan Picks His Spots but Do They Want His Help?," *National Journal*, October 16, 1982, 1745.
57. Rudy Maxa, "Gingrich Hypes Military Column by Constituent," *Washington Post*, October 31, 1982, M2.
58. Adam Clymer, "Campaign Funds Called a Key to Outcome of House Races," *New York Times*, November 5, 1982, A1.
59. Peggy Andersen, "House Votes to Hire Historian," Associated Press, December 17, 1982.
60. "House Votes Itself a $9,100 Pay Increase," *Atlanta Daily World*, December 17, 1982, 1.
61. "Gingrich Votes Against Pay Raise for Congress," *Atlanta Daily World*, December 21, 1982, 1.

CHAPTER 8: A DECADE OF GREAT DEBATES

1. Steven V. Roberts, "One Conservative Faults Two Parties," *New York Times*, August 11, 1983, A18.
2. Newt Gingrich, in discussion with the author, January 9, 2011.
3. Newt Gingrich, "Notes on Self-Government," *Atlanta Daily World*, September 8, 1983, 4.
4. Newt Gingrich, "Notes on Self-Government," *Atlanta Daily World*, April 7, 1983, 4.
5. Newt Gingrich, "Notes on Self-Government," *Atlanta Daily World*, March 31, 1983, 4.
6. Newt Gingrich, "Notes on Self-Government," *Atlanta Daily World*, July 21, 1983, 4.
7. "G.O.P. Elects State Officers; Sees '84 Victory," *Atlanta Daily World*, May 25, 1983, 1.

8. Sandra Evans Teeley, "House Censures Crane and Studds," *Washington Post,* July 21, 1983, A1.
9. Paula Schwed, United Press International, July 18, 1983.
10. *World News Tonight,* ABC News, July 19, 1983.
11. Paula Schwed, United Press International, August 4, 1983.
12. Newt Gingrich, "Notes on Self-Government," *Atlanta Daily World,* August 4, 1983, 4.
13. Newt Gingrich, "Notes on Self-Government," *Atlanta Daily World,* November 3, 1983, 4.
14. David Hoffman, "White House Voices Concern on Waning Latin Policy Support," *Washington Post,* June 25, 1983, A12.
15. "White House Says Public Support Is Slipping on Central America Aid," *New York Times,* June 25, 1983, 3.
16. Ronald Reagan, *The Reagan Diaries,* ed. Douglas Brinkley (New York: HarperCollins, 2007), 123.
17. "House Vote on Nicaragua Covert Aid," *Washington Post,* July 29, 1983, A14.
18. Matt Yancey, "Washington Dateline," Associated Press, June 24, 1983.
19. Newt Gingrich, "Notes on Self-Government," *Atlanta Daily World,* November 17, 1983, 4.
20. William E. Schmidt, "Reagan Incident Figure Is Said to Be 'Troubled,'" *New York Times,* October 24, 1983, A14.
21. Richard C. Gross, "Beirut Bombing Report Withheld Until Next Week," United Press International, December 23, 1983; Terence Hunt, "Reagan, With New Backing, Faces Foreign Policy Decisions," Associated Press, October 31, 1983.
22. Charles J. Hanley, "Major Uncertainties Still Hang over Invasion," Associated Press, November 1, 1983.
23. Newt Gingrich, "Notes on Self-Government," *Atlanta Daily World,* November 3, 1983, 4.
24. United Press International, October 29, 1983.
25. David Hoppe, in discussion with the author, June 14, 2011.
26. Milton Coleman, "To Blacks, GOP Offers Little," *Washington Post,* December 7, 1983, A1.
27. Ibid., A26.
28. William Raspberry, "'Inventing' Black Leaders," *Washington Post,* December 21, 1983, A27.
29. Ibid.
30. Wesley G. Pippert, United Press International, March 23, 1983.
31. Newt Gingrich, "Notes on Self-Government," *Atlanta Daily World,* November 10, 1983, 4.
32. Philip Shabecoff, "Questions Arise Not Just over Watt's Words," *New York Times,* October 2, 1983, E5.
33. Ibid.
34. Dale Russakoff, "Controversy over Watt Remark Continues, White House Is Told," *Washington Post,* September 30, 1983, A4.

35. "White House Begins Watt Successor Search," *Miami Herald*, October 11, 1983, A9.

36. Robert Shepard, United Press International, September 14, 1983.

37. Julia Malone, "More Congressmen Back Reagan on Defense in Wake of Jetliner Downing," *Christian Science Monitor*, September 7, 1983, 3.

38. "Korean Airplane Incident," *MacNeil/Lehrer Report*, September 1, 1983.

39. Phil Gailey, "Conservative Study Gives Reagan a Mixed Rating," *New York Times*, November 25, 1983, B14.

40. Ibid.

41. Lou Cannon and David Hoffman, "White House Staff United by Grim Economic Reality," *Washington Post*, January 9, 1983, A1.

42. Helen Dewar, "The Birth of the U.S. Budget Blues," *Washington Post*, January 10, 1983, A1.

43. Eric Gelman, "Is the GOP Running Scared?," *Newsweek*, March 28, 1983, 13.

44. Evans Witt, "18 Conservatives Attempting New Approach for GOP," Associated Press, August 12, 1983.

45. David Espo, "Conservatives Divided on Support for Reagan," Associated Press, September 11, 1983.

CHAPTER 9: MORNING IN AMERICA

1. "Cong. Gingrich to Start Campaign April 14," *Atlanta Daily World*, March 29, 1984, 2.

2. "Pres. Reagan to Keynote Southern GOP Meet Thurs.," *Atlanta Daily World*, January 22, 1984, 1.

3. "Gingrich Receives Golden Bulldog Award," *Atlanta Daily World*, March 1, 1984, 2.

4. "That 'Dear Comandante' Letter," *Washington Post*, May 3, 1984, A20.

5. "Gingrich Proposes Bill to Prevent Blocking Aid to El Salvador," *Atlanta Daily World*, April 26, 1984, 1.

6. "War on Terrorism; Nicaragua: CIA and Congress; 'Rap' Learning," *MacNeil/Lehrer Report*, April 17, 1984.

7. "Gingrich Proposes Bill to Prevent Blocking Aid to El Salvador," *Atlanta Daily World*, April 26, 1984, 1.

8. Ibid.

9. Newt Gingrich, "Notes on Self-Government," *Atlanta Daily World*, April 29, 1984, 4.

10. Ronald Reagan, *The Reagan Diaries*, ed. Douglas Brinkley (New York: HarperCollins, 2009), 117.

11. Newt Gingrich, "Notes on Self-Government," *Atlanta Daily World*, April 29, 1984, 4.

12. Newt Gingrich, "Notes on Self-Government," *Atlanta Daily World*, May 20, 1984, 4.

13. "That 'Dear Comandante' Letter," *Washington Post*, May 3, 1984, A20.

14. Newt Gingrich, "Writing to Foreign Dictators," *Washington Post*, May 14, 1984, A19.

15. Cliff Haas, "Washington Dateline," Associated Press, January 24, 1984.

16. Tom Raum, "Washington Dateline," Associated Press, January 31, 1984.

17. Steven V. Roberts, "Mired in Fractiousness with Eye on Voters . . . ," *New York Times*, January 26, 1984, B6.

18. "O'Neill Rejects GOP Bid to Debate Hot Issues," *Washington Post*, January 26, 1984, A5.

19. Julia Malone, "One Representative's Attempt to Sharpen the Fuzzy Ideological Lines in Congress," *Christian Science Monitor*, June 27, 1984, 16.

20. "O'Neill Rejects GOP Bid to Debate Hot Issues," *Washington Post*, January 26, 1984, A5.

21. Newt Gingrich, in discussion with the author, December 5, 2010.

22. Ibid.

23. Ibid.

24. James F. Clarity and Warren Weaver Jr., "Briefing," *New York Times*, February 4, 1984, 10.

25. David S. Broder and Amy Rosen, "Numbers and Discipline Contribute to Major Victory," *Washington Post*, March 24, 1983, A1.

26. Tom Shales, "As the Hill Turns," *Washington Post*, May 17, 1984, E8.

27. Stephen Frantzich and John Sullivan, *The C-SPAN Revolution* (Norman, Oklahoma: University of Oklahoma Press, 1996), 33.

28. Ibid., 35.

29. Steven V. Roberts, "Mired in Fractiousness with Eye on Voters . . . ," *New York Times*, January 26, 1984, B6.

30. T. R. Reid, "'Minority Objector' Conscientiously Flays Foes with House Rules," *Washington Post*, March 21, 1984, A3.

31. Bob Walker, in discussion with the author, February 15, 2011.

32. James McCartney, "GOP Rivalries Could Tarnish Second Term," *Miami Herald*, August 26, 1984, A19.

33. "O'Neill Assails a Republican and Is Rebuked by the Chair," *New York Times*, May 16, 1984, A16.

34. "The War on the Floor," *Wall Street Journal*, May 17, 1984, 30.

35. Haynes Johnson, "Small Band of Republican Zealots Evokes Tactic from the Past," *Washington Post*, May 20, 1984, A2.

36. T. R. Reid, "Speaker O'Neill and Republicans Clash Fiercely in House Debate," *Washington Post*, May 16, 1984, A5.

37. *World News Tonight*, ABC News, May 15, 1984.

38. T. R. Reid, "Speaker O'Neill and Republicans Clash Fiercely in House Debate," *Washington Post*, May 16, 1984, A5.

39. Neil MacNeil and Alessandra Stanley, "Tip Topped!," *Time*, May 28, 1984.

40. Howard Fineman, "For the Son of C-Span, Exposure = Power," *Newsweek*, April 3, 1989, 22.

41. T. R. Reid, "It's 'Tip's Greatest Hits,' Electrifying a Closed House GOP Circuit," *Washington Post*, May 29, 1984, A3.

42. Ibid., A1.

43. "O'Neill Assails a Republican and Is Rebuked by the Chair," *New York Times*, May 16, 1984, A16.

44. Steven R. Roberts, "New Conflict a Threat to Old Ways," *New York Times*, May 19, 1984, 7.

45. Neil MacNeil and Alessandra Stanley, "Tip Topped!," *Time*, May 28, 1984.

46. "Republicans Assail O'Neill; Increasing Hostility Feared," *New York Times*, May 18, 1984, A15.

47. Elaine S. Povich, United Press International, May 21, 1984.

48. "The War on the Floor," *Wall Street Journal*, May 17, 1984, 30.

49. *World News Tonight*, ABC News, May 15, 1984.

50. "The War on the Floor," *Wall Street Journal*, May 17, 1984, 30.

51. Ibid.

52. David Rogers, "Assault from the Right: Rep. Gingrich Fights Democrats," *Wall Street Journal*, May 23, 1984, 62.

53. Barbara Rosewicz, United Press International, May 16, 1984.

54. T. R. Reid, "It's 'Tip's Greatest Hits,' Electrifying a Closed House GOP Circuit," *Washington Post*, May 29, 1984, A3.

55. Tom Shales, "As the Hill Turns," *Washington Post*, May 17, 1984, E8.

56. Carol Dimich, "The TV Column," *Washington Post*, May 19, 1984, C6.

57. Associated Press, May 6, 1984.

58. "Transcript of President's Speech on Central America Policy," *New York Times*, May 10, 1984, A16.

59. "House Vote Approving Military Aid for Salvador," *New York Times*, August 11, 1984, 4.

60. Janet Staihar, "House Democrats Considering TV Debates After Reagan Speeches," Associated Press, May 9, 1984.

61. Suzanne Garment, "House Republicans Learn a Few Tricks from the Other Side," *Wall Street Journal*, May 25, 1984, 28.

62. Howell Raines, "Reagan Lays Out the Battle Lines for the Campaign," *New York Times*, August 19, 1984, 30.

63. Newt Gingrich, in discussion with the author, April 7, 2012.

64. "Gingrich Announces Permanent Protection of Workers' Incentives," *Atlanta Daily World*, July 29, 2984, 2.

65. "House Approves Silent Prayer in Schools," *Atlanta Daily World*, July 29, 1984, 1.

66. Tom Raum, "Conservatives Beginning New Drive for School Prayer Amendment," Associated Press, February 28, 1984.

67. "The Legions of the Righteous," *Economist*, March 3, 1984, 40.

68. Maureen Dowd, "Falwell's Forum Opens as Street Melee Erupts," *New York Times*, July 13, 1984, A11.

69. Ibid.

70. Rich Jaroslovsky and Jeanne Saddler, "Conservatives Grabbing Media Attention at Convention in Liberal San Francisco," *Wall Street Journal*, July 16, 1984, 42.

71. Maureen Dowd, "Falwell's Forum Opens as Street Melee Erupts," *New York Times*, July 13, 1984, A11.

72. Elisabeth Bumiller, "Setting the Stage," *Washington Post*, August 20, 1984, C1.

73. Elisabeth Bumiller, Elizabeth Kastor, Myra MacPherson, et al., "Two-Stepping in the Land of Armadillos," *Washington Post*, August 20, 1984, C1.

74. "Gingrich to Co-Chair Education Subcommittee at GOP Convention," *Atlanta Daily World*, August 23, 1984, 4.

75. David S. Broder and Lou Cannon, "Both Wings of GOP Hope to Spice Up a Bland Party Platform," *Washington Post*, July 25, 1984, A3.

76. Gregory Gordon, United Press International, August 9, 1984.

77. David S. Broder and Lou Cannon, "Both Wings of GOP Hope to Spice Up a Bland Party Platform," *Washington Post*, July 25, 1984, A3.

78. "Hammering Out the Platform," *MacNeil/Lehrer NewsHour*, PBS, August 14, 1984.

79. Steven V. Roberts, "Draft by G.O.P. Leaves Opening for a Tax Hike," *New York Times*, August 14, 1984, A20.

80. Jonathon Alter, Thomas M. DeFrank, Eleanor Clift, et al., "Reagan's Roaring Start," *Newsweek*, September 3, 1984, 28.

81. Steven V. Roberts, "Platform Is Seen as Map of Future," *New York Times*, August 19, 1984, 33.

82. Ibid.

83. Bill Peterson, "Olympians' Parade Unwinds Uptight Dallas; Police Reinforced," *Washington Post*, August 18, 1984, A10.

84. Richard Reeves, *The Reagan Detour* (New York: Simon and Schuster, 1985), 63.

85. Steven R. Roberts, "Republicans Cultivating Swing Votes," *New York Times*, September 17, 1984, B8.

86. George F. Will, "Parties of the Extreme," *Washington Post*, August 22, 1984, A27.

87. David S. Broder, "Colossus," *Washington Post*, August 21, 1984, A15.

88. Myra MacPherson, "Party at the Crossroads," *Washington Post*, August 24, 1984, B6.

89. Ibid.

90. "Diversity in Dallas," *Christian Science Monitor*, August 22, 1984, 15.

91. Maureen Dowd, "In Dallas, It's More Than a Feminine Touch," *New York Times*, August 21, 1984, A18.

92. "The Republicans' Embrace," *New York Times*, August 22, 1984, A22.

93. David Hoppe, in discussion with the author, June 14, 2011.

94. Newt Gingrich, "Transition Shaped by an Elite," *New York Times*, August 19, 1984, 19.

95. Michael Barone, "Who Is This Newt Gingrich?," *Washington Post*, August 26, 1984, C8.

96. "Gingrich Rally Set Aug. 25," *Atlanta Daily World*, August 16, 1984, 2.

97. "A 'King' and a Congressman," *Atlanta Daily World*, September 9, 1984, 3.

98. "Ford Pledges Support for Reagan-Bush," *Atlanta Daily World*, August 24, 1984, 1.

99. "3 Run-Offs in Metro Area Sept. 4," *Atlanta Daily World*, August 17, 1984, 1.

100. "'Spirit of America' Fills Gingrich Fundraiser Here," *Atlanta Daily World*, September 18, 1984, 1.

101. "Newt Gingrich Advertisement," *Atlanta Daily World*, November 1, 1984, 6.

102. Steve Schneider, "Nuclear Conflict on HBO's 'Countdown,'" *New York Times*, October 14, 1984, 29.

103. Tom Shales, "Sad Times on the Swinging Scene," *Washington Post*, October 13, 1984, B5.

104. "Citizens Protect Visit of Nicarauguas [sic] Ortega," *Atlanta Daily World*, October 12, 1984, 1.
105. "Newt Gingrich a Leader," *Atlanta Daily World*, October 14, 1984, 4.
106. "Newt Gingrich Advertisement," *Atlanta Daily World*, November 1, 1984, 6.
107. "Selected Grenadian Material Released by State, Defense," *Washington Post*, October 5, 1984, A30.
108. Howard Kurtz and Charles R. Babcock, "Two 'Nonpolitcal' Foundations Push Grenada Rallies," *Washington Post*, October 4, 1984, A32.
109. Steven Strasser, "Reagan: Going for a Sweep," *Newsweek*, November 5, 1984, 24.
110. Fay S. Joyce, "Democrats Seek Cause of Setback in Elections," *New York Times*, November 17, 1984, 15.
111. Robert Byrd, "Conservative Rising Star Feeling Secure These Days," Associated Press, September 21, 1984.
112. Newt Gingrich, "Notes on Self-Government," *Atlanta Daily World*, November 25, 1984, 4.
113. John Malone, "Getting the House in Order: Changes in Rules Proposed," *Christian Science Monitor*, November 21, 1984, 3.
114. "Tip—Fight Him or Love Him," *San Diego Union-Tribune*, November 10, 1984, B16.
115. "Newt Gingrich Tells City Officials Congress Must Get Budget in Order," *Atlanta Daily World*, November 30, 1984, 1.

CHAPTER 10: FAMILY FEUD

1. Margaret Shapiro, "Democrats, Republicans Reelect House Leaders," *Washington Post*, December 4, 1984, A13.
2. Fay S. Joyce, "Democrats Seek Cause of Setback in Elections," *New York Times*, November 17, 1984, 15.
3. Evan Thomas, "Struggling for a Party's Soul," *Time*, September 3, 1984.
4. Fay S. Joyce, "Democrats Seek Cause of Setback in Elections," *New York Times*, November 17, 1984, 15.
5. Ibid.
6. Lou Cannon, "What Lame Duck? Don't Count Out Ronald Reagan Yet," *Washington Post*, January 26, 1986, B1.
7. Ronald Reagan, *The Reagan Diaries*, ed. Douglas Brinkley (New York: HarperCollins, 2007), 277.
8. Rowland Evans and Robert Novak, "Fight Tip O'Neill?," *Washington Post*, November 9, 1984, A27.
9. Elaine S. Povich, United Press International, November 19, 1984.
10. Dan Balz, "GOP Official Critical of '84 Strategy," *Washington Post*, November 16, 1984, A16.
11. Ronald Reagan, *The Reagan Diaries*, ed. Douglas Brinkley (New York: HarperCollins, 2007), 277.
12. Newt Gingrich, "'A Grand Compromise Would Smother a Peaceful Revolution,'" *Washington Post*, November 11, 1984, D8.
13. Sandra Evans and Lou Cannon, "President Will Meet with Tutu," *Washington Post*, December 6, 1984, A1.

14. "South Africa Protesters Take Part in Daily Drama," *New York Times*, December 16, 1984, 26.
15. Helen Dewar, "Republicans Wage Verbal Civil War," *Washington Post*, November 19, 1984, A1.
16. Sandra Evans, "Moves Against Apartheid Urged," *Washington Post*, December 10, 1984, A8.
17. Chuck Conconi, "The Conservatives' Choices," *Washington Post*, December 10, 1984, C3.
18. Kathy Sawyer, "Christian Soldiers March to Different Drummers," *Washington Post*, December 27, 1984, A1.
19. Dennis Farney, "Policy Debate Within GOP to Heat Up Whether or Not Reagan Seeks Reelection," *Wall Street Journal*, January 27, 1984, 58.
20. Rich Jaroslovsky and Jeanne Saddler, "Conservatives Grabbing Media Attention at Convention in Liberal San Francisco," *Wall Street Journal*, July 16, 1984, 42.
21. Robert W. Merry, "The Not So Unified GOP," *Wall Street Journal*, August 20, 1984, 14.
22. "Donald Regan on Reagan Budget; Congressional Budget Reaction; Medicare Fee Freeze?; Hotel Art in New Orleans," *MacNeil/Lehrer NewsHour*, PBS, February 1, 1984.
23. Ibid.
24. Richard E. Cohen, "Frustrated House Republicans Seek More Aggressive Strategy for 1984 and Beyond," *National Journal*, March 3, 1984, 413.
25. "The Legions of the Righteous," *Economist*, March 3, 1984, 40.
26. Robert Byrd, "Conservative Rising Star Feeling Secure These Days," Associated Press, September 21, 1984.
27. Tom Morganthau, Rich Thomas, Gloria Borger, et al., "Reagan: 'I'm Not in a Compromising Mood,'" *Newsweek*, November 26, 1984, 36.
28. Ibid.
29. Ibid.
30. Merrill Hartson, Associated Press, November 28, 1984.
31. Jonathan Rauch, "GOP Conservatives Push Broad Spending Freeze," *National Journal*, December 1, 1984, 2283.
32. George F. Will, "Georgia's Populist of the Right," *Newsweek*, December 3, 1984, 100.
33. Newt Gingrich, in discussion with the author, January 23, 2011.

CHAPTER 11: REPUBLICAN VERSUS REPUBLICAN VERSUS DEMOCRAT

1. Robert W. Merry, "Reagan Calls for Bipartisan Amity, Voices Familiar Themes in Inaugural Address," *Wall Street Journal*, January 22, 1985, 64.
2. William Safire, "Grading the Speech," *New York Times*, January 24, 1985, A25.
3. Robert W. Merry, "Reagan Calls for Bipartisan Amity, Voices Familiar Themes in Inaugural Address," *Wall Street Journal*, January 22, 1985, 64.
4. Newt Gingrich, in discussion with the author, May 9, 2010.
5. Elizabeth Mehren and Betty Cuniberti, "Social Vignettes from an Inauguration Vigil," *Los Angeles Times*, January 22, 1985, E1.

6. Newt Gingrich, "Notes on Self Government," *Atlanta Daily World*, August 4, 1985, 4.
7. "News Briefs: Nicaraguan Debate," *Atlanta Daily World*, February 5, 1985, 1.
8. "Gingrich Defends U.S. Policy in Nicaragua," *Atlanta Daily World*, February 17, 1985, 2.
9. "Gingrich's 'Brilliance' Against Nicaragua's Vice President Applauded," *Los Angeles Times*, February 8, 1985, 2.
10. "Dreaming Spires and Dreamy Dons," *Wall Street Journal*, February 13, 1985, 30.
11. Ibid.
12. "President Says New Aid to Rebels in Nicaragua Essential for Peace," *Atlanta Daily World*, April 19, 1985, 1.
13. "Showdown in Congress Today for Aid to Freedom Fighters," *Atlanta Daily World*, April 23, 1985, 1.
14. Newt Gingrich, "Notes on Self Government," *Atlanta Daily World*, April 28, 1985, 4.
15. "Gingrich Calls Nicaragua Aid Vote 'Dangerous,'" *Atlanta Daily World*, May 7, 1985, 3.
16. William Johnson, "U.S. House Votes to Aid Contras, Reagan Scores Victory with Policy Toward Nicaragua," *Globe and Mail*, June 13, 1985.
17. Mike Royko, "Gung-Ho Wimps Who Ducked War," *Chicago Tribune*, June 17, 1985, C3.
18. Julia Malone, "MX power on Capitol Hill," *Christian Science Monitor*, March 21, 1985, 1.
19. Lois Romano, "Newt Gingrich, Maverick on the Hill," *Washington Post*, January 3, 1985, B1.
20. Ibid.
21. "Gingrich Asks Divorce," *Carroll County Georgian*, July 17, 1980.
22. Ibid.
23. Newt Gingrich, in discussion with the author, December 5, 2010.
24. Newt Gingrich, "Notes on Self Government," *Atlanta Daily World*, March 3, 1985, 4.
25. Rowland Evans and Robert Novak, "The Michel/Gingrich Split," *Washington Post*, March 11, 1985, A15.
26. "Republicans Storm Out of House as Democrats Vote in McClosky," *Atlanta Daily World*, April 26, 1985, 1.
27. Ibid.
28. Mary McGrory, "Capitol Comity," *Washington Post*, May 2, 1985, A2.
29. Dan Balz, "House GOP Agonizes on Protest," *Washington Post*, April 25, 1985, A4.
30. Dan Balz, "Indiana Democrat Wins House Panel's Support," *Washington Post*, April 24, 1985, A4.
31. Dan Balz, "House GOP Agonizes on Protest," *Washington Post*, April 25, 1985, A4.
32. "Republicans Storm Out of House as Democrats Vote in McClosky," *Atlanta Daily World*, April 26, 1985, 1.

33. Ibid., 6.

34. Dan Balz, "Frustrations Embitter House GOP," *Washington Post*, April 29, 1985, A1.

35. "Gerrymandered Dynasty," *Wall Street Journal*, May 1, 1985, 32.

36. Vin Weber, in discussion with the author, June 8, 2011.

37. Dan Balz, "Frustrations Embitter House GOP," *Washington Post*, April 29, 1985, A4.

38. Ibid.

39. Mark Starr, Gloria Borger, and Frank Maier, "Congress: A House Divided," *Newsweek*, April 22, 1985, 29.

40. Ibid.

41. "Bush to Visit April 26th," *Atlanta Daily World*, April 16, 1985, 1.

42. "Gingrich Announces Textile Bill," *Atlanta Daily World*, March 29, 1985, 2.

43. "Now for Reaganism Post-Reagan," *Economist*, March 30, 1985, 44.

44. Newt Gingrich, "Notes on Self-Government," *Atlanta Daily World*, February 26, 1984, 4.

45. Newt Gingrich schedule, private collections of Craig Shirley.

46. "Sam Nunn, Others Disclose Finances," *Atlanta Daily World*, May 26, 1985, 2.

47. Newt Gingrich, "Notes on Self Government," *Atlanta Daily World*, June 2, 1985, 4.

48. Newt Gingrich, "Notes on Self Government," *Atlanta Daily World*, June 23, 1985, 4.

49. Sidney Blumenthal, "2 Congressmen Warned White House About Trip," *Washington Post*, May 1, 1985, A13.

50. Samira Kawar, "U.S. Welcomes Hostages," *Atlanta Daily World*, July 2, 1985, 1.

51. Thomas B. Edsall, "Right Critical of Reagan in Hostage Crisis Longtime Supporters Attack Policies," *Washington Post*, June 29, 1985, A15.

52. Newt Gingrich, "Notes on Self Government," *Atlanta Daily World*, July 21, 1985, 4.

53. Tom G. Palmer, "Future Schlock: Government Planning for Tomorrow," *Wall Street Journal*, June 13, 1985, 30.

54. "Notable & Quotable," *Wall Street Journal*, July 31, 1985, 18.

55. Tom Fielder, "How Budget, Farm Ponds Are Linked in Reagan's Mind," *Miami Herald*, August 11, 1985, B3.

56. Cindy McAfee, "Cong. Gingrich Says AIDS May Cripple Us," *Atlanta Daily World*, December 10, 1985, 1.

57. Ibid.

58. Ibid., 4.

59. Paul Duke Jr., "House Approves Five-Year Farm Bill, Thwarting Move to Limit Price Supports," *Wall Street Journal*, October 9, 1985, 64.

60. Rowland Evans and Robert Novak, ". . . And One Politician's Dilemma," *Washington Post*, August 30, 1985, A23.

61. David S. Broder, "Revolution, Stage 2," *Washington Post*, July 28, 1985, B7.

62. Edward Walsh, "GOP House 'Guerrillas' Soften Their Tactics," *Washington Post*, September 30, 1985, A10.

63. Ibid.

64. Lea Donosky, "Party Lines Broadcast Clearly in House," *Chicago Tribune*, March 24, 1985, C4.

65. Thomas B. Edsall, "Tax Rebuff Engineered by Familiar Alliance," *Washington Post*, December 12, 1985, A6.

66. Anne Swardson and Lou Cannon, "GOP Warned of Backlash If Tax Bill Dies," *Washington Post*, December 10, 1985, A1.

67. Jane Mayer and Robert W. Merry, "Saving Tax Overhaul Will Require the President to Mollify Republicans, Not Alienate Democrats," *Wall Street Journal*, December 16, 1985, 64.

68. Anne Swardson and Dale Russakoff, "Reagan Visit Revives Tax-Overhaul Bill," *Washington Post*, December 17, 1985, A4.

69. United Press International, December 18, 1985.

CHAPTER 12: PLAYING FOR KEEPS

1. John Corry, "The Senate Steps Gingerly into TV's Spotlight," *New York Times*, June 29, 1986, H27.

2. "Tuesday Highlights," *Washington Post*, October 26, 1986, 23.

3. David Espo, "Republicans Told They Must Broaden Party's Appeal," Associated Press, February 2, 1986.

4. Hedrick Smith, "Republicans See Opportunity," *New York Times*, February 4, 1985, A17.

5. Ibid.

6. George E. Curry and Lea Donosky, "Reagan Mends GOP Fences on Hill," *Chicago Tribune*, February 22, 1986, C3.

7. Associated Press, "Washington Dateline," February 22, 1986.

8. John Margolis, "GOP's Kirkpatrick the Belle of the Ball," *Chicago Tribune*, March 5, 1986, C5.

9. "Bitter Battle; Buying Public Opinion; How Safe?; The Senate Reaches Out," *MacNeil/Lehrer NewsHour*, PBS, March 12, 1986.

10. Ibid.

11. Leon Daniel, "Reagan's Contra Aid Package in Trouble," United Press International, March 16, 1986.

12. Christopher Madison, "Does It Matter?," *National Journal*, April 5, 1986, 850.

13. Russell Chandler, "Religious Right Makes Political Arena Its Major Battleground," *Los Angeles Times*, March 29, 1986, 1A.

14. John M. Barry, "Jack Kemp's Presidential Push," *Dun's Business Month*, May 1, 1985, 34.

15. "Kemp Strategy Decisions," February 23, 1988, Newt Gingrich papers, University of West Georgia Archives.

16. "Republicans Like Bush in '88 Race, Then Baker, Dole," *Miami Herald*, July 7, 1985, A6.

17. Eleanor Randolph, "George Will, the Oracle at Strict Remove," *Washington Post*, September 26, 1986, B1.

18. David S. Broder, "A Loyalist's Dilemma," *Washington Post*, March 30, 1986, D7.

19. "GOP Plans Boycott in Indiana Dispute," *Chicago Tribune*, May 2, 1985, M1.

20. Christopher Madison, "Reagan Gets Mixed Reviews for His Loud Speech but Small Stick on Terrorism," *National Journal*, August 3, 1985, 1791.

21. Sandra Sugawara, "Conservative Congressmen Blast Barnes," *Washington Post*, March 13, 1986, C1.

22. Rowland Evans and Robert Novak, "Israel and the Contras," *Washington Post*, March 19, 1986, A19.

23. Rowland Evans and Robert Novak, "Close Call on the Contras," *Washington Post*, June 30, 1986, A11.

24. Cass Peterson, "House Acid-Rain Bill Unveiled," *Washington Post*, April 11, 1986, A5.

25. Paul Davenport, "Call for Increased Volunteer Effort at Community Level," Associated Press, September 21, 1985.

26. Larry Lopez, "Bush Keynotes Meeting of Republican Women," Associated Press, September 22, 1985.

27. Joan Mower, "GOP Members Want to Ban AIDS Kids from Schools, Shut Down Public Baths," Associated Press, October 2, 1985.

28. Joan Mower, "Washington Dateline," Associated Press, October 2, 1985.

29. Norman Ornstein, "But the Austerity Congress Is Limping," *Washington Post*, January 26, 1986, B2.

30. David Maraniss, "The Voice of the Lone Star Populist," *Washington Post*, May 9, 1986, D11.

31. Donald M. Rothberg, "Republican Governors Talk Politics," Associated Press, December 8, 1985.

32. James R. Dickenson, "Major Parties' Activists Vie for Populism Mantle," *Washington Post*, May 10, 1986, A5.

33. Ibid.

34. "Newt Announces for Re-election," *Atlanta Daily World*, June 1, 1986, 3.

35. Ibid.

36. Ibid.

37. "Newt Gingrich Deserves Re-election for Good Job," *Atlanta Daily World*, September 18, 1986, 4.

38. "How Congress Travels on Its Stomach," *New York Times*, April 9, 1986, B6.

39. "Newt Announces for Re-election," *Atlanta Daily World*, June 1, 1986, 3.

40. "Portia Scott Promises Unselfish Service to All in Congress Bid," *Atlanta Daily World*, June 3, 1986, 1.

41. "Cong. Gingrich Applauds Vote to Wipe Out Drugs," *Atlanta Daily World*, September 18, 1986, 11.

42. "Scott Sets Pace for the 5th Congressional Race," *Atlanta Daily World*, August 3, 1986, 1.

43. "Gingrich, Swindall and 20 Others Warn of Daniloff," *Atlanta Daily World*, September 25, 1986, 1.

44. Norman D. Sandler, "President Reagan Stands Firm as Requested by Gingrich and Swindall in Not Compromising," *Atlanta Daily World*, October 2, 1986, 1.

45. David Espo, "Washington Dateline," Associated Press, April 15, 1986.

46. United Press International, April 25, 1986.

47. "Cong. Newt Gingrich Supports Tax Reform," *Atlanta Daily World*, October 5, 1986, 5.

48. Rowland Evans and Robert Novak, "Frozen Republicans," *Washington Post*, September 15, 1986, A15.

49. Rowland Evans and Robert Novak, "Pat Robertson, Kingmaker," *Washington Post*, September 19, 1986, A27.

50. "15,000 Welcome Reagan for Mattingly," *Atlanta Daily World*, October 10, 1986, 1.

CHAPTER 13: END OF THE TRAIL

1. Tom Redburn, "Economic Theorist of 'Public Choice' School James M. Buchanan Wins Nobel Prize," *Los Angeles Times*, October 17, 1986, 1.

2. E. J. Dionne Jr., "'Star Wars' Fight Gives Republicans Way to Attack in 'Issueless' Election," *New York Times*, October 17, 1986, A18.

3. R. W. Apple Jr., "National Role Is Seen for Arizona Nominee," *New York Times*, November 2, 1986, 34.

4. *Statistics of the Congressional Election of November 4, 1986* (Washington, DC: US Government Printing Office, 1987), 10.

5. E. J. Dionne Jr., "Democrats Gain Control of Senate, Drawing Votes of Reagan's Backers," *New York Times*, November 5, 1986, A1.

6. Richard E. Cohen and Dick Kirschten, "An Era of Deadlock?," *National Journal*, January 18, 1986, 126.

7. "President Recommends Investigation of Iran Issue," *Atlanta Daily World*, December 4, 1986, 1.

8. Ronald Reagan, *The Reagan Diaries*, ed. Douglas Brinkley (New York: HarperCollins, 2009), 453, 517.

9. Bernard Weinraub, "At the White House, Suspense, Surprise and Even Optimism," *New York Times*, December 7, 1986, 1.

10. Myra MacPherson, "The Stormy Siege of Don Regan," *Washington Post*, December 5, 1986, C1.

11. Steven V. Roberts, "Baker Courts the Right—and Influences Policy," *New York Times*, May 31, 1987, 5.

12. E. J. Dionne Jr., "Democrats Rejoice at 55–45 Senate Margin but Still Seek Agenda to Counter Reagan," *New York Times*, November 6, 1986, A1.

13. Paul Taylor, "Social Security Overhaul Finds Advocates in GOP," *Washington Post*, November 26, 1986, A4.

14. Ibid.

15. William Safire, "Reagan in the Woodshed," *New York Times*, December 1, 1986, A21.

16. John Dillin, "Iran-Contra Crisis May Have Peaked," *Christian Science Monitor*, January 7, 1987, 1.

17. Marjorie Williams, "The Perilous Rise of Michael Deaver," *Washington Post*, July 13, 1987, B1.

18. Richard E. Cohen and Dick Kirschten, "An Era of Deadlock?," *National Journal*, January 18, 1986, 126.

19. Phil McCombs, "The Library Hearings," *Washington Post*, May 8, 1986, C4.
20. Ibid.

CHAPTER 14: JUST SAY NO

1. "House of Representatives," *Congressional Record*, November 17. 1987, Newt Gingrich papers, University of West Georgia Archives.
2. "Facts on Jim Wright from the Phelan Report for the House Ethics Committee," Newt Gingrich papers, University of West Georgia Archives.
3. "Gingrich Wants Inquiry of Unethical Practices," *Atlanta Daily World*, July 5, 1987, 2.
4. Christopher Callahan, "Conservative House Republicans Urge Review of St Germain Ethics Probe," Associated Press, July 27, 1987.
5. "The St Germain Embarrassment," *Washington Post*, August 9, 1987, C6.
6. George Lardner Jr., "Charges of Favoritism, Tests of Credibility at House Ethics Panel," *Washington Post*, December 15, 1987, A21.
7. Ibid.
8. Paul West, "The Wright Stuff," *New Republic*, October 14, 1985, 24.
9. John M. Barry, "The Man of the House," *New York Times*, November 23, 1986, 53.
10. Ibid., 54.
11. Ibid., 55.
12. Ibid., 59.
13. "Congressman Newt Gingrich Moves Office," *Atlanta Daily World*, February 19, 1987, 2.
14. Newt Gingrich, "Notes on Self Government," *Atlanta Daily World*, March 10, 1987, 4.
15. E. J. Dionne Jr., "The Last Two Years of the 'Reagan Revolution,'" *New York Times*, January 25, 1987, 4.
16. "2 Republican Congressmen Reject 15.6% Pay Increase," *Atlanta Daily World*, April 5, 1987, 1.
17. Paul Taylor, "Will Hart's Demise Give Us the Late, Late Mario Scenario?" *Washington Post*, May 24, 1987, D1.
18. Phil Gailey, "Republicans See March 8 Voting as Opportunity," *New York Times*, May 27, 1987, A16.
19. "House Rejects Outside Ethics Panel," *New York Times*, July 1, 1987, B7.
20. Mike Moran, "Ethics Question Vexes Rep. Lent," *New York Times*, November 29, 1987, L18.
21. "Late TV Listings," *New York Times*, August 16, 1987, 45.
22. Michael Specter and James R. Dickenson, "Politicians Line Up to Admit or Deny Past Marijuana Use," *Washington Post*, November 8, 1987, A1.
23. "Gingrich Announces Hall Conference Plans," *Atlanta Daily World*, March 5, 1987, 2.
24. Newt Gingrich, "Notes on Self Government," *Atlanta Daily World*, June 9, 1987, 4.
25. Ibid.

26. Sidney Blumenthal, "North & the Charge of the Right Brigade," *Washington Post*, August 5, 1987, C1.

27. E. J. Dionne Jr., "Report Seen as Strengthening Democrats for '88 Race," *New York Times*, February 27, 1987, A13.

28. Helen Dewar and Edward Walsh, "Lawmakers Say President Must Take Blame and Reassert Control," *Washington Post*, February 27, 1987, A17.

29. Tim Ahern, "Report Shows Weaknesses in Reagan Management Style, Lawmakers Say," Associated Press, February 26, 1987.

30. Helen Dewar and Edward Walsh, "Lawmakers Say President Must Take Blame and Reassert Control," *Washington Post*, February 27, 1987, A17.

31. George F. Will, "Tear That Embassy Down," *Washington Post*, April 12, 1987, D7.

32. "Presidential Panel Blames Reagan, Aides for 'Chaos' in Iran-Contra Dealings," *Facts on File World News Digest*, February 27, 1987.

33. Charles Krauthammer, "Scandal Time," *Washington Post*, April 12, 1987, D7.

34. "'Ideological Cowboys' and 'Colossal Blunders,'" *Los Angeles Times*, February 26, 1987, 1.

35. Sean McCormally, United Press International, February 26, 1987.

36. "Gingrich Criticizes Wright Meeting with Daniel Ortega," *Atlanta Daily World*, November 24, 1987, 1.

37. Ibid.

38. Newt Gingrich, "Notes on Self Government," November 29, 1987, 4.

39. Richard C. Gross, "Pentagon Widens Rules on 'Sexual Misconduct,'" *Washington Post*, May 11, 1987, A23.

40. Ibid.

41. Newt Gingrich, "Notes on Self Government," *Atlanta Daily World*, November 22, 1987, 4.

42. Tom Kenworthy, "Hill Protests, Pockets Pay Raise," *Washington Post*, July 22, 1987, A17.

43. "2 Republican Congressmen Reject 15.6% Pay Increase," *Atlanta Daily World*, April 3, 1987, 1.

44. Dennis McDougal, "Tea-Bag Protest Hits Federal Pay Hike: Radio Hosts' Lobby Helps Listeners Tune In to Issues," *Los Angeles Times*, February 26, 1989, 1.

45. Jonathan Fuerbringer, "Tax Rise Is Passed by House," *New York Times*, October 30, 1987, D1.

46. Ibid.

47. Newt Gingrich, "Notes on Self Government," *Atlanta Daily World*, November 22, 1987, 4.

48. Eliot Brenner, "Gingrich Questions Wright's Integrity," United Press International, December 16, 1987.

49. Eric Pianin, "House GOP's Frustrations Intensify," *Washington Post*, December 21, 1987, A10.

50. Susan F. Rasky, "Everyone Has Something to Say About Wright," *New York Times*, December 18, 1987, A34.

51. Brooks Jackson, "House Speaker Wright's Dealings with Developer Revive

Questions About His Ethics and Judgment," *Wall Street Journal*, August 5, 1987, 50.

52. Marjorie Williams, "The Message? It's in the Cards!" *Washington Post*, December 24, 1987, D1.

CHAPTER 15: TRUST BUT VERIFY

1. Henry Allen, "The Great Event, Grinding to a Start," *Washington Post*, July 19, 1988, D1.

2. Sidney Blumenthal, "For the GOP's Moderates, a Time of Hope," *Washington Post*, October 12, 1988, D1.

3. Bill Peterson, "Quayle's Service in Guard Stirs Favoritism Question," *Washington Post*, August 18, 1988, A27.

4. Ibid.

5. Robert Byrd, "Politicos, Friends, Family Remember MLK in His Hometown," *Associated Press*, January 18, 1988.

6. Gerald E. Seib and Ellen Hume, "Administration Seems Increasingly Paralyzed In Wake of Bork Fight," *Wall Street Journal*, October 16, 1987, 1.

7. Richard E. Cohen, "The Post-Reagan Right," *National Journal*, February 28, 1987, 488.

8. E. J. Dionne Jr., "The Last Two Years of the 'Reagan Revolution,'" *New York Times*, January 25, 1987, 4.

9. R. W. Apple Jr., "At a Crossroads," *New York Times*, February 27, 1987, A1.

10. Ibid.

11. "Tower Report; Fact Finder; Hill Reaction; Assessing Damage," *MacNeil/Lehrer NewsHour*, PBS, February 26, 1987.

12. Larry Martz, Thomas M. DeFrank, Margaret Garrard Warner, et al., "Reagan's Failure," *Newsweek*, March 9, 1987, 16.

13. Tom Morganthau, Margaret Garrard Warner, Eleanor Clift, et al., "Reagan: Eyes Right," *Newsweek*, March 30, 1987, 20.

14. Ibid.

15. Maureen Dowd, "Is Jack Kemp Mr. Right?," *New York Times*, June 28, 1987, 31.

16. David Shirbman, "Expanded Republican Party Finds Divisiveness May Be Its Biggest Political Headache in 1988," *Wall Street Journal*, April 15, 1987, 72.

17. David Halberstam, "The Vantage Point," *New York Times*, October 31, 1971, 1.

18. John Dillin, "Kemp Calls Plays, but Will GOP Listen?" *Christian Science Monitor*, November 2, 1987, 1.

19. Tamar Jacoby, "A GOP Approach to Immigration," *Los Angeles Times*, April 18, 2012, A11.

20. Hedrick Smith, "Those Fractious Republicans," *New York Times*, October 25, 1987, 30.

21. Julie Johnson, "Pennsylvanian's Case Seen as Big Test for Ethics Unit," *New York Times*, December 10, 1987, B12.

22. Tom Kenworthy, "Counsel to Be Named in Wright Probe," *Washington Post*, July 26, 1988, A12.

23. Brooks Jackson and Jill Abramson, "Chicago Lawyer Named to Begin Wright Inquiry," *Wall Street Journal*, July 27, 1988, 54.

24. "Speaker Wright Used House Employee to Edit and Assemble His Biography," *Wall Street Journal*, June 7, 1988, 74.
25. Steven V. Roberts, "The Foreign Policy Tussle," *New York Times*, January 24, 1988, 26.
26. David Pace, "Ethics Committee Gets Formal Complaint to Investigate Wright," Associated Press, May 26, 1988.
27. Rowland Evans and Robert Novak, "Late-Inning Hardball in the House," *Washington Post*, December 28, 1987, A21.
28. Irvin Molotsky, "Wright 'Very Happy' After Giving His Account to Ethics Committee," *New York Times*, September 15, 1988, A32.
29. Rowland Evans and Robert Novak, "Late-Inning Hardball in the House," *Washington Post*, December 28, 1987, A21.
30. Richard E. Cohen, "Full Speed Ahead," *National Journal*, January 30, 1988, 238.
31. Rowland Evans and Robert Novak, "Late-Inning Hardball in the House," *Washington Post*, December 28, 1987, A21.
32. Peter Osterlund, "House GOP Crucial to Reagan's Vetoes," *Christian Science Monitor*, March 30, 1987, 6.
33. Bob Secter, "Tony Coelho's Dramatic Rise Means a New Style in Democratic Leadership and New Clout for the California Delegation," *Los Angeles Times*, January 11, 1987, 10.
34. Ibid.
35. "House Republican Conference: Thanksgiving Recess Talking Points," Newt Gingrich papers, University of West Georgia Archives.
36. Dave Montgomery, "Gingrich Persists in Angering Foes," *St. Louis Post-Dispatch*, January 2, 1988, 1B.
37. Tom Kenworthy, "Congressional Candidates Ply Convention Crowd," *Washington Post*, July 21, 1988, A29.
38. Dave Montgomery, "Gingrich Persists in Angering Foes," *St. Louis Post-Dispatch*, January 2, 1988, 1B.
39. Bob Livingston, in discussion with the author, February 17, 2011.
40. Letter to Daniel J. Swilliger from Newt Gingrich, January 11, 1988, Newt Gingrich papers, University of West Georgia Archives.
41. "Swindall Vows to Continue; Gingrich Will Investigate," *Atlanta Daily World*, June 21, 1988, 1.
42. Newt Gingrich, "Notes on Self Government," *Atlanta Daily World*, June 5, 1988, 4.
43. Dave Montgomery, "Gingrich Persists in Angering Foes," *St. Louis Post-Dispatch*, January 2, 1988, 1B.
44. Ibid.
45. Newt Gingrich, in discussion with the author, December 5, 2010.
46. Tom Kenworthy, "Democrats Seek Probe of GOP Fund-Raising," *Washington Post*, January 22, 1988, A3.
47. Ibid., A15.
48. Letter to Newt Gingrich from F. H. Panill, Sr., April 20, 1989, Newt Gingrich papers, University of West Georgia Archives.

49. Ibid.

50. "Gingrich Denies Claim He Misused Investor's Money," *Atlanta Daily World*, May 31, 1988, 1.

51. "Gingrich Says Rival Fears Debate in Sixth District," *Atlanta Daily World*, September 23, 1988, 1.

52. Ibid.

53. Tom Kenworthy, "House Ethics Committee to Investigate Wright," *Washington Post*, June 11, 1988, A1.

54. Don Phillips, "Combative Wright Hits 'Flimsy' Case," *Washington Post*, June 13, 1988, A1.

55. Richard L. Berke, "Behind Jim Wright's Book, His Friends," *New York Times*, June 12, 1988, 1.

56. Ibid., 32.

57. Charles R. Babcock and Tom Kenworthy, "Wright: No House Rules Broken," *Washington Post*, June 11, 1988, A6.

58. Richard L. Berke, "Behind Jim Wright's Book, His Friends," *New York Times*, June 12, 1988, 1.

59. Tom Kenworthy, "House Democrats Target Rep. Gingrich for Defeat," *Washington Post*, June 27, 1988, A4.

60. "The Wright Case," *Washington Post*, June 2, 1988, A20.

61. "Bentsen Rally," *Atlanta Daily World*, September 1, 1988, 5.

62. George F. Will, "Snapshot from Florida," *Washington Post*, October 23, 1988, C7.

63. Lawrence L. Knutson, "On Wednesday, George Bush Will Declare Himself Elected," Associated Press, December 27, 1988.

64. E. J. Dionne Jr., "Bush's Bows to the Right," *New York Times*, September 11, 1988, 30.

65. "South," *New York Times*, November 9, 1988, A28.

66. Jon Margolis, "GOP Didn't Deliver Usual Flawless Show," *Chicago Tribune*, August 19, 1988, C1.

67. "Bush Wins Big Victory," *Atlanta Daily World*, November 10, 1988, 1.

68. E. J. Dionne Jr., "Conservatives Find Bush Troubling," *New York Times*, May 14, 1989, 24.

69. Paul A. Gigot, "Guerilla Gingrich Lights a Fire Under the GOP," *Wall Street Journal*, August 19, 1988, 10.

70. Ibid.

71. Newt Gingrich, "Try a Four-Year Plan," *Wall Street Journal*, November 17, 1988, A22.

72. Ibid.

73. Mary McGrory, "Adding Aye of Newt," *Washington Post*, March 23, 1989, A2.

74. *Wall Street Journal*, June 5, 1990.

CHAPTER 16: WRIGHT AND WRONG

1. Paul A. Gigot, "Guerilla Gingrich Lights a Fire Under the GOP," *Wall Street Journal*, August 19, 1988, 10.

2. Maralee Schwartz and Ann Devroy, "The New Regime," *Washington Post*, December 12, 1988, A9.

3. Michael Oreskes, "Congress Opens Session in Spirit of Conciliation," *New York Times*, January 4, 1989, B6.

4. E. J. Dionne Jr., "Something Borrowed, Nothing Blue," *New York Times*, February 10, 1989, A16.

5. Robin Toner, "Tired of Cooling Their Heels, the Republicans Turn Up the Heat," *New York Times*, January 16, 1989, A13.

6. Tom Kenworthy and Don Phillips, "Intrigue in the House: Leadership Choices Loom," *Washington Post*, March 20, 1989, A1.

7. Michael Kranish, "Battle on Tower Is Joined in Senate," *Boston Globe*, March 3, 1989, 1.

8. The eddies and currents of history are too numerous to chart or navigate. It will be forever unknown if Gingrich would have had the chance to eventually lead a revolution that changed history in 1994 had the more popular Cheney remained as Whip, perhaps becoming Speaker in 1995 rather than Gingrich. Or that Cheney, absent his leadership at the Pentagon during the liberation of Kuwait, would have become vice president in 2001. The testimony of Paul Weyrich changed everything.

9. David Hoffman, "Rep. Cheney Chosen as Defense Nominee," *Washington Post*, March 11, 1989, A8.

10. Don Phillips, "Reps. Madigan, Gingrich Vie for GOP Post," *Washington Post*, March 16, 1989, A6.

11. Mary McGrory, "Uneasy Silence over Wright," *Washington Post*, March 16, 1989, A2.

12. Don Phillips, "Piggyback Entry into House GOP Race," *Washington Post*, March 17, 1989, A17.

13. Newt Gingrich, in discussion with the author, December 5, 2010.

14. Robert Smith Walker, in discussion with the author, February 15, 2011.

15. Dan Meyer, in discussion with the author, January 2, 2013.

16. Don Phillips and Tom Kenworthy, "Gingrich Elected House GOP Whip," *Washington Post*, March 23, 1989, A10.

17. Newt Gingrich, in discussion with the author, December 5, 2010.

18. Don Phillips and Tom Kenworthy, "Gingrich Elected House GOP Whip," *Washington Post*, March 23, 1989, A10.

19. George F. Will, "Ethics: 'The Reign of the Accuser,'" *Washington Post*, June 1, 1989, A25.

20. Robin Toner, "Congress," *New York Times*, May 1, 1989, B7.

21. Dan Meyer, in discussion with the author, January 2, 2013.

22. Larry Peterson, "OC Congressmen Cheer Gingrich Win," *Orange County Register*, March 23, 1989, A1.

23. Janet Hook, "Gingrich's Selection as Whip Reflects GOP Discontent," *Congressional Quarterly*, March 25, 1989, 625.

24. Ibid., 627.

25. Newt Gingrich, "Notes on Self Government," January 21, 1988, Newt Gingrich papers, University of West Georgia Archives.

26. Howard Fineman, "For the Son of C-Span, Exposure = Power," *Newsweek*, April 3, 1989, 22.

27. Charles R. Babcock, "Gingrich's Book Venture," *Washington Post*, March 20, 1989, A1.
28. Ibid.
29. Mel Steely, in discussion with the author, November 22, 2010.
30. Irvin Molotsky, "Ethics Panel May Consider Inquiry into Wright Finances," *New York Times*, June 2, 1988, D25.
31. Brooks Jackson and John E. Yang, "Inquiry into Wright's Ethics Is Likely to Be Long, Embarrassing to Democrats," *Wall Street Journal*, June 13, 1988, 40.
32. Brooks Jackson, "New Data Bolster Theory Wright Book May Have Been Route for Improper Gifts," *Wall Street Journal*, June 15, 1988, 60.
33. Dennis Bell and Jack Sirica, "House Ethics Panel Accuses Wright of 69 Rules Violations," *Newsday*, April 18, 1989, 5.
34. Ibid.
35. Robin Toner, "Around Wright, a 'Loyalty Dance,'" *New York Times*, April 7, 1989, A14.
36. "Speaker Wright's Ghostly Ethics," *New York Times*, June 8, 1988, A38.
37. E. J. Dionne Jr., "Wright and His Ethics Case Pose Problem for Democrats," *New York Times*, June 23, 1988, B7.
38. "Project Material Task Force Meeting with Congressional Membership," May 23, 1979, Private Archives Collections of Frank Gregorsky.
39. Ibid.
40. Ibid.
41. Ibid.
42. Letter to Henry Kissinger from Newt Gingrich, February 23, 1988, Newt Gingrich papers, University of West Georgia Archives.
43. Jonathan Fuerbringer, "A House Divided by Political Rancor," *New York Times*, March 16, 1988, A22.
44. Robin Toner, "Around Wright, a 'Loyalty Dance,'" *New York Times*, April 7, 1989, A14.
45. Robin Toner, "Inquiry Report Near, Democrats Fight for Speaker," *New York Times*, April 9, 1989, A23.
46. Susan F. Rasky, "From Political Guerrilla to Republican Folk Hero," *New York Times*, June 15, 1988, A24.
47. John E. Yang, "Politics and Policy," *Wall Street Journal*, May 20, 1988, 52.
48. Michael Oreskes, "Gloom on Wright Shakes Gathering of Key Democrats," *New York Times*, May 18, 1989, A1.
49. George F. Will, "Ethics: 'The Reign of the Accuser,'" *Washington Post*, June 1, 1989, A25.
50. Elliot Brenner, "After Jim Wright's Departure House Hopes for Storm to End; Thomas Foley to Fill Position," *Atlanta Daily World*, June 4, 1989, 1.
51. William J. Eaton, "Wright Resigns, Urges End to This 'Mindless Cannibalism,'" *Los Angeles Times*, June 1, 1989, 1.
52. "Washington's ethical frenzy," *Economist*, June 3, 1989, 17.
53. William J. Eaton, "Wright Resigns, Urges End To This 'Mindless Cannibalism,'" *Los Angeles Times*. June 1, 1989, 1.

54. Dan Phillips, "Republicans Bridle at Wright Speech," *Washington Post*, June 2, 1989, A6.
55. Robin Toner, "Congress," *New York Times*, May 1, 1989, B7.
56. David Osborne, "Newt Gingrich: Shining King of the Post-Reagan Right," *Mother Jones*, November 1, 1984.
57. Tom Kenworthy, "Can Ascension to Whip Cool GOP Fire-Breather?," *Washington Post*, March 23, 1989, A10.
58. Ibid.
59. "Gingrich Holds 'Repeal' Rally," *Atlanta Daily World*, October 13, 1989, 2.
60. Bernard Weinraub, "Bush Fights Perception That He Is Adrift," *New York Times*, March 13, 1989, B5.

CHAPTER 17: TWO IN THE BUSH

1. E. J. Dionne Jr., "Voter-Signup Bill Gains in Congress," *New York Times*, May 6, 1989, 33.
2. Ibid.
3. Newt Gingrich, "Letters to the Editor: The Bush Realignment Is Real," *Washington Post*, March 7, 1989, A24.
4. George C. Wilson, "Cheney Scolds Air Force Chief for Hill Contacts on Missiles," *Washington Post*, March 25, 1989, A1.
5. Paul A. Gigot, "Bush's 100 Days: No-Plan Plan Works, for Now," *Wall Street Journal*, April 21, 1989, A14.
6. Ibid.
7. Sarah Booth Conrov, "Chronicles: Making Their Day by Day," *Washington Post*, January 1, 1989, F1.
8. Chip Kahn, in discussion with the author, November 9, 2010.
9. Robin Toner, "Democrats Weigh the Cost of Defending Their Speaker," *New York Times*, April 16, 1989, E1.
10. E. J. Dionne Jr., "Gingrich, Pursuer of Democrats, Now Finds Himself the Pursued," *New York Times*, June 4, 1989, 34.
11. Newt Gingrich, in discussion with the author, January 9, 2011.
12. E. J. Dionne Jr., "Gingrich, Pursuer of Democrats, Now Finds Himself the Pursued," *New York Times*, June 4, 1989, 1.
13. Mike Feinsilber, "Under Siege, House Democrats Suspect a Plot," Associated Press, June 3, 1989.
14. Walter Goodman, "Many Big News Stories to Tell, but the Biggest of All Is China," *New York Times*, June 5, 1989, A11.
15. Ibid.
16. Newt Gingrich, "The Gingrich Manifesto: The New GOP Whip Says It's Time to Clean House," *Washington Post*, April 9, 1989, B1–B2.
17. Robin Toner, "New Fallout over Ethics," *New York Times*, May 27, 1989, 9.
18. Charles Paul Freund, "Rhetorical Questions: Gingrich and the Centrist Straddle," *Washington Post*, April 11, 1989, A17.
19. Ibid.
20. E. J. Dionne Jr., "Partisan Rancor Fuels Warfare over Ethics," *New York Times*, May 28, 1989, E1.

21. Michael Oreskes, "An 'Evil Wind' of Fear Is Felt in House," *New York Times*, June 1, 1989, D21.
22. Rowland Evans and Robert Novak, "House of Vengeance," *Washington Post*, May 29, 1989, A25.
23. Michael Oreskes, "War Drums in the House," *New York Times*, May 28, 1989, 30.
24. Dirk Johnson, "Constituents Unhappy About Lukens," *New York Times*, June 30, 1989, A12.
25. Michael Oreskes, "Lawmaker Is Accused of Sexual Impropriety," *New York Times*, July 20, 1989, A18.
26. Michael Oreskes, "An 'Evil Wind' of Fear Is Felt in House," *New York Times*, June 1, 1989, A1.
27. Michael Oreskes, "Power of Speaker Already Starting to Pass to Foley," *New York Times*, June 2, 1989, A1.
28. Michael Oreskes, "An 'Evil Wind' of Fear Is Felt in House," *New York Times*, June 1, 1989, D21.
29. Robert Shogan, "Brown Appeals to GOP to Help Draft Code of Conduct," *Los Angeles Times*, June 17, 1989, 20.
30. E. J. Dionne Jr., "President Supports Atwater in Furor over Foley Memo," *New York Times*, June 9, 1989, A23.
31. Richard Cohen, "Foul Rumor," *Washington Post*, June 8, 1989, A23.
32. E. J. Dionne Jr., "President Supports Atwater in Furor over Foley Memo," *New York Times*, June 9, 1989, A23.
33. Dan Balz and Ann Devroy, "Fallout from Foley Memo Puts Atwater on Defensive," *Washington Post*, July 3, 1989, A4.
34. Ibid.
35. Dan Balz, "Votes of Confidence for Atwater and Gingrich," *Washington Post*, June 17, 1989, A11.
36. E. J. Dionne Jr., "President Supports Atwater in Furor over Foley Memo," *New York Times*, June 9, 1989, A23.
37. Dan Balz and Ann Devroy, "Fallout from Foley Memo Puts Atwater on Defensive," *Washington Post*, July 3, 1989, A4.
38. Richard Cohen, "Foul Rumor," *Washington Post*, June 8, 1989, A23.
39. Thomas B. Rosenstiel, "A Case of Blaming Messenger?; Ethics Epidemic: Fingers Are Pointed at the Media," *Los Angeles Times*, June 8, 1989, 1.
40. Richard Cohen, "Foul Rumor," *Washington Post*, June 8, 1989, A23.
41. Ann Devroy and Tom Kenworthy "GOP Aide Quits over Foley Memo," *Washington Post*, June 8, 1989, A10.
42. David E. Rosenbaum, "G.O.P. and Dole Give Strong Backing to Atwater," *New York Times*, 7.
43. Associated Press, March 29, 1991.
44. Confidential interview with the author.
45. Robin Toner, "As Foley Steps In, the House Needs Serious Repairs," *New York Times*, June 11, 1989, E4.
46. Matt Yancey, "Bush Battling Both Parties in House on S&L Plan," Associated Press, June 12, 1989.

47. John J. O'Connor, "What to Do About the Cold War?," *New York Times*, June 21, 1989, C22.
48. William Schneider, "GOP Takes Aim at House Democrats," *National Journal*, July 8, 1989, 21.
49. Robin Toner, "President to Seek Amendment to Bar Burning the Flag," *New York Times*, June 28, 1989, B7.
50. Robin Toner, "Flag Fight: from Rhetoric to Reality," *New York Times*, July 24, 1989, A13.
51. "Toy Congress," *Washington Post*, June 27, 1989, A22.
52. Don Phillips and Tom Kenworthy, "Democrats Brace for Real Battle over Symbolism," *Washington Post*, June 28, 1989, A5.
53. Susan F. Rasky, "Panel Announces Inquiry on Frank," *New York Times*, September 13, 1989, A14.
54. Ibid.
55. "Gingrich Asks Caution in an Inquiry on Frank," *New York Times*, October 4, 1989, A21.
56. Michael Oreskes, "Investigator in Wright Case May Take on Gingrich, Too," *New York Times*, July 18, 1989, A17.
57. Michael Oreskes, "Gingrich's Pay to Aides in 2 Races Raises Question of Rule-Breaking," *New York Times*, July 26, 1989, A1.
58. Michael Oreskes, "Former Employees Say Gingrich Had Workers Do Prohibited Jobs," *New York Times*, September 6, 1989, A23.
59. "Wednesday Evening," *New York Times*, September 10, 1989, 35.
60. Larry Margasak, "Congressman Says Ethics Committee Delaying Decision on Gingrich," Associated Press, October 10, 1989.
61. "Ethics Complaint Filed Against Newt Gingrich," *Wall Street Journal*, April 12, 1989, A16.
62. Michael Oreskes, "Congress: Gingrich Is Learning That He Who Wields the Whip Must Never Get Carried Away with the Task" *New York Times*, July 25, 1989, A20.

CHAPTER 18: A NEW ORDER GOES UP, A WALL FALLS DOWN
1. "CPAC over 30 Years: Conservatives Have Come a Long Way," *Human Events*, February 3, 2003, http://humanevents.com/2003/02/03/cpac-over-30-yearsbrconservatives-have-come-a-long-way/.
2. "House Leaders Rack Up Honoraria," *Washington Post*, March 10, 1989, A7.
3. David Hoffman, "Rep. Cheney Chosen as Defense Nominee," *Washington Post*, March 11, 1989, A1.
4. David S. Broder, "Minimalist Presidency," *Washington Post*, March 26, 1989, D7.
5. Chuck Conconi, "Personalities," *Washington Post*, March 27, 1989, C3.
6. Mark B. Liedl, "Congress's Busywork," *Washington Post*, January 28, 1990, C1.
7. David Shribman, "With Reagan Gone, Conservatives Weigh Strategy to Bring New Energy, Direction to Movement," *Wall Street Journal*, March 2, 1989, A18.
8. "Republicans Throw Down Challenge," *Guardian*, March 23, 1989.
9. Harold Bloom, ed., *Robert Frost* (New York: Infobase Publishing, 2003), 206.

10. Associated Press, "Bush Promises Veto of Tax Increase," September 21, 1989.
11. Robin Toner, "Familiar Partisan Banners Unfurl as Fight over Taxes Takes Shape," *New York Times*, September 22, 1989, D6.
12. Ibid.
13. David E. Rosenbaum, "Victory for Bush: 64 Democrats Join with G.O.P. in Big Setback for Their Leaders," *New York Times*, September 29, 1989, A1.
14. "In Quotes," *New York Times*, October 1, 1989, 16.
15. "Deficit Reduction Bill Signed by Bush," *Los Angeles Times*, December 20, 1989, A18.
16. George Bush, "Statement on Signing the Omnibus Budget Reconciliation Act of 1989," *American Presidency Project*, December 19, 1989, http://www.presidency.ucsb.edu/ws/?pid=17957.
17. Robert P. Hey, "Congress's Ethics on Rise, Obey Says," *Christian Science Monitor*, June 1, 1989, 8.
18. Susan F. Rasky, "The Entire Senate Is About to Have Ethics Problems," *New York Times*, December 31, 1989, E4.
19. Ibid.
20. "Letters to the Editor: The Bush Realignment Is Real," *Washington Post*, March 7, 1989, A24.
21. Rowland Evans and Robert Novak, "No Bush Revolution," *Washington Post*, March 1, 1989, A23.
22. Thomas B. Edsall, "GOP Honing Wedges for Next Campaign," *Washington Post*, February 26, 1989, A6.
23. Ibid.
24. Rowland Evans and Robert Novak, "No Bush Revolution," *Washington Post*, March 1, 1989, A23.
25. Myra MacPherson, "Newt Gingrich, Point Man in a House Divided," *Washington Post*, June 12, 1989, C8.
26. Ibid.
27. Dan Balz, "RNC Waving Red Flag at Democratic Foes," *Washington Post*, June 18, 1989, A4.
28. Mary McGrory, "On the Hill, It's Donkey Eat Donkey," *Washington Post*, June 25, 1989, B5.
29. Bob Beckel, in discussion with the author, October 22, 2010.
30. Tip O'Neill and William Novak, *Man of the House: The Life and Political Memoirs of Speaker Tip O'Neill* (New York: Random House, 1987), 353.
31. Ibid., 355.
32. Maralee Schwartz, "Democratic Debt Triples in 2 Years," *Washington Post*, June 18, 1989, A10.
33. Letter to Newt Gingrich from Nancy Pelosi, October 18, 1990, Newt Gingrich papers, University of West Georgia Archives.
34. Tom Kenworthy, "Ethics Probe, Eastern Strike Pose Worries for Gingrich at Home," *Washington Post*, June 20, 1989, A10.
35. "The Dangers of Playing 'Hardball,'" *Christian Science Monitor*, June 26, 1989, 20.
36. "GA District 6," *Our Campaigns*, http://www.ourcampaigns.com/RaceDetail.html?RaceID=37573.

37. Myron S. Waldman, "Republicans Jockeying for No. 2 Spot in House," *Newsday*, March 18, 1989, 9.

CHAPTER 19: TROUBLE IN PARADISE

1. Bill Dedman, "Barry Takes a Beating in Button Poll," *Washington Post*, April 13, 1989, B3.
2. John Crawley, "Gingrich Predicts Doom for Wright," *Atlanta Daily World*, March 31, 1989, 2.
3. William Schneider, "Jim Wright's Capitol Punishment," *Los Angeles Times*, June 4, 1989, 1.
4. Myron S. Waldman, "Worry over Gingrich Divides Republicans," *Newsday*, July 3, 1989, 14.
5. John Harwood, "Newt Gingrich: GOP's Bare-Knuckles Battler," *St. Petersburg Times*, July 27, 1989, 1A.
6. Jonathan D. Salant, "Boehlert Gives Money Whip a New Reminder of His '92' Supporters," *Syracuse Post-Standard*, April 30, 1989, C7.
7. Jonathan Alter, Howard Fineman, and Eleanor Clift, "The World of Congress," *Newsweek*, April 24, 1989, 28.
8. Josh Getlin, "Gingrich, Right's Bad Boy, Target of Angry Democrats," *Los Angeles Times*, June 11, 1989, 1.
9. "Gingrich Capitalized on Wright Inquiry," *St. Louis Post-Dispatch*, June 15, 1989, 10A.
10. United Press International, "Bush Welcomes Gingrich," April 6, 1989.
11. Charles Fenyvesi, "Washington Whispers," *U.S. News & World Report*, April 10, 1989.
12. Robert Shepard, "House Ethics Committee Embarks on New Probes," *United Press International*, August 19, 1989.
13. Don Phillips, "House Mood Shifts on Sex Cases," *Washington Post*, October 2, 1989, A12.
14. David Pace, "Gingrich Won't Challenge Convicted Republican's Right to Vote in House," Associated Press, June 8, 1989.
15. Ibid.
16. Ralph Z. Hallow and Paul M. Rodriguez, "Frank Is Accused of Silencing House," *Washington Times*, October 13, 1989, A1.
17. Don Kowet, "Late-Night Laughs at Congress' Expense," *Washington Times*, December 1, 1989, E1.
18. Rowland Evans and Robert Novak, "Darman's Dealing," *Washington Post*, April 14, 1989, A27.
19. Walter R. Mears, "Gingrich Choice by GOP May Crimp Bush's Bipartisanship," Associated Press, March 24, 1989.
20. "CB National Press Club Luncheon Speaker Representative Newt Gingrich (R-GA) National Press Club Ballroom," *Federal News Service*, April 27, 1989.
21. Larry Margasak, "Gingrich Complaint, Sex Cases Before Ethics Panel," Associated Press, July 20, 1989.
22. Myron S. Waldman, "Gingrich Charges Weighed," *Newsday*, July 19, 1989, 15.

23. Jim Drinkard, "Gingrich Accused Again," Associated Press, October 25, 1989.
24. Associated Press, "House Votes More Money for Ethics Committee," August 1, 1989.
25. Chuck Conconi, "Personalities," *Washington Post*, September 12, 1989, E3.
26. Rowland Evans and Robert Novak, "Good News to Newt," *Washington Post*, September 25, 1989, A15.
27. Rowland Evans and Robert Novak, "Trouble in Paradise," *Washington Post*, July 31, 1989, A15.
28. Rowland Evans and Robert Novak, "Bush: Tough Backstage," *Washington Post*, August 4, 1989, A23.
29. Brenda Caggiano, "The TV Column," *Washington Post*, August 5, 1989, C6.
30. Don Phillips, "Rep. Gingrich Appears Transformed by the Crack of the Whip," *Washington Post*, August 7, 1989, A7.
31. Rowland Evans and Robert Novak, "A Victory for the New Breed," *Washington Post*, October 2, 1989, A15.
32. "Roll-Call Vote in House on Bill to Cut Capital Gains Tax," *New York Times*, September 29, 1989, D4.
33. Laura K. McFadden, "Justice Has Finally Prevailed," *Newsday*, December 24, 1989, 17.
34. Dan Morgan, "$1.25 Billion Voted for Ex-Internees," *Washington Post*, October 27, 1989, A6.
35. Charlotte Hays, "In and Out, Up and Down in D.C.," *Washington Times*, July 31, 1989, E1.
36. Tom Kenworthy, "Bush Willing to Let Cuts Be Permanent," *Washington Post*, November 2, 1989, A16.
37. Don Phillips, "House Passes Pay-Ethics Bill, 252–174," *Washington Post*, November 17, 1989, A14.
38. Tom Kenworthy, "Gingrich Says Bush Must Choose Between Reform and a 'Second Eisenhower' Era," *Washington Post*, November 28, 1989, A10.
39. Don Phillips and Ann Devroy, "Gingrich Wanted Rollins Fired in GOP Strategy Feed," *Washington Post*, November 30, 1989, A4.
40. Richard Wolf, "Gingrich Hears Rumble at Home," *USA Today*, August 15, 1989, 4A.
41. Ibid.
42. Steven Komarow, "Wright a Major-Non-Subject During Lawmakers' Back-Home Meetings," Associated Press, April 25, 1989.
43. Garry Abrams, "Magazines: The Fat Hits the Fire over Cholesterol," *Los Angeles Times*, September 7, 1989, E1.
44. Ann Devroy, Don Oberdorfer and Tom Kenworthy, "Talking Points: Michigan GOP Chief to Join Quayle Staff, Keeping Party Post," *Washington Post*, December 18, 1989, A13.
45. Danielle Herubin, *State News Service*, October 11, 1989.
46. Suzanne Fields, "What Do Men Want? Answers Are Perplexing," *Los Angeles Times*, December 7, 1989, E24.
47. Donald M. Rothberg, "Coleman Says He Will Seek a Recount," Associated Press, November 8, 1989.
48. Ibid.

CHAPTER 20: BEATING THE BUSH

1. Jeffrey H. Birnbaum, "Gingrich to Be House GOP Whip; Madigan Edged Out in 87–85 Vote," *Wall Street Journal*, March 23, 1989, A26.
2. "New Target of Probe by the House May Be GOP Rep. McDade," *Wall Street Journal*, April 11, 1989, A24.
3. Steve Daley, "Underlying Anger Climbing Up Capitol Hill," *Chicago Tribune*, March 26, 1989, C4.
4. "'Wait' Til Next Year'; Bush; GOP Has Big Losses in 3 States," *Los Angeles Times*, November 8, 1989, P1.
5. "GOP's Defeats Put Heat on Bush Abortion Dtand," *San Diego Union-Tribune*, November 9, 1989, A1.
6. Ann Devroy, "Key Republicans Warn of Political Stampede," *Washington Post*, January 16, 1990, A1.
7. Rowland Evans and Robert Novak, ". . . And Bush's Response," *Washington Post*, January 24, 1990, A23.
8. "Sunday," *Washington Post*, January 20, 1990, C12.
9. Andrew Rosenthal, "Nixon Treated as Hero in Halls of His Disgrace," *New York Times*, March 9, 1990, A12.
10. Michael Oreskes, "Approval of Bush, Bolstered by Panama, Soars in Poll," *New York Times*, January 19, 1990, A20.
11. David S. Broder, "Gingrich Opposes Bush on China Vote," *Washington Post*, January 19, 1990, A13.
12. Helen Dewar, "Senate Returns to Confront Its Turn to Deal with Ethics," *Washington Post*, A1.
13. Michael Oreskes, "American Politics Loses Way as Polls Supplant Leadership," *New York Times*, March 18, 1990, 1.
14. David S. Broder, "Last-Minute Objections Delay Bill to Ease Voter Registration," *Washington Post*, January 31, 1990, A2.
15. Michael Oreskes, "Some G.O.P. Leaders Balk at Registration Bill," *New York Times*, January 31, 1990, A23.
16. Maralee Schwartz, David S. Broder, and Jay Mathews, "Gingrich Rethinking His Stand On Voter-Registration Measure," *Washington Post*, March 11, 1990, A12.
17. James H. Rubin, "Court Strikes Down Federal Law Outlining Burning of Flag," Associated Press, June 11, 1990.
18. Steven Heilbronner, "Gingrich Legal Fees Mounting," *Atlanta Daily World*, February 23, 1990, 2.
19. Newt Gingrich, in discussion with the author, November 22, 2014.
20. Rowland Evans and Robert Novak, "Why Embrace Rosty?," *Washington Post*, March 19, 1990, A11.
21. "Stamp to Honor 'Gone with the Wind,'" *Atlanta Daily World*, March 29, 1990, 8.
22. Richard L. Berke, "Candidates Reach Fund-Raising Peak," *New York Times*, May 8, 1990, A18.
23. Maralee Schwart and David Maraniss, "Gingrich: No More Mr. Nice Guy," *Washington Post*, March 30, 1990, A16.

24. Susan Rasky, "House G.O.P. Chiefs Assail Dole's Stance on Israel," *New York Times*, April 20, 1990, A10.
25. Ibid.
26. Ann Devroy, "Bush Opens Door to Tax-Hike Talks," *Washington Post*, May 8, 1990, A1.
27. Ibid.
28. Ibid.
29. Ed Rollins, in discussion with the author, February 8, 2013.
30. Haley Barbour, in discussion with the author, January 21, 2014.
31. Ann Devroy, "Bush Opens Door to Tax-Hike Talks," *Washington Post*, May 8, 1990, A1.
32. David Wessel and Michel McQueen, "Budget Talks Are Set to Begin at White House," *Wall Street Journal*, May 10, 1990, A3.
33. Alan Murray and Michel McQueen, "Bush Aides Give Mixed Signals on Tax Issue," *Wall Street Journal*, May 11, 1990, A3.
34. Ibid.
35. Ibid.
36. Ibid.

CHAPTER 21: THE "T" WORD
1. Paul A. Gigot, "Potomac Watch: The President Sniffs Out a Budget Deal," *Wall Street Journal*, May 11, 1990, A12.
2. Kerry Knott, in discussion with the author, October 9, 2012.
3. Mary McGrory, "Shaking Hands with Reality," *Washington Post*, May 10, 1990, A1.
4. Ann Devroy and John E. Yang, "White House Shores Up No-Tax Stand," *Washington Post*, May 10, 1990, A1.
5. William Safire, "The Big-Gov Right," *New York Times*, May 11, 1990, A35.
6. Robin Toner, "New Political Realities Create Conservative Identity Crisis," *New York Times*, May 13, 1990, 20.
7. James Pinkerton, in discussion with the author.
8. Robin Toner, "New Political Realities Create Conservative Identity Crisis," *New York Times*, May 13, 1990, 20.
9. Ibid.
10. George F. Will, "He Moved His Lips and Said Nothing," *Washington Post*, June 30, 1990, A1.
11. Terence Hunt, "Bush Concedes That Tax Increases Needed to Decrease Deficit," Associated Press, June 26, 1990.
12. Dan Balz, "President Explains Tax Switch," *Washington Post*, June 30, 1990, A1.
13. "Print Coverage of Tax 'Flip-Flop': 'Read My Lips . . . I Lied,'" *Hotline*, June 27, 1990.
14. Ibid.
15. David Wessel and Michel McQueen, "Bush Reversal on Taxes Spurs Budget Talks," *Wall Street Journal*, June 27, 1990, A3.
16. Steven Komarow, "Washington Today: Tax Issue Gives Gingrich His Ultimate Challenge," Associated Press, July 2, 1990.

17. Richard L. Berke, "Republicans Fear Kiss of Death as Bush Moves Lips on Taxes," *New York Times*, June 27, 1990, B6.

18. Richard L. Berke, "G.O.P. in Revolt on Taxes, Steps Up Criticism of Bush," *New York Times*, June 28, 1990, A20.

19. Ibid.

20. Ibid.

21. Richard L. Berke, "House, 408 to 18, Reprimands Rep. Frank for Ethics Violations," *New York Times*, July 27, 1990, A1.

22. Susan F. Rasky, "President Is Urged to Counterattack," *New York Times*, July 31, 1990, A8.

23. Jeffrey H. Birnbaum, "Gingrich's Conservative Rhetoric Often Conflicts with Role as Representative," *Wall Street Journal*, September 17, 1990, A16.

24. Paul Taylor, "Conservatives Embrace War on Poverty," *Washington Post*, May 19, 1990, A7.

25. Jill Abramson and Edward T. Pound, "Lawmakers Continue to Rake In Spending Fees, with Senators More Cautious Amid Inquires," *Wall Street Journal*, May 31, 1990, A16.

26. Michael Oreskes, "For G.O.P. Arsenal, 133 Words to Fire," *New York Times*, September 9, 1990, 30.

27. David Shribman, "Gingrich to Push His Political Revolt on TV, and in Process Boost Effort to Mold GOP Block," *Wall Street Journal*, May 14, 1990, A18.

28. Mary McGrory, "Shaking Hands with Reality," *Washington Post*, May 10, 1990, A2.

29. "Gingrich Comments on First Budget Meeting," *Atlanta Daily World*, June 5, 1990, 2.

30. David Wessel, "With Exception of Domenici, GOP Lawmakers Limit Role in Deficit Package to Playing Spoiler," *Wall Street Journal*, June 25, 1990, A16.

31. David Wessel and Jeffrey H. Birnbaum, "Bush, Risking Partisan Budget Scrap, Threatens to Stop Being Kinder, Gentler," *Wall Street Journal*, August 2, 1990, A2.

32. John Elvin, "Inside the Beltway," *Washington Times*, June 11, 1990, A6.

33. Judith Colp and Margaret Rankin, "Back-patting, Glad-handing—and $7 Million for GOP," *Washington Times*, June 15, 1990, E2.

34. Dan Morgan, "Cheney Threatens to Act Unilaterally on Pay Issue," *Washington Post*, May 26, 1990, A6.

35. George H. W. Bush, "Address on the End of the Gulf War," *Miller Center*, February 27, 1991, http://millercenter.org/president/bush/speeches/speech-5530.

36. Richard Wolf, "Congress, World: Harsh Reaction; In Washington, Partisan Potshots, Concern," *USA Today*, August 3, 1990, A1.

37. "Review & Outlook: Coca-Cola Classic," *Wall Street Journal*, August 2, 1990, A10.

38. "Friends of Newt Gingrich," *Atlanta Daily World*, June 28, 1990, 3.

39. Larry Haas, in discussion with the author, January 11, 2013.

CHAPTER 22: NERVOUS BREAKDOWN

1. Steven Komarow, "House Rejects Constitutional Amendment to Protect American Flag," *Associated Press*, June 21, 1990.

2. Thomas Ferraro, "Bush Appeals for Public Support on Taxes," United Press International, June 29, 1990.

3. Ralph Z. Hallow, "Damage Is Done, Republicans Say," *Washington Times*, June 27, 1990, A12.

4. Patrick J. Buchanan, "The End of the 'Reagan Revolution,'" *Human Events*, October 13, 1990, 869.

5. Ibid.

6. Ralph Z. Hallow, "Atwater, in Wheelchair, Visits RNC," *Washington Times*, June 28, 1990, A6.

7. RNC News Release, July 20, 1990, Newt Gingrich papers, University of West Georgia Archives.

8. Bob Livingston, in discussion with the author, February 17, 2011.

9. Ibid.

10. Rowland Evans and Robert Novak, "Tax Storm," *Washington Post*, A11.

11. Associated Press, "Gingrich Says He Could Support Tax Increase," July 20, 1990.

12. Letter to Guy Vander Jagt from Newt Gingrich, July 25, 1990, Newt Gingrich papers, University of West Georgia Archives.

13. Letter to Carl Pursell from Newt Gingrich, January 25, 1990, Newt Gingrich papers, University of West Georgia Archives.

14. Jude Wanniski, "Newt Gingrich: World Class Leader," *Polyconomics, Inc.*, October 9, 1990, Newt Gingrich papers, University of West Georgia Archives.

15. Letter to Newt Gingrich from Jude Wanniski, October 23, 1990, Newt Gingrich papers, University of West Georgia Archives.

16. Letter to Jude Wanniski from Newt Gingrich, October 23, 1990, Newt Gingrich papers, University of West Georgia Archives.

17. Tom Redburn, "Attack Democrats on Deficit, Bush Urges," *Los Angeles Times*, August 2, 1990, A17.

18. Rowland Evans and Robert Novak, "Friction in the GOP," *Washington Post*, August 20, 1990, A13.

19. Marshall Ingwerson, "Budget Negotiators Push 'Apex' Summit to the Wire," *Christian Science Monitor*, September 27, 1990, 6.

20. Bud Newman, "Cut Taxes, Don't Raise Them, Gingrich Says," United Press International, August 16, 1990.

21. "Gingrich Breaks with Bush on Taxes," *Orlando Sentinel*, August 28, 1990, A4.

22. John Elvin, "Inside the Beltway," *Washington Times*, June 11, 1990, A6.

23. Ed Rollins, in discussion with the author, February 8, 2013.

24. Ibid.

25. Donald Lambro, "Signals for a New GOP Game Plan," *Washington Times*, August 30, 1990, G3.

26. Newt Gingrich, in discussion with the author.

27. David Wessel, "With Exception of Domenici, GOP Lawmakers Limit Role in Deficit Package to Playing Spoiler," *Wall Street Journal*, June 25, 1990, A16.

28. Ibid.

29. David Wessel and Jackie Calmes, "In Budget Talks, Gingrich Plays Outsiders'

Game While Gramm Is Fast Becoming a Team Player," *Wall Street Journal*, September 17, 1990, A16.

30. Ibid.
31. David Wessel and Jackie Calmes, "Top Leaders Take Over Talks to Cut Deficit," *Wall Street Journal*, September 19, 1990, A3.
32. Scott Sonner, "Anti-Tax Group Says Bush Making Democrats Look Good," Associated Press, August 24, 1990.
33. Robert P. Hey, "Republican Partisanship Flares Up over S&L Debacle," *Christian Science Monitor*, August 2, 1990, 6.
34. David Wessel and Jackie Calmes, "Shift by Bush on Gains Tax Called Possible," *Wall Street Journal*, September 27, 1990, A3.
35. Marshall Ingwerson, "Budget-Summit Agenda Ambitious," *Christian Science Monitor*, September 7, 1990, 7.
36. Marshall Ingwerson, "Budget Negotiators Push 'Apex' Summit to the Wire," *Christian Science Monitor*, September 27, 1990, 6.
37. Ibid.
38. Ibid.
39. Sam Roberts, "Cuomo and Koch Face Off in a War of Printed Word," *New York Times*, April 18, 1984, B1.
40. Frank J. Murray, "Democrats, Deficit Getting Under Bush's Skin," *Washington Times*, August 2, 1990, A2.
41. "Complete Listings of Members, Their Advanced Degrees," *Roll Call*, August 6, 1990.
42. "From Bod to Smile to Ego, We Pick the Best and Biggest in Congress," *Roll Call*, September 10, 1990.

CHAPTER 23: THE WHIP WHO WENT OUT INTO THE COLD

1. "On the House," *Hotline*, September 5, 1990.
2. Federal News Service, "Remarks of Newt Gingrich and Tom Delay Citizens for a Sound Economy Luncheon Speakers: Representative Newt Gingrich (R-GA) Representative Tom Delay (R-TX) Moderator: Wayne Gable, President, Citizens for a Sound Economy J.W. Marriott Hotel, Washington, DC," September 6, 1990.
3. Patrice Hill, "Odds of Budget Success This Weekend Are 1 in 3, House Republican Whip Says," *Bond Buyer*, September 7, 1990.
4. Major Garrett, "Budget Summit Looks Moribund," *Washington Times*, September 20, 1990, A3.
5. John E. Yang and Steven Mufson, "Jump-Start Is Sought for Stalled Budget Talks," *Washington Post*, A7.
6. David E. Rosenbaum, "Accusations Begin in Budget Talks," *New York Times*, September 19, 1990, A26.
7. Ibid.
8. William Schneider, "Putting Aside Party Campaign Scripts," *National Journal*, September 15, 1990, 2224.
9. Richard Wolf, "Bush's Pet Tax Cut Is Elusive; Congress Battles over Capital Gains," *USA Today*, September 21, 1990, 5A.

10. Major Garrett, "Dole Rebukes Gingrich for Hurling a String of Adjectives at Democrats," *Washington Times*, September 17, 1990, A1.

11. John Elvin, "Inside the Beltway," *Washington Times*, September 17, 1990, A6.

12. Kent Jenkins Jr., "John Warner's Charmed Life: The Senator from Virginia, Mastering the Art of Fitting In," *Washington Post*, September 11, 1990, B1; John Elvin, "Inside the Beltway," *Washington Times*, September 17, 1990, A6.

13. Myron S. Waldman, "Fingers Pointing in Budget Talks," *Newsday*, September 27, 1990, 4.

14. Alan Fram, "Budget Plan Would Boost Taxes, Cut Federal Spending," Associated Press, September 30, 1990.

15. Ibid.

16. Tom Redburn and William J. Eaton, "Bush, Top Lawmakers Reach Agreement on Deficit Package," *Los Angeles Times*, October 1, 1990, A1.

17. George Will, "Budget Has Its Chuckles," *Seattle Post-Intelligencer*, October 4, 1990, A13.

18. Susan F. Rasky, "Deadline Extended," *New York Times*, October 1, 1990, A1.

19. Ibid.

20. Gloria Borger, "The Making of a Rebellion," *U.S. News & World Report*, October 15, 1990, 38.

21. Newt Gingrich, in discussion with the author, November 22, 2014.

22. Ibid.

23. Ibid.

24. Ibid.

25. William J. Eaton and Paul Houston, "Gingrich? Few Remain Indifferent," *Los Angeles Times*, October 3, 1990, A20.

26. Susan F. Rasky, "Deadline Extended," *New York Times*, October 1, 1990, A1.

27. Michael Oreskes, "Deficit Pact Blurs Party Boundaries," *New York Times*, October 4, 1990, D22.

28. Bob Walker, in discussion with the author, February 15, 2011.

29. Ibid.

30. Robert Shogan, "Compromise Is Seen as '92 Curtain Raiser," *Los Angeles Times*, October 2, 1990, A18.

31. "Newt Gingrich, Carol Cox on the Budget Plan," *America Tonight*, CBS News, October 2, 1990.

32. Robert Shepard, "Gingrich Causes GOP Leadership Split," United Press International, October 2, 1990.

33. Ibid.

34. Bob Walker, in discussion with the author, February 15, 2011.

35. Dan Balz and John E. Yang, "Bush Makes Appeal for Budget Support," *Washington Post*, October 3, 1990, A1.

36. "Vice President Dan Quayle," *Nightline*, ABC News, October 2, 1990.

37. Ibid.

38. Michael Oreskes, "Deficit Pact Blurs Party Boundaries," *New York Times*, October 4, 1990, D22.

39. Ellen Warren and R.A. Zaldivar, "Bush Asks Nation to Help in Fighting 'Cancer' of Deficit," *Miami Herald*, October 3, 1990, A1.

40. Ibid.
41. David E. Rosenbaum, "Greenspan Calls Budget Proposal a 'Credible' Plan," *New York Times*, October 4, 1990, A1.
42. "Selling the Deal; Tour of Duty; News Maker," *MacNeil/Lehrer NewsHour*, PBS, October 3, 1990.
43. "Gingrich: Nobody's Newtral," *Hotline*, October 4, 1990.
44. Steven Mufson and John E. Yang, "Emotional Pleas Failed to Halt House Revolt," *Washington Post*, October 6, 1990, A8.
45. Ibid.
46. Tom Morganthrau, Thomas M. DeFrank, Ann McDaniel, et al., "Fixing the Big Flop," *Newsweek*, October 15, 1990, 26.
47. John E. Yang and Tom Kenworthy, "House Rejects Deficit-Reduction Agreement," *Washington Post*, October 5, 1990, A1.
48. Susan Page, "House Vote a Big Defeat for Leaders," *Newsday*, October 6, 1990, 11.
49. Ibid.
50. *This Week with David Brinkley*, ABC News, October 21, 1990.
51. R.A. Zaldivar and Charles Green, "Budget Stunner: House Says No 254–179 Vote Rebukes Bush, Leadership Defeat for Compromise Could Trigger Spending Cuts," *Miami Herald*, October 5, 1990, A1.
52. Michael Oreskes, "Budget Boomerang," *New York Times*, October 6, 1990, 8.
53. Maureen Dowd, "Bush Aides' Big-Stick Tactics Drove Away Many in House," *New York Times*, October 6, 1990, 1.
54. Ibid.
55. Thomas B. Edsall, "Political Gridlock: A Symptom of Deeper National Problems?," *Washington Post*, October 7, 1990, A20.
56. Ibid.
57. Thomas B. Edsall and E.J. Dionne Jr., "Democracy at Work: The Tax Revolt of the Masses," *Washington Post*, October 14, 1990, C1.
58. Maureen Dowd, "Bush Aides' Big-Stick Tactics Drove Away Many in House," *New York Times*, October 6, 1990, 8.
59. John E. Yang and Ann Devroy, "House Sustains Veto as Budget Stalemate Continues," *Washington Post*, October 7, 1990, A1.
60. Richard L. Berke, "Debate Brings Delay and Disruption," *New York Times*, October 8, 1990, A14.
61. Maureen Dowd, "The Budget Battle: Impasse on Budget Is Ended; Stopgap Spending Measure Averts Federal Shutdown," *New York Times*, October 9, 1990, A1.
62. David E. Rosenbaum, "Bush Termed Open to Tax Rate Rise on Upper Income," *New York Times*, October 21, 1990, 1.
63. Steven Komarow, "House Approves New Budget Resolution," Associated Press, October 8, 1990.
64. John E. Yang and Steven Mufson, "Divided House Adopts Democrats' Budget Plan," *Washington Post*, October 8, 1990, A1.
65. David E. Rosenbaum, "Tensions Are Eased," *New York Times*, October 9, 1990, A1.
66. Susan F. Rasky, "Dole, in Twist of Fate, Leads Charge for Bush, the Rival He Scorned," *New York Times*, October 17, 1990, A25.

67. William Safire, "Hail to Ginglock," *New York Times*, October 8, 1990, A17.
68. Maureen Dowd, "Helter-Skelter Day Reflects Miscalculations at the Top," *New York Times*, October 9, 1990, A21.
69. Ibid.

CHAPTER 24: FALLOUT

1. Larry Martz, Clara Bingham, Eleanor Clift, et al., "Bush League," *Newsweek*, October 22, 1990, 20.
2. Ibid.
3. George Will, "Deficit Goes Up, Bush Goes Down," *Seattle Post-Intelligencer*, October 14, 1990, D2.
4. Roper Center for Public Opinion Research, "Bush (G. H. W.) Presidential Approval Ratings," *Cornell University*, http://ropercenter.cornell.edu/polls/presidential-approval/.
5. "For the Record," *Washington Post*, October 4, 1990, A26.
6. John Lichfield, "Fighting Bush for the Soul of the Republican Party," *Independent* (London), October 14, 1990, 14.
7. Ibid.
8. "Pump Perk: Congressional Leadership Avoiding $1.41 Gas," *Union Leader*, October 23, 1990, 1.
9. Andrew Rosenthal, "Bush Tries to Quell G.O.P. Rebellion," *New York Times*, October 26, 1990, A22.
10. Otis White, "Georgians Watch Political Cat Fight," *St. Petersburg Times*, November 4, 1990, 3A.
11. Larry Martz, Clara Bingham, Eleanor Clift, et al., "Bush League," *Newsweek*, October 22, 1990, 20.
12. "Gipperdammerung... Ginglock... Send in the Clowns," *Hotline*, October 9, 1990.
13. Ibid.
14. Tom Morganthrau, Thomas M. DeFrank, Ann McDaniel, et al., "Fixing the Big Flop," *Newsweek*, October 15, 1990, 26.
15. Dan Balz, "Bush Seeks Firing of Party Official," *Washington Post*, October 26, 1990, A23.
16. David Lauter, "Aide Says White House Sought 'Congressional Vulnerability,'" *Los Angeles Times*, October 26, 1990, A22.
17. Rowland Evans and Robert Novak, "Bipartisan and Bitter," *Washington Post*, October 8, 1990, A23.
18. "Gipperdammerung... Ginglock... Send in the Clowns," *Hotline*, October 9, 1990.
19. *Hotline*, October 15, 1990.
20. Ibid.
21. Sara Fritz and Dwight Morris, "Campaign Cash Takes a Detour," *Los Angeles Times*, October 28, 1990, A1.
22. Sara Fritz and Dwight Morris, "House Challengers Depend on Ingenuity, Not Money," *Los Angeles Times*, October 30, 1990, A1.
23. Ibid.

24. Tom Morganthrau, Thomas M. DeFrank, Ann McDaniel, et al., "Fixing the Big Flop," *Newsweek*, October 15, 1990, 26.
25. Ed Rollins, in discussion with the author, February 8, 2013.
26. Ibid.
27. Craig Winneker, "Gingrich Budget Defection Is Likely to Sew Up Re-election Bid Despite Worley's Accusations," *Roll Call*, October 18, 1990.
28. Ed Rollins, in discussion with the author, February 8, 2013.
29. Craig Winneker, "Gingrich Budget Defection Is Likely to Sew Up Re-election Bid Despite Worley's Accusations," *Roll Call*, October 18, 1990.
30. *Hotline*, October 19, 1990.
31. Lauran Neergaard, "Gingrich Foe Says GOP Whip Neglecting His District," Associated Press, October 25, 1990.
32. Joseph Mianowany, "Mixed Election Results a Boost for Dems or GOP?," United Press International, November 7, 1990.
33. Major Garrett, "GOP Loses 13 Seats," *Washington Times*, November 7, 1990, A1.
34. Craig Winneker, "Recount Puts Gingrich Up by 972 Votes," *Roll Call*, November 19, 1990.
35. "The South," *Washington Post*, November 4, 1990, A20.
36. Rita Beamish, "In Some Cases, Money Wasn't Everything," Associated Press, November 7, 1990.
37. "1990 'Doublespeak' Prize Awarded to President Bush," *Washington Post*, November 17, 1990, A18.
38. David Braaten, "Foot-in-Mouth Disease an Epidemic in 1990," *Washington Times*, December 31, 1990, A1.
39. David E. Rosenbaum, "Gingrich Assails Bush's Budget Chief," *New York Times*, December 1, 1990, 11.
40. Ibid.
41. Ibid.
42. Robin Toner, "2 Top Republicans Keep on Feuding, and Talking," *New York Times*, December 24, 1990, 10.
43. Dan Balz and Ann Devroy, "Bush's Domestic Policy Seen in Disarray," *Washington Post*, December 20, 1990, A1.
44. David S. Broder, "Quayle Calls for Mending GOP 'Fissures' on Budget, Gulf," *Washington Post*, November 11, 1990, A13.
45. Ibid.
46. David S. Broder and Ann Devroy, "A 'Sobering Experience'," *Washington Post*, November 8, 1990, A44.
47. Bill Tammeus, "Out-of-Control Year Gains Perspective by Quotes from Famous," *Oregonian*, December 28, 1990, C8.
48. David Braaten, "Foot-in-Mouth Disease an Epidemic in 1990," *Washington Times*, December 31, 1990, A1.
49. Lewis Grossberger, "The Rush Hours," *New York Times*, December 16, 1990, 58.
50. David Pace, "Shocked Gingrich Pledges to Renew Ties with District," Associated Press, November 8, 1990.

51. Sandy Grady, "Dan Quayle Is a Bad Joke at Operation Brooke Shields," *Miami Herald*, December 28, 1990, A13.

CHAPTER 25: THE MOTHER OF ALL

1. Joyce Price, "Political Consultants Don Rose-Colored Classes," *Washington Times*, B10.
2. "Bush's Popularity Drops in Face of Crisis," ABC News, *Nightline*, October 16, 1990.
3. Steve Daley, "Bush's Tax Plan Haunts GOP Races," *Chicago Tribune*, October 25, 1990, 1C.
4. David S. Broder and Ann Devroy, "A 'Sobering Experience'," *Washington Post*, November 8, 1990, A44.
5. Ibid.
6. Lucy Howard and Ned Zeman, "Bush: Blocking Newt," *Newsweek*, March 25, 1991, 5.
7. "White House Says War Will Last Months," *St. Petersburg Times*, January 25, 1991, 4A.
8. Michael Barone and David Gergen, "Looking for a Real Anti-incumbent Backlash," *U.S. News & World Report*, February 18, 1991, 43.
9. Ralph Z. Hallow, "Stumbling Blocks Litter Road to '92," *Washington Times*, March 4, 1991, A1.
10. Tom Baxter, "Gingrich Housing No Senatorial Plans," *Atlanta Journal-Constitution*, February 11, 1991, D2.
11. Letter to Dick Cheney from Newt Gingrich, July 27, 1990, Newt Gingrich papers, University of West Georgia Archives.
12. Letter to John Sununu from Newt Gingrich, July 27, 1990, Newt Gingrich papers, University of West Georgia Archives.
13. Letter to Newt Gingrich from Milton Friedman, October 4, 1990, Newt Gingrich papers, University of West Georgia Archives.
14. Letter to Newt Gingrich from George Bush, October 4, 1990, Newt Gingrich papers, University of West Georgia Archives.
15. Letter to "Republican Member of Congress" from Lee Atwater, October 4, 1990, Newt Gingrich papers, University of West Georgia Archives.
16. "Post-War Politics: GOP Attack Dogs—Bark but No Fight?," *Hotline*, March 14, 1991.
17. Tim Curran, "80 GOP War Vets to Run in 1992, Gingrich Predicts," *Roll Call*, March 18, 1991.
18. William Schneider, "Politicizing the Persian Gulf Victory," *National Journal*, March 16, 1991, 674.
19. J. Jennings Moss, "The World After War," *Washington Times*, March 7, 1991, A1.
20. Ibid.
21. Steven Komarow, "GOP Leaders Say Gulf Victory No 'Magic Dust' for Republicans," Associated Press, March 15, 1991.
22. Steven Komarow, "GOP Trying to Capitalize on Gulf War Victory," Associated Press, March 4, 1991.

23. Ibid.
24. Steve Komarow, "Republicans in Congress Move for Wider Influence Over Bush Domestic Agenda," Associated Press, March 16, 1991.

CHAPTER 26: SHADOW OF THE FAT MAN

1. Howard Fineman, "Dream On, Democrats," *Newsweek*, March 18, 1991, 40.
2. Howard Fineman, "Demonizing the Sixties," *Newsweek*, March 25, 1991, 39.
3. George F. Will, ". . . A Serious Candidate," *Washington Post*, March 7, 1991, A23.
4. Ibid.
5. David S. Broder and Thomas B. Edsall, "Democrats See Growing Signs of Trouble in Polls," *Washington Post*, March 22, 1991, A9.
6. Ibid.
7. "Unity Makes Deep Problems," *New York Times*, March 4, 1991, A11.
8. Ann Devroy, "Bush: 'All Is Not Well,'" *Washington Post*, October 5, 1991, A1.
9. Ibid.
10. Tom Baxter, "Political Storm Winds Buffeting Bush," *Atlanta Journal-Constitution*, November 4, 1991, 2.
11. Rowland Evans and Robert Novak, "Tax-Cut Fever," *Washington Post*, November 4, 1991, A21.
12. Confidential interview with the author.
13. Ann Devroy and Eric Pianin, "Bush Refuses to Back House GOP Tax Cut Plan," *Washington Post*, November 26, 1991, A5.
14. "House Backs Bill on Abortion Advice Despite Veto Threat," *Atlanta Journal-Constitution*, June 27, 1991, A10.
15. Bob Livingston, in discussion with the author, February 17, 2011.
16. "Press Conference," *Federal News Service*, June 11, 1991.
17. Jackie Calmes, "In an About-Face, Gingrich Becomes an Apostle of Grass-Roots Politics, Averting Clashes in GOP," *Wall Street Journal*, March 27, 1991, A16.
18. Jaffrey H. Birnbaum, "Ills of Nation's Health-Care System Are Pulling GOP Into Search for Cures," *Wall Street Journal*, June 24, 1991, A12.
19. "Social Swirl," *Atlanta Daily World*, August 11, 1991, 3.
20. Deborah Scroggins, "The Gay Community; Impact in Atlanta," *Atlanta Journal-Constitution*, June 23, 1991, A8.
21. John Elvin, "Newt Lightens Up," *Washington Times*, January 24, 1992, A6.
22. Maralee Schwartz and Tom Kenworthy, "3 Democrats Put on the Line So Gingrich Can Meet Lewis," *Washington Post*, September 7, 1991, A3.
23. Jeanne Cummings, "Pay-Backs, Partisanship Shape Redistricting," *Atlanta Journal-Constitution*, September 8, 1991, D1.
24. Sharyn Wizda, "Gingrich Only One of Area Reps. to Write Rubber Checks," *States News Service*, October 3, 1991.
25. "Kitegate Spills Over," *Wall Street Journal*, October 4, 1991, A14.
26. Craig Winneker, "Drivers for House Leaders Reap Big Payoffs in 1st Quarter of '91," *Roll Call*, September 12, 1991.
27. Ernie Freda, "Capitol Ambulance Now on Call for All," *Atlanta Journal-Constitution*, October 22, 1991, A14.

28. David E. Anderson, "Marshall Resignation Evokes Praise, Dismay," United Press International, June 28, 1991.
29. Greg Henderson, "Danforth: Thomas's Natural Law Theory Does Not Apply to Abortion," United Press International, July 18, 1991.
30. "Did Gutter Politics Get Thomas Confirmed?," *Nightline*, ABC News, October 15, 1991.
31. Ann Devroy, "Gleeful GOP Poised to Exploit Thomas Issue," *Washington Post*, October 18, 1991, A1.
32. Karen Tumulty and Paul Kane, "Republicans Divided on the Importance of an Agenda for Midterm Elections," *Washington Post*, July 17, 2010.
33. "Overheard," *Newsweek*, October 28, 1991.
34. Charles Fenyvesi, "Washington Whispers," *U.S. News and World Report*, September 23, 1991, 25.
35. Frank J. Murray and Michael Hedges, "Records of Calls Sought by GOP," *Washington Times*, September 26, 1991, A1.
36. Ibid.
37. Ernie Freda, "Capitol Ambulance Now on Call for All," *Atlanta Journal-Constitution*, October 22, 1991, A14.
38. Juan Williams, "Sununu on Sununu: What I'm Doing Is Just What the President Wants Done," *Washington Post*, November 24, 1991, C1.
39. John Dillin, "Right's Displeasure with Bush Runs High," *Christian Science Monitor*, January 10, 1991, 1.
40. John E. Yang and Ann Devroy, "Administration Considering Tax Rebate of Up to $300," *Washington Post*, December 18, 1991, A1.
41. John Harwood and Michel McQueen, "Malaise '92: As Bush Ratings Sink, Some Sense Parallels with Carter in 1980," *Wall Street Journal*, March 5, 1992, A1.

CHAPTER 27: ALPHA AND OMEGA

1. Rowland Evans and Robert Novak, "Fire-Eating Advice from Newt Gingrich," *Washington Post*, February 14, 1992, A25.
2. Charles Walston, "Gingrich Hopes to Find Niche in New 6th,"*Atlanta Journal-Constitution*, May 18, 1992, A1.
3. Janice Castro, "With Friends Like These . . . ," *Time*, September 21, 1992.
4. Maralee Schwartz and Charles R. Babcock, "Special Counsel Probe Is Urged of Contributions by Two to GOP," *Washington Post*, June 10, 1992, A14.
5. Ibid.
6. Dorothy E. Clark, "The Whip Becomes a Whipping Boy," *Atlanta Journal-Constitution*, June 15, 1992, A12.
7. Tom Teepen, "Paper's Lewis, Gingrich Coverage Unbalanced," *Atlanta Journal-Constitution*, June 9, 1992, A18.
8. Phillip R. Callaway, "Gingrich Plays Politics with Welfare-Reform Proposals," *Atlanta Journal-Constitution*, June 27, 1992, A16.
9. Kenneth Cooper, "Self-Described 'Reformer' Gingrich Feels Lash of Anti-Incumbent Fever," *Washington Post*, July 16, 1992, A3.
10. Kathy O'Malley and Dorothy Collin, *Chicago Tribune*, June 28, 1992, C5.

11. Bill Lambrecht, "Gingrich in a Fight for His Political Life, House GOP Whip Battling," *St. Louis Post-Dispatch*, September 18, 1992, 1A.
12. John Harwood and Michel McQueen, "Malaise '92: As Bush Ratings Sink, Some Sense Parallels with Carter in 1980," *Wall Street Journal*, March 5, 1992, A1.
13. John Elvin, "Inside the Beltway," *Washington Times*, December 2, 1991, A6.
14. Ralph Z. Hallow, "Gingrich Runs Interference on Bush's Right," *Washington Times*, December 3, 1991, A1.
15. E. J. Dionne Jr., "Buchanan, Like Jackson, Exposes Deep Split in Party," *Washington Post*, March 5, 1992, A1.
16. Jack Anderson, "For IRS, a Junket Takes on New Meaning," *Washington Post*, May 21, 1992, B25.
17. Rowland Evans and Robert Novak, "The Perils of Bashing Pat Buchanan," *Washington Post*, March 11, 1992, A23.
18. John McLaughlin, in discussion with the author, June 13, 2013.
19. *Off the Record*, Fox, December 12, 1991.
20. "Washington at Work," *Washington Post*, March 12, 1992, A25.
21. Rowland Evans and Robert Novak, "Gingrich: Unwelcome Messenger," *Washington Post*, June 12, 1992, A23.
22. Gloria Borger, "Standing Pat? Civil War on the Right," *U.S. News & World Report*, March 16, 1992, 31.
23. "Bush: Signs of GOP Mutiny on the Ship of State," *Hotline*, July 30, 1992.
24. Guy Gugliotta and Kenneth J. Cooper, "String of House Scandals Saps Public Confidence," *Washington Post*, March 11, 1992, A1.
25. Guy Gugliotta and Kenneth J. Cooper, "House Votes to List Names of 355 Who Wrote Bad Checks," *Washington Post*, March 13, 1992, A1.
26. Michael York and Kenneth J. Cooper, "Bank Scandal Spurs U.S. Criminal Probe," *Washington Post*, March 17, 1992, A1.
27. Newt Gingrich, in discussion with the author, February 13, 2011.
28. Adam Clymer, "House Revolutionary," *New York Times*, August 23, 1992.
29. Kenneth J. Cooper, "Foley Plays Down Criminal Probe," *Washington Post*, March 18, 1992, A27.
30. *This Week with David Brinkley*, ABC News, March 15, 1992.
31. Steven Kamarow, "Advantage Republicans. Or Is It Advantage Democrats?," Associated Press, March 14, 1992.
32. Peter Applebome, "Gingrich Tries to Avoid Heat of Voter Outrage He Fanned," *New York Times*, April 18, 1992, 1.
33. Dean Patterson, "Opinions Differ on Importance of House Bank Scandal," United Press International, March 15, 1992.
34. Ibid.
35. *This Week with David Brinkley*, ABC News, March 15, 1992.
36. Kenneth J. Cooper, "Foley Plays Down Criminal Probe," *Washington Post*, March 18, 1992, A27.
37. Clifford Krauss, "Gingrich Takes No Prisoners in the House's Sea of Gentility," *New York Times*, March 17, 1992, A18.
38. *This Week with David Brinkley*, ABC News, March 15, 1992.

39. Ibid.
40. Maureen Dowd, "New Kind of Potomac Fever Is Caused by Spartan Living," *New York Times*, March 22, 1992, 1.
41. Ibid.
42. Ibid.
43. John King, "Western Shootout; Buchanan Back in the Hot Seat," Associated Press, January 14, 1992.
44. Tom Raum, "Buchanan Targeting Georgia Next in GOP Challenge to Bush," Associated Press, February 24, 1992.
45. Dan Balz and E. J. Dionne, Jr., "Insiders Trying to Fathom Outsider Perot's Potential," *Washington Post*, April 22, 1992, A1.
46. Paul Bedard, "Bush Pledges to Fire Leaker of Reilly Note; White House Investigating," *Washington Times*, June 8, 1992, A1.
47. Ann Devroy, "Gingrich Warns Bush Campaign; Political Aides Are Told to Wake Up to Facts of a 'Unique' Year," *Washington Post*, June 7, 1992, A1.
48. Richard L. Berke, "Bush, in Georgia, Questions Clinton's Vision of the Family," *New York Times*, August 23, 1992, 26.
49. Confidential interview with the author.
50. Ernie Freda, "Did Reagan Vote for Clinton?," *Atlanta Journal and Constitution*, January 5, 1993, A5.
51. Ibid.
52. George F. Will, "The Two Roads on Carroll Campbell's Mind," *Washington Post*, December 2, 1993, A21.
53. "Willie Horton: the Mother of All Diversions," *Wall Street Journal*, April 17, 1992, A10.
54. Arthur J. Finkelstein, in discussion with the author.
55. *Capital Gang*, CNN, November 7, 1992.
56. Newt Gingrich, in discussion with the author, January 9, 2011.
57. Ralph Z. Hallow, "Conservatives Rule GOP Roost in House," *Washington Times*, December 9, 1992, A4.
58. "GOP Whip Quits over Right Wing Militancy," *Plain Dealer*, January 6, 1993, 5A.
59. Newt Gingrich, in discussion with the author, February 13, 2011.
60. Mark Shields and Robert Novak, "House Bank Scandal Fallout," CNN, April 18, 1992.
61. "Letters to the Editor: A Three-Party System Would Break Grid-Lock," *Atlanta Journal-Constitution*, September 4, 1992, A15.
62. Bill McAllister, "Term Limits Run Strong in 14 States," *Washington Post*, October 26, 1992, A1.
63. Charles M. Madigan, "GOP Sounds the Attack: Conservatives Lead Assault on Democrats," *Chicago Tribune*, August 19, 1992.
64. Jeff Greenfield, "In Politics, Sometimes Nothing Works," *Chicago Sun-Times*, October 23, 1992, 37.

CHAPTER 28: BLOODY NOSES AND CRACK'D CROWNS

1. Grover Norquist, "It's My Party," *American Spectator*, January 1993.

2. Kevin Merida and Kenneth J. Cooper, "Lobbyists Help Pay for Retreat of House GOP Policy Group," *Washington Post*, February 26, 1993, A14.

3. Paul Bedard, "Conservatives Urge GOP to Create 'Positive Vision'," *Washington Times*, January 24, 1993, A4.

4. Craig Winneker, "Super Bowl for Sale at Party Committees," *Roll Call*, January 27, 1993.

5. James Fallows, "Farewell to Laissez-Faire!," *Washington Post*, February 28, 1993, C3.

6. Ibid.

7. "Dial-In Democracy," *Nightline*, ABC News, February 9, 1993.

8. Frank Luntz, in discussion with the author, July 9, 2013.

9. Gay Gaines, in discussion with the author, March 17, 2011.

10. Ibid.

11. Confidential interview with the author.

12. Frank Luntz, in discussion with the author, July 9, 2013.

13. Ibid.

14. Joe Gaylord, in discussion with the author, June 30, 2010.

15. Lois Romano, "The Reliable Source," *Washington Post*, March 3, 1993, B3.

16. David Warnick, in discussion with the author, March 16, 2011.

17. Jerry Roberts, "The Late Show on C-SPAN—Rep. Dornan Savages Clinton," *San Francisco Chronicle*, October 6, 1992, A4.

18. *Capital Gang*, CNN, November 7, 1992.

19. "Controversy Continues over Gays and Military," *Nightline*, ABC News, January 26, 1993.

20. William M. Welch, "Gingrich Says Baird 'Crossed the Line,'" Associated Press, January 15, 1993.

21. Michael Duffy, "The Incredible Shrinking President," *Time*, June 29, 1992.

22. Adam Clymer, "Lawmakers Revolt on Lifting Gay Ban in Military Service," *New York Times*, January 27, 1993, A1.

23. *CBS Morning News*, CBS News, January 27, 1993.

24. Michael Sangiacomo, "Gingrich Calls Clinton's Stand on Gays 'Bizzare'," *Plain Dealer*, January 30, 1993, 4A.

25. Tom Baxter, "Before Gingrich Challenged Clinton, He Had Tolerant View of Gays in Military," *Atlanta Journal-Constitution*, January 30, 1993, A7.

26. E. J. Dionne, "Clinton and the GOP Options," *Washington Post*, February 16, 1993, A13.

27. Adam Clymer, "Congress and Clinton: A Handshake If Not a Kiss," *New York Times*, January 10, 1993, E5.

28. Newt Gingrich, "Health Care: Time to Get Practical," *Washington Post*, March 9, 1993, A19.

29. George J. Church, Margaret Carlson, Michael Duffy, et al., "A Call to Arms," *Time*, February 22, 1993.

30. John Harwood, "Republican Party Faces Growing Internal Debate over How to Recapture Tax Issue from Democrats," *Wall Street Journal*, March 3, 1993, A16.

31. Ibid.

32. George J. Church, Margaret Carlson, Michael Duffy, et al., "A Call to Arms," *Time*, February 22, 1993.
33. Michelle Ruess, "Ohio's Rep. Boehner Challenges Status Quo," *Plain Dealer*, January 3, 1993, 10A.
34. "House Republicans Manage to Win One Despite Themselves," *Washington Times*, February 7, 1993, B2.
35. Anne Hazard, "Michel Leads Efforts to Thwart Democrats with Suit," *States News Service*, January 4, 1993.
36. Craig Winneker, "Heard on the Hill," *Roll Call*, January 7, 1993.
37. Karen Foerstel, "GOP Wins One-Hour Special Orders Daily," *Roll Call*, January 27, 1993.
38. Bob Walker, in discussion with the author, February 15, 2011.

CHAPTER 29: THE TEMPEST
1. Rowland Evans and Robert Novak, "Clinton Cornered," *Washington Post*, May 10, 1993, A17.
2. Clifford Krauss, "Many in Congress, Citing Vietnam, Oppose Attacks," *New York Times*, April 28, 1993, A10.
3. Tom Kenworthy, "Hill Leaders Talk of Reponse to Iraq," *Washington Post*, May 10, 1993, A11.
4. Marianne Means, "Clinton Sends Just the Right Message," *Miami Herald*, June 30, 1993, A23.
5. Karen Ball, "House Republicans Accuse Clinton of 'Outrageous Lie,'" Associated Press, May 5, 1993.
6. Stephen Labaton, "Prosecutors Reported Seeking to Widen Inquiry on Rostenkowski," *New York Times*, July 21, 1993, A11.
7. "Rostenkowski: House Dems Raucously Keep Record Confidential," *Hotline*, July 23, 1993.
8. Ernie Freda, "Foley Asked to Account for Stock Gains," *Atlanta Journal-Constitution*, July 29, 1993, A16.
9. Tom Baxter, "Storm Clouds Gathering over All in Congress," *Atlanta Journal-Constitution*, August 2, 1993, A5.
10. Joan Lowy, "Partisan Politics Is Taking Mean Turn on Capital Hill," *St. Louis Post-Dispatch*, August 5, 1993, 5B.
11. Susan Headden, Penny Loeb, David Bowermaster, et al., "Money, Congress and Health Care," *U.S. News and World Report*, May 24, 1993, 29.
12. Steven Pearlstein, "Chamber's Shift Hasn't Ended Fight," *Washington Post*, July 20, 1993, C1.
13. Ibid.
14. Robert D. Novak, "GOP: Between Capitulation and Obstruction," *Washington Post*, August 23, 1993, A17.
15. Ibid.
16. Robert D. Novak, "Term Limits: In Trenton . . . ," *Washington Post*, June 24, 1993, A19.
17. Frank Luntz, in discussion with the author, July 9, 2013.

18. Cragg Hines, "Perot Puts the GOP on Horns of Dilemma," *Houston Chronicle*, June 7, 1993, A1.

19. Peter Applebome, "Gingrich Plan for Satellite Lessons Arouses Critics," *New York Times*, September 4, 1993, 6.

20. United Press International, "Teachers Criticize Gingrich Televised Course," August 13, 1993.

21. "Campaign Finance: Jackson Calls Reform This Year 'Dicey'," *Hotline*, August 19, 1993.

22. Thomas B. Edsall, "Christian Political Soldier Helps Revive Movement," *Washington Post*, September 10, 1993, A4.

23. William Claiborne, "Jersey City—Rich in Democratic Traditions—Switches to GOP Portfolio," *Washington Post*, July 4, 1993, A3.

24. "Politics, Policy, and Analysis," *Washington Times*, September 5, 1993, A4.

25. R. W. Apple Jr., "Note Left by White House Aide: Accusation, Anger, and Despair," *New York Times*, August 11, 1993.

26. Ralph Z. Hallow, "Dole Vows GOP Senators Will Bar 'Any New Taxes,'" *Washington Times*, April 27, 1993, A4.

27. "House Narrowly Passes Clinton's Economic Recovery Plan," *NPR*, May 28, 1993.

28. Ed Rollins, in discussion with the author, February 8, 2013.

29. Lance Koonce, "House of Representatives Announces Public Electronic Mail Service," *U.S. Newswire*, June 2, 1993.

30. "Are Republicans Too Mean?," *Capital Gang*, CNN, May 22, 1993.

31. Ibid.

32. "Gay Rights in Georgia," CNN, *The Week in Review*, August 29, 1993.

33. Mary Jacoby, "Bill Trims House Spending by 5.8%," *Roll Call*, June 10, 1993.

34. Ibid.

35. Associated Press, "Washington Dateline," June 12, 1993.

36. Lawrence L. Knutson, "Congressional Diary—Thursday, July 1, 1993," Associated Press, July 2, 1993.

37. "Gingrich: Re-Shaping Image for Leadership Bid," *Hotline*, September 15, 1993.

38. Federal News Service, "News Conference by House Republican Leadership on the Republican Health Care Proposal," September 15, 1993.

39. Kenneth J. Cooper, "Gingrich Claims He Has Votes to Be House Minority Leader," *Washington Post*, October 8, 1993, A6.

40. Dan Balz, "Gingrich Criticizes Clinton's Sales Job," *Washington Post*, October 19, 1993, D4.

41. Kevin Sullivan, "AFL-CIO Official Quits as Democratic Leader," *Washington Post*, November 25, 1993, 1.

42. Al Kamen, "White House Faces a Painful Extraction," *Washington Post*, November 19, 1993, A27.

43. Frank Luntz, in discussion with the author, July 9, 2013; Robert D. Novak, "The Passive Politics of the GOP," *Washington Post*, December 13, 1993, A21.

44. Robert D. Novak, "The Passive Politics of the GOP," *Washington Post*, December 13, 1993, A21.

45. Ibid.

46. David S. Broder, "Gingrich Takes 'No-Compromise' Stand on Health Care Plan," *Washington Post*, December 15, 1993, A11.

47. Merrill Hartson, "GOP Questions Clinton Plan for Health Care Overhaul," Associated Press, September 22, 1993.

48. Federal News Service, "News Conference with Republican Members of Congress on the President's Health Care Legislation," October 27, 1993.

49. Newt Gingrich, "Letters to the Editor: I'm Nihilistic? Check Your Webster's," *Wall Street Journal*, October 26, 1993, A23.

50. Will Shortz, ed., "Crossword," *New York Times*, December 8, 1993, C23.

51. Will Shortz, ed., "Crossword," *New York Times*, December 13, 1993, C18.

CHAPTER 30: WAR OF THE REBELLION

1. E. Michael Myers, "Tributes, Fond Rememberances for Former Speaker O'Neill," United Press International, January 6, 1994.

2. Robert Novak, "High-Stakes Game for the GOP," *Washington Post*, January 27, 1994, A27.

3. Bennett Roth, "GOP Seeks Way to Heal the Split over Health Care," *Houston Chronicle*, January 2, 1994, A1.

4. Ralph Z. Hallow, "Tricky Timing Key to GOP Strategy on Health Plan," *Washington Times*, February 20, 1994, A4.

5. David Hess, "Gephardt Goes After Critics of Clinton's Health-Care Plan, His Targets Were Republicans and Business Groups," *Philadelphia Inquirer*, February 5, 1994, A10.

6. Paul M. Rodriguez, "House to Test Oxford-Style Debate," *Washington Times*, February 8, 1994, A4.

7. David S. Broder, "Is There a Debater in the House?," *Washington Post*, March 6, 1994, C7.

8. Ralph Z. Hallow, "Irked Governors Challenge Clinton; Federal Solutions Foster Resentment," *Washington Times*, January 31, 1994, A4.

9. Alan McConagha, "'No Crisis' Ads,'" *Washington Times*, February 11, 1994, A11.

10. Ibid.

11. Paul A. Gigot, "Why Liberals Really Hate Newtonian Politics," *Wall Street Journal*, October 22, 1993, A14.

12. Morton M. Kondracke, "Powell for Speaker? GOP Is Dreaming of House Control," *Roll Call*, February 17, 1994.

13. Ibid.

14. Ibid.

15. "TV Monitor," *Hotline*, February 23, 1994.

16. Lee Edwards, *The Power of Ideas* (Ottawa, IL: Jamestown Books, 1997), 129.

17. Kenneth J. Cooper, "Rostenkowski Reimburses Government for Supplies," *Washington Post*, February 12, 1994, A3.

18. Ibid.

19. David E. Rosenbaum, "Clinton Seems Willing to Pay a Price to Keep Files on Land Deal Private," *New York Times*, January 7, 1994, A19.

20. Robert Pear, "Congress Asserts Health Proposals Understate Costs," *New York Times*, February 9, 1994, A1.
21. Robert Novak, "Rosty Pal Michel Refuses to Support GOP Ethics Push," *Chicago Sun-Times*, February 13, 1994, 47.
22. "Health Care Budget Criticized," *ABC World News Tonight*, ABC News, February 8, 1994.
23. Eric Pianin, "House Approves Clinton Budget, Tinkers Little," *Washington Post*, March 12, 1994, A11.
24. Tim Curran, "Jones Eyes Comeback Bid Against Gingrich in Georgia," *Roll Call*, February 7, 1994.
25. Mary Louise Kelly, "Ben Jones Makes It Official: He's Going for Gingrich's Seat," *Atlanta Journal-Constitution*, March 3, 1994, C2.
26. Ernie Freda, "Fame and Fortune the New Chapters for Snubbed Guinier," *Atlanta Journal-Constitution*, February 11, 1994, B4.
27. Lois Romano, "The Reliable Source," *Washington Post*, March 11, 1994, G3.
28. Ibid.
29. Ibid.
30. Nita Lelyveld, "Dole Gives Any Health Reform 50–50 Chance of Passage This Year," Associated Press, March 4, 1994.
31. Helen Dewar, "House Democrat Suggests Hearings to Clear Clintons," *Washington Post*, A2.
32. Ann Devroy and Ruth Marcus, "President Revises Whitewater Losses; to Reveal Tax Data," *Washington Post*, March 25, 1994, A1.
33. Mary Ann Akers, "Congressional Republicans Demand Whitewater Hearings," United Press International, March 7, 1994.
34. "Bernie Nussbaum, White House Counsel, to Resign Post in Wake of Whitewater Indiscretions; Dole Questions Shredding of Documents," *CBS Evening News*, CBS News, March 4, 1994.
35. Richard Cohen, "Her Own Worst Enemy," *Washington Post*, March 10, 1994, A21.
36. George F. Will, "Fangs of the Independent Counsel," *Washington Post*, January 7, 1994, A19.
37. Jackie Gingrich Cushman, "Newt Gingrich, Thought Provocateur in Chief," *Townhall*, May 5, 2010, http://townhall.com/columnists/jackiegingrichcushman/2010/05/07/newt_gingrich,_thought_provocateur_in_chief.
38. "Begala and Leach Interview About Whitewater/Madison," *Inside Politics*, CNN, January 4, 1994.
39. Ibid.
40. "Time for a Special Prosecutor," *New York Times*, January 4, 1994, A14.
41. David E. Rosenbaum, "Clinton Seems Willing to Pay a Price to Keep Files on Land Deal Private," *New York Times*, January 7, 1994, A19.
42. David E. Rosenbaum, "G.O.P. Dismisses Qualms About Whitewater Hearing," *New York Times*, March 10, 1994, A20.
43. "TV Monitor," *Hotline*, February 23, 1994.
44. Richard Lacayo, "The Nightmare Before Christmas," *Time*, November 3, 2005.

45. Ibid.
46. Dan Williams and Ann Devroy, "U.S. Policy Lacks Focus, Critics Say," *Washington Post*, April 24, 1994, A1.
47. Jeanne Cummings and Kathey Alexander, "Gingrich Under Fire for Remark: Iraq Tragedy Comment Irritates White House," *Atlanta Journal-Constitution*, April 16, 1994, A8.

CHAPTER 31: THE "GET CLINTON CONSPIRACY" MEETING COMES TO ORDER
1. Richard Cohen, "Hillary Is Her Own Worst Enemy," *Plain Dealer*, March 13, 1994, 6C.
2. Roland A. Taylor, "Rostenkowski: Hearing on Whitewater possible," *Washington Times*, March 7, 1994, A14.
3. Kenneth J. Cooper, "House Approves $28 Billion Crime Bill," *Washington Post*, April 22, 1994, A1.
4. Frances Burton, "Today's Crossword," *Washington Post*, April 1, 1994, E3.
5. Thomas B. Edsall, "As Political Issue, Taxes Are Down," *Washington Post*, April 12, 1994, A4.
6. Associated Press, "Fiske Warns Against Congressional Hearings on Whitewater," March 7, 1994.
7. CNN, "Newt Gingrich Reacts to Lloyd Cutler Appointment," March 8, 1994.
8. Gail Collins, "Hillary Swallowed by the D.C. Tar Pit," *Newsday*, March 8, 1994, 5.
9. "Clinton Appoints New White House Counsel," *ABC World News Tonight*, ABC News, March 8, 1994.
10. Bob Dole, in discussion with the author, March 26, 2013.
11. Federal News Service, "News Briefing with Senator Robert Dole (R-KS) and Representative Newt Gingrich (R-GA) Re: Whitewater And Other Issues," March 14, 1994.
12. "Clinton Appoints New White House Counsel," *ABC World News Tonight*, ABC News, March 8, 1994.
13. Jill Zuckman, "The Moderation of Newt Gingrich," *Boston Globe*, March 12, 1994, 1.
14. Ibid.
15. Federal News Service, "Remarks by Representative Newt Gingrich (R-GA) at the National League of Cities Health Care Reform Conference," March 14, 1994.
16. "Clinton Boosts Health Care in New Hampshire," *Inside Politics*, CNN, March 15, 1994.
17. Anna Quindlen, "Whitewater Offers Lots of Folks a Chance to Look Their Worst," *Chicago Tribune*, March 15, 1994, A27.
18. Ibid., A6.
19. Jill Zuckman, "The Moderation of Gingrich," *Boston Globe*, March 12, 1994, 1.
20. Peter Hogness, "TB or Not TB, That Is the Question," *Newsday*, March 17, 1994, 110.
21. Joe Klein, "The House That Newt Will Build," *Newsweek*, April 25, 1994, 31.

22. Timothy J. Burger, "Gingrich Warns All Ranking Members Not to Take Their Posts for Granted Next Year," *Roll Call*, March 24, 1994.
23. Ibid.
24. Michael McNutt, "Hearings Pressure Grows, Gingrich Says," *Daily Oklahoman*, March 29, 1994, 8.
25. Ibid.
26. Nixon Funeral Cost Taxpayers $311, 039," *Los Angeles Times*, October 4, 1994.

CHAPTER 32: PANIC IN LAFAYETTE PARK
1. "The President's Legal Troubles," *Capital Gang*, CNN, May 21, 1994.
2. Rep. Gingrich Criticizes Nation's 'Sick Culture'," *Plain Dealer*, May 19, 1994, 3A.
3. Ibid.
4. "Clinton Answers Criticism over Whitewater Handling," *ABC World News Tonight*, ABC News, March 7, 1994.
5. "Most Favored Nation and Human Rights in China," *Capital Gang*, CNN, May 28, 1994.
6. Ibid.
7. Ibid.
8. Cal Thomas, "Conservatism Makes Comeback," *Seattle Post-Intelligencer*, June 9, 1994, A15.
9. David Frum, "Wilson? Quayle? Dole? Anyone?," *New York Times*, June 10, 1994, A29.
10. Dan Balz and Thomas B. Edsall, "Democrats Worry South Could Erode Majority," *Washington Post*, May 26, 1994, A10.
11. Ibid.
12. Ibid.
13. Robert D. Novak, "No Health Bill?," *Washington Post*, June 6, 1994, A19.
14. Richard L. Berke, "Democrats Fear That South Will Desert Them for G.O.P. in House Rules," *New York Times*, May 21, 1994, 10.
15. Neil A. Lewis, "Lawmakers Sow Health Bills and Reap Donations," *New York Times*, May 23, 1994, B6.
16. Ibid.
17. "G.O.P. Senators Fail to Reach Consensus on Health Measure," *New York Times*, March 5, 1994, 7.
18. Robin Toner, "Moynihan Sees Danger in Delay on Health," *New York Times*, June 20, 1994, A14.
19. Marshall Ingwerson, "GOP Rep. Gingrich Foresees Sweeping Republican Gains in House This Year," *Christian Science Monitor*, May 19, 1994, 3.
20. Ibid.
21. Jerry Seper and Ralph Z. Hallow, "GOP Tries to Bait Trap for Hearings," *Washington Times*, June 18, 1994, A1.
22. Federal News Service, "News Conference with: Senator Bob Dole (R-KS), Representative Bob Michel (R-IL), Representative Newt Gingrich (R-GA), GOP National Chairman Haley Barbour," May 20, 1994.
23. Ibid.

24. Richard E. Cohen, "House GOP's Takeover Plans," *National Journal*, May 28, 1994, 1252.

25. Ibid.

26. Ibid.

27. Eric Pianin and Kenneth J. Cooper, "In Corridors of Capitol, a Political Death Watch," *Washington Post*, May 26, 1994, A1.

28. Ibid.

29. Gay Gaines, in discussion with author.

30. Gay Hart Gaines, "Rep. Gingrich's Generosity," *Washington Post*, May 14, 1994, A22.

31. David Holmberg, "Palm Beach Dynamo' Sells GOPAC," *Palm Beach Post*, May 8, 1994, 1A.

32. Adrianne Appel, "Central to Health Reform: Who Are the Uninsured?," *Christian Science Monitor*, June 22, 1994, 4.

33. United Press International, "Gephardt: GOP Stalling Health Reform," June 16, 1994.

34. John Aloysius Farrell, "GOP Predicts Its Tactics Will Beat Clinton in '96," *Boston Globe*, June 20, 1994, 1.

35. Jill Zuckman, "Democrat Sees 'Takeover' of GOP," *Boston Globe*, June 22, 1994, 3.

36. Ibid.

37. Alan McCongha, "Gingrich's Lead," *Washington Times*, June 29, 1994, A9.

38. David S. Broder, "How the House Could Roar," *Washington Post*, August 21, 1994, C9.

39. *Parade Magazine*, July 10, 1994.

40. "Mr. Gingrich's Stealth PAC," *Washington Post*, August 1, 1994, A20.

41. Helen Dewar, "Tables Turning on Health Care as Election Issue," *Washington Post*, July 5, 1994, A4.

42. "The Ignorance of the GOP Whip," *Hartford Courant*, June 25, 1994, B8.

43. John King, "White House Allays Some Fears with Promise of Aggressive Campaign Year," Associated Press, June 25, 1994.

44. Ibid.

45. "A President Conservatives Love to Hate in Every Media Form, They Savage Clinton. "It's Intense," Said One Analyst," *Philadelphia Inquirer*, June 26, 1994.

46. Jules Witcover, "Winner Dole Did Not Come for Iowa GOP Straw Poll," *Baltimore Sun*, June 26, 1994, 14A.

47. "It's Called Diplomacy, Senator," *New York Times*, July 12, 1994, A18.

48. Ibid.

49. Ibid.

50. Adam Clymer, "Democrats Issue Draft of Health Plan," *New York Times*, July 27, 1994, A15.

51. David E. Rosenbaum, "A Republican Who Sees Himself as a Revolutionary on the Verge of Victory," *New York Times*, July 24, 1994.

52. Frank J. Murray, "Cutler Hopes Report Silences 'Rumormongers'," *Washington Times*, July 1, 1994, A10.

53. "Employer Mandates: Action On and Off Capitol Hill," *American Health Line*, June 9, 1994.

54. David S. Broder and Dana Priest, "Gephardt Announces Health Plan," *Washington Post*, July 30, 1994, A1.

55. Ibid.

56. Elaine S. Povich, "Democrats Bury Clinton's Health Proposal in Order to Keep It Alive," *Chicago Tribune*, July 24, 1994, C3.

57. Ibid.

58. Katharine Q. Seelye, "Some House Democrats Like Plan but Not Political Risks," *New York Times*, July 30, 1994, 8.

59. Ibid.

60. David Von Drehle, "GOP Borrows $5 Million, Kicks Off $10 Million Drive," *Washington Post*, July 23, 1994, A5.

61. David Von Drehle, "GOP Predicts Huge Midterm Gains," *Washington Post*, July 24, 1994, A20.

62. Michael Barone, "The last Democratic House?," *U.S. News & World Report*, July 18, 1994, 30.

63. *Late Edition*, CNN, July 10, 1994.

64. Ronald Brownstein, "Is the GOP Too Timid to Say No to the Religious Right?," *Los Angeles Times*, July 11, 1994, A5.

65. Alan McConagha, "Hillary's Ratings Drop," *Washington Times*, July 21, 1994, A5.

66. Peter Applebone, "A Suburban Eden Where the Right Rules," *New York Times*, August 1, 1994, A1.

67. Ibid.

68. Ibid.

69. Newt Gingrich, "Cobb County, America," *New York Times*, August 20, 1994, 22.

CHAPTER 33: THE REPUBLICANS TALK CONTRACT

1. Dan Balz and Ronald Brownstein, *Storming the Gates: Protest Politics and the Republican Revival* (Boston: Little, Brown, and Company, 1996), 166.

2. Frank J. Donatelli, in discussion with the author.

3. Dan Balz and Ronald Brownstein, *Storming the Gates: Protest Politics and the Republican Revival* (Boston: Little, Brown, and Company, 1996), 195.

4. George Gallup, Jr., *The Gallup Poll: Public Opinion 1994* (Wilmington, Delaware: Scholarly Resources, Inc., 1995), 28–29.

5. Katharine Q. Seelye, "Crime Bill Fails on a House Vote, Stunning Clinton," *New York Times*, August 12, 1994, A1.

6. Kenneth J. Cooper, "Gun Control Opponents Prevail in Stinging Defeat for Clinton," *Washington Post*, August 12, 1994, A1.

7. R. W. Apple Jr., "A President Staggering," *New York Times*, August 12, 1994, A1.

8. Kenneth J. Cooper, "Gun Control Opponents Prevail in Stinging Defeat for Clinton," *Washington Post*, August 12, 1994, A1.

9. Robin Toner, "Edginess on Capitol Hill," *New York Times*, August 22, 1994, A1.

10. Nita Lelyveld, "Will Partisanship on Crime Sour Health Debate?," Associated Press, August 15, 1994.

11. CNN, "House Whip Newt Gingrich Discusses Crime Bill Defeat," August 12, 1994.

12. Ibid.
13. Ibid.
14. Frank J. Murray and Ralph Z. Hallow, "GOP Hints OK for Modified Crime Bill," *Washington Times*, August 17, 1994, A1.
15. Newt Gingrich, in discussion with the author.
16. "Television," *New York Times*, August 14, 1994, 55.
17. Michael Wines, "Lamenting Petty Politics, Clinton Pushes Crime Bill," *New York Times*, August 15, 1994, B6.
18. "President and Crime Victims Appear in Rose Garden," *CBS This Morning*, CBS, August 16, 1994.
19. Robin Toner, "Senate Now Has Main Role on Health," *New York Times*, August 15, 1994, A12.
20. Frank J. Murray and Ralph Z. Hallow, "GOP Hints OK for Modified Crime Bill," *Washington Times*, August 17, 1994, A1.
21. Sandy Gray, "Better Shaq than Crack," *Baltimore Sun*, August 22, 1994, 9A.
22. Robin Toner, "Edginess on Capitol Hill," *New York Times*, August 22, 1994, http://www.nytimes.com/1994/08/22/us/the-health-care-debate-news-analysis-edginess-on-capitol-hill.html.
23. Sandy Gray, "Better Shaq than Crack," *Baltimore Sun*, August 22, 1994, 9A.
24. George Embrey, "Republicans Refine Their Role in Lawmaking," *Columbus Dispatch*, August 23, 1994, 7A.
25. Dan Balz and Ronald Brownstein, *Storming the Gates: Protest Politics and the Republican Revival* (Boston: Little, Brown, and Company, 1996), 197.
26. George F. Will, "Another Washington Rerun," *Washington Post*, August 21, 1994, C9.
27. Associated Press, "Crime Issue a Bright Spot in Clinton's Dismal Job Rating," August 18, 1994.
28. Ben Smith III and Susan Laccetti, "Health-Care Plan Dead This Year, Gingrich Says; House Minority Whip Cites Battle over Crime Bill," *Atlanta Journal and Constitution*, August 23, 1994, F6.
29. David S. Broder, "GOP Minority Grows Mighty in a Fortnight," *Washington Post*, August 21, 1994, A20.
30. "Lessons of the Crime Bill," *Miami Herald*, August 23, 1994, A10.
31. Michael Barone and Gloria Borger, "The Happy Warrior," *U.S. News & World Report*, August 22, 1994, 32.
32. Ibid.
33. Marshall Ingwerson, "GOP Chances to Win Majority in Congress Distant, but Rising," *Christian Science Monitor*, September 30, 1994, 1.
34. David Broder, "Gingrich Reflects Two Shifts Within GOP," *Dallas Morning News*, August 22, 1994, 13A.
35. Associated Press, "Report Says Seven Gave $200,000 Each to Gingrich PAC," August 18, 1994.
36. "Gingrich's Contributors Include Who's Who of Wealthy, Powerful," *Chicago Tribune*, August 21, 1994, C21.
37. Ibid.

38. Gay Hart Gaines, "Gopac Trains Leaders in Conservative Ideals," *New York Times*, September 7, 1994, A22.

39. David S. Broder, "GOP Minority Grows Mighty in a Fortnight," August 21, 1994, A20.

40. Newt Gingrich, in discussion with the author.

41. "Notes on Bipartisanship," *New York Times*, September 3, 1994, 18.

42. Nita Lelyveld, "Will Partianship on Crime Sour Health Debate?," Associated Press, August 15, 1994.

43. "Taking the Gingrich Pledge," *Washington Post*, September 25, 1994, A2.

44. Mark Shields, "Will Success Foil the GOP?," *Washington Post*, September 15, 1994, A17.

45. Donald Lambro "Clinton's Woes Bode Ill for Democrats in November," *Washington Times*, August 21, 1994, A4.

46. Michael Wines, "In Memoir, Barbara Bush Recalls Private Trials of a Political Life," *New York Times*, September 8, 1994, A1.

47. Ibid., B10.

48. "Joe K's Ex-Maid to Appear on 'Geraldo'," *Hotline*, July 6, 1994.

49. Ibid.

50. Kathey Alexander, "Money Offered for Debate," *Atlanta Journal-Constitution*, July 14, 1994, G10.

51. Robert Novak, "Speaker Gingrich?," *Chicago Sun-Times*, July 10, 1994, 39.

52. Ibid.

53. Bob Dole, "We'll Obstruct What Needs Obstructing," *New York Times*, September 12, 1994, A15.

54. Frank Luntz, in discussion with the author, July 9, 2013.

55. David Hoppe, in discussion with the author, June 14, 2011.

CHAPTER 34: YOU SAY YOU WANT A REVOLUTION?

1. Dana Priest, "Democrats Pull the Plug on Health Care Reform," *Washington Post*, September 27, 1994, A1.

2. "Read Before Signing," *Roll Call*, September 26, 1994.

3. "GOP Contract: 'The Mother of All Photo-Ops'," *Hotline*, September 28, 1994.

4. Lars-Erik Nelson, "GOP's Grab Bag of Gimmicks," *Newsday*, September 29, 1994, A8.

5. Kenneth J. Cooper, "GOP Offers a 'Contract' to Revive Reagan Years," *Washington Post*, September 28, 1994, A1.

6. Kerry Knott, in discussion with the author, October 9, 2012.

7. Ibid.

8. "The G.O.P.'s Deceptive Contract," *New York Times*, September 28, 1994, A20.

9. Ibid.

10. E. J. Dionne Jr., "Aw, C'mon, Newt," *Washington Post*, September 27, 1994, A21.

11. "The GOP 'Contract'," *Christian Science Monitor*, September 29, 1994, 18.

12. Eric Planin, "Some in GOP Don't Buy the 'Contract'," *Washington Post*, September 30, 1994, A10.

13. Ibid.

14. Charles Peters, "Paralysis Resumes," *Baltimore Sun*, September 13, 1994, 9A.
15. Kenneth J. Cooper, "GOP Offers a 'Contract' to Revive Reagan Years," *Washington Post*, September 28, 1994, A1.
16. Newt Gingrich, in discussion with the author.
17. John Dillin, "GOP Has a Shot at House Majority," *Christian Science Monitor*, September 6, 1994, 1.
18. Ibid.
19. Marshall Ingwerson, "Clinton Could Turn Losses to Gains After November," *Christian Science Monitor*, September 26, 1994, 1.
20. George F. Will, "Some Revolution," *Washington Post*, September 1, 1994, A21.
21. "Midterms: Question Is Not Whether, But How Many, Dem Losses," *Hotline*, September 8, 1994.
22. "President Clinton Holds News Conference Citing His Accomplishments and Noting the Problems He's Encountered Since Entering Office," CBS News, *CBS Evening News*, October 7, 1994.
23. Helen Thomas, "Clinton: GOP Contract 'Unfounded Promises'," United Press International, October 7, 1994.
24. "President Clinton Holds News Conference Citing His Accomplishments and Noting the Problems He's Encountered Since Entering Office," *CBS Evening News*, CBS, October 7, 1994.
25. Robert Novak, "President Newt," *Chicago Sun-Times*, October 23, 1994, 47.
26. "GOP '96: Powell Gets the Cover of Newsweek," *Hotline*, October 3, 1994.
27. Ibid.
28. Major Garrett, "Republicans Plan Takeover of House," *Washington Times*, October 8, 1994, A4.
29. Robert Novak, "IRA's Adams Feels Chill at State Dept.," *Chicago Sun-Times*, October 9, 1994, 47.
30. Eliza Newlin Carney, "Leadership PACs Keep the Money Rolling In," *National Journal*, October 1, 1994, 2270.
31. "Open the Books on Newt Inc.," *New York Times*, December 20, 1994, A22.
32. Glenn R. Simpson, "New Addition to Gingrich Family Tree: The Progress And Freedom Foundation," *Roll Call*, September 12, 1994.
33. Associated Press, "FEC Fines Gingrich Campaign $3,800 for Violating Disclosure Law," September 19, 1994.
34. "Open the Books on Newt Inc.," *New York Times*, December 20, 1994, A22.
35. Ralph Z. Hallow, "Gingrich Must Sell Voters on GOP," *Washington Times*, September 19, 1994, A1.
36. Craig Winneker, "Heard on the Hill," *Roll Call*, September 26, 1994.
37. Timothy J. Burger, "Dems Break Silence on GOP 'Contract'," *Roll Call*, September 26, 1994.
38. "Gingrich, Coehlo [sic] Debate Merits of GOP Pledge to Voters," *Inside Politics*, CNN, September 27, 1994.
39. Melissa B. Robinson, "Clinton Rips Republicans on 'Contract with America'," Associated Press, September 29, 1994.
40. *Newsmaker Saturday*, CNN, October 7, 1994.

41. Alan McConagha, "The GOP 'Contract,'" *Washington Times*, September 30, 1994, A5.

42. Susan Page, "The Coattail Curse," *Newsday*, October 10, 1994, A16.

43. "Republicans and the Crime Bill," *StateNet California Journal*, October 1, 1994.

44. Timothy J. Burger, "New World Order for GOP on Committees," *Roll Call*, September 12, 1994.

45. Ibid.

46. Tim Curran, "Paxon: 22-Seat GOP Net," *Roll Call*, September 15, 1994.

47. Ronald A. Taylor, "Republicans Vow to Change Congress," *Washington Times*, September 26, 1994, A4.

48. Ralph Z. Hallow, "Gingrich Must Sell Voters on GOP," *Washington Times*, September 19, 1994, A1.

49. Gary Lee, "Superfund Reform Bites the Dust," *Washington Post*, October 6, 1994, A15.

50. Ann Devroy, "GOP Taking Joy in Obstructionism," *Washington Post*, October 6, 1994, A1.

51. Ibid.

52. "In Congress, 2 Parties Flail Around," *Chicago Tribune*, September 24, 1994, N3.

53. Ibid.

54. "Democrats Attack Clinton's Critics," *Chicago Tribune*, October 3, 1994, N8.

55. Ann Devroy, "GOP Taking Joy in Obstructionism," *Washington Post*, October 7, 1994, A1.

56. Ibid.

57. Don Feder, "AGOP Goes for Gold in House Races," *Boston Herald*, September 26, 1994, 18.

58. *Crossfire*, CNN, October 7, 1994.

59. Major Garrett and J. Jennings Moss, "103rd Congress' Gridlocked End Leaves Many Members Frustrated," *Washington Times*, October 9, 1994, A1.

60. Adam Clymer, "At the Capitol, Much Talk but Hardly Any Action," *New York Times*, October 8, 1994, 9.

61. J. Jennings Moss and Major Garrett, "President Loses Big Down the Stretch," *Washington Times*, October 8, 1994, A1.

62. David Lauter, "As Election Nears, GOP Prospects Even Bright," *Los Angeles Times*, September 25, 1994, A1.

63. Katharine Q. Seelye, "Clinton and Allies Rediscover Their Voice in Writing Epitaph for Congress," *New York Times*, October 9, 1994, 26.

64. Michael Wines, "The President Comes to Town," *New York Times*, October 16, 1994, 41.

65. Paul Bedard, "Clinton Hits Campaign Trail," *Washington Times*, October 8, 1994, A1.

66. Robert J. Vickers, "Clinton Adviser Makes Sales Call," *Plain Dealer*, October 15, 1994, 2B.

67. Marshall Ingwerson, "Democrats Swing Back with Warning of Red Ink," *Christian Science Monitor*, October 14, 1994, 7.

68. Dan Balz, "GOP Plays Hardball with PACs," *Washington Post*, October 13, 1994, A1.
69. Ibid.
70. Ibid.
71. Ann Devroy and Charles R. Babcock, "Gingrich Foresees Corruption Probe by a GOP House," *Washington Post*, October 14, 1994, A1.
72. "Gingrich Talks Tough," *Hotline*, October 14, 1994.
73. Ann Devroy and Charles R. Babcock, "Gingrich Foresees Corruption Probe by a GOP House," *Washington Post*, October 14, 1994, A1.
74. Ibid.
75. "Gingrich Talks Tough," *Hotline*, October 14, 1994.
76. Dan Sewell, "As Gingrich Aims for Speaker, Jones Provokes, Cajoles, Nips," Associated Press, October 5, 1994.
77. "Washington: Latest Survey Puts Foley in Dead Heat," *Roll Call*, October 13, 1994.
78. Frank J. Murray, "White House Launches Anti-Gingrich Campaign," *Washington Times*, October 15, 1994, A4.
79. Ibid.
80. Katharine Q. Seelye, "With Fiery Words, Gingrich Builds His Kingdom," *New York Times*, October 27, 1994, A1.
81. Dan Balz, "The Whip Who Would Be Speaker," *Washington Post*, October 20, 1994, A1.
82. Ibid.
83. Ibid.
84. Karen Tumulty, "Gingrich: At Long Last, Power," *Los Angeles Times*, October 3, 1994, A1.

CHAPTER 35: EVE OF DESTRUCTION

1. John Harwood, "GOP May Push Rivals to Switch Political Parties," *Wall Street Journal*, November 3, 1994, A20.
2. Jim Drinkard, "GOP May Have Problems Luring Converts," Associated Press, November 3, 1994.
3. Karen Tumulty, "Gingrich: At Long Last, Power," *Los Angeles Times*, October 3, 1994, A1.
4. Katharine Q. Seelye, "With Fiery Words, Gingrich Builds His Kingdom," *New York Times*, October 27, 1994, A1.
5. Ibid.
6. Ibid.
7. William Schneider, "Will Obstructionism Be Its Own Reward?," *National Journal*, October 15, 1994, 2434.
8. Bill Hutchinson, in discussion with the author.
9. Marshall Ingwerson, "Democrats Swing Back with Warning of Red Ink," *Christian Science Monitor*, October 14, 1994, 7.
10. Ibid.
11. Timothy Egans, "The No. 1 Congressman and His No. 1 Challenge," *New York Times*, October 29, 1994, 1.

12. Ibid., 8.

13. Bill McAllister, "Individual Expression," *Washington Post*, October 18, 1994, A12.

14. Newt Gingrich, in discussion with the author, May 7, 2010.

15. Ibid.

16. Ibid.

17. Ibid.

18. Charles R. Babcock, "Congressional Campaign Spending Up 18% Since '92," *Washington Post*, November 6, 1994, A34.

19. Jon Sawyer, "Unfinished Business; GOP Confrontation Tactics Bring Gridlock Back to Congress—and the President's Problems Include Some Democrats," *St. Louis Post-Dispatch*, October 9, 1994, 1B.

20. James A. Barnes, "Look Who's Back!," *National Journal*, October 8, 1994, 2371.

21. "Gore Steps Up Campaign Debate," *Washington Post*, October 26, 1994, A8.

22. Judy Mann, "The Cost of the Politics of Meanness," *Washington Post*, October 26, 1994, B10.

23. Dennis Farney and Gerald F. Seib, "Fed Up with Congress, Americans Are Seeking to Break the Gridlock," *Wall Street Journal*, November 7, 1994, A1.

24. Ibid.

25. Al Kamen and Ann Devroy, "Clinton Warns of Horrors If GOP Wins," *Washington Post*, November 3, 1994, A27.

26. Ibid.

27. Ibid.

28. Eric Pianin, "The Social Security Card," *Washington Post*, November 4, 1994, A1.

29. Robert D. Novak, "The Speaker Presumptive," *Washington Post*, November 3, 1994, A23.

30. Helen Dewar and Eric Pianin, "In Switch, Senate Candidates Seek Clinton's Coattails," *Washington Post*, November 4, 1994, A10.

31. Eric Pianin and Bill McAllister, "Gingrich Will Stay Close to Home Through Election," *Washington Post*, November 5, 1994, A6.

32. Kim Masters, "The Politics of Hate," *Washington Post*, November 7, 1994, D1.

33. Ibid., D4.

34. Robert D. Novak, "The Speaker Presumptive," *Washington Post*, November 3, 1994, A23.

35. Ruth Marcus, "Clinton Stumps to the Finish," *Washington Post*, November 8, 1994, A1.

36. Ibid.

37. Ibid., A6.

38. Paul Begala, in discussion with the author, February 23, 2011.

39. Guy Gugliotta, "A Chance to Learn the Hill Game Bit by Bit," *Washington Post*, November 8, 1994, A15.

CHAPTER 36: REALIGNMENT

1. Lloyd Grove, "The Elephant's Roar," *Washington Post*, November 9, 1994, D1.

2. Ibid., D3.

3. Ibid., D1.
4. Ibid.
5. Tom Shales, "CBS Takes the Night in a Landslide," *Washington Post*, November 9, 1994, D1.
6. Katharine Q. Seelye, "With Fiery Words, Gingrich Builds His Kingdom," *New York Times*, October 27, 1994, A26.
7. "Who Won Where: Results in the 435 Races for the House," *New York Times*, November 10, 1994, B1.
8. Kenneth J. Cooper and Eric Pianin, "GOP Rides Wave to Position of Power," *Washington Post*, November 9, 1994, A25.
9. Ibid.
10. Peter Applebome, "The Rising G.O.P. Tide Overwhelms the Democratic Levees in the South," *New York Times*, November 11, 1994, A1.
11. Kenneth J. Cooper and Eric Pianin, "GOP Rides Wave to Position of Power," *Washington Post*, November 9, 1994, A21.
12. Judy Keen, "Clinton Prepares for New Realities," *USA Today*, November 10, 1994, 4A.
13. Dan Balz, "A Party Controls Both Houses for First Time Since '50s," *Washington Post*, November 9, 1994, A1.
14. Newt Gingrich, in discussion with the author.
15. Lloyd Grove, "The Elephant's Roar," *Washington Post*, November 9, 1994, D1.
16. Frank Luntz, in discussion with the author, July 9, 2013.
17. Ibid.
18. Gay Gaines, in discussion with the author, March 17, 2011.
19. Dale Russakoff, "Gingrich Vows Cooperation," *Washington Post*, November 9, 1994, A21.
20. Kenneth J. Cooper and Eric Pianin, "GOP Rides Wave to Position of Power," *Washington Post*, November 9, 1994, A25.
21. Dale Russakoff, "Gingrich Vows Cooperation," *Washington Post*, November 9, 1994, A21.
22. Dan Balz, "Party Controls Both Houses for First Time Since '50s," *Washington Post*, November 9, 1994, A22.
23. David S. Broder, "A Historic Republican Triumph: GOP Captures Congress," *Washington Post*, November 9, 1994, A23.
24. Ibid.
25. Ann Devroy and Helen Dewar, "Clinton Is Poised to Talk Bipartisanship, Act Unilaterally," *Washington Post*, November 9, 1994, A21.
26. Dan Balz, "Party Controls Both Houses for First Time Since '50s," *Washington Post*, November 9, 1994, A22.
27. Lloyd Grove, "The Elephant's Roar," *Washington Post*, November 9, 1994, D1.
28. Ibid.
29. CNN, "Text of the State of the Union Address," January 23, 1996.
30. Frank Luntz, in discussion with the author, July 9, 2013.
31. Bob Walker, in discussion with the author, February 15, 2011.
32. Gay Gaines, in discussion with the author, March 17, 2011.

33. Sean Hannity, in discussion with the author, June 21, 2013.

34. Ibid.

35. Ibid.

36. Ibid.

37. David S. Broder, "A Historic Republican Triumph: GOP Captures Congress," *Washington Post*, November 9, 1994, A1.

38. Ann Devroy and Helen Dewar, "Clinton Is Poised to Talk Bipartisanship, Act Unilaterally," *Washington Post*, November 9, 1994, A21.

39. Ibid.

40. David S. Broder, "A Historic Republican Triumph: GOP Captures Congress," *Washington Post*, November 9, 1994, A1.

41. Ibid.

42. Tom Shales, "CBS Takes the Night in a Landslide," *Washington Post*, November 9, 1994, D2.

43. David S. Broder, "A Historic Republican Triumph: GOP Captures Congress," *Washington Post*, November 9, 1994, A23.

44. Dan Balz, "Party Controls Both Houses for First Time Since '50s," *Washington Post*, November 9, 1994, A22.

45. Newt Gingrich, in discussion with the author, May 7, 2010.

46. David S. Broder, "A Historic Republican Triumph: GOP Captures Congress," *Washington Post*, November 9, 1994, A23.

EPILOGUE

1. John K. Wilson, *Newt Gingrich: Capitol Crimes and Misdemeanors* (Monroe, Maine: Common Courage Press, 1996), 1.

2. Newt Gingrich, in discussion with the author, May 9, 2010.

3. David S. Broder, "Bright, Young Republicans Risk Campaign Dangers," *St. Petersburg Times*, July 2, 1974, 10A.

4. Newt Gingrich, in discussion with the author, April 7, 2012.

5. Dick Williams, *Newt!: Leader of the Second American Revolution* (Marietta, Georgia: Longstreet Press, 1995), 3.

6. Ibid., 4.

7. Newt Gingrich, in discussion with the author, February 13, 2011.

8. Sean Hannity, in discussion with the author, June 21, 2013.

9. Ibid.

10. Newt Gingrich, in discussion with the author.

11. Newt Gingrich, in discussion with the author, February 13, 2011.

12. Frank Luntz, in discussion with the author, July 9, 2013.

13. Ed Rollins, in discussion with the author, February 8, 2013.

14. Bob Livingston, in discussion with the author, February 17, 2011.

15. Vin Weber, in discussion with the author, June, 8, 2011.

16. Heather Cox Richardson, *To Make Men Free: A History of the Republican Party* (New York: Basic Books, 2014), 240.

17. Ibid., 335.

18. Taylor Branch, *The Clinton Tapes* (New York: Simon & Schuster, 2009), 227.

19. Chip Kahn, in discussion with the author, November 23, 2010.
20. Ibid.
21. Nigel Hamilton, *Bill Clinton: Mastering the Presidency* (New York: Perseus Books Group, 2007), 337.
22. Lou Cannon, "Nancy Reagan, an Influential and Protective First Lady, Dies at 94," *New York Times*, March 6, 2016, http://www.nytimes.com/2016/03/07/us/nancy-reagan-a-stylish-and-influential-first-lady-dies-at-94.html.
23. Major Garrett, *The Enduring Revolution* (New York: Crown Forum, 2005), 41.
24. Bob Livingston, in discussion with the author, February 17, 2011.
25. Nigel Hamilton, *Bill Clinton: Mastering the Presidency* (New York: PublicAffairs, 2007), 336.
26. Ibid., 344.
27. David Hoppe, in discussion with the author, June 14, 2011.
28. Bob Dole, in discussion with the author, March 26, 2013.
29. Dick Williams, *Newt!: Leader of the Second American Revolution* (Marietta, Georgia: Longstreet Press, 1995), 149.

BIBLIOGRAPHY

BOOKS

Anderson, Alfred F. *Challenging Newt Gingrich Chapter by Chapter.* Eugene, Oregon: Tom Paine Institute, 1996.

Appleborne, Peter. *Dixie Rising: How the South Is Shaping American Values, Politics, and Culture.* Orlando, Florida: Harcourt Brace & Company, 1996.

Aune, James Arnt. *Selling the Free Market: The Rhetoric of Economic Correctness.* New York: Guilford Press, 2001.

Babbin, Jed. *In the Words of Our Enemies.* Washington, DC: Regnery, 2007.

Balz, Dan and Ronald Brownstein. *Storming the Gates: Protest Politics and the Republican Revival.* Boston: Little, Brown, and Company, 1996.

Barone, Michael, Grant Ujifusa, and Douglas Matthews. *The Almanac of American Politics, 1980.* New York: Dutton, 1979.

Barone, Michael. *Our Country: The Shaping of America from Roosevelt to Reagan.* New York: Free Press, 1990.

Barry, John. *The Ambition and the Power.* New York: Penguin Books, 1990.

Berman, William C. *From the Center to the Edge: The Politics and Policies of the Clinton Presidency.* Lanham, Maryland: Rowman & Littlefield Publishers, 2001.

Bernstein, Amy D. and Peter W. Bernstein, eds. *Quotations from Speaker Newt.* New York: Workman Publishing, 1995.

Black, Earl and Merle Black. *The Rise of Southern Republicans.* Cambridge, Massachusetts: Harvard University Press, 2002.

Bloom, Harold, ed. *Robert Frost.* New York: Infobase Publishing, 2003.

Bollen, Peter, ed. *Frank Talk: The Wit and Wisdom of Barney Frank.* Lincoln, Nebraska: iUniverse, 2006.

Boston, Thomas D., ed. *Leading Issues in the Black Political Economy.* New Brunswick, New Jersey: Transaction Publishers, 2002.

Bourgoin, Suzanne Michele and Paula Kay Byers, eds. *Encyclopedia of World Biography: Ford–Grillparzer.* Second edition. Detroit: Gale, 1998.

Branch, Taylor. *The Clinton Tapes: Conversations with a President, 1993—2001.* New York: Simon & Schuster, 2010.

Brinda, Lawrence. *The Big, Bad Book of Republicans.* Washington, DC: Pazzo Books, 2005.

Brock, David. *Blinded by the Right: The Conscience of an Ex-Conservative.* New York: Three Rivers Press, 2002.

Brock, David. *The Republican Noise Machine: Right-Wing Media and How It Corrupts Democracy.* New York: Random House, 2004.

Brokaw, Tom. *Boom!: Voices of the Sixties–Personal Reflections on the '60s and Today.* New York: Random House, 2007.

Campell, Colin and Bert A. Rockman, ed. *The Clinton Legacy.* New York: Chatham House Publishers, 2000.

Carter, Dan T. *From George Wallace to Newt Gingrich: Race in the Conservative*

Counterrevolution, 1963–1994. Baton Rouge: Louisiana State University Press, 1996.

Carville, James. *We're Right, They're Wrong: A Handbook for Spirited Progressives.* New York: Random House, 1996.

Cheney, Richard and Lynne V. Cheney. *Kings of the Hill.* New York: Simon & Schuster, 1996.

Clinton, William Jefferson. *My Life.* New York: Alfred A. Knopf, 2004.

Connelly, Jr., William F. and John J. Pitney, Jr. *Congress' Permanent Minority?* Lanham, Maryland: Rowman & Littlefield Publishers, 1994.

Crimmins, Cathy and Tom Maeder. *Best of Newt Gingrich's Bedtime Stories for Orphans.* Beverley Hills, California: Dove Books, 1995.

Darman, Richard. *Who's In Control?: Polar Politics and the Sensible Center.* New York: Simon & Schuster, 1996.

Davis, Richard. *The Press and American Politics.* Second edition. Upper Saddle River, New Jersey: Prentice Hall, 1996.

Dean, John W. *Conservatives Without Conscience.* New York: Penguin Books, 2005.

DeLay, Tom and Stephen Mansfield. *No Retreat, No Surrender: One American's Fight.* New York: Penguin, 2007.

Diamond, Edwin and Robert Silverman. *White House to Your House: Media and Politics in Virtual America.* Cambridge, Massachusetts: MIT Press, 1997.

Didion, Joan. *Political Fictions.* New York: Vintage Books, 2001.

Didion, Joan. *We Tell Ourselves Stories in Order to Live: Collected Nonfiction.* New York: Alfred A. Knopf, 2006.

Dodge, Andrew R. and Betty K. Koed, eds. *Biographical Directory of the United States Congress, 1774–2005.* Washington, DC: Library of Congress Cataloging-in-Publishing Data, 2005.

Drew, Elizabeth. *Showdown: The Struggle Between the Gingrich Congress and the Clinton White House.* New York: Simon & Schuster, 1996.

Dubose, Lou and Jan Reid. *The Hammer: God, Money, and the Rise of the Republican Congress.* New York: Perseus Books Group, 2004.

Dwyre, Diana and Victoria A. Farrar-Myers. *Legislative Labyrinth: Congress and Campaign Finance Reform.* Washington, DC: CQ Press, 2001.

Dye, Thomas R. *Politics in America.* Ninth edition. New York: Pearson, 2010.

Edwards, Chris and John Samples. *The Republican Revolution 10 Years Later: Smaller Government or Business as Usual?* Washington, DC: Cato Institute, 2005.

Edwards, Lee. *The Conservative Revolution: The Movement That Remade America.* New York: Free Press, 1999.

Edwards, Lee. *The Power of Ideas: The Heritage Foundation at 25 Years.* Ottawa, Illinois: Jameson Books, Inc., 1997.

Ehrenhalt, Alan, ed. *Politics in America: The 100th Congress.* Washington, DC: CQ Press, 1987.

Eilperin, Juliet. *Fight Club Politics: How Partisanship is Poisoning the House of Representatives.* New York: Rowman & Littlefield, 2006.

Eisenach, Jeffrey A. and Albert Stephen Hanser, eds. *Readings in Renewing American Civilization.* New York: McGraw-Hill, 1993.

Felten, D. Erik. *A Shining City: The Legacy of Ronald Reagan.* New York: Simon & Schuster, 1998.

Fenno, Jr., Richard F. *Congress at the Grassroots: Representational Change in the South, 1970–1998.* Chapel Hill, North Carolina: University of North Carolina Press, 2000.

Feulner, Edwin J. and Doug Wilson. *Getting America Right: The True Conservative Values Our Nation Needs Today.* New York: Crown Forum, 2007.

Forstchen, William R. *One Second After.* New York: Tor Books, 2011.

Frantzich, Stephen and John Sullivan. *The C-SPAN Revolution.* Norman, Oklahoma: University of Oklahoma Pres, 1996.

Frum, David. *What's Right: The New Conservative Majority and the Remaking of America.* New York: Basic Books, 1996.

Gallagher, Bradley N. *Tips from the Top.* Victoria, British Columbia: Trafford, 2003.

Gallup, Jr., George. *The Gallup Poll: Public Opinion 1994.* Wilmington, Delaware: Scholarly Resources, Inc., 1995.

Garrett, Major. *The Enduring Revolution.* New York: Crown Forum, 2005.

Gillham, R. Carroll. *Think or Lose Everything.* North Charleston, South Carolina: BookSurge Publishing, 2007.

Gillon, Steven M. *The Pact: Bill Clinton, Newt Gingrich, and the Rivalry That Defined a Generation.* New York: Oxford University Press, 2008.

Gingrich, Newt and Jackie Gingrich Cushman. *5 Principles for a Successful Life: From Our Family to Yours.* New York: Crown Forum, 2009.

Gingrich, Newt and Nancy Desmond. *The Art of Transformation.* Washington, DC: Center for Health Transformation Press, 2006.

Gingrich, Newt and Terry L. Maple. *A Contract with the Earth.* New York: Penguin, 2008.

Gingrich, Newt and William Forstchen. *1945.* Riverdale, New York: Baen Books, 1996.

Gingrich, Newt and William R Forstchen. *Grant Comes East: A Novel of the Civil War.* New York: St. Martin's Press, 2005.

Gingrich, Newt and William R. Forstchen. *Pearl Harbor: A Novel of December 8th.* New York: St. Martin's Press, 2009.

Gingrich, Newt and William R. Forstchen. *To Try Men's Souls.* New York: St. Martin's Press, 2009.

Gingrich, Newt, Dana Pavey, and Anne Woodbury. *Saving Lives & Saving Money.* Washington, DC: Gingrich Communications, Inc., 2003.

Gingrich, Newt, Robert A. Goldwin, Richard J. Barnet, et al. *Government's Role in Solving Societal Problems.* Washington, DC: Associated Faculty Press, 1982.

Gingrich, Newt. *Drill Here, Drill Now, Pay Less.* Washington, DC: Regnery Publishing, 2008.

Gingrich, Newt. *Lessons Learned the Hard Way: A Personal Report.* New York: HarperCollins, 1998.

Gingrich, Newt. *Real Change: The Fight for America's Future.* Washington, DC: Regnery Publishing, 2009.

Gingrich, Newt. *Rediscovering God in America.* Nashville, Tennessee: Thomas Nelson, Inc., 2009.

Gingrich, Newt. *To Renew America.* New York: HarperCollins, 1995.

Gingrich, Newt. *To Save America: Stopping Obama's Secular-Socialist Machine.* Washington, DC: Regnery Publishing, 2010.

Gingrich, Newt. *Window of Opportunity: A Blueprint for the Future.* New York: Tom Doherty Associates, 1987.

Gingrich, Newt. *Winning the Future: A 21st Century Contract with America.* Washington, DC: Regnery Publishing, 2005.

Greenwald, Glenn. *Great American Hypocrites: Toppling the Big Myths of Republican Politics.* New York: Three Rivers Press, 2008.

Hames, Tim and Nicol Rae. *Governing America: History, Culture, Institutions, Organization, and Policy.* Manchester: Manchester University Press, 1996.

Hamilton, Nigel. *Bill Clinton: Mastering the Presidency.* New York: Perseus Books Group, 2007.

Hilton, Stanley G. and Anne-Renee Testa. *Glass Houses: Shocking Profiles of Congressional Sex Scandals and Other Unofficial Misconduct.* New York: St. Martin's Press, 1998.

Hombs, Mary Ellen. *Welfare Reform: A Reference Handbook.* Santa Barbara, California: ABC-CLIO, 1996.

Johnson, Dennis W. *No Place for Amateurs: How Political Consultants Are Reshaping American Democracy.* New York: Routledge, 2007.

Johnson, Haynes and David S. Broder. *The System: The American Way of Politics at the Breaking Point.* New York: Little, Brown and Co., 1996.

Jones, Charles O. *Clinton and Congress, 1993–1996: Risk, Restoration, and Reelection.* Norman, Oklahoma: University of Oklahoma Press, 1999.

Jordan, Hamilton. *Crisis: The Last Year of the Carter Presidency.* New York: G. P. Putman's Sons, 1982.

Kessler, Ronald. *Inside Congress: The Shocking Scandals, Corruption, and Abuse of Power Behind the Scenes on Capitol Hill.* New York: Pocket Books, 1997.

Killian, Linda. *The Freshmen: What Happened to the Republican Revolution?* Boulder, Colorado: Westview Press, 1998.

Klein, Joe. *The Natural: The Misunderstood Presidency of Bill Clinton.* New York: Doubleday, 2002.

Kuzenski, John C., Laurence W. Moreland, and Robert P. Steed, eds. *Eye of the Storm: The South and Congress in an Era of Change.* Westport, Connecticut: Praeger, 2001.

Lackey, Marcia. *Voices from the Other Side.* Bloomington, Indiana: AuthorHouse, 2005.

Lamb, Brian, Richard Armey, Tuckerman Babcock, et al. *C-SPAN: America's Town Hall.* Washington, DC: Acropolis Books, 1988.

Lamb, Brian. *Booknotes: Life Stories—Notable Biographers on the People Who Shaped America.* New York: Three Rivers Press, 1999.

Laxault, Paul and Richard S. Williamson, eds. *A Changing America: Conservatives View the '80s from the United States Senate.* South Bend, Indiana: Regnery Publishing, 1980.

Lewis, Shelley. *Naked Republicans: A Full-Frontal Exposure of Right-Wing Hypocrisy and Greed.* New York: Villard Books, 2006.

Lichtman, Allan J. *White Protestant Nation: The Rise of the American Conservative Movement.* New York: Grove Press, 2008.

Lind, Michael. *Up from Conservatism: Why the Right Is Wrong for America.* New York: Free Press, 1996.

Lozeau, Pierre-Marie. *Nancy Reagan in Perspective*. New York: Nova History Publications, 2005.

Mann, Thomas E. and Norman J. Ornstein. *The Broken Branch*. New York: Oxford University Press, 2006.

Mayhew, David R. *America's Congress: Actions in the Public Sphere, James Madison Through Newt Gingrich*. New Haven, Connecticut: Yale University Press, 2002.

McCormack, Win. *You Don't Know Me: A Citizen's Guide to Republican Family Values*. Portland, Oregon: Tin House Books, 2008.

Merriner, James and Thomas P. Senter. *Against Long Odds: Citizens Who Challenge Congressional Incumbents*. Westport, Connecticut: Praeger, 1999.

Moore, Michael. *Downsize This!: Random Threats from an Unarmed American*. New York: Random House, 1996.

Moore, Stephen. *Restoring the Dream*. New York: Random House, 1995.

Musgrove, George Derek. *Rumor, Repression, and Racial Politics*. Athens, Georgia: University of Georgia Press, 2012.

Norman, Peggy. *Great Days: Newt Gingrich and the Revolution in Congress*. New York: Random House, 1998.

Novak, Robert D. *Completing the Revolution: A Vision for Victory in 2000*. New York: Free Press, 2000.

Novak, Robert D. *The Prince of Darkness: 50 Years Reporting in Washington*. New York: Crown Forum, 2007.

O'Neill, Tip and William Novak. *Man of the House: The Life and Political Memoirs of Speaker Tip O'Neill*. New York: Random House, 1987.

Pauken, Tom. *Bringing America Home*. Rockford, Illinois: Chronicles Press, 2010.

Peters, Jr., Ronald M. *The American Speakership: The Office in Historical Perspective*. Second edition. Baltimore, Maryland: John Hopkins University Press, 1997.

Pitney, Jr., John J. *The Art of Political Warfare*. Norman, Oklahoma: University of Oklahoma Press, 2001.

Polsby, Nelson W. *How Congress Evolves: Social Bases of Institutional Change*. Oxford: Oxford University Press, 2005.

Rae, Nicol C. and Colton C. Campbell, eds. *New Majority or Old Minority?: The Impact of Republicans on Congress*. New York: Rowman & Littlefield, 1999.

Rae, Nicol C. *Conservative Reformers: The Republican Freshmen and the Lessons of the 104th Congress*. Armonk, New York: M. E. Sharpe, 1998.

Reagan, Ronald. *The Reagan Diaries*. Edited by Douglas Brinkley. New York: HarperCollins, 2007.

Reeves, Richard. *The Reagan Detour*. New York: Simon & Schuster, 1985.

Richardson, Heather Cox. *To Make Men Free: A History of the Republican Party*. New York: Basic Books, 2014.

Rodkey, Geoff, ed. *Newtisms: The Wit and Wisdom of Newt Gingrich*. New York: Pocket Books, 1995.

Rozell, Mark J. *In Contempt of Congress: Postwar Press Coverage on Capitol Hill*. Westport, Connecticut: Praeger, 1996.

Rueter, Ted. *The Newt Gingrich Quiz Book*. Kansas City: Andrews and McMeel, 1995.

Scarborough, Joe. *Rome Wasn't Burnt in a Day*. New York: HarperCollins, 2004.

Schaller, Michael. *The Republican Ascendancy: American Politics, 1968–2001*. Wheeling, Illinois: Harlan Davidson, 2002.

Schantz, Harvey L., ed. *Politics in an Era of Divided Government*. New York: Routledge, 2001.

Schweizer, Peter and Rochelle Schweizer. *The Bushes: Portrait of a Dynasty*. New York: Doubleday, 2004.

Schweizer, Peter and Wynton C. Hall, eds. *Landmark Speeches of the American Conservative Movement*. College Station, Texas: Texas A&M University Press, 2007.

Shirley, Craig. *Last Act: The Final Years and Emerging Legacy of Ronald Reagan*. Nashville, Tennessee: Nelson Books, 2015.

Shirley, Craig. *Reagan's Revolution: The Untold Story of the Campaign That Started It All*. Nashville, Tennessee: Thomas Nelson, Inc., 2005.

Statistics of the Congressional Election of November 4, 1986. Washington, DC: US Government Printing Office, 1987.

Statistics of the Presidential and Congressional Election of November 2, 1976. Washington, DC: US Government Printing Office, 1977.

Statistics of the Presidential and Congressional Election of November 7, 1972. Washington, DC: US Government Printing Office, 1973.

Steely, Mel. *The Gentleman from Georgia: The Biography of Newt Gingrich*. Macon, Georgia: Mercer University Press, 2000.

Strahan, Randall. *Leading Representatives: The Agency of Leaders in the Politics of the U.S. House*. Baltimore, Maryland: John Hopkins University Press, 2007.

Supply-Side Economics in the 1980s: Conference
Proceedings. Westport, Connecticut: Praeger,
1982.

Tanner, Michael D. Leviathan on the Right.
Washington, DC: Cato Institute, 2007.

Theriault, Sean M. The Gingrich Senators: The
Roots of Partisan Warfare in Congress. New
York: Oxford University Press, 2013.

Warner, Judith and Max Berley. Newt Gingrich:
Speaker to America. New York: Signet, 1995.

Weisberg, Herbert F. and Samuel C. Patterson.
Great Theatre: The American Congress in the 1990s.
Cambridge: Cambridge University Press, 1998.

West, Darrell M. Air Wars, 1952—2008. Fifth
edition. Washington, DC: CQ Press, 2010.

White, F. Clifton and Jerome Tuccille. Politics as a
Noble Calling. Ottawa, Illinois: Jameson Books,
1994.

Williams, Dick. Newt!: Leader of the Second
American Revolution. Marietta, Georgia:
Longstreet Press, 1995.

Williams, Robert. Political Scandals in the USA.
Chicago: Fitzroy Dearborn Publishers, 1998.

Wilson, John K. Newt Gingrich: Capitol Crimes
and Misdemeanors. Monroe, Maine: Common
Courage Press, 1996.

PERIODICALS

American Health Line
American Spectator
American Thinker
Atlanta Constitution
Atlanta Daily World
Atlanta Journal
Atlanta Journal-Constitution
Baltimore Sun
Bond Buyer
Boston Globe
Boston Herald
Carroll County Georgian
Chicago Sun-Times
Chicago Tribune
Christian Science Monitor
Clayton News-Daily
Columbus Dispatch
Columbus Ledger-Enquirer
Computerworld
Congressional Quarterly
Daily Oklahoman
Dallas Morning News
Des Moines Register
Dun's Business Month
Economist
Facts on File World News Digest
Globe and Mail
Griffin Daily News
Guardian
Hartford Courant
Hotline
Houston Chronicle
Human Events
Independent (London)
Los Angeles Times
Miami Herald
Mother Jones
National Journal
National Security Record
New Republic
New York Daily News
New York Times
Newman Times-Herald
Newsday
Newsweek
Orange County Register
Oregonian
Orlando Sentinel
Palm Beach Post
Parade Magazine
Philadelphia Inquirer
Pittsburgh Press
Plain Dealer
Roll Call
San Diego Union-Tribune
Seattle Post-Intelligencer
Southside Sun
St. Louis Post-Dispatch
St. Petersburg Times
StateNet California Journal
States News Service
Syracuse Post-Standard
Time
Times Free Press
Townhall
U.S. News & World Report
Union Leader
USA Today
Wall Street Journal
Washington Post
Washington Times
West Georgian News

NEWS WIRES

Associated Press
Federal News Service
United Press International
U.S. Newswire

ELECTRONIC MEDIA
ABC News
CBS News
CNN
C-SPAN
Fox
NPR
PBS

INTERVIEWS
Barbour, Haley. Interview by Craig Shirley. January 21, 2014.

Beckel, Bob. Interview by Craig Shirley. October 22, 2010.

Begala, Paul. Interview by Craig Shirley. February 23, 2011.

Betts, Bonnie E. Interview by Craig Shirley. November 5, 2010.

Brown, Pat. Interview by Craig Shirley. November 5, 2010.

Carter, Jimmy. Interview by Craig Shirley. July 11, 2006.

Cheney, Dick. Interview by Craig Shirley. April 9, 2013.

Christenson, Arne. Interview by Craig Shirley. October 5, 2012.

Dole, Bob. Interview by Craig Shirley. March 26, 2013.

Donatelli, Frank. Interview by Craig Shirley.

Finkelstein, Arthur J. Interview by Craig Shirley.

Gaines, Gay. Interview by Craig Shirley. March 17, 2011.

Gaylord, Joe. Interview by Craig Shirley. June 30, 2010.

Gingrich, Jackie Cushman. Interview by Craig Shirley.

Gingrich, Newt. Interview by Craig Shirley. April 7, 2012.

Gingrich, Newt. Interview by Craig Shirley. December 5, 2010.

Gingrich, Newt. Interview by Craig Shirley. February 13, 2011.

Gingrich, Newt. Interview by Craig Shirley. February 9, 2016.

Gingrich, Newt. Interview by Craig Shirley. January 23, 2011.

Gingrich, Newt. Interview by Craig Shirley. January 9, 2011.

Gingrich, Newt. Interview by Craig Shirley. May 21, 2006.

Gingrich, Newt. Interview by Craig Shirley. May 7, 2010.

Gingrich, Newt. Interview by Craig Shirley. May 9, 2010.

Gingrich, Newt. Interview by Craig Shirley. November 22, 2014.

Gingrich, Newt. Interview by Craig Shirley. October 31, 2010.

Gingrich, Newt. Interview by Craig Shirley. September 23, 2010.

Gregorsky, Frank. Interview by Craig Shirley. February 24, 2011.

Gregory, Carlyle. Interview by Craig Shirley. October 12, 2010.

Gunderson, Steve. Interview by Craig Shirley. January 9, 2013.

Haas, Larry. Interview by Craig Shirley. January 11, 2013.

Hannity, Sean. Interview by Craig Shirley. June 21, 2013.

Hanser, Steve. Interview by Craig Shirley. October 21, 2010.

Hoppe, David. Interview by Craig Shirley. June 14, 2011.

Hutchinson, Bill. Interview by Craig Shirley.

Jackson, Barry. Interview by Craig Shirley. January 4, 2013.

Kahn, Chip. Interview by Craig Shirley. November 23, 2010.

Kahn, Chip. Interview by Craig Shirley. November 9, 2010.

Knott, Kerry. Interview by Craig Shirley. October 9, 2012.

Livingston, Bob. Interview by Craig Shirley. February 17, 2011.

Lubbers, Kathy. Interview by Craig Shirley.

Luntz, Frank. Interview by Craig Shirley. July 9, 2013.

McLaughlin, John. Interview by Craig Shirley. June 13, 2013.

Meyer, Dan. Interview by Craig Shirley. January 2, 2013.

Miller, Zell. Interview by Craig Shirley. November 19, 2010.

Pinkerton, James. Interview by Craig Shirley.

Robinson, Rachel. Interview by Craig Shirley. December 13, 2012.

Rollins, Ed. Interview by Craig Shirley. February 8, 2013.

Steely, Mel. Interview by Craig Shirley. November 22, 2010.

Walker, Bob. Interview by Craig Shirley. February 15, 2011.

Warnick, David. Interview by Craig Shirley. March 16, 2011.

Weber, Vin. Interview by Craig Shirley. June 8, 2011.

WEBSITES

American Conservative Union
American Presidency Project
Congress.gov
Dave Leip's Atlas of U.S. Presidential Elections
Miller Center
New Georgia Encyclopedia
Our Campaigns
Roper Center for Public Opinion Research
U.S. Inflation Calculator

MULTIMEDIA

Johnson, Arte. *The Best of Newt Gingrich's Bedtime Stories for Orphans*. Beverley Hills: Dove Audio, 1995. CD.

Pack, Michael. *The Fall of Newt Gingrich*. Chevy Chase, Maryland: Maniford Productions, 2000. DVD.
Reagan, Ronald. *Freedom's Finest Hour*. Universal City, California: MCA Records, Inc., 1981. CD.

OTHER MATERIAL

Archived Collections, University of West Georgia Archives.
Private Archives Collections of Carlyle Gregory.
Private Archives Collections of Chip Kahn.
Private Archives Collections of Frank Gregorsky.
Private Archives Collections of Karen Tumulty.

INDEX

ABOUT THE AUTHOR

Craig Shirley is the author of three critically praised bestselling books on President Reagan, *Rendezvous with Destiny: Ronald Reagan and the Campaign That Changed America; Reagan's Revolution: The Untold Story of the Campaign That Started It All; Last Act: The Final Years and Emerging Legacy of Ronald Reagan;* and *Reagan Rising: The Decisive Years, 1976–1980.* His book *December 1941: 31 Days That Changed America and Saved the World* appeared multiple times on the *New York Times* bestselling lists in December 2011 and January 2012. Shirley is the chairman of Shirley & Banister Public Affairs, was chosen in 2005 by Springfield College as their Outstanding Alumnus, and has been named the Visiting Reagan Scholar at Eureka College, Ronald Reagan's alma mater, where he taught a course titled "Reagan 101." He is also a trustee of Eureka. His books have been hailed as the definitive works on the Gipper's campaigns of 1976 and 1980 and the post-presidential years. He is a member of the Board of Governors of the Reagan Ranch and has lectured at the Reagan Library. He has spoken at the University of Virginia, Georgetown, Hillsdale College, Regent University, and many other colleges and universities. Shirley, a widely sought-after speaker and commentator, has written extensively for the *Washington Post,* the *Washington Examiner,* the *Washington Times,* the *Los Angeles Times, Town Hall,* the *Weekly Standard, Newsmax, Breitbart, National Review, LifeZette, Conservative News Service,* and many other publications. He also edited the book *Coaching Youth Lacrosse* for the Lacrosse Foundation.

Shirley and his wife, Zorine, reside at "Ben Lomond," a 1730 Georgian-style manor house in Tappahannock, Virginia, and at "Trickle Down Point" on the Rappahannock River in Lancaster, Virginia. They are parents of four children, Matthew, Andrew, Taylor, and Mitchell. Shirley's varied interests include writing, sailing, waterskiing, sport shooting, renovating antique buildings, and scuba diving. He was a decorated contract agent for the Central Intelligence Agency. He is currently writing a biography of Dr. Howard Snyder, the personal physician to Dwight Eisenhower; and a book on the life story of Mary Ball Washington. *Citizen Newt* is his sixth book.

Shirley is considered one of the leading public intellectuals on the history of conservatism and conservative politics in America today.

Scott Mauer is Craig Shirley's primary research assistant. Previously, he had presented and guest-lectured on Soviet and Russian history, as well as other works specializing in Eastern European events. He earned his Master of Arts in History from Hood College in Frederick, Maryland. Mauer has coauthored many articles with Mr. Shirley, and is currently assisting him in his future projects, including a biography of Mary Ball Washington.

Andrew Shirley is a graduate student and contributor with Citizens For the Republic. A former navy Corpsman, he received his undergraduate degree from Marymount University. He is an avid sailor, antique book collector, and mountain climber.